1295

WITHDRAWN

THE
CANADIAN
CORPORATE
ELITE

AN ANALYSIS
OF ECONOMIC
POWER

WALLACE
CLEMENT

With a foreword by John Porter

Carleton Library No. 89

The Carleton University Press
Ottawa, Canada 1986

THE CARLETON LIBRARY SERIES

A series of original works, new collections, and reprints of source material relating to Canada, issued under the supervision of the Editorial Board, Carleton Library Series, Carleton University Press Inc., Ottawa, Canada.

© Carleton University Press Inc., 1986.
ISBN 0-88629-052-X (paperback)

Printed and bound in Canada.

Distributed by: Oxford University Press Canada,
70 Wynford Drive,
DON MILLS, Ontario, Canada,
M3C 1J9.
(416) 441-2941

Acknowledgements
Carleton University Press gratefully acknowledges the support extended to its publishing programme by the Canada Council and the Ontario Arts Council.

Table of Contents

Editor's Foreword

WALLACE CLEMENT'S book is in the tradition of the most dynamic and important studies in sociology, those dealing with social stratification. The attention devoted to the analysis of institutionalized inequalities of condition and of opportunity extends back to the first days of a distinguishable discipline of sociology. Clement's book focuses upon one facet of these inqualities: the concentration and perpetuation of economic power in Canadian society. I believe Clement's analysis to be the most important contribution to the study of concentrated power and elites in Canada since John Porter's widely recognized *The Vertical Mosaic*. (Porter, 1965)

In Canada Porter's work was pathfinding. Indeed, so profound was its impact that for many years the book seemed to have induced a paralysis among Canadian sociologists. The magnitude of Porter's analysis seemed to deter effective critical evaluation, correction, replication, or amplification. Now, however, nine years since the publication of *The Vertical Mosaic*, that hiatus is over. Several works have appeared or are in progress which contribute to the area of enquiry which Porter has dominated (Presthus, 1973; Heap, 1974; Manzer, 1974; Olsen, 1973). Clement's contribution is critical of Porter's work, but no mere criticsm. It is a replication of one aspect of Porter's work, but no mere replication. Rather, in its theoretical statements, data compilation, analysis, and conclusions, this book represents a valuable addition to our knowledge of Canadian society.

Dennis Forcese
Sociology Editor
Ottawa, Ontario

Foreword

When Wallace Clement's book is published it will be twenty years since I began to write about power and inequality in Canada. Its appearance will also mark a decade since the publication in 1965 of *The Vertical Mosaic*. That book had a reception which surprised its modestly confident author and which must have astounded, but increasingly delighted, its cautiously conservative publisher. It received unexpected acclaim both at home and abroad. The expanding number of students who filled our universities in the late sixties made a ready audience. One wonders, why?

There are probably several reasons. Canada was approaching its centennial and occasionally, in the surge of celebration, questions were being asked about the kind of society that had been established. More importantly, perhaps, Canada was being torn by ethnic conflict which no amount of celebration could conceal. The Royal Commission on Bilingualism and Biculturalism was documenting with seemingly ponderous effort the central theme implied by the title, *The Vertical Mosaic*, that is, ethnic disparities in education, income, wealth, and economic power. Finally, although I had much less to say on this matter than others at the time, there was the economic power of the United States, ascendant and ubiquitous.

Also, the late sixties, as we remember from rampages and rhetoric, were a period of rising radicalism amongst students, an occurrence perhaps more American than indigenous to Canada. Disinclined as I am to violence, in our society at least, I have not known whether the appropriate feeling should have been pleasure, embarrassment or anger when students in meetings would denounce university administrators with a hail of invective and with the admonition that if they had read my work the truth would be revealed to them and they would cease to be lackeys of plutocratic power.

While radicals would hurl the findings of *The Vertical Mosaic* at the establishment, that group, which we might loosely define here as the powerful and the privileged, found, too, some use for the evidence presented. If in the storm of radical protest one's feelings might be equivocal about the uses or abuses of one's work, I have little doubt that it was quite proper for me to be amused at the request from a fund-raiser of a private school to quote me in the literature they were preparing for a campaign amongst the wealthy, on the important role of the private, or as they prefer to call themselves, independent schools, in the provision of leadership in Canada. I do not know if they ever did, but I hope I am not to be charged with "selling out" because I agreed.

Radicalism has retreated in our universities, as elsewhere in North America, at a rate which has surprised, and no doubt relieved, those who viewed it with panic and as a permanent feature of academic life. While university administrators are not likely to ask in harmony where all the student radicals have gone, the fact remains that the social criticism expressed by our young people a few years ago seems to have become dulled.

Some of these student radicals have graduated to become faculty members. Still radical, they are now more at home in the library and with the pen than in the lists with their loud-hailers. As scholars their attitude to *The Vertical Mosaic* has changed. Some charge that its errors are egregious, that its author has sinned, to paraphrase at least one meaning of that expression, by missing his Marx.

I have never been dogmatic about the theories and frameworks by which we seek to give order to the facts that emerge from our research. As far as inequality is concerned, the facts often speak for themselves regardless of the framework within which they are presented. I doubt that the picture of inequality which I drew would have been much different or any more demanding of attention if I had had a prime concern for theoretical or definitional purity to the point at which I might have become bogged in a scholastic morass, my data sinking with me.

If my younger critical colleagues speaking with the conviction of evangelists, a happy state of mind denied to me throughout, feel that they have an exclusive hold on truth, I am not likely to challenge them. Rather I would say, "Fine! Go Ahead! Do it your way, but at least do it!" For there is much to be done to demonstrate the pervasiveness and endurance of inequality in Canada. Unless there is some slogging after the facts, theoretical debates are abstract and hollow whether the schoolmen who engage in them are medieval or contemporary. Hence from the point of view of human betterment I view much of the radical criticism as carping rather than constructive.

Wallace Clement is not wholly in the company of the carpers. He is radical in that, like many of us, he does not see the key to human welfare as lying within the institutions of modern capitalism, but he has the good sense to realize that social change depends on the accumulation of evidence that leads us ineluctably to conclude that we must bring it about. He points out what he considers to be the shortcomings of *The Vertical Mosaic*, and goes on from there to present us with an impressive assemblage of information that we cannot ignore if we are concerned about the inequalities that stem from the present concentration of economic power as it is found within Canada, and as it has been created by the investing metropolises of the world.

Mr. Clement's contribution is important in several respects. To me perhaps the most interesting is his meticulous following, within the limits imposed by new forms of data collection, of the same procedures I used twenty years earlier to measure economic concentration and the social origins of the economic elite. I have often been asked if the structure of power and mobility into the elite in Canada has changed since I studied it, the questionner often implying that things must surely have changed because the image of the open society in which he believed he lived, he earnestly wished to retain. Now Mr. Clement has answered that question, as far as the economic and what he calls the media elites are concerned, with evidence that some will find startling but with which few can find reason to be pleased. The economic elite of 1972 is more exclusive in social origins, more upper class and more closely knit by family ties than in 1952. Nor has there been any sizable entry into the board rooms of our major corporations of Canadians who are not British in their ethnic origin. So social structures are slow to change.

By employing the same methods to investigate the concentration of economic power and to identify dominant corporations and trace their interlocking directorships to establish the 1972 economic elite, the author has been able to show a trend and provide the beginning of a time series or a social indicator to tell us something of the direction of social change in the formation of Canada's economic elite. This is a significant advance over the so-called cross-sectional study when only one point in time is considered. It is to be hoped that Mr. Clement will continue and others will follow his example in this important development in Canadian sociology.

Another significant difference which the present study was able to exploit, and which I think is worth noting, is the greatly increased availability of data. The Corporations and Labour Unions Returns Act, requiring both corporations and trade unions to file, if they are federally chartered, as most important ones are, a great deal of information previously held confidential, has meant a great cutting down in time and work required to marshal the facts of economic concentration. Also, some provincial legislation has forced more disclosure through such things as insider trading reports. Gradually Canadians may be becoming aware of the importance of information, collected by governments and other research agencies, for social planning and improving the directing capabilities of our social system. Such information is not important for policy-making and monitoring only, but also in making judgements about the quality of our society.

Another important contribution of this present work is the attempt the author makes to provide historical depth to his analysis. Such a time perspective is essential for thorough class analysis for it is continuity over generations of established families that gives an upper class its tenacity and endurance and accumulated wealth. He adumbrates from Canadian history a pattern of relationships between those who direct economic activity and those who control the major sources of investment, at first in France, then England and finally the United States. Canada's position as a recipient of investment in its staple products and natural resources has given Canadian businessmen an *entrepôt* or go-between role which has in the Twentieth Century given those Canadians, whom Mr. Clement calls the indigenous elite, a continuing control over finance, commerce, transportation and utilities. As a consequence there has been a neglect of entrepreneurial talent, a gap in managerial skill for manufacturing which, as the Herb Gray Report reminds us, persists until today. In all this Mr. Clement is eclectic in drawing upon a growing body of entrepreneurial and elite history both of which represent a new resource for the Canadian social scientist.

In his discussion of what has become the most salient feature of Canadian economic structure, foreign control, Mr. Clement distinguishes between what he calls the indigenous Canadian elite, much confined to its historic go-between role, and the "comprador" elite (a term as delightful for the image it evokes as it is suitable for the relationship it describes), which serves as the agent of foreign, particularly American owners. As decision-makers the compradors are the servants of outsiders who are labelled the "parasitic elite" living off the avails of their investments short of the point where we as hosts are so enfeebled that we can no longer nurture our guests who, for whatever else they produce for us, produce also a national enigma. Contemporary Europe is acquiring a proletariat euphe-

mistically referred to as "guest workers". Canada has acquired a
bourgeoisie of guest owners. But as Mr. Clement points out, the
surviving indigenous elite is also capitalist and many of the comprador elite are capitalists lured by the lucrative take-over bid to transfer their capital to the custody of the foreigner. He provides us with
a fascinating account of his three elite types and leaves us with the
anticipation that there is more to come when he turns his attention
to the "parasites" and the intricate web of multinational enterprises
that make us so much periphery to their centre, hinterland to their
metropolis.

Less striking than the evidence that the economic elite has
become more closed, which I take to be the significant contribution
of this study, is the part of the book that deals with the mass media.
Perhaps that is because it is such a short time since the Senate
committee report, which is drawn upon heavily, brought the picture
of concentration in the mass media up to date. The story is much
the same as with major economic institutions. A higher proportion
than formerly of newspaper circulation, radio listening and television viewing is controlled by the major chains in the hands of upper
class families. That this has taken place in Quebec as well as in
English-speaking Canada is the most important change noted. Very
little is said about public broadcasting or about, for example the
role of Radio Canada in Quebec in the formation of national sentiments in that Province or the emergence of educational television,
or the political struggle for the control of television and cable systems. Nor can we judge from the analysis the effectiveness of the
public control of broadcasting, or whether the public interest is
better served by public regulation as with the broadcast media than
it is with the printed media which has so far escaped public surveil-
lance with those dubious press councils devoted to self-regulation.

Since the author's purpose in this examination of the mass media
is to show that those who own big business also own the mass
media and therefore must use their power to subvert the public
interest, it is surprising that he does not deal with the phenomenon
of the Senate committee itself. He shows the Senate is closely associated with economic power through the number of corporate directorships held by Senators. Why then did they agree to this exposé?
Surely not to satisfy the ego or enhance the career of Senator
Davey.

I suppose I find the mass media chapters less than satisfactory
because, beyond the intrinsic interest of the Senate committee findings, the author argues in them a questionable theoretical point not

unrelated to my earlier references to those radical critics with whom I am reluctant to engage in duals of sophistry about analysing power.

In *The Vertical Mosaic* I adopted what might be called a plural elite model which, very simply, stated that the power of economic, political, bureaucratic, military and other institutions tend to be separated because they perform different tasks for a society and, in so doing, become specialized, and hence there is always a tendency for power also to be separated. At the same time the overall coordinating and guidance needs of the society require interaction between the various elite groups. It therefore becomes a matter of empirical investigation to discover the extent to which these coordinating and guidance needs lead to an aggrandizement of power, to the creation of what might be called a power elite or a ruling centre such as exists, for example, in communist systems where party membership provides the linking mechanism.

In the final chapter, Mr. Clement argues that the links he has shown between the owners of the major mass media complexes and the corporate world and the upper class refute any theory of plural elites because they provide examples of two functionally separated tasks, that is the creation of ideology on the one hand, and sheer economic or money making on the other, which are under the control of the same elite, the corporate. From this position he throws doubt on the separateness of other elites, political, bureaucratic, church, intellectual and so forth, and seems much inclined, in order to conform to a radical orthodoxy, to take as writ that all institutions serve the evils of capitalism. Thus he moves away from his role as a justifiably angered, but reasonably objective investigator.

As to the particular point on which he tries to build his case, the ownership and control of the mass media, the matter is very marginal once the question is asked whether capitalists own the mass media primarily for economic gain or to produce ideology to legitimate their other exploitative behaviour. I suppose the test case would be where capitalists continued to operate newspapers and broadcasting stations at a loss, subsidized from their other activities, to serve their ideological interest. I would think such a case difficult to find. To quote one of his own sources, "Bassett could make more out of a dead *Tely* than a live one."

Other elites, politicians, senior government officials, clergy, intellectuals, generals are not directly linked to profit making enterprises. The degree to which their functional separateness and institutional specialization becomes mitigated because of the over-all coordination and planning of a complex society, should I think remain a problem to investigate rather than be subject to premature theoretical closure, a point which Mr. Clement curiously makes from time to time. If all elites have similar social and educational backgrounds, if they are intermarried or join the same exclusive clubs, all that becomes important evidence to be weighed in making a judgement of how narrowly recruited our elites are, and from which we might infer their broadly similar interests in the survival of a corporate capitalist economy.

We should always remember that to others the evidence might not be so convincing. Thus it seems to me to argue which theory is right, that of plural elites or that of a power elite or that of a ruling class, is futile. Each may have its own particular attraction as a guiding framework for research, but they remain hypotheses to be tested by evidence. Unfortunately, in the study of power, unlike some other fields of inquiry, the evidence is not sufficiently conclusive or generally agreed upon that an hypothesis can be universally accepted or rejected. We might well wish it could be, but our desire for certainty should not overwhelm our critical capacities.

I should not end on a disapproving note lest I should be included with the carpers or vex the reader with theoretical disputation. Mr. Clement's work is impressive and it pleases me that he has found my work a place from which to take off and to make his singular contribution. He will have critics enough with which to deal.

John Porter

List of Tables

List of Appendices

Acknowledgements

A number of people have contributed to making this work possible and I gratefully acknowledge their assistance. Dusky Lee Smith of McMaster University introduced me to the study of elites and provided much of the initial stimulation and encouragement which resulted in my undertaking this work. Small grants were provided by the Department of Sociology and Anthropology at Carleton University; the successive chairmen, Don Whyte and Muni Frumhartz, were responsible for providing this assistance. In various parts of this book material is used which also appears elsewhere. This includes "The Changing Structure of the Canadian Economy" and "Inequality of Access: Characteristics of the Canadian Economic Elite" which both appeared in the *Canadian Review of Sociology and Anthropology*. Also included is some material from "The Ethnic Composition of Canada's Elites 1951 to 1973," a report prepared with Dennis Olsen and submitted to the Secretary of State.

Along the way, Raymond Breton, Joe Smucker, Charles Gordon, Don Whyte and others have read and commented on parts of what eventually appears here. Dennis Olsen has read most of my work and made a very important contribution. In addition, he has been most helpful in sharing his many ideas and concerns with me in our long hours of discussion. Dennis Forcese has contributed greatly both as my editor and by providing encouragement to complete this book. John Hofley of the University of Winnipeg reviewed the original manuscript and provided valuable criticism. Leo Panitch also acted as a reviewer but more than that, he has been an important and continuing contributor to a number of areas of analysis; his criticisms and encouragement have been very important to the final form. Albert Dorland and Jack Wilson of the CALURA Division of Statistics Canada have shared their time and provided important information on corporations which otherwise would have been difficult to develop. Steven King has edited parts of this book and tried to improve what he calls my "austere style" Elsie Clement has given many hours of her time in the thankless tasks of research and typing while at the same time tolerating the drain this work has had on my time.

Finally, special acknowledgement must go to John Porter, both as a teacher and scholar. In addition to opening his data files to me and providing many suggestions, he has initiated an important field of social study and his contribution cannot be underestimated. All of these people have contributed in one way or another to the final form of this book, but final responsibility for remaining errors must be my own.

Carleton University   W.C.
May, 1974

Preface

WRITING almost ten years ago in the preface to *The Vertical Mosaic*, John Porter was able to say, "This book is an attempt to examine the hitherto unexplored subjects of social class and power in Canadian society". In large part because of his seminal study, this statement is fortunately no longer true. Inevitably this work will be considered in light of Porter's and, indeed, this should be the case, but the reader is warned that in many ways it is less ambitious than his while in others more so. Part I of *The Vertical Mosaic* dealt with the issue of class, primarily analysing census data, while Part II analysed the structure of power by undertaking studies of the economic, labour, political, bureaucratic and ideological elites. There is no attempt here to update Part I, and only the economic and media elite studies have been undertaken from the second part. In other words, only four chapters of Porter's book (VII, VIII, IX and XV) could be said to be dealt with here while another two (I and XVII) on social class and power and relations between elites are also examined. This book is, however, more than merely a "replication" of these earlier studies. Rather, there is an attempt to bring Porter's 1951 study of the economic elite up to 1972, synthesize his findings, add them to others which have since become available and move beyond the level and detail of analysis available to him. One further advantage of this study is the examination of two elites at one point in time to understand the extent of overlap between them. While Porter examined both the economic and media elites, his studies were ten years apart (1951 and 1961) and the precise overlap could not be discerned.

Aside from updating Porter's contribution, this book attempts to add several new dimensions to the study of class and power in Canada. If replication is going to be more than merely an exercise, it must inherently contain a notion of social change and this study has, as is evident in Chapters Four and Five, the major purpose of analysing changes within the economic and elite structures over the past twenty years. Moreover, the availability of information does not necessarily follow the actual historical development of a country, and some important studies of Canada's economic history have become available only recently. These recent studies of earlier periods will be tied together in Chapter Two to provide a sense of development and direction to the current situation. Also, more concern is given to economic processes in the formation of a social structure and the way they affect elite configurations. This has led to an increased awareness of the international forces operating which have shaped Canada's past, present and presumably its future.

The existence of Porter's earlier study, and others which have since appeared, allow for a greater depth of analysis. Not only is there more data available but there is now the added responsibility of accounting for changes which have occurred and effects they have had. In addition, several important dimensions have been added, such as a study of regionalism. While Chapter Eight investigates the concentrated structure of the media, Chapter Nine analyses the media elite for 1972 and directly compares it with the economic elite for the same year. The results of this exercise question the degree of separation between these two institutions at the corporate elite level[1].

Acknowledging that this study could have taken several directions other than the one chosen, it was considered a necessary prerequisite before entering such important debates as relations between elites (particularly those of the state system, labour unions and corporate world), that a much more current and thorough analysis of the complex nature of the economic system in Canada be undertaken. After making this initial decision it was recognized that an enormous overlap existed between the privately-owned mass media and those in control of the economic system. Based on this observation, the study was expanded to incorporate the media elite and examine its relationship with the economic elite. Although it does not address systematically the issue of relations between institutionally defined elites[2], it does illustrate that at least two institutional systems—the economic and mass media—are barely distinguishable at the elite level. Furthermore, as will be illustrated in Chapter Six, the degree of interpenetration between state and corporate elites has more than doubled over the past two decades in terms of previous members of the state elite being recruited to dominant positions in the corporate world.

The reader may well ask why this book was written and how have the author's values affected the subject chosen and the way material is analysed. These are reasonable concerns which should be stated at the beginning. In studying stratification in Canada, it was found that as the society matures, its class structure tends to crystallize, thus stifling equality of opportunity and mobility to creative decision making posts within the economy and mass media. As the corporate structure continues to concentrate the structure of power in Canada, the class structure also tends to become more rigid. Furthermore, since so much recent comment has focused on U.S. encroachment into the Canadian economy, there has been a tendency to ignore indigenous Canadian capitalists. Although U.S. economic power has seriously penetrated a good deal of the economy since the early 1950's, there remains a strong Canadian elite of independent and powerful capitalists centered in dominant corporations in the finance, transportation, utilities and the mass media sectors, but with lower participation in manufacturing and resources. The effect of U.S. direct investment has been to create a parallel set of Canadian and foreign elites in branch plants of multinational corporations, particularly in manufacturing and resource sectors. The effect of foreign control is certainly an important theme of this book, as Chapter Three and the overall analysis will demonstrate, but equally important are the much neglected issues of equality of opportunity and equality of condition.

This last issue is basic to the values which underly the following analysis. One difference in focus which stems from the values presented here, as distinct from Porter's, regards the centrality given to concern with condition (the way the society is organized) rather than simply opportunity (the way individuals are able to move within the social structure). The distinction between opportunity and condition will be examined in Chapter One, but for now it is important to see how this differs from Porter's analysis of equality. Having fallen prey somewhat to the inevitability of the "iron law of oligarchy", he concluded his study by saying, "if power and decision-making must always rest with elite groups, there can at least be open recruitment from all classes into the elites" (1965:558). Although it is probably not correct to say Porter abandons the desirablilty of transforming the condition of Canadian society, with this statement he does tend to discount the possibility of doing so. It will be argued throughout this book that retaining the current structures upon which the economic and media elite are based, namely, highly concentrated private corporations, precludes or at least greatly impedes his aspiration of "open recruitment". It will further be argued that opening opportunity channels follows from changes in the structure of society and the former will be greatly retarded unless the latter is accomplished. This has importance for the level of focus which will be evident here, as distinct from a major theme in *The Vertical Mosaic* which sees the educational system as the major institution perpetuating inequalitites.

Although this is not a book about alternative futures or new ways to organize the corporate world, it is about the way it has been structured in the past and at present. If that structure is not changed, equality of condition will not be attained and attempts to move toward equality of opportunity will be greatly hindered. The difference is a matter of focus but has implications for the types of social changes which would be necessary if equality were to be facilitated, as well as the type of society which would emerge.

Basically the values this book embodies are contained within the idea of democracy. There is no one more enlightened on this subject than C.B. Macpherson, particularly in his *The Real World of*

Democracy. He asks what the meaning of democracy is and says that "The answer depends, ultimately, on whether you consider democracy to be a system of government only, or whether you take it to be a kind of society" (1965:18). In capitalist societies such as Canada, democracy is only a kind of government and not a type of society. This particular system of power is known as a "liberal-democracy" where the society and government are "organized on a principle of freedom of choice". The "freedom" of liberal-democracies must, however, be set within the context of basic inequalities which confine that freedom. The state in liberal-democracies is used "to uphold and enforce a certain kind of society, a certain set of relations between individuals, a certain set of rights and claims that people have on each other both directly, and indirectly through their rights to property. These relations themselves are relations of power—they give different people, in different capacities, power over others" (4). Expressing the inequality of liberal-democracy differently, "you cannot have a capitalist market society unless some people have got accumulated capital and a great many others have none, or have so little that they cannot work on their own but have to offer their labour to others. This involves inequality in freedom of choice: all are free but some are freer than others" (7). The power of capital, concentrated into a few private hands, gives a relative few inordinate capabilities for decisions affecting the lives of many. The democracy which is valued here is, in Macpherson's terms, "a kind of society" and not simply "a system of government".

But to say Canada is a liberal-democracy does not mean it cannot be changed nor that the inequalities now present are inevitable. As C. Wright Mills once said: "We study history to discern the alternatives within which human reason and human freedom can now make history" (1959:174). By dispelling current myths and providing an analysis of what exists, the opportunity is provided to critically evaluate the present and generate choices about the future. This book attempts to provide such an analysis of the corporate structure, to separate its components and to put them back together in order that a broader understanding of the type of society Canada is can be debated. It attempts to answer the questions: who are the corporate elite, how and why do they control dominant corporations and what are the consequences for Canadian society?

Notes

[1]Throughout this book the term "economic elite" will be used to denote the uppermost positions in dominant economic corporations while the "media elite" means the corresponding set of positions in dominant mass media com-

plexes. As will be illustrated in Chapter Nine, the current economic elite and media elite are highly overlapping in membership and interaction. Together the economic and media elites will be referred to by the collective term the "corporate elite".

[2]This undertaking awaits Dennis Olsen's completion of his updating of the political, bureaucratic and judicial elites of the federal and provincial levels—in short, the state system, which he is presently engaged in as a PhD. thesis at Carleton University.

Chapter One

Themes and Issues in the Study of Corporate Capitalism

A variety of frameworks have been used to study inequality in liberal-democracies but two of the most useful include the concepts of social class and elites. Both will be used here to analyse the historical development which culminates in the present structure of inequality in Canada's economy. Before undertaking this, some important themes and issues pertaining to the study of corporate capitalism in Canada will be presented. Following this, an analytical framework to be used in studying the relationship between capital, corporations, classes and elites will be provided.

I. Structure and Mobility: The Relationship Between Condition and Opportunity[1]

Canada's economic development involves changes in the way the economy is organized and controlled; these structural changes recast opportunities available to Canadians for upward mobility and access to power. Contained within this statement are two concepts which provide an important theme throughout this book; these are the dual processes of opportunity and condition which "fit" one another in such a way that condition places limits on opportunity.

Frank Parkin argues in *Class Inequality and Political Order* that:

> Inequalities associated with the class system are founded upon two interlocking, but conceptually distinct, social processes. One is the allocation of rewards attaching to different *positions* in the social system; the other is the process of *recruitment* to these positions (1971:13).

Although parallel to Parkin's concepts of "position" and "recruitment", the notions of condition and opportunity are broader in scope. Condition is the framework within which a society is organized and focuses on stable sets of social relations at the structural level. Opportunity focuses on the individual level but the individual as representing certain social types such as members of social classes, ethnic groups, different sexes, region of birth or other ascribed characteristics. Opportunity involves the freedom persons with particular characteristics have to move within settings created by the social structure.

1

In liberal-democracies, where the economic system is predominantly capitalist, condition parallels the class structure and opportunity corresponds to the ability of persons with different class origins to cope with the class structure. The way society is organized provides some with the advantage to accumulate power and privilege then transfer these to their children in the form of wealth, stockholdings, social "position", access to education or "inside" contacts for job placements. The prerogatives of power within capitalism provide that private property and benefits which go along with it represent an important link between condition and opportunity. Private property is at the basis of the economic system in capitalist society and the advantages it affords some are the limits it imposes on others.

Social Forces and Social Change

A static society occurs when there is little vertical mobility between social classes in the sense that between generations there is little social ascent or descent in terms of the relative places subsequent generations hold in the social structure; for example, in a static society a son tends to repeat his father's occupation. There may be horizontal mobility, that is, movement from one similar position to another without corresponding change in the relative place in the social hierarchy. This would occur with a change in the occupational composition of the labour force where, for instance, a farmer's or fisherman's son becomes a factory worker[2], but this does not involve a change in the relative place in the labour force, as would be the case with vertical mobility. In a static society only a minority of the available talent is used since those from lower class origins with high talent will not be recruited to positions requiring high abilities and, conversely, these positions are disproportionately filled by the upper class. In a dynamic society there is a high degree of vertical mobility and a maximum use of talent. Such a society has yet to exist, but theoretically it is known as a "meritocracy"[3]. In such a society it is assumed that there could be both a highly structured society controlled by elites and open recruitment to these elites. In a liberal-democracy based on corporate capitalism this is highly problematic because of the way privilege is transmitted. When condition is structured so private property and prerogatives of power provide advantages to the offspring of the upper class, opportunity is limited to the select. The essential questions are these: what makes a society dynamic, and is it possible to have a dynamic society with a highly structured social system? It will be argued that those who concentrate on making contemporary capitalist societies meritocratic examine only one dimension of stratification, that associated with opportunity. Unless they also understand that condition delimits whether a society will be dynamic or not, they will be frustrated in attempts to gain open recruitment.

The argument pursued here is that new social forces produce changes in condition and open the social structure, thus providing the opportunity for social mobility. This includes downward and upward mobility, each of which occurs if old power holders are displaced by new ones. For instance, if an old elite is replaced by a new one, this transformation will be accompanied by new social types. However, new social forces need not displace traditional ones and may develop parallel structures alongside the old ones, thus expanding the types of structures and avenues available at any time. The effect of this structural expansion would be to create two distinct mobility avenues which may act on different selective criteria. Conversely, the domination of emerging social forces by traditional, established social forces would further consolidate the structure and place additional restrictions on mobility. Consolidation of power can occur in one of two ways. Old social forces can dominate and contain new forces, or social forces can become crystallized whereby the new forces of one era become established forces of the next. This serves to restrict avenues of mobility for new entrants and is analogous with the absence of downward mobility in a stable system. The more hierarchical a social system, the more rigid the structure. This means mobility will be low if the social structure is highly concentrated but mobility will be high if concentration is reduced. Under these conditions mobility would be facilitated by two developments: if a parallel structure emerges or if a centralized structure is decentralized. Either of these developments require initiation by a new social force.

By a social force is meant a source of power; for example, the forces of production are a source of power in that as new modes of production emerge they represent new social forces while old modes of production are established social forces. Power is the capacity to mobilize resources such as capital, wealth, personnel, knowledge, technology, ideology or military force, in the favour and to the advantage of those making allocative decisions. As a social structure stabilizes, the points of access become established, institutionalized avenues become set and those with power are able to dictate the qualities required for entrance. Quite understandably, these qualities tend to resemble the characteristics of those already in power. The limiting case of similar qualities is, of course, common kinship.

Access to corporate power by particular social types can be complemented by other social institutions, such as education. If education is defined as a prerequisite for mobility and if access to education is restricted to certain social types, then this will further restrict mobility to those social types able to gain access to education. Keeping in mind that the powerful are better equipped to have their children go to particular schools (private schools and universities) this further reinforces the probability that subsequent generations of the advantaged will take the ''reins of power''. Education is treated here as a consequence of inequality which appears elsewhere in the society and as an institution which further reinforces inequality but it is not itself the cause of that inequality. For example, it would be argued that if the resources of the society were more equally distributed and privileges eliminated then access to education would become more equal, but the attempt to make access to education equal without redistributing social resources would confront serious barriers.

New social forces represent the emergence of new sources of power. If these emerge and remain autonomous from existing powers, new social types will develop in power positions; but, if new forces are ''captured'' or absorbed by traditional power holders, this will strengthen the traditional elite and further limit mobility for outsiders. This framework will be useful in the analysis of Canada's historical development but the following problem is given for purposes of illustration. If direct investment in Canada by the United States since the early 1950's is viewed as a new social force—new in the sense of the qualitative change in the volume of capital growth since that time —then a number of alternative impacts that this development may have on the Canadian corporate structure and mobility can be analysed. According to the framework presented, one of four things can happen: (i) U.S. investment could be absorbed by traditional Canadian capitalists thus strengthening the position of traditional capitalists and restricting mobility; (ii) U.S. investment could generate a parallel structure thus creating two structures and two elites which would encourage mobility for new social types in the new structure but not in the old one; (iii) related to this, the new social force of U.S. investment could crystallize and after some time restrict mobility similar to the traditional elite; (iv) finally, U.S. investment could displace the traditional Canadian capitalist class, create a new corporate structure and bring with it new social types. Various combinations of these possibilities have, in fact, occurred throughout Canada's development but it must wait until later chapters to analyse these. It is so obvious that a decentralization of the economy has not occurred that this possibility for stimulating mobility will not even be discussed at this time. For now, attention will be turned to the issue of the relationship between the concepts elite and class, as well as a further elaboration of the distinction between opportunity and condition.

II. Social Classes and Elites

The concept "elite" can, and has been, used in a variety of ways by social scholars so it is important to specify the meaning given to it here. Minimally, an elite is a set of uppermost positions within any given institutional sphere that is arranged in a definite hierarchy. In other words, if a given institution were organized on the principle of equality there would not be an elite; however, if the components of an institution were sufficiently differentiated and hierarchically ordered, then a set of elite positions could be identified. To take the economy as an example, if all corporations were roughly the same size but hierarchically ordered within each corporation, then each of the top positions in all corporations would be included in the economic elite. If, however, all corporations were roughly the same size and there was little hierarchical differentiation within them, there would not be an economic elite. Of course, under corporate capitalism neither of these conditions hold. There is both a wide size difference between corporations and high hierarchical differentiation within them. To identify the economic elite it is then necessary to specify both the largest, or what will be called dominant, corporations and positions within these corporations which are uppermost. The basis upon which dominant corporations in the economy and mass media are identified will be specified later and it will be argued in the following two sections that the levels of senior management and directors of corporations are the uppermost decision making positions. The corporate elite is, according to this minimal definition, that set of positions known as senior management and directors within dominant corporations.

However, another aspect of the concept of elite is that elite positions are occupied by "role incumbents" at any given time; for clarity the persons who fill these positions will also be referred to as the elite. To this point the elite has only been specified as a power group, a set of persons who hold powerful positions. These conditions are necessary but not sufficient to also consider the elite as a social group. To demonstrate that a particular elite is also a social group requires that its structure be specified, that members of the group interact and are related to one another sufficiently to say they exhibit solidarity, cohesiveness, coordination, and consciousness of kind[4]. It will be demonstrated that the corporate elite in Canada meets these conditions and may be considered a social group as well as a power group.

What is the relationship between elite and class? Confining the analysis to liberal-democracies, the class structure has a clear role in creating elites and in turn the corporate elite uses its power to reinforce the class structure. Because of their relationship to ownership and control of property, all members of the corporate elite are also members of the bourgeoisie, but all members of the bourgeoisie are not members of the corporate elite. It will be recalled that the elite is defined as the uppermost positions only within dominant corporations, not all corporations. The corporate elite may then be said to correspond to the "big bourgeoisie". The bourgeoisie, as a whole, is part of what will be called the upper class which, in addition to the bourgeoisie, includes their families and elites from other key institutions such as the state and their families. While all members of the corporate and state elites are currently members of the upper class, they may have class origins other than upper class; that is, a person may be working class in origin because he comes from a working class family but may now be a member of the upper class by experiencing mobility into the bourgeoisie through accumulating capital or by being recruited into the elite.

It has been frequently pointed out (Heap, 1972; Hutcheson, 1973) that Porter uses "class" in a variety of ways depending on the type of data at his disposal (census data, income, education, occupation, etc.). Because of his "multi-methodological" approach to class he has to operationalize it in a variety of ways. If forced to operationalize class only once and specify its empirical indicator, he would have been unable to draw on the variety of class-related empirical data available, all of which he did not gather and those who do gather it, such as the state, seldom do so in class categories. In dealing with elites he had somewhat more control over how he would operationalize class but was still limited to some extent by the type of data available. Wherever possible, the position or occupation of the father or a close member of the previous generation was used to determine class of origin. In cases where this was not possible he used education as a proxy for this. For example, attendance at a private school was used to indicate the person was of "upper-middle class" origin because the family had to have sufficient wealth to bear the high costs involved in such an education. In addition, the high rate of attendance by known members of the upper class substantiates that these are upper class institutions and verifies the validity of using such an indicator where others are lacking[5].

Structured Inequality and Inequality of Access[6]

As suggested earlier, there is a further theme which serves to tie the notion of elites to that of class. This is the argument that "inequality of condition leads to inequality of opportunity". The accumulation of privilege associated with dominant positions affords their incumbents advantages which are transmitted to their kin but not available to other members of society. This is transmitted by differential access to the means of mobility such as private and post-secondary education, inherited wealth, career openings, social contacts and a series of advantages perpetuated through class institutions such as private schools and private clubs. This leads to differential class opportunities in favour of the privileged.

As suggested, two distinct dimensions of economic stratification can be explored. One is positions within corporations, their hierarchy and power differentials. The other is recruitment; that is, how the positions become filled. The first is a concern with condition and the second with opportunity. In other words, one is concerned about the structure of inequality while the other is concerned about the process of maintaining inequality. To illustrate that a corporate elite exists involves inequality of condition; to illustrate differential access to elite positions involves unequal opportunity.

This dichotomy corresponds to that outlined by Parkin when he distinguishes between the "egalitarian critique" and the "meritocratic critique". The first "raises objections to the wide disparities of reward accruing to different positions" while the second is concerned about "the process of recruitment to these positions. . . . Seen from this angle, social justice entails not so much the equalization of rewards as the equalization of opportunities to compete for the most privileged positions" (1971:13). Parkin suggests the value of attempting to synthesize the egalitarian critique and the meritocratic critique: "Although the process of rewarding and recruitment are analytically separable they are closely intertwined in the actual operation of the stratification system". One concept he uses to bring the two together is kinship. Families who are able to pass their accumulated advantages on to their kin establish a system of "social self-recruitment within privileged strata from one generation to the next", thus perpetuating class through kinship ties (14).

Of course, it is not kinship *per se* which perpetuates existing class structures. This is accomplished by the persistence of an economic order organized on the basis of corporate capitalism and supported by liberal-democratic states. This structure determines what types of occupations will be created, how many there will be, and conversely, how much unemployment there will be, how the economy will expand, its direction and scope, and the level of technology which will be created and utilized. Class structures are a product of the way a society's economy is organized and class continuity is a product of the way advantages and privilege are transferred. In Canada, as with all liberal-democracies, there is a high correlation between class structures and class continuity: those with advantages are able to pass them on while those without are not able to provide their offspring with the same privileges. By examining inequalities associated with dominant corporations and the perpetuation of class advantages, a Canadian corporate elite with roots firmly embedded in the upper class will be revealed.

Elite Theories

Of the many approaches to social stratification, it is the elite theorists who most consistently take organizations into account. Rather than review the entire elite theory literature, selected examples of the way organizations can be related to social structure will be provided. One of the widest read elite theorists is Gaetano Mosca who, with his student Robert Michels, related stratification to social forces operating in society. Mosca's basic premise was the advantage of position, contending that "all ruling classes tend to become hereditary in fact if not in law" (1939:61). For Mosca, "aristocratic" tendencies referred to societies where the source of elite recruitment was predominantly the upper class while "democratic" tendencies were evident when the entire society was the source. This corresponds closely to the distinction made earlier between static and dynamic societies. It was Mosca's contention that all societies tended to be "aristocratic" since those in power held the advantage of position. Michels took these principles and applied them to organizations thus developing his famous "iron law of oligarchy". He studied revolutionary parties, contending that if any organization was to violate this principle it would be these. In spite of their "democratic guise", it was found they tended to be aristocratic in leadership and oligarchical in form. Although he drew some questionable conclusions about "innate tendencies" in man, he did illustrate his point concerning oligarchy (1962:52). Bureaucratic organizations establish a number of elite positions which are filled, through an absorbing and assimilating process, by new elites with similar social characteristics (34). A basic difficulty with early elite theorists, however, was their assertion that the principles they found are inevitable and inherent in human relations. While it is correct to assert that principles exist, it is quite another matter to make them inevitable and innate.

Mannheim attempted to counter elite theorists by asserting that "the actual shaping of policy is in the hands of elites; but this does not mean to say that the society is not democratic. For it is suffiiient for democracy that the individual citizens . . . have at least the *possibility* of making their aspirations felt at certain intervals" (1953:119). In any form of society "aspirations" can be felt through revolution but this does not seem an adequate definition of democracy. Mannheim does more to compromise the meaning of democracy than challenge elite theorists.

More recent use of the concept elite has tended away from the innateness and inevitability of elite rule, although they have continued to argue that elite dominance characterizes liberal-democracies. There has also been more of an attempt to integrate elite and class analysis. Domhoff, for example, maintains that elites stand at the top of the class structure and can be considered the "operating arm of the upper class" (1970:109). As an approach to the study of elites, Domhoff has developed a methodology he refers to as "the sociology-of-leadership method" which focuses on "sociological background and studies the sociological composition of institutional leadership and of decision-making groups" (1967:145). He contrasts this with the "decision-making approach" which is issue-oriented and examines the actual process of decision-making rather than its structure and participants. Porter's, Mills' (1956) and Domhoff's own work, as well as this study, follow the sociology-of-leadership approach by basing their analysis in key institutions and decision makers. Each of these studies attempts to place elites within the context of the class structure by analysing the extent of particular class membership in various elite positions. This approach allows for analysis of the similarities and differences between various functionally defined institutions, such as the state and corporate worlds, as well as historical changes which occur within and between them.

It is also important to note that current elite studies do not reify organizations since they locate them clearly within the class structure of society and do not assume bureaucracies have "a life of their own" beyond that granted by those who control them. This preserves one of Mills' key points that "far from being dependent upon the structure of institutions, modern elites may smash one structure and set up another" (1956:24). Bureaucracies are not viewed as elements distinct from the social structure but clearly as a means of power which bring together vast resources. Within this framework, any organization can have the following asked of it: Why is it established and for whose purposes? Who controls decisions which direct it? What is the class origin of those in control? These are important questions which will be directed toward corporations operating in Canada.

It should be emphasized that the concept elite is not a substitute for class but complements it. However, if Domhoff's definition of the elite as the "operating arm of the upper class" were strictly adhered to, problems would arise because he defines *a priori* that the elite supports the interests of the upper class. He attempts to resolve this by qualifying the concept as a "power elite", which is the set of elites in control of key institutions. What about elites who are not necessarily in power to support the upper class, possibly the labour union elite or social democratic parties? Domhoff fails to make problematic who the elite supports. Admittedly, he is empirically correct most of the time but, theoretically, one of the key aspects to be determined is precisely what classes are represented in the elite (or various elites) and what class interests they serve. Viewing the problem in this way makes the issue of mobility more central and allows for a discussion of the wider class system by using access to elites as an indication of the rigidity of the entire class structure. It also provides a measure of the way individuals starting with different class origins are able to "make it" into decision making positions of importance. Elites predominantly drawn from one social class indicate the class interests of that elite and the way it will use its power. This is, of course, not the only way class should be analysed—while it does provide an indication of mobility it does not directly address other important issues such as the changing composition of various classes or the relationship between classes based on the extraction of surplus from the workers by the bourgeoisie. These issues require a different methodology than the one adopted here; a great deal more theoretical work and data gathering needs to be undertaken along the line initiated by Leo Johnson (1972).

An Approach to Elites and Class

The opening section to this chapter argued that studying the relationship between opportunity and condition is a fruitful approach to the study of stratification. Furthermore, it was argued that these concepts are ordered in such a way that condition places limits on opportunities. This will now be examined in light of the relationship between elites and class.

Increasing bureaucratization is one way the social structure can become more rigid and this makes breaking out of class bounds more difficult. Porter lends support to this proposition when he argues "increasing bureaucratization of the economic system through the development of the national corporation leads to an increasingly closed system of stratification" (1965:283). How do the effects of class origin operate in a highly structured society dominated by elites and why is it that the more rigid a structure becomes the more closed its mobility? It is important here to specify two related but distinct dimensions of class. Class is defined objectively by relationships to the ownership and control of capital and other valued resources. Added to this, and in many respects contingent upon this objective definition, is class as a social phenomenon as represented by common relationships, backgrounds, residences, intermarriages, associations and ideology. These all serve to create a social bond between members of particular classes and affect the life chances of their members[7]. Social class origins have a strong impact on the way individual biographies intersect with organizations and the positions people hold within these organizations.

Although many sociologists have assumed that the process of bureaucratization and industrialization would break down "particularistic privileged groups" (Parsons, 1947:74), the meritocracy this suggests has not been realized. Sjoberg, for example, in a perceptive passage maintains:

> there are two assumptions that are too readily accepted by scholars, i.e., that a hierarchically ordered system can, and does, provide equality of opportunity and that bureaucrats (i.e. elites) judge persons according to universalistic criteria. In practice, rationality oriented hierarchical systems of bureaucracy have been key vehicles by which various groups (i.e. elites) have sustained, and in some cases increased, their advantages within the broader society. And it is the middle and upper strata who learn to manipulate bureaucracies, e.g., educational structures or special government agencies, for their personal gain (1967:17).

Skills, education and access to organizations are important factors for social mobility but differential access to these valued qualities remains a class phenomenon thus helping perpetuate inequalities and a static society. Advantages deriving from social class origin ease the career avenues to centers of decision making and increase the probability kinship will play a key role in determining life chances. The accumulation of privileges to individuals in upper class positions gives them definite advantages. This appears characteristic not only for Canada but is a generalized condition for many western industrial societies (Pen, 1971:210f).

For the study of inequality in liberal-democracies, the concepts social class and elites are complementary and useful approaches. Viewed in the way they have been in this section, these concepts can be important guides to research and provide ways of analysing information found. Saying classes and elites exist does not imply they should or even have to do so; it simply means this is the way liberal-democracies are structured. It may not be the "best" way or the "fairest" way but the only way these concerns can be evaluated is to understand implications they have for societies and the majority of people who live in them. Adopting these concepts as ways of viewing Canadian society provides a critical perspective from which to make such decisions.

III. Owners, Directors, Managers and Technocrats: The Ownership and Control Debate

Debate over ownership and control of modern corporations can be divided into two issue areas. One involves what may be called the "managerial revolution" argument and the other the "dispersal of stock ownership" argument. Each is intertwined in the continuing debate over the role of private property and who controls the corporation. In this section some of the major figures in the controversy will be presented as well as the responses of some of their critics.

Marx on Managers

In *Capital* Volume III first published in 1894, Karl Marx argued that there were two kinds of capitalists, the industrial capitalist and the money-capitalist (1967:381). With the development of joint-stock companies and credit systems, a separation occurred distinguishing the "work of management as a function from the ownership of capital" (387-388). He called the industrial capitalist the "functioning capitalist" as distinct from the financiers and their managers. The development and differentiation of capitalism permitted the "work of supervision" to be "entirely divorced from the ownership of capital" (386). In Marx's view, the joint-stock company could be controlled either directly by industrial capitalists or indirectly by finance capitalists operating the company with managers. This he compares with similar transformations which occurred within feudalism:

> Stock companies in general—developed with the credit system—have an increasing tendency to separate this work of management as a function from the ownership of capital, be it self-owned or borrowed. Just as the development of bourgeois society witnessed a separation of the functions of judges and administrators from land-ownership, whose attributes they were in feudal times (387-388).

This began the sometimes empirical, sometimes strictly ideological debate over ownership and control of modern corporations.

Tawney on Ownership

R.H. Tawney, writing in 1920, foreshadowed much of the current debate in his *The Acquisitive Society*, where he argued that the role of *rentiers* of capital—that is persons who own capital and receive payment without work—had been expanding with the emergence of corporate capitalism. He predicted a "general tendency for the ownership and administration of property to be separated" (1920:66) as capitalism moved from "individual enterprise" to "joint-stock companies". This process could not continue, he argued, because *rentiers* performed no function in this system: "few working aristocracies, however tyrannical, have fallen; few functionless aristocracies have survived" (67). The "passive property" of the *rentiers* would doom them to extinction since those engaged in "creative activity" would not tolerate being exploited. "The real economic cleavage is not, as is often said, between employers and employed, but between all who do constructive work, from scientist to labourer, on the one hand, and all whose main interest is the preservation of existing proprietary rights" (79).

Tawney was an astute social scholar highly critical of the exploitation he saw in corporate capitalism; he recognized that ownership of capital involved a series of claims which could be distinguished from one another. "Ownership is not a right", Tawney argued, "but a bundle of rights, and it is possible to strip them off piece meal as well as strike them off simultaneously. The ownership of capital involves . . .three main claims: the right to interest as the price of capital, the right to profits, and the right to control, in virtue of which managers and workers are the servants of shareholders" (104). Tawney's proposal was to separate these claims of ownership and convert "industry into a profession" by separating "ownership from management" (161).

It is important to understand that for Tawney this was a remedy to the exploitation of corporate capitalism which required social change through human intervention to be accomplished; it was not something which would happen on its own but something to be done. Some half a century later there have evolved different institutions and sets of people associated with each "right" to ownership he distinguishes. Some gather their surplus through interest bearing capital as portfolio investments, others gain surplus through dividends as direct investments and still others exercise control by virtue of their voting rights. Corporate capitalism has not developed as Tawney would have wished by converting "industry into a profession"; the claims of ownership continue to operate as control although not all ownership is controlling ownership. It will be argued shortly that the three claims of ownership Tawney identifies have changed in their composition somewhat since he wrote. The tendency he identifies for ownership to become separate from management has continued to some extent, although less than commonly supposed, but his desire to have management separate from the control of all ownership has not been realized.

Berle and Means on Ownership and Control

The ownership and control debate got its first empirical examination by Berle and Means who in 1932 published a monumental study entitled *The Modern Corporation and Private Property*. Their work has been seriously misinterpreted and, like so many classics, widely referred to but rarely read. Contrary to popular myths in sociology, Berle and

Means did not argue that power had passed to the "techno-structure" (defined as hired professionals and technicians). Rather, they argued, as did Tawney before them, that power *should* pass to a "neutral technocracy" (1968:312). This recommendation was in response to their finding that "management" was in many instances no longer in the hands of a majority of owners—that is, the majority of stockholders. For Berle and Means, "management" was defined as the board of directors and senior executives of corporations (196). It needs to be emphasized that the "technocracy" of Berle and Means is a recommendation to preserve corporate capitalism in particular and private property in general. They argue that "it is conceivable,—indeed it seems almost essential if the corporate system is to survive,—that the 'control' of the great corporations should develop into a purely neutral technocracy" (312). They even suggest that boards of directors, with the separation of ownership and control, ironically represent the principles of communism:

> this corporate development represents a far greater approach toward communist modalities than appears anywhere else in our system. It is an odd paradox that a corporate board of directors and a communist committee of commissars should so nearly meet in a common contention (245).

They went so far as to suggest the possibility that "by custom the position of director" could become "hereditary" and be "given legal sanction" (305).

Berle and Means were primarily concerned about two developments they observed and were bothered by, namely, the great concentration of wealth in a few giant corporations and the fact that a great portion of stock had become disenfranchised through dispersion among a multitude of small investors, thus separating a large part of ownership from control. Corporations represented great wealth but "control over this wealth has been surrendered to a unified direction" (4). This development destroyed traditional property relations of entrepreneurial capitalism. The "typical" owner had become a mere *rentier* and control had passed to a few "individuals in command of the enterprise" (65). They discuss a series of legal devices through which a few people, holding only a minority of stock, have gained control of the corporation: non-voting stock, voting trusts, minority control, pyramiding and other techniques all gave "working control" through relatively small but strategic holdings (71-75). To find where control rested they examined the election of the board of directors (80). But why has their position been associated with notions like the "managerial revolution"? One answer lies in their use of the word "manager" which recently has taken on a meaning quite different than the one they used. The following is their definition:

> "Management" may be defined as that body of men who, in law, have formally assumed the duties of exercising domination over the corporate business and assets. It thus derives its position from a legal title of some sort. Universally, under the American system of law, managers consist of a board of directors and the senior officers of the corporation (196).

Their protestations were based on the idea that it was somehow "un-American" and against the philosophy of private property for so little ownership to control so much wealth. It would be mistaken to assume, however, that the separation of ownership and control means the separation of *all* ownership from control. What this means is minority ownership, as low as five per cent or even less, is able to control wealth many times its actual value if the remainder of stock is widely dispersed. This together with the concentration of power was Berle and Means' concern.

Burnham on the Managerial Revolution

The position of James Burnham, the real "managerial revolution" theorist, is quite different from that of Berle and Means. Burnham published *The Managerial Revolution* in 1941 and in it argued that a social revolution was occurring which would dramatically change the distribution of social power. One similarity with Berle and Means' position is Burnham's projection of the convergence of the communist and capitalist systems (71-72), but there the similarity ends. The managerial revolution theory holds that the dominant relationship to production is in a stage of transformation from capitalist to managerial. Burnham argues that what is happening "is a drive for social dominance, for power and privilege for the position of ruling class, by the social group or class of the *managers*" (71). This represented, for Burnham, a world wide movement. The economic basis of this relationship was "the state ownership of the major instruments of production. Within this framework there will be no direct property rights in the major instruments of production vested in individuals as individuals" (72).

Contrary to Burnham's projection, it appears that corporate capitalism, in spite of its evolution from entrepreneurial capitalism, has remained capitalist none the less. Ironically, the economic basis for Burnham's thesis has been destroyed by history, but the notion of a managerial revolution, now completely divorced from its original foundation, has remained and is still active in the ideology of managerial theory. With the assumption of capitalism neatly out of the way, Burnham proceeded to argue that "function" would become the touchstone of power and management would become dominant because its function was central to the "technical direction and coordination of the process of production" (77-80). Many years earlier Weber had examined the notion of function and rejected it as the basis for power, as he said: "If 'indispensability' were decisive, then where slave labor prevailed and where freemen usually abhor work as a dishonour, the 'indispensible' slaves ought to have held the positions of power" (1946:232).

For Burnham, the word "manager" was a shortened form for "production management" (80-81). He used the work of Berle and Means but maintained they had "not carried far enough for our purposes", the concept of managerial control. As suggested, far enough for Burnham meant that the state was the owner of the means of production and control had passed to "production management" (89). He introduced the term "technocracy" and argued that the "managerial society" was indeed a "technocracy" but rejected the term because it lacked the proper ideological dressing (203). In a 1959 preface to the book, Burnham denounced his original position as being "too rigid and doctrinaire" and was unable to salvage the main concept (vii), but this has not deterred others from adopting the notion of a managerial revolution and using it for ideological purposes.

Galbraith on the Technostructure

The most current major protagonist in the ownership-control debate is John K. Galbraith who, in 1967 in his widely acclaimed book, *The New Industrial State*, reintroduced the notion of "technocracy" as the basis of power for modern corporations. This was not the first time Galbraith had argued that capitalism had been made safe for common folk: in 1952 he had introduced the notion of "countervailing powers" to show that capitalism was finally safe but, alas, he rejected this in 1967 and replaced it with the "technostructure". Like Berle and Means, Galbraith argues that dominant corporations have become exceedingly powerful and, as his title suggests, have come to dominate modern "industrial" societies—he means, of course, capitalist societies. Unlike Berle and Means, the saving grace is not the hope that a technocracy will evolve but that it has already arrived and that power has now "passed into the organization" and is firmly lodged in the "technostructure". Like Burnham, Galbraith uses the indispensibility of function argument that "power goes to the factor which is hardest to obtain or hardest to replace" (76). In addition to the criticisms made of this position when taken by Burnham, other factors have become prevalent today.

It is at best tenuous to assume that a shortage of technicians exists today; they are produced at a faster rate than ever and there is even unemployment among this group, something unheard of earlier. This does not prevent Galbraith from arguing that knowledge and technical expertise are the "new factors of production". Given this, he maintains that power "extends from the leadership of the modern industrial enterprise down to just short of the labour force and embraces a large number of people and a large variety of talent" (69-70). Power has passed so far into the organization that it seems to embrace everyone short of the supervisor of the cleaning staff (or does it?). Galbraith's all-embracing term seems so broad as to be almost without bounds. He defines the "technostructure" as follows[8]

> it embraces chairman, president, those vice-presidents with im-portant staff or departmental responsibility, occupants of other major staff positions and, perhaps, division or department heads not included above. It includes, however, only a small proportion of those who, as participants, contribute information to group decisions. This latter group is very large; it extends from the most senior officials of the corporation to where it meets, at the outer perimeter, the white and blue collar workers whose function is to conform more or less mechanically to instruction or routine. It embraces all who bring specialized knowledge, talent or experi-ence to group decision-making. This, not the management, is the guiding intelligence—the brain—of the enterprise (82).

But can this conglomeration of people really be the key decision makers in a corporation? No, not even Galbraith would leave it at this. After defining the technostructure, he proceeds to divide this massive set of roles into its important parts. Sometimes owners become part of the technostructure and earn their influence in this way; "Others, through position on the Board of Directors, have power in the selection of management—in decision on those who make decisions" (94). Later he qualifies this again and, this time, rather than being in a position to "make decisions about decisions", as he contended earlier, "the Board of Directors is normally the passive instrument of the management" (159). It seems strange to argue that at one point the board controls management and at another point to reverse this, but Galbraith does this without qualification. He argues that on the "out-ermost circle" of the corporation is the "ordinary stockholder" (being of the position of *rentier*) but the "sizable stockholder", which he does not define, "who sits or is represented on the Board is different" (160).

Presumably the "sizable stockholder" is different because they are in a position of control, but Galbraith does not share this information with us. He proceeds to qualify his original position further by distinguishing levels of power with the terms "inner perimeter", "center" and even "inner circles" (162-163). Presumably, power and decision making are concentrated in this way, but again Galbraith does not tell his readers. It may well be that he is unable to distinguish between influence, authority and power. It may be that the technostructure (if that term is limited to technical expertise) has influence, the managers delegated authority and the board of directors power.

Failure to make important distinctions leaves Galbraith arguing in circles, albeit, with great style. For example, he uses the illustration of a toaster at least twice to show the "power" of the technostructure. He argues that a toaster "must emerge from the teams of scientists, engineers, designers, production experts, market researchers and sales executives. That is why power has shifted to, and into, the technostructure" (319). He had used the example of the toaster earlier (79) to conclude that "managers" did not decide about "important" decisions. Surely managers, directors and the technostructure all deal with the toaster on qualitatively different levels of concern and apply different criteria to evaluate these developments. As Fitch and Oppenheimer argue: "Galbraith's market researchers and engineers work according to the standards set by their sphere of production and distribution" (1970:1, 86), and it is the board which establishes the technostructure's sphere of production and criteria of success. It has the ability to remove the entire technostructure if it does not meet its standards. Power has not passed into the organization, it is still very much where it has been, with senior management and directors. It is necessary to distinguish the types of decisions being discussed. Obviously, technical decisions are made by technicians—that is what they are trained and paid to do—but policy decisions and decisions of importance about production and control are the prerogatives of the board. Failure to distinguish between the importance of a sphere of production and control over it results in making the same kind of mistake Weber warned about earlier. Slaves are a resource; they do not control.

There has been neither a "managerial revolution" nor "a shift of power into the organization", but a managerial reorganization with a change in relationship between the propertied strata and corporate executives.

The Dispersal of Ownership?

The previous discussion focused primarily on the "managerial revolution'' aspect of the ownership and control debate and only briefly on the question of ''dispersal of stock ownership''. The dispersal of ownership has not been as widespread as sometimes suggested; furthermore, the dispersal which has occurred has the effect of increasing the power of capitalists[9] rather than decreasing it. Family controlled firms, as will be demonstrated[10], still have a very prominent place among dominant corporations. Only such dominant firms and upper class families as the Burton's of Simpsons, the Molson's, Eaton's, Woodward's, Weston's, the Bronfman's of Seagrams or the Jeffery's of London Life among many others, need to be mentioned here to illustrate their importance. Within some corporations, however, ownership has become dispersed, primarily within the upper levels of income earners[11], but controlling ownership typically remains concentrated within a few hands. Dispersal of stockholdings which does occur is certainly not evenly spread throughout the population. Indeed, in 1968 only one tenth of all income earners owned as much as one share; the top one per cent owned 42 per cent and the top 10 per cent of income earners about three quarters of all shares (Statistics Canada, 1970: Tables 2 and 5).

Even the fact that only a tenth of income earners owns at least one share does not accurately reflect the actual concentrated control of stock ownership. Is, for example, a person who owns ten shares of Power Corporation the same as as a Paul E. Martin who owns 41,029, a Paul Britton Paine who owns 52,500 or, more especially, a Paul Desmarais or Jean Parisien who own 1,350,765 shares each? Most certainly not. There is a qualitative difference in their relationship to capital and the control they are able to exercise through their ownership. The dispersal of ownership which has occurred is primarily among the middle class whose members tend to have small portfolios valued in the thousands and not tens of millions of dollars. The small or ''typical'' stockholder is a *rentier* whose capital is mobilized as an investment for dividend and capital appreciation but not for control. They are able to sell their shares if they dislike a company's performance but controlling interests are able to get rid of managers and technocrats who do not meet their specifications.

Controlling ownership is usually represented by a block of about 10 per cent or more of the outstanding shares of a company if the remainder of the stock is dispersed. In this situation a block of shares is able to control corporations which exceed many times over the actual dollar value of their investment. One example of a corporation which uses minority holdings to control corporations with assets and revenues greatly exceeding the actual capital investment is Argus Corporation which has the following holdings in important corporations:

B. C. Forest Product	13.4%
Dominion Stores	24.7%
Domtar	16.9%
Hollinger Mines	20.3%
Massey-Ferguson	15.4%
Standard Broadcasting	47.9%

As long as the remaining stock holdings in these companies is dispersed, Argus Corporation controls the key block of voting shares which determines who will be elected to the boards of these companies and who the senior executives will be. Massey-Ferguson will be used as a case to illustrate the relationship between 15.4 per cent ownership and effective control of a corporation. Massey-Ferguson had a total of 18,195,450 outstanding common shares as of May 4, 1971, of which 7,023,204 were held outside Canada and 11,172,037 within. Of these, Argus held 2,850,000 representing a holding valued at about $57 million at the average market price of $20 per common share. This entitled Argus to place six directors from its board on the 18-position board of Massey, including A.A. Thornbrough who is simultaneously a member of the Argus board and president and chief executive officer of Massey. In addition to the corporate holdings of Argus, its board members also have private holdings in Massey which are quite valuable. For example, J.A. McDougald has 120,000 shares valued at $1.2 million while H.J. Carmichael's 30,000 shares are worth $600,000. Each holds a simultaneous position on Massey and Argus. Six of the board members of Massey together privately hold 299,165 shares valued at about $6 million, an average of one million dollars each. These holdings represent only 1.6 per cent of all Massey's outstanding shares but have considerable wealth as well as control value. It is known from the annual report to CALURA (Corporation and Labour Unions Returns Act Division of Statistics Canada) filed May 4, 1971 that aside from Argus, no other corporation or individual holds five per cent or more of Massey's shares. This means Argus' holding of a 15.4 per cent block represents effective control over appointments to the Massey board. If there was a proxy battle it would require a holding of well over $60 million to outvote the shares of Argus and the private holdings of the Argus board. This means with ownership of about $60 million, a corporation with assets valued at over $1 billion and annual sales of about the same value can be controlled. By using minority control, Argus is able to mobilize capital worth many times its actual ownership value.

Tawney's three-fold distinction of ownership rights is important here in terms of the types of claims made by capital. His first distinction concerning rights to interest will be dealt with later along with portfolio investment and financial corporations but the other two distinctions are made clear by the examples given above. The right to profits through dividends is important to about 10 per cent of income earners who own one or more shares but, for the majority, their claims on capital end there. For another group, much smaller than this, the claims of capital on ownership extend to control. The idea that ownership has separated from control is certainly correct for the former group but not for the latter. In fact, the existence of a relatively large number of small stockholders multiplies the power of the small group of large stock-holders by allowing them to control corporations with much smaller amounts of capital than would otherwise be possible.

There is one further aspect of the dispersal of ownership argument which is important, particularly for Canada, but which will only be briefly mentioned here and returned to later. This involves the fact that many corporations operating in Canada are subsidiaries of foreign controlled companies. Under these conditions, subsidiaries are by definition over 50 per cent controlled by the parent corporation thus concentrating ownership in these companies. From the Canadian pers-pective it makes little difference how the ownership of the parent company is dispersed; the fact is in terms of the Canadian operations, a very clearly defined set of people—the board of the parent company —have ownership and control rights over the Canadian subsidiary. This means, for example, that ownership is highly concentrated in about one half the 113 largest corporations operating in Canada simply because they are subsidiaries of foreign controlled multinationals.

Owners, Directors and Managers

Before concluding this section, it is worthwhile to bring together what has been said about owners, directors and managers, and clarify what is meant by the uppermost corporate positions. The board of directors is a synthesis between owners and managers. Typically, senior manage-ment (consisting of the president, vice-presidents and often treasurers, department heads, comptrollers, corporate lawyers and other officials), the chairman of the board and several outside directors make up the directorate of a corporation. Since board members are elected by shareholders it can be assumed, and in many cases demonstrated, that controlling ownership elects either itself or at least its representatives to the board. Moreover, since the board is charged with the responsibility of hiring and promoting senior management it can be argued it repre-sents the focal point of power within a corporation, mediating between controlling ownership and senior management.

As will be shown in later chapters, the outside directors of one dominant company tend to be executives of others[12]. For example,

Alfred Powis is president and chief executive officer of Noranda Mines and therefore a member of the senior executive of that company; simultaneously, however, he is chairman of British Columbia Forest Products as well as acting as an outside director on the Canadian Imperial Bank of Commerce, Gulf Oil of Canada, Sun Life Assurance and Simpsons Ltd. This practice is not exceptional between dominant corporations in Canada. It will be demonstrated later, for example, that there are 1,848 interlocked directorships between the 113 dominant corporations in Canada. Members of the economic elite also hold an additional 839 of 2,066 possible uppermost positions (or 41 per cent of these positions) in the next 175 largest corporations, many of which are executive posts. In other words, it is one thing to say a person is an outside director of a particular corporation and quite another to place that corporation within the entire network of large corporations where they are probably members of the executive of one or more other companies. Members of the corporate elite[13] tend to have several roles simultaneously and many are owners, managers and directors all at the same time. Consequently, by broadening the scope of study, the distinction between these three types tends to lose much of its meaning.

The process identified as "collegiality" by Max Weber in his *Theory of Social and Economic Organization* captures very well the type of decision making processes and forums developed by the corporate elite. Weber argues that "established groups" tend to form "collegial bodies" as forums where a "process of adjustment" can be worked out over "conflicts of interest by compromise" (1947:396). This describes the way boards of directors (and a number of other elite forums) are used by members of the elite to work out and arrive at common understandings and agreements. Unlike the days of entrepreneurial capitalism and rugged individualism where great captains of industry worked on their own, under corporate capitalism the individual has given way to collegial decision making and undertakings. This does not mean the process has become any more democratic, as Weber astutely notes, "Collegiality is in no sense specifically 'democratic' . . . [while collegial bodies] have tended to enforce strict equality within the privileged group they have tended to set up and maintain collegial bodies to supervise or even to take over power" (398). Collegiality is a practice which reinforces existing power arrangements rather than one which democratizes decision making; it does, however, tend to create an equality within the group through a system of mutual reinforcements which makes the overall group more powerful than its individual members. Extensive interlocking between corporations by members of the corporate elite thus has the effect of reinforcing their rule and creating a community of interest between elites rather than the competitive image so frequently portrayed in dominant ideologies. In the following section the phenomenon of corporate power will be examined, both as it is exercised within corporations as well as between them and the wider social system.

IV. Exercising Corporate Power

Corporations are simply structures organized for particular purposes, their prime objective being the appropriation of surplus for the private intentions of the people who control them. The apparent autonomy of corporations has led some to mistakenly attribute to them a quality they do not have; Hobsbawm, for example, says that "Increasingly the real members of the ruling class today are not so much real persons as organizations" (1971:19), and Baran and Sweezy say that "The real capitalist today is not the individual businessman but the corporation" (1966:43). In reacting to the change from entrepreneurial capitalism, dominated by captains of industry, to corporate capitalism, where control is collegial, these authors have over-reacted and reified corporations by abstracting them from their class base and from the people who are still very much in command of them. Organization in general, and corporations in particular, do not have objectives other than those instilled in them by people[14]. They are legal devices created to accomplish certain ends.

Power was defined earlier as the capacity to mobilize resources such as capital, wealth, personnel, knowledge, technology, ideology or military force, in the favour and to the advantage of those making allocative decisions. This definition clearly distinguishes between the base of power as resources organized in particular ways and the exercise of power by those who control these organized resources. Power, then, refers to decision making with consequence; the broader the consequence the more extensive the scope of power. Moreover, at least three dimensions of power are important to distinguish: they involve, firstly, the *structure* of decision making, by which is meant the way power is organized in society in terms of its institutional configurations; secondly, *positions* of power, meaning the way control is exercised within organizations through well established posts which have the capacity to make decisions which others adhere to; finally, the *process* of decision making which refers to information channels and people who can affect those in power and the way those in power can insure that policies they set are adhered to. The most powerful people are those in decision making positions within those organizations which have the widest scope and are able to insure that their policies are carried out.

In liberal-democracies the organizations which most effectively structure resources in the economy are corporations[15]. Those in control of corporations make decisions about the expansion of the economy, its direction, scope and level of technology. With these decisions they determine rates of employment and the types of occupations that will exist in a society[16].

Weber's analysis of bureaucracies applies well to the way corporations are controlled. He argues that those in control

> have the following principal functions: (a) control and possibly a subsequent test of adherence to rules; (b) a monopoly of creation of the rules which govern the action of officials completely, or at least of those which define the limits of their independent authority; (c) above all a monopoly of the granting of the means which are necessary for the administrative function (1947:392).

Weber also argues that bureaucracy "is a power instrument of the first order—for the one who controls the bureaucratic apparatus" (1946:22). Sociological analysis of bureaucracy has relied a great deal on Weber's work but there has been little acknowledgement of statements such as this which place bureaucracy in its social context. Bureaucracy is more than a set of roles and functions; it is a base for action and performs this task most effectively. Besides concentrating power, bureaucracies are mechanisms for control, and bureaucracy itself is a structure based on control. The sets of relationships established in a bureaucracy can be used for a variety of purposes but the direction of that action is determined by policies or goals established and injected by people who direct it.

Business and Management

Tawney has drawn the distinction between "Business" and "Management" as "two compartments . . .within the same economic system". Under corporate capitalism, he argues, these tend to become separate.

> The technical and managerial staff of industry is, of course, as amenable as other men to economic incentives. But their special work is production, not finance; and, provided they are not smarting under a sense of economic injustice, they want, like most workmen, to "see the job done properly". The businessmen who ultimately control industry are concerned with the promotion and capitalization of companies, with competitive selling and advertisement of wares, the control of markets, the securing of special advantages, and the arrangement of pools, combines and monopolies. They are preoccupied, in fact, with financial results,

and are interested in the actual making of goods only in so far as financial results accrue from it (1920:170-171).

As shown earlier in the discussion of Galbraith's "technostructure", the way senior management and directors approach the goals of a corporation are qualitatively different from that of lower level management and technicians. It is important to understand that the latter are accountable to the former.

When tracing accountability within corporations to the group which is accountable to itself, the stopping point is the board of directors and major stockholders. Katz and Kahn refer to this structure as a "set of dyadic power relationships" (1966:216) wherein each level is supervised and directed by a level above it. This is correct for every level except the uppermost and it is therefore important to distinguish between executive leadership represented by the administrative side of the corporation and corporate power which represents control and policy-setting aspects. These are related but distinct components of corporate control: administration is the carrying out of decisions which have been made, but administration is established, the personnel selected and accountability demanded by those in power.

Some have argued the process of decentralization circumvents traditional authority structures, but the case of General Motors —considered by many to be a model of decentralized operations —illustrates otherwise (Harbison & Myers, 1959:43f). The structure involved is what G.M. describes as "Decentralized operations and responsibilities with co-ordinated control" (*Fortune*, 1956:145-146). Neufeld provides an illustration from a Canadian case of decentralization in a directive from Massey-Ferguson's executive:

> The organizational structure that best serves total corporate interests will be a blend of decentralized and centralized management. Marketing and manufacturing activities together with some supporting service functions, should be organized in a way that would bring them as close as possible to the local market situation. On the other hand, the activities that determine the long-range character of the Company—such as control of product line, facilities, and money, and planning the strategy of reacting to changes in the patterns of international trade—should be handled on a centralized basis (1969:227).

Decentralization is a management technique, not a reallocation of power. The division of technical, management and control levels remain intact in each of the above cases. Policy making is still at the top and policy represents what is deemed "valued" by the corporation. As

Blau and Scott contend: "each official in the hierarchy has his value premises supplied by his superior"; and following this procedure, organization serves to "limit the scope of the decisions that each member must make" (1962:36-38). This is a key point in corporate structures. The range of discretion is determined by policy established at the top, be this a wide or narrow range; discretion is delegated and established but accountability maintained.

Decision Making Processes

Corporate decision making focuses on policy making and involves three elements: the ability to initiate decisions, approve recommendations and coordinate the corporation's activities with the objectives of those in control. These are the prerogatives of the board of directors and the greater the resources which are, or can be, mobilized by the decision making process, the greater their power. To the extent that power derives from the decision making process, it is organized. This distinguishes, for example, boards of directors from consumers with respect to economic power. Although consumers can *influence* decision making, the board actually makes decisions and need only take into account, more or less, consumer demands as part of their decision. This points out the importance of distinguishing between being present in the arena where decisions are made and exercising outside influence. Decision makers maintain control—this is what Mills meant when he spoke of the "institutional base" of power (1956:10-11).

It is structure which defines channels of communication, action and division of labour but it is decisions which activate the structure. As Berle and Means suggest: "At the very pinnacle of the hierarchy of organization in a great corporation, there alone, can individual initiative have a measure of free play" (1968:307). At every other level the nature and destiny of activities are subject to higher levels of control. "The consequences of bureaucracy depend therefore, upon the direction which the powers using the apparatus give to it" (Weber, 1946:230). Mills puts it even more forcibly:

> The ends of men are often merely hopes, but means are facts within some men's control. That is why all means of power tend to become ends to an elite that is in command of them (1956:23).

Social scientists tend to lose sight of the fact that organizations are a means, an apparatus of power, designed to accomplish tasks. Consequently they become reified and abstracted from their social settings. Decision making is the mechanism which mobilizes corporations; it is the ability to cause responses to values interjected at the top. In other words, policy decisions commit corporations to a course of action. This is clearly contrary to Galbraith's notion of the technostructure where "power passes into the organization" (1967:80): the technostructure represents administrative and technical authority but not policy making power. In the hierarchy of modern corporations, top positions maintain control over all echelons below them. In terms of three dimensions of decision making outlined by Katz and Kahn: "the level of generality of abstraction of the decision; the amount of internal and external organizational space affected by the decision; and the length of time for which the decision will hold" (1966:259), the technostructure has very limited decision making powers indeed—it is the board of directors which best fits the characteristics of these criteria. Again the case of Massey-Ferguson serves as an illustration:

> Massey-Ferguson has accepted the principle that operations units should enjoy maximum responsibility and authority and that exceptions to this should be defined and understood. Massey-Ferguson Limited, the parent company, has been transformed into a holding company and its executives constitute the corporate group. The North American operations unit has the same relationship with the corporate or parent company executives as do operations units in the rest of the world. True, corporate executives retain some detailed line responsibilities and, in emergency cases, temporarily assume others in individual operations units. But generally their role is to examine and eventually approve annual plans of operations units, to examine performance against plans, and to plan long-term strategy for the continuing development of the company's world-wide operations (Neufeld, 1969:389-390).

"Concrete decisions" generally involve formation of goals, procedures to achieve these goals, selection of key personnel and financial control. Desirable levels of profit returns are set, investment decisions made and entrepreneurial action is undertaken by the top levels. Generally it can therefore be said that the board is engaged in the allocation of values and the distribution of valued resources.

In summary, the corporate elite may think they are being "good corporate citizens"—for the most part, within the assumptions of corporate capitalism, they are—but decisions are still being made by a select few within the corporation and these decisions are based on their view of what the world is and should be. The corporate elite operate from their own social perspectives and backgrounds and monopolize key economic decisions. They reflect the selection process by which they come to have access to the positions of command and are able to allocate vast resources through the corporate mechanisms they control.

And, of course, one of the prerogatives of power holders is to deny that they have power. Earle McLaughlin, chairman and president of the Royal Bank, maintains that:

> Power is something political. What we have is *responsibility* . . . I don't believe that I have any power at all, though I do have a lot of responsibility. I'm frightened of losing business. Being a banker you can't exercise any power; all you can do is fulfill the responsibility you feel to your depositors, shareholders, staff and the public at large (quoted by Newman with emphasis in original, 1972a:22-24).

Despite McLaughlin's "feeling" about his power, he remains one of the most powerful men in the Canadian corporate world: he is chairman and president of the Royal Bank, Canada's largest bank, and also sits on the board of Power Corporation, Genstar Ltd., Metropolitan Life Insurance, the Algoma Steel Corporation, Canadian Pacific and is on the board of the largest corporation in the world, General Motors Corporation (Detroit). To deny that he has power is ideology— ideology which camouflages the reality of his power.

Managers or Directors?

There has recently been a study of managers in Canada by William Daly who modeled his study after the Warner and Abegglen approach used in *Occupational Mobility in American Business and Industry* (1955). Daly, using a collage of criteria for selecting them, argued that 332 corporations represented the largest corporations operating in Canada. He then used the 1967 *Directory of Directors* to select the three "top" managers from these firms, arriving at a total of 978 to whom he mailed questionnaires, receiving usable returns from just under half. He found that 71 per cent of these managers were born in Canada with the proportion from the U.S. accounting for about 16 per cent (1972:95). Two findings which are of interest from this study are that by separating the presidents and chairmen of the companies from whom he received returns, 11.8 per cent had relatives as "influential connections in the present firm", 13.7 per cent had friends and 17.1 per cent had business associates in their present firms before they entered them (76). Another is the relatively high class origins of this group. "Over 70% of the respondents came from managerial or professional origins. In relation to population, [sic] he was over eight times as likely to have a father in the managerial or owner classification of the census and almost four and a half times one from a professional occupation" (91).

Daly's thesis is concerned with what he calls an "occupational elite" (1), the senior managers from 332 corporations.[17] He did not take into account the boards of directors of the corporations he studies, for they would not be an "occupational elite" but an elite of decision makers. His very weak defence of this decision refers to John Porter's earlier work, stating that "His [Porter's] original study of directors tended to overlook the influence of full-time company officials in determining company policy. In his later book he recognized the concentration of control in the hands of management" (15-16). Daly footnotes at this point, a reference to Porter's *The Vertical Mosaic* (1965:252) but does not quote from Porter. An examination of what Porter says on this page suggests why Daly does not provide a quotation—Porter states very emphatically here exactly the opposite to what Daly says he does:

> The notion that directors are a kind of window dressing arranged by management follows from the theory of management control. Whether or not this situation applies to American industry as a consequence of the separation of ownership and control is not our concern here. It is doubtful, however, that it satisfactorily describes Canadian corporate power. *It would be quite wrong to select a group of senior managers of Canadian corporations and describe them as the economic elite* (emphasis added).

It is to the boards of directors which Daly mistakenly ignored that attention will be turned.

The central concept related to the board of directors' function is that of corporate control; the board is the formalized means of establishing power relations. As stock ownership became widely dispersed, major owners were forced to formalize their control through this body[18].

In Canada John Porter has shown "that the relationship between investors, directors, and managers in the structure of power is a very close one" (1965:242). As has been argued, these divisions are closely linked socially and economically to the structure of corporate capitalism. Each relates to the corporation and derives its power from this relationship. Although it is the office or corporate position which is the base of power, by holding these positions power becomes translated to collegial groups of individuals and to the social class which serves as the recruiting base to fill these positions. As Parkin notes, the concept of power is important to stratification studies but, as earlier sections have shown, "we have to specify what it is that accounts for variations in men's ability to stake successful claims to rewards" (1971:20). In Canada, the ability to rise to positions of power is primarily a class phenomenon. When boards are examined it should be remembered that they are a legal device for class power and not isolated positions distinct from social class relationships.

Just as it is important to relate directors to social class, it is equally important to relate them to stockholders, managers and other institutions (Porter, 1965:22). In light of the ideological tendency to personify the corporation by giving it a "soul" or a "conscience", it is important to keep the structure of the corporation distinct from the real personalities which activate this structure. The corporate elite "are not merely 'bureaucrats': they command bureaucracies" (Mills, 1956:286). This point is made forcibly by E. Palmer when he asserts that "a corporation does not control its directors, rather the directors control it" (1967:367).

All this boils down to a rather simple, though exceedingly important point: "Directors control the resources of corporations through particular legal instruments which give them the right to do so" (Porter, 1965:229).

The Relative Power of Corporations

In concluding this section one final aspect of corporate power should be discussed—the distinction between corporations based on their relative size. One of the dominant social forces operating today is the trend toward increased consolidation of social activities into large-scale organizations. In the economy this is represented in the centralizing tendencies of accumulation and concentration which slowly reduce each major economic sector to a few dominant companies. Classical definitions of firms as small autonomous units relating on the market place and engaged in some kind of dynamic equilibrium guided by an "invisible hand" are opposed by more recent analysis which takes into account financial and corporate blocks that, rather than being controlled by the market, control it (Baran & Sweezy, 1966; Galbraith, 1967, 1973)

There are roughly three levels operating in the economy: those "dominant" corporations powerful enough to establish the "tone" and direction of particular segments of the economy and together the general direction of the entire economy; the "middle range" economic powers which conform to the "tone" established by the dominants but which generally benefit from doing so and are not powerful enough to contradict the direction of the dominants; those who are affected by the policies and direction of each of the above, like small businessmen and consumers[19]. For this reason it is appropriate to apply what Juran has called the "Pareto principle", meaning the "principle of separating the vital few from the trivial many" (1964:44). It is reasonable to separate dominant corporations for purposes of analysis since they have a qualitatively different effect than do others. Some of the largest corporations, for example, wield more power than do some nation states (Child, 1969:2).

Berle and Means recognized that "competition is no longer among the many. And competition among the few is a radically different thing" (1968:xxxiv). The centripetal force of concentration has been operating for at least the past 75 years and has had a definite impact on the relationsip between corporations in terms of competition and their relationship to the market. Some prefer to characterize a concentrated economy as a "duopoly" (Berle & Means, 1968:45), others as "oligopoly" (Galbraith, 1967:195) and still others as "monopoly" (Brady, 1943:259; Aaronovitch, 1955:12; Baran & Sweezy, 1966:6). Regardless of the term selected, each refers to what Perroux calls the "domination effect" which means that a "firm can alter, for its own benefit the structure of competitive or allied firms" (1971:56-61). Dominant firms then, are those which can exercise the "domination effect".

Concentration establishes a few dominant corporations with the ability to control the resources of the economy—this is what is meant by economic power. Accumulation and concentration, as principles involved in the power of capital, are processes Marx emphasized throughout *Capital* (1967:I, 625; II, 233; III, 264). But whether this is "inherent" in corporate capitalism or "inevitable" is not at issue; the fact is, the history of corporate capitalism is to concentrate. Why this is so relates to the advantages giant corporations have over others —including an abundance of capital with access to credit, experienced management, a large and effective sales apparatus, and large research and development resources and facilities.

V. Canada's Economic Boundaries

Before finally bringing the arguments presented thus far into a conceptual framework which will be used to analyse the development, structure and composition of the Canadian corporate elite, this section will examine some issues regarding the boundaries of Canada's economic system.

The issue of boundaries is crucial to a study of the Canadian economy as it exists and as it has developed. Canada's economic fate has been embedded in the economy of the North Atlantic triangle. This results in a discontinuity between the political system and the economic system in the sense that they do not match: the parameters of the economic system of which Canada is currently a part extends into the continental context (North America) and in some cases beyond, but the parameters of the political system are set and have historical continuity with distinct state jurisdiction. To the extent the state and economic systems are necessarily tied together, then there are contradictory parameters.

It is agreed that the Canadian corporate elite is committed to the capitalist mode of production and that international movements of capital are a logical extension of this commitment. Porter's argument is that "Because the nationalities of the actors in the system have no place in the instrumental norms of capitalism it is difficult to see how nationality affects the behavior of those who govern a capitalist economy" (1965:269-270). However—and here there is a departure from Porter—while it is correct to maintain there is basic agreement on the rules of capitalism and its desirability by the Canadian corporate elite, there are some important differences between members of the Canadian corporate elite and others which must be taken into account. This difference hinges on the issue of "territory". The strength of Canadian capitalists, today and historically, lies in the finance, transportation and utilities sectors of the economy. This is their "turf" and where their greatest strength lies both nationally and internationally. This is true for Canadian banks, life insurance companies and utilities such as Brascan. It is out of their powerful national base in these sectors of the economy that most of the Canadian corporate elite operates. This is evident, for example, in the reaction and subsequent legislation in the mid-1960's when foreign firms attempted to expand their takeovers of insurance companies and were prevented from doing so. One of the best illustrations is the Mercantile Bank affair and the confrontation between Walter Gordon, then Minister of Finance and a solid member of the traditional upper class, and J.S. Rockefeller of the First National City Bank (Citibank). Citibank took over the Mercantile Bank from a Dutch group in 1963 through a legislative loop-hole. The financial elite quickly reacted and insured that Citibank would reduce its holdings to 10 per cent and be restricted in its growth[20]. Foreign control is greatest in the surplus creating sectors of manufacturing and resources but Canadian control is dominant in the "service" sectors and areas of circulation such as finance, utilities and trade.

It is within this context that the replication in Canada of the Big Three U.S. automakers and the international oil concentration should be analysed. Only in this way can the resistance to moves into the "turf" of Canadian capitalists in finance, transportation and utilities be understood while foreign control is encouraged in other sectors. It is from their carefully guarded base of operation that the Canadian corporate elite is able to enter into an alliance with foreign capitalists in other sectors.

This issue of boundaries will be a particularly important theme throughout the following chapters on Canada's economic development and current structure. For the present, it is sufficient to argue that the nation-state is a reasonable unit of analysis, even if it does not contain the entire economic system, simply for political reasons if no other. Nations are arrived at after long and bitter struggles, negotiations and planning, and they also have historical continuity. To say nation-states are becoming obsolescent or that one state is subservient to another does not resolve the problems of people living within these political units. Although it will be emphatically argued in subsequent chapters that Canada's economic system is not separate or detached from a wider capitalist system, it is none the less valuable to examine Canada's place within the wider system and analyse the implications of this for Canadians. For now it is sufficient to note that the issue of whether Canada is "dominated" by U.S. capitalists or in a "junior partnership" with them is at least problematic and much more complex than these simple assertions suggest. While this is probably correct for what will later be called the comprador elite, it does not accurately describe the traditional indigenous elite[21]. The indigenous elite is better understood as being in an alliance with foreign capital as a full partner resulting from an historical divison of labour. The difference between these two ways of understanding the impact of foreign investment has important implications for the study of Canadian society and will be elaborated elsewhere.

In conclusion, the five initial issues and themes important to the study of corporate capitalism are the distinction between condition and opportunity, the relationship between class and elites, the debate between ownership and control, the exercise of corporate power and finally, the question of economic boundaries. These issues, plus several others, will now be integrated into a conceptual framework useful for analysing the relationship between capital, corporations, classes and elites.

From Capital to Elites: An Analytical Framework

It is necessary to develop an analytical and conceptual framework encompassing various social processes and relating them to patterns of economic power in Canada. This will involve beginning with capital formations and economic processes and relating these to various types of organizations and generally to the social strucutre. This will make possible an examination of patterns of stratification and structures of decision making. For reasons already specified, it will also be important to introduce the issues of boundaries into the analysis. And resources, technology and ecological considerations are also important because of the constraints or advantages they impose. Finally, the historical dimension is important since it includes changes involved in the above considerations.

Capital Formations and Economic Processes

Two key processes involved in capitalism are concentration and accumulation; they refer to the tendency of capital to attract more capital and concentrate in fewer and larger units, thereby centralizing the means of production. Some implications of these processes have already been examined in the analysis of opportunity and condition. Another important distinction is between merchant, financial and industrial capital[22]. Naylor maintains the following:

> Finance [sic] capital emerges not from industrial capital, as is usually supposed, but from merchant capital, through the pooling of merchants' resources and their development of a banking structure, and through the earnings of the entrepôt trade. Like merchant capital, finance capital is a low-risk type of venture; but, unlike merchant capital, it is long-term (1972:13).

This encompasses Marx's position regarding the evolutionary link between merchant and financial capital (1967:III, 267-337). In Canada the transition from merchant to financial capital will become apparent in the movement from mercantile-based fishing and fur trading activities to investment houses, banks and insurance companies. The type of investment favoured by financial capital, stable and long-term, will be evident with the canal and railway booms undertaken by Canadian mercantile elites.

Financial capital is linked with portfolio investment and industrial capital with direct investment. The former gains returns through interest while the latter generates its surplus through dividends. Another way of making this distinction is by identifying commercial and industrial activities. Commercialism encompasses both merchant and financial capital since each involves a ''go-between'' relationship rather than one based on production[23]. In this sense, merchant and financial capital are different levels of development of commercialism with merchants' capital being based in trade where the merchant acts as ''middle-man'' in distribution, while financial capital institutionalizes these functions into a developed credit system of banking and other long-term financial institutions. Industrialism represents direct and long-term investment in the means of production; that is, it is engaged in the process of transforming resources by using the labour-power of others.

Direct and portfolio investment are related to different economic processes and forms of control. Portfolio capital is interest bearing capital which is loaned and can be repaid by using earnings from investment; it is, therefore, "self-liquidating". Direct investment is capital which controls the means of production, whether industrial or resource-based. Unlike portfolio investment, direct investment tends to accumulate and expand, maintaining control while repaying the owner with dividends rather than interest. While portfolio investment can be repaid, direct investment remains established unless it becomes bankrupt, repatriated, confiscated or natural resources become exhausted. Although it is important to maintain the distinction, the control associated with portfolio investment should not be minimized because of the "service" costs associated with repaying debts. This is particularly true when interest rates are high and return on investment low. In addition, those who own portfolio capital have discretion over who they will loan it to, under what conditions and at what interest rates, and ultimately they also have the power to recall loans.

Historically, there has been a dramatic shift in the relative prevalence of these two types of capital. It has been calculated that "in 1914 ninety per cent of all international capital movements took the form of portfolio investment by individuals and financial institutions, whereas today seventy-five per cent of the capital outflows of the leading industrialised nations are in the form of direct investment by companies" (Tugendhat, 1972:17). This reflects an historical shift from financial to industrial capital in international capital flows. Also reflected is a change from the U.K. as the dominant exporter of portfolio capital to the U.S. as the dominant exporter of direct investment, particularly following the Second World War.

Social Structures and Organization

Organizational forms are intimately related to the type of capital employed and organizational structures reflect the capital base they are constructed upon. While portfolio investment is 'loaned' to organizations or individuals for reinvestment, direct investment involves a total "package" of capital, management and technology. Foreign direct investment has as its primary *modus operendi* the multinational corporation, operating through branch plant subsidiaries or affiliates (notable Canadian exceptions being United States equity control of International Nickel and Alcan). For example, expressed in terms of direct investment abroad by Canadian firms for 1969, 92.5 per cent was carried through subsidiaries, five per cent through affiliates and 2.5 per cent through unincorporated branches (Information Canada, 1971:82). Direct investment illustrates preference for control over investment within the context of corporate structures, rather than using the 'market' as a mechanism for buying and selling raw materials and industrial goods, since it allows vertical and horizontal integration within one corporate structure. Multinational corporations arose out of foreign direct investment but, as the United Kingdom experience illustrates, it does not necessarily follow that multinationals are the inevitable consequence of foreign investment, and, in fact, there is a choice involved in the form of organization selected and type of capital employment.

As suggested, capital formations have a direct bearing on the organization of production; an additional factor is the economic sector within which investment occurs. It is important to distinguish these economic sectors; for example, within Canada distinctions must be made between resource, industry and finance (put another way, between primary, secondary and tertiary sectors). By making these distinctions it is possible to analyse degrees of development within each sector. It is possible that the finance or tertiary sector of the Canadian economy is, and has been historically, overdeveloped by enjoying a powerful position within Canada and with its relationship to outside powers. An overdeveloped financial structure does not indicate that industrial or resource sectors are developed to the same extent—indeed, the Canadian case indicates otherwise.

Elites and Decision Making

The way production is organized provides the structure within which economic decision making occurs. The exercise of economic power involves access to organizations through which power can be realized; in liberal-democracies this means control over the decision making apparatus of dominant corporations. It is through organizational structures, and the distribution of power within and between these organizations, that economic dimensions of stratification become operative. Elite models base their analysis on dominant positions within dominant institutions to focus on the upper levels of stratification. Elite studies are, therefore, concerned with the institutional structure of society and questions related to class recruitment to positions of power.

From the perspective of the nation being studied, it is important to distinguish between national or *indigenous elites* who may operate primarily within the particular nation or be based in the nation but operate internationally through multinational corporations, satellite or *comprador elites* who operate branch plants of foreign multinational corporations and may be either nationals or imports from the headquarters and, finally, the foreign or *parasite elites* who are the heads of multinational corporations outside the host country. Each is related in the sense of being allied or competitive with one another. Moreover, they involve patterns of relationships between corporations and the internal workings of corporations. This latter aspect has received much less emphasis than has the former yet it is a significant dimension of analysis, particularly from the perspective of an interest in stratification. For example, comprador elites are the counterpart of parasite elites[24]: comprador elites are top ranking managers and directors of branch plants who follow the policies of parasite elites based in the parent corporations. Since structures involve relationships, they change over time and it is important to analyse these structural changes. This is suggested, for example, in the transition from charter companies to small-scale entrepreneurial firms, to joint-stock companies of a national scale, to modern multinational corporations.

For present considerations, it will be important to distinguish between particular bases of power and the nations in which they originate. Ideally, this involves not only corporate but other bases of power as well (including, for example, military, political and religious bases), but the parameters of this study are limited to corporate power with only peripheral reference to the others. It is argued that international dimensions of power are particularly relevant to the study of relations between, and comparison of, the United Kingdom, the United States and Canada, since imperial linkages between these areas have important implications for their internal stratification structures.

One of the central points of elite studies is the assertion that power "is exercised, not so much by individuals as by collectives" (Porter, 1955:504). This clearly forms the link between social structure and social stratification. Previous analysis has shown social class to be very much a hereditary phenomenon—particularly related to inherited wealth and accumulated advantage such as social conditioning, opened avenues, access to education and skills, etc. Just as an analysis of social class position requires understanding career patterns and social origins, so an analysis of social class and power on a macro-level requires analysis of the "career" of the social structure as it affects the development of current structures of inequality.

Boundaries (Spatial Dimension)

Boundaries refer to the parameters under consideration and what can be thought of as representing a "system" for analysis. For example, the parameters for the following discussion include the North Atlantic triangle since this represents the economic system of which Canada is, and has been, a part. The pulls between the continental and Atlantic economies in terms of economic and political orientations have represented two of the most powerful social forces interacting throughout Canada's history. Whether in terms of the United Kingdom or the United States, Canada's economy has been international, and this provides the minimum frame of reference for an analysis of social change and economic development. It is within this context that the hinterland/metropolis, center/periphery or development of under-development models[25] prove useful. The traditional focus on staples provides a helpful transition into these models. The staples theory includes an assumption that "staple exports are the leading sector of the economy and set the pace for economic growth" (Watkins, 1967:53). More fundamentally, it is a theory of "imperial relationships"; as Watkins argues, "What Innis was talking about is areas where the growth process is led by primary exports and the dominant elite within the colony is committed to exports" (1970a:40). As the nature of the export changes, so will the relationship of capital, social structure and stratification. Old staples were oriented toward merchant capital, e.g. fish, furs and timber, with short-term, high-turnover of capital; but new staples require more direct investment, e.g., pulp and paper, minerals, gas and oil, hydro, etc. This change in the nature of staples and type of capital and organizational requirements is reflected in the different relationship Canada formed with the United States as opposed to the United Kingdom. It also establishes the central proposition of the metropolis/hinterland model; that is, an "imperial relationship". As Archibald suggests, "The essence of the satellite-hinterland model is concerned with the development of the western economy as a total system" (1971:111). The hinterland/metropolis, center/periphery and satellite/metropolis dichotomies each represent a similar relationship, while the development of under-development model, although similar, builds in an emphasis on the relationship as a form of exploitation. Each model is based on relationships of power and class with each including a conflict of interest between the two analytical poles. Naylor posits that "while the internal dialectics of class and of capital accumulation may determine the nature of metropolitan expansion, the social structure and the structure of capital in the hinterland cannot be regarded as independent of the metropole. On the contrary, internal changes in the metropole are the immediate causes of socio-economic reorganization in the hinterland" (1972:2). It becomes necessary when dealing with imperial relationships to examine patterns of stratification and the form of capital structure in the center as well as the periphery. These relationships are of historical concern in Canada and remain a central issue in the current era of multinational corporations.

Resources, Technology and Ecology

Resources refer to the particular natural resources an area has at its disposal; for example, in Canada fish, fur, timber, oil, minerals and hydro power. These are important resources and, as suggested previously, the nature of the staple dictates to some extent the form of organization used to extract the staple. Technology refers to the ability to exploit resources and the skills required to accomplish this task. Technology will affect the kinds of resources that can be exploited, the type of organizations possible for conducting exploitation and, to some extent, the level of demand for resources; for example, oil and gas related to heating and automobiles or pulp and paper related to mass printing techniques. Ecology represents a slightly different dimension as it refers to the natural advantages or disadvantages a particular area offers; for example, the waterways of the St. Lawrence or the climate and soil of the Prairies. These dimensions are more frequently taken for granted in analysis than integrated because they represent limiting or advantage-producing contexts for other points of analysis. However, technology in particular can be seen as a social force which enhances particular means of production and influences the development of new forms of organization. It is apparent, for example, that multinational corporations are enhanced in their potential scope of operation by developments of technology, particularly in transportation and communication. Economic control of existing technology and facilities to develop new technology are important aspects of power; historically the technology required for industrialization in Canada has often been controlled by the United States and United Kingdom.

Technology has a direct impact on the types of organizations selected to undertake production but, like raw materials, technology is property and, as such, is controlled as capital and reinforced by the state through devices such as patents and copyrights. Advanced technology provides potential for development but, as private capital, it provides this opportunity only to those who own and can afford to employ it. The relationship between technology and multinational corporations is of particular importance since control of technology has encouraged and enhanced the tendency toward concentration of capital and allowed the development of integrated world-wide systems. For example, technology allows for enormous control of operations beyond a scope previously possible, as in the case of companies like Shell and Standard Oil which have installed computer networks for the control of their wide-ranging operations (Turner, 1970:7). Another instance is rapid transportation such as air travel: Keegan's study of 13 multinationals reveals that their executives averaged travel budgets of $10,000 per year with some running as high as $25,000 (1968:35-41). These developments dramatically enhance the modern multinational's position in terms of world-wide control of their operations, and represents an important feature not present during earlier imperialism.

Historical Framework (Temporal Parameters)

This refers to the historical interaction of economic processes, social structure, patterns of social stratification and spatial parameters within the limiting or advantage producing context of particular resources, technology and ecology. In the following chapters there is an attempt to integrate each of these levels into an analysis of historical process rather than trap history in events or personalities. An understanding of the current configuration of Canadian corporate institutions and the class base of these institutions requires an analysis of social forces and institutions which shaped the class structure of previous periods. Since a theory of social change is a theory about historical process, concern here is with social forces which operate at particular periods and lead to changes in the type of society. Sociological analysis can provide an examination of contemporary social structure and process but, without an historical dimension it is at a loss to provide analysis of social change.

This chapter has attempted to set out a series of themes and issues important to the study of corporate capitalism generally and particularly as it relates to Canada. The main focus has been on the way changes in the structure of the economy affect social mobility. The concepts social class and elite are complimentary approaches to a critical study of inequality in liberal-democracies. In the economic domain each is related to the institution of private property which sustains the basis upon which the economic structure is built and provides a major means for transmitting privilege and power. As this illustrates, to attempt an analysis of social mobility without understanding the structures within which this occurs and institutions which support it, tends to by-pass many of the crucial issues upon which unequal opportunities are based. Far too often sociological analysis has failed to place the process of inequality within the context of the structures which create and sustain it. The rest of the book will show that as long as economic power is allowed to remain in its present concentrated state, there appears to be no hope for equality of opportunity or equality of condition in Canada.

Notes

[1]This discussion is drawn in part from a paper entitled, "The Changing Structure of the Canadian Economy" which I have published in the *Canadian Review of Sociology and Anthropology*, Special Issue: Aspects of Canadian Society (1974a).

[2]For an excellent discussion of these types of changes in the class structure, see Leo Johnson's, "The development of class in Canada in the twentieth century" (1972).

[3]For an interesting and informative satirical examination of meritocracy, see Michael Young's, *The Rise of the Meritocracy* (1958).

[4]Elite theory is *not* based on a notion of history-making as either conspiracy or corruption. This is not to say these do not exist but they are not inimical to their basis of power and decision making. Rather, elite theory analyses the system within the "rules of the game" accepted as legitimate by the elite (legitimate, of course, because the elite generally make the rules).

[5]This problem of using educational attainment as a proxy for class of origin will be returned to in Chapter Five.

[6]Much of the following section is drawn from my paper, "Inequality of Access: Characteristics of the Canadian Corporate Elite," which appears in the *Canadian Review of Sociology and Anthropology*, Volume 12, Number 1.

[7]To the extent that mobility does occur and it is "selected mobility" (that is, those in control are able to "sift out" those they wish), so rule is reinforced rather than threatened. Marx observed that "The more a ruling class is able to assimilate the foremost minds of a ruled class, the more stable and dangerous becomes its rule" (1967: III, 601). The crucial element here is "assimilation" since it implies the absorption of those outside the ruling order without transforming the basic character and purpose of rule itself. Moreover, this process reinforces the strength of those in command and engulfs the ambitious outside existing power bases.

[8]In his most recent book, *Economics and the Public Purpose*, Galbraith defines the technostructure much more narrowly, in terms of the corporation, but broader in terms of other institutional spheres: "The technostructure consists of corporation executives, lawyers, scientists, engineers, economists, controllers, advertising and marketing men. It has allies and satellites in law firms, advertising agencies, business consulting firms, accounting firms, the business and engineering schools and elsewhere in the universities" (1973:162).

[9]Lenin recognized that dispersal of stock ownership with maintenance of a block of shares is "one of the ways of increasing the power of the financial oligarchy" (1969:55).

[10]See, for example, the analysis of family controlled corporations in Chapter Four and the analysis of elites who have had their main careers in family firms in Chapter Five. In these chapters it will be demonstrated that the role of family controlled firms among the elite has increased over the past twenty years rather than declined.

[11]It was observed some time ago by Marx that the number of stockholders would increase with corporate capitalism. He said, "With the growth of material wealth, the class of money-capitalists grows; on the one hand, the number and the wealth of retiring capitalists, rentiers, increases; and on the other hand, the development of the credit system is promoted, thereby increasing the number of bankers, money-lenders, financiers, etc" (1967:III, 510).

[12]Indeed, it will be shown that 60.3 per cent of the executives in dominant corporations hold an outside directorship in at least one of the other 113 dominant corporations in Canada.

[13]The use of the term corporate elite as a collective term for the economic

and media elites illustrates the overlap between them. It will be shown, for example, that about one half of those identified as the media elite are simultaneously members of the economic elite.

[14]For example, Marx says in *Capital*, Volume III, that the capitalist is "personified capital endowed with a consciousness of its own and a will" (1967:289-290).

[15]The subject of ideological power controlled by the mass media will be the subject of Chapter Seven.

[16]With regard to determining the types of occupations and the effects this has on the class structure, see Johnson on the decline of the petty bourgeoisie and the rise of a new middle class (1972) and also Miliband (1969:15ff).

[17]This is about three times the number of dominant corporations to be found in Chapter Four.

[18]One of the difficulties with this subject is the diverse way the term "management" is applied. For example, Burnham and Galbraith use the term to denote administrative and production functions but Baran and Sweezy use it synonomously with the board of directors (1966:15). Management is used here in the former sense, thus keeping it distinct from the board of directors.

[19]A detailed examination of the process of concentration and accumulation and an analysis of Canada's economic world is provided in Chapter Four.

[20]Canadian financiers have been successful in maintaining control of banking. Foreign control accounts for only .6 per cent of the assets and .5 per cent of the income of all chartered banks in Canada. This phenomenon will be developed in Chapter Four.

[21]For definitions and elaborations of these terms, see the discussion of "Elites and Decision Making" in the following section on the analytical framework and in Chapter Three.

[22]There is some confusion, perpetuated by Naylor and others, over the terms "finance capital" and "financial capital." Naylor confuses the two terms by meaning to use "financial capital" but instead using "finance capital." *Finance capital* means, essentially, what is herein being called "corporate capitalism" as opposed to "entrepreneurial capitalism." Lenin says, "The concentration of production; the monopolies arising therefrom; the merging or coalescence of the banks with industry—such is the history of the rise of finance capital and such is the content of this term" (1969:52-53). Similarly, Perlo defines "finance capital" as "the linking of banking and industrial monopolies and monopolists into supermonopolies which tower over even the greatest of the industrial combines" (1957:17). Similar statements can be found in Aaronovitch (1961:43) or Fitch and Oppenheimer (1970:v, 97). *Financial capital*, however, is the counterpart of "industrial capital;" that is, it is capital in the sphere of circulation rather than production. Financial capital is an extension of merchant's capital; in Marx's words, merchant capital "is older than the capitalist mode of production . . . merchant's capital is penned in the sphere of circulation, and since its function consists exclusively of promoting the exchange of commodities, it requires no other conditions for its existence . . . outside those necessary for the simple circulation of commodities and money" (1967:III, 325). With the development of capitalism and a credit system, merchant capital becomes transformed into financial capital. Together financial capital and merchant's capital may be referred to as commercial capital; that is,

capital engaged in circulation rather than production. Leo Panitch privately pointed out these important distinctions.

[23]Marx says, "Commercial capital, therefore—stripped of all heterogeneous functions, such as storing, expressing, transporting, distributing, retailing, which may be connected with it, and confined to its true function of buying in order to sell—creates neither value nor surplus-value, but acts as a middleman in their realization and thereby simultaneously in the actual exchange of commodities, i.e., in their transfer from hand to hand in the social metabolism" (1967:III, 282).

[24]The concepts comprador and parasite are developed fully in Chapter Three and placed within the social and elite structures.

[25]The hinterland/metropolis model has been developed by A.K. Davis in his paper, "Canadian Society and History as Hinterland Versus Metropolis" (1971), following A.G. Frank's thesis in "The Development of Underdevelopment" (1966) and *Capitalism and Under-Development in Latin America* (1967). E. Fossum develops the center/periphery model in "Political Development and Strategies for Change" (1970).

Chapter Two

Socio-Economic Forces, Institutions and Elites in Canada's Development

FOUNDATIONS for the present structure of economic institutions were established in the nineteenth century and major social and economic forces which shape present institutional configurations have their roots in this early period. To understand the current basis of social stratification, these forces need to be taken into account. By analysing economic dimensions of history within their social and political context, the task of this chapter is to establish an outline of major economic forces, institutions and elites which culminate in the current structure of inequality. Although the patterns of history examined focus on economic aspects of stratification and power distribution, some relations with social and political spheres and their implications for social and political development will also be incorporated. The tendency to concentrate on economic dimensions of stratification at the elite level does not mean to reject other important aspects; it simply represents the frame of reference selected for the present study.

The time frame of this chapter is from 1600 to the early 1950's, but equal importance will not be placed on each period; this being a sociological rather than "historical" account, the purpose will be to abstract trends and forces related to stratification at selected periods. Where an historian's attention might be on the detail and sequence of events or an economist's on production, allocation and distribution of resources, concentration here will be on social institutions, stratification and power distribution.

Economic organizations will be of central concern since they are embedded in the social structure and act as transfer mechanisms for elite decisions. For this reason their internal organization and distribution of power to various positions acts as an indicator of stratification at a societal level. The analysis will, therefore, be concerned with the organization of economic activity and the social structure within the context of a history of investment, ownership and control of the Canadian economy. Development of, and investment in, resources, finance, service (e.g., transportation, utilities) and manufacturing will also be examined.

This necessarily involves placing Canada within the framework of the North Atlantic triangle and analysing relationships this has involved. Canada's economic system has historically been trans-national and never totally independent of powerful "partners", either in trade or capital investment, thus resulting in a configuration of economic power intimately integrated with the economies of the North Atlantic triangle to which Britain and the United States represent counterparts to Canada. Initial binding ties were with the United Kingdom, forming a trans-Atlantic alliance with Canada trading off natural resources for British portfolio investment. More recent binding ties have been continental, with Canada again exporting natural resources, but with United States direct investment both controlling large portions of the means of production and transforming these resources at home and within Canada.

An analysis of Canada's development in ten periods to 1951 will be developed. This will be followed by an examination, in Chapter Three, of trends since 1951. The position implicit here is that each successive phase of capitalist development in Canada is built upon previous ones, and that outside forces have had important consequences for Canada's development which have relevance for the contemporary situation.

Historical Process: The Evolving Canadian Social Structure[1]

I. Foundings of Colonial Rule (1600-1763)

Multinational corporations were not the first organizations to penetrate the world economy; this was accomplished by the European mercantile thrust in the 15th Century. Initial operations were primarily trading but soon evolved into colonial rule. Based on state power, mercantilism equated economic power with national power, thus encouraging the development of a strong commercial class (see Easterbrook & Aitken, 1956:19). This commercial or merchant class generated profit by providing intermediary services between world resources and the home country. While English and Dutch efforts were undertaken by a mercantile oligarchy, the French relied on state power to practice mercantile activity thus placing more emphasis on military and religious aspects of colonialism. In England, mercantilism was supported by the British aristocracy and financiers who were excited at the prospect of economic gain from the colonies; this was "reinforced by the aggressive spirit of Restoration imperialism—a desire to extend Britain's commerce, a curiosity about places still unknown, a zest for discovery and exploration—particularly, in this case, the search for a northwest passage to the Pacific" (82). English merchants enjoyed an extremely powerful position in government but in France the state dominated commerce. As a maritime nation, England was forced into a position where trade provided an essential basis of wealth and power, consequently, they were more "outward looking" than continental France. English mercantile philosophy was summarized by Sir Walter Raleigh when he said: "Who rules the trade of the world rules the wealth of the world and consequently the world itself" (16). The world, it has been said, was ruled by the Bank of England which was established in 1694 and provided the center for British mercantilism.

Colonization and settlement were not priorities for the English in North America, and France, initially, had great difficulty in encouraging her charter companies to establish permanent settlements. Charter companies were only interested in settlement to the extent that it would enhance extraction of key staples. Fishing involved removal of resources with little or no settlement or indigenous involvement, but the fur trade was forced to rely on Indians, voyageurs and some clerical workers indigenous to Canada. Fishing expeditions involved small enterprises with low organizational and capital requirements; they "were unincorporated associations of merchants formed to raise a common fund to finance each expedition and they divided their profits at the end of each voyage" (Labrie & Palmer, 1967:33). While early fishing involved little "spin-off" for North America, fur trading was organized by royal charter and monopoly, thus providing a degree of leverage, particularly in France, for state encouragement of settlement. For instance, the Rouen merchants' Compagnie du Canada was established in Quebec in 1608 under a royal charter which demanded settlement. Settlement for the French was an attempt to "transplant" feudalism which, in its distorted form, was the basis of the social structure under colonial New France.

As fur trading became established and local animals scarce, it was necessary to penetrate the continent in search of new supplies. Although Montreal remained the entrepôt, posts became located throughout the continent with voyageurs acting as carriers and Indians as trappers (occupying the lowest rung of the social structure). The St. Lawrence was established as the main trading route providing a fur trade organized by Montreal financiers and, by involved trading structures and charters, they established the fur trade as a monopolistic enterprise controlled by Montreal financiers working in partnership with interior traders.

During the French regime, fur trade remained the central activity, accounting for over 70 per cent of the colonies' exports (Pritchard, 1972:27). Rigid French mercantilism prevented greater economic diversification and created a distorted social structure where the colonial elite was part of the colonizing elite, with the colonial elite dominating economic, political and military affairs. Colonial traders tended to be related through marriage and commerce to the French merchants and aristocracy. This was encouraged by the need for access to capital controlled in France. As Pritchard has concluded, "These merchants were not colonists in the accepted sense of the word, for they always maintained their metropolitan connections, frequently crossed the Atlantic, and sometimes after decades of residence in New France, returned home permanently" (1972:37). This did not prevent the emergence, as Guindon argues, of "an indigenous middle class recruited from the various indigenous groups, a middle class whose status, power, and prestige were derived from its formal though subordinate participation in the expanding institutions of the imperial regimes. While the newly acquired status of the middle class was honored by its co-nationals, it was bestowed upon them by the ruling aliens" (1968:37). Although the colonial regime was controlled from outside thus limiting mobility to the topmost positions for the indigenous population, the effect of developing government and administration within New France was to change the indigenous class structure by creating an indigenous middle class. This development is analogous with the effect of multinational corporations creating branch plants in Canada many years later. In both cases, there is external control, but each has the effect of transforming the Canadian class structure by enlarging the middle class and using it as a recruitment base for their Canadian operations[2].

In addition to providing furs, New France was strategically important for rivalry with Britain, but the Conquest of 1755 settled that issue and North America became a British possession, and with its domination, brought a new social structure. As typically happens, this was super-imposed on the remnant French colony following Conquest. Conquest, Guindon says, "involved the takeover by the British of the political and economic institutions of New France. This was greatly facilitated by the massive exodus of the middle-class entrepreneurs and political administrators of New France" (1968:52). One colonial rule gave way to another, and both new and old forces were external to Canada so indigenous mobility was not facilitated by replacing one set of rulers by another.

Characterized by "aggressive commercialism" as opposed to the "inflexible centralism" of France, the British colonial system relied on a system of colonial trade designed for the advancement of the home country. Under British rule, fur trade was dominated by great trading companies, particularly the North West Company (NWC) and the Hudson's Bay Company (HBC), each with quite different structures. The NWC was "a distinctively Canadian concern" organized by a group of Montreal merchants to counter the dominant position of the HBC. A syndicate was formed in response to increasing capital requirements of extended continental trade and this association of small ventures centered its trade on the St. Lawrence corridor to the interior.

As a joint enterprise, it resembled early fishing expeditions which gathered capital to finance expeditions and split profits at the end of a period. Its organization required constant refurbishing by expanding trade, and, unlike the HBC, did not form a rigid bureaucratic framework extending back to the United Kingdom. The "wintering partners" who travelled into the interior maintained a powerful position in determing the direction of the organization (Easterbrook & Aitken, 1956:166-167). Its flexible structure allowed it to absorb competitors rather than engage in competition. Internal organization involved partners who received profits on a share basis, clerks who worked for a wage but were allowed to become partners after a five to seven year apprenticeship and voyageurs who worked on a contract basis (172-173).

The HBC, however, involved a much more rigid organization and expanded into the continent at a slower pace under the control of a centralized authority, resident in England, with branch headquarters and a governor in Canada. Organized by British merchants and supported by the aristocracy, it involved a syndicate of 13 men who obtained a royal charter in 1670. Unlike the NWC, the HBC was a syndicate of owners and this syndicate was not internal to the organization. Easterbrook and Aitken argue that "In terms of the general trend of English commercial organization and policy, it was distinctly a throw-back to an earlier era . . .an era when all of England's overseas commerce had been organized under great companies" (1956:82). However, this "throw-back" managed to dominate much of the commerce in Canada until 1867 and remains powerful in a revised form today.

It is important to contrast the effects of capital accumulation by these two companies and effects they have had on Canadian capital formations and elite configurations. The HBC "profits on the originally subscribed capital stock, actually paid up, of between 60 and 70 per cent per annum from the years 1690 to 1800" (Myers, 1972:42-43) were returned to England (47). On the other hand, "profits of the North West Company were derived from great fortunes which later were conspicuous in banks, steamboats, railways, and other capitalist channels" (61-63). These two types of capital formations represent the difference between the future development of an indigenous economic elite in Canada and an external elite in Britain, both of which were based, to a large extent, on capital appropriated in Canada. These patterns illustrate the importance of relating stratification to the means of capital accumulation. Although each relied, to some extent, on foreign capital, operations of the HBC were directed from Britain with capital flowing back along the same path; the NWC used its own capital and borrowed some from the United Kingdom[3], thus retaining capital accumulation and control within Canada to form the basis of an indigenous capitalist class. The NWC can be regarded as a new indigenous social force which emerged parallel to the external colonial powers represented by the HBC. The NWC provided an avenue to power for indigenous Canadians distinct from the colonial power of the HBC. The effects can still be seen today with capital accumulated through the NWC providing an initial basis for developing an autonomous financial and transportation structure while the HBC, still owned primarily by equity control from the U.K., is now engaged in retail and wholesale trade, as well as gas and oil leasing from properties initially received under colonial rule. This provides the pattern for the development of stratification in Canada.

II. Colonial Social Structure and British Mercantilism (1763-1837)

Early industrialization in Britain focused on textiles and railways financed by surplus accumulated through merchant activities. Once these industries developed there remained, for a period, a low capacity for further capital absorption and the colonies provided receptive markets for investment and outlets for early manufactured goods. With a tight association between merchants, landed interest and the state, industrial capital was still dependent on this class. After acquiring large amounts of surplus, merchants evolved into financial capitalists, maintaining the same "middleman" function as before but now oriented toward more long-term ventures and organized in banking houses and insurance companies. These nascent financiers provided early portfolio investment so important to Canada's early transportation projects. Block emphasizes that "over-capitalization" within British industry, combined with low technical development, produced, for a time, a gap in the pace of Britain's industrialization. Surplus available as a result encouraged its "outward thrust" (1970:139).

As a colony, Canada had to fit the dominant mode of production prevalent in the U.K. at the time. Mercantilism provided English fur trading merchants in Canada with capital securing advantages which French merchants, remaining after the Conquest, lacked. Alliance between English-speaking Montreal merchants and English commercial interests provided a strong and complementary power base on both sides of the Atlantic. The export of staples from Canada's abundant natural resources was beneficial to both and reinforced colonial dependence. This mercantile empire was strengthened by legislation known as the Acts of Trade, designed to continue import of colonial staples and export of British capital. Canada developed within the framework of British navigation laws and trade preferences and these provided the operating assumptions of politicians and business interests in Canada.

The St. Lawrence provided a ready channel to bind colonial resources to the colonizers' capital, but industrialization in the colonies was stultified by the mercantile empire with its focus of circulation rather than production and a policy[4] prohibiting export of "manufactured machines and the emigration of skilled artisans". This maintained dependence and "continued domination of merchant capital at the expense of industrial capital, which would compete with Britain. The merchant class and rich Loyalists in Canada aligned themselves with the colonial ruling class, the church, and the land-owning elites" (Naylor, 1972:6).

These developments are reflected in the Canadian colonial structure at the time, particularly the "Family Compact" of Upper Canada, the "Chateau Clique" of Lower Canada and the merchants of the Maritimes. These associations of power cannot be divorced from colonial design, as S.D. Clark notes:

> Land grants to favoured individuals or organizations, financial subsidies, preferments in political appointments, or measures restricting the operation of competitive interests were means employed to build up privileged social institutions such as an aristocratic class or established church. The object was to assure the loyalty of frontier populations to the mother country, and such aids therefore served the same purpose as military garrisons or police forces (1970:181).

The social structure developed as a means of social control and was encouraged by Britain and taken advantage of by the emergent Canadian elite. By giving the Governor General the power to appoint officeholders in the colonies, the Constitutional Act of 1791 provided the foundation for half a century of domination by small powerful enclaves (Teeple, 1972:47-48). The ruling classes of Upper and Lower Canada formed a tight set of family relations and were firmly based on a union of interlocking interests. Alliance was formed through political, religious and financial control which united them into a single social class active as an "elite of office" and represented in the inner circles of the Executive Council by a "power elite" (Saunders, 1967:17f). Their power was political as much as economic and they enjoyed the advantages of both through land grants and access to capital but they were not engaged in industrial pursuits, choosing rather to build on merchant capital. Each group must be examined separately since they represent somewhat different power bases. Initially, each filled a "political vacuum" but by accumulating advantages evolved into a rigid structure commanding political and economic power which remained dominant for some fifty years.

In Upper Canada the "link of executive and legislative power was the key to the position of the Family Compact" with executive positions representing a "small charmed circle" (Saunders, 1967:17-19). This association remained in power until the Act of Union in 1841 when the basis of political office was changed. They were linked by education and "cultivation" which limited mobility into the oligarchy and served as exclusion mechanisms. Although business was not as dominant in the Family Compact as in the Chateau Clique, the financial power of men like William Allan, first president of the Bank of Upper Canada in 1821, first president of the British American Assurance Company in 1833, Commissioner of the Canada Company and member of the Executive Council in 1825, illustrates its more than marginal importance (Saunders, 1967:18). The principal alliance, however, was political, bureaucratic, religious and professional with a class base in the quasi-aristocracy of Upper Canada. Lord Durham's statement is a classic summation of the Family Compact:

> For a long time this body of men, receiving at times accession to its members, possessed almost all the highest public offices, by means of which, and of its influence in the Executive Council, it wielded all the powers of Government. . . . Successive Governors, as they came in turn, are said to have submitted quietly to its influence, or, after a short and unavailing struggle, to have yielded to this well-organized party the real conduct of affairs (quoted by Myers, 1972:80).

Durham says further that they controlled the bench, the church, owned the land, the chartered banks and "almost exclusively all offices of trust and profit".

In the Maritimes the situation was slightly different. Enjoying rapid expansion due to the U.S. Embargo Act of 1807, which forced almost all North American trading to be conducted through its ports, a closely-knit Maritime group enjoyed a rapid surge of power. Representing what has been referred to as the "Atlantic edition of the Family Compact," the Maritime oligarchy was centered in the Council of Twelve in Halifax and the Halifax Banking Company. More commercially oriented than the Family Compact, the "ruling faction in Nova Scotia was an amalgam of colonial-military officialdom with a closely-knit group of merchant-bankers possessing strong ties with London commercial houses. The Executive and Legislative Councils were made up of the same twelve men, not one of whom owed his position to election" (Ryerson, 1968:194). Among them was Sir Samuel Cunard, famous for his shipping lines and close ties with Britain.

The most powerful commercial association in the colony was centered in the Chateau Clique of Lower Canada. Like the Maritime group, it was closely allied politically and economically with Britain and formed an association closely resembling an aristocracy of power. For example, of the twelve office-holders in the 1830 Legislative Council, seven were "large landed proprietors" and three were merchants (Ryerson, 1968:50). By 1812, this English-speaking group was centered in the three mercantile activities of fur trading, timber and export/import commerce (Easterbrook & Aitken, 1956:158). These men were "go-betweens" rather than independent men of power, as Mackenzie's critical remarks suggest: "Few of these Montreal commission merchants are men of capital: they are generally merely the factors or agents of British houses, and thus a chain of debt, dependence and degradation is begun and kept up" (quoted by Ryerson, 1968:107). Within the context of colonial rule, they were the most powerful indigenous force but their power was subservient to the wish of the colonizer.

The position of French Canadians during this period was clearly weaker than the English. Under the British regime, the clergy controlled education and collected tithes, the seigneurs owned land and held some administrative positions but the English dominated the commercially-based economy and executive posts of government. The English took over the role of the bourgeoisie and formed an alliance with the high clergy and remnant French aristocracy to form an "aristocratic compact" (Rioux, 1971:18-20).

Common to all three oligarchies was a commitment to British rule and advantages they attained from the prevailing mercantile system. Each had, as their economic foundation, mercantile pursuits acting as mediators between the staples of Canada and United Kingdom commercial houses. None had a vision of developing a strong indigenous industrial system, since, under the protection of British mercantilism, their needs would be met by the colonizers' industrial structure. Their interest was in developing a strong transportation system for their mercantile trade. Efforts in this direction focused on the St. Lawrence and development of a canal system and, later, a trans-continental railway. One major undertaking was William Merritt's creation of the Welland Canal Company whose board was dominated by members of the Family Compact. They were not involved because of their personal expertise but because of legitimacy they lent to the project and access they had to sources of capital (see Aitken, 1967:64-70). The project was also supported by John Galt who, as head of the Canada Company, was also involved in another important economic activity of the period, land grants. A.T. Galt, John Galt's son, was commissioner of the Northwest Land Company, Lower Canada's counterpart to the Canada

Company. On the promise of promoting settlement in the colony, these companies were granted enormous tracts of land around London and in the Eastern Townships. While restricting distribution of free land to immigrants, the companies did generate a great deal of capital, later to appear in "promoting or getting control of banks, railroads, cotton and woolen factories, mines and other concerns" (Myers, 1972:86).

Later in the period trade in square timber gained importance as a staple, filling the slack between the decline of the fur trade and the boom of wheat. Initially, timber trade was organized by small firms but, as capital requirements increased, only branches of British firms were able to survive. These "were usually managed by a relative of one of the partners in the British firm, a son or a cousin, who ran the business in North America" (Easterbrook & Aitken, 1956:194), thus resembling the structure of control evident in New France with links back to the center. During its brief importance, timber established several important fortunes, not the least of which was the Price Brothers' firm, still dominant in Canadian timber.

This period was also noted for the genesis of banking in Canada. Early banking functions were undertaken by Montreal merchants as credit channels from Britain and, as early as 1792, private banks led by merchants in Montreal began to petition for chartered status, although it was not until 1817 that the Bank of Montreal, Canada's first chartered bank, was established. The early banks were closely aligned with merchant and commercial interests; they specialized in fish, fur and wheat commerce and did not engage in industrial loans. Each bank was closely associated with the dominant power interest in its province: the Bank of Montreal was controlled by the Chateau Clique and was the official government bank; the Bank of Commerce and Bank of Upper Canada were the Family Compact's response to the Bank of Montreal; the Halifax Banking Company (later the Bank of Nova Scotia) was the Maritime's answer. Dominance remained, however, with Montreal mercantilists. As Acheson illustrates, York's entrepreneurs of the 1820's were primarily trade merchants who lacked an adequate financial structure. The Bank of Upper Canada, established in 1821, was controlled by the local state; "of the original fifteen directors, nine were members of the executive or legislative council or were civil servants" (1969:423). Disagreement among its founders failed the merchants' needs and, unlike the Chateau Clique with its powerful commercial association, the Family Compact was a weaker economic alliance.

In 1821, one of the great rivalries of early Canadian history ended with the takeover of the North West Company by the Hudson's Bay Company. This was a strong blow to the Montreal merchants who waged a determined battle but lost to their English counterparts who were able to muster greater financial strength. On top of this severe setback, developments in England were soon to be even more serious. English industrialization was gaining strength and industrial interests were beginning to push for free trade which would mean the end of imperial preference—the basis of Montreal's mercantile strength.

III. Nascent Industrialization and the Shopkeeper Aristocracy (1837-1854)

The West Indies were a testing ground for struggles between the imperial power of Britain and the upstart imperialist United States. The outcome of this confrontation was to change the direction of Canada's alliance. The U.S. sought equal opportunity to trade with the West Indies while the U.K. mercantilists stood strongly for maintainance of imperial preference. Struggle between the imperial powers was waged on an economic front and political solution simply marked economic victory. "It was the ability of the United States to carry through a programme of commercial retaliation on the classic mercantilist pattern which compelled Britain to modify its imperial trade policy" (Easterbrook & Aitken, 1956:238). The U.S. emerged victorious from this test of strength in 1830, marking a radical departure in the world forum of economic power and the beginning of the end to British colonial hegemony and the emergence of an American economic empire.

With the rise of U.S. industrialization and demands this created for westward expansion, a dilemma was created. On the one hand, the first continental market for Canadian staples, particularly lumber, was created but at the same time, transcontinental expansion created within Canada a series of what Aitken describes as "forced moves" of "defensive expansionism" to prevent U.S. encroachment on Canada's western territory. These events, he argues, stimulated rapid extension of transporation systems within Canada and strengthened political union within the provinces to provide the basis for "very large public investment and has brought the political leadership into the intimate alliance with influential business groups" (1965:496-497). Canada's forced expansion strengthened the business-government alliance which remained important throughout Canada's development. Based on imperial preference, the "first commercial empire of the St. Lawrence" was destroyed but a second empire would soon emerge in its place.

Expensive transportation systems were demanded by the staple economy but financing for these expenditures could not be found within the colony. It required looking outward for support from British financiers. High capital requirements brought promoters and politicians together to petition the British financial houses which demanded state-guaranteed loans. With completion of the Erie Canal in 1825, and redirection of trade, business and political interests again found it profitable to create a common front, businessmen to protect their hinterland and politicians to protect their territory. Predictably, the Montreal merchants were the most avid supporters of canal construction—as they were for later railways. In Upper Canada, agricultural and timber interests strengthened these demands; for instance, the Lachine Canal completed in 1821 and the 1828 completion of the Welland Canal satisfied the Montreal and Niagara merchants, respectively. Unable to sustain the maintenance costs of the Welland Canal, its founders called upon the provincial government to take it over, partially in 1836, and completely in 1841. With this experience, the London-financed government undertook the Cornwall Canal construction as a state project. Reluctant public ownership in support of merchant interests had begun, not by design but by default. The canal boom was a forerunner of the railway boom so prevalent from the 1850's to the early 1900's.

Responding to commercial demands, the provinces of Upper Canada and Lower Canada were united in 1840. This increased state power through its ability to secure loans from England and extract customs duties to finance the heavy capital requirements of canal construction. Representing more of a commercial alliance than a political design, union was engineered by Montreal and Toronto capitalists. As Naylor points out:

> Behind the Act of Union and the merging of the debts of the two provinces were the machinations of the merchant oligarchy who needed access to further funds to complete the St. Lawrence canal system, and of the Baring Brothers, a merchant banking house in London which saw in Union a means of ensuring the value of Upper Canadian securities by redistributing the burden of the debt over the more populous Lower Canada (1972:8-9).

As a strategy to have the populace finance canal construction, the union further reinforced the unity of merchant and political interests against each province's agricultural hinterlands. In Lower Canada this added another element of exploitation to the national issue.

Concurrent with these developments in the east, the Hudson's Bay Company was solidly in command of the west, having its licence renewed in 1838 for another 21 years. Although it prevented settlement near its trading posts in the remainder of the west, in 1835 the company assumed direct control of the Red River settlement and began to establish its own form of "self-rule", appointing "governors, legislators, judges and other authorities" who "made the laws, and executed their own sentences" (Myers, 1972:140). The company had diversified from fur trade and was now concentrating on land ownership and retail sales from its 115 outposts. Donald Smith, chief executive officer of the company in North America, had done a little diversification himself by investing part of his sizable fortune in the Bank of Montreal. In British Columbia the company's factor, James Douglas, had taken a different course and became governor of the colony in 1858.

Several well documented accounts of Canada's social structure exist for this period, particularly for relations between the political and economic elites who, for the most part, were one and the same people, thus forming a ruling class[5]. For example, Minister of Finance A.T. Galt was issued charters for the St. Lawrence and Atlantic Railroad, Montreal and Kingston Railroad and the Grand Trunk Railway, in addition to being a commissioner of the British North America Land Company, Bank of Montreal, Northwest Coal and Navigation Company and President of Canada Guaranty Company. The existence of a ruling class based in commerce and politics can be contrasted with the nascent industrialists described by Ryerson, while the social origins of the ruling class can be determined from Tulchinsky's study of Montreal merchants. The composition of this elite explains why the Canadian economy continued to be based on staple export and why it failed to diversify into industrial activities, so prevalent in both the U.K. and U.S. at the time. It was within an economy dominated by imperially-oriented merchants that the emerging industrialists had to struggle. The ruling class was the old, established social force based in commerce and the state, while the nascent industrialists were an emerging social force. This "shopkeeper aristocracy", as it was described by Judge Thorpe, stifled the emergence of the indigenous manufacturing entrepreneurs.

Ryerson documents the "embryonic industrial bourgeoisie" in the Maritimes and in Upper and Lower Canada. Development in Lower Canada followed three paths according to Ryerson: "growth of the timber trade" focused in "sawmills and ship yards", "establishment of manufactories and machine shops" and "small scale consumer-goods enterprises" responding to local markets (1968:39). In Nova Scotia there were 1,114 sawmills, each employing two to three persons in 1871; the Maritimes generally were characterized by "small-scale individual capitalist enterprises" (215). In Upper Canada the situation was somewhat different; while there were 1,618 sawmills in 1851 producing 400 million feet of lumber, the introduction of "steam-driven machine production meant *concentration* of production and of capital" so that by 1871, almost the same volume was produced by only six mills, controlled in large part by U.S. capitalists (259). Railway construction created the conditions for the development of equipment and stock; in 1853 the first locomotive was built in Toronto thus initiating a heavy industry base for the colony (260). Ryerson stresses that development of "incipient industrialism" was greatly retarded by the existence of a Canadian ruling class based in mercantile capital who, in Teeple's words, "preferred to trade [their] articles rather than produce them" (1972:61). Manufacturing developed at a pace and direction desired by a mercantile oligarchy who preferred to extract its surplus through commerce rather than production. To the limited extent that the ruling class entered manufacturing, it was in those activities directly contingent to their mercantile pursuits— including ship building and railway rolling stock. With these developments, there begins to be created within these industries a labouring class indigenous to Canada. This foreshadows later developments which displace independent commodity producers for the capitalist labour market. The concentration Ryerson shows in lumber mills between 1851 and 1871 also has an important effect on the labour force. Instead of two- or three-man operations, the larger firms were beginning to create an industrial work force—a proletariate.

Tulchinsky's excellent study of the Montreal-based merchant class for the period 1837-1853 describes it as one of "significant growth of new insurance, banking and telegraph companies, as well as capital expansion amongst the older banks". In addition to developing a St. Lawrence canal system, the period saw introduction of steamer service to the U.K. and the beginning of railways to service the "Montreal argonauts" quest for "commercial ties with her restless hinterland" (1972:125). Although personal investment in the commercial activities of the city was a prerequisite of membership, "prominence, reputed wealth, service in organizations like the Board of Trade or in provincial or municipal politics seem to have been other important criteria for directorships in the companies" (129-130). Three families provided leadership—the McGill's, Molson's and Torrance's. The "cadre of leaders" was of upper class background:

> most prominent members of the Montreal commercial fraternity were favoured with considerable advantages. Family business connections in Montreal combined with some experience, and often backed by grammar school (or collège classique) education, paved the way for their easy entry and accelerated advancement to positions of leadership in the city's commercial affairs. In most cases, too, it seems that they were in command of or had access to substantial capital (130).

Tulchinsky emphasizes the relationships between particular types of commercial activities such as merchants, ship builders, import/export dealers and railway promoters, arguing the same people were inter-locked in each and that none expressed much interest in other indus-tries. Interlocking interests were reinforced by membership in common associations such as the Montreal Board of Trade and the Board of Brokers (138-141). Most prominent businessmen were Scottish in origin with American representing the second largest group followed by English, Irish and English-speaking Canadians. ''While French-Canadians were not numerous as directors of, or large investors in many joint-stock companies, they were nevertheless a significant ele-ment in the business community, though not all were themselves in commerce''. More were likely to be in medical or legal professions and ''among commission merchants and agents, for example, there were practically no French Canadians'' (132-133).

In contrast, McCalla's study of the Toronto Board of Trade from 1850-1860 found them cut off from the powerful Montreal finance center. It was organized by merchant capitalists with limited capital resources, especially lacking access to powerful banks. Also absent was the national political power at the command of its Montreal rival. According to McCalla:

> the board's membership was dominated by the city's wholesalers who, throughout the period 1845-1860, comprised over one-half of both the total membership and the executive. . . . The board was very much an organization of traders. Trade, of course, was the primary way to fortune in Toronto (1969:52-53).

Although they formed a fairly closed circle among themselves, the Toronto merchants were not part of the powerful. ''Lawyers, most bankers, and the 'gentlemen' sons of the old 'compact' families were the elements of that leadership which did not participate in the board's activities. Not many manufacturers could yet be considered big businessmen and of those few who were, several were members of the board'' (53).

Tulchinsky's findings, when combined with the political connec-tions and activities of the ruling class presented in Appendix i and McCalla's study of the Toronto Board of Trade, give a fairly com-prehensive outline of the economic structure in the colonies at the time. It is quite clear that the nascent industrialists presented in Ryerson's analysis had quite formidable opposition to their new task of diversify-ing the Canadian economy. They were, however, soon to be given a hand by events occurring outside the colony.

British industrialization brought an end to imperial preference and an expanding market for Canadian staples. A shift from mercantile to free trade offered both advantages and drawbacks for Canadian development. The evolution of classical political economy was to create an aura of u. certainty in the colonies as industrial capitalists in England struggled with the vested interests of mercantilism for tariff reform. The Reform Bill of 1832 and repeal of the Corn Laws in 1846 signifies the transformation within Britain. The reaction within Canada was an increasing orientation toward the U.S. and, to a limited extent, stimulation of industrial development within Canada.

IV. Reciprocity and the Continental Context (1854-1867)

This period begins with the Reciprocity Treaty of 1854 which marks a shift in economic terms from the United Kingdom to the United States. Although ties remained strong with England, the treaty denoted both an end of the British outward thrust and an increasingly internal focus on her own industrialization as the new "frontier". Industrialization in the U.S. and the U.K. changed Canada's economic orientation from the imperial context of British mercantilism to an increasingly continental orientation with the advent of free trade. Symbolized most dramatically by the Montreal businessmen's Annexation Manifesto of 1849, and later, the call for commercial union by Henry W. Darling, president of the Toronto Board of Trade and the influential continentalist, Goldwin Smith, the future of Canadian commerce was seen in her ability to tap into the United States industrial boom. This movement culminated in establishing the Reciprocity Treaty which D.C. Masters argues was "a more moderate scheme than Commercial Union" but "the Liberals were unable to avoid the charge that they were really trying to lead Canada into political union with the United States" (1965:15). In terms of the Canadian economy, the elite decided its fate was vested with continental growth and, if annexation was not possible, reciprocity was a strong second best.

  Although not without resistence in Canada, especially from the Maritimes who had lost some of their fishing rights in concessions to the U.S., the Reciprocity Treaty signalled the future direction of Canada's economy. Support for it came mainly from Upper Canada's grain, agricultural and lumber businessmen, represented by A.T. Galt and W.H. Merritt, who saw reciprocity providing a vast market for their goods. Masters suggests that "the desire for reciprocity was a projection of colonialism. Having relied on a projected British market and lost it, the colonists now hoped to lean on the United States market" (1965:3). The implications of reciprocity, however, were not only an outlet for Canadian products and resource, but a reciprocal "invitation" to powerful U.S. manufacturing interests to enter Canada with the effect of leaving Canada's nascent industrial class unprotected from booming industry to the south. By focusing on export of raw materials and importing industrial goods, it signifies to Aitken that "central Canada and the Maritimes seemed content to accept the status of an economic satellite of the United States" (1967:203).

Reciprocity did not involve forging totally new relationships with the U.S.; rather, it meant strengthening existing patterns, many of which were further reinforced during the American Civil War when many small industries were initiated in Canada to feed the war effort (see Masters, 1965:8). Simultaneously, western settlements on the Red River and in British Columbia were becoming increasingly drawn into U.S. influence following trade patterns established during the early 1840's.

Coincident with loss of imperial preference was the upsurge in the movement west; outlying areas became important as sources of staples and internal markets for goods. The rise of "continental imperialism" had begun. Penetration of the west required heavy capital investment in transportation, especially the railway boom which dominated the attention of politicians and businessmen alike for more than half a century. Threatened by U.S. railways entering their hinterland, Montreal commercial interests demanded a system of railways be developed to maintain the St. Lawrence corridor as its main trading route for Canadian staples. This coincided with the political interest of maintaining sovereignty and national unity. In spite of distractions, "the Canadian westward movement was a planned and directed process" (Creighton, 1970:26) with state and business interests allied in an attempt to penetrate the western hinterland. Acting simultaneously as "an instrument of colonialism" and as "engines of industrialization", railways absorbed the resources and energy of the ruling class (Ryerson, 1968:258). In 1850, Canada lagged well behind the U.S. in miles of railway tracks, with only 66 compared to over 9,000 miles in the U.S. (Easterbrook & Aitken, 1956:294-295). If this deficit was to be overcome to maintain a competitive position in the west, great capital investment would be needed. Railway promoters turned to the state for capital and obtained the Guarantee Act of 1849 which committed it to a one-half subsidy of all railway contstruction. The tradition of government as financial backer of transportation facilities was extended from canal to railway construction.

Most important among the many rail lines initiated during this period was the Grand Trunk Railway. With the government acting as mediator between British finance houses and Montreal promoters, the Grand Trunk began by taking over smaller lines and consolidating them with new construction. At the onset, nine of its directors were members of the Canadian cabinet and later, six of the twelve directors had the dual roles of cabinet ministers and board members of the Grand Trunk. Also represented on the board were London bankers and the Bank of

Montreal (Easterbrook & Aitken, 1956:307-308). By 1867 the Canadian government had "loaned" the company $26 million, all of which was "forgiven". Confronting the Hudson's Bay Company, which owned much of the land needed for railway expansion, E.W. Watkin, as president of the Grand Trunk and with the aid of London financiers, bought it out in 1863. Under new ownership, the Hudson's Bay Company surrendered its charter in 1869 for which it was compensated $1.5 million and one twentieth of "all the extraordinary fertile expanse from the Red River to the Rocky Mountains" which, over the next twenty years, yielded $15.6 million for the sale of less than one third of its land grant (Myers, 1972:143-148).

Heavy capital grants to railways placed the government deeply in debt and committed it to a series of long-term obligations. Debt was soon to be one of the major forces behind the move to confederation of the provinces. A beginning in this direction is reflected in the need to meet these debts through imposition of customs duties; as A.T. Galt said in 1862 as Minister of Finance: "The government has increased the duties for the purpose of enabling them to meet the interest on the public works" (quoted by Innis, 1956:71). Indeed, by 1866 customs duties accounted for 66 per cent of the government revenue with a further 17 per cent gained through excise taxes (Rowell/Sirois Report, 1963:48-49). The ruling finance/railway/political oligarchy committed itself to heavy capital outlays and now it had to prove to the London banking houses that it could make good on its promises.

Railways were not the only commercial activities engaged in by leading political figures of the day[6]; many were also involved in insurance companies and banking, both of which are commercial. As Aitken notes, the state was not accessible to all business interests but only to commercial elites at the exclusion of many small entrepreneurs (1965:495). Naylor argues the following:

> The list of eminent financiers and railwaymen of the period is a veritable "who's who" of Canadian politics for two generations. And without exception, the linkage runs from merchant capitalism to finance, transportation, and land speculation (1972:17).

These changes between the old mercantilists and the new commercial activities controlled by the ruling class reflect its institutionalization of traditional economic pursuits. Ryerson's study of the "new ruling class" leads him to conclude that the most powerful interests were centered in the Grand Trunk and Bank of Montreal group centered in Montreal[7]. A second group was beginning to emerge in the Toronto-Hamilton area which he divides into three subsections: first, those associated with extractive industries and closely tied to the U.S.;

second, an "up-and-coming manufacturing group" which was forming its own financial base; and a third group associated with government and the railways (1968:277).

This ruling class was showing signs of independence from Britain, unlike earlier oligarchies, and was beginning to launch a campaign of economic expansion into the west and development of an indigenous economic force. For example, by 1857, "the Bank of Montreal was larger than any American bank and probably the largest and most powerful transacter in the New York money market" (Hammond, 1967:167). The indigenous elite was weakened, however, by its failure to diversify. Concentration remained in staple production and commerce which continued to tie it to external economies through trade, thus making it highly vulnerable to international economic conditions. In the United States, industrialization was leading to greater diversification, but Canadian manufacturers remained small and only incidentally protected from U.S. manufactured goods. United States manufacturers were also beginning to move into Canada on a small scale; for example, Hiram Walker moved from Massachusetts in 1857 and established his distillery. This kind of encroachment on manufacturing was responded to with pressure from the Toronto-Hamilton manufacturers and, in 1859, Alexander Galt introduced the first "industrially-based tariff in Canada" to protect these interests (Easterbrook & Aitken, 1956:373).

In response to an attempt to create a unified economic system and a strong central government for promoting westward expansion, Confederation was expected to strengthen Canada's position in the international money and trade markets as well as promote inter-provincial trade for a strenghened local market. The result was "a commercial state" (Naylor, 1973:45); that is, a state which would serve the ends of the dominant commercial ruling class. This was the design of elites from both Canada's and the Maritime provinces, all of whom felt they would benefit by the union. As Tupper of Nova Scotia said: "The possession of coal mines, together with other natural advantages, must, in the course of time, make Nova Scotia the great emporium for manufacturers in British America" (quoted by Creighton, 1965:462-463). His assumptions were shared by the business interests of each province. Confederation was to strengthen the economic position of all concerned and generate a new industrial center. The aspirations of early Canadian businessmen were high and not without foundation.

V. Expansion of Canadian Commercialism (1867-1900)

With Confederation "colony had given way to nation", but had the

Toronto-Montreal ruling class itself not become a colonizer and the west its hinterland? Torn between British capital and American markets, the Canadian ruling class generated "the National Policy" of 1879, a policy which asserted the independence of Canada from the encroachment of U.S. westward expansion and declared that central Canada was to rule the western hinterland. In the age of its greatest autonomy Canadian financiers, allied with the state, continued to assert a vision of Canada placing the St. Lawrence region at the center of an east-west nexus of trade. Working as a unit, the economic and political ruling class prepared themselves for the extraction, transportation and exportation of Canada's staples. Contrary to the idea of the National Policy as a popular nationalist movement, Watkins asserts it "was the ideological content of the new technology of the railway wedded to the old river economy of the St. Lawrence. As a manifestation of nationalism and as an instrument of nation-building, the National Policy was more of the commercial imperialism of the St. Lawrence merchants than a broad-based mass movement" (1970:287).

Assuming the central role of the Toronto-Montreal axis, the policy of continental expansion maintained that rail transporation was a prerequisite to extracting Canadian staples and moving them to the markets abroad. Railways and other activities, it was argued, would "spin off" a series of financial and industrial benefits which would project Canada into a leading industrial nation by the twentieth century. Protection of indigenous development would be provided by protective and revenue producing tariffs which would strengthen the financial position of the state and provide a capital base for expansion. The strengthened state would then be in a better position to tap the financial resources of the London money market. The debate between Sir John A. Macdonald with his policy of protectionism and the free trade economic philosophy of Sir Wilfrid Laurier was won by the protectionists. Laurier's prophesy that this policy would reinforce the power of the vested interests in support of Macdonald has been borne out in history (Rae & McLeod, 1969:204). As Underhill asserts, the forces behind the National Policy were "the interests of the ambitious, dynamic, speculative or entrepreneurial business groups, who aimed to make money out of the new national community or to install themselves in the strategic positions of power within it—the railway promoters, banks, manufacturers, land companies, contractors, and such people" who all thought they would gain (Underhill, 1964:25). Some proved to be right and others dead wrong.

As ambitious and confident as they were, achievement of these aspirations of power were detached from the reality of their position in the North Atlantic triangle. Their strength, as mediators, still depended on outside links to support their adventures and absorb the staples they wished to market. The grand design was inherently vulnerable to the world situation and the implications of their actions for the development of a strong indigenous industrial base were to prove deceptive. Failure to develop autonomously from either the U.S. or U.K. has been a flaw in Canadian development which has often made the ruling elite in Canada susceptible to external forces. This relationship was inherent in the course of development chosen with its emphasis on staple extraction and export with the failure to generate a strong indigenous industrial base.

It cannot be asserted enough that early railway promoters and politicians—including cabinets and prime ministers—were intimate. Not only were they from the same social class, as occurs frequently in later years, but they were often the same people. Based in railway promotions, construction and finance, their accumulated wealth and advantage allowed them to become leading capitalists in other spheres. Documentation is provided by Myers, among others, to illustrate that Canada, up to the early 1900's, was dominated by a select group of people who could correctly be called a ruling class representing the dominant political, economic and military forces of their time. Each of these institutions was dominated by an interlocking network of the same men, holding positions in each simultaneously and throughout their careers. This was an era in Canadian history when it could correctly be said that an economic class ruled politically. The marriage of politics and business, evident at the executive level, also occurred in the legislature as a survey by Myers for 1878 shows: in the legislature, "there were 56 merchants, 55 lawyers, 12 gentlemen of leisure, and an assortment of manufacturers, insurance company presidents, ship building and lumber capitalists, contractors, and a few journalists, physicians and farmers" (1972:265-266). The differentiation of political and economic elites, more prevalent today, had not occurred at this time. This was not simply characteristic of the Macdonald government, as Creighton argues, the "Laurier Plutocracy" was composed of the same "bankers, engineers, corporation lawyers, railway builders, mining promoters, pulp and paper producers, and public utility entrepreneurs" (1970:108). Even exposure on the scale of the infamous "Pacific Scandal" was not sufficient to keep the powerful interests who supported Macdonald out of office in 1878. "Business and politics" was an accepted developmental strategy. The close relationship between George Stephen (of the Bank of Montreal and major promoter of the Canadian Pacific Railway) and Macdonald continued as "one of the closest political-business friendships in North American history", even after Macdonald was forced to resign office and then later returned. Stephen contributed one million dollars to Macdonald's cam.

paign fund (Bliss, 1972:177). It is within the context of these power alliances that the transcontinental railway was constructed.

Confederation had promised commercial interests from central Canada two railways, one from the Maritimes and the other transcontinental. Maritime interests felt a railway from central Canada to the east coast would promote industrialization, thereby opening the markets of the center to its manufactured goods, coal and lumber. In fact, the railway was to have the opposite impact by serving as a drain on the Maritime economy in favour of the center. The transcontinental railway, on the other hand, was designed to drain the western hinterland of her staples and, when finally completed, accomplished this task.

Keeping with the National Policy of defensive expansion, the government insisted that the transcontinental line be built completely within Canada. This proved more difficult a task than anticipated and the bargaining of the railway promoters for added concessions delayed commencement of the project. Insisting that the road was to be built by private capitalists and financed by government land grants and loans, Macdonald was forced to reluctantly initiate construction on a limited basis without private capitalists in order to fulfill the political promises he had made. When agreement was finally reached, Montreal promoters received more than generous concessions. Myers rhetorically asks of the Canadian Pacific charter, "When had any Company, except the Hudson's Bay Company, been invested with such extraordinary privileges and powers, immunities and rights?" (1972:266). The contract involved a direct subsidy of $25 million in cash, 25 million acres of "suitable" land along the rail line, land for roadbeds and stations, complete turnover of existing rail lines valued at $37.8 million, plus concessions on taxation of land, capital stock and no duties on imported materials for construction. In addition to other concessions and grants made later, the government agreed to give the company a "free hand" at setting freight rates until it had made a 10 per cent profit on its capital (Easterbrook & Aitken, 1956:428-429). Welfare capitalism had begun. By forming its own construction company in conjunction with the Bank of Montreal, the railway syndicate was able to make an initial $10 million profit and with the formation of a land company, to dispose of the generous land grants, additional capital was also raised (Myers, 1972:273-282).

Railways placed a heavy burden on the resources of the federal government; by this time three quarters of all federal debt was incurred through support of railways and other transportation facilities (Rowell/Sirois Report, 1963:45-46). Tariffs, designed to create revenue were supposed to serve both commercial interests and nascent manufacturers by simultaneously providing a financial base and "protection" from some foreign goods, In the seven years following Confederation, customs revenues increased by 60 per cent. "Dominion Government was proving to be a magnificent financial instrument for creating the new British North America of which the Fathers had dreamed" (81), the Rowell/Sirois Commission noted. The tariff policy associated with the National Policy was not intended to prevent foreign capital from entering the country; rather, it was designed to promote a Canadian market and industrialization within Canada. The "protective" dimensions of the tariff were created between 1879 and 1887 with the intent of developing an inter-provincial trading system, obviously to the advantage of the commercial elite. With implementation of the tariff in 1879, investment from the U.S. was actively encouraged to enter Canada, and this policy met with some success producing what Naylor has called, "Industry in Canada but no Canadian industry" (1972:25). Naylor is overstating his point; of course, there was some Canadian industry prior to, and catalysed by, the policy but most industrial pursuits were not led by the ruling class. Powerful Canadian interests chose rather to engage in traditional commercial pursuits of finance and transportation. Industrialization was undertaken by smaller Canadian entrepreneurs and already developed firms from the United States. Scheinberg notes that the National Policy intended to develop foreign investment behind the tariff walls but "foreign economic domination was never perceived as a real threat during that period. American investment was stimulated, but not in amounts that would raise fears. Macdonald, of course, does not bear the responsibility for the failures of twentieth-century Canadian leaders to readjust to changed economic circumstances" (1973:222). Scheinberg may be overly generous to Macdonald and his associates but he is correct in the failure of later elites to adjust. However, Macdonald and his associates also failed to adjust their own commercial assumptions to an industrial age. They preferred to import "wholesale", an industrial system from the U.S. rather than support the nascent entrepreneurs already present. In other words, traditional dominant interests in Canada failed to encourage and sustain new indigenous social forces in manufacturing. Rather, it chose to dominate and contain them by taking advantage of their weak capital and market position by moving in and consolidating industrially-based entrepreneurial firms into joint-stock complexes suited to the purposes of financial capitalism.

Acheson demonstrates how the National Policy, in the short term, generated within the Maritimes a developing industrial structure that emerged from the limited capital of second-generation Maritime merchant families. But, as he illustrates, they had neither the capital reserves nor control of market outlets which rested in Canada with the powerful Montreal-centered ruling class[8]. The desire and ambition of early Maritimers was to generate a powerful industrial system led by the East, as in the U.S. model. The power of the Montreal ruling class proved too great an obstacle to such high aspirations. Acheson shows that "the decade following 1879 was characterized by a significant transfer of capital and human resources from the traditional staples into a new manufacturing base which was emerging in response to federal tariff policies" (1972b:3). Maritime entrepreneurs were too limited in their capital reserves, according to Acheson, to survive the recession of 1885 and "acquiesced in the 1890's to the industrial leadership of the Montreal business community" (4). Their success to that point under the National Policy, however, was substantial. By 1885 the Maritimes, with under a fifth of Canada's population, "contained eight of the twenty-three Canadian cotton mills—including seven of the nineteen erected after 1879—three of five sugar refineries, two of seven rope factories, one of three glass works, both of the Canadian steel mills, and six of the nation's twelve rolling mills" (14). Reliance on the Montreal entrepôt for inter-provincial trade limited the Maritimes' control over its own development. Moreover, Montreal interests entered actively into the Maritimes' taking control of major coal fields and railways and, as Acheson says, "the community manufactory which had dominated the industrial growth of the 1880's ceased to exist in the 1890's" (19). There was a "growing shift from industrial to financial capitalism. Centered on the Montreal stock market, the new movement brought to the control of industrial corporations men who had neither a communal nor a vocational interest in the concern" (23-24). As intended, the National Policy did produce industry within Canada but the ruling financial elite failed to allow its development. It stifled emerging entrepreneurial talent by maintaining tight control of capital sources and taking over control of firms after they developed. With the shift in manufacturing from entrepreneur-controlled firms engaged in production to financier-controlled conglomerates, companies themselves became commodities to be bought and sold[9]. This limited, once again, the entrepreneurial talents of Canadian industrialists. Acheson concludes that "the National Policy simply represented to the entrepreneur a transfer from a British to a Canadian commercial empire" (28). The emerging social force was literally absorbed by traditional power holders within Canada.

It is interesting to note that many initial large-scale industrial pursuits controlled by Canadians in central Canada, as will be shown for companies like The Steel Company of Canada, were also consolidated by finance capitalists (see Kilbourn, 1960:18, 48ff). They were developed in response to the need to supply rail lines and rolling stock and, not initially at least, for independent industrial activity. Rather, as in the case of Maritime industry, financiers such as Max Aitken amalgamated several developing manufacturing firms into giant empires dominated by the ruling elite. Small nascent industrialists were unable to resist the thrust toward corporate capitalism.

By 1867 there was only $15 million in U.S. direct investment and $815 million in bonds from the U.K. in Canada. Only $30 million in portfolio investment came from the United States[10]. This pattern of investment, U.K. protfolio and U.S. direct, was to be persistent throughout Canadian history[11]. The implications of these types of investments are most apparent in the type of institutional structures which developed and the nature of elites heading these organizations. "With portfolio investment, there is a transfer of bond which gives the holder a claim to a sum of money and interest payments—it does not involve ownership of physical assets" (Naylor, 1973:45). This creates institutions within the economy headed by indigenous entrepreneurs able to form an indigenous capitalist class. Direct investment brings with it direct control and foreign capitalists. Foreign direct investment, while creating economic activity, does not create an indigenous capitalist class.

Both types of investment were active at the same time but not necessarily in the same quantities. The trend, however, is toward an increasing proportion of direct to portfolio. Between 1867 and 1900, the percentage of direct to total investment increased from 7.7 per cent to 18.5 per cent. The other trend to be noted is the tendency for U.S. investment to be direct and U.K. investment to be portfolio. It is at the level of capital formation that the basic difference between Canada's relationship with the United Kingdom and the United States exists. One relationship breeds increasing independence, the other dependency.

Increasing interpenetration of the continental economies was occurring not only at the level of capital, but also in terms of trade. Growth within the U.S. increasingly pulled Canadian staples into its industrial system thus increasing regionalism within Canada. The north-south pull, previously evident with the Red River settlement and British Columbia, was beginning to rival the projected east-west trajectory of the National Policy. In pursuit of outlets for natural resources from the hinterland, commercial interests of central Canada promoted this development in areas of forest products and non-ferrous metals. Some of the new companies associated with this trade were also off-shoots of earlier commercial corporations: the Nanaimo coal mine operation was initiated by the Hudson's Bay Company.

In the early post-Confederation period, world trade was prosperous and Canada's position reflected this general boom. Between 1868 and 1874, exports rose from $58 million to $89 million while imports increased from $73 to $128 million. Exports doubled during this time to the United Kingdom and they increased by one third to the United

States (Easterbrook & Aitken, 1956:389). With a slump in 1873 and depressions in 1876 and 1879, the situation stimulated protectionists' policies in the U.S. and U.K. and slowed down the boom in Canada.

The predominant characteristics of industry at the time of Confederation were that they were small, rural and had low capital investment. In 1870 there were 38,898 establishments engaged in manufacturing, employing 181,679 people, or an average of less than five persons per establishment, with an average capital investment of only $1,900. One quarter of the net value added by these enterprises came from leading urban centers (Creighton, 1970:6-7; Rowell/Sirois Report, 1963:24). This reflects the "agricultural" character of manufacturing (80 per cent of the population was rural) with concentration on blacksmith shops, handicrafts and agricultural implements. Over one half the population was engaged in agriculture, lumbering and fishing while only 13 per cent was involved in manufacturing and handicrafts (Ryerson, 1968:443). This phase would not last much longer.

Myers dates the beginning of corporate concentration in 1879 with the absorption of a series of small railways by the Grand Trunk and later by the Canadian Pacific. The tariff served to increase the number of mergers, particularly in textiles, where many small manufacturers gave way to two giants by 1892. With the tariff and increasing entry of United States firms into the domestic market, concentration proceeded to consolidate the multitude of small firms. These developments should be placed in the context of dominance by commercial interests over industrial entrepreneurs and the effect they had on the underdevelopment of an industrial base in Canada[12]. In this context it is understandable that industrial pursuits were stifled and left for the most part to well capitalized United States industrialists and newly arrived industrialist immigrants from the United Kingdom.

Acheson's study of the emerging industrial elite [13] between 1880 and 1885, provides a contrast between the commercial interests of the ruling class and nascent industrial entrepreneurs who were mainly immigrants from the U.K. and U.S. He argues that 168 industrialists dominated manufacturing between 1880 and 1885[14]. Social mobility for the industrial elite was intimately linked to immigration— immigrants composed more than half of the elite in 1885. This varied with each region:

> Virtually all of the successful Maritime entrepreneurs were native-born, as were nearly half of those of the St. Lawrence region. By contrast, more than three-fifths of the Lake Peninsula leaders were foreign-born (1972a:147).

Moreover, four fifths of the elite had fathers who were foreign born, "a proportion which would rise to nine out of ten if the Maritimes were excluded" (148). Occupational inheritance was prevalent among the elite; "it would appear that most Canadian industrialists inherited rather than acquired their status in society: nearly one-third were sons of manufacturers, more than a fifth were raised as children of men engaged in a variety of other business occupations" (150). Seen in the context of the high immigration, this group imported their skills and capital to Canada to take advantage of the growing opportunities. Rather than representing social mobility for indigenous Canadians, the new industrialization represented "horizontal mobility" from a similar social position in their place of origin (151). Acheson did find "mobility on a more modest scale was also evident among the number of the native-born members", citing examples of Hart Massey and Alexander Gibson as exceptional (155).

The elite was composed of three groups:

> The smallest consisted of a group of old Canadian industrial and commercial families often of several generations standing in British North America. The largest contained a number of individuals of British, American and German backgrounds, scions of industrial or commercial families in their native lands who succeeded in transferring their status to the new society through a form of horizontal mobility. Finally, a third group, largely of Scottish or native-Canadian farm or minor industrial origins, succeeded over a lifetime in achieving a significant degree of vertical mobility (171).

Acheson maintains that only in the case of tariff policy in the 1880's was this group able to be effective politically[15]; in fact, outside their own industrial sphere this group was powerless, considering themselves the "working class" of businessmen[16] (151). Their relatively low place in terms of wealth is evident in a survey Acheson reports:

> In a survey of Canadian wealth conducted in 1892, the *Canadian Journal of Commerce* gave pride of place to the transportation entrepreneurs whose personal resources frequently exceeded several millions of dollars. The remaining Canadian millionaires were all "merchant princes"—wholesalers and shippers (164).

By his calculation, Acheson found that "the 'typical' industrialist of the period was a man whose personal fortune, largely invested in his physical plant, probably amount to $100,000 to $300,000—a modest sum when measured in either international or national business terms" (166).

It is evident that a larger part of the industrial elite of the period was not only separate from the ruling class, but did not contend meaningfully with it for political power. The likes of Donald Alexander Smith of the CPR, governor of the Hudson's Bay Company, president of the Bank of Montreal and member of parliament; Sir Herbert Holt, financier and railwayman and Sir Hugh Allan of steamship, banking, insurance, telegraph and railway fame, were the type of commercial capitalists who dominated Canada at the time. They established policy for the country and provided the restrictive framework within which the emerging industrialists had to contend. It was only immigrant capitalists and extensions of industrialization from the U.K. and U.S. who could provide their own capital and markets that were able to survive. Operating as mediators in the North Atlantic triangle, commercial interests concentrated on developing staples to serve the industrialists of the United Kingdom and United States. Their profits were in the international market, not in limited native markets. It is this international character of Canadian capitalism, unable to contend with trade restrictions and international fluctuations, which dominated Canadian political economy.

VI. From Entrepreneurial to Corporate Capitalism (1900-1913)

Between 1879 and World War I, Canada's industrial structure underwent great transformations with the earlier era characterized by small establishments averaging one to two thousand capitalization and the latter, by joint-stock companies and the rise of corporate capitalism. Acheson shows, for instance, that the "real value of output increased from $423,000,000 in 1880 to $1,527,000,000 in 1910" (1973:189n). Following his study of the 1885 industrial elite, he repeated his procedures for 1910 to capture the effect of transformations in the industrial structure on recruitment to the elite. Only 51 per cent of the industrial elite in 1885 were native born but by 1910 this increased to 74 per cent; the proportion of fathers who were native born increased only slightly from 22 per cent to 27 per cent (193,195). Many of the 1910 elite were sons of the immigrants so prevalent in the 1885 study.

> About half of all the industrialists of 1910 entered businesses —manufacturing, mercantile, financial, transportation, or construction firms—which were owned or controlled by their fathers or uncles. Some of these concerns were already large joint stock corporations; most were relatively small family firms which were used as a base from which the entrepreneur later expanded his activities. Most of the remaining industrialists, and particularly

those of more limited means, began their careers in the service of one of the joint stock companies (202-203).

The transformation from entrepreneurial capitalism to corporate capitalism[17] studied by Acheson was not without important effects for mobility into the elite. Simultaneous with the concentration of the corporate structure from small enterprises to joint stock companies was a closure in access to decision making positions. This is documented in Table 1.

TABLE 1
Social Origins of the Industrial Elite, 1885-1910

Father's Occupation	1885 Elite	1910 Elite
Professional	8%	15%
Businessman	23%	32%
Manufacturer	32%	28%
Manager	5%	9%
(Sub-total)	(68%)	(84%)
Farmer	26%	15%
Craftsman	6%	1%
Labourer	0	0
Total	100%	100%
Total cases	105	129

(Acheson, 1973:206, Table 12).

While in 1885, 68 per cent of the industrial elite's fathers were professionals, businessmen, manufacturers or managers, by 1910 this climbed to 84 per cent. Correspondingly, the 32 per cent whose fathers were farmers or craftsmen had been cut by half to 16 per cent, thus representing a decline in the ability of the petty-bourgeois to make the move into the bourgeoisie. At neither point did any of the elites have fathers who were labourers (206). Of the 129 members of the industrial elite,

At least fifty-three members of the elite of 1910 were clearly identifiable as sons of leading Canadian industrialists or merchants. In addition to these, some twenty-one members of the 1885 elite remained among the 1910 industrialists. Still another indication of the hardening social fabric was the growing incidence of intermarriage among the offspring of leading entrepreneurs. In all, at least fifteen marriages, each involving two leading industrial families, occurred among the members of the elites of 1885 and 1910 (206-207).

Consistent with other findings reported, Acheson's study verifies the increasingly important component of financiers among the industrial elite in 1910. This indicates that the ruling class of financiers, railway magnets and members of the state elite were moving into manufacturing concerns after they had been established by entrepreneurs. The effect of this was to close off opportunities for others in the field without upper class backgrounds. During one brief period the manufacturing sector was open and immigrants with skills and some capital were able to establish themselves as a new social force but as the ruling class moved in and consolidated these emerging firms, avenues began to close, manufacturing became concentrated and opportunities were limited. Acheson notes that "as the strength of the finance industrialist grew within the [industrial] elite, and as that of the manufacturer industrialist waned, the opportunities for vertical social mobility became increasingly narrowed" (209-210). Several indications of upper class activities by the industrial elite not evident earlier are private schools, notably Upper Canada College (201), and private men's clubs. Although he notes:

> all industrialists generally participated in the club movement, merchants, financiers and construction and transportation entrepreneurs among the elite were more likely to be found in clubrooms than were manufacturers . . .an interlocking corporate elite of Montreal and Toronto entrepreneurs generally held memberships in the Mount Royal and St. James clubs of Montreal, the Rideau of Ottawa, and the Toronto and York clubs of Toronto (214-215).

Even the short period when the structure was open did not provide mobility for many indigenous Canadians, particularly French Canadians. The industrial elite, like the ruling class, was overwhelmingly Anglo. With only 7 per cent French Canadians in 1885, this had dropped to 6 per cent by 1910 in spite of French Canadians being 29 per cent of the population (197).

Several processes which characterize the period can be summarized. Earlier small scale manufacturing enterprises were now consolidated into joint stock companies and as this occurred they were increasingly taken over by members of the traditional ruling class. Finance capital tended toward secure investment with a profitable return while industrial capital attempted to secure profits through

production which was initially more venturesome and required entrepreneurial skills. As industries became established and profitable as
joint stock companies, financiers tended to move in with capital resources and secured control. Finance capitalists entered after the initial
enterprise proved viable but did not themselves initiate industrial
development[18].

Simultaneously, there was the phenomenon of foreign investment
and a branch plant economy. Moving in behind tariff barriers, there
were 450 such operations by 1913, among them Singer Sewing
Machines, Edison Electric, American Tobacco, Westinghouse, Gil-
lette and International Harvester (Bliss, 1970:31-32). These tended to
be larger and more self-sufficient than their Canadian counterparts.
There was also the beginning of what later became known as the
"sell-out" of Canadian industry by such sectors as the automobile
industry, once Canadian controlled, now integrated with U.S. industrial giants. "In 1907 Sam McLaughlin of Oshawa began assembling
Buick automobiles on license. The weakness of his operation was that
while he owned it, he was forced to import his engines from Detroit. He
did the same thing with Chevrolet after 1914. Then, in 1918 he sold
both companies to General Motors and General Motors of Canada was
formed" (Laxer, J., 1973:32). These developments illustrate the
economic environment within which Canadian manufacturers had to
cope. The financial ruling class was engaging in taking control and
consolidating firms which became profitable, powerful U.S. industrialists to the south were moving their own concentrated industrial
system into Canada through branch plant operations and buying out
viable firms to consolidate them on a continental basis. An industrial
structure did exist at the turn of the century in Canada which was
independent of the United States and the ruling financial elite but it
lacked the power, especially in terms of capital and market access, to
survive within this environment. Only a few were able to independently
survive as viable operations.

The shift from entrepreneurial to corporate capitalism was accomplished by two distinct social forces. One was the movement of branch
plants into manufacturing with U.S. corporate capitalism's extention
into Canada, while simultaneously there was the internal shift so well
documented by Acheson. Each combined to actively consolidate the
numerous small manufactures which existed only a few years earlier.
Although it is difficult to distinguish the external and internal forces in
the consolidation movement, Reynolds provides an observation on
their combined effect:

The years 1909-12 were marked particularly by mergers in the
heavy industries. Canada Cement, Amalgamated Asbestos,

Canadian Car and Foundry, Dominion Steel Corporation, and The Steel Company of Canada date from this period. Important textile, tobacco, brewing, milling, and paper combinations were also formed, however, and nearly every industry in the country was affected (1940:6).

With the emergence of corporate capitalism there was, for the first time, the beginning of an industrial system developing, although at a cost to entrepreneurs. Canadian participation in industry was increasingly confined to members of the ruling class who were able to control corporations through stock ownership in a way not possible during the entrepreneurial phase.

The effect of the merger movement and organization of production through corporate capitalism was for increasing participation by the dominant Canadian commercial interests in manufacturing but at the ownership and control level through consolidation, and not in entrepreneurial activities. Moreover, the industrial structure was considerably different by 1910 than it had been even twenty years earlier; there were now U.S. controlled branch plants to contend with and this restricted the manufacturing areas that Canadian industrialists were able to move into. The consequence for mobility, within Canadian controlled firms at least, was a general shift in the class of origin toward more upper class, both through the domination by the traditional ruling class and the absorption of older manufacturing families. Acheson says, "In firms, such as Massey and Harris, which had been transformed into joint stock companies, individual families were usually still able to dominate corporate proceedings" (1973:191). The result of integrating leaders of Canadian manufacturing with commercial interests was an interpenetration of both the top-most manufacturing families and the traditional ruling class. Alongside this alliance was the beginning of another emerging group, those associated with U.S. branch plants. In between there was little room for the entrepreneur from outside the upper class; they were squeezed out of the now concentrated market, and mobility to the top within the new corporate giants was limited.

An excellent illustration of the development of indigenous industrial capitalism on a large scale is to be found in the origins of The Steel Company of Canada. Unlike earlier ventures, Stelco was backed by the indigenous ruling class. Created by merging the industrial efforts of the Bigelow and Hersey families, which Kilbourn characterizes as standing "in the tradition of rugged individualism and the small self-made entrepreneur" (1960:18), the marriage was performed by members of the ruling class. As Kilbourn states:

The Montreal Rolling Mills was born not in a blacksmith's shop, but in the counting house of a wealthy merchant. It had the benefit, from the beginning, of distinguished god-parents and influential uncles, among whom were numbered important members of the Conservative Party and the leading families of Montreal. It was a harbinger of finance capitalism and the large corporation. It was ultimately to be the means by which a young financier named Max Aitken put together the many-sided industrial empire of the Steel Company of Canada (18).

Kilbourn's detailed historical-journalistic account of these early days of Canadian large-scale manufacturing is ridden with illustrations of the friendships and fortunes which forged this giant corporation and the concessions, exemptions and bonuses offered by the city of Hamilton to early steel interests and later to U.S. giants, Westinghouse and International Nickel (48). He describes how the influential Senator Wood, a financier and "prominent Liberal", persuaded the Cabinet to grant trade and tariff concessions to the steel makers (50). The early company ran into early financial difficulty but was "tided over by a large personal loan from George Gooderham, the Toronto banker and whisky distiller and a friend of some of the company's organizers" (50). The value of being "well connected" within the ruling class was evident in the entire range of transactions which occurred before Stelco could be successfully formed. Little wonder the smaller nascent industrialists were not able to develop given their distance from the inner circles of power. Stelco's creation was not industrial, it was financial and political.

Built as a "spin off" from the railway boom, the early steel producers were heavily dependent on the ruling commercial elite; it is understandable they would engage in steel production above other industrial pursuits. This is reflected in the enormous increase in production during the early period. "Between 1901 and 1911, iron and steel and their manufactures became Canada's foremost industry. Steel production jumped from 29,000 to 882,000 tons a year, pig iron from 252,000 to 923,000 tons" (54). This was not the manufactory of the previous period nor were the men who ran it the earlier manufacturers. Kilbourn is worth quoting at length to illustrate exactly who the men were that controlled this early industrial venture by indigenous capitalists. He says the board of directors included men like:

. . . William Molson, president of Molson's Bank and of the Champlain Railway Company, director of the Grand Trunk, Governor of McGill University, and scion of the brewing family which was so successful at breeding generations of able sons. And there was Peter Randolph, of the sugar refinery and many other commercial interests, a member of one of those Transatlantic Montreal families which still maintained their social roots and business ties on both sides of the water. The company's board would include in the future several distinguished and influential senators. Among its future presidents, besides Molson and Redpath themselves, would be the shipping magnate Andrew Allan, and Sir Edward Clouston of the Bank of Montreal, the accepted financial oracle of his day. These were men of substance whose advice was based on experience in many fields. They could talk on equal terms with Cabinet ministers. And they would bring back valuable intelligence and tangible support from their friends in the City of London on their regular visits to the world's financial capital (20-21).

This does not exhaust the powerful connections that this early enterprise enjoyed; there were also men like "William McMaster, distant younger relative of a more famous Scot with the same name, the Toronto Liberal Senator who built a dry goods business, a university, and the Canadian Bank of Commerce"; E.R. Wood of Dominion Securities and his associates "Senator Cox of Canada Life and Sir Edmund Walker of the Canadian Bank of Commerce"; Sir Edmund Osler, president of the Dominion Bank, and his brother Dr. William Osler; W.D. Matthews, a director of the CPR and vice-president of the Dominion Bank (23-24, 64-72). The list goes on and on, all the evidence pointing to the fact that these men were not industrial entrepreneurs but financiers and political men who had entered the industrial world to further integrate their already tight control on the railways which they felt were the life-blood of their commercial livelihood. The Steel Company of Canada was not alone in this process of consolidation; for example, "The Dominion Textile Company was formed in 1905 by a syndicate of 16 men, including Sir Herbert Holt and Sir Charles Gordon, to take over four existing cotton companies" and others like the Canada Cement Company formed in 1909 consolidated eleven cement companies (Reynolds, 1940:177-178).

The Canadian social structure of this era is an extension of that from post-Confederation. The alliance of transportation, banking and political interests remained and was strengthened by economic boom. Wealth was increasingly concentrated with "less than 50 men" controlling "$4,000,000,000 or more than one-third of Canada's material wealth as expressed in railways, banks, factories, mines and other properties and resources" (Myers, 1972:xxxi). The famous "Eighteen Liberals of Toronto", among them "bankers, corporation lawyers, manufacturers and merchandisers", were deciding government policies and Canada's future (Creighton, 1970:124). By 1907 the yearly sales of Eaton's was over $22 million and their empire, with that of Simpson's and Hudson's Bay, was extending into the west to capture growing markets. Behind the federal government and the railways, Eaton's was the third largest employer (Starowicz, 1972:7-8). Overarching the entire social structure remained the oligarchy of business and government working on commercial assumptions and guided by a colonialist National Policy. Projecting itself into the world market, the stability of the ruling class, and with it the fate of the Canadian economy, depended on outlets for Canadian staples. They may have controlled the political and economic situation within Canada, but within the world market, they remained vulnerable.

Scattering to service the industrial centers of the world with staples, the Canadian ruling class was obsessed with railways and the prosperity they would bring. Using the instruments of land grants and subsidies, the government commissioned a second transcontinental railway and, as before, used private capitalists and public money to fund the venture. In the years before 1913, the government had supported railways to the extent of 56 million acres of prime land valued at over $1,121 million in addition to cash subsidies of $224 million and bonds valued at $245 million, an average subsidy of $50,000 per mile of railway (Myers, 1972:151). By committing itself to construction of the second transcontinental railway, the government found itself in a position of being forced "more by accident than design", to quote the Royal Commission on Transportation, to take over the disastrous CNR. Mackenzie and Mann, the two major promoters of the CNR, were able to make sizable fortunes from the project in spite of its failure. Afraid of the implication of bankruptcy for their international credit position and the effect it would have on the Bank of Commerce at home, the state invented another form of what Creighton calls "railway dole" —nationalization. Rather than running counter to capitalist sentiments, nationalization of the CNR was clearly supportive of capitalism, following the tradition of welfare capitalism so prevalent throughout Canada's economic history. Characterized by the Rowell/Sirois Report as a "great holding company", the federal government had increased its revenues from $63 million to $253 million between 1896 and 1913, only to increase its debt to $521 million by 1913, most of which was attributable to transportation facilities (Rowell/Sirois Report, 1963:56, 95, 98). With $2 billion dollars invested in railways, expansion west began to tap into the wheat boom which had now become a staple central to Canadian agriculture and export policy. The wheat boom stimulated immigration and migration west as it did industrialization, central Canadian industrialization that is.

Just as the tariff policy had the effect of creating a branch plant situation in central Canadian industry, it had its counterpart in the west.

Innis maintains that the wheat boom encouraged many farmers from the United States to take up their vocation in Canada's west; "grain firms followed the settlers from Minneapolis to Winnipeg with the expansion of the Winnipeg grain exchange. American capital and technique seized on the advantages of a potential expanding market and branch plants were established in Canada in increasing numbers" (1956:167).

Events within the U.K. and U.S. at this time generated a situation of readily available capital and Canada was one of the main outlets for this surplus, thus increasing foreign capital investment by $2,545 million between 1900 and 1913. With the crest of the industrial boom reached at home, the United Kingdom increased foreign investment capital from 8 per cent to 48 percent of total British investment (Easterbrook & Aitken, 1956:402). This investment was mainly divided between railways (41 per cent) and government stocks (30 per cent) with limited investment in finance (8 per cent), mining (7 per cent), industry (6 per cent) and other activities (Block, 1970:161n). In Canada new British portfolio investment amounted to $1,618 million between 1900 and 1913 with only $135 million in direct investment. United States investment for the same period was $285 million portfolio and $345 million direct. Once again, the different forms of investment reflect the different economic philosophies; as Creighton suggests, "The basic principle of the nineteenth century British Empire, in economics as well as in politics, had been devolution—the encouragement of local initiative and the grant of local autonomy. The hard foundation of the twentieth-century American empire was to be centralized control" (1970:181). Reflecting the tariff barrier and the nature of direct investment, the phenomenon of branch plants began to take on real significance. Although they reflect the industrial strength of the United States at this time, they also indicate the chosen policy of development envisioned by the ruling economic and political interests who assumed that the jump over the border would result in the "Canadianization" of these industries. What was ignored, however, was the fact that these corporations were vertically and often horizontally linked with their U.S. counterparts and unlike portfolio debts, the debts of direct investment do not go away but instead strengthen. Regardless, manufacturing grew rapidly during this period, surpassing agricultural output after 1910 but remaining concentrated in central Canada. In 1911, four fifths of manufacturing output was in Ontario and Quebec; this was consistent with the centers of power and the National Policy of an east-west nexus. From 1900 to 1910, the net value of manufacturing had increased two and a half times, as had textiles, while iron and steel increased over three times and flour and grist mills more than five times. There was also the start of pulp and paper, coal, and lumber mills (Easterbrook & Aitken, 1956:485).

The decades surrounding the turn of the century were crucial to Canada's economic history. They mark the extension of dominance by the commercial ruling class, the demise of the entrepreneur, and the penetration of U.S. direct investment through branch plants. Two new social forces, both centered in manufacturing, had emerged; one was smashed and consolidated with the traditional center of power while the other grew and increased in power alongside the established powers. Canadian manufacturers could not survive because the commercial ruling class did not allow them to; U.S. manufacturers were much more advanced and had the support of their parent companies.

VII. More Mergers and the First World War (1913-1926)

War stimulated the economy; in the west, wheat production was intensified to meet growing food demands and in the east, munitions plants were established. Munitions sustained the industrial sector which developed to support railway requirements but had shown signs of a slow-down with most of the capital requirements of railway construction satisfied. The First World War provided an important boost to manufacturing; for example, the "total annual value of manufactures more than doubled in the decade 1910-20, to almost a billion and a half dollars. The country's steel capacity also doubled to two million tons, one-quarter of it accounted for by Stelco" (Kilbourn, 1960:107). In a detailed examination of the impact of the First World War on the position of Stelco, Kilbourn describes how war production doubled the ingot capacity, increased profits, financed expansion of plants and equipment, and expanded the number of employees almost two-fold from 4,400 to 7,800. He goes on to say, "More lasting and far more significant than mere expansion in size was the fact the new prosperity enabled the company to improve its position as an integrated steel-making enterprise. It could add new areas to its finishing work and move towards self-sufficiency in ore, coal, and coke-making" (102-103). In other words, growth and profits as a key war industry allowed Stelco to expand, vertically integrating various elements of production which otherwise may have been developed by resource-based companies. Rather than encourage the development of an independent resource sector, the industrial sector expanded its operations into this area in order to "sell" to themselves.

War had a particularly strong impact on non-ferrous metal extraction, especially copper, zinc and nickel. These resources were mainly for export, however, with these items accounting for an export increase from $14 million to $23 million between 1911 and 1921. Most dramatic was the increase during a similar period from $19 million to $150 million in pulp and paper (Easterbrook & Aitken, 1956:488). The war boost was to end in 1920 with another withdrawal of the world economy but some residual effect was to be felt.

Laxer illustrates both the growth of automobile manufacturing in the 1920's—U.S. control having bought out Sam McLaughlin a decade earlier—and the importance of tapping into the British Empire market. He says, "In 1929 Canada's American-owned auto industry produced the second largest number of cars of any country in the world and exported over 100,000 automobiles out of the quarter million produced. These exports were mainly to other British Empire countries. 1929 was, in fact, the high point of the Canadian auto industry in relation to production in other countries" (1973:33).

The policy of production decentralization throughout the Commonwealth during the war also stimulated indigenously financed industry in Canada. On the other hand, war produced a substantial strengthening of the state with over $2,100 million in war loans attained from within Canada, of which "from 80 per cent to 85 per cent of the War loan bonds were purchased by business organizations, financial institutions, and individuals with substantial incomes" (Rowell/Sirois Report, 1963:125). The federal government took a new interest in industry during the war and, using powers conferred by the War Measures Act, created the Board of Commerce which was active until its existence was declared unconstitutional in 1922 (122). The Rowell/Sirois Commission argued that "growing concentration of control in industry and finance and the large profits made by individuals and corporations out of the War-time prosperity, enlarged the pools of wealth which could be tapped by corporation taxes and eventually by succession duties" (1963:130-131).

The post-war period also experienced investment patterns different from early staples with the new staples of pulp and paper and minerals. In terms of economic importance, the United States surpassed the United Kingdom during the period. By 1921, 60 per cent of trade was conducted with the United States. Industrialization had begun on an enlarged scale in Canada but the small Canadian firms were not in a strong position to compete with their giant United States counterparts.

It is interesting to note the change in the nature of capital investment at the time. Heavy war demands forced some U.K. investment to withdraw, but in the U.S., the war had a different impact by stimulating industrialization and creating a surplus. Although U.K. direct investment increased by $136 million between 1913 and 1926, portfolio investment declined by $317 million. Contrary to early and later patterns, the United States actually had more portfolio investment in Canada in 1926 than direct investment ($1,793 million compared to $1,403). United States investment as a percentage of foreign investment increased from 21.5 per cent in 1913 to 53.0 per cent in 1926. This reflect two patterns in Canada-U.S. investment relations during the period. Simultaneously, U.S. corporate giants were establishing branches in Canada and an indigenous industrial base, using, in part, U.S. portfolio investment, was also beginning to show signs of strength. Paradoxically, Canada was showing both signs of dependence and independence but, in either case, it had now become almost totally committed to the continental economy in terms of imports and exports, portfolio and direct investment. The era of United Kingdom supremacy in Canada was over.

New relationships in economics were to be felt in the political world as well. For the next 21 years Canadian political life was to be dominated by Mackenzie King, the first Prime Minister to be raised on U.S. political culture, having spent a good deal of his early life in the United States working for the Rockefeller family. King's orientation reflected Canada's. In a rather poetic passage, King captures both the international flavour of Canadian capitalism during the period and the forces of concentration at work.

> The world-wide nature of forces at work upon Capital is reflected in the world's commerce. It also, like a mighty tide sweeps now in this direction, now in that; deepening or deserting former channels; nowhere constant, everywhere seeking or forsaking anew. Captial has sought in different ways to fortify itself against the cross-currents of this ceaseless change. At first, its countless competing units struggled one against another; little by little, they began to coalesce, and the process has so continued. Industry no longer resembles the innumerable stars of the sky by night, as it once did with its distribution of power in a multitude of hands (1918:29-30).

Reynolds provides empirical verification to King's observations. Between 1900 and 1933, there were 374 consolidations of which 58 were during 1909 to 1912 and 231 between 1925 and 1930 (1940:6n). For example, "British Empire Steel Corporation was incorporated in 1920 to consolidate all of the steel and coal interests of Nova Scotia, including Dominion Steel Corporation, Dominion Coal, Nova Scotia Steel, and Halifax Shipyards. . . . Moreover, the companies included were themselves the result of previous mergers" (179-180).

Consolidation was occurring in banking as well as in industry. From a high of 51 banks in 1874, there were only 36 by 1900 and 11 by 1925, reflecting the increasing concentration of power in the financial field. In 1895, only the Bank of Montreal, with 18 per cent of the total resources of banks and the Commerce with 9 per cent, were exceptionally large. By 1927, the situation had changed dramatically with the Bank of Montreal accounting for 26 per cent, as did the Royal Bank, and the Commerce had 17 per cent. Between them, the three largest banks accounted for about 70 per cent of the total Canadian bank resources; financial interests had become centered in three major banks and seven smaller ones by 1928[19]. Prosperity brought consolidation to the financial elite and the forces of accumulation and concentration were very much at work.

VIII. Depression and Withdrawal of the World Economy (1926-1939)[20]

The height of the wheat boom in Canada was reached in 1928 when it accounted for more than 50 per cent of world export in this staple. In Canada, wheat accounted for 32 per cent and pulp and paper for 15 per cent of exports; each of these commodities was dependent on world trade conditions for their success. Due to Canada's dependence on world markets, the world-wide Depression of the 1930's was particularly severe. By 1932, the pulp and paper industry had fallen to 53 per cent capacity and mineral exports had dropped by more than 60 per cent. Overall capital expenditures dropped by 70 per cent (Creighton, 1970:200-201). These developments levelled a severe blow to emerging industrialists, particularly independent Canadian operations which were always in a weak market and capital position. The level of industrial development reached between 1926 and 1929 was not to be achieved again until after the Second World War. Depression brought with it a withdrawal of the world economy and an end to free trade.

By 1930 the average capital investment in an establishment was $217,000 compared to only $1,900 in 1870. Depression further increased concentration by eliminating the smallest firms and increased reliance on commercial capital. The state became increasingly important in the economy, even more than during the First World War, but this time, involvement was in terms of salvaging the commercial empire it had helped develop. Between 1932 and 1934 the state paid 40 per cent of the transportation costs for use of the CNR, but in spite of these efforts, the economy was in worse shape in 1939 than it had been when the period opened.

Outstanding in an otherwise largely unexplored era of Canadian history is Lloyd G. Reynolds' study of *The Control of Competition in Canada* for the Depression years. His results, drawn largely from the Royal Commission on Price Spreads, confirm the trends outlined earlier regarding mergers but in addition, he is able to show the consequences of this for the concentration of Canadian industry. As suggested earlier, concentration was a product of two forces—one

TABLE 2

Industrial Concentration in the 1930's by Control of Output in Selected Manufacturing Industries

Industry	Cumulative percentage of output controlled by:				
	1 Firm	2 Firms	3 Firms	4 Firms	5 Firms
Automobiles	40	65	89	—	—
Ammunition, explosives, ammonia, chlorine	100	—	—	—	—
Agricultural implements	—	60	—	75	—
Brewing (Ontario & Quebec)	—	—	—	—	—
Cement	90	—	—	—	—
Copper	53	83	—	93	—
Canning (fruit & vegetables)	67	—	—	—	—
Cotton Yarn & Cloth	48	—	79	—	—
Electrical equipment (heavy)	—	—	100	—	—
Fertilizer	—	—	70	—	—
Lead	91	—	—	—	—
Meat Packing	59	85	—	—	—
Milling	—	—	—	—	73
Nickel	71	—	—	—	—
Oil	55	—	—	—	—
Pulp and Paper	—	—	—	—	90
Rubber Footwear	39	50	61	72	—
Silks (real)	23	42	61	—	—
Silk (artificial)	66	100	—	—	—
Sugar	—	—	—	—	100
Tires	—	—	—	—	65
Tobacco	70	90	—	—	—
Zinc	74	—	—	—	—

(Source: Lloyd G. Reynolds, *The Control of Competition in Canada*, 1940, Table I:5).

foreign and the other indigenous—which combined to squeeze out smaller manufacturers. Reynolds notes that concentration in many industries, particularly "automobiles, tires, gasoline, tobacco, rayon, aluminum" and others, was a product of importing concentration from the U.S. market into Canada (1940:xii). He says,

> The extension of many large United States producers into Canada . . . has operated as a check on competition. Perhaps the most notable examples are Imperial Oil (formed in 1880 as a Standard Oil subsidiary) and Imperial Tobacco . . . Canadian Celanese, Canadian Westinghouse, Canadian General Electric, Aluminum Limited, International Harvester, the 'big three' automobile companies and the 'big four' tire producers occupy the same dominant position in Canada that their parent companies enjoy in the United States (6-7).

As has already been illustrated, concentration was also facilitated by indigenous forces led by dominant commercial interests. With examples too numerous to list here, Reynolds notes that, "Few of the leaders of Canadian industry reached their present position by growth alone. Most of them are the result of a merger or a succession of mergers" (175). Again, similar to what has already been illustrated, he notes the effect of the merger movement is that "control of industry, too, tends in the process to be transferred from men experienced in production to men experienced in finance, as owner-managers are superseded by boards of directors composed of promoters and bankers . . . Financially-minded directors tend to regard a corporation primarily as a source of interest payments and commissions" (181-182). Table 2 provides a comprehensive outline of concentration within industries following from both the U.S.-based force toward concentration and the equally effective indigenous one led by commercial interests.

Reynolds is also able to illustrate that concentrated industries earned substantially higher rates of profits than all manufacturing companies in either Canada or the U.S. "Canadian monopolies earned 12.2 per cent annually on stockholders' investment over the ten years 1928-37. Over the comparable period 1927-35, manufacturing companies generally were able to earn only 4.0 per cent in Canada and 6.3 per cent in the United States" (60-61). Moreover, concentrated Canadian industries were not hit nearly as hard as others by the Depression. For example, in 1931 their rate of return remained at six per cent while all Canadian manufacturing fell to 1.9 per cent and U.S. manufacturing to 0.3 per cent (60, Table 3). The overall effect of the Depression was to eliminate smaller and weaker companies and further reinforce the dominant position of a few large firms. Although there is no data available to confirm this, it would be anticipated that the effect was to further restrict mobility into elite positions as the social structure became further concentrated. This projection arises from the theory outlined in Chapter One on the relationship between opportunity and condition plus the support this theory was given by Acheson's study on the effects of similar transformations between 1880 and 1910.

One trend concerning the relationship between economic and political elites should also be noted at this point. While it was demonstrated for earlier eras that there was a ruling class of political and economic interests who in large part were the same, there was a gradual shift in the relationship between these sectors occurring since the turn of the century. These two institutions were gradually becoming separate but related spheres of activity. Although not exclusively, there was evolving a division of labour between them and a set of norms which prevented the simultaneous holding of political office and key corporate positions. Other types of activities were created, however, which substituted for the earlier practice of holding positions in each institution simultaneously. In addition to the interchange of persons from one institution to another accompanied by a rite of passage which stripped earlier offices, there was also the practice of lobbying. As Reynolds points out, "Lobbying activity, instead of being concentrated on committees of the legislature, as in the United States, tends to be focused on Cabinet members. Sponsors of a measure try to secure the support of Cabinet members, and particularly of the Prime Minister, through visits, letters, petititions and other means" (1940:260). This was not a difficult process and doors were always open to the economic elite; moreover, "Cabinet members do not need to be bribed to accept the business viewpoint. They already think like businessmen" (262). This was not to say that the relationship was not constantly reinforced by exhibitions of power by the economic elite; indeed, Reynolds demonstrates businessmen "have been willing and able to spend large sums of money in advancing their claims. Permanent lobbies in Ottawa, innumerable special delegations, the unifying influence of conventions and trade journals, the molding of public opinion through newspapers and other media, contributions to party funds—all these investments have yielded an abundant return" (272). The difference in the way political and economic interests relate to one another since the turn of the century will be elaborated later. For now it is important to place Canada within the North Atlantic triangle and changes occurring there.

Canada still remained tied to the U.S. empire and maintained its tariff policy on the basis that it was bringing U.S. branch plants into Canada, 92 in 1931 alone (Naylor, 1972:29). Overall, the Depression finalized the end of the British empire and decreased the total amount of foreign investment entering Canada. The decline of the U.K. and U.S. investment slowed down Canadian industrialization. British investment declined during the period and U.S. investment increased only slightly, representing its lowest period of growth since Confederation, with $477 million in portfolio and an equal amount of direct investment. The central characteristic of the direct investment was its concentration in manufacturing, particularly automobiles, and mining, particularly iron ore. It took the Second World War to provide a stimulus to the Canadian economy and generate a program of industrialization.

IX. The Second World War, Government and Industry (1939-1946)

The Second World War had a ''similar though quantitatively much greater effect'' on industrialization in Canada than the First War. Manufacturing, especially in areas of tool-making, electronics, chemicals and aluminum, began to blossom while the steel industry increased its output by over 120 per cent and aluminum grew by 500 per cent between 1939 and 1942 (Easterbrook & Aitken, 1956:520). These developments reflect the different character of the Second from the First War, where much greater mechanism and motorization became important. Canadian plants concentrated on airplanes, ships, tanks, and cars—producing one million motor vehicles during the war alone (Creighton, 1970:249). The war also affected the reintegration of the Canadian economy with the United States economy which emerged as the strongest world economy in the capitalist system after the War. Canada was actually a net exporter of capital during the war as the amount of total United Kingdom investment in Canada dropped by $777 million. United States portfolio investment increased by only $359 million and direct was up by $547 million. This was the beginning of the reintroduction of direct investment as the major means of U.S. investment in Canada but the proportions were still not as great as they would be soon.

The government reintroduced its earlier concern with wheat during this period and, in 1935, the Canadian Wheat Board was reinstated and, with the outbreak of war in 1943, became the only marketing agent for wheat in Canada. Similar to the conditions of crisis which caused the government to take over the CNR, the Wheat Board came under government control only after it was illustrated that private capitalists were unable to cope with existing trade conditions (Easterbrook & Aitken, 1956:502-503). The Bank of Canada established in 1935 as a private corporation to manage the monetary system, was nationalized in 1938 to provide an over-arching agency to maintain financial stability and deal with matters of foreign exchange. It was also in this period that the Industrial Development Bank was established to provide industrial loans, an area of finance lacking in indigenous support up to this time.

Two of the most powerful organizations ever to exist in Canada were instituted during the Second World War. These were the Wartime Industries Control Board under the direction of C.D. Howe and the Wartime Prices and Trade Board directed by Donald Gordon. Each board was vested with dictatorial powers over the direction of Canada's economy. As C.D. Howe said in his preface to their official government history, the period when these boards were in power was "one of the more important eras of Canadian history, the years during which the country emerged from its position as a producer of basic supplies to that of a highly industrialized state" (Kennedy, 1950:v). From the corporate world[21] and upper levels of the state bureaucracies, some of Canada's most powerful men were recruited to establish policies and oversee the administration of the boards and, with them, the entire Canadian economy. When the boards were dismantled after the war, the individuals who had held powerful positions again re-entered the corporate and state bureaucracies with many contacts, lasting friendships and an intimate knowledge of Canada's corporate and state structures and personnel. Many members of the present economic elite who emerged in the post-war period after tenure on these boards were in much more powerful positions than before they entered.

Although some areas of production were established on the basis of crown corporations, in areas where firms were already established they were "induced" through such measures as direct payments by the government for capital equipment, payments for the expansion of facilities which were later sold back to the companies for nominal sums, and fast write-offs of capital equipment over only three years was granted, thus providing great quantities of capital for expansion. Kilbourn discusses the effects of these measures on the steel industry, declaring that they provided the greatest expansion ever occurring within the industry, before or since the war (1960:175-176). Neufeld describes a similar phenomenon in the Massey-Ferguson organization which benefited from contracts, not only with the Canadian government but those of the U.K. and U.S. as well. He says the company's sales were $21 million in 1939 (none from war production) and by 1942 sales had climbed to $58 million, of which 49 per cent was from war production. By 1945 sales were up to $116 million with war production up to 58 per cent. Even with price controls in effect, "over the six-year period, 1940-1945, Massey-Harris' net profit before taxes amounted to $25.6 million, half of which reflected profits from war production" (1969:45-46). As with the steel industry, there were added advantages of fast write-offs for capital investment, expanded production and new technology which helped the company's position well after the war was over. Similar developments occurred in all major industries within Canada, including, for example, Molsons Breweries (see Denison, 1955:354).

The war is of importance in this discussion for two reasons: firstly, it was a time when most of the present dominant industrial corporations enjoyed their greatest expansion and movement into positions of importance within the Canadian economy. Under the direction of C.D. Howe there was, for the first time in Canada, the start of development of an industrial system; that is, an integrated set of companies which perform a variety of functions. Although surplus is extracted on a firm-by-firm basis, the lucrative survival of one firm is often based on the complementary activities of others. Secondly, wartime mobilization provided a period of great mobility for many of the present corporate elite, providing them with experience and contacts important in the upper levels of power. This will be returned to in a later discussion when mobility into the current elite and the phenomenon of elite forums are analysed.

X. Early Post-War Boom and the Rise of an Industrial Structure (1946-1951)

On the back of the war boom, and receiving additional stimulation by government spending on the Korean War, industrialization grew rapidly immediately following the war. The period saw a striking shift in the nature of Canada's exports; pulp and paper and related products had captured 34 per cent of the export market by 1954, agricultural products declined to nine per cent while new growth in non-ferrous metals was evident with its 17 per cent contribution to the market. Iron ore production also increased from under 2 tons to 21 tons. In 1947 oil was first struck in Leduc and in the following ten years, crude petroleum increased from eight billion to 220 billion cubic feet. Before this, 63 of the 71 million barrels of crude used in Canada had been imported. Limited oil extraction had been taking place earlier and existing firms moved into large-scale Canadian production following the finds. Canadians had formed Imperial Oil in 1880 but by 1898 John D. Rockefeller's Standard Oil had gained a majority interest in the company. Since then it consolidated a number of other firms and with their find at Leduc became the most powerful company in mineral fuels (Easterbrook & Aitken, 1956:545-546; Creighton, 1970:283-284). Reliance was still on natural resources but there was emerging a diversification not characteristic of early staples. The Korean War stimulated government spending on defence with an increase from under $400 million in 1949 to almost $2 billion in 1952. "The newly established Department of Defence Production, over which the energetic and ruthless C.D. Howe presided, stimulated the revival and expansion of the aircraft and electronics industries and brought shipbuilding back to something like its level of importance during the Second World War" (Creighton, 1970:284).

Investment patterns reflect the great boost of growth in this era, particularly through U.S. direct investment. By 1952, United Kingdom direct investment totalled only $544 million and portfolio investment was at a low ebb totalling only $1,340 million. The great boost was from the United States, where portfolio investment increased by $737 million to total $3,466 million and direct investment increased by $2,104 million in only six years to total $4,532 million by 1952. While direct investment accounted for 39 per cent of all foreign investment in Canada in 1946, this increased to one half by 1952, and United States foreign investment, as a percentage of all, stood at 77 per cent.

It was for the period 1948-1950 that John Porter drew his list of dominant corporations as the basis for his economic elite study. Just at the beginning of the fantastic on-slaught of U.S. capital, the study captures the situation at the peak of the post-war industrial boom. The economic elite, Porter argues, was based in:

> a group of 183 "dominant corporations" . . . responsible in the period 1948-1950, for 40 to 50 per cent of the gross value of production in manufacturing, 63 per cent of the total value of metal production; 90 per cent of railway transportation; 88 per cent of the gross earnings of telegraph and cable services; 82 per cent of the total revenue of Canadian air carriers; 83 per cent of telephone revenues; and 60 to 70 per cent of the hydro-electricity produced by privately-owned companies, as well as a large but undetermined proportion of other industries such as industrial minerals, fuels, water transportation, and retail distribution (1955:508).

Manufacturing corporations, he notes, were highly influenced by U.S. control, accounting for 40-50 per cent of their gross value. Financial institutions, however, represented a very different pattern with only five U.S. residents and one from the U.K. out of 203 bank directors. Bank directors held 23 per cent of all directorships in dominant industrial corporations while dominant insurance directors totalled 134 and held 14 per cent of the industrial directorships. Insurance directors also held 27 per cent of the bank directorships while bank directors held 41 per cent of the dominant insurance directorships (1956:211). Of the total elite, 23 per cent were U.S. dominated; that is, either U.S.

residents or Canadian residents in U.S. subsidiaries, while only four per cent were U.K. dominated. These findings suggest that U.S. capitalism made significant inroads into the Canadian corporate structure, but the Canadian component remained powerful in the financial sector, its traditional strength. Initially, it would seem that a parallel structure had emerged with U.S. control in large parts of manufacturing and Canadian control of its traditional financial forté.

Porter's study provides an analysis of the Canadian resident members of this elite for 1951. He finds that "the professional and financial groups make up almost 60 per cent of the economic elite. Another 14.8 per cent of the elite are individuals who were born in or close to it" thus indicating mobility was strongly biased toward those from finance backgrounds and limited to those from advantaged social origins (1957:380-381). Only 6.7 per cent of the elite were French Canadian (one third of the population) while other ethnic groups represented insignificant numbers in the elite (one fifth of the population) and the rest were Anglos (1965:286). This illustrates that ethnic differentiation remained as significant for access to the economic elite in 1951 as it had in 1885 and 1910. Whatever the effect of U.S. investment, it did not change the ethnic balance in Canada at the upper levels of economic power; nor did it undermine the class base of the elite. The upper class, composed of the kin of earlier elites and big businessmen, still held a predominant place in the power structure. Porter found 38 per cent of the elite had upper class origins with this increasing to 50 per cent when those attending private schools were also included as upper class[22]. The middle class accounted for 32 per cent and only 18 per cent were lower than middle class. Class of origin shifted significantly higher when only the most powerful members were included. For the top 100 members of the elite, 67 per cent were upper class in origin, including those attending private schools: the 100 most powerful members of the elite themselves accounted for 25 per cent of the directorships in industry, 29 per cent in banks and 23 per cent in insurance companies, thus representing a sizable amount of power beyond the 10 per cent of the elite they represented (1957:391n).

The high interlocking Porter found within economic institutions is matched by elite cross-membership in terms of kinship, common educational backgrounds in private schools, a few key universities and law schools as well as in social groups such as private clubs (394). He also describes a number of relationships members of the economic elite have with one another and members of other, particularly political, elites (1965:430-41, 526-529). Porter maintains the following:

> Social goals are now established by a much smaller number than in the days of entrepreneurial capitalism. Because of the traditional

rights of private property, enshrined in the myth that corporations are individuals, the corporate elite hold the creative privileges available (1961:34).

It is the economic elite which determines much of the making of history in Canada, Porter argues, because they, unlike the political elite which lacks continuity, have had continuous control of major economic enterprises which guide the making of history within a capitalist economy. It is the economic elite which makes decisions about development within Canada and it is this group which has chosen to base itself in traditional commercial pursuits while, in large part, ignoring the industrial potential of the country. Porter's findings indicate that by 1951 corporate capitalism had become well entrenched in Canada and a financial elite still based in an upper class with strong political connections remained the keystone to the economic system. There are indications, however, that significant inroads had been made by U.S. industrialists into the manufacturing sector, traditionally the weakest sector as far as the Canadian economic elite were concerned. The period just following Porter's study confirms the trend to increased U.S. control of industry and also indicates it has made intrusions into the resource sector as well.

Rapid growth of U.S. direct investment during the following two decades increases the number of U.S. dominated members of the elite and integrates to an even greater extent the Canadian economy within the continental context. These developments will be analysed in subsequent chapers, but for now, the historical processes discussed thus far will be summarized.

Opportunity and Condition in Canada's Development: A Summary to 1951

It was stated earlier that "Canada's economic development involves changes in the way the economy is organized and controlled; these structural changes recast opportunities available to Canadians for upward mobility and access to power". In the process of analysing Canada's economic history, information was gathered on changing structures and their implications for mobility. The social forces involved and their effects will be summarized before proceeding with developments of the 1950's and 1960's.

From the perspective of Europe, Canada was an extension of social forces operating there and, initially at least, the social structure was imported so the uppermost positions were firmly attached to the European ruling classes. This nullified the possibility of indigenous mobility to the top but did create a middle class within Canada to serve the foreign masters. Similar structures developed with such enterprises as the Hudson's Bay Company while others, like the North West Company, represented for the first time, indigenous structures and capital accumulation which allowed the emergence of an indigenous capitalist class. The capitalist class which developed was commercial, mediating between the resources of Canada and the markets of Britain. Colonial power reinforced this commercial class to the exclusion of indigenous manufacturing. This is apparent in the powerful enclaves built up around the colonial offices in Canada which emergent commercial elites took advantage of by aligning themselves with these externally controlled powers. Initially brought into being by external social forces, the indigenous commercial class eventually attained independence with changes in Britain and crystallized into the most powerful social force in Canada. Over time it solidified and thus limited mobility into its inner circles. Emerging social forces such as small manufacturers were initially serverly limited in their growth and later tended to be absorbed by either dominant Canadian commercial interests or emerging industrialists from the U.S. who themselves represented yet another new force. The traditional ruling class and the new industrial social force from the U.S. combined, around the turn of the century, to create the merger movement and concentration of entrepreneurial firms into corporate capitalism. The effect was increasing dominance by the traditional ruling class and, parallel to this, a strong and growing U.S. component in manufacturing. Consolidation of corporate structures resulted in a decline in both upward mobility and vertical mobility through immigration from outside North America.

During the course of development, since the turn of the century, the two main forces established were first, Canadian commercial interests who had expanded somewhat into manufacturing with the advent of corporate capitalism and, secondly, U.S. industrialists who grew in strength rather erratically over the next fifty years. Of the two forces, the Canadian commercial class was dominant; it was, however, a vulnerable class because its fortunes depended on external markets and it had failed to energetically enter into manufacturing and resource sectors. Having stultified indigenous entrepreneurs by dominating them, the commercial class set the tone for post-war development. The next two decades were to see the growth of the U.S. industrial social force on a scale qualitatively greater than ever before.

Notes

[1]Parts of this chapter appear in my paper, "The Changing Structure of the Canadian Economy," *Canadian Review of Sociology and Anthropology*, Aspects of Canadian Society, 1974.

[2]This will be expanded on in Chapter Five.

[3]Easterbrook and Aitken have a detailed discussion of how the NWC raised its capital. They say in 1775 four sets of traders joined to pool their stock for a year and split profits at the end of the period. By 1779, the agreement, which lasted four years, included eight firms whereby "they would carry on the fur trade as one firm. The profits were divided at the end of each year, and there was no share capital as we understand the term today" (1958:166). By 1790, the company evolved a system of obtaining credit from English firms and was using its shares as a means of "absorbing" rival companies (167-169).

[4]The development of strong mercantilists and weak industrialists are not unrelated. As Marx noted, "The less developed the production, the more wealth in money is concentrated in the hands of merchants or appears in the specific form of merchants' wealth" (1967:III, 326). Consequently, the imperial policy prohibiting exporting—the bases upon which an industrial system could be created—and facilitated development of greater wealth in the mercantilists' hands.

[5]This is illustrated in Appendix I, which documents some charters issued by the government to sitting legislators for the period 1845-1858. As well as listing these charters, the appendix gives a breakdown of some of the activities of leading political/economic elites of the period.

[6]Appendix I gives some indication of the range of these activities.

[7]Although commercial activities remained dominant, Ryerson does mention some important indigenous industrial capitalists beginning to emerge as part of the "new ruling class." These included "the Gooderham's (distillers), the Molsons (brewers), Ogilvy's (flour mills), the Paxton's (Montreal Steam Cooperage, 1857), Warden King iron founders (1852)" (1968:276).

[8]Acheson says, "Most Maritime manufactories suffered from two major organizational problems: the continued difficulty faced by community corporations in securing financing in the frequent periods of marginal business activity, and the fact that most firms depended upon Montreal wholesale houses to dispose of their extra-regional exports" (1972:15).

[9]Acheson provides numerous examples of this consolidation process in the Maritimes between 1880 and 1920, whereby external financiers bought and sold firms using the bond and stock markets of Montreal (1927b:15-27). Consolidating firms and turning them into joint-stock companies served the *modus operandi* of the financiers who extracted their surplus on transactions of capital and stocks.

[10]See Appendix II for investment information. Sources are Levitt, 1970 and Information Canada, 1972.

[11]If A loans B $100 (portfolio) at a 10 per cent interest rate, and B invests that $100 in production (direct) from which B obtains a 16 per cent return per year with which B pays off the debt ($11 per year over 10 years), B obtains $16 the first year and pays out $11, reinvesting the $5. After the first year, the investment is $105; after the tenth year, the portfolio investment is eliminated but the direct investment is worth over $150 without any outside claims.

[12]As Naylor notes: "Industrial capital needs cheap raw materials, easy credit conditions, and low transport costs; merchant capital relies on regional scarcities of raw materials and goods to obtain high prices extracted through credit costs, transportation rates, and merchandise mark-up. Merchant capital,

typified by a low ratio of fixed to circulatory capital, also needs rapid turnover, and cannot undertake long-term risky investment. It is, therefore, oriented toward abetting the quick extraction of staple output, rather than industrial processing'' (1972:21).

[13] Acheson's studies, it should be noted are of the industrial elite. He says, "Industrialist is used in this study to refer only to those figures who played leading roles within the manufacturing sector'' (1973:190). There is contained within his studies a direct analysis of industrialization in early Canada and not directly an attempt to study finance and transportation elites.

[14] He drew his population from trade journals of the period, records of the Canadian Manufacturers Association and biographical dictionaries (1972a:144-145n).

[15] The tariff policy, as part of the National Policy, was certainly important but was also in the interest of the ruling commercial class. The consequences of this policy, as will be shown, were in the long run, more in line with the ruling interests than those of early manufacturers.

[16] Marx has a similar comment on the role of industrial entrepreneurs: ''The industrial capitalist is a worker, compared to the money-capitalist, but a worker in the sense of capitalist, i.e., an exploiter of the labour of others'' (1967:III, 387).

[17] Entrepreneurial capitalism is characterized by innovative individuals who organize, own and manage relatively small businesses engaged in competition on the marketplace with numerous other small concerns in a high risk situation. Corporate capitalism, the product of the centripetal movement of centralized capital, is characterized by joint-stock companies which are large, highly concentrated and controlled by ownership of shares; management is often hired by controlling ownership and a few large corporations have the majority of the market thus reducing risk and competition.

[18] The ''merger movement'' in Canada, like that occurring simultaneously in the U.S., was undertaken by finance capitalists. The difference, however, is that in the U.S. finance capitalists were just emerging into a dominant position at the turn of the century while Canadian financiers had been dominant for some time.

[19] As Appendix III illustrates, the concentration in 1928 has not changed much to the present.

[20] There is an absence of elite studies between the 1910 study by Acheson and the 1951 study by Porter. This important period, therefore, has not been studied in the same detail as earlier and later periods. Although the logical time to focus the study would be 1930, mid-way between the existing ones, there is some problem here because of the Depression. For this reason, it would probably be wise to design two studies, one for about 1925 and the other about 1935. This would leave an equal period between existing studies and also capture the effect of the Depression on elite composition.

[21] For example, E. P. Taylor, one of Canada's most powerful capitalists who had the distinction of holding the most dominant directorships in 1951 (10), became one of C. D. Howe's ''dollar-a-year men.'' His father-in-law had the distinction of being in charge of Canadian shipbuilding during the First World War.

[22] Private schools of the Headmasters' Association in English Canada and

classical colleges in Quebec were institutions where upper class children received their education. The high cost of sending children to these privileged establishments restricted access to those whose parents were wealthy enough to pay high tuition and boarding costs. The class of origin of the 1951 elite are compared with the 1972 corporate elite in detail in Chapter Five.

Chapter Three

Parasites, Satellites and Stratification: Current Trends in Canada's Economy

EMBEDDED in the capitalist economic order of Canada and perpetuated through the sanctity of private property, the economic elite, during the post-World War II period, has concentrated its base of power and consolidated avenues of access into its inner circles. Important transformations have occurred in the economic structure and rapid industrialization has been evident but the elite remains as closed as it was in 1951, even tighter in some key respects. Contrary to liberal ideology which holds that greater mobility will characterize "post-industrialism", Canada remains capitalist, industrial and closed at the upper levels of corporate power. Many sociologists who celebrate existing structures, assert that corporate capitalism, with time and industrialization, will reduce inequalities based on ascription. Parsons, for example[1], argues that religion, ethnicity, regionalism, and social class based on ascriptive characteristics "have lost much of their force" (1970:14-15). Evidence now exists that this is not the case for Canada between 1951 and 1972. Although only the upper levels of corporate power are examined here, other recent studies find that increasing inequality is a general phenomenon penetrating the entire social structure.

Johnson has recently shown that income inequality between 1948 and 1968, and especially for the last ten years of the period, has involved a proportional shift of income distribution from the bottom income earners to the top. Over the twenty-year period, "the only people who have received a disproportionately increased percentage of national income have been the richest one-third of Canadian income earners. The lower income workers have been the sufferers" (1973:5). Recognizing that an overall shift has occurred in the amount of income received, Johnson focuses on the way this income is distributed and finds, for example,

> in the 1958-1968 period, the bottom ten per cent of income earners suffered a loss in purchasing power of 35.6 per cent, while the second decile lost 6.6 per cent. On the other hand, the top deciles of income earners greatly increased their purchasing power . . . the top decile received, in addition to a 51.4 per cent increase in

purchasing power, 72 per cent of all capital gains from the appreciation of share capital (3-4).

Although members of the corporate elite are defined in terms of power and not by wealth, there exists a high correlation between the two in Canada. For example, a recent study of the presidents of Canadian corporations by Heidrick and Struggles, Inc. found that three quarters of the presidents in corporations with sales of over $100 million had salaries over $100,000 (1973:6).

Enormous inequality in the distribution of income is not alleviated by the existing regressive tax structure, as a recent study by Maslove for the Economic Council of Canada discovered. His examination of taxation found that "the overall effective tax pattern is highly regressive to a Broad Income level of $5,000-$6,000. Taking Full Income as the base, regressiveness is evident up to an income level of $3,000-$4,000"[2] (1972:64). Given that 46 per cent of all family incomes in Canada are included in the under $6,000 income class for 1969, the regressive tax structure affects a very large proportion of the population. Contrary to the ideology of progressive taxation[3], the 8.3 per cent of family units which received over $15,000 income in 1969, paid a rate of only 1.4 per cent higher than the average based on Full Income and 8.4 per cent *less* than those earning under $2,000. Based on Broad Income, this highest group actually paid a lower proportion than did the average (108-109, 128-129). In other words, the tax structure is hardly even proportional at the upper levels and not progressive. Maslove summarizes his findings as follows: "The extremely regressive nature of the tax system at the low end of the income scale and the lack of progressivity over the remainder is the predominant conclusion to emerge from this Study" (77).

It would not be correct to argue that the wealthy are paying higher taxation rates through the corporate structure. In fact, the corporate contribution to the total tax revenue has been rapidly declining in recent years. Deaton shows:

> Between 1962 and 1970, the corporate share of all Federal income revenue *fell* by roughly 38% while the individual share of Federal income tax revenue *increased* by over 23%. With respect to all Provincial income tax revenue between 1962 and 1970 the corporate share *fell* by over 60% while the individual share *increased* by roughly 83% (1972:32).

The burden of taxation has been shifted from the corporate world to the individual. Given that individual taxation in Canada is regressive, this represents a further step in the direction of inequality in favour of the rich and powerful.

The trends outlined here of an increasing disparity in income distribution, a regressive taxation system and an increasing shift in emphasis of taxation toward individual as opposed to corporate taxation combined with increasing closure of the corporate elite and increasing concentration of capital, to be discussed, provide a sense of uneasiness, not only about sociological theory but about the direction of Canadian society. These developments, and others to be outlined, should lead to a basic questioning of the future in store for Canadians if substantial social change does not occur.

Post-War Developments in the Canadian Economy

Based on the historical development of a strong indigenous financial elite and a weak indigenous industrial elite, the 1950's witnessed the development of foreign control in manufacturing and resource sectors. Representing a strong social force in Canadian society, foreign controlled multinational corporations have a prominent place among dominant corporations. This serves to dislodge a portion of the indigenous economic elite and create a unique set of relationships among elites. The expansive powers of European capitalism at an earlier period and U.S. capitalism in recent times, extend beyond national bounds and create a system of internationalized capitalism at once rooted in nation states and at the same time independent of them. The practice of trans-national corporations is not entirely new: in 1932 Berle and Means characterized the American Telephone and Telegraph Company as "an empire bounded by no geographical limits, but held together by centralized control" (1968:5). What has recently changed is the scope and dimensions of their activities. For example, Berle has recently maintained that these corporate giants must be put in a framework "in somewhat the way we have heretofore thought of nations" (1957:15), and Child characterizes corporations such as British Petroleum and Unilever as "supra-national organizations" whose "internal decisions may have as much impact on patterns of trade and international relations as decisions taken by governments" (1969:1). These developments have concerned Canadian politicians, as the following statement by John Turner, Minister of Finance, illustrates:

> Next to the nation state, the international corporation is today's most influential institution. It commands vast resources, stretches across countless boundaries, directs the fate of millions of world's citizens and carries a common culture which has been labeled

"coca-colonization". We have no international institutions to control the power of the multinational corporation (*Toronto Star*, October 3, 1968).

There has been great unease in Canada over what has been termed its "branch plant" condition or "miniature replica" economy. Decision making in foreign subsidiaries is undertaken by the parent corporation outside the nation where the branch plant is located and positions of power are predominantly held by non-residents (Litvak & Maule, 1971:22f). Effects of this extend beyond the economy and into the political domain in terms of the types of economic policies which can be carried out (Hymer, 1972:60; Behrman, 1972:143).

The way multinational firms are organized affects the power of branch plant boards of directors. For instance, C.M. Harding, chairman and chief executive officer of Harding Carpets, director of Union Gas of Canada, Confederation Life and The Toronto-Dominion Bank, refers to the "invisible boards in Canada" when discussing the foreign parents of Canadian subsidiaries (McDougall, 1969:26). Referring to proposed Ontario legislation governing Canadian representation on subsidiary boards, Mitchel Sharp, former Minister of Trade and Commerce and now Minister of External Affairs, suggests this is ineffectual, stating the federal government "was aware that a firm required to alter the composition of its board by law might seek out passive directors. And it was aware that key decisions are often taken not by the board of a subsidiary but by the board of the parent company itself" (*Globe & Mail*, June 21, 1972). Earlier in the year, Sharp told the Vancouver Board of Trade that "Every Canadian should pray every morning and evening that the United States' economy will continue to prosper" (*Globe & Mail*, January 18, 1972). Sharp's own career in the corporate world as vice-president of Brascan, and his position as a member of the political elite, make him qualified to understand where power is held. With the prevalence of multinational corporations, a portion of the economic elite will be foreign to Canada's stratification system; this has not reached the stage where it could be said there is no economic elite in Canada but it is important enough to have a substantial part in stratification analysis.

Continental integration, particularly trade, had been strong since 1854 and it increased rapidly after the early 1920's but capital and resource integration took on a different face in the early 1950's, particularly under the guidance of the American import to the Liberal St-Laurent cabinet as Minister of Trade and Commerce and Defence Production, C.D. Howe. Possibly the most dramatic event illustrating the changing nature of Canadian-U.S. economic relations and C.D. Howe's part in these developments is the natural gas/Trans-Canada pipeline deal he engineered in 1956. Guided by the Albertan and Federal governments, the privately-owned Trans-Canada Pipe Lines Company was formed to transmit natural gas from the west to eastern Canadian and U.S. markets. Although involving both a Canadian company and U.S. subsidiary, the project was controlled by Americans. The natural gas supplier was also U.S.-controlled. The pipeline company requested a $275 million bond issue from the Canadian government to fund the project but there was strong opposition by the Conservatives, press and public as well as the Minister of Finance, Walter Harris. Howe, a powerful cabinet minister and active continentalist, decided to fight all opposition and began to mount an attack to push legislation through the House which would subsidize the project. Opposition was strong but the Liberals employed closure four times to push it through: "On six of the seven clauses proposed by the government at the resolution stage, the entire discussion consisted of 207 words uttered by Howe himself!" (Creighton, 1970:295). This was a project which Prime Minister St-Laurent had declared to be of such import as to rank with construction of the Canadian Pacific (293). In light of developments since, with natural gas[4] and the general pattern of U.S. ownership, control and use of natural resources, this deal must, indeed, rank high in historical significance. Creighton places Howe's role in the development this way:

> The close integration of Canada into a North American economy dominated by the United States was, to a very large extent, a development of the two decades in which he [C.D. Howe] had watched over Canada's economic progress; and Canada's new continental orientation was in effect a gigantic amplification of his own continental outlook (1970:294).

Supported, in large part, by wartime expansion and the program of industrialization introduced by Howe, the Canadian economy became totally integrated as the resource producing appendage of the North American economic system. Unlike an earlier debate over the CPR, there was no government opposition to building part of the pipeline through the U.S., nor was there opposition to the U.S. companies who owned the oil reserves of the west and proposed to sell the oil to the U.S.; on the contrary, it was the U.S. government which proposed quotas in 1958 but the Canadian government protested and was able to attain an exemption (Aitken, 1965:507). The U.S. controlled refineries in the east preferred to use Canadian oil as a reserve, first drawing on the cheaper and less stable "foreign" resources.

As a utility, policy on natural gas was quite different with the Canadian government deciding in 1953 that it would impose quotas on its export. Actually, the ruling was designed to insure that central Canada was well supplied with cheap natural gas essential to its industrial needs and not for the purpose of creating Canadian reserves (Aitken, 1965:509). Using the method of a Crown Corporation to build the costly northern section of the gas line and subsidizing to the extent of 90 per cent of the western section, the government continued in the Canadian tradition of allying itself closely with business interests[5] and taking financial responsibility for transportation and utilities. The same is true of government ownership in air travel which C.D. Howe argued private enterprise could not afford to finance but from which they would greatly benefit (Rae & McLeod, 1969:172-173). Government continued its policy of providing the economic sub-structure upon which business could construct profitable enterprises and, in particular, profitable for central Canada. Continental integration was continuing not only in ownership but also for trade. In 1950, two thirds of Canada's exports went to the U.S. and the same proportion of imports was received from there (Easterbrook & Aitken, 1956:576). The 1950's also represented a dramatic inflow of U.S. capital into Canada on a scale quantitatively greater than any previous period. Between 1952 and 1960, U.S. direct investment rose by $6,017 million to total $10,549 million while U.S. portfolio investment increased by $2,703 million to total $6,169 million. This is compared to the $1,535 million in U.K. direct investment and $1,824 million in portfolio investment held by the U.K. in 1960. It is this more than twofold increase in U.S. direct investment, carried mainly through multinational corporations, in the span of only eight years which had a great effect on the Canadian economy and social structure. More U.S. direct investment existed in Canada in 1960 than the total of all types of investment which had entered Canada up to 1952.

This great influx did not occur because of capital shortage in Canada; indeed, in 1957 Canada had $4.6 billion invested in portfolio investment in the U.K. and $2 billion in direct investment—$1.2 billion of this in the U.S. (Easterbrook & Aitken, 1956:573-574). Between 1946 and 1958 domestic savings accounted for 75 per cent of all capital investment in Canada (574). The explanation lies as much with the type of traditional Canadian commercial capitalists as the aggressive industrialists of the United States.

(i) Concentration in the 1950's

In a study of corporate concentration based in the mid-1950's, Rosenbluth found there were about 100 corporations with assets over $100 million, 57 of which were non-financial (1961:198). These 57 corporations accounted for 38 per cent of the "real" assets of all non-financial corporations but this percentage actually under-estimates concentration since private companies like Eatons and General Motors did not publish their financial statements (199-200). In the manufacturing sector, 28 corporations accounted for 29 per cent of the assets, again under-estimating actual control concentration because subsidiaries were not consolidated with parents (200). Concentration was lower in retail, wholesale and service sectors (201). The CNR and CPR accounted for 89 per cent of railway revenue while their subsidiaries had 69 per cent of the assets of the air transport industry. Bell Telephone alone had 66 per cent of the operating revenue of all telephone companies while in oil pipelines, the Interprovincial and Trans Mountain companies had 72 per cent of the assets (201-202). In finance the degree of concentration was high, as it had been for some time[6], with nine banks accounting for almost all the assets while the same number of insurance companies held 75 per cent of the total assets in that sector (202). Table 3 indicates the high degree of concentration prevalent during this period in manufacturing and resources plus the extent of foreign, particularly U.S., ownership.

As this table illustrates, by 1954 the largest companies in both manufacturing and resources were fairly evenly split between U.S. and Canadian control, with about 10 per cent of the companies controlled elsewhere.

Rosenbluth illustrates the rapidity with which foreign, mainly U.S., control came to the manufacturing sector. While in 1946 only 35 per cent of that sector was foreign controlled, by 1953 this had jumped to 50 per cent and to 56 per cent by 1957. In the space of 10 years, manufacturing had changed from predominantly Canadian to foreign dominated. The same pattern, although occurring more dramatically, was apparent in mining and smelting where foreign control represented only 38 per cent in 1946 but 57 per cent in 1953 and 70 per cent by 1957 (206). Of the 60 largest manufacturing concerns studied, Rosenbluth found 30 (50 per cent) were Canadian controlled but accounted for only 42 per cent of the investment while 23 (38 per cent) U.S. controlled corporations accounted for 52 per cent of the total investment. The four (6 per cent) U.K. companies represented only six per cent of the total investment for the year ending 1953 (205). This illustrates clearly that the U.S. controlled more than one half of the manufacturing in 1953 and they were much more concentrated than their Canadian controlled counterparts.

What should be noted is the dramatic change in the structure and concentration of the Canadian economy in the decade of the 1950's. John Porter's study of the 1948-1950 structure of corporate capitalism captured the situation just prior to a great surge of U.S. direct investment and rapid growth of the 1950's and 60's. The period of 1948-1950

TABLE 3

Foreign Control and Concentration of Canadian Resources and Industries, 1954

Industry	% Value-added Accounted for by six largest firms	Country of control of six largest firms		
		U.S.	Other Foreign	Canada
Crude Petroleum	68	5	1	—
Petroleum Refining	93	4	1	1
Mining, Smelting and Refining				
Nickel-Copper	100	3	—	3
Lead-Zinc	86	1	1	4
Copper-Gold	88	2	—	4
Iron Ore	100	3	—	3
Aluminum (one company)	100	1	—	—
Asbestos	94	2	1	3
Gypsum	97	3	1	2
TOTAL RESOURCE		**24**	**5**	**20**
Manufacturing				
Pulp and Paper	46	1	1	4
Fertilizers	92	2	1	3
Acids, Alkalis, Salts	63	3	2	1
Electrical Apparatus	52	2	2	2
Primary Iron and Steel	84	6	—	5
Automobiles	97	3	—	—
Railway Rolling Stock	84	3	—	2
Synthetic Fibers (5 only)	100	—	—	6
Other Primary Textiles	90	2	2	4
Agricultural Implements	91	—	—	—
Rubber Goods	77	4	—	1
TOTAL MANUFACTURING		**29**	**8**	**28**

Adapted from Rosenbluth, 1961:207, Table III. Original I. Brecher and S.S. Reisman, *Canada-United States Economic Relations*, 1957:278-285.

was one of relatively high Canadian autonomy with about one quarter of the elite foreign controlled. With the rapid introduction of direct investment from the U.S. and the concentration of this investment in the largest manufacturing and resource corporations, an increase in the number of members of the economic elite which fall under U.S. dominance has occurred[7]. Low foreign investment in utilities, transportation and financial institutions suggests this section of the elite still remained predominantly Canadian controlled during the 1950's, similar to the situation existing when Porter conducted his study (Levitt, 1970:61). The decade of the 1960's saw the emergence in dominant form, of multinational corporations thus adding a totally new dimension to the study of economic elites in Canada.

(ii) The Decade of the Multinationals (1960's)

Multinational corporations are a response to two developments characteristic of contemporary capitalism. The first is the marked tendency for accumulation and concentration of capital within the most advanced capitalist economies. This is illustrated by the U.S. where there emerged several giant corporations which have at their disposal resources enabling them to carry out large-scale operations, frequently integrated vertically and horizontally. This first characteristic of corporate strength operates alongside a second development, interpenetration of the various national economies through the initiative of multinationals and the encouragement, or lack of resistance, by host countries. Multinationals are not exclusively a phenomenon of the 1960's; it is only that they gained a predominant position during this period. The two characteristics of corporate concentration and strength, along with interpenetrating economies, highlight the Canadian situation in the 1960's. Multinationals did not initiate the interpenetration of the North American economy but have followed the path set by prior trade and investment patterns.

It is the multinational corporation, as a way of organizing economic activity, which distinguishes the original mercantile period from so-called "neo-mercantilism"[8], a period like its namesake which is characterized by one nation state operating in another for the purpose of bringing resources and capital to capitalists of the home country. Another similarity to the earlier period is the close relationship between business and politics evident through state support of corporations with economic agreements and intervention by the state in support of imperialist pursuits. Also characteristic of "neo-mercantilism" is asymmetry in "negotiations" between the political and economic elites of the home and host countries. Kari Levitt describes the U.S. appropriately as the "super-metropole" of "new mercantilism" and she draws an interesting comparison between the recent vintage and the original.

> In the new mercantilism, as in the old, the corporation based in the metropole directly exercises the entrepreneurial function and collects a "venture profit" from its investment. It organizes the collection or extraction of the raw material staple required in the metropolis and supplies the hinterland with manufactured goods, whether produced at home or "on site" in the host country (1970:24).

Clearly, the multinational corporation is a much more efficient instrument of "neo-mercantilism" for the U.S. empire than was the charter company of the British empire. In each case, however, the instruments of empire have maintained close links with the financial interest of the home and host countries while at the same time generating a good deal of its investment capital from the earnings of its own operations. The simple process of extraction and export of early chartered companies has been replaced by a more sophisticated system of branch plant operations, marketing in the host country and capital, as well as resource export to the home country. Existence of branch plants and "on site" processing or production is important for a number of reasons, not the least of which is the creation of an indigenous labour force that can act as a taxation base for income tax purposes and, as an indigenous market for goods and serivces.

World Corporations

The top 100 industrials outside the U.S. are comparable with the top 150 U.S. industrials, as ranked by *Fortune* in 1971, with the 100th outside the U.S. corporation having sales of $818 million compared to 150th U.S. corporation having sales of $830 million. In other words, of the top 250 world industrials in 1971, three fifths are U.S. based and two fifths are outside the U.S. Table 4 illustrates the distribution of the top 250 world industrials.

The three Canadian corporations in the top 250 world corporations are Alcan Aluminum (58/100 non-U.S.), Massey-Ferguson (84) and Canada Packers (91). The second hundred non-U.S. corporations includes a further seven Canadian corporations, as does the third hundred. It is interesting to note that the largest "Canadian" industrial, Alcan, is not controlled in Canada since it has 51.2 per cent foreign ownership—39.4 per cent of which is in the U.S. Similarly, the fourth largest "Canadian" industrial, The International Nickel Company of

TABLE 4

Top 250 World Industrials by Nation, 1971

United States	150	Australia	2
Japan	21	Belgium	2
Germany	20	Netherlands	2
Britain	19	Neth.-Britain	2
France	14	Brazil	1
Italy	4	Luxembourg	1
Switzerland	4	Mexico	1
Sweden	3	Britain-Italy	1
Canada	3	TOTAL	250

Canada, is 70 per cent controlled outside Canada with over 50 per cent of the total ownership located in the U.S.

The volume of multinationals makes them a powerful force in the economy of the entire world. The enormousness of these enterprises is illustrated by Rotstein:

> The value of the production of all multinational corporations in countries outside their home base in 1967 exceeded $214 billion. This makes the aggregate production of these corporations abroad the third largest economy in the world, second only to the domestic economies of the United States and the Soviet Union (1970:211).

The power of multinationals comes not only from the size of the resources they command but also from the flexibility they have through world-wide operations. This means that investment decisions are made on the basis of "an overall assessment of the firm's international position" thus adding a dimension of flexibility absent in national corporations, not only in terms of investment decisions but also in dealing with politicians (Block, 1970:152). An example of this is the ability of mining companies to shift operations to avoid taxes (Information Canada, 1972:304). The size and flexibility of multinationals combined with their close financial connections gives them added strength in capitalizing on credit opportunities, often to the detriment of small-scale national companies. Draining capital reserves from financial institutions of both the home and host countries creates a situation which, in Block's terms, is "ironic" in advanced nations but "tragic" in under-developed nations. The government study *Foreign Direct Investment in Canada* identifies two characteristics of multinational corporations which further adds to their strength relative to national corporations, particularly Canadian industries. These are "distinctiveness"—the ability of multinationals to manufacture for a much larger market, both in the home and host nations—and "backward vertical integration"—the ability to take advantage of resources available in the host country because they "feed" the industrial capacity at home (32,45).

Multinationals are not really so "multinational" at all; in fact, they are extensions of predominantly U.S. corporations into the world economy and are more accurately analysed as U.S. national corporations with international operations. Some recent data from the *Foreign Direct Investment in Canada* study illustrate this point:

> (i) The book value of United States foreign direct investment increased from approximately $7.5 billion in 1929 to $70.8 billion in 1969.
>
> (ii) Sixty-two of the top 100 United States corporations have production facilities in at least 6 foreign countries and 71 of the top 126 industrial corporations for which information is available are reported to have one-third of their employment abroad.
>
> (iii) It is estimated that about 80 per cent of all United States foreign direct investment is accounted for by some 200 firms (e.g., General Motors, Chrysler, Ford, Singer, Esso, ITT, etc.) (1972:52).

The dominant position of multinationals also has an important effect in the area of trade. With multinationals, "trade" by-passes any notion of a market since the majority of transfers involve intra-company movements of raw materials from subsidiaries to parents. What once was a market situation is now an administrative exchange within one organization extending over national boundaries. In 1969 exchanges between subsidiaries and parents accounted for 75 per cent of all "trade" conducted by foreign controlled companies in Canada (Information Canada, 1972:171). This is encouraged by the state through such agreements as the Auto Pact between Canada and the U.S. which explicitly sanctions the continental nature of the North American economy. Other inter-governmental agencies like IMF, GATT, and IBRD reflect similar assumptions (Godfrey & Watkins, 1970:223). Free trade is the economic philosophy of multinationals since it serves to open new markets and impose fewer restrictions and duties while protectionism remains the philosophy of smaller national industrial entrepreneurs. This is most evident in the different positions advocated by two major economic associations in Canada: the Canadian Manufacturers Association advocates strong tariffs (1969:207) while the Canadian-American Committee strongly favours tariff elimination (1969:210). Regardless of which philosophy prevails, as the National Policy of Macdonald illustrated in 1879, tariffs do not change the nature of dependence, they only shift the location of plants.

Canadian Capital and Concentration

It is often argued that multinationals bring extensive investment into capital poor areas, either geographically defined or developmentally defined, but the example of Canada suggests otherwise. Between 1960 and 1967, new capital inflow from the U.S. amounted to $4.1 billion but counter to this, outflows in the form of remittances to U.S. parents amounted to $5.9 billion, a net outflow of capital from Canada to the U.S. of $1.8 billion during this period (Levitt, 1970:94).

The argument that U.S. investment comes to Canada because capital is scarce in this country runs counter to the evidence. In addition to the net outflow of funds from subsidiaries to parents of $1.8 billion between 1960 and 1965, most of the foreign capital for expansion is obtained within Canada. Capital sources for expansion of foreign controlled firms totalled $43.9 billion between 1946 and 1967 of which only $9.7 billion or 22 per cent was from foreign sources. For the more recent period of 1960-1967, this decreases to only 19 per cent (Information Canada, 1972:25). This indicates that mostly Canadian capital, or capital generated from retained earnings by Canadian operations of foreign firms, finances large amounts of foreign investment. In addition, a good deal of Canadian capital, particularly that held by financial institutions, is invested outside Canada as portfolio investment. This has increased rapidly during the 1960's. "As recently as 1960, major Canadian financial institutions held only 10 per cent of their stock portfolios in foreign equities; the proportion had risen to 24 per cent by 1966" (Levitt, 1970:139). Pension funds have also tended to place their portfolio investments in foreign firms, amounting to $600 million between 1962 and 1969 while during the same period mutual funds invested $1 billion abroad (Information Canada, 1972:81). These forms of investment do not involve Canadian control of foreign enterprises, rather they tend to be interest-bearing portfolio investments.

Financial institutions in Canada have traditionally been oriented to long-term, stable investment and, therefore, tend to avoid "venture" loans to newly-emerging industry. In some cases the legal structure, particularly in the case of insurance companies, prohibits what may be called "venture capital". This problem has been compounded by the concentrated nature of Canadian financial institutions. The degree of concentration in finance is illustrated in Table 5 for the year end December 1969:

TABLE 5

Concentrations in Financial Organizations (1969)

Financial Sector	Per Cent of Assets Controlled by the *Five* Largest Corporations
Chartered Banks	93
Life Insurance	63
Trust Companies	61
Mortgage Loan	61
Sales Finance	68
Consumer Loan	88
Investment Dealers	49

Constructed from data in *Foreign Direct Investment in Canada* (1972:101f).

These figures actually under-represent concentration because of the relationships between corporations in these various sectors.

Concentration in Canadian industry is greater than their counterparts in the U.S.; for example, three quarters of the shipments from manufacturing firms originate in industries where eight or fewer firms represent 80 per cent of the shipments while in the U.S. the corresponding figure is only 13.7 per cent (Information Canada, 1972:217). This does not measure actual corporate concentration which is much greater since several firms are frequently owned or controlled by the same corporation, but it does give a point of comparison between Canada and the U.S. A good deal of concentration in Canada can be directly attributed to the presence of U.S. giant corporations operating in Canada; for example, the average assets of foreign owned nonfinancial firms in Canada for 1971 was $9.3 million compared to $2.5 million for Canadian owned firms (CALURA, 1974:44, Statement 19). In manufacturing alone, even more startling differences exist with foreign firms in 1968 averaging $12.11 million sales and $11.44 million assets compared to corresponding figures of $3.03 and $2.58 million for Canadian controlled firms (Information Canada, 1972:214). In mining, foreign firms are about five times larger than Canadian firms (assets of $17 million compared to $3.8 million in 1967). Although foreign controlled firms represent only 11.5 per cent of all the firms in mining, they account for 60 per cent of the assets. Other resource sectors represent much the same situation:

The big foreign controlled firms are particularly concentrated in petroleum and coal products (24 firms with average assets of $198 million), smelting and refining (28 firms with average assets of

$86 million), primary metals (60 firms with average assets of $52 million), and metal mining (63 firms with average assets of $31 million). The eight largest firms in petroleum accounted for over eighty per cent of industry sales in 1968. The four largest firms in primary smelting and refining accounted for nearly ninety per cent of production (224).

Again it should be emphasized that concentration in terms of firms under-estimates concentration in terms of control, with one corporation operating several firms in one sector and even several firms in more than one sector. The point to be made, however, is that foreign firms tend to congregate in the most concentrated industries, particularly manufacturing and resource industries, and tend to be much larger than their Canadian controlled counterparts. As a government report on foreign investment suggests, ''much foreign investment merely represents the extension of foreign oligopoly and world concentration into Canada'' thus creating an investment situation unfavourable to indigenous capitalists (Information Canada, 1972:43).

Table 6 representing U.S. direct investment throughout the world illustrates the central position Canada has in the U.S. empire, especially in the 1950's and 60's, surpassing U.S. direct investment in even Latin America by 1964.

TABLE 6
U.S. Direct Investment (in billions)

	1924		1958		1964		1967	
	$	%	$	%	$	%	$	%
Europe	.9	17	4.4	16	12.1	27	17.9	30
Canada	1.1	20	8.9	32	13.8	31	18.0	31
Latin America	2.8	52	12.7	43	10.3	23	10.2	17
Other	.6	11	1.1	9	8.1	19	13.2	22

(Drache, 1970:25; Turner, 1970:5).

The shift from under-developed areas of the world to the less under-developed by U.S. direct investment suggests a further characteristic of multinational corporations: the tendency to enter manufacturing sectors rather than strictly seeking out natural resources. There tends to be a greater integration of resource exploitation and manufacturing production within companies. For example, in 1897 resources accounted for 59 per cent of U.S. foreign investment with only 15 per cent in manufacturing while in 1969, 42 per cent was in manufacturing and 36 per cent in resources (Information Canada, 1972:52). This reflects the more sophisticated organization of multinationals discussed earlier and their ability to tap local markets and local labour with branch plant operations.

Foreign investment in Canada during the 1960's followed much the same pattern as the previous decade, again with rapid inflow and concentration on U.S. direct investment. From 1960 to 1965, U.S. direct investment increased by $3,391 million while U.K. total investments increased by only $139 million. U.S. portfolio investment also increased in significant quantities to add $3,196 million during the period. The proportion of direct to total foreign investments appears to have levelled at about 58 per cent, by far the highest proportion of direct investment in Canada's history. The percentage of total investment accounted for by U.S. investment also increased to a high of 79 per cent. It does not appear from these statistics that there has been any decline of U.S. direct investment; indeed, the tendency is for continually higher levels of both U.S. and direct investment.

Changing Corporate Elite in the 1960's

Each of these developments in capital investment, organizational structures, and degree of concentration give an indication of the type of social structure which has developed in Canada since 1950 and particularly in the 1960's. One point of analysis insisted on by elite theory is that it is not adequate to examine the underlying economic processes and institutional structures alone but analysis must be extended to the level of relationships between people, particularly those who hold the command posts of the dominant institutions and have the means of exercising power under their control. Essential to elite analysis is the structure of decision making and study of those holding key positions. It is only at this point that the structure of inequality can be analysed in terms of social stratification. For example, to argue that multinational corporations dominate the Canadian economy would be incorrect. Elite theory would insist it is the men who head these corporations that command the resources of these organizations and, therefore, control the economy. It is this essential de-reification of corporate structures which is essential to an analysis of stratification.

Based on calculations from a 1962 CALURA study of the 217 largest mining and manufacturing corporations, the following tables give an indication about the residence and nationality of directors from leading non-financial corporations in Canada. It shows that 60.3 per cent of the directors in these firms with assets over $25 million in 1962 were Canadian citizens and 66.7 per cent of the directors were residents of Canada. It is obvious from Table 7 that higher percentages of directors were non-residents in corporations with higher degrees of non-resident ownership.

Performing additional calculations on this data the following can be determined: corporations which are foreign controlled (over 50 per cent non-resident ownership) account for 62 per cent of the directors of corporations with assets over $25 million while only 38 per cent of the directors are in corporations controlled in Canada. This 38 per cent declines slightly if non-resident directors were excluded. These figures indicate that by far the highest proportion of directors in the largest mining and manufacturing corporations were controlled outside Canada as of 1962. This suggests that the proportion of directors controlled outside Canada had increased substantially since 1948-1950 when John Porter found that a total of 27 per cent from all sectors were foreign controlled (23 per cent U.S. and 4 per cent U.K.). Although the corresponding proportion for 1962 appears from these calculations to be 62 per cent, this over-states actual control because finance and utilities, two key Canadian controlled sectors, were not included in the CALURA study while they were in Porter's.

Because of the way CALURA data is reported the breakdown between U.S. and U.K. cannot be determined. On the basis of investment patterns, however, the distribution would be even greater in terms of U.S. dominance than in 1948-1950. Table 8 presents these calculations in table form.

These data indicate that the degree of truncation which has occurred in the Canadian economy as a result of the introduction of multinational corporations has had a significant effect on the structure and distribution of members of the economic elite. By far the majority of top decision making positions in the largest mining and manufacturing corporations in 1962 were held by people who were either in non-Canadian controlled corporations or were not Canadian citizens or residents. In terms of the structure of the economic elite for these sectors during 1962, the majority held "comprador" positions and a minority were "indigenous". Limitations on this kind of survey should be noted. Since it is a sample of corporations with assets of $25 million or more, the study does not indicate the different degrees of ownership by assets. There may be a substantial difference between corporations which have assets of only $25 million and a group with assets over $250 million[9]. Since data was collected on a corporation by corporation basis, no interlocking directorships are taken into account, so the number of directorships is not the same as the number of directors. There is no differentiation between different spheres of the economy; nor is there representation from the finances, utilities and trade sectors.

TABLE 7

Directorships of Mining and Manufacturing Corporations with over $25 Million Assets (1962)

% Non-resident Ownership	No. of Corp.	Total Directors	Directors Resident in Canada	%	Directors Can. Citizens	%
95% or over	94	841	391	46.5	317	37.7
75-94.9%	21	232	145	62.5	123	53.1
50-74.9%	23	259	165	63.4	152	58.7
25-49.9%	22	236	192	81.4	186	78.8
5-24.9%	39	439	399	90.9	392	89.3
Under 5%	18	155	150	96.8	148	95.3
TOTALS	217	2,162	1,442	66.7	1,304	60.3

(Based on CALURA Report for 1962:34-35)

TABLE 8

**Resident/Non-Resident Distribution
of Directors of Mining and Manufacturing Corporations
with Assets over $25 Million (1962)**

	No. of Corp.	No. of Directors	Per Cent Directors	Per Cent Directors with Canadian Citizenship
Over 50% Non-resident controlled corporations	138	1,332	62	44
Over 50% Canadian controlled corporations	79	830	38	88
TOTALS	217	2,162	100%	60% (average)

(Calculated from Table VIII)

In spite of its limitations, the study does give an indication of foreign domination in major decision making posts in the surplus-generating sectors of the Canadian economy.

It is appropriate to group members of the economic elite who sit on boards of foreign controlled firms as comprador elites because their appointments are determined by the foreign parent and, with the centralization of decision making in multinational corporations, few decisions of consequence are made by board members of branch plants. This view is supported by the government study of *Foreign Direct Investment in Canada* (1972:140), popularly known as "The Grey Report". This study also notes a number of other situations which follow from Canada's particular position in the continental economic system: "under-development of the Canadian techno-structure" because much of the research and development activity is carried on in the U.S. (297); large payments made to non-residents for management fees ($72million in 1964), royalties ($69 million), rent ($49 million) and research and development ($34 million) (203); U.S. manufacturing establishments tend to be more capital intensive and create less jobs, for instance, U.S. manufacturers employed 30 per cent of the workers but held 60 per cent of the assets (214).

One of the most interesting sociological reasons the government study gives for the high degree of foreign investment is the "social rigidity" of the Canadian social structure. It notes that "Canadian society has tended, particularly in the past, to be dominated by an establishment based more on social connections than ability and providing only limited scope for social mobility" (296-297). At another point, it explicitly mentions financial institutions as being particularly closed, even to other businessmen, and "restricted to individuals having the right social connections" (40). Finally, the authors of the study argue, implicitly using an elite model, that:

> It was not very long ago that large portions of Canada's population were effectively frozen out of top jobs in Canadian business. Persons who were not of Anglo-Saxon extraction appear to have had more difficulty in penetrating the senior levels of many corporations. They often found it difficult also to obtain the support and assistance for their own smaller businesses from the large corporations, further stultifying their growth capabilities (139-140).

Understandably, the government attempted to suppress the document before it was exposed through a leak to the *Canadian Forum* and published as "The Grey Report". From a sociological perspective, no more damning document of the Canadian social structure exists than the information contained in this report[10].

Canada in the 1960's witnessed a great transformation in its economic power structure. Primarily using the multinational corporation, U.S. economic elites have penetrated the Canadian power structure and created a distorted elite formation[11] at the top of the economic hierarchy. Three major elites have been identified for analytical purposes, although it remains to be demonstrated that they exist as distinct social groups. First is the indigenous elite, closely associated with dominant Canadian controlled financial, utilities, and transportation corporations, with smaller representation in the manufacturing and resource extraction sectors. Second, is a comprador elite, the senior management and directors of dominant foreign controlled branch plants, mainly in manufacturing and resource sectors. This group is subservient to the third group, the parasite elites, who control major multinational corporations which dominate important sectors of the Canadian economy through branch plants. They focus on resource and manufacturing sectors and operate their enterprises as part of an integrated organization. The relative power of each group in this particular historical phase of Canadian development will be examined subsequently.

(iii) Overview and Implications for Analysis

As argued throughout this and the previous chapter, Canada has experienced a qualitatively different type of economic relationship between the U.K. and U.S. imperial systems. The different impact of these two imperial "policies", one primarily commercial and the other industrial, is attributable to the nature of capitalist development in each country at the time they penetrated the Canadian economy. This evolution of the internal organization of the two major imperial powers and a comparative analysis of each is detailed in Block's "Expanding Capitalism: The British and American Cases" (1970:165) where he presents a strong case for analysing imperialism in terms of stages of development within the home and host nations. In this and the previous chapter, the difference between the two systems has been illustrated with particular reference to the type of investment used by each and the economic spheres within which investment took place. For example, U.K. investment has been focused in the tertiary sector of the economy, mainly transportation, finance, and other "support" services, while U.S. investment was initially in natural resources, as early as the 1800's in timber, and later expanded to industry. Appendix II (a & b) clearly illustrates the changing volume of capital from the U.S. and

U.K. and provides the essential distinction between portfolio and direct investment with evidence for the high correlation between portfolio U.K. investment and direct U.S. investment. From 1867 to about 1962, portfolio investment has always been greater from the U.K. than has direct investment and in the post-1962 period, little total investment has been of U.K. origin. U.S. portfolio investment, compared to direct, was greater from the period of the early 1920's to about 1950, at which time a great boom in U.S. direct investment took place pushing U.S. investment as a percentage of total investment from 60 per cent in 1939 to 72 per cent in 1956 and 77 per cent in 1960. Rapid introduction of U.S. capital increased the percentage of direct relative to all foreign investment for the same years from 33.5 per cent to 39 per cent and 50 per cent, respectively, apparently stabilizing at about 58 per cent by 1960. The introduction of $6,107 million in U.S. direct investment alone between 1952 and 1960 is almost twice the total of all U.K. investment present in Canada at any point in history.

It is within the North Atlantic triangle that Canada, as a national entity, must be analysed and it is first to the U.K. and later to the U.S. that Canada has had the role of an economic "satellite" in terms of trading natural resources and importing manufactured goods. In terms of investment, it may be accurate to describe Canada's relationship with the U.K. as 'satellitic' since it was U.K. portfolio investment which developed an indigenous economic elite. However, the notion of "satellite" does not accurately capture the quality of Canada's relationship with the U.S. in the post-war period. The U.S. case involves direct control and development of a "satellite" elite within Canada but this elite has only secondary power within the overall multinational framework. The powerful elite associated with U.S. direct investment is actually a foreign elite more appropriately described as a parasite[12]. The appropriation of capital and stultification of indigenous elites in the industrial and resource spheres has left Canada in a situation of dependence on the U.S. in these sectors and has not produced adequate returns to Canada from this asymmetrical relationship[13]. Although a satellite elite has developed with U.S. direct investment, the absence of power within this group creates a situation wherein major decisions in the area of resources and manufacturing accrue to heads of multinational corporations based mainly in the U.S. The removal of power from Canada, contrary to the U.K. era, follows from the type of capital investment and organization associated with multinational corporations. With direct investment, dependency and control increase over time, as in a parasitic relationship; it does not generate a situation where debts are paid off whereby indigenous control increases over time, as in portfolio investment. The parasitic elite gathers in capital and resources from Canada and in turn is able to reallocate this surplus into further control. Parasitism is the *modus operandi* of multinational corporations. They receive support from comprador elites from within the nations they operate in while at the same time preserving and increasing their advantage through maintenance of control and expropriation of capital to their elite in the center nation. Comprador elites are top ranking managers and directors of branch plants who follow directives and policies of multinational headquarters. Their functions are mainly advisory and administrative since they manage and conduct the affairs of subsidiaries of parent corporations (branch plants being subsidiaries of parent corporations which are located in nations other than the parent corporation and, as such, subject to the same constraints as other subsidiaries). The origin of the term comprador emerges from an analysis of China about 1850 where there was a "hybrid society" of the Imperial system and foreign powers which used compradors as a way of mediating, or as a "wedge" for their interests to conduct business within the country[14].

Elite formations in a situation of high foreign control include parasite elites who control parent multinational corporations, comprador elites who manage branch plants and an indigenous elite which controls national corporations and may or may not be linked with foreign corporations, in addition to their primary activities. Further elaboration of this structure would exist where, for example, the indigenous elite is also itself multinational in character and acts as a parasite elite toward another nation. More complexity may also be introduced where the elite structure becomes international and members of the indigenous elite cross national boundaries and sit on the boards of foreign controlled parents.

Compradorization creates a situation where capital, entrepreneurial talent and investment potentials are eliminated from the "host" country with the effect of decreasing, rather than increasing, autonomy with development. British investment, since it was portfolio, increased autonomy over time and permitted the emergence of an indigenous Canadian elite. U.S. investment has reversed the development toward autonomy and instead has brought Canada into a situation of greater dependency than during previous periods. This confirms Innis' perceptive statement that "Canada moved from colony to nation to colony" (1956:405). In terms of the power to decide about the allocation of resources in Canada, there has been a regression to the under-development of decision making (although not total under-development of "material" well-being)[15], with loss of control over the future of development, over stability built on an indigenous base, and over the retention and allocation of surplus.

It should be emphasized that these remarks refer exclusively to those sectors of the Canadian economy dominated by multinational corporations, particularly natural resources and manufacturing, and not to the other sectors, such as finance, transportation and utilities which were once associated with U.K. portfolio investment but are now controlled by indigenous elites. This reflects the change from mercantilism with the rise of industrialization and the introduction of branch plants into manufacturing. It is important to examine U.S. control but it is equally important to locate precisely where this control is dominant, as in oil and automobiles. The fact that there is a core of Canadian capitalists who are powerful within Canada and world capitalism as a whole—such as Canadian financial capital in banks and insurance companies but also in utilities such as Brascan and even some manufacturers like Massey-Ferguson or Moore Corporation—suggests that compradorization has occurred alongside the traditional elite rather than displacing it.

Early mercantilism was also associated with parallel economic and political penetration thus being more "formal". As Watkins argues, "neo-mercantilism" has a different character suggesting "a new colonialism that replaces formal empire with informal empire and tolerates political independence but not economic independence . . . informal empire turns formal, however, when the chips are down. That's what the U.S. marines are all about in this hemisphere" (1970:134). One of the greatest advantages to multinational corporations is Canada's receptiveness to their presence and the lack of hostility they encounter in terms of expropriating natural resources.

As argued in Chapter One, the nature of capital, the form of organization used to organize production, and the social structure, are each related to one another. To examine patterns of stratification, particularly at the elite level, requires an analysis of the capital formations, organizational forms and social structure in an historical perspective. Canadian entrepreneurs evolved from the British mercantile empire into a position of relative autonomy, although there has been heavy reliance on staples designed for the industrial centers of the U.K. and U.S. Interlock within the North Atlantic triangle in the interim between old mercantilism and "neo-mercantilism" was based on trade with mostly portfolio investment providing capital requirements and relatively low levels of direct control from outside Canada. This permitted and encouraged the development of an indigenous economic elite, an elite which traditionally has centered its resources in commercial activities such as transportation, finance and trade, while virtually ignoring the industrial development of the country. The indigenous industrial elite which has emerged since Confederation did not enjoy a position of power like the commercial elite, nor did it enjoy the benefits of government support to the extent the established traditional elite did. Indigenous industrialization experienced periods of boom during the first and second wars, but it was not sufficiently developed to withstand the brunt of "neo-mercantilism". Emerging as the most powerful capitalist nation after the Second World War, U.S.-based industrial interests were able to follow the path of earlier penetration and establish branch plants within Canada to capture large parts of the Canadian market and buy out many existing firms. The fate of the industrial sector followed the prior course of resource industries which were integrated with the U.S. This further weakened the Canadian industrial elite, never a very powerful group, but representing the potential for an indigenous industrial system.

The traditional commercial elite has never been threatened in its stronghold by the burst of U.S. direct investment and, in fact, enjoyed a favourable position of servicing[16] the industrial boom stimulated by U.S. controlled industrialization. Even in the few instances where their autonomy has been challenged, as in the Mercantile Bank affair and insurance company take-overs in the early 1960's, close alliance with the state allowed them to capitalize on this position and brought pressure to bear for legislation insuring their protection. With U.S. dominance in resources and industry emerged an elite centered in these areas which was subservient to the needs and demands of a foreign elite. Using natural resources and capital withdrawn from Canada, this parasitic elite reinforced its position of dominance in the capitalist world and particularly in Canada. The comprador elite is composed of both foreign nationals and others drawn from within Canada. This elite is most aptly described as management in terms of its function and is not the decision making and policy setting sector of the elite[17], a function reserved for the parasite elite. The comprador elite is continentalist in its orientation, occasionally having career patterns which take them into dominant positions within the foreign elite.

The fragmentation of the elite which has resulted does not necessarily breed conflict. On the contrary, the position of the traditional indigenous elite is reinforced by the industrial development occurring with U.S. direct investment. It is the smaller Canadian entrepreneurs based in industries which have not established themselves as dominant who feel the squeeze of U.S. penetration. They find themselves in a position of conflicting interests because of their weaker capital and market position. Unable to maintain their autonomy, this group is frequently forced to sell out their interests and join the ranks of the comprador elite.

In the meantime, other interests, not as well developed as the predominantly Anglo-Saxon elites, are still struggling to participate in economic decision making. These include, for example, French-Canadians, members of "third" ethnic groups, people from the under-developed regions of Canada such as the Maritimes and the West, and other members of regional and social hinterlands, not to mention the majority of the population not from the upper class. The following chapter will analyse the structure of corporate capitalism in Canada for 1972 and examine the interlocking relationships between dominant corporations. Later chapters will then analyse the economic elite which controls these corporations.

Notes

[1]For an excellent summary and discussion of similar positions taken by a variety of sociologists, see John Goldthorpe's, "Social Stratification in Industrial Society" (1966).

[2]According to Maslove's definitions, "Broad Income is a pre-government comprehensive income concept. It is equal to Full Income minus transfer payments. Thus it approximates what income would be before taxes and before government expenditures." Full income "is the sum of family money income plus certain nonmoney (imputed) income components. Included in the latter are such items as the rental value of owner-occupied dwellings, food and fuel produced and consumed on farms, and imputed interest. Corporate retained earnings and the unshifted portion of the corporate profits tax are also included because, if corporate taxes are deemed to be paid by individual shareholders, then, for consistency, the corresponding corporate earnings must be included in their incomes. Finally, included here are supplementary labour incomes minus the portion of social security contributions that is shifted to consumers" (1972:11-12).

[3]A progressive taxation is where the higher the income the higher the *rate* of taxation. In Canada the overall tax structure is regressive at the under-$6,000 level (that is, the lower the income the higher the taxation rate) and only proportional above $6,000 (the same rate over a range of incomes). Maslove's study was "designed to bias the results in favor of a progressive system," thus understating the actual regressiveness (1972:77-78).

[4]See, for example, Laxer (1970) *The Energy Poker Game*.

[5]The movement between business and industry at the upper levels is common for men like Louis St-Laurent, Mitchel Sharp, Robert Winters and James Richardson but the zeal of C. D. Howe seems to outshine them all; at his death in 1961 Howe was "chairman of Ogilvie Flour Mills Ltd. and a director of the Bank of Montreal. He also held directorships in National Trust Co. Ltd. and the Crown Life Insurance Co., was chairman of Price Brothers & Co. Ltd., a director of Dominion Tar & Chemical Co., Ltd. (the latter a Taylor-Argus company, and the Taylor interests having a substantial holding in Price Brothers), Atlas Steel Ltd., Rio Tinto Mining Co. of Canada Ltd., Hollinger Consolidated Gold Mines . . . (etc.). . . . Howe also held directorships in the following U.S.-controlled firms: Aluminum Ltd., RCA Victor Co. Ltd., and two New York-controlled investment trusts: Canadian Fund Inc. and Canadian Investment Fund Ltd." (Park& Park, 1962:58-59).

[6]See Appendix III.

[7]In Chapter Four it will be shown that foreign control has increased from 27 per cent of the elite positions in 1951 to 40 per cent in 1972. It will also illustrate the concentration of foreign control in manufacturing and resources and Canadian control in finance and utilities.

[8]"Neo-mercantilism" is sometimes used to describe the political economy of multinational corporations but a distinction between the current stage and its namesake lies in the creation of an indigenous labour force since the earlier form was primarily in the sphere of circulation while the latter is in production. This has important implications for the structure of the labour force which develops. Leo Panitch has made this point privately.

[9]In Chapter Four it will be shown that the minimum asset size of dominant corporations in 1972 was about $250 million.

[10]In a rather strange way, Neil McKinnon, chairman of the Canadian Imperial Bank of Commerce supports the view that the tightly controlled financial structure in Canada has been the main source of capital. "Canada has always been under-capitalized because most of the industrial development here took place during and after World War II, when the welfare state had started. In the U.S., on the other hand, most of the growth took place during the 19th century when large pools of private capital could still be collected. Here, the large pools of capital have had to be provided by financial institutions, particularly the banks, rather than individuals" (quoted by Newman, 1972a:23). McKinnon's analysis that "the welfare state" somehow has confiscated the pools of capital held by Canadian capitalists is subject to question but his general point that the banks have been key institutions for capital sources is well taken.

[11]"Distorted elite formation" in the sense that typically, the economic elite would be contained within a national economy and controlled by citizens and residents of that nation.

[12]Parasitism, according to the dictionary, is "a parasitic mode of life or existence" with a parasite something which receives advantage from its "host" "without giving any useful or proper return" thus reducing the host's potential for development. Typically, a parasite does not eliminate its host; if it did, it would destroy its own source of nourishment. In a curious way a parasite is dependent on the survival of the very thing from which it takes for its own well being. What is important for present purposes is that this concept describes a particular relationship, a relationship where actions of one party serve its own self-interest to the detriment of other parties. It will be argued that this relationship most aptly describes how multinational corporations relate to structures of decision making and potential for development.

[13]Because the parasite elite draws more from Canada (revenue, resources, decision making power, etc.) than it puts in, does *not* mean all groups are adversely affected. Indeed, the financiers gain through interest on bonds and their portfolios, transportation interests gain to the extent their services are used as do those in utilities. What is lost must also be measured in terms of *potential*. For example, those in manufacturing lose potential markets and "room" for expansion and the possibility that indigenous interests would emerge is reduced. In resources, the expansion potential is lost, moreover, the Canadian nation-state loses in terms of depleting resource reserves and Canadian workers lose in terms of potential jobs in refining and manufacturing when raw materials are shipped outside for these operations.

[14]Moore says the following of China: "a new hybrid society had already emerged in which power and social position no longer rested securely in the hands of those with a classical education [the Imperial system]. After the conclusion of the Opium War in 1842, the *compradores* spread through all the treaty ports of China. These men served in a variety of capacities as intermediaries between decaying Chinese officialdom and the foreign merchants. Their position was ambiguous. By shady methods they could accumulate great fortunes to live a life of cultivated ease. On the other hand, many Chinese condemned them as servants of the foreign devils who were destroying the foundations of Chinese society" (1966:176).

[15]If the "de-industrialization" thesis of the Waffle is correct, then there would be a decline in the number of jobs and standard of living in Canada. The "de-industrialization" thesis is that in recent years there has been a withdrawal of U.S. manufacturing plants from Canada to the U.S. The evidence to support the thesis is only slim at this point, restricted to a small region of Canada, and not sufficiently developed to be considered a trend. See *(Canada) Ltd., The Political Economy of Dependency* (1973).

[16]In addition to providing capital backing to foreign firms—both parents and branch plants—the indigenous elite has been active in supplying utilities such as natural gas and hydro electric power, providing extensive transportation services such as ship lines and railways, communications networks such as telephones and telecommunications, not to mention the services of trust and mortgage companies.

[17]The comprador elite is created either by development of new production facilities in Canada which are foreign controlled or by buying out existing firms. If the second occurs, the existing owners are then displaced and make a ready pool of managers to take on the role of compradors. This process is the same whether it occurs across boarders or within nation-states. As Marx observed, "After every crisis there are enough ex-manufacturers in the English factory districts who will supervise, for low wages, what were formerly their own factories in the capacity of managers for the new owners" (1967:III, 387).

Chapter Four

Structured Inequality: Dominant Corporations and Their Interlocks

CANADA has been and remains a society controlled by elites. Moreover, its present class system, as the culmination of a long historical development, reflects not a random but a structured inequality. The overseers of this carefully maintained domination, in its economic aspects, at least, are the economic elite. They preside over the corporate world, using as their means of power, the central institutions of the Canadian economy—113 dominant corporations, their subsidiaries, affiliates, investments, interlocking directorships with smaller corporations, family ties and shared class origins. Their power is reinforced by control over the major sources of capital, especially the key banks and insurance companies, and over the paramount positions within most of the central economic sectors. With increasing economic concentration over the past twenty years, the structure has become increasingly closed thus making it more difficult for those outside the inner circles of power to break through.

A variety of separate organizations and relationships cross-cut the corporate world, obscuring the fact that at the top a small number of people with common social origins, common experiences, and common interests oversee the direction of economic life. The inner circles of power are almost impenetrable and it is clear that their tight control of the legal fictions, known as corporations, denies most members of Canadian society any influence or participation in the fundamental economic decisions that affect the future and direction of the Canadian nation-state. This chapter will attempt to penetrate the "corporate mirage" of competing, struggling corporations which obscures the reality of elite power and masks over-riding factors which bring those at the top together to govern these legal fictions.

I) Identifying Dominant Corporations

Identification of the economic elite depends on an analysis of the structure of economic power as represented by the extent of concentration within a few dominant corporations. Over the last two decades since John Porter identified the central corporations in Canada, mergers and acquisitions have been prevalent among dominant corporations. For example, Domtar, itself an affiliate of Argus Corporation, has acquired three other dominant corporations as defined in 1948-50; John Labatt's has acquired three others while Power Corporation has acquired four. Most active in the merger movement has been George Weston Ltd. which represents no less than six earlier dominant corporations. Overall, of the 183 dominant corporations identified by Porter, no less than 41 have been reduced to 17 current companies through acquisitions and mergers[1]. It should be remembered that this consolidation is only among the very largest companies of twenty years ago and does not include the multitude of smaller companies which have also been absorbed.

Since mergers typically occur within sectors of related economic function, they are an important source of concentration and the most effective means of eliminating "competition". Moreover, all forms of increased concentration need not involve destruction of old organizations, as Neufeld illustrates with the case of Massey-Ferguson: "Legally, a new organization was not formed. Rather, Massey-Harris Company Limited issued shares to Harry Ferguson and merely changed its corporate name to Massey-Harris-Ferguson Limited" but "within a year even Harry Ferguson had left the company, and had sold his stock to the Argus group, the shareholders who had been close to Massey-Harris for many years" (1969:47). Although technically a merger, those in control of Massey-Harris in fact took over the Ferguson organization, one of the few other corporations in the farm implement business.

The centripetal movement of merger and acquisition centralizes economic power, especially that of the economic elite. The result has been to create a situation wherein a few large corporate complexes dominate each key sector of the economy with some conglomerates dominating more than one sector simultaneously. While horizontal mergers absorb similar organizations and vertical mergers integrate over several aspects of production (e.g., raw materials or transportation or refining or production or distribution), conglomerates are purely capital oriented in the sense that relationships exist not at the level of production between subsidiaries, but at the level of control[2].

The sociologist's concern about monopoly differs from that of, for example, the economist, whose concern is with competing economic units rather than with similar social types and their control of "competing" economic units. This position suggests that the traditional economist's focus on monopoly is too sector-specific and, since capital (e.g., assets and profit) cuts across sectors, what should be focused on is the overall structure of power. This assumes that the major way capitalists relate is through capital and not necessarily, as the conglomerate illustrates, through similar production activities. In other words, capital as an indicator of economic power, has implications for determining which corporations become defined as dominant. When, for example, "value-added" or "number of hands employed" is used to indicate relative concentration, they are necessarily biased towards production-based companies and even within these companies, towards particular ways of producing profits. For instance, "number of hands employed" is biased towards labour-intensive industries and understates the power of capital-intensive operations. If it can be agreed that increased revenues or profits, and with that, control over sources of capital, is the goal of capitalism, then it is more appropriate to focus on the goal rather than the means. More general statistics such as assets, revenue and net income cut across all sectors and, since oriented toward the actual goals of capitalism, are more appropriate to a focus on general economic power.

Appendix IV, entitled "Relative Position of Canadian Corporations as Identified by Porter c̄ 1950 and Position in 1971", illustrates both the mergers which have occured during recent times and, to some extent, the implications of defining dominant corporations differently than did Porter. Generally, the finance corporations have remained stable with two amalgamations involving four banks increasing concentration within the already highly centralized banking community and two dominant insurance companies becoming subsidiaries of a holding company. Industrial corporations have also become more concentrated with most of those corporations identified as dominant by Porter either directly represented in the current set of dominant corporations or represented through being merged with current dominant corporations. Those corporations which were identified by Porter as dominant but are not now within this group are typically the smaller ones within his original categories. They have either failed to grow at the same rate as other corporations or have been eliminated in the change of criteria from "number of hands employed", as used by Porter, to proportion of assets and sales, as used in this study[3]. The decision to change the criteria from "number of hands employed"[4] to one which combines sales and assets was made in large part because of the increasing availability of data since Porter completed his study. More corporations now publish financial statements and, for many of those which do not, financial statements can be purchased from Consumer and Corporate Affairs. Exceptions still exist (such as Canadian International Paper, which has a provincial charter and does not file with Consumer and Corporate Affairs) but these exceptions have only a minimal effect on overall availability and are not sufficient to warrant using alternative criteria.

By arguing that power stems from command over resources, there are still several types of resources which can be selected as criteria. "Number of hands employed" is biased towards production and labour extensive corporations so it understates the power of finance-based and capital-intensive corporations. Assets have as their base of power, control over property commanded (in the sense of capital). Assets, however, tend to be biased toward finance corporations because of the extensive capital they command. Operating revenue or income (under certain circumstances defined simply as sales) represents power in terms of a type of "market" situation. Revenue measures not only direct sales but also incorporates income from investments and subsidiaries which for some corporations represent substantial portions of their returns. But revenue tends to be biased towards production types of operations which have both high income and high overhead. Net income is another criteria which could be used to represent power in terms of flexibility and growth but it is so subject to bookkeeping techniques and investment patterns that it is overly volatile to use as an indicator of corporate power except over an extended period of time. From some of these possibilities mentioned, sales or revenue and assets together best approximate an operationalization of the concept of power which is defined as command over resources. Therefore, to minimize biases toward either production or finance types of operations, a combination of revenue and assets was selected, forming what is called a composite rank[5]. Dominant corporations were then defined using two points of reference: first, within particular functionally defined sectors, by the amount of revenue or assets accounted for, and secondly, in the context of all other corporations outside that functionally defined sector in order to balance the importance of each sector against all others. For reasons stated above, it was decided to report net income rather than incorporate it as part of the criteria for selection.

Based on a study of all corporations for which data was available, the following guidelines were established: a corporation was defined as dominant if it had assets of greater than $250 million and income of over $50 million and as middle range if over $50 million assets and $10 million sales but not meeting the criteria for dominance. These guidelines remained flexible so that within particular functionally defined sectors, such as banking and insurance, when the largest corporations accounted for 80 per cent or more of all sales and assets within that sector, only these were selected[6].

One additional decision related to subsidiaries requires explanation. As was argued in earlier chapters, boards of subsidiaries are appointed by and subject to the whim and will of the parent corporate board. As such, their power is delegated and, according to the rules of power, less powerful than those who do the appointing. Consequently, subsidiaries are reported within particular sectors when their parents do not consolidate their assets and revenues in their own statements; however, only the boards of parent corporations are selected as dominant. Notable exceptions are the boards of foreign controlled subsidiaries: since the parameters of power are defined within the Canadian nation-state, only the boards of foreign subsidiaries operating in Canada, and not the foreign-based parent boards, are included in the present study—except to the extent that Canadian boards and foreign boards overlap. This necessary exception itself indicates the inadequacy of abstracting Canada as a nation-state from Canada as part of a larger economic system, a problem discussed extensively earlier.

TABLE 9

Assets and Revenue of 113 Dominant Corporations in Canada by Sector as a Per Cent of All Assets and Revenue, Year End 1971*

Sector	Per Cent Assets	Per Cent Revenue
Finance		
Banks	90	91
Life Insurance	86	81
Sales Finance	90	—
Mortgage & Trust	80	—
Trade		
Retail	39	45
Wholesale	15	11
Transportation & Utilities		
Utilities	66	81
Railways	89	87
Transportation (including pipelines)	90	31
Communications	97	93
Mining		
Metal Mining	56	64
Mineral Fuels	48	40
Manufacturing		
Paper Products	52	57
Food and Beverages	66	56
Petroleum	90	94
Non-metallic Minerals	44	30
Primary Metals	55	57
Transportation Equipment	59	59
Machinery	66	58
Electrical Products	35	31
Other Manufacturing	29	43

* For a detailed breakdown, see Appendix VII.

The result of these criteria when applied to corporations operating in Canada are presented in Appendix VII as "Corporation Tables and Notes" and summarized here in Table 9. The very high percentages in these sectors, as defined by Standard Industrial Classification, illustrates the enormous amount of power concentrated in only 113 dominant corporations. A breakdown of assets and sales by each sector is provided in Appendix IX, "Distribution of Sales and Assets for Industrial Corporations by Sector expressed in Dollars and Percentages, 1971 year end". The sectors which contribute the greatest proportion of assets and sales for industrial corporations are included as dominant, thus meeting the criteria mentioned earlier of comparability between sectors. This appendix also illustrates differences between sectors in terms of all industrial corporations on the two criteria. For example, retail trade accounts for only 8.4 per cent of the assets and 16.2 per cent of the sales for industrial corporations while communications industries account for 5.3 per cent of assets and only 1.3 per cent of sales. The amalgamation of these two criteria provide a better index than do each of them separately from the perspective of measuring control over resources. If assets were used alone then retail trade would be under-represented or, if sales alone, then the communications industry would be understated.

But the percentage control reported above for the 113 dominant corporations should be regarded as conservative since they understate the actual control exercised. It does not include hundreds of smaller businesses which are only nominally independent of these central corporations either as suppliers or retailers[7]. Nor does it include the control of subsidiaries which are smaller than "middle range" since they are excluded from the present analysis. It does not measure the power exercised by directors of dominant corporations in other middle range and smaller corporations by their presence on the boards of directors[8], nor does it give an indication of the amount of power exercised beyond their immediate corporations by "setting the pace" for various industries because they are the largest and most important corporations within these sectors. A further way in which these corporations compound their control beyond their immediate assets and income is the method known as pyramiding whereby control is compounded through less than 100 per cent ownership yet control enough ownership to maintain effective control[9]. Each step away from the original investment expands the amount of control exercised by that investment thus "pyramiding" the actual amount of control the investment gives. The Argus example of control with less than 50 per cent ownership presented in an earlier chapter illustrates another form of pyramiding control.

It was stated at the beginning of this chapter that the economic elite exercise power through a "corporate mirage", a web of interlocked networks which weave throughout corporations operating in Canada. In addition to interlocking directorships and common social origins, which will be examined later, a series of other relationships can be described which serve to unify the top of the corporate world beyond the 113 dominant corporations.

Some companies, particularly from the United States, have more than one subsidiary operating in Canada but have no legal connection in Canada, sharing only the foreign parent in common. For example, Ford of Canada and Ensite are both subsidiaries of Ford Motor Co., the United States parent; General Motors (U.S.) operates both General Motors of Canada and GM Acceptance Co.; Celenese Corp. of America operates two major Canadian subsidiaries, Celenese Canada and Columbia Cellulose; IT&T operates several independent subsidiaries in Canada including Rayonier, Sheraton Hotels and Avis Rent-A-Car. Each of these corporate mirages creates problems of classification since Canada is viewed here apart from its North American context. In terms of decision making it would be correct to take only the boards of parent companies, such as General Motors (U.S.), and not the boards of both General Motors of Canada and GM Acceptance but since each operates in separate sectors and each subsidiary is comparable with other dominants in its sector, the boards of each were selected. Another example of vertically integrated operations across several sectors is the oil industry where exploration, drilling, refining, transportation through pipelines or ships, wholesale and retail trades are all related operations. Within the Canadian Gas Association, for instance, several industrial sectors are integrated, the current president being A.R. McMurrich, vice-president of the Steel Co. of Canada, a major pipeline producer. It is reported that the presidency "rotates among the component groups that make up the $6-billion natural gas industry in Canada—the producers, the pipeliners, the utilities and the makers of gas appliances" (*Globe & Mail*, May 31, 1972).

Other legal fictions include joint ventures such as the Gas Arctic Group which is composed of Texas Eastern Transmission Corp., Canadian National Railways, Columbia Gas System of Delaware, Northern Natural Gas of Omaha and Pacific Lighting Corp. of Los Angeles or the Northwest Group composed of Humber Oil and Refining Co., Trans-Canada Pipelines Ltd. of Toronto, Atlantic Richfield Co. of New York, Standard Oil (Ohio) and others (*Globe & Mail*, June 9, 1972). Joint ventures appear to be on the increase with even such long established firms as Eatons joining with the Steel Co. of Canada and TRW Inc. to form the Canada Systems Group (EST) Ltd., a computer services company (*Financial Post*, April 1, 1972). Other companies with wide participation are Brinco, made up of seven companies; RoyNat Ltd., a term financing company for land and buildings involving four companies; Syncrude Canada is the product of four partners, all large in the oil sector which joined to develop the Alberta Tar Sands in a $800 million project and another joint venture is the Orion Banking Group, a London-based multinational banking company of which Royal Bank was a founding member. Relationships such as those between buyer and seller, producer and distributer, financier and producer, and a host of others—even joint media campaigns such as the extensive advertisements carried out in major Canadian papers sponsored jointly by the Aluminum Co. of Canada, American Can of Canada, Dominion Foundaries and Steel, and the Steel Company of Canada, telling the reader of the merits of disposable cans (*Globe & Mail*, May 2, 1972:33)—indicate only a few additional ways in which major corporations work together rather than compete with one another. The idea that each corporation is an independent empire unto itself, fiercely struggling with all other corporations, is a myth. Separate corporate structures are a legal screen which clouds the interwoven extension of the economic elite into the highest levels of the Canadian economy.

II) Corporate Sectors

Corporate sectors are divisions constructed with Standard Industrial Classifications (SIC) based on an analysis of the major activity of the corporation in some production or financial function. Although there are difficulties with this type of classification[10], there appears to be no more satisfactory method available if aggregate financial statistics are desired. That is, since government publications of financial statistics for corporations use SIC, it is necessary to replicate their classifications[11]. The following sections will discuss, in a more detailed manner, the various sectors and the percentage of assets and sales accounted for by dominant corporations. Statistical calculations reported here can be found in Appendix VII.

(i) Banks

Five dominant banks are at the center of indigenous capitalism in Canada, providing both financing for other central corporations and, as will be illustrated later, their board rooms provide the main focal point for meetings of the economic elite.

Chartered banks are among the oldest and most powerful of Canada's corporate institutions: all of the five dominant banks or their successors were founded before or just following Confederation. Since that time, the five have risen to places of ascendency within their field, accounting between them for 90 per cent of the assets and 91 per cent of the income of all banks and thus representing one of the most concentrated banking structures in the world. All five are national banks, unlike four out of the five middle range banks which are regional in character and scope. A fifth middle range bank, the Mercantile Bank, is the only foreign controlled bank to break into the banking community in recent years. Barclay's Bank of Canada, an English subsidiary, was established in 1929 but it was bought out by the Imperial Bank in 1953. The Mercantile Bank was established by a Dutch Bank in the same year Barclay's was bought out, with control later passing to the First National Bank of New York[12].

Since 1951, there have been two mergers involving four banks, aside from Barclay's. In 1955, the Bank of Toronto and the Dominion Bank amalgamated to form the Toronto-Dominion Bank and in 1961, the Bank of Commerce and the Imperial Bank joined to form the Canadian Imperial Bank of Commerce. This left only eight banks until the establishment of the Bank of British Columbia in 1968. The only shifts in relative power of the banks since 1951 have been due to the amalgamations mentioned, thus further concentrating the already tight banking establishment.

Reflective of their great stability and power is the fact that a bank has not failed in Canada since 1923, a situation very different from the United States where a small bank drops off every two weeks on the average. Their survival is partially due to the very tight control by senior executives and directors, who directly pass on new loans exceeding a million dollars.

Three of the five dominant banks have their head offices in Toronto and the Royal Bank and Bank of Montreal, which have their head offices centered in Montreal, are reported to be shifting more of their operations toward Toronto in recent years. This phenomen appears to be related to a general shift of power away from Montreal to Toronto, but it is not known whether the banks are part of the cause of the shift or are responding to other forces.

Recently, banks have entered the mortgage lending business, many of them forming subsidiaries directly for this purpose since 1963. In 1963 banks, along with three trust companies, formed RoyNat to engage in financing, development and rental of commercial real estate. Similar ventures have occurred in the mutual fund field (Neufeld, 1972:131-132). Although there has been a long association between banks and trust companies, the 1967 Bank Act required that banks reduce their equity boldings in these companies to 10 per cent but the close association remained. Regulations also provide that banks—the

Mercantile being a notable exception—remain Canadian controlled in terms of both equity participation and directorships (Galbraith, 1970:24-25).

(ii) Life Insurance

Very similar to the chartered banks, the life insurance companies are well established institutions of power within Canada. All of the dominant Canadian controlled life insurance companies were established in or before 1900 with only a few of the middle range companies being established after this date. Among the 13 dominant insurance companies, three are foreign controlled, the Metropolitan Life and Prudential Life being controlled in the U.S. and Standard Life from the United Kingdom. Two other dominant insurance companies, Great West Life and Imperial Life, are both subsidiaries of Power Corporation. This leaves only eight independent Canadian controlled dominant companies. Although slightly less concentrated than the banks, dominant life insurance companies still account for 86 per cent of the total assets and 81 per cent of income of all the companies in this sector. Canadian companies control 82 per cent of all assets and 80 per cent of all income for life insurance companies operating in Canada. Unlike banks, the number of life insurance companies has been steadily increasing in Canada with 24 at Confederation, there were 59 by 1925, decreasing to 57 in 1945 but then increasing rapidly to 98 by 1960 and 129 by 1970. But in spite of the increasing numbers of companies operating in Canada there has been very little change in the relative dominance of these companies since 1900 when Canada Life, Sun Life, Confederation Life and Mutual Life emerged as the central companies. At that time, these four companies alone accounted for about 78 per cent of all the assets of life companies (Neufeld, 1972:247). All ten companies identified by Porter in 1950 as dominant remain dominant today with the only additions being three foreign controlled companies which were also comparable with those identified as dominant then.

The origins of life insurance companies certainly were not humble: "Manufacturers Life was founded by the Gooderham family in 1887. First president was Sir John A. Macdonald, who assumed the post while *still Prime Minister*. He served as president until his death in 1891" (emphasis added, *Financial Post*, August 12, 1972). Currently several life insurance companies remain dominated by families, London Life and the Jeffery family and Crown Life and the Burns family being examples.

Since 1961, following seven foreign takeovers and several others imminent, legislation has been in force to insure Canadian control and participation in the life insurance business. This was further reinforced in 1965 with legislation similar to that protecting the banks (Neufeld, 1972:246-248). Both life insurance companies and banks, two sectors dominated by long established Canadian controlled firms, have enjoyed government protection from foreign takeovers while most other sectors have not. It is not unexpected then, that the life companies and banks together form the nub not only of Canadian finance but of indigenous Canadian capitalism.

(iii) Investment Companies

Investment companies represent a collage of corporations operating in several different sectors. The one thing they do have in common is that their main activity is that of holding companies, with assets in more than one sector. Most of the companies defined as dominant in this sector are either parents of corporations dominant in other sectors (for example, Anglo-Canadian Telephone, the Canadian subsidiary of the U.S. General Telephone and Electronics controls both British Columbia Telephone and Quebec Telephone) or they are themselves subsidiaries of dominant corporations from other sectors (for example, Canadian Pacific Investments acts as a holding company for Canadian Pacific, dominant in transportation). Other companies, like Moore Corp., have extensive operations outside Canada and as such do not fit standard classification procedures used by CALURA.

Two companies which are exceptional in this sector are Power and Argus Corporations. Each is fairly unique to the Canadian corporate scene and each extremely powerful within the corporate world. Power Corporation is controlled by Paul Desmarais, a Sudbury-born financier, through a series of other holding companies[13]. Some of Power's holdings are run as independent operations, such as the Canada Steamship Lines run by Paul Desmarais's brother, Louis, while others such as Laurentide Financial Corp. and Union Acceptance Corp. operate through an integrated management function called Laurentide-Union Management Corp. Argus is similar to Power but rather than running its conglomerate on majority control, as does Power, it uses minority holdings to control. As E.P. Taylor, the architect of Argus, once said, "I look for companies that will not grow with the country, but faster than the country. . . . I look for companies where no very large shareholder exists. With my partners, I buy enough stock to give us effective control. Then the company holds our view. . . . It's our policy to find the right executives, to put them at the top, then to leave them alone to appoint their own employees right down the line" (quoted by Newman, 1959:224-226). With companies such as Argus and Power

searching for other large companies which are "management controlled", a tight rein over corporate holdings is obviously going to be
the result.

(iv) Other Finance Companies

There remains to be considered other finance companies which exist in
sectors not included by Porter in 1948-50, such as sales finance and
consumer loans, trust and mortgage companies. The introduction of
these new sectors is not simply an alteration in the methodology but
represents an actual increase in the growth and importance of these
sectors over the past 20 years. It would not be argued that they have
gained nearly the same stature as dominant banks or insurance companies but the "near banks" have developed to the extent that they are
highly comparable to other dominant corporations.

Eight consumer loans and sales finance companies are included as
dominant with one, Laurentide Finance, being a subsidiary of Power
Corporation. General Motors Acceptance is a subsidiary of General
Motors Corp. of Detroit, just as is General Motors of Canada, but it is
organized in such a way that the board is accountable to the parent
rather than to the Canadian subsidiary. General Motors Acceptance
was organized in 1953 to provide financing for GM dealers. Ford
established Ford Motor Credit Co. of Canada in 1962 and Chrysler
organized Chrysler Credit Canada Ltd. in 1966 but because of the way
they organized their ownership, only the boards of Ford and Chrysler
corporations are included.

Based on various calculations by Neufeld, it is estimated that
approximately 90 per cent of the assets of the sales finance and consumer loans sector are accounted for by the companies classified as
dominant[14]. In a detailed examination of this sector, he suggests that
"significant structural changes have occurred in the consumer credit
industry since the end of the Second World War" noting that they made
a dramatic increase in the mid-1950's but that they have become
endangered in recent years because of competition from more established financial institutions (1972:324-325). The development of this
sector has been stimulated by Canada's geographic and economic
proximity to the United States. The early companies were associated
with the U.S. automobile industry. Even IAC, the largest company in
this sector, began in 1925 as a U.S. subsidiary but in the early 1930's
was bought out by Canadian interests. Although U.S. ownership is
significant in this sector, federal intervention into the proposed
takeover of Traders Group in 1969 has helped maintain the majority of

the sales finance sector (about 57 per cent) under Canadian control: of the eight key corporations, four are Canadian controlled and four U.S. controlled companies.

Just as problems of classification prevent establishing a precise figure for sales finance and consumer loans companies, this also creates a problem in the trust and mortgage field. However, based on Neufeld's calculations, it is estimated that over 80 per cent of the assets in this sector are accounted for by the five trust and four mortgage companies identified as dominant[15].

Bond and Shearer maintain that trust companies act as two companies in one, both administering trusts and estates (that is, other people's holdings) and acting as "true financial intermediaries" by accepting deposits and making investments (1972:215). They have been active in the mortgage field and have a relatively free hand in the type of investments they are able to make. Neufeld documents three cases of close relationships between banks and trust companies: Royal Trust and the Bank of Montreal, Montreal Trust and the Royal Bank, and National Trust and the Canadian Bank of Commerce. Since 1971, however, they have been prohibited by legislation from interlocking directorships and limited in equity participation to 10 per cent (1972:295)[16].

Mortgage companies have also experienced rapid growth in the post-war period, with Neufeld reporting that "the growth rate of the mortgage loan companies from 1944 to 1968 exceeded that of the total of all financial intermediaries combined" (1972:216). Bond and Shearer argue that the function of mortgage loan companies "are practically indistinguishable from the trust companies" except for the specifically trust functions (1972:220). In fact, one of the largest mortgage companies, Canada Permanent, also operates one of the largest trust companies and, as their annual report spells out: "There are few financial companies whose services are so widespread as those of Canada Permanent. . . . it is one of Canada's largest financial complexes". The report also states that in addition to their own assets of $1,552 million they administer an additional $2,025 million. Another company in the mortgage sector is Investors Group, a subsidiary of Power Corporation. The only foreign controlled company in this sector is Crédit Foncier which is controlled from France. A very old company founded by special legislation in Quebec in 1880, the company is national in scope and not regionalized in Quebec as the name would suggest. The company also operates two subsidiaries, one in the real estate field and a second in the development field, "mainly in the field of natural resources" according to their annual report. The annual report also provides a breakdown of the distribution of loans with 37 per

TABLE 10

Total Retail Trade in Canada, 1971 year end

	Foreign	CANADIAN		Unclassified	TOTAL
		Private	Government		
Assets	22%	55%	2%	21%	100%
Sales	22	55	5	18	100%
Profits	14	27	49	9	100%

CALURA, Part I Corporations Report for 1971 (March 1974).

cent in Quebec, 21 per cent in Ontario and nine, five and four per cent, respectively, in Alberta, Manitoba and Saskatchewan.

(v) Trade

As Table 10 illustrates, the majority of retail trade is controlled by private companies within Canada. There is, however, a large unclassified component of corporations (see CALURA, 1974:61) and a large profit classified as controlled by the Canadian government which, for CALURA's purposes, apparently includes co-operatives.

In the retail trade, 11 companies are classed as dominant, with one, Loblaw Groceterias, being a subsidiary of Loblaw Companies, in turn a subsidiary of George Weston Ltd. which is dominant in food and beverages. These 11 dominant corporations account for 39 per cent of the assets and 45 per cent of the sales of all retail companies. This, however, understates the actual control exercised in the retail business because motor vehicle dealers, which are mainly controlled through franchise relationships with one of the dominant automobile manufacturers, are excluded. According to published figures motor vehicle dealers had sales of $4,925 million in 1971 representing approximately one quarter of all retail sales. If this figure were added to the already identified retail companies, they would account for almost three quarters of all retail sales (*Economic Review*, April 1973:93).

Among the dominant retail companies are those which specialize in food distribution and those mainly oriented to dry goods. All of the companies were established during or before 1931 with the exception of Simpson-Sears, which is a joint venture of Simpsons and Sears-Roebuck of the United States, which, of course, are themselves very old firms. The joint venture gave the U.S. company an avenue into the Canadian retail market and the Canadian company greater buying contacts in the U.S.

Retail companies employ a tremendous number of people; for example, Eatons employes 50,000, Hudson's Bay Company 17,000, Simpsons-Sears 22,000 and Simpsons 9,000. Between them, these four companies employ about one hundred thousand people, more if part-time seasonal help were included.

Family enterprises dominate in retail trade. For example, of the four largest retail companies, the Weston family dominates Loblaws, the Eaton family, Eatons, the Burton family, Simpsons, and the Steinberg family, Steinbergs. Eatons is "really owned by four beneficiaries and they are run by a group of trustees who, in fact, administer on behalf of the beneficiaries the shares of the T. Eaton Co. The four beneficiaries are the four sons of John David Eaton", according to John Picton, President of Eatons since 1969. He also states that: "No

TABLE 11

Total Wholesale Trade in Canada, 1971 year end

| | Foreign | CANADIAN | | Unclassified | TOTAL |
		Private	Government		
Assets	33%	52%	7%	8%	100%
Sales	29	61	2	8	100%
Profits	31	55	7	7	100%

CALURA, Part I Corporations Report for 1971 (March 1974).

management of Eatons have any shares in the company'' (*Globe & Mail*, June 15, 1972:B5).

The Hudson's Bay Co., which was discussed as being of such historical importance in earlier chapters, remains an important retailer. According to its annual report, furs constitute only one per cent of its total sales with retail sales accounting for 80.2 per cent and wholesale for the remaining 18.8 per cent. Early land grants provided the company with sufficient capital to establish itself as dominant in retail trade and its ventures into the oil business through the affiliated Hudson's Bay Oil and Gas Co. directly stem from the original land granted under the Deed of Surrender in 1870.

Another dominant retail company is Dominion Stores, an affiliate of Argus Corporation. Four other companies are subsidiaries of United States parents, including Woolworth's, Canada Safeway, Kresge's and Zellers. Rather than independent Canadian operations, these companies might better be regarded as extensions of U.S. marketing schemes into the North American economy. Their operations are integrated with those of the U.S. parent's and their Canadian operations are designed to capture part of the Canadian market by taking advantage of "spill-over advertising".

As is evident in Table 11, the majority of wholesale trade is controlled within Canada by private companies with slightly higher U.S. control of assets and sales than in retail trade.

The wholesale trade is composed of companies which are related to retail operations, such as Canadian Tire, Oshawa Group and M. Loeb as well as two wholesalers of oil. The seven dominant wholesalers, including Kelly Douglas, a subsidiary of George Weston, account for 15 per cent of assets and 11 per cent of sales. Once again, family firms dominate this sector, for example, the Weston's through Kelly Douglas, the Wolfe family in Oshawa Group, the Billes family in Canadian Tire, the Loeb's in M. Loeb, the Irving's in Irving Oil and the Richardson's in James Richardson.

Two of the dominant wholesale companies are tied in with the over 1,400 IGA retail stores. M. Loeb, which sells both in Canada and the eastern United States, has a franchise with IGA in addition to owning 42.6 per cent of IGA Canada Ltd. Similarly, the Oshawa Group has an IGA franchise and owns 42.6 per cent of IGA Canada Ltd. According to ''Canadian Stock Comment 26-Oshawa Group'' prepared by Merril Lynch, Royal Securities Ltd., 54 per cent of Oshawa Group's food sales in 1971-72 were to IGA and food accounted for 72 per cent of Oshawa's total sales for the same period. Similar data is not available for M. Loeb but based on the data regarding ownership and the sales of Oshawa Group, it can be stated that the separateness of these companies is another instance of ''the corporate mirage'' dis-

TABLE 12

Total Utilities in Canada, 1971 year end

	Foreign	CANADIAN Private	CANADIAN Government	Unclassified
Assets	8%	33%	58%	—
Income	11	46	38	5%
Profit	20	68	10	2%

CALURA, Part I Corporations Report for 1971 (March 1974).

cussed earlier. Further examples of this appear in a recent *Financial Post* article which reports that George Weston was attempting to gain control of M. Loeb. In addition to being of interest from the perspective of how stocks can be manipulated to maintain control, the article illustrates how some "customer" relations corporations establish with one another operate. The article states that Garfield Weston personally flew to Canada from his estate in England to make an offer to the Loeb family, but a price could not be agreed on so Weston began to buy up stock on the market, managing to acquire 13.6 per cent. In order to protect themselves, the Loeb's began to use a third company, Horne & Pitfield which they controlled, to which it issued additonal shares deflating the Weston ownership, which had grown by this time to about 24 per cent down to about 14 per cent. One would expect by this time that some competitive fervor would have arisen but the *Financial Post* reports: "Not so, says Bertram Loeb: 'There is little likelihood of their losing us as a customer. We buy from each other because it suits us.' 'Our relationship is good', Creber (President of George Weston) chimes in" (February 1973:15). Even after one company tried to take over the other against the owner's will, it was "business as usual".

(vi) Transportation and Utilities

The transportation and utilities sector differs from others in that there are high degrees of government participation, particularly through crown corporations such as the Canadian National Railway, discussed in earlier chapters, and in government controlled hydro electric projects.

From Table 12, it is obvious government enterprises have, on the aggregate, high investments but very low returns, making this a highly subsidized sector of the economy. While the government controls 58 per cent of the assets, it receives only 38 per cent of the income and 10 per cent of the profits. As suggested in the historical analysis, foreign control is low in this sector.

The communications sector is very highly concentrated with only two dominant corporations and their subsidiaries accounting for 97 per cent of the assets and 93 per cent sales. Bell Canada commands the field with Anglo-Canadian Telephone, a subsidiary of General Telephone and Electronics from the U.S., being the only other major participant in the field. Each is a long established firm with Bell incorporated in 1880 and the Anglo-Canadian subsidiaries established during or before 1927. Being government regulated corporations, together they have a *de facto* monopoly of the communications industry.

The other utilities sectors are highly concentrated as well, with

TABLE 13

Total Mining in Canada, 1971 year end

| | Foreign | CANADIAN | | Unclassified |
		Private	Government	
Assets	69%	29%	1%	1%
Sales	76	23	—	1%
Profits	79	23	—	-2%

CALURA, Part I Corporations Reports for 1971 (March 1974).

five corporations in the electric power, gas and water utilities sector accounting for 66 per cent of assets and 81 per cent sales. The only foreign controlled firm in this sector is Canadian Utilities, a subsidiary of International Utilities of the United States. Canadian Utilities also controls two middle range corporations, Northwestern Utilities and Canadian Western Natural Gas. Most of the corporations in this sector are involved in natural gas transportation. The largest company, Northern and Central Gas, according to its annual report, has the following distribution of sales: oil and gas exploration and production 21 per cent, industrial gas 32 per cent, commercial gas 13 per cent and residential gas 28 per cent.

CALURA aggregates pipelines and railways so it is difficult to present individual percentages, however, using the Statistics Canada Publication, *Railway Transport*, it is possible to determine that two railways, the Canadian National (CN) and Canadian Pacific (CP), account for 89 per cent of assets and 87 per cent of income between them. When railways and pipelines are combined under the heading "transportation", 86 per cent of assets and 31 per cent of revenue becomes accounted for. While the railways are Canadian owned, CP privately and CN as a crown corporation, the pipelines present a different case. Exceptional in the utilities sector, U.S. control dominates in the pipeline sector with only TransCanada being controlled in Canada. This can be accounted for by the fact that pipelines are part of an integrated oil operation ruled by U.S. control. In fact, each of the central oil producers is affiliated with one of the key pipelines[17]. Unlike any other sector examined to this point, the pipeline business is very young, dating from the early 1950's. It is in this area of new growth that U.S. capital has been able to gain ascendency just as it has in most other sectors of the Canadian economy whose growth dates from the postwar period.

(vii) Mining

Of the nine dominant mining corporations, seven are controlled in the United States and two in Canada. This includes four corporations in metal mining, two of which are U.S. controlled, and five from mineral fuels, all U.S. controlled. This foreign mastery is reflected in the aggregate statistics for mines with 68 per cent of all assets, 73 per cent sales and 72 per cent profits controlled outside Canada. About 80 per cent of the foreign control is American. As Table 13 illustrates, there is very low Canadian participation and this is reflected in the dominant companies in this area. In the mining sector, foreign controlled companies pay only 14 per cent tax on profits while Canadian companies

TABLE 14

Total Manufacturing in Canada, 1971 year end

	Foreign	CANADIAN		Unclassified
		Private	Government	
Assets	58%	39%	1%	2%
Sales	57	39	1	3
Profits	66	33	—	1

CALURA, Part I Corporations Report for 1971 (March 1974).

pay 21 per cent—a significant form of subsidy to mining companies when compared to other sectors of the economy.

Dominant corporations in metal mining account for 56 per cent of all assets and 64 per cent of sales with the corresponding figures being 48 per cent and 40 per cent for mineral fuels. The two capital intensive mining sectors date from quite distinct periods. The key metal mines are somewhat older, originating around 1920, while the younger mineral fuels sector did not develop in any extensive way until about the Second World War. While there are high degrees of U.S. ownership in the metal mining sectors, these are not integrated with U.S.-based operations; rather, they tend to be fairly independent Canadian operations responsive to particular Canadian resources. On the other hand, mineral fuels represent an extension of U.S. giants into the Canadian resource base. Each of the dominant corporations is a subsidiary of its U.S. parent operating within a continental framework[18]. Regardless of whether Canada's government has a continental energy policy or not, it is clear that the U.S. oil giants have just such a policy, integrating their Canadian subsidiary operations with their U.S. headquarters.

(viii) Manufacturing

About three fifths of the entire manufacturing sector is foreign controlled while Canadian participation is only about one third. Foreign corporations pay somewhat less tax—44 per cent compared to 48 per cent by Canadian controlled companies. There is, however, substantial variation within the subdivisions of manufacturing with respect to foreign control.

In the paper products sector there are six dominant corporations, the largest four of which are Canadian controlled with one each of the remaining two controlled in the U.S. and U.K. Dominant companies in this sector were established mainly between the First World War and the Depression, making this a well established industry. The dominant corporations in this sector account for 52 per cent of assets and 57 per cent sales. Since 1950 this sector has become much more concentrated with the present six dominant companies accounting for 13 companies identified by Porter. The greatest expansion has occurred by Domtar which accounts for four corporations dominant in 1950. Pulp and paper is the oldest resource-based manufacturing sector in Canada. The predominance of Canadian control in this sector can be linked to its early origins, when British portfolio investments provided the major source of financing. This is unlike most of the other manufacturing and resource sectors which were established in the era of U.S. direct investment.

Wood industries are smaller than paper products with only two dominant corporations, one controlled in the U.S. and the other a consortium of U.S. and Canadian companies. These are both younger companies being established in the post-war period. Between them, they account for 19 per cent of the assets and 11 per cent of sales indicating that although these two companies lead the field, there is substantial participation by smaller concerns.

Just as in the mineral fuels sector, the petroleum sector is an exclusive preserve of foreign corporations, the majority of which are controlled in the U.S. Also similar to mineral fuels, foreign firms pay only 19 per cent tax while lack of Canadian participation prevents a corresponding figure for Canadian controlled firms. Between them, the eight dominant corporations in this sector account for 90 per cent of all assets and 94 per cent of all sales, making it among the most concentrated industries. It should be noted that this is concentration from outside Canada and reflects the state of the world oil industry and not any indigenous forces. The largest of the firms are older and well established within Canada but many did not experience rapid growth until the post-war period. Although the four largest companies were identified as dominant in 1950, the four smaller dominant companies have attained this position since that time.

The food and beverage industry is dominated by Canadian dominant corporations and U.S. middle range companies. This pattern exists because the industry is continental in scope with U.S. giants in the field extending their operations into Canada, very similar to the pattern in retail trade. Because they are primarily U.S. extensions and not independent operations, they tend to be smaller than their Canadian counterparts. Only recently through the sale of Canadian Breweries to Rothman's has any of the dominant companies come under foreign control. Many key companies in this sector are also controlled by well established family firms and no dominant companies were established after 1930. The largest companies account for 66 per cent of the assets and 56 per cent of sales in this sector while a series of middle range companies add an additional 16 per cent and 19 per cent respectively. Rapid concentration has occurred in this sector since 1950; the present seven dominant companies representing 23 companies identified as dominant by Porter.

The primary metal sector is dominated by four companies, three of which are steel producers with high Canadian participation and the fourth, the U.S. controlled Aluminum Co. of Canada. Between them, the four companies account for 55 per cent of the assets and 57 per cent of the sales in the primary metals sector. Once again, they are older companies, well established in the industry. This sector has also become more concentrated since 1950: four companies now accounting for seven companies identified by Porter as dominant about twenty years ago. This occurred during the same period when the industry experienced rapid growth as well as the introduction of blast furnaces and oxygen steel making. Simultaneously, the companies began expansion into integrated operations through the purchase of several mining companies and secondary manufacturing concerns such as Dofasco's purchase of National Steel Car.

The transportation equipment sector is dominated by the three giant U.S. automakers which between them account for almost the entire automobile manufacturing in Canada and 59 per cent of the assets and sales of the entire transportation and shipment sector. These three companies have extensive economic power within Canada; for example, General Motors employs 28,000 people and spends $650 million with Canadian suppliers, consequently controlling resources well beyond those indicated by its individual assets and sales. For instance, two of the middle range companies, Ensite and Budd Automotive, are integrated with the dominant companies. As in many of the other sectors discussed, the automotive industry is continental in scope. Total U.S. dominance occurred during the rapid growth of the industry in the early 1900's when the few indigenous Canadian manufacturers—Sam McLaughlin is the most notable example—sold out to the U.S. giants. Since that time, the three, reinforced in large part by government support such as the Auto Pact, have monopolized the industry and no company has even approached the inner circle.

The machinery sector is dominated by one company in each of two fields, with Massey-Ferguson dominating the farm implement field and IBM Canada the computer industry. Together they account for 66 per cent of the assets and 58 per cent of the sales in this sector.

Sectors not discussed to this point include two dominant companies in the electrical products sector with one, Northern Electric, a subsidiary of Bell Canada[19] and the other, Canadian General Electric, a subsidiary of the U.S. parent General Electric. Together these companies account for 35 per cent of the assets and 31 per cent of the sales in this sector. Other manufacturing companies classed as dominant include Imasco and Rothman's, both foreign controlled, which monopolize the tobacco products industry. In chemicals, only Canadian Industries, controlled in the U.K., is classified as dominant while a series of U.S. companies control the middle range companies in this sector. As with retail and food and beverages, there is a continental network centered in the U.S. which has branch plants in Canada integrated with the parent operations. The existence of these capital and high-skill companies on a continental basis inhibits the development of indigenous outlets for highly qualified manpower and at the same time reduces the research and development potential of the nation.

The final sector to be discussed is real estate, a relatively recent

growth industry in Canada. Generally, real estate companies themselves do not have the assets or revenue to be considered dominant, but,
during the past few years, dominant corporations have established
several subsidiaries in this field. As referred to earlier, many of these
new ventures are part of mortgage and trust companies, but other
companies such as Power Corporation, Distillers-Seagrams through
Cemp Investments, and even the very old family firm of Eatons have
entered this field significantly. The evidence suggests that rather than
being taken over by "new blood", this emerging industry is in fact
controlled by the established economic elite.

Before leaving this section and turning to the issue of directorships, a general comment is needed. Recent discussions of the Canadian economy have focused on the issue of U.S. ownership. Ideologues
of all persuasions have latched onto this issue as being central in any
discussion of corporate capitalism in Canada. While it is correct to state
that U.S. control monopolizes the resource and much of the manufacturing sectors, not all of the control over the Canadian economy is in the
hands of U.S. corporate capitalists. Foreign control is greatest in the
surplus creating sectors (manufacturing and resources) but Canadian
control dominates in "service" sectors and areas of circulation (finance, utilities and trade). Indeed, indigenous Canadian capitalists
have been ignored while a smokescreen of nationalism shrouds their
existence. Throughout the focus on foreign investment, the Canadian
economy remains controlled in large part by a set of families who have
been in the past and still remain at the core of the Canadian economy.
Very little discussion has been concerned with the extent of democratization in Canadian institutions and very few remarks can be heard about
equalizing access to places of decision making in the Canadian
economy. The indigenous elite based in the upper class remains unchallenged by champions of "Canadian control" like the Committee for an
Independent Canada.

III) Directorship Positions

Directorship positions represent the actual number of openings on
boards of corporations and are not equivalent to the number of persons
since individuals may, and often do, hold more than one position
simultaneously. Examining directorships, including senior management, defined as dominant in 1951, Porter found that 170 dominant
corporations included 1,304 positions held by Canadian residents and
an additional 306 held by non-residents. In 1972, 113 dominant corporations included 1,454 positions held by residents of Canada with an
additional 301 held outside Canada. This represents an overall expansion in the number of elite positions by about nine per cent since 1951

but a contraction by almost a third in the number of dominant corporations. Two facts account for the larger number of positions now. First, several new sectors in finance, including sales finance, mortgage and trust companies, have come into prominence and these tend to have larger boards than most companies. Another factor is that corporations defined as dominant in 1972 are relatively larger than those of 1951 and this typically means a larger board is created. It is important to note that aside from minimal legal requirements, the size of the board and number of senior management positions is based on decisions by those in control of the corporation.

The total number of foreign resident directorships has remained stable over the 1951 to 1972 period, shifting only slightly from 306 to 301, in spite of rapid increases in the amount of foreign investment and control. This indicates that a simultaneous shift has occurred in the way foreign investment is now controlled. Rather than coming to Canada from foreign residences to board meetings, an increasing proportion of the foreign subsidiaries are managed by inside directors, both Canadian and foreign born, resident in Canada. In other cases Canadian participation is substantial in these subsidiaries, as will be evident when interlocks are examined. An increased number of directors of foreign boards are members of the indigenous Canadian economic elite and there has been more delegation of administrative responsibilities to foreign and Canadian born executives who head subsidiary boards and report back to the parent board. This indicates that in a large number of cases, very direct control is exercised outside the country and the boards are strictly administrative in Canada with policy direction emanating from the parent.

All foreign residents are not members of foreign subsidiaries in Canada; in fact, a substantial number are recruited as contacts for indigenously controlled boards. For example, there are 23 foreign residents on the boards of the Canadian controlled dominant banks. These are powerful foreign capitalists who have been recruited to the bank boards because they provide essential contacts and legitimacy for the multinational operations of the Canadian banks. Similar situations occur on other Canadian controlled boards of Canadian multinationals, all of which emphasizes the international scope of capitalism.

But there are some problems in using residence as a criteria for highly mobile elite members. For example, John Angus McDougald, chairman and president of Argus, reports two residents, one in Ontario and the other in Florida. In these cases even if one residence was reported as Canadian, the individual was classed as a resident. Similarly, the use of birth place as an indicator of early experience is ambiguous. The decision was made to define as Canadian born, anyone actually born in Canada or born to parents normally resident in Canada

TABLE 15

Residence and Control of Dominant Directorship Positions by Sector, 1972*

Residence & Control	Finance	Utilities	Trade	Manufacturing	Resource	All
Canada	79.6%	75.3%	51.7%	44.7%	24.0%	60.0%
U.S.	12.1	22.4	37.9	32.3	52.6	26.0
U.K.	7.0	1.2	10.4	12.0	8.4	7.7
Other	4.0	1.2	0.0	11.1	15.0	6.3
TOTAL	100%	100%	100%	100%	100%	100%
N	(852)	(170)	(174)	(226)	(333)	(1755)

* Joint ventures have been included by residence of director without control differentiation. "Residence & Control" includes the positions occupied by persons who are resident in the area indicated or are Canadian residents in foreign controlled firms. For example, "Canada" includes persons resident in Canada in Canadian controlled firms while "U.S." includes those residents in the U.S. and comprador positions in Canada in U.S. controlled firms.

but temporarily absent because of schooling or a placement. Two assumptions had to be made in instances where adequate data was not available: they were assumed to be born in Canada if presently resident in Canada and those now resident outside Canada were assumed to be born in the country of their present residence. These assumptions affect only a very few cases and cannot alter the basic pattern.

Each corporation and the major sectors were broken down by the residence and birth of their directors. This table, presented in Appendix XII as "Distribution of Directorships by Corporation, Residence and Birth, 1972" shows that 1,277 positions are held by persons born in Canada while 301 are held by persons born in the U.S., 113 in the U.K. and 64 born elsewhere. This leaves the impression that Canadian born members dominate the board rooms; but when residence and birth are combined with control, a different situation becomes evident for some sectors.

Porter found that in 1951 a total of 27 per cent of the positions in dominant corporations operating in Canada were held by foreign residents or Canadian residents in foreign controlled corporations, but by 1972, this had increased to 40 per cent. And when birth rather than residence is used as the criteria, the extent of foreign birth and control increases to 46 per cent of the positions.

These figures represent the total of all sectors combined but when the analysis becomes sector-specific, some important differences emerge which support the previous analysis concerning the particular concentration of traditional indigenous elites and the location of new social forces controlled outside Canada. Table 15 presents the residence and control of directorship positions subdivided by the five key sectors discussed earlier in this chapter.

The wide variance between sectors and areas of control illustrates the validity of making the distinctions. Canadian residents and Canadian controlled companies account for about three quarters of the directorships in both finance and utilities (including transportation) while U.S. residents and U.S. control account for only 12 per cent in finance (the lowest U.S. participation of any sector) and 22 per cent in utilities, most of which is in pipelines. It is evident that the core of indigenous Canadian capitalism is centered in its traditional forté of finance and utilities, accounting between them for three quarters of all positions which are Canadian controlled and resident. Canadian control and residence account for about half the positions in trade while the U.S. participation increases to almost two fifths and the U.K. about one tenth. Canadian participation in manufacturing drops to 45 per cent, most of this being accounted for by involvement in either pulp and paper or food and beverages; U.S. participation increases to about one third while the largest differences from other sectors occurs in those

TABLE 16

Birth and Control of Dominant
Directorship Positions by Sector, 1972*

Birth & Control	Finance	Utilities	Trade	Manufacturing	Resource	All
Canada	68.0%	65.3%	47.7%	41.2%	22.8%	53.7%
U.S.	16.4	28.8	39.1	34.5	53.5	29.2
U.K.	10.7	4.1	10.9	13.2	8.7	10.0
Other	4.9	1.8	2.3	11.1	15.0	7.1
TOTAL	100%	100%	100%	100%	100%	100%
N	(852)	(170)	(174)	(226)	(333)	(1755)

* Joint ventures have been included by birth of director without control differentiation. Canadian born is defined as born in Canada or to parents temporarily resident outside Canada (e.g., schooling, temporary placement). The assumption is made that those for whom data is not available, are born in Canada and the further assumption is made that foreign residents were born in the country of present residence. See also note to Table 15.

director's resident or controlled outside Canada, the U.S. and U.K. with these accounting for about one tenth of all the positions, similar to the amount accounted for by the U.K. Most significant of all is the fact that over half the positions in the resource sector are controlled by U.S. residents or ownership while less than one quarter of the positions are Canadian resident and controlled. U.K. participation remains at about one tenth but the 'other' areas increase to 15 per cent, the sector of their highest participation. When birth is substituted for residence the amount of Canadian participation drops even further.

As Table 16 illustrates, Canadian born and control still dominate the finance sector although there is a drop of almost 10 per cent from when residence was used as a criteria. The difference is picked up almost evenly by the U.S. and U.K. with each increasing by about four per cent while the 'other' category remains stable. Very similar shifts occur through the table with the general trend of decreased Canadian born and controlled participation and a shift upwards for the U.S. and U.K. The ''other'' category remains fairly stable between the two tables, indicative of the low levels of elite mobility into Canada from areas outside the U.S. and U.K. The only area where any noticeable differences between the two criteria with respect to ''other'', is a slight increase in the trade sector (from no participation based on residence to 2.3 per cent based on birth). This phenomenon will be examined in the following chapter. Otherwise the effect of immigration (the difference between birth and residence) is confined to the North Atlantic triangle.

On the aggregate, the difference between birth and residence as criteria decreases overall Canadian participation from 60 per cent to 53.7 per cent and increases U.S. participation from 26 per cent to 29.2 per cent, as does that of the U.K. from 7.7 per cent to 10 per cent. The best overall indicator of the extent of compradorization which has occurred remains the difference between 27 per cent foreign controlled positions based on residence in 1951 to the 40 per cent by residence and 46 per cent by birth in 1972. While it does indicate a significant increase in the amount of foreign control, a substantial segment still remains under Canadian control and an important indigenous elite still exists, in spite of the erosion of power in industrial and resource sectors.

IV) Corporate Interlocks

Interlocking directorships are of interest because they are concrete expressions of social and economic networks, indicating common commitments and shared relationships. Those members of the corporate elite who sit on more than one dominant board do so because they are recognized by their peers as men of power and import. The practice.

of interlocking directorships serves to further concentrate power even beyond the already highly concentrated corporate structures of the 113 dominant corporations. At the pinnacle of the economic elite are those members who sit on the boards of one of Canada's five dominant banks or eleven dominant insurance companies—or even both, as is frequently the case. Since interlocks with dominant banks and insurance companies are of such import for access to capital, the essence of economic growth, they will be analysed separately before an analysis of other interlocks is presented.

(i) Dominant Bank and Insurance Interlocks

In 1951 Porter found that the nine largest Canadian banks had 55 interlocks with the 10 largest Canadian insurance companies. In 1972 the largest five Canadian banks, when interlocked with the eight independent Canadian controlled dominant insurance companies, produced a total of 51 interlocks. Since insurance companies are prohibited from interlocking with other insurance companies and banks with other banks, each bank and each insurance company can only interface once. In 1951, 90 interfaces (10 banks times nine insurance companies) produced 55 interlocks; in 1972, only 40 interfaces (five banks times eight insurance companies) produced 51 interlocks representing a substantial increase in the "density" of interlocking between dominant Canadian banks and insurance companies. If the number of insurance companies is expanded to include all dominant insurance companies operating in Canada (eight controlled in Canada, two U.S., and one U.K.) then this total of 11 insurance companies has 59 interlocks with the five dominant banks with still only 55 interfaces. To this point, the two subsidiaries of Power Corporation, Great West and Imperial Life, have been excluded. They have a total of six interlocks with dominant banks bringing the total to 65 interlocks between dominant insurance companies and banks. In contrast, the five other "Canadian" banks have only three interlocks with the eight dominant Canadian insurance companies and two more with the two dominant subsidiaries of Power. They do not interlock at all with the three foreign controlled insurance companies.

Not all dominant insurance companies are equally interlocked with the dominant banks. The three foreign controlled insurance companies have only eight interlocks with the five giant banks and four of these are between Standard Life (U.K.) and the Bank of Montreal. Sun Life, the largest insurance company, has a total of 14 interlocks with dominant banks including four with each of the Royal Bank and Canadian Imperial Bank and five with the Bank of Montreal; in other words, 70 per cent of the directors of Sun Life also hold a dominant bank directorship.

The nine chartered banks identified as dominant by Porter in 1951 had 203 directors, including five U.S. residents and one resident of the U.K. In 1972 the five dominant banks had a total of 231 directorships which included seven U.S. residents, 10 U.K. residents and six others. Although there are three times as many foreign resident directors in the dominant banks now as in 1951, they still account for only nine per cent of all directorships in the dominant banks. Porter also found that 197 Canadian residents with bank directorships held 297 directorships in the dominant corporations of the Canadian economy, representing 22.7 per cent of the total positions. In 1972, the 231 elite members with bank directorships held 306 other dominant directorship positions, accounting for 25.1 per cent of all these positions held by Canadian residents. This represents an increase in the scope of members of the economic elite with dominant bank directorships over the past twenty years. In addition, more than one quarter of the bank directorships are held by members of the elite who also hold directorships in one of the 11 dominant insurance companies.

The extensiveness of interlocking between banks and other dominant companies is of importance both from the perspective of the companies many of the directors represent, and the operations of the banks themselves[20]. Charles Rathgeb, president of Comstock International, director of Algoma Steel, IAC Ltd., and a recent appointee to the Royal Bank has said, "For a Canadian, becoming a bank director is the summit of one's business career. The banks are very powerful in the sense that no individual in Canada, in my mind, can do much without the support of the chartered banks." From the banker's point of view, John Coleman, Royal's deputy chairman and director of Calgary Power, Chrysler Canada, TransCanada PipeLines and Chrysler Corp. (Detroit), has said, "Our directors are of considerable help to management. The product of banking is the same, so it's the personal contact that counts. If we hear of some corporate business coming up, if necessary we'll look at the names of the company's directors and try to get at them through our own directors and *their* connections. If we heard a big deal was coming up in the West, we wouldn't hesitate a minute to call up one of our prairie directors to see if he could get us some of the action" (quoted by Newman, 1972b:30, 74). These examples illustrate that bankers and outside directors operate in a corresponsive relationship, mutually supportive and gaining from the contacts and capital of the other. The two routes to the board rooms of the dominant banks, one being the long haul into executive positions through the banks themselves, and the other as an outside director brought in because of power and position gained in other corporate sectors, are complimentary associations: one group has capital to invest and the other desires capital to expand present operations and engage in new undertakings.

A strong explanation of why capital is difficult to secure for new ventures not undertaken by members of the elite is that the banking circles are so much a part of the established dominant corporate world making it almost impossible for outsiders to ''break in.'' The economic elite has both contacts and legitimacy required for access to capital. Access to banks and insurance companies provides the advantage necessary to avail themselves of new investment opportunities. A tight system insures that investments by banks will be fairly stable and secure but at the same time prohibits those outside the small charmed circle from breaking into the elite. For this reason, it is argued that the banks with their extensive contacts in the economic elite provide the focal point for elite continuity and operate as a major exclusion mechanism.

Operating on a very similar basis as the most powerful banks, the key life insurance companies are also extensively interlocked with other dominant corporations. The 10 insurance companies identified by Porter in 1951 included 134 directors who held 178 directorships in other dominant corporations thus accounting for 14 per cent of all top directorships. In 1972, 145 directors of the 11 most powerful insurance companies had a total of 220 directorships in other dominant corporations. These directors account for 17 per cent of all dominant director-ships. Just as in the banks, the density of interlocks between the top insurance companies and other dominant companies has increased over the past twenty years. While the directors of dominant insurance companies accounted for 27 per cent of the directorships in the banks in 1951, this has remained stable with 28 per cent of the bank director-ships in 1972. However, the directors of dominant banks hold 41 per cent of the directorships in dominant insurance companies in 1972, the same proportion as in 1951. The percentage of bank directors holding directorships in key insurance companies is greater than the opposite relationship because of the relatively smaller number of insurance directorships (145) compared to bank directorships (208). Because of the very tight relationship between dominant banks and insurance companies, with a large portion of each sector's boards represented in the board rooms of the other, the tight circle mentioned in the discus-sion of bank interlocks becomes even tighter and encompasses the second major source of capital in Canada, the life insurance companies. The implications of this highly concentrated and exclusive set of people controlling the major sources of capital extend far beyond the financial circle alone. Without the cooperation of this group, capitalists in any sector of the economy would find it extremely difficult to secure adequate sources of financing to fund large-scale undertakings. It is this set of people who control the future expansion and new areas of growth within the private sector of the Canadian economy and the worth of any new venture is a matter for their judgment.

Since both the banks and insurance companies act as funnelling devices, diverting the excess capital of corporations and the savings of people into their own reserves, control over decisions about reallocating these funds gives those in command great power. By mobilizing the capital of others, the financial elite is the central node intermediating between accumulation and investment. It does not use its own capital; on the contrary, its specialty is gathering together the reserves of even the lowest classes through such devices as pension funds, savings accounts, life insurance policies and innumerable other devices to centralize the control of reserve capital. This is the enormous power concentrated at the top of these institutions in the hands of the economic elite.

(ii) Interlocking Directorships Among 113 Dominant Corporations

There are a total of 1,848 interlocked directorship positions within the 113 dominant corporations in Canada. This enormous web of interconnections cuts across the formal structures of each dominant corporation; it is the existence of these multiple exchanges in the arenas of decision making which permit the analysis to move from separate corporate entities to an interacting set of powerful people, the economic elite, who really control and direct the future of these dominant companies and with that the Canadian economy.

A detailed presentation of interlocks is included in Appendix XI entitled ''Interlocking Directorships of Dominant Corporations, By Sector and Control, 1972.'' This table records the relationships between individual dominant corporations and other dominant corporations within the various sectors. Although it presents all the interlocking directorships between dominant corporations, it does not indicate all interlocks between dominant companies. For example, James C. Thackray, an executive vice-president of Bell Canada is also a director of Canada Permanent Mortgage, but the relationship is not recorded because he is not a director of Bell, although from within Bell's executive ranks. This type of case is not very common but does provide a set of links between upper levels of dominant companies in addition to interlocking directorships.

Although the appendix does provide a detailed breakdown of each corporation's interlocks, it is necessary to reconstruct these exchanges in order to analyse relationships between key variables. This will be

FIGURE 1

Density of Interlocks Between Corporate Sectors, 1972*

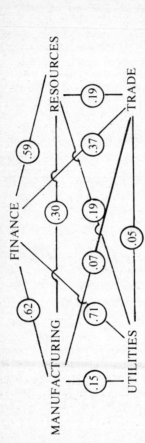

* Density of interlocks is the actual number of interlocks divided by the potential number. This represents a summary of the detailed interlocks reported in Appendix XI, "Interlocking Directorships of Dominant Corporations, By Sector and Control". If the index were 1.0 then all positions in one sector would be filled by persons who simultaneously hold positions in another sector. If .50 then one-half the potential number of interlocks do in fact occur.

done by first examining the relationship between the five economic sectors outlined earlier in this chapter and secondly, by analysing the variable of area of control of dominant corporations in order to determine the extensiveness of relationships between groups of corporations.

One indicator of the degree of interlock between sectors is the size of company boards. Since the number of directorship positions are based on decisions by those in control of the corporation, those who choose to create larger boards do so in order to increase the number of contacts with other corporations. As would be expected, finance has the largest boards with an average size of 19.8 directorship positions, followed by utilities with 14.2, resources with 13.3, manufacturing with 12.6, and trade has the smallest boards with 11.6. When they interlock with other sectors and corporations within their own sector, it is the finance-based corporations who have the highest density and absolute numbers of interlocks. Density of interlocks is defined as the potential number of interlocks divided by the actual number of interlocks. The potential number is the limitation imposed by the total number of directorship positions within a particular sector. For example, there are 122 interlocks between the utilities and finance sector and although there are 852 positions within finance, there are only 170 in utilities, consequently, a limit on the number of interlocks is imposed by the number of positions in the utilities sector. When 170 (the potential number of interlocks as represented by the number of board positions within utilities) is divided by 122 (the actual number of interlocks between finance and utilities) it is found that .71 of the positions are interlocked thus providing an indicator of the density of the interlock, which, as would be expected in this case, is very high because of the known strong relationship between finance and utilities for indigenous capitalists in Canada.

Finance has the strongest relationship with each of the other sectors both in terms of density and actual interlocks. In addition to the .71 relationship with utilities, finance has a .62 relation with manufacturing, .59 with resources but only .37 with trade. In the relationship with every other sector, trade has the lowest density and actual number of interlocks, with only .05 with utilities, .19 with resources and .07 with manufacturing. In addition to those mentioned, utilities have a .15 relation with manufacturing and a .30 relation with resources while manufacturing and resources have a .19 relationship. The evidence is that while every sector is related with every other one, they do not all have the same density of relationships, with the finance sector consistently the most frequent interlocking sector and trade the least. Between these outer limits, the resource and utilities sectors are very similar in the density of their interlocks while the manufacturing sector has somewhat lower overall density.

Within the finance sector, it is the banks and insurance companies, along with the trust and mortgage companies, which have the most extensive interlocks, while the consumer loans companies are much lower. Within the investment companies, four in particular stand out as having high interlocks with banks, insurance, and trust and mortgage companies; these are Brascan, Argus Corporation, Power Corporation and Moore Corporation. As the four Canadian controlled companies within this sector they further reinforce the power of Canadian financiers. Within trade, the wholesale business has the lowest interlocks. This can be attributed to the fact that they are firms which tend not to be part of the national economic elite[21]. Of the five companies in wholesale, there is only one interlock with a dominant bank and two interlocks with dominant insurance companies. Although generally lower than other sectors, retail trade has more extensive interlocks than does wholesale, this being particularly the case with Simpsons-Sears, Hudson's Bay, Simpsons, and Dominion Stores. The U.S. controlled retail stores such as Zellers, Kresge's, Safeway, and Woolworth's have very low interlocks. Interestingly, Eatons has only seven interlocks but four of these are with dominant banks; presumably Eatons can afford to be selective.

In utilities it is the long established Canadian controlled companies which are most strongly interlocked—a clear indication that the U.S. controlled companies are not interlocked as strongly with other companies. It is interesting to note that the few interlocks the U.S. controlled companies do have are concentrated in finance, particularly with the dominant banks.

In the resource sector, the pulp and paper companies, those which are Canadian controlled, have the strongest interlocks. The metal mines also have high interlocks and to a lesser extent, the petroleum industry which is split between three with high interlocks and three with low. This is similar to mineral fuels where two have high interlocks and the others do not.

In the manufacturing sector, it is primary metals which are highly interlocked, as is the case with machinery companies. Transportation equipment and tobacco industries do not interlock extensively with other dominant corporations, although Ford does have more interlocks than the other two U.S. controlled automobile giants. There is a definite split in the food and beverage industry, between the beverage industry[22] which is strongly interlocked and the food industry which is not.

From the above discussion it is evident that sector has a strong part in the relationships between various corporations and the people who control them. But another variable, not unrelated to sector, as was argued earlier in this chapter, is the origin of control of the corporation. Table 17 summarizes the number of interlocks each corporation has with other dominant corporations and separates them on the basis of the country or origin of the controlling interest. Appendix XIII provides a more detailed breakdown.

TABLE 17

Corporate Interlocks Between Dominant Corporations by Area of Control, 1972

Interlocks	Canada	U.S.	U.K.	Other
25 or over	41.4%	5.8%	10%	14.3%
10-24	29.3	22.8	40	57.1
less than 10	29.3	71.4	50	28.6
TOTAL	100%	100%	100%	100%
N*	(58)	(35)	(10)	(7)
Average	23.4	7.0	9.6	16.3

* Total of this table is 110 corporations since the three joint ventures are excluded. For a more detailed breakdown, see Appendix XIII.

It is clear from this table that Canadian controlled companies are the greatest interlockers with other dominant companies. Core corporations with the highest interlocks are at the center of the economic elite, providing historical continuity to the entire elite. An examination of which companies are the largest interlockers verifies this position: the five most interlocked companies with over 50 interlocks are the Canadian Imperial Bank of Commerce (90), the Bank of Montreal (73), the Royal Bank (63), Canadian Pacific Railway (61), and Sun Life (60). These corporations stand above all others as the core institutions of the economic elite.

Not far behind the core institutions already mentioned are the Toronto-Dominion Bank, Bell Canada and Domtar, each with 46 interlocks with the other dominant corporations. The foreign controlled corporation with the largest number of interlocks is International Nickel (34), putting it in the same category as the Bank of Nova Scotia, Canada Life, Brascan, Argus, Huron & Erie Mortgage, Dominion Stores, TransCanada Pipe Line, Consolidated-Bathurst, John Labatt, Steel Company of Canada, and Massey-Ferguson. With between 25 and 29 dominant interlocks are the three foreign controlled companies of Gulf Oil, Hudson's Bay Co., and Canada Cement Lafarge while the Canadian controlled Power Corporation, National Trust, Simpsons, Abitibi Paper and Molsons Industries are also in this range.

At the other end, there are 17 Canadian firms with less than 10 interlocking directorships each, and nine of these are family firms, including six of the eight having less than five interlocks. More than half the U.S. controlled companies fall into this category of less than five interlocks while only 30 per cent of the U.K. companies and none of the companies controlled elsewhere have less than five. Most of the U.S. companies in the less than five category are those which operate as continental companies with branch plant subsidiaries which are tightly controlled by the parent company in the U.S. Those with five or more interlocks tend to be companies with substantial operations in Canada and appear to have more administrative power than the others.

The strong similarity between the Canadian controlled family firms and U.S. subsidiaries, both of which tend to have low interlocks, could be accounted for by the fact that tight control is exercised in both cases with low outside or "public" participation in the shareholdings. The existence of outside shareholders may mean that greater legitimacy is required in order to sell shares whereas in the tightly-held companies, only the family members and inside executives need sit on the board.

When the average number of interlocks by area of control is examined, it is apparent that companies controlled in the United Kingdom (with an average of 9.6 interlocks) and those from outside the North Atlantic triangle (with 16.3) have more autonomy and are more highly integrated with the Canadian economic elite than are the companies controlled in the United States (with 7.0). The Canadian companies, as would be expected have the most extensive interlocking networks (with 23.4). It may be that companies controlled in the United Kingdom and elsewhere have greater Canadian participation because they are not operating in a continental economy as many of the U.S. controlled firms are. Consequently, although they are foreign controlled, they operate within Canada on a more independent basis with the Canadian operations acting more as self-contained units than the vertically and horizontally integrated North American operations of many U.S. corporations.

(iii) Dominant Interlocks with Other Prominent Corporations

It would be mistaken to conclude that the economic elite interlocks only within dominant corporations; rather, it penetrates other spheres of the economy and corporations smaller than dominant. It is important to recognize that the dominant corporations in Canada's economic structure are not isolated from middle range or smaller corporations. Many of these companies provide complementary activities and are integrated into the social network of the elite. Just as many executives from dominant corporations are recruited to sit on the boards of smaller companies, so does the reverse process occur with frequency. This penetration serves to have the economic elite as part of the total economy and not simply sitting atop it. Many members of the elite also sit on the boards of key subsidiaries; just as Canadian boards of foreign controlled corporations serve to provide advice, guidance, contacts and legitimacy to the operations of these companies, so too the boards of important subsidiaries within Canada engage in the same practice. Although ties are obviously strong with the parent or controlling corporation, high degrees of outside recruitment from other elite members is also prevalent. Subsidiaries and middle range corporations are important not only from the perspective of control but also act as a further meeting place for elites and in some cases may even be considered important "breeding grounds" or mobility avenues for entrance into the elite.

In Appendix X, "Selected Prominent Corporations and Institutions and their Interlocks with the Economic Elite, 1972," 175 of the largest middle range and smaller corporations and other prominent institutions are listed with reference to the total board membership, number of elite directors (representing the degree of elite penetration) and executive positions within the corporations held by members of the economic elite. A survey of this list indicates that the degree of penetration is very extensive and proves that the power of the elite is not confined exclusively to dominant corporations. For instance, of the 2,066 uppermost postions within these 175 corporations, members of the economic elite hold 839 posts or 40.6 per cent of the total. If there were some way of incorporating the degree of control exercised over these corporations, the percentage of particular sectors controlled by the elite outlined earlier in this chapter would be greatly increased.

There is also an indication in Appendix X of the continuing importance of those corporations included by Porter in 1948-50 as dominant but excluded as dominant in the current study. The evidence indicates that since they were dominant in the past they are still very much within the cadre of the economic elite today. This is verified by the high numbers of directors from these corporations which are still included in the elite by other board memberships[23]. Although these corporations are currently excluded as dominant, it is very much in evidence that the corporations identified by Porter were and still are part of the operating base of the economic elite.

Another interesting point made from Appendix X is the over-representation of those members of the economic elite who already have more than one directorship among dominant corporations. Of the

839 directorships held by members of the elite in other than dominant corporations as listed in the appendix, 385 (45.9 per cent) are held by members of the economic elite with one dominant directorship, 23 (2.7 per cent) by members of the foreign elite not resident in Canada and 431 (51.4 per cent) by members of the elite with more than one dominant directorship. The multiple dominant directorship group is very much over-represented in these non-dominant corporations and prominent institutions compared to their numerical representation in the elite as a whole which is only 28.9 per cent. This phenomenon will be returned to in the next chapter.

Another important meeting place for members of the economic elite is on the advisory boards of dominant trust companies spread throughout the country. For example, Canada Permanent has 150 individuals on its advisory boards throughout Canada. Of these, 23 are also members of the elite with three members on the St. John's, Newfoundland board, five on the Halifax board, two on the Saskatchewan board, three on the Calgary board, and four on the Vancouver board. Similarly, Royal Trust has 173 individuals on its advisory boards, including 37 members of the elite, three of whom are in Toronto, four in Winnipeg, three in Calgary, three in Edmonton and five in Vancouver. Although these positions are advisory and not in themselves elite positions, it is evident that they do provide a further extension of elite power and interaction.

(iv) Multiple Directorships

The hierarchy within the economic elite in terms of those who hold multiple directorships was alluded to earlier but merits further attention[24]. In 1951 Porter found that 203 members of the economic elite, representing 22 per cent of the total elite, held more than one dominant directorship; together they held 600 or 46 per cent of all dominant directorships (1965:589). This pattern is still evident in 1972, only more so. The proportion of directorships accounted for by people holding multiple dominant directorships has increased from 46 per cent in 1951 to 54 per cent in 1972, indicating an increase in the degree of corporate interaction at the upper levels of power during this period. That an increased portion of the elite engaged in interlocking directorships over the same period is also evident, with an increase from 22 to 29 per cent, Table 18 breaks down these interlocks in detail.

The direction indicated by a comparison of Porter's 1951 table and the present findings is an overall increase in the number of multiple directorship holders. For example, in 1951, 91 directors held three or more directorships, accounting for 28.8 per cent of all dominant directorships, while those in the same category now number 119 and hold

TABLE 18

Distribution of 1,454 Canadian Resident Directorships of 113 Dominant Corporations Among 946 Residents of Canada, 1972*

No. of Directorships held by one Person	Total No. of Persons	Total No. of directorships	No. of Persons	Per Cent	Cumulative No. of directorships	Per Cent
8	1	8	1	.1	8	.1
7	6	42	7	.7	50	3.4
6	6	36	13	1.4	86	5.9
5	20	100	33	3.5	186	12.8
4	28	112	61	6.5	298	20.5
3	58	174	119	12.6	472	32.5
2	155	310	274	29.0	782	53.8
1	672	672	946	100.0	1,454	100.0
TOTAL	946	1,454				

* A total of 287 foreign residents (195 from the U.S., 55 from the U.K., and 37 others) held an additional 301 directorships in dominant corporations. Total boards for all dominant corporations are included.

32.5 per cent of all dominant directorships. The implications of this shift argue for a further concentration of power at the top of the economic elite over the past twenty years and not a decentralization of power and opening up of the elite.

Two major processes have been occurring throughout Canada's economic history and particularly during the past two decades. Between 1951 and 1972, there has been a marked tendency for an increasing centralization and concentration of capital into fewer and larger firms, and secondly, an increasing penetration of the economy by foreign, especially U.S., direct investment. These processes are associated with two social forces, one traditional and the other new. Traditional social forces are represented by the indigenous elite and are concentrated in finance, utilities and to a lesser extent, in specific parts of the manufacturing and resource sectors. The new social force is represented by a comprador elite, the Canadian counterpart of a foreign based parasite elite, concentrated in manufacturing and resource sectors.

Analysis presented previously illustrated that during earlier periods, particularly in the 1880's, the social structure was relatively open and recent immigrants could enter manufacturing. However, as accumulation and concentration took effect, financiers consolidated smaller firms thus closing avenues and limiting access. Since then, it has become increasingly difficult for other than the dominant Anglo upper class to enter the elite. The transformation of the economic structure, particularly since the 1950's with branch plants, has an effect on the elite structure. This new elite has concentrated in sectors traditionally ignored by the indigenous elite. The comprador elite parallels rather than displaces the traditional elite since it remains sector-specific[25]. Since the traditional Canadian elite chose to gather its surplus in the role of mediator rather than producer, it has committed itself, and Canada with it, to an economy wherein U.S. industrial capitalists represent the leading industrial edge. The power of the traditional indigenous elite has not been eroded in the process; quite the contrary, it has further consolidated its position in traditional activities.

Extremely high interlocks between the two major sources of capital, banks and insurance companies, as well as the extensive web between Canadian controlled companies illustrates that as the corporations themselves become more concentrated, so does the interaction between elites. Indeed, the fact that 29 per cent of the elite hold 54 per cent of the positions, indicates that extensive elite interaction has been taking place among indigenous corporations in spite of the new social force represented by U.S. direct investment and the comprador elite. It should not be surprising to find that avenues to the traditional elite have become closed in the process; it will be interesting to find out if the new social forces bring new social types. The next chapter will provide the answer.

Notes

[1] For a summary of what has happened to the 183 dominant corporations in 1948-50, see Appendix IV.

[2] Other evidence exists which illustrates that there has been an increasing rate of concentration within the manufacturing sector. See Concentration in Manufacturing, 1971:5ff.

[3] Further reference to corporations identified by Porter and still operating but not included as dominant in 1972, appears near the end of this chapter.

[4] For a detailed description of the criteria and sources used by Porter to identify dominant corporations in 1948-50, see "The Concentration of Economic Power," Appendix II of *The Vertical Mosaic* (1965:570-580).

[5] For a detailed explanation, see the Introduction to the "Corporate Statistics Tables," Appendix VI.

[6] The uses of assets and income introduces a slight bias by overrepresenting Canadian, as opposed to foreign, control. Using data provided by *Foreign Direct Investment in Canada*, for overall levels of non-resident ownership (defined as over 50 per cent voting stock held outside Canada) indicates that foreign ownership accounted for 39.6 per cent of assets, 43.2 per cent of equity, 35.1 per cent sales, 43.8 per cent profits and 47.7 per cent taxable income. Therefore, use of assets and sales, the two lowest indicators of foreign control, tends to understate the impact of foreign control as compared to equity or profits and taxable income (1972:17). Additional factors related to foreign investment will be discussed elsewhere in this chapter.

[7] One example being franchise relationships such as the ones many retail automobile dealers have with automobile manufacturers.

[8] This will be further examined later in this chapter.

[9] For example, Canadian Pacific Ltd. holds 90.1 per cent of Canadian Investments Ltd. which in turn controls Cominco Ltd. through 53 per cent holding which in turn controls Pacific Coast Terminals Co. Ltd. through a 78.2 per cent holding.

[10] These are discussed in Appendix V.

[11] Fortunately, the CALURA Division of Statistics Canada was kind enough to provide SIC numbers and other information for a large number of corporations.

[12] Canadian controlled charter banks control 99.4 per cent of the assets and 99.5 per cent of the income in this sector.

[13] Power's major holdings are presented in "Notes to Corporate Tables," Appendix VIII, as are those of Argus Corporation.

[14] See table entitled "Sales Finance and Consumer Loans," in Appendix VII.

[15]See corporation tables and footnotes in Appendix VII for a description of the calculation.

[16]It is also suggested by Neufeld that trust companies have enjoyed high degrees of growth in the post-war period (1972:319). This is particularly true in the real estate field. A closer examination of Royal Trust, the largest in its sector, provides an indication of the types of activities and power of all trust companies. Their annual report for 1971 states that they have a total of 76 offices and 3,114 employees, making it a sizable operation. Royal's assets are broken down as follows: mortgages 51 per cent, securities 19 per cent, Canada Bonds nine per cent, secured loans six per cent, and cash or equivalent 15 per cent; this compares with the entire industry which has 75, 14, 6, 1, and 4 per cent, respectively, for each of these categories. This same report also provided a detailed breakdown of the services provided for individuals (among them estate planning, executor and trustee services, investment management, and retirement plans) and for corporations (among them transfer agents, trustee services, real estate agents, property management, and collection services for charitable organizations). The *Financial Post* states that the Royal controls assets greatly beyond those reported because of its administering accounts valued at $9,325 million (August 5, 1972). It is also interesting to note that in 1973 Power Corporation, through its subsidiary Investors Group, acquired 51 per cent of the equity in Montreal Trust making it a subsidiary, thus even further concentrating the corporate world.

[17]See Pipelines table and endnote #3 in Appendix VII.

[18]For a good survey of the resource industry in Canada, its history and foreign control, see Mel Watkins (1973:126), "Resources and Underdevelopment."

[19]For an excellent discussion of Northern Electric and Bell Canada, see *Last Post*, Volume 3, Number 8.

[20]In a recent interview, Allen T. Lambert, president and chairman of the Toronto-Dominion Bank, was asked: "Why do banks need such large boards of directors—and so many interlocking directorships?" His response was: "When one considers the essential need for regional representation and the large number of regular meetings, the board of directors of the Toronto-Dominion Bank is not particularly large. Our board has only some 38 members. These gentlemen are charged with the responsibility of evaluating management's performance and are all senior businessmen who bring with them a great deal of ability to evaluate management and aid in making our decisions." He was then asked: "Why are senior executives seldom promoted to the boards, as they are in many other companies?", to which he responded: "We have at present, three of our senior officials who are members of the board of directors. To fill the board of directors with senior bankers would detract from the board's independence and ability to give management an independent judgment and ability to judge management decisions" (*Globe and Mail*, April 12, 1972).

[21]The national economic elite, as separate from regional or ethnic elites, will be discussed in the following chapter.

[22]With the exception of the Bronfman controlled Distillers-Corporation Seagrams, which will be discussed in the next chapter.

[23]A few examples will illustrate the point: Wabasso's 14-position board has seven members of the economic elite, including the chairman and president;

all seven of these directors have more than one dominant directorship. Union Carbide of Canada has four members of the economic elite on its 11-position board, including the president; Standard Brands has four of 13, including the chairman; Sidbec has three of 12, including the president and general manager; Rio Algoma Mines has five of 15, with six of those not in the elite being foreign residents; RCA has four of 19; Polymer five of 11; Ogilvy Flour five of eight; Robert Morse five of 12; Maple Leaf Mills four of 12; MLW-Worthington three of 11; Hollinger Mines five of 10, including the chairman, president and chief executive officer, vice-president and chairman of the executive committee; Goodyear Tire and Rubber has four of 12, including the president and chief executive officer; Fraser Companies ten of 14, including the chairman and chief executive officer; Dominion Textiles five of 11; Canron seven of 14, including the chairman and chief executive officer plus the vice-chairman; Asbestos Corporation has four of 12, including the vice-chairman and general counsel.

[24]In the following chapter this will provide an important variable in the analysis of class origins and social backgrounds.

[25]However, as was argued earlier, the parasite elite and its Canadian extension, the comprador elite, does prevent the emergence of an indigenous elite in manufacturing and resources. It does displace a portion of the indigenous elite by buying out established dominant corporations but this has largely occurred outside traditional areas of Canadian control. It is from the sectors owned by smaller manufacturers unable to compete in the international market that cries of nationalism can be heard since they are threatened by the onslaught of foreign dominants.

Chapter Five

Inequality of Access (I):
Careers, Class Origins and Avenues to the Economic Elite

BASED on the dominant corporations identified in the previous chapter, the Canadian economic elite over the past twenty years has become a more exclusively upper class preserve. Since 1951, crystallization of the upper levels of power beyond the already rigid power structure identified by Porter has made it evident that several important transformations have occurred in the career patterns and class origins of the economic elite. These will be analysed in this chapter and related to changes in the economic structure already outlined. As may be anticipated, increasing concentration of economic power into fewer and larger corporations, along with the development of a parallel set of foreign controlled corporations, particlarly in manufacturing and resource sectors, have been the two major developments affecting access to the economic elite since the early post-war period. It will be important, therefore, to identify the way in which these developments have been consequential for access to the economic elite and their implications for Canadian society.

The present analysis is based on a study of the directors and senior executives of the 113 dominant corporations operating in Canada and only those members of the elite resident in Canada will be included, although in some specified instances only the Canadian born component of this elite is analysed.[1] Although biographical data could not be found for all members of the elite resident in Canada, the sample accounts for 88 per cent of the elite positions and 82 per cent of the individuals occupying elite positions, a somewhat higher coverage than Porter found in 1951[2].

I. Avenues to the Elite: Career Patterns of the Economic Elite

Most of the means used to gain access into the economic elite can be identified as falling into one of the eight categories, not all of which are related to any "functional" specialization. Three of the distinctions are based on particular skills, including the technical specialties of engineering and science, knowledge of the law and lawyers and finally, administrative skills and commerce. Four further distinctions involve particular connections and/or corporate specializations. These include financiers and financial executives whose task it is to have access to capital, individuals whose main career had been in another elite and thus providing extra-corporate careers, individuals whose main career has been in the finance department of a substantial business thus giving them knowledge of and experience in matters related to investments, and those whose main reason for entering the economic elite is based on the strongest contact of all, kinship, which is to say, a career in a family firm. A final characterization is based on an individual or set of individuals "making it on their own account". This refers to the fact that they have created and developed substantial businesses within one generation which forms the basis for their entrance into the economic elite. Table 19 provides a breakdown of members of the economic elite, as far as was possible, into these categories and compares the current pattern with 1951. Some individuals could fit into more than one category but the one which best characterized their total career was selected.

The final category represents the remainder of individuals, who did not readily fall into any of the other eight divisions. The figure for their category is slightly lower than that reported by Porter for 1951, one reason being the introduction of a new category, "commerce", in the present study. Reasons for this change will be discussed under that classification.

In addition to providing the distribution of career patterns for the current economic elite, Table 20 includes a breakdown of the distribution of directorships held in the dominant banks, insurance companies and all dominant corporations for each career type. The final column gives the number of directorships held on the average by each member of the particular career types. Some career types tend to hold more directorships in dominant corporations than others; for example, commerce, career in family firm, main career in another elite and financiers and financial executives tend to be over-represented in the number of directorships held compared to their proportion in the elite as a whole, while finance department, engineering and science, those who made it on their own account and, to a lesser extent, those with training in law, tend to be under-represented in terms of the number of directorships held compared to their overall proportion in the elite. Each of these will be discussed in detail in the following sections.

(i) Technical Training: Engineers and Scientists

The proportion of the economic elite with specialized skills in the technical fields of science and engineering has declined over the past twenty years, both for the Canadian born and for the entire Canadian resident elite. Together they hold less dominant directorships than their

TABLE 19

Main Career Patterns of the Economic Elite, 1951* and 1972

Main Career Avenues**	Canadian Born			Canadian & Foreign Born		
	1951 %	1972 %	1972 N	1951 %	1972 %	1972 N
Engineering & Science	19.3	12.1	(81)	22.3	13.9	(108)
Financier & Finance Executive	18.0	17.9	(120)	16.7	17.9	(139)
Law	17.7	21.7	(146)	14.2	19.0	(147)
Finance Department	6.0	6.6	(44)	6.7	7.6	(59)
Main Career in other Elite***	2.1	6.5	(43)	1.8	5.8	(45)
Career in Family Firms	16.8	18.8	(126)	14.9	17.2	(133)
Own Account	7.5	2.1	(14)	7.6	2.2	(17)
Commerce	—	4.6	(31)	—	4.4	(34)
Unclassified	12.4	10.1	(68)	15.6	12.0	(93)
TOTAL	100.0	100.0		100.0	100.0	
N	(611)	(673)		(760)	(775)	

* See Porter, 1965:275. Table XXVII.

** As will be noted in the discussion, these categories are not necessarily mutually exclusive. Individuals were allocated by their main career pattern; that is, where they spent the majority of their working lives. If there was no main career pattern which could be determined, they were left unclassified.

*** "Main career in other elite" does not include the media elite for reasons to be specified in Chapter Nine.

TABLE 20

Proportion of Dominant Directorships Held by Career Patterns for Residents of Canada, 1972

Dominant Directorships

Main Career Avenue	Bank %	Insurance %	All %	Career Patterns %	Dominant Directorships Per Person
Engineering & Science	15.5	11.4	12.9	13.9	1.52
Financier & Finance Executive	16.5	32.1	18.5	17.9	1.70
Law	18.5	12.9	18.3	19.0	1.59
Finance Department	3.0	3.6	6.8	7.6	1.48
Main Career in other Elite	5.0	6.4	6.2	5.8	1.76
Career in Family Firms	23.0	21.4	18.7	17.2	1.80
Own Account	1.5	—	2.0	2.2	1.53
Commerce	5.5	5.7	5.1	4.4	1.91
Unclassified	11.5	6.4	11.5	12.0	1.58
TOTAL	100%	100%	100%	100%	1.65 (mean)
N	(200)	(140)	(1,276)	(775)	

proportion of the entire elite would warrant, although they are some-what over-represented in bank directorships. The 15.5 per cent of bank directorships is similar to the proportion held twenty years ago while the proportion of insurance directorships declined from 17 to 11.4 per cent. Overall, they hold fewer directorships than do the financial executives, lawyers, or those whose main career has been in a family firm. The declining proportion of technical people suggests their increasing specialization in lower levels of the corporation which is no longer as suitable for the generalist perspective required of policy makers. While in an earlier era those in science and engineering were provided with a wider education and were involved in a broader range of activities within the corporation, the current moves to specialization in the educational system and within the corporation, tends to "block" them into these roles. As will be seen, lawyers now tend to have taken over the more generalist role once held by the technically trained people thus suggesting a shift from technical to legal expertise as important functions in the elite.

Of the 81 Canadian born technically trained elite, there are 59 engineers, 14 chemists, six with other science training and two whose training has been in technical schools beyond the secondary level. All 27 of the foreign born have attended university with 18 engineers and nine with science degrees; of these, 16 were born in the U.S., nine in the U.K., and two elsewhere. The 25 per cent of this category who are foreign born residents of Canada represents somewhat of a decline from the 30 per cent of twenty years ago, but still accounts for a substantial amount of foreign recruitment in this area. Fewer Canadian born members took their college training in the U.S. than twenty years ago, with a decline from 31 per cent to only 11 per cent currently. McGill has declined as the predominant place where the Canadian born were educated, accounting now for only 15 per cent compared to 36 per cent in 1951. The University of Toronto has remained about even over the period (from 30 per cent to 27 per cent) while the University of Alberta has become more popular with 10 graduates (12 per cent), of whom seven graduated after 1935. The rest are fairly evenly spread among the major Canadian universities with five each at Queens and the University of British Columbia. One indication of the increasing Canadian participation in this area is the fact that 25 per cent of the Canadian born and only 11 per cent of the foreign born were born after 1920. This suggests the Canadian content of the engineers and scientists is becoming increasingly prevalent for the youngest age group.

Only 16 per cent of the Canadian born had the advantage of attending a private school while 26 per cent of the foreign born, all from the U.K., had this advantage. For the most part, the engineers and scientists are of solid middle class origin[3] with just over two thirds of the Canadian born from this class. Technical training requires extensive post-secondary education which, particularly before the Second War, although still the case today[4], was a privilege reserved for the middle and upper classes. One further notable characteristic of this category is that it is almost exclusively Anglo (98.8 per cent) with only one French-Canadian and two "third" ethnics. Clearly the technical field has not provided an avenue of mobility for other than the dominant Anglos. The almost total absence of French-Canadians must be attributed to the lack of institutionalized French language educational avenues in these fields; the low "third" ethnic participation is consistent with their general position in the economic elite[5].

(ii) Financiers and Financial Executives

Although the overall proportion of the elite classified as financiers and finanacial executives has increased somewhat, the Canadian-born component has remained steady. The number of senior executives from chartered banks has increased from 23 to 29, but there are now 30 senior insurance executives, which is three times the 1951 figure. In addition, there are 50 financiers and 30 executives from other financial institutions, such as trust companies.

In 1951 only 45 per cent of the financiers and financial executives attended university; this has increased to 60 per cent of the financiers, 70 per cent of the insurance executives and 57 per cent of the other financial executives. Only a quarter of the bank executives have attended university but this seven represents a substantial increase from the one in 23 who had gone in 1951. Two of the banking executives have attended Harvard at the post-graduate level and another went to the London School of Economics. Ten of the financiers have also had post-graduate training, four of them at Harvard; seven insurance executives have had the same advantage with three of them attending the University of Toronto for their post-graduate training. Executives from the other financial corporations have had extensive training in law, with nine out of 30 having degrees in this field.

Financiers and financial executives do not interlock quite as extensively as they did in 1951 although they still hold a disproportionate number of directorships, particularly in insurance where they have 32 per cent of all dominant directorships. Porter indicates that 39 per cent of the financiers had elite connections in 1951 with this being most prevalent among the youngest group. This is borne out in the present set of financiers, 46 per cent of whom have family connnections in the elite. Bankers also have high (35 per cent) elite connections, while only 17 and 13 per cent, respectively, of the insurance and other finance executives have elite kin. The elite connections of this group is borne out in their high class origins. For example, 58 per cent of the financiers, 43 per cent of the insurance executives and 52 per cent of the bankers are upper class in orign. There is, however, an important difference between them in terms of working class origin. While 10 per cent each of the financier and insurance executives are from working class origins, 34.5 per cent of the bankers have made the long crawl after early careers in small-town banks. As will be demonstrated later, however, the practice of local recruitment and working their way through to organization is now being discontinued and replaced by university trained executives thus cutting out one of the traditional working class avenues into the elite.

Private school attendance is high amoung this group with 23 (46 per cent) of the financiers enjoying this advantage, five of them attending Upper Canada College (three at the same time) while another four went to University of Toronto Schools. There were also nine (31 per cent) bankers with the same advantage (two also attending Upper Canada College at the same time), seven (23 per cent) insurance executives and 11 (37 per cent) other financial executives. Private schools have provided large numbers of the people in this category with common experiences at an early age, as well as presenting the opportunity for extensive contacts to be developed with other upper class peers. These initial contacts have been fostered in later life within the confines of one or more of the exclusive national men's clubs (the Rideau, Mt. Royal, St. James, York, Toronto and National)[6]. Sixty-six per cent of the financiers, 90 per cent of the bank executives, 47 per cent of the life insurance executives and 70 per cent of the other financial executives belong to one or more of these six clubs.

There are a few French-Canadians in the financier and financial executive category, with five financiers, two bank executives, two life insurance executives and three other financial executives of French origin; there is only one Jew and one other of "third" ethnic origin (both financiers). Anglos dominate as financiers (86 per cent), bankers (93 per cent), insurance (93 per cent) and other (90 per cent) executives.

(iii) The Lawyers

There has been a substantial increase in the number and proportion of lawyers in the economic elite with this change coming almost exclusively from those who have law degrees but chose to work their way into the elite via the corporate rather than legal world. While there were 108 lawyers in 1951 (all Canadian born), this increased to 146 Canadian born and one other born outside Canada by 1972. Law as a route to the economic elite remains, with one exception, the preserve of Canadian born members thus reflecting the territorial base of the legal profession.

While only 10 (9 per cent) came through corporate legal departments in 1951, 35 (24 per cent) are now internal recruits. This suggests an increasing number who have chosen law as a general education suited to the corporate world and not primarily as a means of entering private practice, as was the case twenty years ago. Although lawyers still tend to interlock extensively, the increased number of internal lawyers tends to deflate the proportions somewhat. While accounting for more dominant directorships now than twenty years ago (16 to 18.5 per cent), there has been a slight decline in their proportion of bank directorships (19 to 18.5 per cent) although they still have nearly the highest proportion[7] (second only to the proportion accounted for by those in family firms). They now hold fewer insurance directorships than earlier, declining from 19 per cent in 1951 to 13 per cent in 1972.

While only 49 of those from law firms (44 per cent) report political affiliations, there is a considerable difference in their party affiliation. Porter reported that the 61 who declared their affiliation in 1951 were about equally split between the two major parties. In 1972, however, 28 per cent of those associated with law firms report Liberal affiliation and only 16 per cent report Conservative. An additional four of the internal lawyers report Liberal affiliation and there are no Conservatives in this category. This shift seems to reflect the long pattern of dominance by the Liberals in federal Canadian politics.

Porter reports that there were 13 sets of partners among the lawyers associated with law firms in 1951, while in 1972 there were 23 firms with more than one member of the economic elite; together they include 60 partners and 106 dominant directorships. One Montreal firm—Ogilvy, Cope, Porteous, Hansard, Marler, Montgomery and Renault—alone has seven members in the economic elite, all of whom had taken law at McGill University. Another firm from Quebec City, St-Laurent, Monast, Desmeules, Walters and Dubé, has only two members in the economic elite but between them nine directorships. These are André Monast with six dominant directorships, including the CNR, Canadian Imperial Bank of Commerce, Dominion Stores, Canada Cement Lafarge, Confederation Life and Noranda Mines, adding a seventh, IBM Canada, in 1973; Renault St-Laurent, son of the late Prime Minister Louis S. St-Laurent and also a lawyer, is the other partner, with three dominant directorships including again the CNR plus IAC Ltd. and Rothmans of Pall Mall in addition to sitting on the U.S. parent board of Scott Paper. Although these are just a few examples, the fact that 106 dominant directorships are held by members of 23 law firms serves to illustrate that this provides an additional area where dominant directorships become further concentrated.

All the lawyers are trained in Canada with half attending Osgoode Hall and about on fifth going to each of the University of Toronto and McGill; Dalhousie, University of Manitoba, Laval and University of Montreal are also important. Many of the lawyers share common social experiences in their educational careers; for example, four went to the University of Toronto Schools for their private schooling together, each of them going on to the University of Toronto for their LL.B's and then on to Osgoode. This includes one pair of twins, John A. and James M. Tory who followed their lawyer father's footsteps, taking, between them, five of his dominant directorships.

The experience of private schools is not uncommon to lawyers in the elite, with 46 per cent of those in law practice having this advantage compared to only 29 per cent of the internal lawyers. Of those in law firms, four attended the Collége Sainte Marie, as did three of the internal lawyers, seven the University of Toronto Schools, five Upper Canada College, four St. John's-Ravenscourt, four Trinity College and three Lower Canada College. One difference between lawyers associated with firms and the internal lawyers in terms of class is the fact that practicing lawyers are more upper class with 63.4 per cent compared to 54.3 per cent of the internal lawyers who are upper class in origin.

Law is the career pattern with the greatest representation of French-Canadians; it includes 14 associated with firms (12.5 per cent) and seven internal lawyers (20 per cent) with 14.3 per cent of all those trained in law being French-Canadian in origin. Five Jews, all in law firms, have also gained their mobility into the elite through law, of which three, associated with Phillips & Vineberg, account for only four dominant directorships between them. The Jews account for 4.5 per cent of those associated with law firms, but since there are none among the internal lawyers, their overall proportion is only 3.4 per cent. Anglos remain the predominant group, accounting for 82.3 per cent of all the lawyers in the elite.

Consistent with the high upper class origins of the lawyers associated with law firms is the fact that 23 have inherited positions from their fathers. This includes 14 who inherited positions in law firms, 19 who inherited directorships and 10 who inherited both. This does not count the Jeffery family, associated with Jeffery and Jeffery and London Life, who will be discussed under family firms. Altogether, 38 per cent of those in law firms and 23 per cent of the others have some family connection in the elite.

(iv) Mobility Through the Finance Department

Careers in finance departments account for similar proportions in both periods. Of the 44 Canadian born, 33 are chartered accountants, nine have economics or administrative training and two appear to be inside-trained, both of them entering the corporate world after attending private schools. Only four of the 15 foreign born are chartered accountants, the others working their way up as treasurers or comptrollers. About half the entire group has made it to the top after a "long crawl" of at least 15 years before gaining a directorship or executive position. Of the Canadian born members, 45.5 per cent are upper class in origin with about one third attending private schools. Only two members of this category inherited directorships and nine have families in the elite. Forty per cent have memberships in one of the six exclusive national men's clubs.

As in all of the career patterns, Anglos dominate with 89.9 per cent of the entire group while there are only five French-Canadians (8.5 per cent) and one representative from a "third" ethnic group. For the most part, those entering the elite through the finance department have been inside directors and remained there, having low levels of inter-locks compared to other career patterns.

(v) Commerce

Porter did not include commerce as a career pattern into the 1951 economic elite, noting that "Comparatively few persons in the elite have been trained in commerce or business administration" (1957: 381). Many of the "new breed" (actually bred from old "blood") tend to be more oriented toward commerce degrees than twenty years ago. For example, Paul Desmarais graduated from Ottawa University with a degree in commerce, as did his brother Louis from McGill, while their father was a lawyer.

Those whose main careers have involved commerce training and careers number only 31 of the Canadian born members of the elite and 34 when Canadian and foreign born are combined, but together hold somewhat higher proportions of the directorships in dominant corporations, banks and insurance companies. An additional 30 members of the elite also received commerce degrees but their main careers have been classified in other sections.

Many members of the commerce section have had common educational experiences. For example, six members of the elite had their initial commerce training at McGill with four of these later going on the Harvard to obtain MBA's. Of the 11 who attended Harvard, eight graduated between 1947 and 1951. The following example illustrates how common educational experience can lead to common social types. Ian A. Barclay and Gordon S.J. Bowell both received MBA's from Harvard between 1947 and 1949. Both now live in Vancouver, each belonging to both the Vancouver and Shaughnessy Clubs. Mr. Barclay is president and chief executive officer of British Columbia Forest Products while Mr. Bowell is president and chief executor officer of Weldwood of Canada, each gaining their present positions within a year of the other.

Those in commerce tend to be younger than the rest of the elite, most enjoying high class backgrounds with 53 per cent having upper class origins. Half belong to one or more of the six exclusive national men's clubs. One similar characterisitic of this group to the lawyers is the relatively high participation by French-Canadians (high, that is, for the economic elite since they are still well below their third of the population) with 14.7 per cent compared to 85.3 per cent Anglo. Since this is a relatively new avenue it may well be that commerce may provide in future an avenue into the elite for French-Canadians.

(vi) Main Career in Another Elite

More people have been classified as having their main careers in another elite than by Porter for 1951, partially because of a redefinitional of what constitutes having a main career in another elite. Only 14 persons (1.8 per cent) transferred to the economic elite after having their main careers in the political, bureaucratic or military elite in 1951, whereas in 1972, 5.8 per cent of the economic elite entered by way of the other elites[8], including 18 from the bureaucratic elite and 17 from the political elite as defined by Porter (1965) and Olsen (1973)[9]. An additional 10 are classified as academic elite, including university deans, presidents and prominent professors, particularly from business schools. There are no members classified as having their main career in the military.

Even using only the political and bureaucratic elite, the numbers are more than doubled compared to Porter's, representing a greater degree of interlock between the economic and the state elites than had existed twenty years ago. This phenomenon can be referred to as "career overlaps", the individuals being "elite switchers". Among the members of the political elite are eight former federal cabinet ministers, five former provincial premiers, including one from each of Quebec, Alberta, Manitoba and two from Ontario, one former prime minister and three other provicial political elites. Some examples from the bureaucratic elite are Graham Towers, Governor of the Bank of Canada from 1934 to 1954 (director of Canada Life and Moore Corp.); W.J. Bennett, President of Atomic Energy of Canada for 1946 to 1958 (president of Iron Ore Co. of Canada and director of Canadian Pacific); K.R. MacGreggor, Superintendent of Insurance from 1953 to 1964 (president of Numac Oil & Gas, director of Canadian Utilities and Polymer); Dr. A.J.R. Smith, Chairman of the Economic Council of Canada from 1967 to 1971 (director of IBM Canada); and D.B. Mansur, President of Central Mortgage and Housing from 1946 to 1954 (president of Kinross Mortgage, director of Consumers' Gas and Guarantee Trust).

A recent announcement in the *Globe and Mail* provides a case where both the head of a firm and his successor have their main careers outside the corporate world:

> J.V. Clyne yesterday announced his retirement as chief executive officer of MacMillian Bloedel Ltd. but will remain at the request of the directors as unpaid chairman of the company. . . . Mr. Clyne, a justice of the Supreme Court of British Columbia before he joined the company in 1958, has been chairman and chief executive officer since 1960. Later, the board announced the appointment of Robert W. Bonner as president and chief executive officer of the company. Mr. Bonner, 51, had previously been vice-chairman. He is a former Attorney-General of British Columbia who entered government with the Social Credit Party in 1952, serving in various Cabinet posts. In May, 1968, he resigned from the Government to join MacMillan Bloedel as vice-president, administration, and later was appointed a director. He was named vice-chairman in April last year (April 27, 1972).

Overall, those from other elites account for a higher proportion of the dominant directorships than their representation in the elite suggests since they tend to have high interlocks between dominant corporations, each member holding an average of over one and three quarters dominant directorships. Just under half (46.7 per cent) are of upper class origin. Only one Jew (2.2 per cent) and six French-Canadians (13.3 per cent) entered the elite through this route while it provided an avenue for 38 Anglos (84.4 per cent). The question of interchanges between elites and their relationships will be returned to in following chapters.

(vii) Career in Family Firms

The 133 individuals who have been characterized as gaining access to the elite through family firms have spent the majority of their business careers in corporations in which their father, or in five cases maternal grandfather, held a key corporate position. This career pattern does not include all those from upper class origins, nor does it include those who gained their mobility in their father-in-law's firms. Some members classified here have had training in one of the other sectors already outlined but the *main* reason for gaining an elite position is kinship.

There are more individuals classified as having their main career in family firms now, with 133 (17.2 per cent), than in 1951, when there were 113 (14.8 per cent). The current figure includes 126 Canadian born (18.8 per cent) and only seven foreign born (6.8 per cent).

Most of the foreign born having careers in family firms are from the United States but some, like Thomas J. Bata who began in his father's Bata shoe factory in Czechoslovakia, were born elsewhere. In 1929 Bata travelled to England as an assistant general manager in his father's firm, coming to Canada and construcing a shoe factory in 1935, of which he still retains the presidency. However, he is included in the elite because of a directorship in IBM Canada and not because of Bata Shoes. Nathanael V. Davis has been associated with Alcan since 1939, as president from 1947 to 1971 and now chairman and chief executive officer, taking over from his father, Edward Kirk Davis, who had been president since Alcan's organization in 1928. Although Nathanael V. attended both Harvard and London School of Economics, it would be difficult to argue that the reason he followed in his father's footsteps was *primarily* because of this education in commerce; rather the commerce degree allowed him to take advantage of the position open to him because of birth. Davis now holds directorships in Canada Life and Bank of Monteal as well. Certainly his U. S. birthplace has not been an impediment to gaining the top position in the multinational Alcan.

Of the 126 Canadian born members, 66 have some training or position which otherwise may have classified them in previous categories. There are 16 with under-graduate degrees in science, including 11 engineers all of whom have gained their mobility in "non-technical" departments of corporations their fathers were associated with. There are 10 with law degrees, only three of whom are associated with law firms; these three are the Jeffery brothers—associated with both their father's law firm and London Life. The other seven have law degrees but have been associated with family firms most of their lives (for example, Arthur Simard and Allan Bronfman). Commerce degrees are held by 11 with, for instance, Alan Young Eaton attending the University of Toronto, Cambridge and Harvard where he obtained an MBA, G. Drummond Birks obtaining a B. Comm. from McGill, and H. Arnold Steinberg going on to Harvard from McGill for an MBA. There are 26 financiers and financial executives, most of which are investment dealers but also including, for example, John Kenneth Macdonald, chairman of Confederation Life as were his father and grandfather before him, and A. Bruce Matthews, who succeeded his father as President of Excelsior Life. Three had careers in finance departments, with, for instance, Harland de M. Molson joining Clarkson McDonald Currie and Co. as a junior in 1926, becoming a chartered accountant in 1933, a director of Molson's in 1938 and secretary in 1946 and now holding the position of chairman in the family firm in addition to his directorships with the Bank of Montreal, Sun Life and Canadian Industries.

Within this group of 126 Canadian born with their main careeers in family firms there are 24 current father/son combinations and 32 current brothers. The fact that inheritance plays a predominant part in the mobility of this group is reflected by the fact that many in it are much younger than those in other sections discussed, with 55 born after 1920, four of these after 1935, and 55 between 1905 and 1919, while only 16 were born prior to 1905.

Examining the entire group of 133, it is evident that private schooling plays a large part among those who inherit their positions—85 (65 per cent) attend private schools. There are also 108 who attended university (81 per cent), plus one other who went to a technical institute. About one quarter of the group enjoyed the advantage of having an international education. Sixty members of this group (45 per cent) belong to one of the six national men's clubs and 25 belong to clubs outside Canada, indicating that there is high participation in both the national and international upper class circles. While there are only 10 French-Canadians in this group (7.5 per cent), there are two (Bata and Koerner) from Czechoslovakia and 15 Jews (making this at 11.3 per cent, the area of greatest mobility for Jews). There are in contrast, 106 Anglos (79.7 per cent) dominating this avenue, as they do every other.

The power of this group extends further than does any other group in terms of interlocking directorships. While representing 17.2 per cent of the elite, they account for 18.7 per cent of the directorships in all dominant companies, 23 percent of the directorships in the key banks (with 35 per cent of the members of this group holding a bank directorship) and 21.4 per cent of the insurance directorships (with 23 per cent of the group holding an insurance directorship). On the average, each member of the elite classified here has one and four fifths dominant directorships, second only to the much smaller group with commerce degees. Between them, they hold about one fifth of all dominant directorships.

Many Canadian firms have been and remain dominated by particular families, quite contrary to the ideology of managerial revolution theorists, the post-industrial thesis, and those who argue that "power has passed to the technocracy". Long lists of prominent family firms could be provided; for example, C.L. Burton became president of Simpson's in 1929, succeeded by his eldest son Edgar with his youngest son Allan also holding a vice-presidency in the company. The fifth generation of Molson's are still in control of what is now called

Molsons Industries, having expanded their brewing operation. Five Eatons have been president of Eaton's since Timothy Easton first opened a store in Toronto in 1867 and two sons of John David Eaton (John Craig, chairman of Eaton's of Canada, and Fredrik Stefan, president of the same company) still run the company. Similarly, Chuck Woodward's paternal grandfather built his first department store in 1892 in Vancouver and now this has expanded to include 77 retail stores. Woodward has a double advantage; his other grandfather left him one of the largest ranches in North America covering one half a million acres with 10,000 cattle. Chuck Woodward is reported to have said that he resisted taking over the family empire but, "I didn't want to hurt my father, and because I was the last male Woodward left I had a duty [so] I came down to work" (*Macleans*, June 1973:42). To look after the family fortune and carry on the family name is perceived as a "duty", not only for the Woodward's but for many of those who inherit their positions. The family remains important in Canadian life—at least at the top of the class structure.

W. Galen Weston became chief executive officer of Loblaw Cos. at the age of 30, after sitting on the board of George Weston Ltd., Loblaw's parent company founded by his father, since he was 27 years of age. According to reports filed with the Ontario Security Commission, W. Galen Weston holds 66,425 shares in George Weston Ltd. valued at over $1,325,000 at current prices. There are five Bronfman's also associated with Distillers-Corporation Seagrams. The Bronfman's also control Cemp Investments. A recent report provides some insight into how family fortunes are maintained inter-generationally and how they are run:

> Cemp Investments Ltd. provides a partial glimpse into the fortune that has been built from profits in huge, world-wide Distillers Corp-Seagrams Ltd., controlled by the Bronfman family of Montreal. Distillers' sales run to over $1.5 billion a year. Cemp is owned by four trusts established by the late Samuel Bronfman —creator of the world's largest distilling organization—for his four children and his grandchildren. The name is taken from the first name of Bronfman's four children: Charles, Edgar, Minda and Phyllis. Charles runs the Canadian operations of the Distillers Corp-Seagrams; Edgar, based in New York, is president of the big firm; Minda is married to a French baron; and Phyllis is a Chicago architect (*Toronto Star*, April 15, 1972).

Not all of the family firms which have provided members with access to the elite are dominant. For example, Carl A. Pollock is in the elite because he is a director of the Royal Bank, but he is also the chairman of Electrohome Ltd., a firm established in 1907 by the grandfather of John Pollock, who is now president at 36. John Pollock is quoted as saying: "I wouldn't say that because my name is Pollock it hasn't helped me get on. It has. But I think the days of that degree of nepotism are over" (*Globe & Mail,* August 22, 1972). It would appear that either Mr. Pollock is blind to the facts of inheritance or he has been so well socialized into the upper class that he believes everyone enjoys the same advantages he does. (Is not passing on of position the highest form of nepotism?) Other examples of middle range family firms which have provided avenues to the elite would have to include the Birks. G. Drummond Birks, president and chief executive officer of Henry Birks & Sons Ltd. is in the elite because of his directorships on the boards of Standard Life and the Royal Trust. His access to the elite has been through the family-run firm established in Montreal in 1879 with a tradition of centuries of family involvement in the silversmith business in England before that.

All of the examples have not been exhausted; just to mention the Billes' of Canadian Tire, the Burns' of Crown Life, the Loeb's of M. Loeb, the Scott's of Wood Gundy, the Steinberg's of Steinbergs or the Wolfe's of Oshawa Group would all indicate that the extent of family control over the corporate world in Canada is far from insignificant. It is as powerful, even more powerful, than it ever was.

(viii) Own Account

In stark contrast to those who have made it into the elite through family firms are those who manage to establish firms on their own and gain the stature in one generation of becoming members of the economic elite. Porter reports for 1951 that 7.6 per cent of the elite made it on their own account, a total of 58 people. He noted that several of these built smaller regional firms and subsequently have been recruited to the boards of dominant companies. One of the strongest indicators that the structure of power in the Canadian economy has become more rigid over the past twenty years is the fact that only 26 members of the present elite have made it into the elite group on their own account, representing only 2.2 per cent of the entire group. These people only account for 2.0 per cent of the dominant directorships, only three directorships in the banks (1.5 per cent) and no directorships in dominant insurance companies.

All of those who moved into the elite by initiating substantial businesses of their own were born before 1930, with 11 of the 17 born before 1920. Indicative of the fact that not all of the members in this group started at the bottom of the class structure is the fact that eight people between them attended private schools (5) or university (6). Some, however, did start out near the bottom.

More than half the group are members of regional firms who have been recruited into the board rooms of dominant corporations. This includes the only French-Canadian in the group, J.C. Hebert, who established Transpaper Products in Montreal in 1947 and sold the company in 1966 at which time he was sole owner. He is in the elite because he sits on the board of Power Corporation.

The outstanding feature of those who have made it on their own account is the fact that three Jewish families, the Steinberg's, Loeb's, and Wolfe's, each established firms of national scope. All these firms are in the trade sector. Two of the firms, M. Loeb and Oshawa Group, are in large part based on one organization, IGA Canada Ltd. Nonetheless, it is significant that eight Jews have been able to break into the economic elite within one generation. The relationship between Jews and other members of the elite will be examined in the following chapter.

It should be noted that once a firm of national scope has been established, it is only the founding generation which makes it on its own account. It may well be that Max and Maurice Wolfe struck out in 1911 with $64 capital to establish what has become a half-billion dollar empire (see *The Oshawa Group Annual Report 1972*), but their sons and grandsons enjoy an advantage they did not: their fathers established the business. If the firm is then passed on to the second generation, as is the case with the present dominant firms in this category, the structure once more becomes solidified and access for outsiders more difficult. For example, Charles L. Gundy inherited eight directorships from his father, James Henry Gundy, including seven dominant corporations and the chairmanship of Wood Gundy. James Henry may have made it on his own account (his father being a Methodist minister), but the same cannot be said of Charles L. who obviously was born into the upper class. As the corporate structure becomes more concentrated and the class structure more rigid, it becomes increasingly difficult for those outside the inner circles of power to break in and mobility becomes stifled. The dramatic closing off of this avenue of mobility into the economic elite since 1951 illustrates that mobility into the upper levels of power in Canada is becoming much more difficult as the corporate structure becomes more concentrated. It was shown earlier that of the 183 dominant corporations in 1951, 41 have been reduced through merger and acquisition to 17 current companies. Now it has been illustrated that the counter process, that is major corporations emerging within the space of one generation, has also declined over the same period. The net effect of these developments is to further reinforce existing dominant companies and limit the ability of others to emerge.

II. Mobility into the Economic Elite: Class and Economic Power

Class origins of the economic elite are important from a number of perspectives. They show the extent of mobility existing at any given time and, if more than one time-frame is available, relative changes in class access to elite positions. One assumption of a concern with mobility is that talent is distributed throughout all classes in society and if everyone had equal opportunity for access to the elite, the total society would be better served. The perspective of liberal-democratic theory is concerned with the value that everyone in a society should have equal opportunity to realize their potential with the freedom to exercise this potential in the management and direction of a society's future. From the social structural perspective, class access to the elite is an important indicator of the degree of openness present in the flow between different classes or, put differently, the extent of class crystallization there is in a society. The more difficult it is for people outside the upper class to enter the elite and, conversely, the greater the proportion of elite members recruited from the upper class, the greater the concentration of power in a particular society. With greater concentration of power there is less opportunity for those outside the inner circles of power to express their concerns and desires, thus stifling equality of opportunity which forms the basis of liberal-democratic ideology. As has been suggested before, the predecessor to inequality of opportunity is inequality of condition. The more highly concentrated the economic structure, the more difficult it will be to have open recruitment since, in a capitalist economic order, the prerogatives of power provide unequal advantages to the few at the expense of the many. The concentration of the economic structure since 1951 has already been documented; now its implication for mobility will be presented.

(i) Class Origins of the Economic Elite

Class origins of the economic elite in 1972 compared to their origins reported by Porter in 1951 are summarized in Table 21 and appear in detail in Appendix XIV. These data provide conclusive evidence that access to the economic elite has become more exclusively the preserve of the upper class over the past twenty years. Using the same criteria and indicators as Porter, the present study replicates as close as possible both the spirit and methodology used in the earlier study.

Of the 673 Canadian born members of the economic elite, 28.5 per cent had fathers, or in a few cases uncles[10], in the economic elite. This represents an increase of 6.5 per cent from 1951 in the proportions of the elite enjoying the advantage of family origins directly from the inner circles of the corporate world in the previous generation. When it is recalled that less than 700 Canadian qualify as members of the economic elite at any time over the past twenty years, there is a very high degree of elite continuity when 192 members of the current elite replicate their fathers' positions. Adding 16 other members of the elite with fathers in either the political or bureaucratic elite, as previously defined, increases to 30.9 per cent the present elite who had fathers in one of the three dominant Canadian elites. Compared to the 24 per cent found by Porter twenty years ago, this means that almost seven per cent more of the current elite had early direct elite connections and are now themselves members of the economic elite. An additional 39 not already included married into a family where the father was a member of one of three elites discussed above. In other words, 247 members of the current elite embarked on their careers with the initial advantage of elite connections. This still represents about six per cent increase since 1951. Another 68 not thus far included had fathers in substantial businesses, which, as far as could be determined, were not dominant but of sufficient size to provide an initial upper class avenue into the elite. This means that 46.8 per cent of the present economic elite began at or near the top of the class structure[11], thus bringing the difference between the 1951 findings to a full 9.8 per cent more with this initial advantage.

Of the remainder, 85 had attended private schools. This was used by Porter to indicate that the class origins of this class were "upper-middle class"[12]. In the preceding section, it was shown that 65 per cent of the current members of the elite who had their main careers in family firms attended private schools. Evidence to be provided later illustrates both that the cost of sending a child to private school and the environment of such schools, provide upper class backgrounds for the potential elite. The additional 85 who attended private school brings to 400 the number with upper class origins, which represents 59.4 per cent of the elite—still significantly more than the 50 per cent with the same origins twenty years ago.

A further 57 had fathers engaged in middle class occupations such as engineers, doctors, lawyers, ministers and managers. This brings the total to 457, accounting for almost 68 per cent of the elite. There are also 177 not included to this point who attended university. Given that only about eight per cent of the male population in the current elite's age group had even some university training, it is reasonable to assume that using university education as an indicator of middle class is still confining class origins to fairly near the top of the class structure.

Addition of the university trained members brings the proportion to 94.2 per cent while the same indicators accounted for only 82 per cent of the entire economic elite in 1951. It is assumed that the remainder includes those who have made it into the elite with less than middle class origins. In 1951, 18 per cent of the elite were in this bottom category, but only 5.8 per cent of the present elite are in the same position. Every indicator shows that the current elite is of higher class origin than twenty years ago. The class structure of Canadian society has tightened in terms of gaining access into the economic elite, becoming much more impermeable for anyone of less than middle class origins.

Table 21 illustrates that particularly the upper class, but also the middle class, are over-represented compared to the Canadian population. Moreover, this over-representation has increased over the last two decades. While there is no reason to believe there has been any significant changes in the size of the upper class, the proportion with upper class origins in the elite increased by 9.4 per cent during the period. Middle class origins increased by 2.8 per cent while working class origins represent a significant decline of 12.2 per cent. The major difference between the two periods can be found in the 6.5 per cent increase in the proportion with fathers in the economic elite and particularly those with careers in family firms, as discussed earlier.

Comparison of class origin with the population is complicated by the fact that not all of the population is "at risk" in terms of recruitment into the elite. However, by defining the population "at risk" there is a tendency to suggest it is the population who should be eligible for recruitment to the elite rather than the one who in fact is. For example, mobility into the corporate elite is not a "risky business" for women since only six of 946 members of the elite (.6 per cent) are women. Since women in Canada tend to attend university much less than their male counterparts, the effect of including them in the population "at risk" would mean the proportion of the population classed here as middle class would decline. This does not mean to suggest that women should not become members of the economic elite; it simply reflects the fact that for the most part they have not. Similarly, the selection of the occupational structure in Canada for 1941 reflects the census year closest to the mean age at which the current elite entered the labour force and does not mean to imply that younger or older people should not be recruited. As can be seen from this discussion, the problem of assigning a proportion to the population as being middle class is not easily resolved, so the 15 per cent figure should be considered as an approximation based on the assumptions specified[13]. The specification of the proportion of upper class in the population is less problematic since it is so small that the 1-2 per cent estimate probably overstates the

TABLE 21

Class Origins of the Canadian Born Members of the Economic Elite, 1951 and 1972

	Population (approximately)*	Economic Elite		(Per Cent Change 1951 to 1972)
		1951	1972	
Upper Class**	1-2%	50%	59.4%	(+ 9.4)
Middle Class	15	32	34.8	(+ 2.8)
Working Class	85	18	5.8	(−12.2)
N		100% (611)	100% (673)	

* The population "at risk" breakdown is based on a calculation of occupations in 1941, the census year closest to when most members of the current elite entered the labour force. At that time, 12 per cent of the labour force was engaged in middle class occupations including professional, managerial and proprietary. Only eight per cent of the male population of the age group of the current elite had even some university. Given the high known overlap between sons of the middle class and entering university the proportions from middle class origins would approximate 15 per cent of the population. Working class origins are less than middle class thus including manual, service and primary occupations. Upper class includes members of one of the economic, political, or bureaucratic elites, fathers with large but not dominant corporations, and their families. Also see private schools in note below, and note 2 in Appendix XI.

** Includes attendance at one of the Headmasters' Association private schools or classical colleges. See Appendix XI for a detailed breakdown of class categories.

actual case. Working class is used here as a residual. In a more detailed analysis of the class composition[14] there would have to be much more refinement used to denote the components of this class.

Another signficant fact is that these population breakdowns do not conform to the "felt class status" of the Canadian population. Rich Van Loon, for example, found in a 1965 survey of 2,741 Canadians that 10 per cent identified themselves as "upper-class", 40 per cent as "middle-class", 49 per cent as "working-class" and one per cent as "lower-class" (1970:384). According to the criteria of middle class used above, only about 20 per cent of the population in 1965 would be middle class based on the employed population classified as managerial, professional and technical (this having risen from the 12 per cent in the same classification in 1941) (see Kalbach & McVey, 1971:257; Canada Year Book, 1972:831ff). Middle class as used here does not mean the "middle-majority" of the population. Although there is no problem in assigning class of origin when the occupation of the father could be determined, the use of university attendance is admittedly imprecise as an index of origin since it is based on performance rather than birth but as a proxy, it proves to be a sound criteria of middle class origin given its high correlation with class origins found elsewhere (Porter, 1965:183).

It should be remembered that the indicators used here are for class of origin and not the class structure of the current society, so they attempt to replicate the structure for a much earlier period. Therefore, indicators such as private school or university attendance carry even more meaning as class proxies for the earlier periods than they do today. Most of the current members of the elite attended private schools between 1930 and 1935 and university between 1935 and 1940—the period, it will be recalled, of the Great Depression. It is evident that only the most affluent could consider sending their children to fee-paying private schools during that era. The fact that only eight per cent of the male population the same age as the elite attended university, plus the finding that even by 1965 only four per cent of the population over 17 years of age had university degrees and a further 5.4 per cent had some university, suggests that post-secondary education remains a rather exclusive preserve in Canada. At the same time in the United States, for example, 19.2 per cent of a similar age group had at least some university while the corresponding proportion in Canada was only 9.4 per cent (Special Labour Force Study, 1966, Table 15:8).

In spite of problems associated with the class of origin for the population, the origin of the elite for 1951 and 1972 are compared to each other on identical criteria. While it may be correct to argue the 2.8 per cent increase of the elite with middle class origins results from a shift in the class structure, this would not account for changes in the upper class or the working class. The proportion of the population with upper class origins certainly did not increase by 9.4 per cent over the past twenty years. Explanations other than the changing composition of the class structure must be used to account for this shift. After examining in the following sections some of the components which went into creating this shift, an analysis of its causes will be provided.

(ii) Continuity in the Economic Elite Over Twenty Years

Within the present elite there is a core of 76 members who have survived over twenty years; that is, they appear in both the 1951 and 1972 economic elites. Analysis of the class origin of this group found that it differed substantially from both the 1951 and 1972 elite. Exactly one half of this group had fathers who themselves were in the economic elite in an earlier period. This includes 38 individuals of whom 35 directly inherited directorships from their fathers. Inheritance is substantially more prevalent in those lasting over twenty years than in either of the overall elites in 1951 or 1972. A further indication of their upper class origins is the fact that over half (54 per cent) had attended private schools. In Table 22, the high upper class origin of this group is borne out.

TABLE 22

Class Origins of Members of the Economic Elite Lasting Over Twenty Years

Class	Core Group	Elite 1951	Elite 1972
Upper Class	68.5%	50%	59.4%
Middle Class	28.9	32	34.8
Working Class	2.6	18	5.8
TOTAL	100%	100%	100%
N	(76)	(611)	(673)

Although almost 10 per cent higher in upper class origin than the 1972 elite, the core group lasting over twenty years is almost 20 per cent higher than the 1951 elite in this respect. Moreover, only about half as many compared to the 1972 elite and one seventh as many compared to the 1951 elite are of working class origin. This suggests not only that upper class members of the elite move to the top of the corporate world at an earlier age, but they also last longer, thus providing greater historical continuity than even their high proportions in the elite as a whole would imply. It also adds weight to the argument that private property in the form of inheritance is a major legal device members of the upper class have for staying in powerful positions, and that they use this to pass privileges on to their offspring.

A further characteristic of this core group worth noting is that there are only three French-Canadians (less than four per cent) and two members from "third" ethnic groups (2.6 per cent) while the remaining 93.4 per cent are Anglos. This illustrates that French-Canadians and members of "third" ethnic groups do not have the same degree of historical continuity within the economic elite as do Anglos. This could be due to the fact that French-Canadians enter the elite at a later age but, as will be illustrated, this is not the case. A more probable explanation is that they do not control the same amount of capital in terms of ownership of major corporations and consequently are not able to pass advantages inter-generationally to the same extent as Anglos. This parallels the finding earlier that the French tend to concentrate in law rather than in other career patterns, such as careers in family firms which require transmission of capital. The issue of ethnic participation will be returned to in the next chapter but for now it is important to note that the upper class enters the elite at an earlier age and lasts longer than do either the middle or more especially, the working classes.

(iii) Mobility and the Banks

Traditionally the long crawl through the banks was one institutional avenue for those starting at or near the bottom of the class structure to enter the economic elite. Many bank executives used to begin at a very young age as clerks in local banks and work their way up over an average of 40 years into the executive ranks. To some extent this avenue of mobility remains, but over the past twenty years it has become restricted with more current executives coming from upper class families, having gone to private schools and university and entered the executive ranks at a much earlier age than was previously the case. For example, nine of the 29 bank executives (31 per cent) from the 1972 corporate elite attended private schools and ten (35 per cent) have family connections in the elite. Three of the executives have gone on to post-graduate training, two at Harvard and one at the London School of Economics, with seven having undergraduate degrees. Class origins of the banker represents quite a different pattern from the overall economic elite and is reflective of changes occuring within the recruitment pattern. While not quite as high in upper class origin as the overall 1972 elite with 52 per cent compared to 59.4 per cent, the current bankers are more upper class than the 50 per cent of the overall 1951 elite. This differs from the traditional image of the bankers long crawl. However, this image is not without foundation since 34.5 per cent of the bankers are of working class origin, substantially higher than the 5.8 per cent of the overall elite. Why do the bankers have both high upper class and, relatively at least, high working class origins? The answer is to be found at least in part in the changing recruitment pattern. The upper class bankers tend to be younger and recruited from university immediately into the executive ranks. Older bankers, remnants of the time when executives were recruited internally, tend to be much more working class in origin. The transformation takes some time to work itself through but the direction of change is obvious.

The "new breed" of bankers take less time to get to the top, at least in part, because of their class advantage. While the average to get to the top was 40 years from the time of entering the bank, this long wait has now been substantially shortened. For example, W. Earl McLaughlin had upper class advantages and it took him only 24 years to become president of the Royal Bank at the age of 45. Another excellent illustration is the case of Harold Wilfred and Richard Murray Thomson, a father and son who have both become bank executives. Harold W. entered the Imperial Bank in 1921 working his way up to becoming a director and vice-president in 1962 after the amalgamation with the Commerce, and vice-chairman in 1963, before retiring in 1971. His son, Richard M., went to the University of Toronto, graduating in 1955 and going on to Harvard to get an MBA in 1957 and to Queens in 1958 to take a banking course, after having joined the Toronto-Dominion Bank in 1957. While it took his father 29 years to become assistant general manager, the son attained the position after only eight years and became chief general manager in his eleventh year with the presidency following 15 years after entering the bank at the age of 40. It had taken his father 42 years just to become vice-chairman.

The tightening up of the upper levels of the banks is part of the general trend in this direction. With more upper class recruitment into the elite and with this one avenue closing off to the lower classes, it indicates that the future will involve even greater monopolization of positions of power by the upper class. In terms of the framework outlined earlier, the development in the banks whereby the upper class is increasingly capturing the executive positions represents an extension of the traditional, dominant social force thus "cutting off" a route previously used by members of the working class for mobility. The earlier structure has become crystallized and opportunity restricted. It should also be noted that the effect of bankers entering the executive ranks younger and staying longer, cuts off the "circulation" of people able to move into these positions.

(iv) New Sectors and Old Elites

It is of interest, from the perspective of social change, to determine what effect expanding the scope of activities covered by dominant corporations has on the composition of the elite. As discussed earlier, three new sectors have been introduced to the analysis since 1951; the trust companies, the mortgage companies and the sales finance and consumer loans corporations. By examining the class origins of elite members from these "new" financial fields it is possible to determine if their presence has had an effect on class access to the elite. Those individuals with directorships *only* in one of these three sectors and holding no other dominant directorships will be examined. It was expected that class origins would tend to shift lower since virtually all those with multiple directorships are excluded by definition, because if an individual has a directorship in one of the other dominant corporations they would have been included within one of the sectors used by Porter. Since those with multiple directorships are on the whole from higher class origins[15] this removes many members of the upper class from the subset under consideration.

In spite of these qualifications, the class distribution remains high, in fact much higher than Porter found for the entire economic elite in 1951 and even slightly higher than the overall 1972 elite. Of the 138 Canadian born members of this subset, 33 per cent have the advantage of elite connections before embarking on their careers compared to 37 per cent for all of the current elite. While 50 per cent of the 1951 elite and 59.4 per cent of the 1972 elite are upper class, 60.2 per cent of this subset from "new" financial sectors have this advantage. At the other end of the class structure only eight per cent of the "new" group started with working class origins while 5.8 per cent of the entire 1972 group were in the same situation and 18 per cent of the 1951 elite. The evidence reveals that no inroads have been made into the elite because of the increasing importance of these "new" sectors; quite the contrary, since nearly one quarter of these "new" positions are filled by sons of previous elites. This suggests that expansion of the scope of the economic elite does not mean that new social types are necessarily recruited to fill the positions, but rather the evidence illustrates that they tend to be filled by the same old elite. Another potential resource of lower class mobility is cut off and control by the upper class becomes more pervasive. While these sectors can be considered "new" social forces in the sense of coming into prominence over the past twenty years, the positions created have been overwhelmingly filled by the upper class. Their rapid entry into this area can be attributed to the fact that the finance sector is their "turf" and the activities of these are amenable to their commercial assumptions. Absorbing these sectors

TABLE 23

Career Avenues of Canadian Born Members of the Elite by Corporate Sectors and Area of Control, 1972

Control	Finance	Utilities	Trade	Manufacturing	Resource	All
Canadian	94.6%	92.1%	88.0%	58.3%	38.3%	75.1%
U.S.	3.6	7.9	6.0	27.1	53.1	18.7
U.K.	1.2	—	6.0	6.3	3.7	3.2
Other	0.6	—	—	8.3	4.9	3.0
TOTAL	100%	100%	100%	100%	100%	100%
Distribution	38.8%	8.8%	11.8%	22.2%	18.7%	100%
N	(168)	(38)	(50)	(96)	(81)	(433)

has added strength to their traditional finance forté and limited "outside" entrants.

(v) Career Avenues, Class and Corporate Sectors

Of the 673 Canadian born members of the economic elite, 63 per cent or 433 can be classified as having primarily used one corporate sector as an avenue into the elite. Of the remaining 37 per cent, 127 used law as their main avenue and 35 came from other elites. A further 78 could not be classified as having entered the elite primarily through one of the five sectors. These include some from construction, engineering firms, accounting firms, the media, architects, real estate, advertising and other activities plus some who switched between sectors.

In Table 23, sectors were divided into the major divisions used in the last chapter and separated by control in order to determine what main corporate avenues have been used by the Canadian born elite to gain their present positions. Of the 433 who could be classified, nine per cent came through utilities, 39 per cent through finance, 19 per cent through resource, 22 per cent through manufacturing and 12 per cent through trade. When separated by control, this same group included three quarters who came through Canadian controlled firms, about a fifth through U.S. controlled companies and three per cent each through U.K. and "other" controlled.

The findings indicate that Canadian controlled finance corporations are by far the greatest corporate avenues into the elite, with 37 per cent of all those classified using this route. Within the transportation and utilities sector, 92 per cent used Canadian controlled firms while the remaining avenues were U.S. controlled. This increases to 95 per cent through Canadian controlled finance companies. Canadian controlled companies in trade were also the main avenue with 88 per cent. In manufacturing the situation begins to change with only 58 per cent using Canadian controlled companies and 57 per cent of these are in food, beverage and related products. U.S. controlled manufacturing accounted for 27 per cent while U.K. and "other" control included six and eight per cent, respectively. In the resource sector U.S. companies provided the greatest career avenue accounting for 53 per cent while U.K. and "other" companies accounted for four and five per cent, respectively. The resource sector accounts for over half of all those who have their main career in U.S. controlled companies. Canadian controlled resource firms accounted for only 38 per cent of the avenues in this sector with 68 per cent of these in pulp and paper.

Aside from U.S. resource companies which provided an avenue for 10 per cent of the Canadian born elite classified and, to a lesser extent, U.S. manufacturing companies which provided an avenue for

TABLE 24
Class Origins of Canadian Born Members of the Elite by Corporate Sector, 1972

Class	Finance	Utilities	Trade	Manufacturing	Resource	All
Upper Class	65.9%	60.2%	64.8%	61.5%	59.0%	59.4%
Middle Class	27.9	32.4	29.7	32.5	35.4	34.8
Working Class	6.2	7.4	5.5	6.0	5.2	5.8
TOTAL	100%	100%	100%	100%	100%	100%
N*	(454)	(108)	(91)	(117)	(154)	(673)

* The total cases across sectors totals 924 and not 673 since each case is allowed to fall into the sector where they have a position; that is, the categories in this table are not mutually exclusive because a multiple directorship holder may appear in more than one sector.

about five per cent of the total, foreign firms have not been major avenues to the elite for Canadians. Canadian controlled companies, particularly in finance, utilities and trade have been much more common routes. The degree of foreign dependency must be questioned when only a quarter of the elite used foreign controlled firms as a means of passage into the elite. The evidence suggests that there remain independent, Canadian controlled avenues of access open to at least upper class Canadians. To argue that all the Canadian elite is in a dependency relationship with foreign capitalists would be mistaken. There is still a core of Canadian elites very much in control of access into their select ranks.

It is of interest to see if any particular sector of the economy is more open to mobility than any of the others. Table 24 presents the class origins of the economic elite by sector for Canadian-born members. This represents the class origin of the elite if only any one of the five sectors had been chosen to examine elite mobility rather than the total set of sectors. The distribution of the total elite is presented in the final column as all corporate sectors. It will be noticed that all sectors except resources have higher upper class origins than the overall elite. This is because each position which fell into any of the sectors was included thus weighting the overall pattern toward mutiple directorship holders who, as will be illustrated shortly, tend to be more upper class thus weighting the individual sectors toward higher upper class origins. Weighting was only allowed to occur between sectors and not within sectors; in other words, someone with both bank and insurance directorships was only counted once in finance but someone with both bank and oil directorships is counted in both finance and resource.

The most striking feature of the table is the similarity of each of the sectors; in other words, someone with both bank and insurance in finance to a low of 59 per cent in resource, a difference of some seven per cent. For the middle class the range difference is only 6.5 per cent and for the working class only 2.2 per cent. This suggests there are really no sectors particularly open to other than the upper class although the resource sector, as the newest area of economic activity, is relatively more open to those outside the upper class than are any of the others. As would be expected, the finance sector has the highest upper class representation since it is the oldest, traditional forté of the upper class. Since there is such a high relationship between the resource sector and foreign control, the lower proportion of upper class in this sector suggests there may be more mobility occurring in foreign controlled companies than in others. The following section on comprador elites will, indeed, demonstrate this to be the case.

(vi) Comprador Elites and Mobility

In Chapter Four, it was shown that only 53.7 per cent of the positions in dominant corporations are controlled by persons born in Canada while 29.2 per cent are U.S. born or controlled, 10 per cent U.K. and 7.1 per cent other. It was emphasized that this referred to positions and not to people. In other words, these proportions are reflective of the extent of structural compradorization since a member of the indigenous elite may, and often does, sit on the board of branch plants. For example, Neil J. McKinnon sits on the boards of Ford Motor Co. of Canada and Falconbridge Nickel Mines, both of which are U.S. controlled. Does this mean that he is a comprador elite because he holds comprador positions? Not in this case, because his main corporate affiliation is as chairman of the Canadian Imperial Bank of Commerce as well as being a director of Canada Life Assurance Co., Brascan, Trans Canada PipeLines and MacMillan Bloedel. Because of the practice of indigenous elites often holding comprador positions simultaneously with indigenous positions, there will be a difference between structural compradorization and individual compradorization.

The concept comprador elite is operationalized as those members of the elite who identify their main corporate affiliation[16] as a Canadian subsidiary of a foreign controlled parent, or in a few cases where the "principal occupation" was other than corporate, as in the case of a law firm, the designation was based on which country of control the individual held the majority of his dominant directorships.

When all the Canadian born members of the economic elite are analysed, it is found that 76 per cent are indigenous Canadian elites, 15.8 per cent U.S. controlled comprador, 5.6 per cent U.K. and 2.6 per cent "other" comprador. Once again, there is strong evidence that the indigenous economic elite is strong and not totally dependent on foreign capitalists. While only 53.7 per cent of the positions based on birth and control are Canadian, 76 per cent of the Canadian born elites are indigenous and have an autonomous Canadian base of power. Since it is important to establish some direction to the process of individual compradorization, the age of the two elites will be used to establish this direction.

When the various elites are divided by age as in the Table 25, an interesting pattern emerges. The oldest group has the highest indigenous elite but the middle group is the highest comprador, a drop of over 10 per cent from the older group; the youngest group begins to reverse the age relationship. The increasing compradorization of the economic elite is represented by the shift from the oldest to the middle group but this general trend is counteracted by the youngest group which has the highest degree of inheritance and consequently enters the elite earlier.

TABLE 25

Age Distribution of the Canadian Born
Indigenous and Comprador Elites, 1972

Year of Birth & Age

Elite	Before 1905 (over 65)	1905-1920 (50-65)	After 1920 (under 50)	All
Indigenous	84.9%	73.2%	76.0%	76.7%
Comprador				
— U.S.	12.6	17.0	15.8	15.5
— U.K.	1.7	5.6	5.6	4.9
— Other	.8	4.2	2.6	3.0
TOTAL	100%	100%	100%	100%
N	(119)	(358)	(196)	(673)

In spite of the high degree of inheritance within the youngest age group, there are still 8.9 per cent more comprador elites in this group than in the oldest while the 11.7 per cent difference between the middle and oldest remains the greatest gap. Although the overall trend in the past twenty years has been toward increasing compradorization of the Canadian economic elite, there still remains a strong and vigorous core—as evident in the existence of the youngest group—of indigenous capitalists.

As Table 26 demonstrates, there is a very interesting and important difference between comprador and indigenous elites with respect to class origin. While only 17 (or 10.6 per cent) of the comprador elite had fathers who were in the economic elite for an earlier period[17], 175 (or 34.2 per cent) of the indigenous elite have the same advantage. Approximately 20 per cent more of the indigenous elite are upper class and about 20 per cent more of the comprador elite are middle class. In other words, just over half the comprador elite are middle class in origin compared to only 30 per cent of the indigenous elite. Comprador elites are both more middle class and more "meritocratic" than indigenous elite members. At the lowest level there are actually more indigenous Canadians than comprador, accounted for predominantly by Canadian institutions like banks which have tended in the past to recruit some of their executives from the working class.

Compradorization has permitted some members of the middle class, but not the working class, participation in the arenas of power; this is unlike the indigenous elite which has higher class origins and tends to exclude even the middle class. The process of compradoriza-

TABLE 26

**Class Origins of the Canadian Born Members
of the Comprador and Indigenous Elites, 1972**

	Comprador Elite	Indigenous Elite	% Difference of Comprador & Indigenous Elites
Upper Class	45.3%	63.9%	18.6%
Middle Class	50.4	29.9	-20.5
Working Class	4.3	6.2	1.9
	100%	100%	
N	(161)	(512)	

tion is primarily a phenomenon of the middle class and does not have the same extent of participation from the upper class as the indigenous elite. Although the comprador elite has power within the Canadian context, or at least represents the power others exercise in Canada, within the continental or North Atlantic triangle framework this so-called elite is without power. The middle class members of the comprador elite only have the power of an agent since they are subject to the dictates of the parasite elite. Just as the operators of the fur trading posts may have been powerful vis à vis the native people, they were not powerful vis à vis the governor of the Hudson's Bay Company. The "power" of the middle class in the board rooms of branch plants may in fact be a sham, masking this class's participation in the economic field. The numerous lawyers and technicians who make up the majority of the comprador elite are in fact without power when viewed in a larger framework which includes the North Atlantic triangle.

Two important processes concerning compradorization are occurring. First, structural compradorization is occurring much more rapidly than is individual compradorization. While 46 per cent of the dominant positions based on foreign control and birth are comprador, only 24 per cent of the Canadian born elite are comprador. In other words, comprador positions are filled by both comprador elites and indigenous elites. While it was demonstrated in Chapter Four that foreign controlled firms are not interlocked as tightly as Canadian controlled ones, they were nonetheless substantially related through interlocks. Moreover, it was demonstrated in Table 23 that Canadian controlled companies provided three quarters of all the corporate career avenues into the elite. While it would not be correct to say the upper class has "captured" all the comprador positions, there is clearly a tendency to ally themselves with foreign capitalists by sitting on the boards of branch plants. The second tendency is the more open mobility to comprador positions than indigenous positions. As has been demonstrated, the comprador elite is much more likely to be middle class than is the indigenous elite. Two developments have been simultaneously occurring with compradorization. On the one hand, many of the indigenous elite have taken on comprador positions in addition to their Canadian controlled ones; on the other hand, "new recruits" to comprador postions, particularly to executive posts, has opened an avenue for the middle class. The emergence of a new comprador structure has meant that some new social types have been allowed to emerge while at the same time the traditional indigenous elite has entered into an alliance with this new social force.

While there are new social forces in operation which tend to bring with them new social types, as can be detected when the comprador elite is separated from the indigenous elite, the old traditional established social force is also moving into these new positions thus nullifying in large part the gains which would have been made in terms of mobility if the two structures (the traditional indigenous one and the new comprador one) had been kept separate. The effect of an alliance between them is to limit the new mobility possibilities opened by the new social force. Before moving to the last section of this chapter on size and concentration within the economic elite, the relationship between kinship and class will be discussed.

(vii) Elite Family Connection

Inheritance is a subset of social class in that it entails a direct relationship consisting of an inter-generational transfer of property or position. Class involves a more general notion of "inheritance" in that its reference is the social structure and the position of a family within that social structure. A person's class origins are determined by the ascribed characteristics from the family of birth. A person's class position after "leaving" the family of birth is, in a qualified way, achieved. Achieved in the sense that the person is equipped with certain attributes which must then be applied. The qualification is that within Canadian society, and in other liberal-democratic societies, ascribed class position by birth determines in large part the attributes with which a person is "equipped", thus determining to a great extent the ability to achieve.

What may be called the accumulation of privilege is the differential ability of those from the upper class to provide their offspring with advantages unknown or unavailable to the lower classes. No one would argue the elite is not well "equipped" in terms of education, experience, capital or contacts; quite the contrary, they are very well endowed in these respects and that is why they become elites. The argument is that their initial advantages to obtain these attributes, some achieved and some ascribed, places them in a privileged position relative to others not so endowed. The elite is not a leisure class in the sense that they are mere *rentiers* sitting back and simply reaping returns on investments. They are also the active makers of decisions, thoroughly involved in the operation of the economy. They are using the endowments or "equipment" imparted and entrusted to them by their parents.

The problem is that everyone is not equally well endowed with these privileges at birth, nor are they imparted with the same advantages. It is differential access to advantages based on a hierarchically structured society which serves to perpetuate inequality. The idea that Canada is a free society with everyone equally competing on some great marketplace for the positions and prerogatives of power is a good ideology for the elite and the privileged but it is *not* good sociology.

Up to this point, class has been used to focus on the general social structure. In this section, the phenomenon of inheritance is examined. Inheritance refers to the inter-generational transfer of property or position directly from a person's father, mother, maternal or paternal grandfather, uncle or father-in-law. Although it may be correct to consider intra-generational transfers between siblings as a form of inheritance, they are excluded in this discussion because they are not inter-generational. It has been found that more than one quarter of the Canadian born members of the elite have directly inherited positions from kin in the corporate or legal world. Many have inherited from more than one kin, consequently, the following totals add to more than the 184 individuals who have inherited important positions. The greatest amount of inheritance comes from fathers with 164 individuals directly inheriting directorships from their fathers with more than one directorship per inheritance frequent. Since inheritance often goes back three generations or more, there are eight people who inherited directorships from their maternal grandfathers and 27 who inherited directorships from their paternal grandfathers. A further 14 inherited directorships from their fathers-in-law. There are also 17 members of the elite who inherited law firms from their fathers, typically inheriting directorships at the same time. Being born into families which are able to provide these types of advantages is the experience of very few Canadians.

A further aspect of family connections which serves to tie the elite together not only historically, as does inheritance and generally class, but on a day to day basis, is current family connections within the elite. Although the elite includes only a very small number of people, there are numerous kinship ties, possibly as many as would be found in the adult population of a small town of comparable size. Current kinship ties provide channels of communication between various sectors and corporations within which the elite operates. They can also provide avenues of access and means of legitimacy between elite members because kinship links provide familiarity and with familiarity confidence in the actions of others. There are 40 members of the current elite who are part of a father-and-son combination. There are also 50 members of the elite who currently have brothers in the elite. Another nine members currently have fathers-in-law in the elite with two separate cases of two elite members each having the same elite fathers-in-law. There are also 31 members who have an uncle, cousin, son-in-law or brother-in-law in the current elite. It appears that kinship plays more than a passing role in integrating the economic elite.

Both by providing historical continuity to the elite and a strong current network. kinship ties the economic elite together. It is at the core of the social basis of the upper class, providing an interacting set of people with cohesion, continuity and consciousness of kind. Inter-generational transfer of private property provides guaranteed access to the elite for the privileged few fortunate enough to be born into it.

This section has provided an analysis of the class origin of the economic elite from a variety of perspectives by making distinctions based on length of time in the elite, the mobility afforded by various economic sectors within the elite and differences between comprador and indigenous elites. It has demonstrated that the elite itself is not homogeneous and even within it, there are some important distinctions to be drawn. In the following section there will be an elaboration of these distinctions and an attempt to make some refinements based on the types of activities elite members undertake as well as address the question of heirarchy within the elite and its size.

III. Elite Size and Concentration

The economic elite itself is not an undifferentiated set of people. Comprador and indigenous elites have already been discussed as one major division within the elite. In this final part of the chapter, several other ways of sub-dividing the economic elite will be analysed —including corporate positions, hierarchical distinctions within the elite and the elite as a changing dynamic set of people who have been captured at only one point in time in this study and at an earlier point by Porter.

(i) Executives, Insiders and Outsiders: Corporate Positions

Executives are defined as members of the economic elite holding one of the following posts within a dominant company: chairman, president, chief executive officer or vice-chairman; inside directors are either vice-presidents or hold a senior management position within a dominant corporation. Outside directors hold one or more directorships in dominant corporations and are not simultaneously executives or insiders in another dominant company, although they may be in a middle range or smaller company[18]. A person may simultaneously be an executive or insider in one company and an outsider in another but for present purposes an individual classed as an insider or executive will not be included in the analysis of outsiders, thus making each category mutually exclusive.

Within the economic elite a fairly substantial difference exists between Canadian and foreign born members in terms of the corporate positions they hold. For the Canadian born members, 21 per cent are executives, 22 per cent insiders and 57 per cent outside directors. In contrast, among the foreign born, 28 per cent are executives, 22 per cent insiders and 50 per cent outside directors. In other words, there is a seven per cent difference between Canadian and foreign born with respect to being executives or outsiders. The difference is accounted for by the fact that a good number of multinational companies operating in Canada still prefer to send their chief executives from the home base. Consistent with their roles within corporations, there is a large difference in the extent that various positions interlock with other corporations. For example, only 18.9 per cent of the insiders hold directorships in other dominant companies, 30.3 per cent of the outside directors do the same but 60.6 per cent of the executives hold more than one dominant directorship. This verifies the earlier argument that a member of the executive of one company is frequently an outside director in another.

Of the Canadian born members of the economic elite, the inside directors tend to be youngest and the outside directors oldest, with executives in between. Of those born before 1905, there are 10 per cent of the executives, eight per cent of the insiders and 24 per cent of the outsiders and of those born after 1920, there are 30 per cent of the executives, 43 per cent of the insiders and 23 per cent of the outside directors. This indicates that the insiders are usually much younger, particularly when it is known that most of the eight per cent of the insiders born before 1905 are either "parachuted" into vice-presidency's after careers elsewhere or have spent their entire career with the firm and are now rewarded with the position, essentially at the end of their career. Somewhat correlated with the age factor, but mainly related to the character of their career, is the fact that only 19 per cent of the inside directors have more than one directorship in dominant corporations. As their name suggests, inside directors are oriented toward the internal workings of the corporation, albeit, from a policy level. The fact that only about one fifth of the elite are inside directors attests to the fact that the elite is not made up primarily of bureaucrats but of policy makers sitting atop the bureaucratic apparatus. As Porter has said: "While it is correct to describe the modern corporation as a vast bureaucracy in the classic sense in which Max Weber used the term, its highest government is not in the hands of men best described as bureaucratic" (1965:281).

Few members of the elite could be said to have been selected meritocratically in the sense that they have worked their way up through the corporate bureaucracy without the advantage of high class origins. Even all of the inside directors are not meritocratic. They are rather composed of two types: sons learning the family business and those engaged in a long or relatively long crawl to the board room. Based on an analysis of the difference between the class origins of insiders and executives, it can be said that even at the upper levels of power those with class advantage are more likely to make the break from the insider to executive level.

It is evident from Table 27 that insiders are at least 15 per cent lower in the upper class category compared to either the executives or outsiders. If the sons who have careers in family firms were separated from the other insiders, only 31 per cent would be of upper class origin. It is evident that it is primarily sons learning the business and those of upper class origins who make the shift into the executive ranks from within the bureaucracy and similarly into the circle of outside directors. Given this phenomenon it is doubtful that many of the insider comprador elites will break into the executive ranks of the multinational corporations they work for.

(ii) Elite Divisions by Activity

One distinction within the elite which has been discussed earlier under the heading ''career patterns'' is the ''functional'' or task differentiation within the elite including technical men, financiers and financial executives, lawyers, those trained in commerce and those whose main experience has been in corporate finance departments. In the previous section on corporate positions, the differences between executives, inside directors, and outside directors was discussed. If the task and position of elites are combined it can be argued that four major, although not mutually exclusive, divisions can be drawn. These would include an elite of managers including inside directors and some executives who themselves do not have major holdings in the corporations they work for. A second division includes a wealth elite which is composed of large stockholders who either hold executive positions or sit on the board as outside directors. At present, it is a difficult and involved task to establish who within the elite is a member of wealth or large owner class; however, plans are now under way to conduct a study which would allow this to be determined. A third division is an honourific elite characterized by horizontal mobility from other elites including the political, bureaucratic, military and academic world. At this point it is difficult to say just how much power these people have after they enter the corporate board rooms, although minimally, they provide contacts with other important elites within Canada and at the same time give legitimacy to the operations of the corporations. At least some elite switchers—for instance, John Robarts, former Premier of Ontario, now a partner in two law firms and director of five dominant corporations—have moved into economic elite at a relatively young age and are now engaged in an active economic career. The relative power of each of these groups within the economic elite and in relations

TABLE 27

Class Origin of the Canadian Born Economic Elite by Corporate Position*, 1972

Class	Executive	Insider	Outsider	All
Upper Class	62.0%	46.7%	63.5%	59.4%
Middle Class	30.3	44.6	32.6	34.8
Working Class	7.7	8.7	3.9	5.8
TOTAL	100%	100%	100%	100%
N	(142)	(148)	(383)	(673)

* Each category has been made mutually exclusive by including anyone who may be an executive or insider in the appropriate category and not including them among the outsiders even if they hold an outsider directorship in addition to the other position. These categories refer exclusively to positions in dominant corporations.

between elites is also the subject of future inquiry (see Clement and Olsen, 1973). Under the honourific elite, particularly in terms of the legitimation aspect, there would be included the very few women who now appear in the elite (six in the entire set of directors, each holding one position). The practice of having a token woman on the board is now prevalent in the U.S. but this practice is just beginning to take hold in Canada. A fourth division is the expertise elite, including the professionals, technicians, lawyers and accountants. In a few cases these would include some advisors and consultants to the elite and in other cases they involve elite members who themselves are trained in these fields but whose main activity is policy making within the elite. Each of these four groupings may, and probably do, have differential power within the elite but it is difficult to assign them different degrees of power in this type of analysis. As Porter has said: "Given secrecy and the collective responsibility which operates in all these elite collectivities, it must be assumed that all members have some power" (1955:508).

(iii) The "Top 100" Directors and Multiple Directorship Holders

Porter introduced into his study the divisons of the "Top 100" which has been replicated here. Another basis of differentiation has also been introduced which distinguishes between those with multiple dominant directorships and those with only one. These two methods of dividing the economic elite hierarchically will be examined, particularly with reference to class origins.

As Porter has commented, the notion of the "Top 100" involves an "unavoidable arbitrariness in attempting to rank members of the elite" (1965:295). It does, however, provide a useful distinction when the criteria for selection are spelled out. The "Top 100" were selected in this, and in Porter's study, on the basis of holding top executive positions, particularly presidencies and chairmanships, within the largest of the dominant corporations; they hold multiple directorships which include more than one of the largest dominant corporations, or a combination of each of these, a situation Porter mentions is common in 1951 and one which is repeated in 1972.

The "Top 100"   Although including only about 10 per cent of the entire elite, as they did in 1951, the "Top 100" have a scope well beyond their proportional representation. They hold 342 of the dominant directorships (24 per cent) held by Canadian residents; 59 of the directorshps in the five big banks (28 per cent) and 36 insurance directorships (25 per cent). These are about identical percentages to those reported by Porter for the "Top 100" in 1951 with the corresponding figures being 25, 29 and 23 per cent, respectively. One difference between the "Top 100" in 1951 and in 1972, is that there were 88 Canadian born in the group in the earlier period but only 80 now. This reflects the general trend reported throughout the analysis.

Multiple Directorship Holders   Although there are 274 multiple directorship holders resident in Canada, adequate biographical data could be found for only 267 of these, thus representing a coverage of 97.5 per cent. These 267 individuals constitute 34.5 per cent of the total number of elite members resident in Canada. Although Porter did not use multiple directorship holders as analytical distinction[19], he did report that 22 per cent of the Canadian residents had a total of 46 per cent of the dominant directorships in 1951. This does not exclude the few for whom biographical coverage was not adequate. Multiple directorhsip holders in 1972 account for 53.8 per cent of all dominant directorships held by Canadian residents, 58.6 per cent of all insurance directorships included and 68.3 per cent of the directorships in the five key banks. This represents an increased number and scope over a similar group for 1951. Enormous power is concentrated within these 267 individuals who hold more than one dominant directorship. Over half of them hold a directorship in one of the key banks, together holding over two thirds of these key directorships. These are people who are the interlocks analysed earlier. They move between dominant corporations carrying with them a knowledge of the corporate world much broader than those who hold single directorships. They have much more extensive contacts within the elite than any other group and they have been recognized by their peers as men of power by being invited to sit on more than one dominant board. This indeed is a very select group.

The core of the elite are the members of the "Top 100" and those who hold multiple directorships. Since only 15 members of the "Top 100" do not overlap with the multiple directors there is a core of 282 persons who, between them, wield tremendous corporate power, even relative to the other members of the economic elite.

(iv) Class Origin of the "Top 100" and Multiple Directorship Holders

Tables 23 and 24 provide a breakdown of the class origin for various subgroups within the 1951 and 1972 economic elites, respectively. There is a high similarity between the class of origin of the Canadian born "Top 100" in both 1951 and 1972 with about two thirds upper class in each, although the working class has dropped by over one half in 1972. The most important finding is that almost three quarters of the multiple directorship holders in

1972 are of upper class origin, exactly 20 per cent more from the upper class than the single directorship holders and even eight per cent higher than the "Top 100".

In 1951, there was only a four per cent difference between single and multiple directorship holders, a difference which has increased to 20 per cent by 1972 compared to both the multiple directorship holders in 1951 and the single directorship holders in 1972. While in the earlier period it made little difference in terms of class of origin whether a member of the elite was upper class or not in terms of holding more than one dominant directorship, by 1972, being upper class is almost a prerequisite. Even the single directorship holders are now almost identical in upper class composition to the multiple directorship holders of twenty years ago.

Once again the class barriers become important within the economic elite, even much more than they were twenty years ago. Those members of the elite with upper class origins have a much stronger probability of becoming multiple directors than do those from the lower classes. This verifies the value of upper class connections and the social network operating at that level. Because they have been at the top from an early age and because their kin are well known within the corporate world, members of the upper class have a much more comprehensive set of connections which are reflected in their being invited to sit on more than one dominant board. Also evident from these findings is the fact that the power of the upper class within the elite is much more pervasive than even their numbers would indicate. It should be remembered that while this select group of multiple directors makes up only 29 per cent of the total elite, it controls 54 per cent of all directorships, 59 per cent of those in insurance companies and 68 per cent of those in banks. Enormous power is concentrated in these few members of the elite, almost three quarters of whom are upper class in origin.

Another fact which verifies the vitality and power of the core group of indigenous capitalists is the fact that 86 per cent of those with multiple directorships are Canadian born. As the evidence accumulates, it becomes clearer that there is a solid core of elites in Canada firmly rooted in the upper class which is not dependent on foreign capitalists. It is independent and powerful in and of itself, and able to operate in the continental and North Atlantic framework on its own strength. Evidence of this strength is the fact that at least 15 of the 80 "Top 100" born in Canada sit on the parent boards of multinational corporations based outside Canada. Between them, these 15 hold 26 directorships on these foreign boards, including 23 in the U.S., one in the U.K. and two elsewhere. This includes two on the board of General Motors of the U.S., that nation's largest corporation. Other foreign

TABLE 28

Class Origins of the Canadian Born Economic Elite By Sub-Groups, 1951*

	All	Top 100	Single Directorships	Multiple Directorships
Upper Class	50%	67%	48.8%	52.9%
Middle Class	32	18.2	33.3	30.0
Working Class	18	14.8	17.9	17.1
TOTAL	100%	100%	100%	100%
N	(611)	(88)	(418)	(193)

* The 'Single Directorships' and 'Multiple Directorships' were recalculated for use here from the original data. Others from Porter, 1965:292, Table XXVIII.

TABLE 29

Class Origins of the Canadian Born Economic Elite By Sub-Groups, 1972

	All	Top 100	Single Directorships	Multiple Directorships
Upper Class	59.4%	65%	52.8%	72.8%
Middle Class	34.8	28.8	41.1	22
Working Class	5.8	6.2	6.1	5.2
TOTAL	100%	100%	100%	100%
N	(673)	(80)	(443)	(230)

boards include the Bank of New York, IBM, Chrysler, Honeywell, Continental Oil, Union Carbide and even the controversial Texasgulf[20]. There are also at least 24 members of the multiple directorship group who have directorships on foreign boards. This evidence proves that the core of Canadian capitalism is not weak, nor is it unable to operate outside Canada in the rest of the capitalist world. The periphery of Canadian capitalism has been sold out to foreign, particularly U.S., capitalism but this has had a greater effect on the power of the middle class than on the upper class, since it was illustrated earlier that compradorization is primarily a middle class phenomenon.

(v) The Elite as a Changing Group

The economic elite as captured in this study is for one point in time, 1972, as was Porter's study which was also based at one point in time, 1951. These "bench marks" fail to acknowledge the different points in the careers of various elite members. To some extent the analysis of those who have remained in the elite over the past twenty years illustrates that there are people of different ages and points in their careers within the overall group called the economic elite. The preceding section discussed the active core of the elite which holds more than one dominant directorship but it should be recognized that some members in the rest of the elite are also on their way into this core as well as some who have been in the core but are now retired or in the process of retiring. For example, E.P. Taylor is "phasing out" his corporate activity after holding 10 dominant directorships in 1951; he "only" holds three in 1972—Massey-Ferguson, Argus and the Royal Bank. One indication of those near the end of their career is that when asked to state their "principal occupation", 34 or 4.4 per cent of the elite indicated they were "retired".

As Table 30 illustrates, fewer members of the over 65-year old group were born into the upper class, with 49.6 per cent of the group in this situation compared to the under-50 group, where 67.4 per cent were born into the upper class while 55.6 per cent of the middle aged group had this advantage. This illustrates that upper class members of the elite are able to break into elite positions at an earlier age than the middle and working classes. The middle and working classes are in the positions where, if they are to make it into the elite at all, they must endure the long crawl. The long crawl is not simply a waiting period; it is also a socialization and "testing" period within which the middle and lower class members must compete with one another and prove to those at the top that they are "worthy" by spending most of their adult life struggling to the top "learning the ropes". Once they have been effectively socialized, a few of the corporate men break into the elite.

TABLE 31

**Age and Class of Origin
for the Canadian Born Economic Elite, 1972**

Year of Birth & Age

Class	Before 1905 (over 65)	1905-1920 (50-65)	After 1920 (under 50)	All
Upper Class	49.6%	55.6%	67.4%	59.4%
Middle Class	43.7	36.9	30.6	34.8
Working Class	6.7	7.5	2.0	5.8
TOTAL	100%	100%	100%	100%
N	(119)	(358)	(196)	(673)

The case of the banks, as detailed earlier, is the classic example of effective socialization. Only two per cent of the under-50 group has made it into the elite with lower than middle class origins while they make up 7.5 per cent of the 50-65 age group and 6.7 per cent of the over-65 group. At the highest level, almost 40 per cent of the under-50 group had fathers directly in the economic elite while only 22 per cent of those between 50 and 65 years had the same advantage and 30 per cent of the oldest group.

With the upper class entering the elite at a younger age and staying there longer, it serves to further concentrate their power over time since someone in the elite for twenty years or more obviously has more impact on the direction of the Canadian economy than someone staying for, say, only five years. On every variable examined, it is the upper class which has the greatest concentration of economic power: they enter the elite at a younger age; they hold more bank and insurance directorships; they have more multiple dominant directorships and they stay longer. They also tend to pass their accumulated advantages on to their offspring who then repeat the process all over again.

Before proceeding to a discussion of further aspects of the inequality of access into the economic elite, it is worthwhile to briefly summarize some of the major findings and arguments presented in this chapter. Beginning with career avenues into the elite, it was shown that there has been a decline in the proportion of "technical men" but an increase in the proportion of lawyers, particularly those who have come through the corporation rather than by way of the law firm. Career patterns also provided the first indication of an increase in the amount of inheritance and upper class recruitment into the elite with the finding that the proportion having their main career in family firms had increased since 1951, while the proportion who had made it on their "own account" had declined. In addition to the 1,848 interlock positions among the 113 dominant corporations found in Chapter Four, it was shown that law partnerships add another dimension to interlocking. Twenty-three partnerships were found which had more than one partner in the elite. Between them, the 60 partners held 106 dominant directorships.

Focus was then turned explicitly to the class origins of the elite, showing that three fifths of the present elite came from upper class origins. This was an increase of almost 10 per cent from the origins of the economic elite twenty years ago. Members of the current elite who also appeared in Porter's study of 1951 were examined separately and it was shown that half of this group had fathers in the economic elite, and over two thirds were upper class, illustrating that upper class members of the elite tend to last much longer in the elite than do those of the middle class. One partial explanation of the crystallization of the class structure was offered in a closer examination of the banks which have traditionally been wide avenues of lower class recruitment but recently have become closed off. In another section, it was shown that three financial sectors which had come into importance since 1951 did not provide mobility for middle and working classes on any different basis than any of the older sectors.

Attention turned to five corporate sectors to analyse which had provided mobility into the elite and who controlled them. It was found that the main avenue was through Canadian controlled corporations in the finance sectors and that few had actually made it into the elite by way of foreign controlled firms. The only notable exceptions were a total of 15 per cent who made it through U.S. controlled resource and manufacturing corporations. An analysis of corporate positions found that there was stratification within the elite itself with few inside directors without upper class origin able to break into the executive ranks or the circle of outside directors. Mobility was examined explicitly in terms of the indigenous/comprador dichotomy illustrating that compradorization was primarily a phenomenon which affected the middle classes and had little impact on the core of the indigenous elite which remains firmly rooted in the upper class. The parallel comprador elite did indeed provide mobility for a number of middle class Canadians but many of the positions were also occupied by the traditional upper class indigenous elite who had entered into an alliance with foreign capitalists. It was argued that inheritance was a major means of perpetuating class privilege by illustrating that more than one quarter of the present elite had inherited important positions from previous generations. It was also illustrated that current kinship connections are prevalent within the elite, serving to unify it beyond its already concentrated state.

The size of the elite was examined showing that stratification occurs within the elite, particularly for those holding multiple directorships who make up only 29 per cent of the elite but hold 54 per cent of the positions in dominant corporations and 68 per cent of the bank directorships. Almost three quarters of this select group were found to be upper class, making them substantially more upper class in origin than those having only one dominant directorship. This brings the discussion to the preceding section which argued that the elite, as defined in this and Porter's study, represented only two points in time and that within the elite there are a variety of ages and career differences which reflect the changing character of the elite. Given that the youngest members of the group had the highest social class, it should not be expected that the class structure will become more open in the forseeable future, barring a major social upheaval. The analysis in the following chapter turns to some major social variables such as regionalism, ethnicity, religion and education and then finally, an examination of relationships members of the economic elite have "beyond the board room".

Notes

[1]Directors and senior executives of the 113 dominant corporations were identified from *The Financial Post Directory of Directors 1972* and in a few cases from reports filed with the Department of Corporate and Consumer Affairs. This provided the names and corporate directorships of 946 individuals resident in Canada holding a total of 1,454 corporate directorships in the dominant corporations. Adequate biographical data was found for 775 (81.9 per cent) of the corporate elite. The 81.9 per cent of the elite for whom data was available include 1,276 of the positions (87.8 per cent). This compares favourably with Porter's coverage of 77.2 per cent of the elite members and 82 per cent of the positions. Half of the 171 for whom data was not available were inside directors, indicating that these are mainly new entrants into the elite who have not yet made it into the biographical sources examined. Only nine of those missing held executive positions in dominant corporations. Adequate data could not be found for four of the six women who appear in the elite. Only residents of Canada were included in the present study, with the 287 foreign residents holding 305 dominant directorships excluded from the present analysis. Of the 287, 195 are U.S. residents, 55 in the U.K. and 37 resident elsewhere.

[2]Biographical sources include *Canadian Who's Who*, various years; *Who's Who in Canada*, various years; the *National Reference Book*, various years; *Biographies Canadiennes Francaises*, various years; *Who's Who in Canadian Jewry*, 1965; regional *Who's Who's*; *The Canadian Directory of Parliament, 1867-1967*; American and British *Who's Who*; *The Canadian Who Was Who, 1875-1937*; *Poor's Register of Corporations, Directors and Executives*; *A Cyclopedia of Canadian Biography*, 1919; *Macmillan Dictionary of Canadian Biography*, 1963; *Directory of Directors*, various years; *Morgan's Canadian Men and Women of Their Time*, 1912; *Encyclopedia Canadiana*; newspapers and magazines, particularly the *Globe & Mail* and *Financial Post*.

[3]Class origin will be defined and operationalized later in this chapter.

[4]See Porter's *Does Money Matter?* (1974) where he demonstrates post-secondary education remains a middle class preserve. He argues that expansion of post-secondary education since the war has been primarily by the middle class females.

[5]This will be demonstrated in Chapter Six.

[6]Elite membership in these clubs will be examined in detail in Chapter Six.

[7]Included here are seven lawyers on the board of the Bank of Montreal, six on Canadian Imperial Bank of Commerce, six on Bank of Nova Scotia, eight on Toronto-Dominion and ten on the Royal Bank.

[8]"Career in other elite" does not include the mass media elite. As will be demonstrated in Chapter Nine, one quarter of the media elite which overlaps

with the corporate elite has their main career in the media compared to 70 per cent of the half which does not overlap. If the media elite was included as "other" elite, this would raise the Canadian born proportion of "main career in other elite" to 8.2 per cent. This was not included, however, because there is too much overlap between the economic elite and media elite to consider them as other than one, the corporate elite.

[9]Porter's political elite includes federal cabinet ministers, all provincial premiers, justices of the Supreme Court of Canada, presidents of the Exchequer Court, plus provincial chief justices (1965:604), while Olsen includes the above plus selected cabinet ministers and judges from the four largest provinces. Porter's bureaucratic elite includes "senior federal public servants of the rank of deputy minister or the equivalent, associate and assistant deputy ministers or the equivalents, directors of branches in the more important departments and senior executives of Crown corporations" (608). Again, Olsen includes these positions plus their counterparts in the four largest provinces.

[10]Uncles were used as equivalent to fathers in cases where the position of the uncle provided an indication of the family origin. For example, the case of Henry Borden, whose uncle was used as being equivalent to having a father in the political elite. "Borden is a nephew of Sir Robert Borden, who was like a father to young Harry, and in 1918 the then Prime Minister of Canada took the boy to the Imperial War Conference in London to meet the British elite" (*Last Post*, 1973:39). Henry Borden is now a member of the executive committee and director of both Brascan and Bell Canada as well as director of IBM Canada, Massey-Ferguson and Huron & Erie Mortgage Corp., all of which are dominant, in addition to being chairman of the Canadian Board of Norwich Union Life Insurance and a director and member of the executive committee of Brinco. His meeting with the British elite with his Prime Minister uncle seems to have served him well.

[11]"At or near the top" refers to those people who began their careers with the advantage of having kin from the previous generation in one of the three elites or in a substantial business. A substantial business is defined as one which may have been dominant in an earlier period but minimally would have been "middle range" as described earlier. Upper class encompasses those included as "at or near the top" and their families plus members of other elites such as the military, ideological or honorific, and wealth elites and their families. Also included as upper class are those who have attended one of the Headmasters' Association private schools or a classical college.

[12]For clarity of presentation, those included as "upper-middle class" by Porter by virtue of their attending a private school, will be collapsed into the upper class. This makes no difference in terms of the relative comparison between 1951 and 1972. For example, excluding this category would mean 37 per cent are upper class in origin for 1951 and 46.8 per cent in 1972, a difference of 9.8 per cent increase. By collapsing, the 1951 upper class origin is 50 per cent and the 1972 is 59.4 per cent, a difference of 9.4 per cent. The net effect is to decrease the change by only .4 per cent.

[13]The assumptions specified above and those in the footnotes to Table 21 and Appendix XIV.

[14]See, for example, Johnson (1972).

[15]The higher class origin of multiple directorship holders will be demon-

strated in a subsequent section of this chapter.

[16]This is a self-defined affiliation as reported in the *Directory of Directors* which sends each person a listing of their corporate directorships and asks them to indicate which was their "principal occupation."

[17]Six sold out family firms and joined the comprador ranks while the other eleven have taken on executive positions similar to those held earlier by their fathers.

[18]See Appendix X, where the interlocks between the economic elite and 175 small companies are examined. It is shown that the elite controls 829 of the 2,066 (or 40.6 per cent) highest positions in these firms.

[19]The multiple directorship holders have now been calculated from Porter's original data of the 203 multiple directorship holders in 1951; adequate biographical data was available for 193, representing 95.1 per cent coverage.

[20]Prior to the Canada Development Corporation buying shares.

Chapter Six

Inequality of Access (II):
The Private World of Powerful People

THIS chapter will be divided into three sections. First, some further social background characteristics of the economic elite such as regionalism, ethnicity, religion and educational attainment. Next, there will be an analysis of the private world of powerful people: the private schools, exclusive national men's clubs, and trade associations. Finally, the relationship between the economic and state elites will be examined, including party affiliations, elite forums and interchange between these two most powerful elites. Some additional class related variables will also be examined as they relate to the areas outlined here.

I. Social Background Characteristics of the Economic Elite

(i) Regionalism and Class Origins

Regionalism in Canadian society is a social issue which has received a good deal of attention from social analysts, but regional inequities have seldom been examined from the perspective of class origins. By using birth place rather than present residence, a stronger indication can be obtained for the opportunities members of various classes born in the major regions of Canada have of entering the economic elite. If residence were used, it would be too susceptible to the clustering of elite members in the metropolitan centers of Toronto and Montreal after migration from their places of birth consequently ignoring the origin features important for understanding life chances.

Of the Canadian born members of the elite, 68 per cent were born in Ontario or Quebec, 23 per cent in the western provinces and only nine per cent in the Maritimes. When this is compared to the 1921 distributions of population, the census year closest to when most of the present elite were born, it is found that the central provinces are overrepresented by about eight per cent while the West is underrepresented by five per cent and the East by three per cent. Given the high degree of elite recruitment from the upper class, these differences would be expected to exist because of the historical differences in the development of the economic structures in these regions. This is in the same sequence as the development af Canada occurred; the Center established first, soon followed by the Maritimes and, not until much later, the West. It also matches the center/periphery analysis now popular in many discussions of regionalism in Canada with a difference of 13 percentage points between the Center and the Western periphery and 11 points between the Center and the East with the Center over-represented in each case.

One obvious difference between the regions accounting for this differential representation is the economic structure within each region and, related to that, the different class structures of each region. By analysing the class origins of elite members born in the three regions, it is possible to determine the extent of differential class recruitment within the regions, aside from their disparities in numerical distribution.

As would be expected, Ontario and Quebec, with their longer established and more crystallized class structures, have more elite members born in the upper class with 62.7 per cent while the Maritimes are next with 59.3 per cent and the West with the lowest proportion at 50 per cent. As is evident in Table 31, there is a substantially greater difference between the West and Center, with a 12.7 per cent upper class difference, compared to the East and the Center, with only a 3.4 per cent difference.

The findings[1] suggest a high degree of similarity between the Center and the East, based on the older established class structures of those two regions. The West, on the other hand, as an immigrant society, did not have a rigid class structure relative to the other parts of Canada when the present elites were growing up the 1920's and 1930's or even when they were embarking on their careers in the 1940's. An important conclusion which can be drawn from this is that as social structures mature and become more established, the chances of those outside the upper class entering elite positions declines. This is similar to the finding already presented regarding the general crystallization of the class structure since 1951. In each case, the direction associated with maturing societies is toward a more rigid stucture which permits less and less mobility. Without any great social upheavals in the society, it seems that the class structure continues in the direction of less, rather than more, equality. At one point in Canada's development, the West could be regarded as a new social force thus providing greater mobility than the older traditional forces of the Center and the East. As the West becomes transformed, and the social structure coalesces, it will come to resemble the other regions of Canada where mobility already has become restricted. Indeed, at this point, the class origins of those from the West resembles closely the pattern found for 1951, each having half from the upper class. The West is twenty years behind but rapidly catching up.

The small difference between the Center and the East also indi-

TABLE 31

Regionalism and Social Class of the Economic Elite, 1972

Class	Birth Place			All
	West	Center	East	
Upper Class	50.0%	62.7%	59.3%	59.4%
Middle Class	44.3	31.8	32.2	34.8
Working Class	5.7	5.5	8.5	5.8
TOTAL	100%	100%	100%	100%
N	(158)	(456)	(59)	(673)

cates that it is not so much the level of development within the region as the maturity of the class structure which determines mobility. Measured in terms of economic development, the East would be more similar to the West than to Ontario and Quebec. The major determinant of mobility would then seem to be the length of time the class structure of a particular region is allowed to survive without encountering social upheavals, rather than strictly the level of economic development within that region. As class structures develop, the upper class is able to construct institutions of exclusions, for example, private schools and clubs, which serve to protect their privileges from encroachment by the middle and lower classes. Even an underdeveloped region like the Maritimes can still retain a rigid class structure which retards mobility and perpetuates privilege. These findings bring into question whether either development or under-development affect mobility. It would seem that it is the character of the social structure, particularly the structure of stratification within a society, which is the major determinant of mobility. The more hierachical the social structure, the less chance for mobility, regardless of the so-called "opportunity structure" which is frequently said to be correlated with the level of development in society. A higher "standard of living" or GNP does not equate to higher mobility or more equitable distributions of power. As the West begins to mature, another avenue of access to elite positions from less than upper class origins will again be cut off.

The middle and working classes of Ontario and Quebec have a lower probability of entering the economic elite than do their counterparts in the West, not because they are more poorly "equipped" to do so, but because they have to "compete" with an established upper class while in the West this class did not exist to the same extent in the 1920's to 1940's. An upper class did, however, exist in the Maritimes during this period, consequently, the other classes had less of a chance to enter the elite.

There is other evidence that the West differs substantially from other regions of Canada. By examining corporate sectors where the Western-born hold their directorships, and the extent of compradorization, it will be demonstrated that the West, with its higher middle class origins (over 12 per cent higher than either of the other regions) is more dependent on the U.S. than other regions with an established traditional indigenous elite. First, the corporate sectors that elites born in the various regions have positions in, will be examined in Table 32.

The Western-born are over-represented both in terms of their proportion of the total elite and their 1921 population base in both utilities and resources. The reason for the utilities over-representation in pipelines and resources is because of oil and gas. In other sectors, particularly manufacturing and finance, they are under-represented.

TABLE 32

Regionalism and Corporate Sectors for the Economic Elite, 1972

Sector	Birth Place			Total		(Number of Positions*)
	West	Center	East	Total		
Finance	21.4%	70%	8.6%	100%		454
Utilities	34.3	56.5	9.3	100		108
Trade	23.1	74.7	2.2	100		91
Manufacturing	17.9	74.4	7.7	100		117
Resources	31.8	59.7	8.4	100		154
Total Elite	23.4	67.8	8.8	100		924
Population (1921)	28	60	12	100		
N	(158)	(456)	(59)	(673)		

* Number of positions does not total to 673 because one person may hold a position simultaneously in more than one sector.

The East never reaches its proportion of the 1921 population and only in utilities, slightly surpasses its proportion of the elite. The Center, on the other hand, is over-represented in terms of the 1921 population base in all sectors except utilities; in terms of its proportion of the elite, it is also under-represented in resources. It is highly over-represented in trade, manufacturing and finance. The fact that the West is lowest in manufacturing, 10 per cent lower than its proportion of the population, reflects the historical development of manufacturing in Central Canada and the lower structural possibilities for mobility in this sector by those born in the West. Their high concentration in resources and utilities, particularly those related to gas and oil, suggests their association with U.S. controlled companies in these fields and their ability to take advantage of the post-war development occurring in these areas. As will be seen in Table 33, this is indeed the case.

Westerners are much more likely to be U.S. comprador elites than those born anywhere else in Canada; indeed, they are almost identical to the foreign born, with about one quarter of each as U.S. compradors. On the other hand, Eastern-born are most likely to be U.K. comprador elites, again almost identical to the foreign born proportion. Each of these findings reflect the historical associations these regions have had outside Canada—the West with the U.S. and the East with the U.K. The Center, however, is almost 80 per cent indigenous and the East is also more indigenous than the West. As would be expected, the foreign born are almost half comprador, reflecting intra-company transfers within multinational companies to comprador positions within Canada, probably for a relatively short time before being transferred back to the parent company. This is particularly evident in the over a quarter who are U.S. compradors.

As the higher middle class origins within the West and their tendency to concentrate in sectors associated with oil and gas suggested, the Westerners turn out to be substantially more likely to be comprador than either the Center or the East. Association with U.S. controlled development in the West has provided the middle class there with greater mobility possibilities than they would have in the more established regions of Canada. Once again, the East is much more similar to the Center thus lending support to the argument made earlier that it is not the level of development within the region but the crystallization of the class structure which determines the amount of mobility available. U.S. penetration of the West to exploit gas and oil has occurred primarily in the post-war period and as a new social force, it has opened the class structure there for a new social type—the middle class. Will this new social force also crystallize and form a class structure similar to the other regions? It is too soon to be able to answer that yet, but it is certainly aimed in that direction.

TABLE 33

Regionalism and Compradorization of the Economic Elite, 1972

Elite	Birth Place					
	West	Center	East	Canadian Born	Foreign Born	All
Indigenous	70.3%	79%	76.3%	76.7%	52.9%	73.2%
Comprador						
— U.S.	23.4	13.4	10.2	15.5	25.5	17.2
— U.K.	5.1	4.4	8.5	4.9	8.8	5.4
— Other	1.3	3.3	5.1	3	12.8	4.3
TOTAL	100%	100%	100%	100%	100%	100%
N	(158)	(456)	(59)	(673)	(102)	(775)

(ii) Ethnicity and Inequality of Access

In Canada, as in many modern societies built on conquest and immigration, ethnicity is interwoven into the class system so that it provides advantages to the conquerors while keeping the conquered and newly-arrived at the bottom of the so-called "opportunity structure". Two elite systems based on the two chartered groups provide their members with differential access to the elite with the "third force" of other ethnic groups not even having an elite of their own which operates in the national arenas of economic power.

The Historical Participation of Ethnic Groups in the Economic Elite[2]

Commerce in New France was dominated by merchants from France (Pritchard, 1972) but Conquest by the English in 1755 drove most of these early entrepreneurs back to their mother country and they were replaced in economic activities by British immigrants (Guindon, 1968). Strengthened through their ties with Britain, the Anglo elite dominated commerce while the French lacked the advantages of capital and market access associated with the Empire. The trans-Atlantic alliance between Canadian and British mercantilists effectively stifled mobility into dominant economic activities for others. For example, Tulchinsky's study of the Montreal business community from 1837 to 1853 finds few French-Canadians in commercial occupations. They tended to be concentrated in medical and legal professions (1972:132-133.). Further evidence of Anglo dominance is provided by Acheson's detailed study of the industrial elite in Canada between 1885 and 1910 which again finds French and "third" ethnic groups under-represented. French-Canadians had only seven per cent of the elite positions in 1885 and this dropped to six per cent in 1910 in spite of their representing about 29 per cent of the population. About 16 per cent of the population was accounted for by "third" ethnic groups, but only four and three per cent, respectively, of the industrial elite. Porter found only 6.7 per cent of the economic elite to be French-Canadian (a third of the population by then) while "third" ethnic groups represented insignificant numbers in the elite (but one fifth of the Canadian population) and the remainder were Anglos (1965:286). In other words, since the Conquest and through the next two centuries until mid-way into the present century, French-Canadians and "third" ethnic groups have been effectively restricted in their access to top decision making positions in the Canadian economy.

Why have there been so few French and "third" ethnic group members in the upper levels of economic power? Since the Conquest, Canada's economic development relied heavily on British capital and markets. Early migrants from the United Kingdom tended to bring their

TABLE 34

Proportion of Ethnic Representation in the Economic Elite, 1951 and 1972

| | Economic Elite | | Canadian Population | |
	1951	1972	1951	1971
Anglo	92.3%	86.2%	47.9%	44.7%
French	6.7	8.4	30.8	28.6
Other	1*	5.4	21.3	26.7
TOTAL	100%	100%	100%	100%
N	(760)	(775)		

* Porter says .78 per cent of his sample is Jewish; other 'third' ethnic groups "were hardly represented at all" (1965:286).

own capital plus contacts with the financial houses of Britain. Using primarily British portfolio investment, first and subsequent generations of Anglo extraction were able to establish and maintain a commercial empire which eventually provided them with autonomy and control in financial, transportation and utilities sectors of the economy. This indigenous capitalist class formed a closed circle of powerful and wealthy men who excluded outsiders, among whom were included French-Canadians and newly-arriving ethnic groups. Control of the economic sector has remained with Anglos over the years because of their ability to gain access to sources of capital. More recently, the Canadian economy has become continental in focus and the Canadian Anglos were established in a stronger position linguistically and through their accumulated capital to transform their power into an alliance with the United States industrial capitalists. As a society based on conquest and immigration, Canada developed a high correlation between ethnicity and social class (hence Porter's title, *The Vertical Mosaic*). With this strong relationship, it is difficult to distinguish between the effects of social class and ethnic origin for mobility into the economic elite. Regardless, the combined effects have been sufficient to maintain Anglo dominance in the upper class and in elite positions within the economy.

French-Canadians[3]

Although French-Canadians constitute just under one third of the Canadian population, only 65 members of the current economic elite could be classified this way, making the French component of the elite only 8.4 per cent. In 1951, Porter found 51 French-Canadians representing only 6.7 per cent of the elite at that time. This means a net increase of only 14 more French-Canadians or 1.7 per cent more of the elite population over the past twenty years. These have not been uneventful years in French-Anglo relations; quite the contrary, they were supposed to contain the "new awakening" (a loaded phrase which somehow assumes the French have themselves been their own barrier to gaining equality and not their position vis à vis the dominant Anglos) and the "quiet revolution" of the 1960's and the not-so-quiet revolution of recent years. In spite of ideological statements to the contrary, the French have not made significant inroads into the economic world.

Some may argue that the French may not have made it to the very top of the corporate world but they have at least made gains in the middle range and smaller corporations. Once again, the evidence is to the contrary. A recent study based on 12,741 names of executives from some 2,400 companies operating in Canada listed in the 1971 *Directory of Directors*, found only 9.48 per cent to be French-Canadian (Presthus, 1973:56). This is only about one per cent more than are to be found in the economic elite and includes many corporations much smaller than the 113 dominant ones which are the basis of this study.

TABLE 35

Index of Ethnic Representation* in the Economic Elite, 1951 and 1972

	Economic Elite	
	1951	1972
Anglo	1.93	1.93
French	0.22	0.29
Other	0.05	0.20

* A figure of over 1.00 denotes over-representation and an index below 1.00 shows under-representation. This index is arrived at by dividing the population into the elite representation thus standardizing over time for changes in the ethnic composition of the population. It is a ratio of the ethnic proportion in the elite divided by the corresponding proportion of the Canadian population for the same time. The basic data is drawn from Table 34.

As is evident in Table 35, French-Canadians have made some ground over the past twenty years with their proportion of the elite increasing slightly while their proportion of the population fell slightly. Nevertheless, they still remain very much under-represented in both periods, in fact, almost as under-represented by 1972 as "other" ethnics. In the process, however, the Anglos have not lost any ground. From Table 34 it appears that Anglos have declined but the drop from 92.3 per cent in 1951 to 86.2 per cent in 1972 is deceptive. In fact, when compared to the decline in the population base, as in Table 35, the apparent decline disappears. For Anglos the index of representation is identical for each period (1.93 in 1951 and 1972). In other words, their decline in the proportion of the total Canadian population and the change can be explained simply in demographic terms and is not due to inroads made by either French or "third" ethnics.

One of the key issues of French-Anglo relations is the different proportions of French in the various elites. It has already been stated that they represent only 8.4 per cent of the current economic elite. This is still well below the 13.4 per cent Porter found for the bureaucratic elite in 1953 and the 21.7 per cent of the political elite from 1940 to 1960 (1965:389,441). Moreover, it is well below the French proportion found in the current state elite by Dennis Olsen, who says 23.2 per cent of the bureaucratic elite in 1973 and the 24.7 per cent of the political elite between 1961 and 1973 are French (Clement and Olsen, 1974). It is evident in comparison with the two state elites that they have a much higher French representation, although still never reaching their proportion of the population. This suggests that the historical division of labour between the two charter groups is still very much in evidence.

It was already stated that only three French-Canadians (3.9 per cent) were included in the group of elite members who have survived twenty years or more in the economic elite. This suggest they lack the same historical continuity in the corporate world as do Anglos. With access to the upper levels of the economic domain so dependent upon inheritance of position through both capital and social networks, it is understandable that French-Canadians are under-represented in the present elite. Previous generations of French-Canadian elites did not accumulate large amounts of capital, consequently, they were not able to transfer the same privileges to their offspring as were the Anglos. This is not to say that there is not a well-defined class structure within French Canada; it only means that that structure is not primarily based on control over economic institutions. At the top of the French class structure there are only a few families—like the Simards—who control very tightly what French corporate activity there is.

The class structure of French Canada is even more rigid than for all Canada, as was suggested in the earlier findings on regionalism. In fact, while 59.4 per cent of the elite as a whole are upper class, 87.6 per cent of the French in the elite have this distinction. Part of this is due to the effect of the classical college system and this being included as a criteria of upper class. However, even when only those born at or near the top (which excludes private schools) are examined, it is found that 50.8 per cent of the French are in this category compared to 46.8 per cent of the Canadian born elite as a whole. Only one French-Canadian has less than middle class origins and he was born in the United States. While there may not be a great deal of room for many French-Canadians in the economic elite as it now stands, there is certainly room made for the upper class French. This difference will be returned to later but for now it may be suggested that the different ethnic participation in the elite may not be due to "discrimination" but in fact may be a product of the different sizes of the various classes in each of the ethnic groups. That is, it may be that the French have a proportionately smaller upper class compared to their population base than do the Anglos and their 8.4 per cent proportion of the economic elite may resemble their proportion of the Canadian upper class[4].

The French tend to be younger than the elite as a whole but this reflects their higher class origins rather than their only slightly increased participation in the corporate world. While 18 per cent of the entire Canadian born elite was born before 1905, only 11 per cent of the French fell into this category; forty per cent of the French were born after 1920 compared to 29 per cent of the entire elite born in Canada.

Most of the 65 French were born in Quebec (58) with only four in Ontario, two in the U.S. and one in France. This suggests that almost 90 per cent of the French-Canadians had avenues into the elite within the institutional structure of Quebec society[5]. There is a difference with respect to compradorization between the French and others in the elite. While 76.9 per cent of the French are indigenous elites, this is 4.1 per cent more than the non-French. The major difference is between the U.S. comprador group where only 7.7 per cent of the French are found but 18 per cent of the non-French. To some extent, this accounts for the higher French proportion of upper class since the Anglos have experienced greater compradorization and, as has been shown, this means greater mobility for the middle class.

A major avenue of mobility for French-Canadians into the economic elite has been through connections with the state. Of the French in the current elite, there are three Senators, an additional three from the political elite, including two former federal elite members and Jean Lesage, a former Premier, and three from the bureaucratic elite. Between them, they account for 14 per cent of all the French in the economic elite. In addition, seven have close relatives who are in the state elite and 19, not included in any of the categories listed thus far, sit on key government boards or organizations such as crown corporations. Altogether this includes 54 per cent of all the French in the elite. This suggests that the French have been successful in using the state as a means for access to the economic elite and that they have strong relations with the state after gaining access.

Law, one of the major institutional links between the corporate and state systems, is also a major avenue of mobility for French-Canadians. There are 16 associated with law firms (24.6 per cent) and an additional 12 who have law degrees (18.5 per cent) representing a total of 43 per cent of the French members of the elite with training in law. This in considerably more than the one third of the French-Canadians in the 1951 economic elite trained as lawyers or the 19 per cent of the entire 1972 economic elite with training in law.

Education has been important for French-Canadian members of the elite with 75.4 per cent attending private schools, particularly the College Ste. Marie and College-de-Brèbeuf, with 11 members of the current elite attending each of them. Common educational experience within the upper class educational institutions of Quebec makes for lasting association; for example, four members of the elite attended both classical colleges mentioned above and all went on to the University of Montreal, with two of them now sitting on the board of Royal Trust together. University education has also been important to French-Canadian elites, with 83 per cent attending university (54) of which 43 went on to advanced degrees including 28 in law and 13 in commerce, of which six went to Harvard. Of the 54 attending university, 22 have their first degrees from the University of Montreal, eight at each of McGill and Laval, and four at the University of Ottawa with only 12 going elsewhere.

Club life is important among French-Canadians with only eight of the 65 not reporting any club membership. Most popular is St. Denis, with 27 elite members (41 per cent). There are 43 per cent of the French-Canadians who belong to one of the six national exclusive men's clubs with 17 belonging to the Mt. Royal, 19 to the St. James and five to the Rideau, but only one to each of the three Toronto clubs. This illustrates that there is a high degree of social separation at the club level between the French-Canadians and Anglos outside Quebec, although they do come together in the Montreal clubs.

"Third" Ethnics

Although over one quarter of Canada's population is made up of ethnic groups other than the two charter groups (26.7 per cent), they have almost no representation in the economic elite, except for Jews. From the non-charter groups, there are only 32 Jewish-Canadians (4.1 per cent) and 10 from other "third" ethnic groups (1.3 per cent). In 1951 there were only six Jews (.78 per cent) in the elite thus indicating they have made significant inroads into the elite over the past twenty years. None the less, "third" ethnic groups still remain the most under-represented ethnic category in the elite, as can be seen in Table 35. They have made limited gains in the elite while simultaneously their proportion of the Canadian population also increased by over five per cent in the last twenty years.

There are, however, several factors associated with the Jewish representation worth noting. It has already been discussed that most of the inroads have been on their "own account", indicating that the avenue of mobility into the elite has not been through established corporations but through firms which have been established and grown to national scope within one generation. A closer examination of the firms with which they were associated explains why they are 4.1 per cent of the elite and only 1.4 per cent of the population. Of the 32 Jews, 28 are associated with one of the five corporations, with one of five a long established corporation in the beverage industry, three in trade and one primarily in real estate. These are tightly-held family firms with only six families accounting for 25 of the 32 Jewish members of the elite. Outside these family firms, Jews have much less economic power in dominant financial corporations, holding only five of the dominant bank directorships (2.4 per cent) and two dominant insurance directorships (1.2 per cent). In other words, their representation in financial corporations is well below their proportion of the entire economic elite.

Outside the board room there is not very much participation by Jews in the private world of the economic elite, with only two belonging to one of the six national exclusive men's clubs. There are, however, Jewish clubs to which they belong, particularly the Montefiore with 10 members and the Elmridge with eight. Rosenberg provides an excellent discussion of the Jewish cultural and social associations, mentioning in particular that "the Montefiore Club is the second home of the vast majority of Jewish community leaders" (1971:143-144). In an earlier discussion, Rosenberg provided a detailed discussion of Jewish participation in various corporate sectors; the essence of his discussion, as with the findings of the present study, is that Jews have not, and do not, play a dominant role in the economic elite in Canada. Their participation is, for the most part, peripheral to the economic elite and located in the high risk sectors of trade and real estate (1939:215). Although in proportion to their representation in the population Jews are over-represented in the elite, this participation is so confined to a very few family firms that it does not give an adequate indication of their participation in the elite as a whole.

Although not exclusively, there is a tendency toward social separation in the philanthropic, cultural and honourific activities of the Jewish members of the elite. These are for the most part institutions associated within the Jewish tradition and community. With few exceptions, these 32 individuals are more correctly understood as an elite of the Jewish community, separate yet interlocking in a peripheral way with the national Anglo-dominated elite.

While Jewish-Canadians are somewhat over-represented in terms of their population base, other "third" ethnics are extremely underrepresented with only 1.3 per cent of the elite and 25.1 per cent of the Canadian population. Members of the other "third" ethnic groups stand in sharp contrast to the Jews. With one exception, the 10 members of the elite from other "third" ethnic groups are not participants in the cultural or philathropic associations of their ethnic groups and unlike the Jewish members are not associated with a particular set of elite corporations. The only case of overlap is two members on the CNR, a federal crown corporation. Unlike the Jews who have made it on their own account within Canada, members of these other ethnic groups have mainly transported family businesses from elsewhere to Canada (for example, Bata, Prentice and Koerner from Czechoslovakia) or transferred their high class position to Canada within multinational corporations (for example, A.A. Franck of Genstar). In other words, these few members of other ethnic groups have not, for the most part, "made it" within Canada but have been horizontally mobile from high class positions outside Canada.

Implications of Ethnic Representation in the Economic Elite

Ethnic representation in the economic elite satisfies neither of the two "official" models of Canadian society—"biculturalism" and "multiculturalism". Neither in the 1951 or 1972 economic elite was there anything close to approaching the proportions required to say there was sufficient French representation for the bicultural model; nor was there sufficient "third" ethnic participation for the multicultural model. The conclusion must be that the economic elite is characterized by Anglo dominance in both periods. The limited "third" ethnic penetration which has occurred with Jewish-Canadians has not been through integration with the dominant Anglos; rather, it has been by creating a parallel elite within a few corporations which for the most part are separate from the mainstream of economic power. Members of other "third" ethnic groups remain virtually absent from the elite, never reaching close to two per cent while about a quarter of the Canadian population. Later, the issue of ethnic representation in the elite will be raised in connection with the mass media and the relationship between language, legal and capital bases of power by the various ethnic groups will be examined.

(iii) Religious Affiliation of the Elite

In Canadian society it is difficult to separate the effects of religion in terms of elite membership from the effects of ethnicity. Jews, with four per cent of the Canadian born elite and 4.9 per cent of the foreign born, illustrate the extreme case where ethnicity and religion are one in the same. To a lesser extent, this is also true for French-Canadians and Catholics. While there are 85 Canadian born Catholics (12.6 per cent) and 13 foreign born (12.8 per cent), the 65 French-Canadians alone account for 58 of those who reported Catholic as their religious affiliation, with the other seven not reporting any affiliation. In other words, about two thirds of the Canadian born reporting Catholic are French-Canadians while the remainder are spread throughout the country. Anglos are also associated with one of the three major Protestant religions, Anglican, United, or Presbyterian. It would be difficult to argue that ideological differences between the major religious groups in Canada were somehow determinant of elite membership apart from other social and ethnic groups.

The 12.7 per cent Catholics of the total 775 Canadian resident members of the elite in 1972 is slightly more than the 10.3 per cent in 1951 but still well below their 46.2 per cent of the total population in Canada. This dramatic difference between the population and the elite would seem to extend beyond the under-representation caused by the

French factor and somewhat into the "other" ethnic exclusion from the elite, particularly European, but it is not possible to isolate these factors in this study. The under-representation of Catholics may also be related to the differential educational experiences of many Catholics and Protestants but again, this is difficult to isolate. Anglicans remain the dominant religious affiliation with 25.5 per cent in 1951 and 25.3 per cent in 1972, despite a drop in the total population over the same period from 14.7 per cent to 11.8 per cent. When only those with multiple directorships are considered, the Anglicans increase to 32 per cent. This increase for multiple directorship holders is associated with the high class position of Anglicans in Canada and the U.K. The United Church representation is substantial with 17.3 per cent currently and 17.6 per cent two decades ago. about equal to the present Canadian population with 17.5 per cent. Although Presbyterians have declined from 11.3 to 7.1 per cent, they are still over-represented compared to their four per cent of the population. Baptists and "other" Protestants are all under-represented; with only 2.6 per cent of the present elite and 2.5 per cent in 1951, they make up almost eight per cent of the population. Many report their religious affiliation simply as "Protestants" (eight per cent compared to 8.7 per cent earlier) while many others do not bother to report any affiliation at all, 23 per cent compared to 23.3 per cent in 1951. There does not appear to be any significant differences in the overall distribution of religious affiliation since 1951 which does not reflect population changes with the exception of the Anglicans and Uniteds, who have held steady in spite of declining numbers in the population at large.

Particularly in terms of education, religion serves as a method of creating social networks. When private shcools are run on a denominational basis, such as Appleby College, Ashbury College, Trinity College or Ridley College, which have all been Anglican-affiliated, this promotes association and friendships among the upper class based on common social experiences. It is because Anglican institutions have been established as class institutions and exclusion mechanisms that a disproportionate number of Anglicans appear in the elite and not because there is some "ethnic" associated with this denomination which creates elites.

(iv) Education: Training and Social Networks

Less than 10 per cent of the male population in the same age group as the economic elite have had any education past secondary school and only about five per cent have university degrees; the few who do have the advantage of higher education are indeed privileged. Of course, if females of the corresponding age were included, the proportion of the total population who attended university would drop even lower since only about two per cent of the women of this age have had the same advantage. The economic elite, in contrast to the Canadian population, has two distinct advantages; it is almost exclusively male[6] and most of its members have graduated from university.

Universities in Canada have always operated as effective screening devices to keep the lower classes[7] from competing for high skill and high paying jobs. With university education increasingly becoming a prerequisite for elite membership, particularly if there is no family firm to inherit, the university as a selection device, is accomplishing many of the former tasks of personnel departments by weeding out lower class members. In 1951, 58.3 per cent of the elite were university educated with an additional 5.4 per cent having some other higher education past the secondary level such as chartered accountancy degrees or technical training. By 1972, this had increased to 80.5 per cent of the elite with the university training and an additional four per cent with other post secondary education[8]. In other words, only 104 (15.5 per cent) of the Canadian born members of the elite did not have more than post secondary education.

The interesting question becomes not how many were educated at university but, how did those who were not manage to get into the elite? Of the 104 who did not have post secondary education, one quarter (26) attended private schools and a further one fifth (21) inherited their positions. In other words, almost half had upper class advantages and did not require university training as an avenue to the elite. Of the remaining, 14 spent an average of 40 years in the banks before attaining an executive position after beginning on the average at 16 years of age, two through insurance or other finance companies, eight financiers, six on their own account, two from the political elite and 18 from a variety of other routes. As discussed earlier, even the banks are now using the universities as screening devices, having given way to their own internal selection system and letting the state educational system do their inital socialization for them.

Not only is university education important but it appears that even post-graduate training and professional degrees are also rapidly becoming prerequisites of elite membership. Of the Canadian born, 280 have additional training beyond their under-graduate degrees, accounting for 41.6 per cent of the entire Canadian born elite. Of these, 183 have law degrees, including 15 who have other post-graduate degrees aside from law with 10 attending Harvard for MBA's. Altogether, 53 of those with post-graduate degrees went to the U.S. for their education and 34 of these to Harvard for MBA's. An additional 14 went to the U.K. and two to France for their post-graduate training while the rest obtained their degrees in Canada.

Age has an effect on whether the elite member attended university with 73.1 per cent of those over 65 attending and 79.3 per cent of those between 50 and 65 compared to 87.3 per cent for those under 50. Together with the difference for the entire elite between 1951 and 1972, this provides conclusive evidence of the increasing importance of university education to elite membership.

From the perspective of Canadian educational institutions, it is important to know how many of the Canadian born members were educated in Canada[9]. Very few of those who attended university went exclusively to foreign universities with 10.7 per cent of those who obtained only under-graduate degrees going to universities outside Canada and 7.8 per cent of those who went on to post-graduate work obtaining their first degrees outside Canada. Of those attending university, 84 per cent went exclusively to Canadian universities. When private schools are included, 16.4 per cent of the present elite who had attended university enjoyed the advantage of being educated outside Canada. Although foreign institutions of education have an important part to play in the educational careers of many members of the elite, particularly the MBA programme at Harvard, it is still primarily Canadian institutions of higher learning which do most of the selection of Canadian born elite members.

Not all universities in Canada are equally endowed with the ability to pass on elite membership. Actually, only four universities between them passed on three fifths of the elite attending university. Of those attending university, 27.1 per cent had their under-graduate education at the University of Toronto while another 15.7 per cent went to McGill. While almost half of those attending university obtained their degrees in one of these two places of higher learning, there are eight other universities with between three and 5.4 per cent of the elite passing through their gates at an under-graduate level, together accounting for only 34.7 per cent of those attending university. Obviously, not only attending university, but which university, makes a considerable difference for movement into the elite.

The value of university attendance extends well beyond the training gained there. It is also a breeding ground for elite connections and lasting associations. One recent case will illustrate some of the added benefits of attending one of the two top Canadian universities had for E. Leo Kolber, president of Cemp Investments and director of Distillers Corporation-Seagrams and the Toronto-Dominion Bank:

> During his law school days, Mr. Kolber on his own had six houses built in the Montreal Island municipality, the Town of Mount Royal; they are still there. His friendship with Charles Bronfman, whom he succeeded as president of Cemp, dates from their days at

McGill University about 20 years ago. The first deal he and Charles Bronfman did together was in 1953, the year after Mr. Kolber's graduation from law school, when he got capital backing from Mr. Bronfman to buy some property in the Montreal Island City of Westmount. The deal was quite profitable but would have been more so had they held the land longer than they did . In 1957, when Mr. Kolber was in his late twenties and had practiced law for a few years, the late Samuel Bronfman brought him in as a managing director of Cemp which, under several previous managers, had "not done much". Mr. Kolber says "Mr. Sam" was like a father to him (*Globe & Mail*, January 5, 1972).

Obviously not from the bottom of society when he began (being able to buy six houses in Mount Royal while still in law school!), E. Leo Kolber was able to make it into the big time because of the friendship established with Canada's elite at McGill, even being "adopted" into the family. It is not known just how often these types of lasting friendships are established during the university years but, at least attendance at the University of Toronto and McGill suggest there is ample opportunity for this to occur.

II. The Private World of Powerful People

At the upper levels of power in Canada, there is a society very different from the rest of Canadian society. At the higher circles is a society of "joiners"; a set of people who become involved at the executive level in a range of philanthropic and cultural activities ranging from the Boy Scouts to the boards of governors of Canada's major universities. From private schools to private clubs, they lead a life quite apart from, although very much affecting, the existence of the vast majority of Canadians. The "private world of powerful people" is not an anonymous group, at least for its participants. A Canadian textile executive who is also a director of several corporations is quoted as saying: "They all know each other or of each other. It's really like a small community where there are no strangers, although they might live far apart. Nowadays, that doesn't matter. They're linked together by telephone and jet" (*Executive*, 1973:33). The social circles of the upper class are not simply confined to the economic elite, although it is certainly a core institution. Through a series of elite forums and political connections, the economic elite makes decisions well beyond those confined to the dominant corporations where they gain their power. This section will examine part of this private world of powerful people.

(i) Private Schools: Preserves of the Upper Class*

Although they may be examined as educational institutions, private schools are most appropriately understood as class institutions designed to create upper class associations and maintain class values both by exclusion and socialization; that is, exclusion of the lower classes and socialization of the potential elite. Private school education is a life-long asset for the select few experiencing it. As Mills has said: "The one deep experience that distinguishes the social rich from the merely rich and those below is their schooling" (1956:63). The thousands of dollars it costs the upper class to send their children to private schools pays off many times over in the "social capital" they accummulate during those formative years. These select few are indeed the "social rich" as Mills maintains. What Porter refers to as "an item within the common experience of class" (1965: 528), is the total package of upper class training which occurs not only in private schools but through the experiences gained by living in the exclusive residential areas of Canada's metropolitan centres like Forest Hill, Westmount, or Rockcliffe Park, vacations at exclusive resorts in Canada and abroad, plus a host of other experience known to only the upper levels of the class structure.

Attending "dad's" old school is another form of inheritance preserving the continuity of the elite. The fee-paying schools of eastern Canada are institutions which stem well back into Canada's history with some, like Upper Canada College founded in 1829 and Trinity College School founded in 1865, providing common class experiences for many generations of Canada's upper class.

The pervasiveness of private school attendance is on the increase in the elite. While 34.2 per cent of the Canadian born elite attended the private schools in 1951, this increased to 39.8 per cent or 267 of the elite in 1972. Included are 49 of the 65 French-Canadians who attended classical colleges, about the same proportion as the 42 who did the same in 1951. Of those attending English-speaking private schools, elite members went almost exclusively to one of the 16 members of the Headmasters' Association and within this group, primarily to the older schools of eastern Canada[10].

The Headmasters' Association is an organization formed in 1936 modeled after the English Headmasters' Conference of about 200 "public" schools including 133 privately funded schools based on foundation money of which only nine, called the "Clarendon Schools", are most important (Sampson, 1965:202-203). The Headmasters' Association (Canadian Independent Schools), as it is formally called, helps coordinate activities between its member schools thus extending the tight school network. The private schools which are members of the association are not supported by state funds, much to the chagrin of Ned Rhodes, Jr., chairman of the board of governors of Ashbury College. Speaking recently about his school's planned expansion from its present 262 enrolment of boys from grades five to 13, to a capacity of 320 (smaller than many public schools but including four years of primary and five years of secondary students, averaging about 30 students entering and graduating each year), Rhodes said: "The fact that no recognition in any financial way is made of these schools is discrimination of the most flagrant scale" *(Ottawa Journal,* June 9, 1973). Members of the upper class seem upset that private schools, unlike most activities of the economic elite, are not subsidized by the state. Chairman Rhodes insists the state support one of the most glaring bastions of upper class privilege with public money and dares to call it "discrimination"; the only discrimination involved is the unequal treatment private schools receive compared to other activities of the elites. It appears they have come to expect the Canadian people to pay for their children's private education in addition to all the other surplus they extract. In 1938, it cost $675 per year to send a child to a private school; now the costs are well over three thousand dollars per child. This is more than the total income of a quarter of the families in Canada and the fathers of these boys can afford to send their sons to these schools and Chairman Rhodes calls it "discrimination".

Money is not the only thing needed to get into private schools —although it helps with fees ranging between $400-plus to $825 in 1938 when most of the current elite were attending these schools[11]. Mount Allison Academy advertised the following admission procedure in 1938: "Application for admission should be made to the Headmaster. Those seeking admission must present certificates of standing from their previous school and *certificates of character* from the minister of their church, and from the principal of the school last attended" (emphasis added, Stephen, 1938:53).

Classical Colleges[12] are the French-Canadian counterpart to the English-speaking private schools. These are private fee-paying institutions in Quebec, many of them residential as are their English counterparts, operated by the Catholic clergy. They used to mediate between elementary education and university attendance, lasting about eight years and costing an average of $325 per year for tuition fees for years 1-4 and $400 from 5-8 plus between $400 and $500 per year for room and board, a total cost of about $1,000 per year per son (85 per cent of those attending were male). Unlike their English equivalents, the state in Quebec supported classical colleges with an annual grant *(Encyclopedia Canadiana,* 1968:volume 3:20).

It is evident why almost two thirds of the elite members who had careers in family firms attended private schools. Providing the aspiring elite with a total environment for usually eight of the most formative years, the sons of the upper class are taught the values appropriate to their position; they have "strong characters built" and have the opportunity to build lasting friendships with other upper class boys they will later meet in the board rooms of Canada's largest corporations. As was already suggested, the pervasiveness of private school attendance within the elite has increased since 1951 but at the same time concentration into fewer of the "finer" schools has also been occurring. While 29 members of the elite in 1951 had attended Upper Canada College, by 1972 this had increased to 38 elite members. Other elite schools include the University of Toronto Schools with 28 of the present elite, Trinity College School with 21, and 10 others with between seven and 13 each. Since many of these schools were originated as extensions of the Anglican church, it is understandable that 38 per cent of the Canadian born elite members attending private schools would be Anglican, 47 per cent if French-Canadians are excluded.

Common private school attendance is only the beginning of many careers which lead along very similar career paths. For example, of five elite members who attended Appleby College at the same time, four went on to the University of Toronto, including two of them by way of the Royal Military College. Five members of the elite followed a path which leads directly from Upper Canada College (UCC) to the University of Toronto to Osgoode Hall, while an additional 12 stopped short of Osgoode and went directly into the corporate world. Three UCC alumni are on the board of Crown Life together, and two of these are also on the board of the Bank of Montreal where they met a third former UCC graduate. There are also five UCC graduates on the board of National Trust, four of whom appear to have attended their alma mater at the same time. These are not uncommon occurrences within the board rooms of dominant corporations; there are at least two former UCC students on no fewer than 18 dominant corporations, including six which have three former UCC students and others with more than three. This is not unique to UCC by any means; for example, seven present members of the elite were at Ridley College at the same time and between them hold 25 dominant directorships.

Private school connections do not end after graduation since many of the students return to sit on their board of governors, overseeing the next lot of potential elites and ensuring class continuity. Others prefer to get together at alumni meetings such as the Selwyn Old Boys Association. Still others are able to help their "old schools" out in other ways; for example, Maxwell A. Bell who was appointed by the federal government as chairman of Hockey Canada, was able to gather funds to help out his old school with the assistance of some other members of the elite, as the following account relates:

Mr. Bell joined former National Hockey League president Mervyn (Red) Dutton and Supply Minister James Richardson to help finance an Olympic-size hockey arena in Winnipeg in memory of two of Mr. Dutton's sons, killed in action in the Second World War. The arena was ostensibly built for St John's-Ravenscourt school for boys but was used by the national team as training headquarters. Mr. Bell attended St. John's before it was amalgamated with Ravenscourt (*Globe & Mail,* July 29, 1972).

St. John's-Ravenscourt, a member of the Headmasters' Association, is not simply a "school for boys" as the article suggests; it is a school for 348 sons of the upper class.

After attending private school and typically going on to the University of Toronto, or possibly McGill, the sons of the upper class are ready for the corporate board rooms. Like their fathers, they then enter another private world—the exclusive men's clubs.

(ii) Private Clubs, Bastions of the Elite

While the "country club" is a mark of status for the middle class family, it is not the same as an exclusive gentlemen's club which is just that, the preserve of the upper class male. Providing more than simply status to the upper class male, "the club" is a meeting place, a social circle, where businessmen can entertain and make deals. It serves as a badge of "social certification" but is more, in that "the club" is a place where friendships are established and old relationships nourished. A person's "contacts" are important in the corporate world because they affect the ability to have access to capital, to establish joint ventures and to enter into buyer and seller relationships with the men who control the nation's largest corporations. To participate in the club life is to be known "by those who count" and, moreover, to have their sons known. Particularly, in the six national exclusive men's clubs, there is an opportunity for the economic elite to come together socially at the national level thus transcending metropolitan and even regional class systems. These six Canadian clubs are one of the key institutions which form a interacting and active national upper class.

Three of Canada's national clubs are located in Toronto, including, appropriately enough, the National Club founded in 1874, the York Club established in 1909, and the Toronto Club whose origins are the oldest of all the national clubs, dating back to 1835. In Montreal are the Mount Royal Club founded in 1899 and the St. James' Club instituted in 1857. The sixth is the Rideau Club of Ottawa, established two years prior to Confederation by Sir John A. Macdonald; although not central to the economic elite, national because of its location and heritage. Over one half of the economic elite (51.1 per cent) belong to one or more of these six clubs with members from across Canada belonging to each of them. Between them the 396 members of the economic elite belonging to one or more of these six clubs hold 689 memberships, an average of almost two each. The total membership of these clubs is not large, averaging 578 in 1947 and 644 in 1957, the last year for which total records are available. Based on the projected growth, it is estimated that they average just over 700 members currently. In 1957, they ranged in size from 390 members, in the York Club, to a high of 1,127, in the National Club.

As an indicator of the relative importance for each of the clubs, the present elite membership can be compared with that found by Porter in 1951. This is suggestive of the relative importance each center has for the current economic elite as a social meeting ground. The St. James' Club has had a stable number of elite members over the past twenty years with 146 in 1951 and 133 in 1972, and the total membership has remained unchanged with members of the economic elite accounting for about 18 per cent of the total membership. The Mount Royal has also been consistent in the number of economic elite members with 150 in 1951 and 148 in 1972, but its total membership has increased over the same period bringing the elite proportion from 34.5 per cent in the earlier period to about 27 per cent now. In Toronto, the situation is somewhat different. The Toronto Club has had an increase from 105 to 152 elite members over the twenty years while its membership has remained stable and the elite proportion increased from about 30 to 35 per cent. A similar increase has occurred at the York Club, with an increase from 92 to 101 and a steady membership with the economic elite accounting for 31 per cent in 1951 and 34 per cent in 1972. The National Club, with the largest membership of all, has fallen off somewhat from 115 to 105 while the total membership has increased, substantially reducing the proportion of elites from 13 per cent to about eight per cent. The movement of the National Club away from the general trend of more elite participation in the Toronto-based clubs may be due to a "dilution" factor of too many outsiders. The most significant change occurs in the Rideau Club. Porter mentioned that the Rideau Club, with 81 members of the economic elite, was located "off the path of industry and commerce" (1965:305). While the total membership in the Rideau Club has been growing substantially over the years, it now has only 50 members from the economic elite, less than half that of the other national clubs and 31 less than in 1951. This would suggest that the Rideau, or more significantly the federal government, may have declined as a key social domain for the economic elite.

There are other clubs with substantial numbers of elite members but they are not as important to the national upper class. For example, the Granite Club has 82 members from the elite but over 6,000 total membership. Several other clubs are more regional in scope, each having between 20 and 50 elite members. These number 21 with some like the St. Denis of Montreal having 27 members who are from the French-Canadian economic elite (41 per cent of all French-Canadians) being quite specialized. Others like the Halifax Club, the Hamilton Club, the London Club, Calgary Petroleum, the Ranchmen's Club or the Vancouver Club are more closely meshed with the local rather than the national upper class, although leading members of the local upper class also tend to participate at the national level as well.

As in most activities they engage in, members of the economic elite tend to congregate in the decision making levels of the clubs with many having held directorships and executive positions in the clubs over the years. In one recent example, members of the economic elite hold five of the 13 directorships in the National Club (*Financial Post,* June 30, 1973).

Another interesting aspect of club life is the international circuit. With much of their business outside Canada, it is important for the economic elite to maintain social contact with the elite of other countries. In the economic elite, 109 current members have club memberships outside Canada, several in more than one country. These include 88 with club memberships in the U.S., 18 in the U.K., and 20 elsewhere. Most popular, appropriately enough, is the Canadian Club of New York with 31 members of the elite while others like the Links of New York and Rolling Rock of Pennsylvania with seven each, are also important.

As with private schools, the private clubs are kept exclusive by regulating memberships and high initial membership fees and annual dues. These costs can be set aside, however, by free memberships in one of the exclusive clubs as part of the compensation attached to corporate positions[13].

Social Class as Exclusion and Inclusion

Recapping the analysis, the economic elite was initially defined as a set of positions which sit atop dominant corporations in Canada. The question of the degree and type of interaction existing between the men who filled these positions was then posed. It was shown that this set of men are similar social types by examining their origins on a number of variables such as class, ethnicity, and education. The preceding analysis has now shown that they are not only of similar social origins and types, but collectively, they are an interacting social entity; they operate at the national level within the context of class institutions established inside and outside the corporate world.

It becomes increasingly evident that the men who fill elite positions are predominantly from the upper class originally, or have become accepted into the upper class in terms of life style and social circles. The process by which the upper class is able to maintain itself may be understood as one of co-optation and selection. As Porter has argued: "Class continuity does not mean that there is no mobility. Rather it means there is sufficient continuity to maintain class institutions" (1965:285n). As long as the upper class is able to keep its social class institutions such as private schools and clubs intact, it will be able to maintain its monopoly of power by selecting those members of the middle class, and occasionally lower class, deemed acceptable and excluding those who are not. This means accepting the life-style, attitudes and values of the upper class. As guardians of the institutions of power and the avenues of access, they are able to dictate that the system should operate as they see fit; that is, a system of exclusion and monopoly for their own privileges and prerogatives of power.

With clearly defined avenues of mobility into the elite, it is possible to regulate key gate-keeper institutions in such a way that class continuity will remain unchallenged. As Mills has argued, nowhere is class consciousness so evident as within the elite. "For by class consciousness, as a psychological fact, one means that the individual member of a 'class' accepts only those accepted by his circle as among those who are significant to his own image of self" (1956:283). The economic elite in Canada is that section of the upper class which operates the major institutions of the economy on behalf of, and in the interest of, the upper class. As will now be seen, they operate more than just the economy.

(iii) Philanthropic and Trade Associations

Members of the economic elite engage in activities which extend well "beyond the board room", as Porter would say, into a variety of other positions in society. Some, such as the honourific roles to be discussed in this section, are merely prestige appointments which provide status and legitimacy to the office holders and the institutions they are associated with; others, such as the trade associations also included here, are more directly related to the corporate world and serve to coordinate activites within that realm. Later, members of the elite will be examined to understand how elite forums and associations with the state serve to cut across functionally defined spheres of power.

Philanthropy and Prestige

It should be clear that as used here, the term elite has as its referent positions of power within key decision making institutions, and not to an "elite of prestige"; this is not the same as saying the elite is without prestige. Bierstedt makes the point that power and prestige are separate variables but "prestige is frequently unaccompanied by power and when the two occur together, power is usually the basis and ground of prestige rather than the reverse. Prestige would seem to be a consequence of power rather than a determinant of it or a necessary component of it" (1950:731). Prestige, then, is a luxury item among the package of upper class privileges and not central to the maintenance of class institutions or elite power. Status, however, is valued and serves the elite in several ways by providing legitimacy and operates as a motivational device for many aspiring to elite positions. It can also serve to widen the social circle of elite members and provide an avenue of access for some into the elite.

As Aileen D. Ross has found in a study of philanthropy in Canada, philanthropic activity "not only facilitates business careers in ways well recognized by the fraternity of successful buisnessmen, but also enters as a substantial ingredient in the public relations programs of modern corporations" (1968:284). She goes on to argue that philanthropic activities open avenues into "other positions of importance in the community". This is reflected in her finding that mobility within the philanthropic world parallels that in the corporate world since it represents coming closer to the inner social circles thus providing "contact with men who are influential in business" (285).

University and Hospital Boards

Among the most notable of philanthropic activities which make up the honourific roles of the elite are the boards of governors or guiding bodies of universities, private schools and other institutions of learning plus similar positions in the hospitals of major metropolitan centers. Porter noted that 80 elite members held governing positons in the major 15 universities in 1951. In 1972 this remains an important acitivity with 240 elite members (31 per cent) holding, at some point, a governing position in one of the private schools, universities or other institution of higher learning. Hospital boards are also important in this respect with over one quarter of the elite holding an equivalent position in one of the major hospitals. The overlap of 13 per cent who hold positions on both, indicates that this is indeed a tight social circle. A host of other positions at the executive level are also held by members of the economic elite: including a variety of societies, exhibitions, Air Cadets, the Salvation Army, art galleries, United Appeals, Boy Scouts, operas, foundations, the Red Cross and a multitude of others.

A recent development has been the establishment of advisory groups for the faculties of business administration at leading Canadian schools of business, such as those at the University of Western Ontario and the University of Toronto. Following is a recent announcement for one of these boards:

> University of Toronto's new Faculty of Management Studies this week announced formation of a Management Advisory Council drawn from leading business, professional, government and labor people. Chairman of the council will be W.O. Twaits, chairman and chief executive officer, Imperial Oil Ltd. The council was formed to ensure effective liason between the faculty (formerly the School of Business) and the community it serves (*Financial Post*, October 28, 1972).

Evidently, the "community it serves" is defined in quite narrow terms. As well as the chairman, 18 members of the advisory board are members of the economic elite including 13 who hold multiple directorships. The remaining 22 members come from academic circles, smaller corporations, top bureaucrats and only two from unions. This is similar to the advisory committee of the School of Business at the University of Western Ontario where 22 members of the elite, including 13 with multiple directorships, sit on the 39-position board. These represent direct extensions of the economic elite into positions of importance in major gate-keeping institutions, maintaining the tradition established in the boards of governors of the key Canadian universities. For example, the University of Toronto, most important of all Canadian elite universities, has 13 members of the economic elite on its 21-member board;† eight of the 13 are multiple directorship holders. Some elite members are more active than others in this respect; for example, John J. Jodrey, a member of the economic elite as was his father, sits on the board of governors of Acadia University, Dalhousie University and King's College School, a member of the Headmasters' Association.

It is not only boards within academia which provide meeting places for members of the elite. For example, in a recent seminar held by the School of Business Administration of the University of Western Ontario, the proceedings of which appear in a collection edited by W.J. McDougall entitled *The Effective Director,* there were a total of 54 participants from academic, political and corporate spheres. Of the 54, 20 were members of the economic elite, 15 holding more than one dominant directorship. Universities not only provide a meeting ground for potential elites during their school days, but continue to act in this capacity even after they have actually entered the elite—providing meeting places on their boards and establishing elite forums where elite members can work out their common concerns.

Foundations

Unlike studies of the upper class in the United States (Domhoff, 1967; 1970), very little is known about foundations in Canada and a great deal more research is needed in this area. While this still remains uncharted ground, some insights are provided in a recent article by Allan Arlett, "Our foundations now easier to find". In this article, he tells who has established some of Canada's larger foundations, maintaining that some are large even within the world context.

> Founded in 1937 and headquartered in Montreal, McConnell ranks amongst the 25 largest in the world. A listing of Canada's largest foundations would include the following: J.W. McConnell, Garfield Weston, Eldee, R.S. McLaughlin, Donner, J.P. Bickell, Vancouver, Atkinson, Physicians & Surgeons, Beaverbrook, Molson, Sir James Dunn, Laidlaw, Richard Ivey, Levesque and Winnipeg. Between them they hold over $700 million in assets. The McConnell and Garfield Weston foundations alone account for about $300 million in assets. Foundations have been established by a number of different methods, but the majority were founded by individuals or families. Those endowing Canada's larger foundations developed their wealth in a variety of ways. Newspapers played an important part in the fortunes of McConnell, Atkinson and Beaverbrook; industrial investments for Garfield Weston, automobiles for McLaughlin, steel for Donner and Dunn; breweries for Molson; lumber for Laidlaw, law and investments for the Ivey's and mining and investments for Bickell (*Financial Post*, June 9, 1973).

At another point in the article Arlett discusses the Bronfman family's foundation as well as those of the Eaton's, Birk's, Zeller's, and other upper class family foundations; prominent among those who have endowed these foundations are the names of current and earlier elites. The ability to develop and fund a foundation is limited to only a few of the wealthiest families, even within the elite. Through foundations, elites are able to determine what type of grants and to whom they should go. Through these legal devices, they can keep family fortunes intact over generations thus having a social impact well after they are dead. It may well be that foundation life in Canada is as central to its upper class as that of the United States but without additional work in this area, no conclusive answer is available.

Trade Associations

More directly related to the organization of corporate power than are philanthropic and foundation activities are the trade associations. Some are professional associations like the 748-member Canadian Institute of Actuaries, with members mainly in the insurance field but also in pension plans and working with government social security schemes. As in most of these associations, the executive is composed of members of the economic elite. For example, Robert C. Dowsett, president of Crown Life has just succeeded John C. Maynard of Canada Life in the position of president of the Canadian Institute of Actuaries (*Financial Post*, May 26, 1973).

Chambers of Commerce are other associations in which elites are active, generally following the pattern of movement from the local to provincial to national and even the international level, as they proceed in their careers. Boards of Trade are also popular, many of them having existed for some time, such as the Ottawa Board of Trade founded in 1857, or the Montreal Board of Trade, recently celebrating its 150th anniversary with the appointment of Kenneth A. White, president of Royal Trust, as its new president (*Globe & Mail*, May 6, 1972). Even trade associations establish joint ventures; for example, the Canadian Tax Foundation is sponsored jointly by the Canadian Bar Association and the Canadian Institute of Chartered Accountants and is sponsored by over 700 corporations (*Financial Post*, April 1, 1972).

Another organization of importance is the Canadian Bankers' Association, founded in 1900. It brings chartered banks together to deal with common problems related to banking operations and the government. The association has a full-time staff of 30 employees and an executive director. Galbraith says that it provides:

> a useful channel of communication with the government, for suggestions on regulations or other matters that the government may wish the banks to cooperate on or carry out. Indeed, the executive council of the Association at its regular quarterly meetings always arranges to meet with the Governor of the central bank—the Bank of Canada—and senior officials of the Department of Finance for a mutual exchange of ideas and views (1970:35).

This association is but one of the direct channels the economic elite has open to the federal government. For example, in a summary of the witnesses appearing before the standing committee on Trade, Finance and Economic Affairs, it is reported that 32 per cent of the witnesses are representatives of individual companies, including Alcan, Bell Canada, Imperial Oil, INCO, Shell Canada and Stelco, among others, as well as an additional 35 percent of the witnesses who represent industrial, commercial and financial associations (Lewis, 1972:101). All of these, whether through trade associations or directly by representatives of dominant corporations, are channels which serve to bring the state and economic elite together at the top of the decision making posts of each sphere. This issue will now be examined.

III. Relations Between Elites

One of the most crucial issues in the study of social class and elites is the relationship between various key bases of power. In liberal-democracies these include the economic world, the state, the mass media and, in some cases, labour unions. In the next three chapters, the mass media and its relationship with the economic elite will be examined in detail. The relationship between labour unions and the economic elite will not be dealt with here. In this section, and to some extent in the concluding chapter, the relationship between the economic and state elites will be examined. As in any relationship there are, of course, two sides. In this book only the perspective of the economic elite will be undertaken; that is, the movement of members from the state elite into the economic elite and positions held by the economic elite in the state system. A detailed analysis would require a similar examination from the perspective of the state elite and an evaluation of the role of state fiscal policy on the operation of the economy[14]. In this section elite forums created and frequented by members of the state and economic elites will be examined, as will the political affiliations and relationships of members of the economic elite. Finally, a brief case study of one of the most interesting corporations in Canada, Power Corporation, and its relationship with the state will be provided.

(i) Elite Forums

Sprinkled throughout the institutional structures of Canadian society are a collage of organizations which may be referred to as elite forums. These meeting places of elites from the corporate, state and other key institutional spheres are open to and created by men of power. They are not public forums but forums for Canada's elites. In them policies are formulated and opinions made known to other men of power. Within their closed confines differences can be resolved and compromises made. It is within these varied associations of elites that the corporate world dominates. They are avenues of contact and channels of communication between diverse sections of the elite. Although their stated purposes are varied and their organizations, at times, quite dissimilar, they have one thing in common; they are all dominated by the economic elite.

Canadian Executive Service Overseas (CESO), founded in 1967, provides volunteer businessmen to foreign countries. Funded by the Canadian International Development Agency, CESO pays the travel costs of executives and their wives to other countries which in turn pay expenses during their stay. According to the annual report: "Canada wins new friends and international respect as more and more CESO volunteers work in overseas nations" (CESO Annual Report, 1971-2:3). More than "winning new friends" and "respect", Canadian corporations gain new sources of materials and customers for Canadian goods. They also do their part in spreading capitalism to newly emerging nations. Of the 105 members of the board of directors of CESO, there are a total of 71 members of the economic elite —including both the chairman, Fraser W. Bruce of Alcan Aluminum, and the vice-chairman, Paul G. Desmarais of Power Corporation. Of these 71 directors, 36 hold more than one directorship in dominant corporations.

The *Canadian-American Committee* is an association of Canadian and U.S. elites and labour union leaders. In light of the continental economy which each shares, associations of this type are required as forums between the two elites and as pipelines into their respective state elites. As Dr. Wallace Sterling, a member of the U.S. component of the committee and former president of Stanford University has said: "I think it is fair to say that the members have not been without rather acute influence on their respective governments" (*Globe & Mail,* August 13, 1971). Some of the Canadian members of the committee include J.L. Walker, president of the Bank of Montreal; T.N. Beaupre, chairman of Domtar; John Clyne, chairman of MacMillan Bloedel; Paul Desmarais, chairman of Power Corporation; Paul Leman, president of Alcan; W.O. Twaits, chairman of Imperial Oil and Adam Zimmerman, vice-president of Noranada Mines. Each of the corporations these men represent have extensive interests in the U.S. either because they are U.S. controlled, have operations there, or sell substantial parts of their products in the U.S. One half of the Canadian-American Committee are from the economic elite and one half of these are individuals who hold more than one dominant directorship. They include among them, as the above list suggests, the most powerful businessmen in Canada.

The *Ontario Research Foundation* was formed in 1928 by the then Premier, G. Howard Ferguson, with $1-1/2 million from industry and $1-1/2 million from the Ontario government, in response to the post-war need for research facilities.

In addition to carrying on research from its endowment, the foundation also conducts research for industry, operating as a type of cooperative at the elite level by providing expertise in highly technical fields. The board of 22 has 13 members of the economic elite[15], including the chairman and two vice-chairmen. Of the 13 there are seven with multiple directorships.

Other forums of importance would include the 18-year old *Conference Board in Canada*, a branch of the U.S. based Conference Board, headed by Arthur J.R. Smith as president; he is the former chairman of the Economic Council of Canada and currently a director of IBM Canada. The *Canada Committee*, founded in 1964, defines its purpose as a "One United Canada" and has a number of prominent French and English members of the elite on its board of governors, including R.C. Scrivener, president of Bell Canada, director of Power Corporation and the Imperial Bank of Commerce; Arthur Deane Nesbitt, chairman of Nesbitt, Thomson and Co. as well as director of Power Corporation, TransCanada PipeLines, Manufacturers Life and Consolidated Bathurst; and Louis Hebert, chairman and president of the Banque Canadienne Nationale and director of Sun Life and Noranda Mines. Another elite forum is the 41-member *Advisory Council to Industry, Trade and Commerce*, a body which has been established for four years to "Examine and keep under review the policies, programs, and services of the department, advise on the adequacy and recommend improvements or new activities" (*Ottawa Journal*, April 21, 1973). The corresponding body in Quebec is the *Conseil de l'Industrie*, a 58-member board of leading members of the economic elite active in Quebec, including six members of Power Corporation's board of directors. Another forum includes the *Canadian Association for Latin America* made up of the 60 largest Canadian-based corporations and designed to increase trade relations with Latin America. These are just some of the scores of boards and associations which have been created over the years to coordinate elite activities.

Other types of ad hoc elite associations include a recent "mission" of Canada's economic elite to meet with the U.S. state elite. In February of 1973 a contingent of 80 "top Canadian business executives" went on a "remarkable mission" to Washington to meet for two days with top ranking U.S. politicians and bureaucrats. Of the 80, 35 were executives from Canada's dominant corporations and of these, 18 were holders of more than one dominant directorship (see *Financial Post*, February 24, 1973). Another recent "workshop" involving the economic elite also occurred but little is known about the proceedings because it was private, in spite of the fact that it was sponsored in part by the federal government:

Herman Kahn and his Hudson Institute set up shop here Sunday for a three-day conference that will see some impressive brain-power focused on "The Corporate Environment, 1975-1985". But the participants will be keeping most of their superthoughts to themselves. The conference is the 11th to be held as part of the institute's three-year corporate environment study sponsored by about 60 corporations. Since two federal government departments and 10 Canadian corporations are among the sponsors much of the three-day meeting will focus on Canadian problems. The meetings are closed and "off the record", the institute says. Canadian participants include Bell Canada, Hydro-Quebec, MacMillan Bloedel, Power Corp., John Labatt Ltd. and Royal Bank of Canada. The federal government departments are Industry, Trade and Commerce and the Ministry of State for Science and Technology (*Ottawa Journal,* March 5, 1973).

Another elite forum recently established by the federal government with an initial grant of almost $1 million with promises to match an expected $10 million endowment over the next seven years is the *Institute for Public Policy Research,* "Canada's first independent think tank". Designed to produce long term research into Canadian "social problems", the institute "will not depend on governments for annual votes to support its operations and will not be subject to the political hazards and time pressures of internal govenment research"; it will rather be accountable, according to R. S. Ritchie, head of the institute, *"to a board of directors who will be self-replacing as are the boards of most voluntary institutions in our society"*. In this case, the board of directors includes J.V. Clyne, chairman of MacMillan Bloedel Ltd. and director of Canadian Pacific Ltd.; John Robarts, former premier of Ontario and presently director of Power Corporation, Metropolitan Life, Canadian Imperial Bank of Commerce, Bell Canada and Abitibi Paper; Mrs. Jeanne Sauve, now a federal cabinet minister and wife of Maurice Sauve, a former federal cabinet minister and now vice-president of Consolidated-Bathurst and director of BP Canada Ltd.; and Ronald Ritchie, vice-president of Imperial Oil and the "driving force behind the institute". Ritchie is no stranger to government circles, being an executive director of the influential Royal Commission of Government Organization (the Glassco Commission), serving on the Wartime Prices and Trade Board and a director of Imperial Oil since 1963 (emphasis added, *Globe & Mail,* February 15, 1972; March 8, 1972).

Ritchie's remark that the board of directors of his institute would be "self-replacing as are the boards of most voluntary institutions" is important since it illustrates how elite control of these forums is maintained over time. Unlike corporations where stock ownership can change hands and the entire board of directors replaced by the new controlling interest, once these forums are established they become self-perpetuating institutions of elite power and privilege accountable to no one, not even the state. By loading the board with solid elite members from the beginning, and giving it self-selecting power, insures that the board will remain an elite institution, barring very bad judgment or poor certification procedures for future elites.

(ii) Political Relationships and Affiliations of the Economic Elite

Political relationships of the economic elite have been alluded to at various points throughout but in this section a specific analysis of party affiliation, elite switchers from the political to the corporate world, corporate relationships with government and, finally, a case study of Power Corporation's relationship with the state will be presented.

Political Party

In 1951 Porter was able to determine the political affiliation of 203 members of the economic elite. He found a distribution of 85 Conservatives and 86 Liberals among the Canadian born; when the foreign born were included, there were 92 Liberals and 106 Conservatives. In the present study political affiliation could be determined for only 159 members of the elite with a distribution of 76 Liberals and 70 Conservatives among the Canadian born and 80 Liberals and 77 Conservatives when the foreign born are included. An additional four declared themselves to be independent while there were two Social Credits, both from the political elite (E.C. Manning of Alberta and R.W. Bonner of B.C.). Although there are a few more Liberals proportionately among the present elite than in 1951, the low coverage does not warrant drawing confident conclusions based on the data. The only finding which is of significance is the fact that in 1951 Porter found biographical sources reporting political affiliations for 26.7 per cent of the elite, while in 1972 this is reported for only 20.8 per cent. Since the elites of each period had the same opportunity, this would indicate that declaring affiliation is of less importance to the economic elite now than it was twenty years ago. When the few for whom party affiliation is available are analysed in terms of the indigenous/comprador dichotomy, a slight difference occurs with more Liberals as U.S. comprador elites but again the findings should not be pushed too far because of the low coverage.

Elite Switchers

Porter noted that "37 Liberals and 19 Conservatives had been politicians at some stage of their career", going on to note that there were 17 Liberal senators included in this group (1965:298). In 1972 there were only 19 Liberal who had been politicians, 10 Conservatives and two Social Credits. This includes 17 who were members of the political elite and 13 Senators (11 Liberals, one Conservative and one Social Credit). Another two senators did not declare any affiliation[16].

While the number holding political office was 56 in 1951, this had dropped to 33 by 1972, a fairly substantial movement away from the total who had held political office. However, it should be recalled that earlier it was argued that in 1951 only 14 people had their main careers in other elites (including the political, bureaucratic and military) while in 1972 it was found that 17 had their main careers in the political elite[17] with another 18 in the bureaucratic elite, more than double the numbers from 1951. A closer examination is required to reconcile this finding with the fact that more members of the economic elite held political office in 1951 than in 1972. Only a small part of the difference is accounted for by the fact that there were 17 Senators in 1951 and 15 in 1972. The difference becomes evident when those holding elite offices are compared. While only 14 members of the economic elite in 1951 had their main careers in either the political, bureaucratic or military elite, there were 56 politicians, 39 if the senators were excluded. In other words, more members of the economic elite entered the political world at non-elite levels during the earlier period while in 1972 only a few members of the economic elite moved into the political world[18], with most of the movement being from the state elite to the corporate world. Only three Conservatives and none of the Liberals from the 1972 economic elite held political offices which were not either elite positions or in the Senate. This illustrates that there is less exchange at the lower levels of the electoral political life but much greater switching at the top from the political to the corporate world than earlier.

A similar phenomenon has occurred with the bureaucratic elite; while there are now 18 members of the present economic elite who had their main careers in the bureaucratic elite[19] and another two who held elite positions within the bureaucracy; in 1951, only "in one or two cases persons . . . made the big jump in their careers after serving in the federal bureaucracy, particularly during the war" (Porter, 1965:281). In addition to the 20 members of the present elite who were clearly in the bureaucratic elite, there are 35 who held key, but probably not elite, positions during the war in the federal bureaucracy. Including all present members of the economic elite, it is found that 49 served in the war on either the Wartime Industries Control Board, the Wartime

Prices and Trade Board or one of the agencies under the command of these two[20] and followed their minister, C. D. Howe, into the corporate board rooms following the war. All 49 were born before 1920, putting them in an age bracket which typically has fewer upper class members than the elite as a whole. When the class origins of this group are examined separately, it is found that a similar proportion were born into the upper class (53 per cent) compared to the Canadian born economic elite (59 per cent). The difference is that only one half of the proportion of those from the bureaucracy during the war had fathers in the economic elite (14.3 per cent compared to 28.5 per cent) while more had fathers who were in other elites or married into elite families (22.4 per cent compared to 8.2 per cent). This would indicate that upper class members who were not sons of members of the economic elite tended to be recruited into the federal bureaucracy. Typically, sons of the economic elite were engaged in working for family firms during this time while other upper class sons without this avenue readily open to them were ''eligible'' to be recruited into the bureaucracy. One example of this would be Henry Borden who was mentioned earlier in connection with his Prime Minister uncle:

> When war broke out in 1939, Henry Borden offered his services to the Canadian government. Among the positions he occupied over the next six years are general counsel for the Department of Munitions and Supply, Co-ordinator of Controls for the Department of Munitions and Supply and chairman of the Wartime Industries Control Board. . . . Borden came to Brazilian Traction in 1946 as president, a position he held for the next 17 years. He was chairman of the board for a further two years, and is still a director and member of the executive committee (*Last Post*, 1973:39).

Crown corporations frequently recruit members of the economic elite to their board rooms with a total of 52 members of the economic elite having this type of relationship with the state[21]. Included here are 42 members of the elite not accounted for above as being in the political or bureaucratic elite, in the Senate or in the bureaucracy during the war. Royal Commissions are another way members of the economic elite are recruited to state service with a total of 24 members of the current economic elite having been on at least one Royal Commission, some on as many as three. Of the 24, there are 14 who are not included above. There are also a series of govenment boards and commissions to which the economic elite belongs including among them the National Research Council, the Atlantic Provinces Research Council, a series of harbour commissions and port authorities, National Advisory Commissions on Petroleum or Mining, the Government Export Advisory Commission and a number of other similar bodies. Altogether, 78 members of the economic elite sit on these boards or commissions, including 62 not included above.

Another group of the economic elite are not themsleves involved with the state but have close kin who are; for example, 32 have kin in the political elite, 20 have kin in the Senate, eight with kin in the bureaucratic elite, 18 with kin in the House of Commons or Provincial Legislature and another five with kin known to be on government boards or who are Lieutenant Governors. Altogether this represents 95 members of the elite with kin in state positions. Of these 95, there are 56 not included in any of the above categories. When these relationships are viewed cumulatively, it is found that 2.5 per cent of the economic elite were once in the political elite; adding the Senate, this increases to 4.9 per cent; two Lieutenant Governors bring the cumulative total to 5.2 per cent and 20 from the bureaucratic elite increases the total to 8.2 per cent; bureaucratic war service to 13.4 per cent; crown corporations to 19.6 per cent; Royal Commissions to 21.8 per cent; other government boards or commissions to 31.1 per cent and close relatives holding one of the above positions brings the total proportion of the elite with some present or previous contact with the political world to 39.4 per cent.

Although the evidence does not indicate that the state elite, and the economic elite, overlap extensively at one point in time, when elite-switchers and other relationships between the state and the corporate world are included there is ample evidence to support the position that they operate within a very similar set of social circles. The economic elite interacts extensively on the level of boards and commissions as well as having close kin in or close to the state elite. A few examples will illustrate the importance of state connections through kinship links for the economic elite. Among these include: the Hon. Maurice Sauve (vice-president of Consolidated-Bathurst and director of IBM Canada), former federal minister, whose wife Jeanne is now Minister of Science; the Hon. Louis-P. Gelinas (director of John Labatt's, Canada Cement Lafarge and Distillers Corporation-Seagrams) who married Juliette Taschereau, daughter of the Hon. L.A. Taschereau, one-time Minister of Public Works; the Hon. Eric Cook (vice-president and director of Crown Zellerbach) whose father, the Hon. Sir Tasker Cook, was Prime Minister of Newfoundland; the Hon. Richard Stanbury, Senator, (director of Beneficial Finance Co.) whose brother, the Hon. Robert Stanbury is Minister of Communications; Hon. James Sinclair, former federal cabinet minister (deputy chairman of Canada Cement Lafarge, director of the Bank of Montreal, Sun Life, Canadian Industries, and Alcan) whose daughter Margaret married Prime Minister P.E.

Trudeau; the Hon. Jacques Flynn, Senator (director of Canada Cement Lafarge) whose grandfather was Premier of Quebec; Claude Pratte (director of Canadian Pacific and the Royal Bank) who married Frances, daughter of the Hon. Ouesime Gagnon, minister in the Bennett cabinet; Col. Maxwell Meighen (vice-president of Argus Corp. and Huron & Erie Mortgage and director of Dominion Stores, Algoma Steel, Domtar, Massey-Ferguson and Canadian General Electric), son of the Rt. Hon. Arthur Meighen, former Prime Minister; Renault St-Laurent (director of the CNR, IAC Ltd. and Rothmans of Pall Mall), son of the Rt. Hon. Louis St-Laurent, former Prime Minister; Richard Gavin Reid (vice-president of Imperial Oil), son of the Premier of Alberta with the same name; George Taylor Richardson (president of James Richardson and Sons, governor of Hudson's Bay Co., director of Canadian Imperial Bank of Commerce and INCO.), brother of the Hon James Richardson, Minister of National Defence; Arthur Simard (chairman of Marine Industries and director of Power Corporation), father-in-law to Robert Bourassa, Premier of Quebec; D. D. Lougheed (vice-president and general manager of Imperial Oil), brother of Peter Lougheed, Premier of Alberta. These examples illustrate that kinship links between the corporate and political world are important beyond the direct exchange of personnel between the two domains.

Patronage may or may not be involved in political or bureaucratic transfers and relationships between the corporate world[22]. What is more important sociologically, is to recognize that patronage is a subset of social networks between elites; that is, contacts based on positions of importance in any of the elites involves exchange of information, influence and personnel. The fact that "ex-Premiers' conferences" are held in the board rooms of some dominant corporations (for example, the Hon. Duff Roblin and the Hon. Jean Lesage are both on the board of Montreal Trust while the Hon. John Robarts and the Hon. E.C. Manning meet on the board of the Canadian Imperial Bank of Commerce) attests to the fact that these men have connections valued in the economic elite. It need not indicate that they have given special privileges to these corporations beyond the enormous privileges they gave to other corporations while in office. It does illustrate the general unity between these two institutional spheres.

(iii) Political Power and Power Corporation

Power Corporation is probably the most powerful corporate complex in Canada. The conglomerate is organized as a holding company with controlling interest of 36.5 per cent in Consolidated-Bathurst, a giant pulp and paper company; 52.2 per cent interest in Campeau Corporation, a dominant real estate company; 99.6 per cent of Canada Steamship Lines which, besides owning a fleet of freight vessels, also operates grain elevators and ship building yards; 56.7 per cent of Dominion Glass, which operate glass and plastic container plants and has interests in Alberta gas well properties; 53.3 per cent of Laurentide Financial Corporation, a dominant finance and loan company; 51.2 per cent of Imperial Life, a dominant insurance company; 50.2 per cent of Investors Group, "the biggest mutual-fund organization in Canada", which in turn holds 50.1 per cent of Great-West Life, another dominant insurance company, and in 1973, acquired 51 per cent of Montreal Trust Company, also dominant in its field. Besides the two interlocking directorships Power Corporation has with each of the Royal Bank and the Canadian Imperial Bank of Commerce, it has, according to Paul Desmarais, its chairman and chief executive officer, strong relations with the Bank of America which have "introduced a new dimension to the financial group" (*Globe & Mail*, May 31, 1972).

The Power Corporation conglomerate has strong ties with the federal and Quebec Liberal parties which has prompted some questioning recently about the $10 million in federal grants received by the company between 1968 and 1972 (*Ottawa Journal*, May 19, 1973). Some of these connections include the Hon. Maurice Sauve, former Liberal cabinet minister and now vice-president of administration in Consolidated-Bathurst; Paul E. Martin, son of Paul Martin who is now Liberal leader in the Senate, who is a vice-president of Consolidated-Bathurst, vice-president of Power, chairman of the executive committee and director of Dominion Glass and director of Canada Steamship Lines, Davie Shipbuilding and St. Maurice Capital Corporation; Claude C. Frennette, former president of the Quebec wing of the federal Liberal party and now a vice-president of Power; Tony Hampson, a former Power director and now chairman of the government's newly instituted Canada Development Corporation; Jean-Luc Pepin, Minister of Industry, Trade and Commerce from 1968 to 1972 and defeated in a recent election, is now a director of Power; Maurice Strong a former president of Power, is now Undersecretary-General of the United Nations and a close friend of Anthony Hampson; Louis Desmarais, brother of Paul Desmarais, who is chairman of Power Corp., is himself a director of Power and president and chief executive officer of Canada Steamship Lines as well as being recently appointed to the deputy chairmanship of Canada Development Corporation; Alfredo F.M. Campo is chairman and chief executive officer of Petrofina Canada and a director of Power, a member of the General Council of Industry (Quebec) and a member of the National Advisory Committee on Petroleum (federal); J. Claude Hebert, a director of Power and member of the National Productivity Council (federal); Jean-Paul Gignac, brother of Jacques G. Gignac, the Libyan Ambassador since 1970 and Chief of Cultural Affairs in Ottawa 1967-1970, was himself commissioner of Hydro-Quebec from 1961 to 1969 and is now president of Sidbec (Quebec Crown Corporation) and a director of Power; Arthur Simard, chairman of Marine Industries as was his father Joseph before him, is father-in-law to Premier Robert Bourassa of Quebec, and a director of Power. Based on this evidence, some would conclude that Power Corporation supports the Liberal party. This would not be correct. Power Corporation is attracted to power. Only because the Liberal party has held political power during recent years in Quebec and Ottawa is there such a high inter-change between Power Corporation and the Liberals. Evidence that Power Corporation is attracted to power and not the Liberal party is the fact that the Hon. John P. Robarts, Conservative Premier of Ontario from 1961 to 1971 also sits on the board of Power Corporation in addition to the boards of Abitibi Paper, Bell Canada, Canadian Imperial Bank of Commerce, and Metropolitan Life. Power transcends political affiliation.

This chapter has explored a number of social background characteristics of the economic elite and the private world of powerful people. For instance, regionalism was examined and it was found that those born in the West and East are under-represented in the elite compared to the Center in terms of their population base. The West, however, has provided greater mobility to the middle class then either the Center or the East. This provided further evidence that as Canadian society matures, its class structure becomes more rigid and access to the elite further confined to those with upper class origins.

As in 1951, French-Canadians were very much under-represented in the economic elite while members of other non-Anglo groups were virtually excluded. Porter's position that Canada is *The Vertical Mosaic*, continues to stand as the most apt characterization of ethnic stratification from the perspective of the economic elite. An examination of the education of elite members illustrated that the proportion of the economic elite attending university or other post-secondary institutions had increased to 85 per cent of the elite while about three fifths of the elite had the same advantage in 1951. The University of Toronto and McGill continue to be the key universities in Canada for educating the elite with Harvard becoming important on the post-graduate level.

In an examination of the ''private world of powerful people'', it was found that private schools and private clubs are of continuing importance as class institutions in the social life of elites, as are the activities associated with trade associations and philanthropic activities. Through elite forums the power of the economic elite becomes extended into other important spheres of social life. This becomes particularly evident when political relationships of the economic elite are examined. It was illustrated that while party affiliation is of declining importance, ''elite switching'', membership on key state-created elite forums and kinship relations between elites illustrates that the political, bureaucratic and economic elite generally move in the same social circles in Canada. While it was not possible to determine the precise overlap between the state and the economic elites at this time, this can now be done for the economic and media elite. Before doing so, it will be important to develop some theoretical concerns related to the mass media and its power base as well as concentration within media complexes. When this is done, a study paralleling this and the previous chapter on inequality of access for the economic elite will be presented for the media elite.

Notes

[1]This argument assumes that there are regional class structures as well as a national class structure within which potential elites compete for access.

[2]Parts of the following analysis also appear in a report submitted to the Secretary of State by Clement and Olsen, entitled ''The Ethnic Composition of Canada's Elites, 1951 to 1973'' (May, 1974). The historical perspective is a summary from Chapter Two.

[3]There is, of course, an issue as to the ''degrees of Frenchness'' actually apparent in the 65 members of the elite defined here as French. The criteria used to decide whether a person was to be categorized as French include: (i) membership in French-speaking clubs, (ii) association with known French social service or philanthropic organizations, (iii) ethnic origin of the father, (iv) mother and (v) wife, if their name appeared in (vi) *Biographies Canadiennes Francaises*, (vii) if educated in French-speaking institutions, particularly the classical colleges and French-speaking universities, (vii) if Catholic in religion, (ix) birth in Quebec or known settlements of French in the rest of Canada and (x) an historically French name. These ten criteria tend to cluster so that a person meeting one of the criteria usually has the rest as well. In marginal cases, if the person met any three of the ten criteria they were considered to be French. This means that some of those included were educated in English-speaking schools, had a mother who was Anglo and in several cases, wives who were Anglo (including an Eaton!).

[4]This discussion will be developed in Chapter Nine where the question of French-Canadian ownership of capital will be again raised.

[5]The Desmarais brothers of Sudbury are a notable exception.

[6]Women are probably the most under-represented social type in the economic elite. Of the total 946 persons holding elite positions, only 6 or .6 per cent of the total are women. Of these six, adequate biographical data was available for only two. This finding supports the *Report of the Royal Commission on the Status of Women in Canada* which examined 5,889 directorships and 1,469 senior executive positions in Canadian corporations and found women holding only 41 or .7 per cent of the directorships and eight or .5 per cent of the

executive offices (Information Canada, 1970:28). Although women do have lower education, this still cannot account for the wide discrimination found.

[7] Actually the working class hardly ever get into university, having been screened out in secondary school.

[8] Even when the foreign born are included the proportion with more than post-secondary education drops by only .7 per cent compared to a corresponding drop of 1.2 per cent in 1951.

[9] A recent survey by Heindricks and Struggles of the presidents of the 255 largest companies in Canada found similar results reporting that "the vast majority (82 per cent) of the presidents surveyed who received a B.S/B.A. did so at a Canadian undergraduate school. Advanced degrees, however were awarded in nearly equal proportions by institutions in Canada and the U.S." (1973:8). They note that the University of Toronto awarded the most undergraduate degrees but was second to Harvard for most graduate degrees.

[10] There are of course, other private schools in English-speaking Canada, many of them religious affiliated but these are not considered here as private schools. The *Canada Year Book* notes: "Approximately 2 p.c. of all elementary-secondary school students were enrolled in private schools in 1970-71 compared with 4 p.c. in 1960-61. . . . Ontario is the major exception; in that province the number of students in private schools increased gradually over the decade from 26,175 to 44,116" (1972:400).

[11] Material from the 1930's is used here because this is the period when the current elite attended these schools. The cost of attending one of the Headmasters' Association schools now is over $3,000 per year per child.

[12] The classical college system was eliminated in the early 1970's in Quebec. The effect of this and whether alternative upper class institutions will develop is not known. Of course, this does not affect the current elite.

[13] A membership in the Rideau Club, for example, consists of a $550 initiation fee plus $275 annually. This cost is not borne as a personal expense by most executives, as a recent survey of presidents of Canadian companies found: "More than 9 out of 10 presidents hold a town club membership at company expense. . . . A majority of the presidents of Canadian companies also receive a country club membership, an automobile without driver and a stock option plan. Among the larger industrials, a majority of responding presidents also receive an auto with driver, financial counselling and a deferred bonus" (Hendricks & Struggles Inc., 1973:6).

[14] It will be possible to undertake such an analysis in the not too distant future when Dennis Olsen completes his study of the state system in Canada.

[15] Five new members of the Board of Governors of The Ontario Research Foundation were recently announced (*Ottawa Citizen*, January 8, 1974:11). Of the five, four are members of the economic elite.

[16] The 15 Senators in the current corporate elite is well below the total proportion of Senators from business, industry and finance. Presthus reports that this type made up from 37 per cent of the 102-member Senate with law accounting for 30 per cent, government and politics 16 per cent, professions (other than law) nine per cent, agriculture six per cent and labour one per cent (1973:28).

[17] These figures are continually changing. For example, during the course of this study, Joe Green joined the board of Petrofina Canada and Jean-Luc

Pepin the board of Power Corporation, both being former ministers in the Trudeau cabinet and, consequently, from the political elite but not included in these tabulations.

[18] According to a recent article, it was found that only two per cent of Canada's M.P.'s are "from the senior executive ranks of big business" (*Impetus*, May 1973:9). If those M.P.'s who are in the cabinet were excluded even this low two per cent would drop, indicating that very few members of the upper levels of the corporate world enter electoral politics at other than the cabinet level. A notable case is James Richardson, Minister of National Defense, who had to drop 13 directorships including his family firm, now run by his brother, to enter the cabinet. Mitchell Sharp, Minister of External Affairs, is another frequently noted case illustrating the same phenomenon.

[19] A notable example of movement from the bureaucratic elite into the economic elite is K.R. MacGregor who was Superintendent of Insurance with the rank of Deputy Minister from 1953 to 1964 and in 1964 became president of Mutual Life and later added the positon of executive officer; he is also a director of the Huron & Erie Mortgage Corporation. Another case is Vincent William Scully who headed Victory Aircraft, a Crown corporation during the war, becoming Deputy Minister of Reconstruction (1945-48) and Deputy Minister of National Revenue (1948-51). Leaving the bureaucracy, he came to Stelco in 1951, becoming president in 1957. He is now chairman of the executive committee and director of Stelco in addition to being a director of Sun Life and Moore Corp., adding Gulf Oil of Canada late in 1972.

[20] An important historical footnote directly related to the wartime bureaucratic elite and the implications for future corporate relations is provided by the Argus take-over of Massey-Harris. Discussing the reorganization of Massey, Neufeld recounts how E.P. Taylor first became interested in the company: "There was one interesting and historically important sidelight to the reorganization, for with it began the direct participation of E.P. Taylor and W.E. Phillips in the affairs of the company. Duncan wanted to strengthen his board and thought of Taylor. The two had been neighbours and friends in Toronto. Since both were in the service of the government of Canada as 'dollar-a-year' men in the early war years, they had further opportunity to meet. Duncan returned . . . to Massey-Harris in early 1941, and on one of his trips to Washington where Taylor was located as chief executive officer of the British Supply Council, Duncan asked him to come onto the Board" (1969:42).

[21] Included among the Crown corporations are Air Canada, with seven of its nine board members in the economic elite; Atomic Energy of Canada, two of ten; the Bank of Canada, four of 15; the Canada Development Corporation, seven of 21; Eldorado Nuclear, four of seven; the Industrial Development Bank, three of 14; Polymer (now Polystar), five of 11; Sidbec, three of 12; and all the board of the Canadian National Railway, which is included as a dominant corporation.

[22] For example, is the fact that "a supply company, owned 23.7 per cent by Premier Bourassa's wife, has received 41 government contracts worth a total of $1,019,790 since the Liberals came to power in April, 1970" because of patronage or because the Bourassa's and Simard's own so much of Quebec that

it is hard to do business without running into them? "Only one of these contracts was awarded through public tenders. Another 23.7 per cent of the company's shares are owned by Mrs. Bourassa's brother, Claude Simard, who also happens to be a tourism minister in the premier's cabinet" (*Ottawa Journal*, April 19, 1974:7).

* The most recent advertising brochure of The Canadian Headmasters' Association, 1973-74 shows that the number of member schools had increased to 24 with a total of 8,407 students and 713 teaching staff. There are an average of 350 students and 30 teachers per school resulting in a student/teacher ratio of 1:11.8. Eleven of these schools are located in Ontario, five in Quebec, four in B.C. and one each in Nova Scotia, New Brunswick, Manitoba and Alberta. They are very proud of their students who have become members of the elite, including testimonials from former students and a list of graduates in such activities as academia, business, law and the state. Several statements from this brochure reinforce what has been said earlier: "if one examines the Graduating Classes of the entire membership over the past two years, one will find that 90.4% of all the students in these classes proceeded to Degree-granting Universities." Under the heading "The Business World and the Independent School" the explicit ideology of these schools is stated: "Naturally, the schools have a sympathetic understanding of the free enterprise system and this is passed on to their students."

† Regarding the University of Toronto Board, this data refers to the Board of Governors for 1971. Since then a 50-member 'governing council' with eight students, 12 faculty and 30 administrators and government appointments, has been created.

Chapter Seven

The Media Elite: Gatekeepers of Ideas

JOHN PORTER undertook a study of the media elite in Canada for the year 1961, arguing this institution represented a separate dimension of elite activity from the economic, political, bureaucratic and trade union sectors. There is no need to argue with Porter's point that these key institutions should be regarded as analytically separate areas of social study. The burden of proof that various combinations of these may be controlled by the same or similar sets of people should remain an empirical proposition. The media, Porter found, are like the Minotaur. They are partially like the economic sector in that they are organized primarily as corporations and as such seek profits, but they are more: they are also organizations whose major activity is the dissemination and reinforcement of ideologies and values. Although Porter was able to answer one of the major questions he began with, namely what is the structure and function of the mass media in Canada, he was not able to answer, in a precise way, the other major issue which is of wider theoretical and social concern: how much overlap, if any, is there between the economic and media elites and, indeed, are they empirically separate in terms of who controls them? This was not possible because his study of the economic elite had been undertaken 10 years earlier, in 1951. This and subsequent chapters will attempt to address both types of questions, first by an analysis of the structure and function of the media, and second, making a comparison of the extent of overlap and similarity of the economic and media elites. Before this is undertaken, some theoretical and analytical issues will be raised.

(i) Ideology and the Media

Ideology is a framework of assumptions, ideas and values incorporated into the perspective an individual or collective uses to guide analyses, interests and commitments into a system of meaning. In the words of C.B. Macpherson: "Ideologies contain, in varying proportions, elements of explanation (of fact and history), justification (of demands), and faith or belief (in the ultimate truth or rightness of their case)" (1969:301). One important aspect of the sociology of knowledge is examination of the social basis of ideology; that is, the way ideologies emerge from and respond to the social order. Ideologies are part of the superstructure of society, as opposed to the socio-economic foundations which form the base. The superstructure develops from the base but in turn modifies and strengthens its genitor. A study of ideology from a sociological perspective implies that the analysis focuses not only on ideas per se, but their development and active relationship with their base. In arguing that there is an interactive relationship between the base and superstruture, it is being claimed that ideologies *arise* and are *maintained* by social conditions but become embodied in human relationships which in turn provide a system of explanation and orientation which directs the activities of people. Ideologies, it is important to remember, are promoted by and reflect the interests of particular groups within society. Typically, specialized conductors of ideologies become organized within social institutions, such as the mass media in industrial society, which have as one major purpose the generation and dissemination of ideas and information.

Mannheim

In his attempt to elaborate a sociology of knowledge, Karl Mannheim argued, in *Ideology and Utopia,* that it was important "to comprehend thought in the concrete setting of an historical-social situation" since each individual finds himself within "an inherited situation" which he did not create but is forced to take into account; moreover, the "patterns of thought and of conduct" the individual must use to cope have also been pre-formed (1936:3). In what he calls "a well stabilized society", the upper class "has little cause to call into question its own social existence and the value of its achievements" and it is only with democratization that "the techniques of thinking and ideas of the lower strata are for the first time in a position to confront the ideas of the dominant strata on the same level of validity" (8-9). He goes on to argue that behind the "façade" of ideologies are the actual life-situations of those who espouse them (56), and in particular, it is in the interest of those in command to present the existing order "as absolute and eternal" in an attempt to maintain their stability (87). In his *Essays On Society and Social Psychology,* Mannheim argued that "the key to the understanding of changes in ideas is to be found in the changing social background, mainly in the fate of the social groups or classes which are the 'carriers' of these styles of thought" (1953:74). From Mannheim's work, it can be maintained that ideologies arise and are formed in groups both on the basis of the situations into which they are born, and the experiences they accumulate within a given social order. In a class-based low mobility society, there will be a corresponding relationship between birth and experience.

Although individual biographies are widely varied, there remains a basic commonality to many of their experiences within a given social structure. These would include, among others, common educational experiences within similar educational settings and institutions, common work experiences through similar occupations and, today, the common experience of mass media exposure—particularly newspapers, magazines, radio and televison. Many of these experiences are variable by social class and, especially in Canada, by the factor of ethnicity. For example, most everyone experiences primary school, the working class less secondary education and even less university, while the private school is an upper class milieu. Similar divisions occur by ethnicity with the added dimension of French language educational institutions including, until recently, classical colleges as the private school counterpart. Occupational differentiation obviously provides varying work situtations and divergent life styles. Given the high relationship between many of these factors or experiences, there emerges a structural division within society in which individuals find themselves in similar social "locations".

Ideologies represent an interdependent set of ideas which become embodied in various social groups arising out of their "locations" and serve to defend, orient and direct the interests and actions of these groups. Ideologies which represent the *status quo* position and, by definition, are the most powerful at any time, are referred to as "dominant ideologies". Dominant ideologies are formations of groups used to preserve and maintain existing institutions and social stability while "counter ideologies" seek to change existing arrangements thus disrupting stability. For Mannheim, those who espouse counter ideologies would be considered "utopian" since they seek to change the prevailing order. He would argue that "ideologists", who are attempting to maintain the existing order, would employ various "social techniques" (means of social control) to reinforce their positions of dominance. When two concepts in Marx's writings are combined a similar position emerges.

Marx

Mannheim's point concerning being born into an already existing situation is paralleled by Karl Marx's statement that: "Men make their own history, but they do not make it just as they please; they do not make it under circumstances chosen by themselves, but under circumstances directly found, given and transmitted from the past". With this, Marx argues that each generation is confronted with the advances, institutions and ideologies of prior generations. These in turn affect the consciousness of each emerging order. For Marx, the "relations of production" are the "real foundation" of ideas because they establish the "general character of the social, political, and intellectual processes of life. It is not the consciousness of men that determines their existence, but on the contrary, their social existence determines their consciousness'' (*A Contribution to the Critique of Political Economy*, 1970a:20-21). It is interesting to note how Marx responded to an objection to his position in a footnote to the first volume of Capital:

> In the estimation of that paper, my view that each special mode of production and the social relations corresponding to it, in short, that the economic structure of society, is the real basis on which the juridical political superstructure is raised, and to which definite social forms of thought correspond; that the mode of production determines the character of the social, political, and intellectual life generally, all this is very true for our own times, in which material interests preponderate, but not for the middle ages, in which Catholicism, nor for Athens and Rome, where politics reigned supreme . . . the middle ages could not live on Catholicism, nor the ancient world on politics. On the contrary, it is the mode in which they gained a livelihood that explains why here politics, and there Catholicism, played the chief part (1967:82n).

This provides some idea of the variety of circumstances within which Marx argued his proposition held. Although the mode of production was always at the basis of the social order, he did not see an inactive role for political or ideological orders. Indeed, at times they could play ''the chief part''.

These statements should be understood in light of his famous statement in *The German Ideology* that: ''The ideas of the ruling class in every epoch, i.e. the class which is the ruling *material* force of society, is at the same time its ruling intellectual force. The class which has the means of material production at its disposal, has control at the same time over the means of mental production, so that thereby, generally speaking, the ideas of those who lack the means of mental production are subject to it'' (1970b:64). It is apparent that Marx conceived of ideology as a social force which can be used to affect the actions of people contrary to those coincident with their social position[1]. Obviously, part of what is being alluded to is class consciousness. This will not be pursued further here except to mention that Miliband has an excellent discussion of ''levels'' of class consciousness and comes to the conclusion, as have others, that it ''is more commonly found among members of a privileged class than among members of a subordinate one'' (1971:22)[2]. It is important to note, and this will be pursued further, that there is an interactive relationship between the ideological level and social conditions which generate ideological positions. Ironically, if it is the ruling class which alone is able to attain and sustain class consciousness, it may well be that the advantages coinciding with that position may be sufficient to counter the development of alternative ideologies from subordinate classes.

(ii) Ruling Ideas and Counterforces: The Mass Media

Mass media as a "social technique", to use Mannheim's term, has the potential of being a conductor of ruling ideas *par excellence*. This represents a concentration of the means of conducting ideologies more powerful than Marx or Mannheim conceived and a counterforce to ideologies associated with subordinate social positions. It may be that the "end of ideology" espoused by many defenders of the existing order in fact means an end of a prevalent ideology *in opposition to* the dominant ideology, thus providing a lack of contrast needed to make apparent the dominant ideology. It may be a product of the mass media and control over its use by those who hold the dominant ideology.

Increase in the means of mass communication in a society does not necessarily imply increased communication if communication is taken to mean two-sided or equal exhange of information. By using the qualifying concept of "mass", communication is transformed into a one-sided input from a small number of people who control much of the social distribution of information by controlling key points of distribution. Mass media actually decreases the communications relationship, reducing the number of sources and increasing the number of recipients thus reducing the *variety* of communicative relationships. This argument runs contrary to the usual position that the increasing complexity of the social structure generates more "constellations" of ideas and belief systems by increasing the number of kinds of relationships (Dibble quoted by Curtis and Petras, 1970:9).

Media influences values and affects conformity and the more effective this is, the less need there is to use coercive means of social control. Behaviour can be affected by either subtle or blunt means —socialization is a subtle means of conducting ideology. Although not the only means of insuring conformity (threat and force being other examples), over time socialization may be more effective. A person is born into an ongoing social structure which contains, in an already developed form, social classes and, if the social structure is not in a state of social upheaval, a dominant ideology. Thus the individuals' social situation exists prior to their arrival. Their socialization is based on the existing class and ideological situation and as such is initially conducted by way of the existential position of the previous generation. There is from the beginning in stable societies a strong social force, although not the only force (the existential position being at least one important possible counterforce), in the direction of the powerful definition of reality as presented by the mass media. The totality of forces operating on individuals throughout their lives, including the mass media, involves what Mills has called "the cultural apparatus" of society. The mass media may initiate particular ideological positions but, for the most part, they operate as a reflexive mechanism which selects or screens information; it is simultaneously part of the "cultural apparatus" and reflective of it.

What, then, is the relationship between the everyday experience of people and the view of the world they receive via the media? Frank Parkin's position is that there are three alternative "meaning systems" or perspectives operating in industrial society. These are: (1) the dominant which "derives from the dominant institutional orders of society, and presents what might be called the 'official' version of social inequality", (2) the subordinate which "derives from the working class community setting, and promotes various modes of adjustment or accommodation to subordinate status", and (3) the radical which "has its source in the mass political party of the subordinate class and presents an oppositional view of the reward system" (1971:10, 81-83). The subordinate perspective emerges from the cross-pressure of the dominant meaning system which is accomodated to the social position of those outside the inner circles of power thus conforming to what Marx called the "ruling ideas". Parkin suggests that "the extent to which values are legitimized in society is largely a function of institutional power. Values are much more likely to flow in a "downward" than "upward" direction . . . normative consensus is better understood in terms of the socialization of one class by another, rather than as independent class agreement or convergence on values" (81). The subordinate perspective is a "mirror image" of the dominant meaning system which presents the most powerful definition of reality. For this reason potential conflicts over prevailing inequalities may be minimized. This argument assumes that there are divergent interests between class in society and that the upper class is most powerful since it is able to "label" particular situations in a way which reflects its interest and have those "labels" stick. In this way the dominant ideology becomes instilled in the lower classes contrary to their existential position. Parkin's point is that:

> those groups in society which occupy positions of the greatest power and privilege will also tend to have the greatest access to the means of legitimation. That is to say, the social and political definitions of those in dominant positions tend to become objectified and enshrined in the major institutional orders, so providing the moral framework of the entire social system. It is not of course necessary to posit any monolithic social or normative unity to the

groups which cluster at the apex of the dominant class. Undoubtedly they display variations in political and social outlook—as, for example, between aristocratic or traditional *élites* on one hand and managerial or entrepreneurial *élites* on the other. However, these differences are not likely to be fundamental with regard to the values underlying class inequality and its institutional supports (83).

Parkin does not wish to argue that the subordinate value system becomes identical with the dominant one or in his words, an "outright endorsement" of it. He rather views it as a "negotiated version" between unequal sources of influence. The dominant ideology is not able to negate totally experiences encountered. He notes particularly attitudinal studies of the working class that find, on general questions, that there is a tendency to identify with the dominant values but in situationally specific ones, attitudes are more in line with existential positions (95). He draws the conclusion that "the subordinate value system restricts man's consciousness to the immediacy of a *localized* setting; and the dominant value system encourages consciousness of a *national* identity; but the radical value system promotes the consciousness of *class*" (97)[3].

Dominant ideologies are founded on relationships of inequality in the economic and political realms which become translated into ideological dominance. Galbraith has argued that: "It is possible that people need to believe that they are unmanaged if they are to be managed effectively" (1967:288). This is part of the power inherent in dominant positions. The dominant ideology is "real" to the extent that it affects behaviour, including acceptance. This does not mean that counter ideologies do not exist; it only means that they exist in unequal proportion to their counterparts[4].

(iii) Existential and Ideational Perspective

It is argued here that ideas come into being within the context of a definable set of situations and institutions. It has been stressed that the interactive relationship between ideas and existence does not occur within a vacuum but within a society characterized by inequality in the economic and political sectors as well as inequality in terms of access to the major means of transmitting ideology.

Two major positions develop from the discussion to this point, one is existential and the other ideational. (1) A group's social origins and social position affect their perception of the world, their evaluations and generally their ideology. (2) A group's understanding of the world will be affected by access to information they receive and the form in which they receive it. It has been argued that the second may dominate the first if the person or group is primarily a recipient of information while the first will affect the second if they are mainly transmitters of information or their social position conforms to the dominant ideology. Given that the mass media is primarily a one-way means of communication, it can be argued that if the upper class is in the position of transmitter and the lower classes in the position of receivers, the validity of Parkin's point that a subordinate or accommodative meaning system is prevalent in the working class is reinforced. Control over the mass media is a key point of controlling much of the information which permeates society and forms a major medium of socialization. It is by no means the only medium, only education, religion, or the family need be mentioned as others, but it is one of the major sources and is increasingly taking over many of the functions once held by these other institutions.

Porter has argued for the Canadian case that the ideological elite can be designated as "those at the top of ideological institutions, specifically in the modern period, the mass media, the educational system, and the churches" (1965:460). This does not mean that other institutions such as the economic, political, legal or military do not engage in and engender ideologies, certainly they do. Each corporation, for example, has its own means of projecting ideology, the public relations department. What is argued here is that these other institutions specialize in ideology creating and sustaining activities. In the present analysis, the mass media will provide the focus for identifying the media elite component of the ideological elite.

The evolution of control over means of communications is not "natural" or "accidental" but can be identified as an important institution and analysed in the context of the social structure. Porter maintains:

> The consensus which is necessary for the maintenance of social structure does not come about through some metaphysical entity of a group or social mind, or a general will. Rather, the unifying of value themes is achieved through the control of media of communications, and therefore the structure of the ideological system becomes articulated with other systems of power. The ideological systems must provide the justification for the economic system, the political system, and so forth, and this it does by attempting to show that the existing arrangements conform with the traditional value system (460).

It is possible to identify the media elite by examining control over the dominant organizations involved in mass communications. Individuals identified can then be examined in terms of their social origins and social positions, particularly as they relate to other elites and as they reflect the characteristics of the entire social structure. The power of the media elite is in terms of control over access to decision making and control over the content of the media, or at least control over selection of those who determine the content of the media. They represent what Bertrand Russell has called "the forces which cause opinion" (1938:93).

(iv) The Role of Mass Media

The mass media is the dominant means of articulating opinion today. Ralph Miliband insists that the media are "functional" in modern capitalist societies but "functional" for the existing order. He argues:

> There is nothing particularly surprising about the character and role of the mass media in advanced capitalist society. Given the economic and political context in which they function, they cannot fail to be, predominantly, agencies for the dissemination of ideas and values which affirm rather than challenge existing patterns of power and privilege, and thus to be weapons in the arsenal of class domination (1969:236).

C. Wright Mills, in his chapter on "The Mass Society" (1956) and Miliband, in his chapters on "The Process of Legitimation" (1969), each place a strong emphasis on the role of the mass media and other institutions of ideology. Each argues that the pervasive *image* of society, as emanating from a variety of sources, does not correspond to its reality but the image has the effect of reinforcing stability and prevailing forms of inequality. Mills argues that the basis of liberal ideology is justification by, on behalf of and in the name of the "public" which "is held to be the very balance wheel of democratic power" (298). This ideology, Mills maintains, has as its primary assumption a climate of discussion and organization based on public action to initiate and respond to social issues. "This eighteenth-century idea of the public of public opinion parallels the economic idea of the market of the free economy" (299). A free market, he argues, which is not monopolized by a few dominant interests. Mills found that this primary assumption of liberal theory was in fact an ideal, itself acting as a legitimation and not a correct reflection of the existing arrangement of power. This raises for Mills the problem of accountability; for as he says, if an "elite is truly responsible to, or even exists in connection with, a community of publics, it carries a very different meaning than if such a public is being transformed into a society of masses" (302).

Characteristic of industrial societies as the dominant mode of communication, he argues, is a system of mass media which structures out the possiblity of "answering back" and therefore, cuts the population off from participation as a public. In this situation, "opinion-making becomes an accepted technique of power-holding and power-getting" (310). He further argues that the media "guide our very experiences. Our standards of credulity, our standards of reality, tend to be set by these media" (311). If access to the media is open and competition exists between them, the possibility for diversity remains but if this is restricted to those already in power, it means their stability is greatly reinforced.

Miliband starts from the general model provided by Mills and applies it to an examination of the media in modern capitalist societies. For example, he focuses on business and "its power of advertisement, which is also self-advertisement" (215). This is not simply the public relations type of media content but the pervasive impact constant bombardment of brand names and consumer products through the media has on every-day meanings and life styles. He notes that there is an appearance of great diversity and openness, particularly compared to "monolithic" nations. His argument is that:

> the notion of pluralist diversity and competitive equilibrium is, here as in every other field, rather superficial and misleading. For the agencies of communication and notably the mass media are, in reality, and the expression of dissident views notwithstanding, a crucial element in the legitimation of capitalist socity. Freedom of expression is not thereby rendered meaningless. But that freedom has to be set in the real economic and political context of these societies; and in that context the free expression of ideas and opinions *mainly* means the free expression of ideas and opinions which are helpful to the prevailing system of power and privilege (220).

Miliband goes on to examine various media from a variety of perspectives to show their role in maintaining stability. One of the most interesting points he notes is the limited access to the "means of mental production", as he calls the media. They are primarily privately controlled but more important is the finding that "these agencies are in that part of the private domain which is dominated by large-scale capitalist enterprise. Even more notably, the mass media are not only business, but big business" (227). This means the media are controlled by the most powerful segments of the business community; the "right of ownership confers the right of making propaganda, and where that right is exercised, it is most likely to be exercised in the service of strongly conservative prejudices'' (229). Control over the media in capitalist societies, whether by the state or big business, places them squarely in the realm of the dominant interests already powerful in other fields. This reduces their critical possibilities and diminishes the possibility that alternative conceptions of reality will be provided. Highly concentrated means of mental manipulation provide the conditions wherein dominant classes can reinforce and sustain their hegemonic position. It is a form of power on a par with coercion but clearly better suited to long-term stability and the ideology of liberalism.

Gerth and Mills have collected together various terms used to describe symbol manipulation which justifies rule:

> Mosca's ''political formula'' or ''great superstitions'', Locke's ''principle of sovereignty'', Sorel's ''ruling myth'', Thurman Arnold's ''folklore'', Weber's ''legitimations'', Durkheim's ''collective representations'', Marx's ''dominant ideas'', Rousseau's ''general will'', Lasswell's ''symbols of authority'' or ''symbols of justification'', Mannheim's ''ideology'', Herbert Spencer's ''public sentiments''—all testify the central place of master symbols in social analysis (1953:277).

Selznick suggests ideologies, like the process of cooptation, are ''self-defence mechanisms'' used by people in coming ''to terms with major social forces'' (1948:34). Ideologies are used to condition the environment and are part of ''the folklore of capitalism''. Arnold has suggested: ''Organizations which exercise governing powers of a permanent character do not maintain their power by force. Force is entirely too exhausting. They do it by identifying themselves with the faiths and loyalties of the people'' (1973:193). In terms of capitalist society, the most reinforcing ideology is that of ''the rights of property'' which are intimately ingrained in the value system. Some have attempted to generate an ideology by introducing the concepts ''corporate conscience'' and ''corporate soul'' but, in their more vulgar face at least, they have not caught on[5]. The idea of ''countervailing powers'' and the related concept of ''veto groups'', as well as the latest invention of the ''technostructure'', have all been tried.

Each of these concepts refers to the way elites use ideas to establish and reinforce their power. The mass media is now one of the major methods used to accomplish this and is a much more sophisticated technique than many of the earlier authors were ever able to perceive. John Galbraith, for example, has noted the crucial role the media has come to play in corporate capitalism. He speaks, as do Baran and Sweezy (1966:115f), of the ''sales effort''. The point made by both sets of writings is that corporate capitalism, in its effort to plan, has developed the "need to control consumer behaviour" (1967:211). The "management of demand" is accomplished through sales strategies designed "to shift the locus of decision in the purchase of goods from the consumer where it is beyond control to the firm where it is subject to control" (215). Galbraith calls this "the revised sequence" where there is the ability to control demand (the market), contrary to "the accepted sequence". In other words, the "invisible hand" of the market is replaced by the manipulations of advertisement. To accomplish this, extensive use of the media is required.

Another way to analyse this phenomenon is as the ideology of consumerism, an ideology which seems prevalent in all advanced capitalist societies and even in periphery nations touched by capitalism and its techniques of consumer control. Consumerism also operates as a means of social control by the creation of artificial needs. This involves the dissemination of corporate propaganda aimed at all society's members for goods and services beyond actual needs (sexy cars, pore-clogging deodorants for various parts of the body, vitamins shaped like cartoons, etc.). It involves social control because it directs human energy in both the acts of consumption and the "need" for production to satisfy erroneous needs. The ability to create demands for the products of capitalism becomes another important role of the mass media. Baran and Sweezy have noted a further implication of advertising, its affect on income distribution. They argue: "The costs of advertising and selling are borne by the consumer, it is held that the proliferation of advertising causes a redistribution of income: the income of consumers is reduced while that of advertisers and of the advertising media is increased by the same amount" (123).

As Porter has pointed out, the mass media are "important instruments of opinion-making and they establish the climate of thought in the society" (1965:216). One of the effects of the mass media is to perpetuate the myth that society's advantages are widespread and enjoyed by all. It is frequently suggested that Canada could do better by the Biafrans or the children of India, but how often are the native peoples of Canada or the children in the slums of Canada's major cities subject to the same kinds of national campaigns? Read the *Real Poverty Report* or the *Poverty Wall* to find out if distribution of wealth and advantage is widespread: however, the ideology of corporate capitalism is one of abundance and stability requiring wide acceptance of this ideology. Ideology is used to create an environment favourable to the elite and it is necessary that this be done, if the elites' legitimacy is to be maintained. Public relations is a means of making ideology palatable[6]. Surette has developed what he calls a "Law of Increasing Returns" which states that: "The quality of public relations increases in direct proportion to the gravity of the problem" (1973:36). This is an apt way to characterize the way the economic elite uses its power to manipulate the ideological climate.

More fundamentally, Porter argues that the major task of ideologies, and particularly the mass media, are "the problems of internal cohesion, and the maintenance of social values and of the institutional forms that the values support" (1965:457). For "cohesion" and "consensus" to be maintained, members of a society must be socialized into a system of values which provide a bond. This is not to say that these are necessarily values consistent with the position of all groups or that they have the same reflection in all groups, as Parkin's analysis has shown; but for the stability and predictability to continue this activity must be accomplished. In an unequal society this means justification of inequality; in an exploitive society this means the rationalization of exploitation. Porter argues that: "Like other institutional systems [the ideological system] acquires some degree of autonomy from which it acquires a power of its own" (460). It is precisely this degree of autonomy which will be empirically examined here —like other institutional spheres the extent of autonomy should be made problematic and resolved by empirical investigation of the relationships involved and the degree of overlap.

To digress for a moment, the concern here is not about the production of knowledge *per se*, but the selective transformation of knowledge into "news". In capitalist society news has become a commodity which sells products and is itself a valuable commodity. By this is meant that "news" is treated as a means to attain an audience and the audience to sell products.

The media elite, for the most part, are not themselves generators of ideologies. They rather act as gatekeepers, performing the function of selection and screening alternatives by establishing limits of tolerance. In this role they are not so much involved in changing ideologies as reinforcing existing ones. In this role, they are very much involved in exercising an important form of power. In the words of the Senate Committee on Mass Media: "The power of the press . . . is the power of selection" and as it argues about the media owners: "They're *not* spectators. They control the presentation of the news, and therefore have a vast and perhaps disproportionate say in how our society defines itself" (I, 1970:7-8). In Mills' terms, "The media not only gives us information, they guide our very experiences" (1956:311). The structure of the media is such that "men live in second-hand worlds" fabricated by what he calls "the cultural apparatus" which is composed of "the observation posts, the interpretation centers, the presentation depots" (1963:406). The importance of this fact is compounded by the central place "news" has in society. Some time ago. Park noted that: "In the modern world the role of news has assumed increased rather than diminished importance as compared with some other forms of knowledge" (1940:686).

To summarize briefly this section, it can be argued that the task of the media in contemporary industrial society is translating information to the public. If this is to be an objective undertaking, at least two factors must be present. (1) The media elite must be sufficiently autonomous from other elites in society to provide a detached perspective on their activities and present a critical accounting of the policies and persuasions of these other elites; that is, a pluralist social structure must exist at the elite level. (2) The media elite must contain within it representations from all major social groupings in proportion to their occurrence in the population at large; that is, equal access to decision making positions must prevail. It is questionable whether these conditions can be met in a society where capital controls the major media. Freedom of the press in capitalist society means, in the words of an "eminent publisher" appearing before the Senate Committee on Mass Media: "The right of the public to buy a newspaper each day if they wish, to write letters to the editor, or to start a paper of their own if they don't like it" (I:8). Given the unequal distribution of capital to Canadians, his arrogant remarks give little solace to those unable to "start a paper of their own".

(v) Elites and Elective Affinity

Before proceeding to the models to be used, it is useful to introduce a concept which has been alluded to in various ways. This is the notion of elective affinity as originated by Max Weber. Elective affinity can be applied in two ways in this study. First in terms of selection and presentation of "news" and second, in terms of the selection and recruitment of the media elite and their employees. For Weber "elective affinity" (*Wahlverwandschaft*) expresses the way ideas and material interests "seek each other out" in the ongoing processes of society (1946:280). It involves the selective perception of previously generated ideas to suit the current position of the actors. There is a selection from the range of alternatives available which suit the situation of those engaged in the selection. Meanings and contexts are changed through the reinterpretation of ideas which bear an "affinity" to those in a position to "elect". In the study of mass media, this can apply to those who are in the situation of selecting from available information what they consider to be "news" and to frame that information in a context which suits their view of the world. It also applies to the audience which selects sources and types of "news" which coincides with their existing perceptions. In this way there is a built-in conservatism in the impact of the media by tending to reinforce whatever presently exists. The propensity to accept any given information depends upon the ability to fit it into an existing framework and equally important, the previous evaluation of the source of the information. Those whose opinion is highly valued will have a greater impact on the audience than the opinion of others lacking such legitimacy. The process of recruitment also operates in a similar manner. Those in the position to decide on recruitment will most likely select those with whom they have an "affinity". Moreover, this will tend to encourage, within the aspiring, views which are similar to those in command.

Throughout, there has been an elite model implicit in the argument. By using Maurice Pinard's work, this model will be summarized before proceeding with the analysis of the media. Pinard argues the following: "The values and interests of the elites are more important than those of the lower classes to explain the conservative and nationalist character of Quebec politics" (1970:87). Arguing against the traditional "cultural interpretation" of ideology in Quebec, he poses a model of elites and masses, saying that "Class sentiments among the masses are not necessarily actualized and reflected in class organizations and class parties, because of the power of the elites and their ability to redirect working-class sentiments and interest" (88). Elites are able, according to Pinard, to "mediate" and "translate" the values and ideologies prevalent in that society. He goes on to formulate a theory about relationships between elites which affect the response of the mass:

> If the culture of the elites represents a highly monolithic and closed system and if little dissension is tolerated among the elites, it is very likely that the organizations of the lower classes will be controlled by typical members of the elites and imbued with middle-class and elite values; a great amount of re-direction of class sentiments will tend to take place. On the other hand, in societies in which a greater degree of ideological pluralism prevails among the elites and where segments of them become aliented and are at liberty to desert their class to work for the defence of lower-class interests, the chances are greater that the translation will be more faithful, even though some "adjustments" are likely to take place (106).

It is the class which holds the power bases of society (including the means of communication) which are able, in large part, to influence and direct the ideology of the population. This is particularly the case when there are a lack of alternatives open to people, as in a "monolithic" culture with poorly articulated alternative ideologies. Pinard, for example, argues that it is the ideology of the elite segment of society which should be used to account for the failure of the working class to develop an ideology which reflects their interests. This does not mean there are no class differences and class conflicts; it means that many of these class interests have been effectively contained and directed by powerful interests.

To summarize the relationship between ideology and elite structure, it can be said that (i) the more monolithic a social structure, the more likely that elites are able to redirect interests and prevent conflict; (ii) elites act as mediators and are able to "translate" class interests; (iii) in a pluralist elite structure increased possibilities are available for lower class interests to be accurately manifest, and (iv) there is no need for value consensus among classes if there is a fairly unified system of elites since they would be capable of redirecting these interests in ways which are adjusted to elite values, thus defusing a source of opposition. From this it is possible to empirically examine the extent of separation between the media and economic elite. The higher their overlap, the greater the possibility that a monolithic structure exists at the elite level and the lower the opportunity for other segments to present alternative ideologies and values.

Another point which relates to the relations between elites is the fact that the media elite acts as a control point or a "funnel" of information, consequently, it must first gain information which may be blocked. Indeed, the information may be regarded as secret so the economic, judicial, bureaucratic or political elites may control what information they will release. Only upon disclosure is the media elite in a position to select from the hundreds of events, announcements, etc. what will be presented, how it will be presented and where (headlines, features, cover story, etc.). Only then is it in the position to select and amplify the information received thus affecting the perceptions of the world by those receiving the news.

The ideas of legitimacy and stability have long been important to understanding the phenomenon of dominance. Reliance on force as a mechanism of social control for long periods taxes too heavily the productive capacity of a regime. Justification though legitimizing rule has proven a much more effective way to achieve and sustain stability. In the following chapters, Canada's media will be examined, first from the perspective of the degree of concentration within it and the way it is organized and, following this, who controls it and, particularly, its relationship with the economic elite.

Notes

[1] In contemporary terms, Mandel has captured this notion that counter-forces are operating which affect ideologies: "Which forces will turn out to be stronger in determining the worker's attitude to the society he lives in, the mystifying ideas he receives, yesterday in church and today through the T.V., or the social reality he confronts and assimilates day after day through practical experience?" (1971:185).

[2] Hobsbawm has arrived at a similar conclusion (1971:8).

[3] "National", as used by Parkin is not meant to convey the notion of "nationalism" but refers to the nation-state as a level of analysis rather than a community or social class level.

[4] Laski came to similar conclusions some time ago arguing as follows: ". . . freedom of opinion under capitalism has always seemed less real to the working-classes than it has to the employer or to the intellectual. The implications of intellectual freedom to each are so different that the interpretation they will give to its operation sometimes seem to proceed from different worlds" (1935:210).

[5] One interesting ideology of corporate capitalism is the contention that capitalism is not an ideology at all. Before the American Newspaper Publishers, Henry Ford II delivered a speech entitled, "An Incentive-for-Everybody Economy" in which he said: "We must recognize that *American* capitalism is not an 'ism' in the accepted sense. It is practical and unsentimental. It deals with man as he is and as he, perhaps, should be. It does not in other words, lend itself to glorious over-simplification and grandiose, utopian dreams" (emphasis added, 1963:295).

[6] In *The Hidden Persuaders*, Vance Packard quotes an advertising specialist from the "Public Relations Journal" as saying: "One of the fundamental considerations involved here is the right to manipulate human personality" (259).

Chapter Eight

Structure and Concentration of Canada's Mass Media

JUST as it was necessary to analyse the process of concentration in the economic world, so is the study of concentration within the media central to identifying the dominant media complexes and the media elite. Unlike corporations in the economic world which were differentiated on the basis of control over capital measured in terms of assets and revenue, dominant media complexes must be identified in terms of the control they exercise over the dissemination of information. The best indicator of this is "circulation"; that is, how much of the population is reached by any particular media mode and within that by particular media complexes. It will be demonstrated that the process of concentration in the economic domain again re-occurs in the mass media. The three most important media modes in Canada are newspapers, radio and television. However, media complexes do not always divide neatly into these three categories since they may, and often do, control means of communication in two or even all three modes. This, it will be shown, is simply a further means of concentration.

This chapter will be divided into two major sections. First, the aggregate concentration within the various modes of communication and then, on the basis of each of the dominant media complexes identified. These dominant media complexes will provide the basis for selecting the media elite much the same way dominant corporations in the economy were the basis for identifying the economic elite.

I. Structure and Control of the Media

(i) Concentration and Chains

It was argued earlier that for diversity to occur in the ideology presented to the public there must be diversity of media sources and some form of ideological competition whereby one position was not capable of totally overwhelming alternative positions. In other words, it is necessary that there is an open "market" situation and not one monopolized by a few dominant sources. However, Warnock has argued that in North America, the overall trend is a "decline of competition and the growth of monopoly and oligarchy" (1970:120). Moreover, Monroe has shown that concentration of ownership in the media was not confined just to concentration within the major media (newpapers, television and radio) but across the media as well. He found that the largest publishing interests also held numerous broadcasting outlets. For example, Southam Press has 26 broadcasting outlets, Thomson 10, Sifton and Maclean-Hunter nine each. There was also concentration within the broadcasting companies without publication interests; for example, Moffat Broadcasting has 10 outlets (1967:42).

The phenomenon of concentration is not all that recent in Canada; as Wolfe (1973:25-26) has pointed out, many reports of increasing concentration in the media have been provided but since these early warnings the trend towards concentration has continued. The most recent study of this is provided by the Senate Committee on Mass Media which published three comprehensive volumes of data and warnings. Their study will provide the basis for examining the current concentrated condition of the media in Canada.

The Senate Committee report states that:

> the trend towards fewer and fewer owners of our sources of news and information is already well entrenched. There are only five cities in the country where genuine competition between newspapers exists; and in all five cities, some or all of these competing dailies are owned by chains. Seventy years ago there were thirty-five Canadian communities with two or more daily newspapers; today there are only fifteen—and in five of these cities, the two dailies are published by the same owner (I:5)[1].

Although concentration was evident some time ago, it has increased very rapidly within the past twelve years. For example, the largest chains (Thomson, Southam and F.P.) controlled 25 per cent of daily circulation in 1958 but by 1970 this increased to 45 per cent. The Senate report argues that the structure of the media has changed but the mythology surrounding it has not; "conventional wisdom still cherishes the image of the 'independent' owner-editor, a tough but kindly old curmudgeon who somehow represented the collective conscience of his community. If this image ever had validity, it hasn't now. Your average daily newspaper editor is the hired branch-manager for a group of shareholders who typically live somewhere else" (I:5).

Their study covers 116 daily newspapers, 66.4 per cent of which are owned by groups; 97 private TV stations, 48.5 per cent group-owned; and 272 radio stations, 47.4 per cent group owned[2]. The actual concentration of circulation is higher than the proportion group owned because the establishments controlled by groups tend to be larger and with wider circulation. Of the 103 largest communities in Canada, it was found that "there are 61 where groups or independents own two or more of the community's media outlets" (I:19). What is the explanation offered for this trend? "In the case of broadcasting, federal licensing policy protects broadcasters against excessive, uneconomical competition. In the case of newspapers, the circulation wars of yester-year have created monopoly or near-monopoly situations which now confer large benefits on the survivors" (I:63). In other words, what the forces of accumulation and concentration did in publishing years ago, the forces of government "regulation" have been able to accomplish for broadcasting today.

As Table 36 illustrates, except for Nova Scotia, groups account for the majority of circulation within each of the provinces.

TABLE 36
Percentage Circulation Controlled by Newspaper 'Groups' in Canada, 1970

British Columbia	95%	Quebec (French)	50.6%
Alberta	95%	(English	97.5%
Saskatchewan	100%	New Brunswick	92.7%
Manitoba	88.3%	P.E.I.	72.6%
Ontario	75.9%	Nova Scotia	9.0%
		Newfoundland	81.1%

(see Senate Report on Mass Media, II:60)

Broadcasting interests have been somewhat more diversified but the clear trend is towards greater concentration. For example, "Over the last decade, nearly a dozen television stations that were once controlled by local interests or in which local interest had substantial minority interest, have come under the control of major broadcasting groups" (II:63). Moreover, there are other factors such as network affiliations (CTV and CBC) which provide additional unity between even "independent" broadcasters.

The Senate Report suggests a number of additional factors which enhance the trend toward concentration. They argue that access to capital is a major reason large corporations are able to raise the necessary capital to continue and expand while smaller operations lack this advantage (II:267). Circulation battles are also noted where larger corporations are able to withstand short-term losses and wipe out independents (II:268-269). Higher profit returns by larger companies are also noted. In radio, for example, 221 stations which were separate from television interests were examined and only 22 stations (8.4 per cent) accounted for over 69 per cent of the revenue. Similarly, with television there were 29 stations separate from radio and eight of these

(27.6 per cent) accounted for 92 per cent of the revenue (II:354). In the printing and publication industry the situation is much the same. There were 545 establishments with over $25,000 in revenue; of these, 22 (four per cent) had over $5 million revenue and accounted for 53.5 per cent of the employees and 63.7 per cent of the revenue (II:223).

It is interesting to examine what a member of the media elite thinks about such developments. Lord Thomson speaking about the recent sale of the *Telegram*'s assets said: "It amused me to see Honderich come off his high horse about unlimited competition and about great political room for everybody to move and all the rest of it. When the crunch came he wasn't ashamed to make a deal that was very much in his own interests" (*Globe & Mail,* December 6, 1971:7). Lord Thomson, of course, has been making deals to take control of newspapers in Canada for decades. It is interesting to note that "competition" is not problematic for him, nor is "political room". He defines control over newspapers in terms of the interests of the owners and not in terms of the public. His own 27 dailies in Canada give him a good deal of "interests".

Porter noted cases of relationships between various groups, particularly in terms of joint undertakings. For instance, he notes: "The Sifton and Southam newspaper groups have been two major shareholders in All-Canada Radio Facilities Ltd., a management company for advertising sales and the supplying of transcriptions to twenty-nine stations across the country" (1965:468). Today these examples can be multiplied many times over. Examples are "the eight-year partnership of the Thomson group and the Toronto *Star* in the ownership of a limited number of small daily and weekly newspapers"; "the long-standing common interest of Southam and F.P. Publications in the Vancouver *Sun* and *Province*"; the "joint venture launched by the Toronto *Star* and Southam in forming Southstar Publications Limited, which publishes and distributes the *Canadian* and *Canadian Homes* to thirteen papers"; furthermore, in 1969, Southstar papers became printed by Montreal Standard Publishing, the same company which publishes *Weekend*, the "competitor" of the *Canadian*. "The two competitors also joined forces to form MagnaMedia Limited, a new company whose function is to sell advertising for the publications of both companies" (II:22). With these types of overlapping ownership patterns it is difficult at times to distinguish between even the major complexes.

(ii) Access to Media and Who's Vulnerable

Given the concentrated structure of mass media in Canada an important issue becomes who has access to positions of decision making within them. In the capitalist or private media, ownership insures rights of access plus a veto power over others who seek access. This will be examined later but for now another issue of access and vulnerability will be analysed. The Senate Report has observed that: "It is apparent that it is possible in the communications media for conglomerate owners to be employed—either directly or indirectly—to further or protect the other interests of the conglomerate. In Canada, there are a number of such conglomerates with extensive interests in the mass media" (II:16). Their argument is that conglomerates (a series of companies operating in various sectors and held together at the top by a holding company) such as Power Corporation or Argus, which have important holdings in the media, are able to use these to "protect" other diverse interests. If it can be demonstrated that there is an extensive interpenetration of the economic elite into the media, the same argument would apply there as well. It will be demonstrated that just such a situation exists in Canada[3].

Another aspect of vulnerability is the phenomenon of public relations. Most corporations employ public relations men and even have entire departments devoted exclusively to the task of news management. As one public relations man told the Senate hearings: "A public relations man's practice of public relations is inside his organization, rather than outside" (I:250). His argument being that his task is to mediate between corporate executives and media to ensure that the "right" information is released and that it will carry the "proper" connotations. In Canada, there are 1,350 full-time public relations men with nearly 1,000 of them belonging to the Canadian Public Relations Society. They are in the employ of those capable of paying them. Another public relations man said he is engaged in "various shades of seduction. The PR man uses his skills with the news media on a very personal basis to get his [*sic*] story across to alleviate criticism. The newsmen try to use this personal relationship to dig out the stories they really want from the PR man and *his masters*. If the PR man falls for this and gives out the 'inside' story he will probably lose his job or his client" (emphasis added, I:252). The role of the secret is important in powerful circles and it is the powerful who are best able to protect themselves from public scrutiny.

(iii) Content

Freedom of the press must be placed within its economic and political context to have any meaning. Diversity of opinion is clearly evident within the media and liberal-democracies, unlike totalitarian states, pride themselves on their "openness". To place the media in its context means to understand who has access to the media and who is vulnerable. In other words, power in other spheres of society have their reflection in the content of the media. The *major* identification of the media, for a variety of reasons to be examined, is with liberal-democracy and capitalism. Put another way, this means identification with the prevailing political and economic orders. Miliband has argued that the primary concern of the private media is profit but, "making money is not at all incompatible with making politics, and in a more general sense with political indoctrination. Thus the *purpose* of the 'entertainment' industry, in its various forms, may be profit; but the *content* of its output is not therefore by any means free from political and ideological connotations" (1969:225).

Calling on Weber's notion of elective affinity, which is being defined as the selection of ideas from those available which "match" or "fit" the existential position of the people using them, it is argued here that media men, as mediators and conductors of events and ideas, also practice this, wittingly or not. Even the most "objective" of all media, the scientific journals, have been shown to operate according to the principles of elective affinity. Diana Crane examined the academic backgounds of the editors of three established scientific journals and found over-representation of papers submitted by colleges from universities where they were trained with a correspondingly higher rejection rate for those from other institutions. Curtis and Petra have argued that: "Her data tend to substantiate the appraisal that journal editors operate as 'gatekeepers' of science by selectively screening the information that is permitted to circulate through these journals in the scientific community" (1970:44). If this principle operates in the scientific community where objectivity is its hallmark, it can be expected to operate to an even greater extent in the mass media where such values are not so explicit.

Jill Armstrong's work on the F.L.Q. crisis is Quebec sheds some light on the role of the media during such times. Liberal-democracies have generally permitted, in varying degrees, opposition to the prevailing order; however, when threats, factual or contrived, attain serious proportions, the forces of repression are set in motion. Witness, for instance, the mobilization of political, military and ideological forces in Canada during October 1970. Armstrong argues that: "There must be a popular acceptance of the over-all legitimacy of the authorities and the regime. The public response in the Quebec crisis was generally that of unquestioning acceptance and a failure to challenge government policy" (1972:302). Her argument is that: "The official definition of the situation must provide the means for individual actors to identify themselves. . . . Ordinary members weigh the statements of opinion leaders and heed those they see as trustworthy" (303). The role of symbol manipulation is evident in times of crisis. For example, the funeral of Laporte was used as a means to gain overall legitimacy for politicians. "His widow had asked that the funeral be private, but her needs were secondary to those of the state. The ceremony symbolized him as a dedicated representative of the government's policies vis-à-vis French Canada" (303). The media was used very effectively in this event to "mobilize fear" among the populus. Armstrong argues that this is accomplished by "reduction of a complex phenomenon to a readily identifiable and threatening entity. . . . Canadians were given a legitimate target against which to seek retribution" (304). This was designed to gain support for the government. Her explicit purpose in this study was to examine the role of the media, maintaining:

> The media provide a crucial influence on the climate in which members of the public come to form opinions on an issue, since they are the primary sources of information and interpreters of events. The abundant support for the government and the hunt for ideological defectors was undoubtedly affected by editorial treatment of events in Quebec (305).

Contents of letters to the editor revealed the reflexive character of the pro-government writers in terms of repeating the very words used by political leaders. For example, "Almost to a man, the opponents were called 'bleeding hearts', echoing the words of the prime minister in a television interview" (312). Some of the most interesting results from this study were the "consistent findings that trust in the leaderships appeared to be almost automatic suggesting that Canadians eliminated themselves as social actors when faced with events of crucial significance" (323). Her study illustrates that in times of crisis, it is the political leadership which is given access to the media and the media for the most part, gives overwhelming support to that leadership. The rapid translation of government opinion to the public through the media tends to establish particular opinions in the public which in turn supports the government but remains passive in the process, being manipulated both by political power centers and the means of communication.

There is also some evidence concerning content[4] on the level of policy and direct intervention. Floyd S. Chalmers of Maclean-Hunter, the biographer of Col. Maclean, says that: "The Colonel believed that every reputable publication should have well-defined policies, which would provide a strong guideline in every editorial decision. There should be no deviation from basic principles" (1969:252). As owner of the company, it was, of course, Colonel MacLean who set the policy and rigidly enforced it. The Colonel, in fact, was so set on his policies that he resisted attempts by particular advertisers to influence *his* editorial policies.

The Senate Report provides another more specific example of the powerful intervening in the content of the media.

> On the occasion of his retirement as president of Eaton's, in August 1969, John David Eaton was asked if he had ever tried to use his power and influence to quash newspaper stories. "Instead of answering directly, John David countered: 'Wouldn't you?' There were all sorts of things from their private lives that people wouldn't want to see in the paper" (II:148-149).

Another example which relates directly to Eaton's remarks—and explains why in fact powerful people seldom have to intervene—is provided by the Haggart case. Haggart tells of columns he wrote in both the Toronto *Star* and *Telegram* being killed and of explicit instructions from John Bassett of the *Telegram* that anything he did on the Eaton's had to be approved by him before Haggart could even write it (McDayter & Elman, 1971:46; *Last Post*, 1972:29).

The case of *La Presse*, recently acquired by Power Corporation's Paul Desmarais, is also of interest. As "the largest French language daily newspaper in North America, its editorial viewpoint is clearly identifiable with the politics of the Liberal establishment" (Littleton, 1972:16). This should not be surprising in light of the extensive relationships Power has with the Liberal governments of Quebec and Ottawa demonstrated earlier. This editorial stance was accomplished through the "house cleaning" of dissident editors and reporters during the famous *La Presse* strike just after Desmarais took over control of the company.

The Senate Report recognized that the view presented by some owners of media complexes that their separate editors have full autonomy from head office is, at least in part, a justification hinging more on public relations than on reality. The view of the media complex owners "may be tempered somewhat by the awareness that head office is able to influence, at least within certain limits, editorial approach through its power over the appointment of individual publishers and its control over their operating and capital budgets" (II:9). As will be illustrated later, if the editors are not in fact part of the controlling family, as is often the case, they tend to be long-time employees who have spent their entire careers with the company. In the long process before being selected by controlling interests to become an editor, they come to learn the "rules of the game" through the long socialization and selection process. If they suddenly become unruly they can be replaced. Have you ever heard of an editor replacing an owner?

There is another aspect to the content of the media which is not typically considered in these terms: advertising. Advertising affects both the other content and is itself part of the content of the media. In terms of the first point, the Senate Report puts it very succinctly: "What the media *are* selling, in a capitalist society, is an audience, and the means to reach that audience with advertising messages" (I:39). From the point of view of the advertiser, content "is nothing more than the means of attracting the audience". To use the words of the Association of Canadian Advertisers: "Essentially, the national advertiser views any medium simply as a vehicle for conveying his advertising message. . . . He is very definitely interested in the editorial information or program content of any medium, because of course, the nature of the content determines the particular segment of the public likely to be reached" (I:40). What this means is the quite obvious point that the advertiser is indeed concerned about whether his product is sandwiched between a tribute to Lenin or Marcus Welby. It also suggests the obverse as well; that is, the editor or producer is also sensitive to the wants of the advertisers and is very much concerned about their opinion of the media. Any other view in a capitalist society would run the editor or publisher into problems gaining revenue, the backbone of their existence.

(iv) Advertising

It was noted earlier that the management of demand by corporate capitalists, as argued by Galbraith, Miliband, Baran and Sweezy, is an important aspect of distribution for corporations. It should also be noted that it is the crucial aspect of the livelihood of corporations in the media business. It is, in fact, their major source of revenue. Both are dependent on the mass media establishing an audience to which they can sell their products or services. A major consequence of this is to breed political and social indifference among the audience, a development long ago recognized by Weber who said: "Our great capitalist newspaper concerns, which attained control, especially over the "chain newspapers", with "want ads", have been regularly and typically the breeders of political indifference" (1946:97). In any society political indifferences lead to brokerage politics—a politics of acceptance vested in the stability of the ruling order. In other words, political indifference is itself a political action in that it sanctifies those who presently hold power.

Audiences in liberal-democracies have come to accept advertising as part and parcel of the media but this acceptance only accredits the effectiveness of the media in having its audiences accept this form of indoctrination. Today this has achieved such proportions that it might be argued that "news is something written on the back of an advertisement". Indeed, according to Warnock's calculation, "The average daily newspaper today devotes over one-half of its space to advertising'' (1970:122). According to the Senate Report: "The major source of . . . revenue is advertising, and the economics of advertising ultimately determine all other decisions basic to the operation of a newspaper or broadcasting station" (II:119). The symbiotic relationship between the media and advertisers is clear. Each is dependent on the other. It would be absurd to take the position that the presence of advertising as the major source of revenue does not affect the content of the media. In fact, in large part, it has become the content.

It is not necessary to argue that the advertiser directly determines the content of the media. It is enough to know that media owners are very aware of the limits of tolerance and they need to remain within these limits. In this sense, even the state controlled media are not exempt. The Senate Report tells of "a classic case of advertising nervousness" occurring "when the CBC rescheduled a particular episode of its series *Quentin Durgens, MP,* to avoid its coinciding with the introduction of a new line of automobiles. This particular episode was about auto safety. General Motors was the sponsor of the programme" (II:149). But this is simply a single episode within a sea of programming which works within a capitalist framework.

Within recent history this dependency has increased greatly; for example, in 1954 only $8.6 million in advertising revenue was received in television but by 1968 it had increased to $118 million, an increase of 1,272 per cent in 14 years (II:289). The 1971 figures for the newspaper and periodical industry indicate that 73.3 per cent of its revenue was derived from advertising while only 26.8 per cent from sales. The Senate Report maintains that "93% of the gross income of the private broadcasting industry" is from advertising (I:243).

It is often felt that because corporations "subsidize" the media through advertising that the audience gets its entertainment free. This could explain the high levels of tolerance in terms of advertising saturation people endure. But nothing could be further from the actual situation. As Judy LaMarsh has pointed out: "The public does not seem to appreciate that it also pays for the cost of private T.V. . . . by its purchase of the advertiser's products or services" (1969:261). To think that the cost of advertising is borne by corporations is sheer lunacy. Each dollar is transferred to the consumer who is at one and the same time the audience. If they ever came to realize how much they are really paying to listen to the radio, watch television or read a newspaper or magazine, they may demand quality but as it is the cost remains hidden behind a charade of the corporation paying the piper; the corporation calls the tune but the consumer pays.

Finally, and this is the key to the question "Do advertisers control and manipulate the mass media?"; the question boils down to the answer given by the Senate Report: "The point, of course, is that they do not have to; because broadly speaking the advertisers, their agencies, and the media owners are all the same kind of people, doing the same kind of thing, with the same kind of private-enterprise rationale" (I:244). As the study of the elites will show, not only are the media elite the same "kind" of people as the economic elite, in large part, *they are the same people*.

(v) Foreign Impact on the Mass Media

Similar to the finance, transportation and utilities sectors of the Canadian economy, there is very little foreign control of the mass media. This is in contrast to the industrial and resource based sectors where there is very high foreign, particularly U.S., control. This has not developed "accidentally" or without reasons. In fact, these sectors with Canadian control have developed together, being financed and controlled by the same people. In each there has been a high degree of government intervention and assistance. In 1968, following the lead established in the finance sector, the state intervened and has limited foreign ownership in broadcasting to 20 per cent[5]. The newspaper industry, with the notable exception of Thomson Newspapers, which is as much Canadian as British, has traditionally been and remains controlled within Canada. This does not mean there is not a high degree of U.S. influence in the media available in Canada. But this is due more to the geographical proximity and overwhelming power of the U.S. vis à vis Canada and the high degree of penetration in other spheres of the economy than to direct ownership of the media.

Although the percentages vary somewhat, the Senate Report suggests that 68 per cent of Canadians can receive U.S. television broadcasts and obviously a greater proportion can receive radio. Peers says there are "twenty-three U.S. television stations lined along the border" (1970:150). With the extension of cable television into more northern areas it can be expected that this will increase. In spite of this, 83 per cent of the viewing time by Canadians was on Canadian stations in 1968 (151). However, a great deal of the content of the media presented on Canadian stations originates in the U.S.

The periodical business which publishes in the U.S. but circulates in Canada is an important example of U.S. penetration of the media market. The most notable example of this are the *Time* and *Reader's Digest* periodicals (see *Last Post,* May 1973). Similarly, Warnock has illustrated that a great deal of the content of newspapers, especially the "boilerplate", is of U.S. origin (1970:125). This is also true for many syndicated columnists, and even some editorials and political cartoons. U.S. control is felt in other ways as well; for example, the Institute of

Canadian Advertising, whose members conduct between 85 and 90 per cent of all advertising agency work in Canada, has 13 of its 49 members which are U.S. owned. This 26 per cent of the companies are, on the whole, larger than their Canadian counterparts since they conducted 36 per cent of the business (II:136).

Although it is important to note that a great deal of the content and advertising revenue comes from the U.S. or through U.S. controlled companies, it should also be kept in mind that actual ownership and control of the media in Canada remains very firmly with the Canadian media elite. That they decide to use a great deal of U.S. content reflects the similarity between Canada and the U.S. elites in terms of their values and cultural orientation. To note that a great deal of the advertising revenue is U.S. based is simply to acknowledge the obvious that Canada and the U.S. operate in a continental capitalist economy. What is important however, is to recognize that the Canadian media elite is in a position of importance within this continental framework. The media elite are not mere agents of U.S. multinational corporations any more than are the Canadian banks and life insurance companies. They all operate on a common set of capitalist assumptions which places them in a cooperative relationship with one another and not necessarily a subservient one. The Canadian media elite, as with the economic elite in certain sectors, uses the state to preserve its interests. These interests are not contradictory to the interests of U.S. capitalism. Rather, they mesh into a common ground of understanding and operation which maintains each in their positions of dominance.

(vi) The Media's Audience

What is the scope of the media in Canada? If many members of the country were unable to receive the content of the media it would be difficult to argue that it has much impact, regardless of its concentration. The evidence is, however, that most everyone in Canada is reached by the mass media. Ninety per cent of Canadians claim they read a newspaper daily, 95.8 per cent have televisions, and 97.6 per cent have radios, according to the 1972 figures released by Statistics Canada. In fact, more Canadian households in 1972 were without hot and cold water supplies, without baths or showers, without telephones or automobiles than were without televisions; there were even more without toilets than without radios (Information Canada, May 1972). In other words, access to the media seems to be a very high priority for Canadians and access to the media means that the media has access to Canadians as well.

Newspapers   Canada's first newspaper, the *Halifax Gazette*, was founded almost 100 years after the first U.K. paper and almost 50 years after the first appeared in the U.S. Since then several processes have been operating. In 1900, there were 121 dailies and the peak was reached in 1913 when there were 138 but, at that time, there were also 138 publishers. In 1930, 99 publishers controlled 116 dailies. By 1953 there were 89 dailies but only 57 publishers, the period with the fewest dailies and publishers. In 1966, this had increased to 110 dailies and 63 publishers. However, intertwined with the concentration of dailies and publishers is another phenomenon, that of group ownership. By 1970, 12 groups controlled over two thirds of the 116 dailies. While three groups (Southam, Thomson, and FP) controlled about 20 per cent of the circulation in 1958, in 1970 their control had increased to 47 per cent, including 49 of 116 dailies (Senate Report, I:19 and II:60; Kesterton, 1973:19). There is another way of examining concentration and that is a comparison between number of dailies and circulation. In Table 32 the number of dailies and total circulation are traced over a 50-year period. It should be remembered that the phenomenon of groups is occurring in addition to the concentration which appears here.

TABLE 37

Daily Newspapers in Canada (French and English) and Their Circulation, 1921 to 1971. (1921 base year)

Year	Number	Per Cent	Circulation	Per Cent
1921	111	100	1,716,000	100
1931	111	100	2,233,000	130
1941	103	93	2,378,657	139
1951	95	86	3,556,320	207
1961	109	99	4,064,461	237
1971	114	103	4,692,170	273

(Source: *Canada Year Book*, various years)

What these intervals indicate is that the number of dailies over the long term has not increased while, as already pointed out, group ownership has been steadily reducing the independence of these dailies; that is, two thirds of the dailies in 1971 are controlled by only 12 groups while in 1921, the 111 dailies were all independent. While the number of dailies has remained steady with only a three per cent increase in 50 years, the circulation has increased almost three-fold. Nearly the same number of dailies control a much wider circulation than earlier, thus representing concentration several times greater than was evident in 1921.

TABLE 38

Proportion of Daily Newspaper Circulation, 1970

Company	Circulation	% Canadian Total	Cumulative %
1. F. P. Publications	855,170	18.2	18.2
2. Southam	849,364	18.0	36.2
3. Thomson	400,615	8.5	44.7
4. Toronto Star	395,210	8.4	53.1
5. Desmarais-Parisien-Francoeur	319,770	6.8	59.9
6. Telegram*	242,805	5.2	65.0
7. Montreal Star	195,696	4.2	69.6
8. Sifton	115,785	2.5	71.6
9. Irving	104,442	2.2	73.9
TOTAL	3,614,354	73.9	
Total Canadian	4,710,865		

(Table 33 is based on Table 13 of the Senate Report, II:60 with calculations)
Telegram folded in 1972.

Table 38 illustrates the extent of group ownership and concentration for 1970.

These nine groups, all with circulations of over 100,000, control almost three quarters of the total circulation of daily newspapers in Canada. The next five largest complexes control only an additional 2.8 per cent of total circulation between them. As will be seen shortly, many of the companies in these newspaper complexes also have extensive holdings in broadcasting. These nine complexes plus seven others with extensive broadcasting interests, again with circulations over 100,000, are identified here as dominant media complexes and form the basis for identifying the media elite. The forces of centralization and concentration did not end with the Senate Report; as Senator Davey recently said:

> While we were preparing the report, the St. John's *Evening Telegram* was swallowed up by the Thomson chain and Southam acquired the Owen Sound *Sun-Times*. Since we tabled our report, the Cape Breton *Post* became part of the Thomson chain. F.P. Publications added the Montreal *Star* to its chain of big city dailies. Thomson bought the Belleville *Intelligencer*, and the Summerside *Journal-Pioneer*. Southam acquired the Brantford *Expositor*, the Montreal *Gazette* and that lively independent Windsor *Star*. Most recently the Thomson chain purchased the Niagara Falls *Review*. And on and on it goes (1973:3). (1973:3).

By 1972 all of the figures based on concentration in 1970 have become conservative. It is hard to keep pace with the centralization tendencies in Canada's media.

Wire Services   A further way news is concentrated in Canada, beyond the limited number of dailies and media groups, is through The Canadian Press (CP) wire services. This is a news gathering cooperative with 104 of the 114 dailies in Canada belonging to it in 1971 (Canada Year Book, 1972:973). In addition to the local reporting by member papers, the CP has its own news staff and is linked by Teletype to its fellow members. The cost is shared as a ratio of circulation and operates non-profit. According to the Senate Report, "More than 70 papers rely on CP for *all* the news they publish beyond what is written locally by their own staffs" (I:230). Socialism exists in Canada but it is at the top of the largest newspapers in the country! The basic source of news for most of the newspapers in Canada turns out to be identical for each of them.

Television Networks   Television was not introduced to Canada until 1953 and since then it has remained highly concentrated. Since television broadcasting is capital intensive, only those with large amounts of capital could afford to enter the field. Private broadcasters set-up in metropolitan areas but as access to television became defined as a right, the state, through the CBC, became involved to provide service to outlying and less profitable areas. The CBC will be examined more extensively in a moment. The CTV network is set up as a central programming center for its twelve member stations which originate programming and 77 private stations. Air time and advertising time are divided between local stations and the network. Its audience includes over half the households in Canada. The French counterpart to CTV is Tele-Metropole Corporation which has three affiliates. Overall, there are 18 CBC stations (13 English and five French) which originate programming. In addition, there are 40 private stations (32 English and eight French) which are CBC-affiliates. Aside from CTV and T-M Corp., there are only eight independents without network affiliation (Canada Year Book, 1972:64).

Other Media   Radio, which began in Canada in 1918, is less concentrated than either newspapers or television. This is due to the low capital cost of establishing a station. But lower concentration does not mean to say that it too is not concentrated. For example, of the 272 radio stations in the Senate study, 129 (47.4 per cent) have group interests. Of the 103 communities examined, 34 had groups owning two or more stations and 26 where independents did the same. In terms of revenue the concentration is even more apparent. For 1968, only 8.4 per cent of the radio stations controlled 68 per cent of the revenue (I:16; II:345).

Cable television is also becoming a growth area in the media with a little over one quarter of urban households subscribing in 1971. This industry is also highly concentrated and a number of the complexes defined as dominant in other media areas have entered the field. Concentration is indicated by the fact that 11 of 261 companies (4.2 per cent) control 47.2 per cent of sales revenue, 54.6 per cent of net profit, 57.5 per cent of total assets and 45.7 per cent of subscribers (Information Canada, December 1972).

The magazine business, as has been stated, has extensive foreign participation with only one large Canadian company. *Time* and *Reader's Digest*, between them, account for 41 per cent of advertising revenue while Maclean-Hunter has 46 per cent, leaving only 13 per cent for all others (Wolfe, 1973:26)[6].

(vii) State Involvement and Regulation

Of the major media, newspapers have the greatest degree of autonomy from the government. However, like the corporate world, there are a number of pressures which cut across their "autonomy". For example, it was argued earlier that the state, like corporations, engages heavily in news management by employing public relations experts and to some extent politicians themselves are public relations men whose task it is to sell themselves and their policies. Since much of what is defined as "news" concerns legislative matters, the media are dependent on the state to supply their information and similarly, both at election times and during the course of debate, politicians are dependent on access to the media and desire a favourable light shed on themselves and their policies. Another area of mutual relationships where the media desires a strong relationship with both the state and political parties is in advertisement. Since the state uses a great deal of advertisement and a great deal is also used at election times by political parties, the media is interested in maintaining cordial relations with those handing out the funds. A further area which brings them together, and this will be explored shortly, is in the interchange of personnel or those who have been called "elite switchers".

The CBC was established by the state in 1936, initially for radio then later for television. Until 1958, it also served as a regulatory agency but then was replaced by the Board of Broadcast Governors (BBG) in this capacity. As the regulatory functions were removed and private broadcasting became more powerful in Canada, the CBC was forced to move away from the British model of state subsidy to the U.S. model of commercial criteria. Porter has argued, and current evidence substantiates his point, that: "The power of the privately owned stations in their struggle against the CBC does not arise from concentration within the broadcasting industry, but rather it arises from the close links between private broadcasters, publishers, and large corporations" (1965: 470).

For the first few years after the BBG was established, the CBC remained the only television network but soon the CTV network was established and with large amounts of U.S. content, began to capture much of the advertising revenue. This ended the financial independence of the CBC and forced it to rely heavily on Parliament for funding (see Monroe, 1967:42). Additional factors entered as access to the media became defined as a right. The CBC, as a public company, had to take responsibility for outlying areas which were not profitable for private companies thus filling in the gaps left when the profitable areas were saturated. According to Judy LaMarsh: "There has been no noticeable move by privately owned facilities to go into uneconomical

TABLE 39

Sources of Revenue for Canadian Radio and Television, 1970
($ millions)

| | Radio | | | | Television | | | | |
| | Private | | CBC | | Private | | CBC | | |
	$	%	$	%	$	%	$	%
Advertising	111.813	97.6	1.854	4.9	95.906	86.3	34.711	21.1
Other	2.735	2.4	.021	.1	15.259	13.7	.993	.6
Parliament	—	—	35.896	95.0	—	—	128.811	78.3
TOTAL	114.548	100	37.711	100	111.165	100	164.515	100
No. of employees	6,278		1,830		4,149		7,319	

(Canada Year Book, 1972:969 with calculations) .

markets for small numbers of households, so that the burden falls on the public corporation [CBC]'' (1969:246). It also began to take responsibility for providing media in the two official languages. The Senate Report illustrates the effect this has had on advertising revenue in television. For example, ''from 1963-1968, the CBC's network revenue grew by 22.1 per cent. During the same time, the private network revenues grew by 74.3 per cent. The introduction of competition from CTV was largely responsible for the slowness in the growth of CBC revenue'' (II:291). In radio the shift has been even greater. Over the same 1963-1968 period, CBC advertising revenue dropped by 23.1 per cent while private broadcasters have increased by 63.8 per cent (293).

In radio the CBC is almost totally dependent on Parliamentary grants for its source of revenue. CBC radio accounts for 23 per cent of the employees in radio and 24 per cent of the revenue from all sources. In television, on the other hand, CBC has 64 per cent of the employees and 60 per cent of the revenue. The CBC sources of revenue differ between radio and television, with Parliamentary grants accounting for 95 per cent of the former and 78 per cent of the later. Private broadcasting is almost totally dependent on advertising which makes up 98 per cent of radio revenue and 86 per cent of television.

Although there appears to be some variation in the way the CBC is controlled, depending on who is president, Judy LaMarsh's autobiography clearly tells who was in charge when she was Secretary of State. She says that the CBC reported through her ''as a sort of conduit-pipe'' to parliament. But, as she says, this was only on paper; in fact, J. Alphonse Ouimet had direct access to Prime Minister Pearson and only came to her office ''once or twice and only when summoned'' in her final year (1969:252). According to her: ''Ouimet ran the Board of Directors without any question. They did exactly what he required of them. As its Chairman, he alone was responsible for the agenda. . . . Apparently Ernest Bushnell disputed something Ouimet had told the Board. After the meeting, the President took Bushnell to lunch and carefully explained that hereafter there would be only one view put forward to the Board, and it would be his, Ouimet's'' (253). Generally the CBC has a good deal of autonomy from the government but control is exercised over the appointment of the key positions. LaMarsh's writings illustrate that the particular relationship between the CBC and the Cabinet regarding funding, controversy and appointments makes this public corporation very different at the top than private corporations.

Another important government body is the Canadian Radio-Television Commission (CRTC) which was formed in 1967 to replace the BBG. Its task is a licencing agency. According to the Senate Report, this body has a great deal of impact on entry into the broadcasting market and as such, is responsible in large part for the present concentration in this field. "The granting of greater freedom of entry into the market could conceivably result in increased competition and also somewhat wider diversity of ownership, presuming that the proportion of group-owned stations newly licenced is not large" (II:27). In other words, under the present system existing broadcasters operate in a controlled market and it is up to the CRTC to grant further entry. LaMarsh's autobiography also provides details of the careful selection of people to fill the positions on the CRTC board (1969:255-257) and the network of friends or friends of friends operating in recruitment.

In the newpaper field, the Senate Report points out that it is not so much government action as inaction which has led to the present concentration. "On no known occasion in Canada have the joint resources of the Combines and Investigation Branch and the Restrictive Trade Practices Commission prevented a newspaper sale, consolidation or merger" (II:422)[7]. In the following section, the extent of ownership by the largest media complexes will be examined along with some information on who controls these complexes.

II. Dominant Media Complexes

An extensive study of media ownership has recently been undertaken by the Special Senate Committee on Mass Media and will provide the basis for selection of dominant media complexes for this study. The study identified "twenty groups holding extensive media interests in Canada" (1970, II:75). Additional analysis of these complexes indicates that four are substantially smaller as measured by circulation controlled than are the other sixteen and have been dropped from the present study while one other, Moffat Communications, could not be located in either the *Directory of Directors 1972* or through the CALURA reports filed with Consumer and Corporate Affairs in Ottawa. This leaves fifteen corporate complexes which form the base of what is being called the media elite. Each of the groups will be examined in turn, but first, those excluded will be briefly discussed.

Of the twenty groups identified, the following were excluded as too small based on their circulation: The Crépault Group, The Dougall Family, Rogers Broadcasting, and The Pratte, Baribeau and Lepage Group. The Crépault Group controls six radio stations with a total circulation of 693,700 and is controlled by Raymond Crépault. The Dougall Family controls five radio stations with a circulation of 106,500 and a television station with 87,000. Rogers Broadcasting Ltd. has four radio stations with a circulation of 327,900 and four cable companies which are "controlled by shares held in two Rogers' family trusts, its president being Edward S. Rogers''. The fourth group does not have its circulation published in the Senate Report and all that is said is that: "The Pratte, Baribeau and Lepage families have extensive and often intricately interlocked broadcasting interests in Quebec" (II:97). It is evident that the effect of excluding these four smaller complexes reduces the extent of family ownership and control within the media elite. Consequently, everything said in the next section on elite composition should be regarded as "conservative" in this respect.

(i) *The Bassett-Eaton Group*

This complex was best known for the Toronto *Telegram* which recently folded with a circulation of 242,805 but remains powerful operating through Baton Broadcasting Inc., which controls two television stations with a circulation of 1,343,600, including CFTO-TV of Toronto. "Shares are held in trust for the three sons of Toronto publisher John W.H. Bassett and the four sons of John David Eaton" (II:76). Interestingly, "Baton Broadcasting Limited also controls Israel Canada Production, based in Tel Aviv and responsible for producing 80 per cent of Israeli television" (II:76). Eaton family holdings are well known in retail trade as are the Bassett interests in Maple Leaf Gardens, the Toronto Maple Leaf Hockey Club and the Argonaut Football Club.

The following account of the death of the Toronto *Telegram* places in perspective the basis of the sale:

> Bassett could make more out of a dead *Tely* than a live one. The negotiations between Bassett and Honderich (of the Toronto *Star*) which had been carried out (since July or spring, no one is certain) by Walter Gordon. On September 14, the negotiations culminated in a peculiar deal. The *Star* purchased the *Telegram*'s subscription list of about 84,000 names for $10 million. Just the list. The *Star* leased the *Tely*'s presses for two years for $1 million a year. Add $2 million. The *Globe* & *Mail*, in search of a new printing plant and office, agreed to purchase the *Tely* building for a reported minimum of $7 million (one account has it as $12 million). Add a minimum of $7 million. Total value of the *Tely* dead: $19 million *at least*. Total value of the *Tely* alive, if sold, $11 million. For Bassett, the decision was clear (*Last Post*, 1972:31).

Three generations of Bassett's have been dominant in the media. John Bassett was president and publisher of the Montreal *Gazette* while Major John White Hughes Bassett, who purchased the Toronto *Telegram* in 1953, is presently the chairman and president of Baton Broadcasting. His son, John F. Bassett, is now a vice-president and director of the company. J.W.H. Bassett is also chairman of the Argonaut Football Club while his son, J.F., is a director and president of Agincourt Productions. The family has private school links and memberships in key national exclusive men's clubs. For example, J.W.H. attended Ashbury College School before receiving his B.A. from the University of Bishop's College in 1936 and has memberships in the Toronto, York, St. James', Mount Royal and Layford Cay (Bahamas) clubs.

Also linked with the company is the Eaton family represented on the board of Fredrik S. Eaton, an Upper Canada College graduate and fourth generation Eaton in the elite. He also has a membership in the Toronto Club. Another directorship link with Eaton's is Allan Leslie Beattie, Q.C., a partner in Osler, Hoskin and Harcourt of Toronto and also a member of the Toronto Club, having attended St. Andrew's College private school, the University of Toronto and Osgoode. He is the son of Robert Leslie Beattie, a former executive of the International Nickel Co. and director of the Bank of Toronto. Another lawyer, Edwin A. Goodman, Q.C., also a graduate of the University of Toronto and Osgoode, and member of Goodman and Goodman of Toronto, provides a link with the John Labatt Ltd. where he is a director as he is with Cadillac Development Corp. and United Trust. He is former executive director of the P.C. Party of Ontario and presently chairman of a Committee for an Independent Canada. Charles L. Dubin, Q.C., a third lawyer on the board, also graduated from University of Toronto and Osgoode; he is with Tory, Tory, DesLauriers and Binnigton of Toronto, and is also director of the Argonaut Football Club. Charles Fowler William Burns is also a director as well as chairman of Crown Life, as was his father before him who was also associated with the Bank of Nova Scotia and National Trust. His father-in-law, Norman F. Wilson, was a member of the Senate and director of Crown Life. C.F.W. Burns also attended Upper Canada College and Trinity College School as well as the University of Toronto. Presently, he is a member of the Toronto Club and York Club as well as the Rolling Rock in Pennsylvania. He is also a director of the Argonaut Football Club, Algoma Central Railway, Canada Permanent Trust and Mortgage, The Ontario Jockey Club, and Denison Mines. Finally, Foster W. Hewitt, who broadcast the first hockey game in Canada in 1923, is a vice-president of the company and chairman of Radio Station CKFH. He also attended Upper Canada College, the third member of the board to do so, and the University of Toronto, the fifth board member having done so. He holds a 16.6 per cent interest in the company.

(ii) *Bushnell Communications*.

Bushnell has diverse media interests, including twelve radio stations of which seven have 406,900 circulation (unknown for the other five) and six television stations of which five have a circulation of 1,217,100 in addition to four cable companies. A good deal of Bushnell's power in the media is directly related to government action. For example, federal legislation forced Canadian Marconi to reduce its broadcasting holdings because it was British controlled and the CRTC approved Bushnell's takeover of the company's interests for almost $23 million. "The approval was very important, apart from any other consideration, because it placed two major CTV affiliates and programme-production centers under the same direct control. This required the CRTC to overlook the policy laid down in 1966 by the BBG prohibiting any further multiple interests in CTV" (II:77-78). Once again, control is tightly held, 78.5 per cent through a voting trust whose trustees are E.L. Bushnell, G.E. Beament and A. Martineau.

Since 1969, Ernest L. Bushnell has been chairman of the company. A former member of the bureaucratic elite, having spent many years with the CBC and resigning as a vice-president. He is a member of the Rideau Club and son-in-law of Edward Wood who was president of Dominion Securities, vice-president of National Trust, director of Canada Life, Canadian Imperial Bank of Commerce and Brazillian Traction. Also listed as a director is the Hon. Jeanne Sauve, now a Minister in the federal cabinet as was her husband, the Hon. Maurice Sauve, who is presently associated with Power Corporation as a vice-president of its subsidiary, Consolidated-Bathurst. He is also a director of BP Canada. O. John Firestone is another former bureaucratic elite member associated with the federal government for 18 years and now a professor of economics and vice-dean on the faculty of social science at the University of Ottawa. Clarence Edward Atchison, a vice-president of The Investors Group, another Power Corporation subsidiary, is a director of Bushnell as well as Montreal Trust and Great-West Life, two further Power subsidiaries. Willard Estey, Q.C., a lawyer with Robertson, Lane, Perrett, Frankish and Estey of Toronto provides a further political link. His lawyer father was a Liberal Minister of Education for the Province of Saskatchewan.

(iii) *CHUM Ltd*.

Allan F. Waters controls CHUM Ltd. which includes six radio stations with a circulation of 967,800 and a television station with 219,000. Allan Frederick Waters, in addition to being president of CHUM Ltd., is a director of the CTV Television Network. He is also a director of the recently created Canada Development Corporation. Ralph Trapnell Snelgrove, chairman of Barrie Broadcasting is a vice-president and director. His father-in-law, J.G. Fraser, was a vice-president of Barrie Broadcasting and a vice-president of Victoria and Grey Trust. Another director, R.M. Sutherland, Q.C., a partner in Fashen and Calvin of Toronto is also a director of Collier-Macmillan of Canada and Kennecott Canada. Arthur Deane Nesbitt provides a directorship link with Power Corporation, as well as TransCanada PipeLines, Manufacturers Life and Consolidated-Bathurst. He is also a chairman and chief executive officer of Nesbitt, Thomson & Co., investment dealers, as was his father before him, who organized Power Corporation in 1925 and was an associate of Sir Herbert Holt, president of the Royal Bank. A.D. is son-in-law of D. Ross McMaster, director of Standard Life, the Bank of Montreal and Steel Co. of Canada and brother-in-law to A.C. McKim, a director of National Trust and Consolidated-Bathurst.

(iv) *Paul Desmarais, Jean Parisien and Jacques Francoeur.*

As of 1970 this complex controlled newspaper circulation of 319,770 including four dailies of which *La Presse* (Montreal), taken over in 1967, was the largest, twelve weeklies and five weekend magazines. In addition to this, two radio stations with a circulation of 25,700 and a television station with 122,500. According to a recent *Financial Post* story on the pending sale of the family-owned *Le Soleil*, a major Quebec City daily: "The pending purchase is a particularly important and sensitive one in Quebec since Power Corp. currently holds five of the province's French-language daily publications. Should it also own *Le Soleil* and its affiliate, it would control some 70 per cent of the province's French-speaking circulation" (September 22, 1973:5)[8]. Paul Desmarais, according to the Senate Report, "owns just over 30 per cent of Power Corporation" (II:82), certainly sufficient to exercise control over this widely diversified and powerful corporation. Power Corporation is used as the holding company for these interests.

In 1965, Porter argued that there were no chains in the French newspapers and there "appear to be no substantial interlocking interests between newspapers and television" (1965:487-488). The entry of Power Corporation, under the direction of financier Paul Desmarais, has changed both these positions. As shown above, this group now owns five of the seven French language papers in the province and is in the process of acquiring a sixth (see *The Citizen*, December 12, 1973:11). This has all occurred within the space of about five years. Another development, to be explored in more detail under Télémédia

(Quebec), changes the second point described by Porter that the French publishing and broadcasting interests are separate. The recent acquisition of controlling interest in Télémédia by Power through its subsidiary Montreal Trust rounds out its extensive media interest in the province.

Power Corporation's extensive non-media holdings and state connections need not be elaborated again here. Paul Desmarais, son of a Sudbury lawyer, graduated in commerce from the University of Ottawa and is a member of the St. James' Club, is chairman and chief executive officer of the company. He is also director of Brascan, Consolidated-Bathurst and Montreal Trust. Along with his brother, Louis, he is also a director of *La Presse*. Louis, a commerce graduate from McGill, is president and chief executive officer of Canada Steamship Lines as well as director of Power. He is also vice-chairman of the Canada Development Corporation. As mentioned earlier, A.D. Nesbitt is simultaneously director of CHUM Ltd. and Power. Arthur Simard, Q.C., related to Robert Bourassa, Premier of Quebec, is a product of the classical college system and graduate from law at the University of Montreal. He is a third generation member of the Quebec bourgeoisie, following the tradition of his grandfather, Capt. Joseph, the famous merchant capitalist and his father, Joseph, who held directorships in seven dominant corporations. Jean-Paul Gignac, another classical college graduate, is president and general manager of Sidbec and Sidbec-Dosco, Quebec crown corporations. In addition to his Power directorships, he is on the board of Brinco Ltd. His brother, Jacques, also has a distinguished bureaucratic career as former vice counsel in Boston and presently Libian Ambassador. Several lawyers also sit on the board, Paul Britton Paine, Q.C., is general counsel, vice-president and director while Wilbrod Bherer, Q.C., is a partner in Bherer, Bernier, Cote, Ouellet, Morin and Huot of Quebec City. Both belong to the St. James' Club. The third lawyer is the Hon. John Robarts, former Premier of Ontario, who is now partner in two law firms and director of Abitibi Paper, Bell Canada, Canadian Imperial Bank of Commerce, and Metropolitan Life in addition to Power. Peter D. Curry, graduate of Ridley College and Bishop's University, is chairman of The Investors Group and Cablecasting Ltd., as well as a director of Power, Northern and Central Gas, Molsons Industries, The International Nickel Co., and Ford Motor Co. W. Earle McLaughlin, chairman and president of the Royal Bank, is director of Power, Metropolitan Life, Algoma Steel, Canadian Pacific, and Genstar Ltd. He is also a member of the board of General Motors Corp. (Detroit) and has club memberships in the York, the Toronto, Mount Royal, Rideau and St. James' clubs. Robert

Carleton Scrivner, President of Bell Canada, is also on the board of Power and the Canadian Imperial Bank of Commerce, holding club memberships in the St. James' and Mount Royal clubs. Alfredo Campo belongs to the same clubs and, in addition to being on the board of Power, is chairman and chief executive officer of Petrofina Canada. His father-in-law, H.H. Bradburn, was vice-president and director of McCall-Frontenac Oil. The examples of Power directors with private school education, elite inheritance, dominant directorships and exclusive national men's clubs goes on and on.

(v) *F.P. Publications*.

Holding 18.2 per cent of all daily newspaper circulation in Canada with circulation of 855,170, F.P. Publications is the largest corporation in its field. In addition, it has interests in two cable companies. Its newspaper interests include eight dailies, the most notable of which are the *Globe & Mail* in Toronto and the Vancouver *Sun*.

Brig. Richard Sankey Malone, son of Lt. Col. Willard Park Malone, is president and general manager of F.P. Publications while also acting as president and publisher of the Winnipeg *Free Press*. He is also chairman and chief executive officer of The Journal Publishing Co., executive vice-president of Sun Publishing and director of several subsidiary papers such as the *Globe & Mail*. A graduate of the University of Toronto Schools and Ridley College, he also belongs to the Rideau Club. He has a long career as a reporter and acted as staff secretary to the Minister of Defense during the war in charge of such things as public relations for the Normandy Campaign. R. Howard Webster took over control of the *Globe & Mail* in 1955 and now holds the post of chairman in that company and is deputy chairman of F.P. Publications. He is also president of Imperial Trust, a position he has held since 1961. In addition to a number of directorships on subsidiary newspapers, he is chairman of Quebecair, the Windsor Hotel, Penobscot Building and president of Detroit Marine Terminals, while holding directorships in Burns Foods and Holt-Renfrew and Co. He is a graduate of Lower Canada College and McGill University. Like his brother, Colin Wesley, who has directorships on Domtar, Massey-Ferguson, Pacific Petroleum, Hawker Sidley, Royal Bank and Sun Life, he carries on the tradition of their father, Hon. Lorne Campbell, who was a Senator and attained his initial wealth in the St. Lawrence Coal Business becoming President of Town Publishers and director of Imperial Trust, Holt-Renfrew & Co. and Dominion Steel and Coal. Donald C. McGavin, Q.C., formerly a partner in Aikins, MacAulay, Moffat, Dickson, Hinch and McGavin of Winnipeg, is now general solicitor for the International Nickel Co. of Canada and director of both

F.P. Publications and *The Globe & Mail*. James Stuart Keate, publisher of the Vancouver *Sun* and vice-president and director of Sun Publishing also sits on the board. He has a long career in journalism. He married the daughter of financier Hugh E. Melicke, son of Senator Emil J., and was president of Great Northern Investment Co.

(vi) *The Irving Group*.

"The greatest regional concentration of mass media ownership in Canada is to be found in New Brunswick. All five of the English-language daily newspapers in the province are controlled by K.C. Irving" (II:86). This includes five daily newspapers with a circulation of 104,442 plus a radio station with circulation of 52,700 and two television stations with 296,200. "In addition to the media outlets which it controls, the K.C. Irving Group has probably the most diverse non-media interests of any conglomerate organization in Canada. . . . By any standard, the interests of the Irving family are large. They assume gigantic proportions, however, in a province that lags behind many other parts of the country in industrial development" (II:87).

K.C. Irving's interest ranges over a number of corporations in the petroleum, lumber and publishing fields, and in 1972 had "left his business empire valued at $500 million by many in the hands of his three sons". They are John E., who "acquired the Moncton Publishing Co. and University Press of N.B. . . . and will own the companies outright"; James K., who "acquired 40% interest in New Brunswick Publishing Co." and; Arthur L., who "acquired 40% interest in N.B. Publishing". In the words of Beland Honderich, publisher of the Toronto *Star*: "Mr. Irving has in effect, created a private empire of New Brunswick, complete with its official press—print and electonic" (I:70).

(vii) *Maclean-Hunter Limited*.

With diverse media interests in the publication field and broadcasting, Maclean-Hunter is described by the Senate Report as "a major mass-communications conglomerate" which includes "three English-language and two French-language consumer periodicals, with a total circulation of 2,262,800; a weekly, the *Financial Post*, with a circulation of 154,000; forty-six English-language and ten French-language business periodicals with a total circulation of approximately 516,000; and twenty-one annuals". In addition, it controls two television stations with a circulation of 300,000 and six radio stations of which five have a circulation of 416,500 plus sixteen cable companies. "The largest single block of stock is held by the Hunter family" (II:90).

In 1973, the company purchased Macmillan of Canada. According to the company's *Annual Report for 1972*: "This acquisition combined with the company's interest in New Press and the works published under the imprints of Maclean-Hunter Learning Materials Company and Maclean-Hunter Limited, itself, created a significant new Canada-oriented force in the book-publishing industry". Over the past five years the interests of the company have been diversified. For example, in 1968, publishing accounted for 73 per cent of revenue while this declined to 55.7 per cent in 1972, broadcasting remained fairly even with 10 per cent earlier and 12.7 per cent currently. The major shift occurred in cable TV where the proportion of revenue rose from 2.6 per cent to 12.3 per cent.

Maclean-Hunter represents an interesting case of "inheritance". Left without a living son, Col. Maclean "adopted two or three dozen young men as his 'children'. He often called them just that" (Chalmers, 1969:viii). Actually, he "adopted" only Hunter to pass the company on to. In 1920, he sold 30 per cent of the company to him and "he initiated an arrangement whereby Hunter could eventually acquire, from the Maclean estate, enough shares to represent full voting control" (321-322).

President of Maclean-Hunter is Donald G. Campbell, a long-time employee of the company and director of CTV Television Network as well as serving in various capacities on the boards of many of the Maclean-Hunter subsidiaries. Control of the company rests with Donald F. Hunter, a graduate of Upper Canada College and University of Toronto. He is son of Horace T. Hunter, who was president of Macleans in 1933, and chairman of Maclean-Hunter in 1952, as well as director of the Toronto Bank. Donald F. is now chairman of Maclean-Hunter and director of the Toronto-Dominion Bank. Most of the board members are long-time employees of the company: James Lindley Craig, executive vice-president and director of the company since 1964 who joined in 1930. He is a member of the National Club; Floyd Sherman Chalmers began with the company in 1919 acting for 17 years as editor of the *Financial Post* and becoming president from 1952 to 1964, continuing to 1969 as chairman. He is a member of the York Club, Chancellor of York University and author of *A Gentleman of the Press*, the biography of John Bayne Maclean, founder of the company. Also on the board are a number of editors and publishers of the company's major publications; for example, Doris Hilda Anderson has been editor of *Chatelaine* since 1958. Others include Paul Septimus Deacon as editor and publisher of the *Financial Post*. He attended the University of Toronto Schools, as did his three brothers, all of whom have been associated with their father's stock brokerage firm, F.H.

Deacon. Brother Donald Mackay is a Liberal MLA in the Ontario legislature. Paul S. graduated from the University of Toronto with his M. Comm. whereupon he joined the *Financial Post*. Another director is Peter C. Newman, publisher and editor of *Maclean's* magazine. He is a graduate of Upper Canada College and University of Toronto where he received his M. Comm. He is also a member of the Rideau Club.

(viii) *The McConnell Family*.

Based in the Montreal *Star* with a circulation of 195,696 and *Weekend* magazine with 1,805,839, the McConnell family fortune built by J.W. McConnell is kept intact through a complex financial arrangement. "At the apex of the McConnell family holdings are 88 per cent of the shares of the Commercial Trust Company Limited held by the Montreal Trust Company as part of a voting trust agreement under which the shares are voted at the direction of J.G. McConnell and Mrs. P.M. Laing during their lifetimes" (II:95).

The Montreal *Star* was acquired by John Wilson McConnell in 1925 who became president of the company in 1938 when the earlier publisher died. He was also president of St. Lawrence Sugar Refinery. He was active in the Montreal financial world as president of the Bank of Montreal and with directorships in Montreal Light & Heat, Holt-Renfrew, Brazillian Traction, Canada Steamship Lines, Ogilvie Flour Mills, Sun Life, International Nickel and Royal Trust. The presidency was later acquired by his son, John G. McConnell, who attended Lower Canada College, McGill and Cambridge. Having since retired from the presidency, he remains a director of the company, also acting in that capacity with St. Lawrence Sugar and as chairman of Commerical Trust. He is a member of the Mount Royal, St. James', The Brook (N.Y.) and Sunnydale Gold (England) clubs. The current president and chief executive officer is Derek A. Price who married Jill McConnell in 1954. He is a graduate of Bishop's College School and Princeton. Derek A. is one of the long line from the Price family in the elite. His uncle, Arthur Clifford, is director of Royal Trust and The Price Co., being chairman from 1961 to 1965. Derek A.'s father, John H., also graduated from Bishop's College School and was associated with The Price Bros., Saguenay Power, CHRC, International Power and, Quebec Pulp and Power. His father was Sir William Price, also of Bishop's College School, and president of Price Bros. as well as vice-president of the Union Bank and director of Montreal Trust. He was also an MP in the House of Commons. Kathleen G. Laing, daughter of John Wilson McConnell, is also a director as is her husband, Peter Marshall Laing, Q.C., who had a private school education in England and graduated from McGill and Oxford. He is now a partner in Laing, Weldon, Courtois, Clarkson, Parsons, Gouthier and Tetrault of Montreal. Another former president and long-time employee of the company, now acting as a director, is Robert Lawrence Brown who is a member of the St. James' Club. Another lawyer, R.E. Parsons, Q.C., of Smith, Anglin, Laing, Weldon & Courtois of Montreal is also on the board as well as on the board of Sheraton Ltd.

(ix) *Moffat Broadcasting*.

Although it was not possible to determine the directorship holders of Moffat Broadcasting, the company has media interests extensive enough to be considered dominant. It holds seven radio stations with a circulation of 701,900 and a television station with 325,000 as well as two cable companies.

(x) *The Sifton Group*.

Operating as the Armadale Communications Ltd., the Sifton family represents a long tradition in the media. The group owns two newspapers with a circulation of 115,785, four radio stations with 513,000, two television stations, one of which has 191,100 and a magazine with 32,000.

Armadale Communications represents three generations of control in the media elite by the Sifton family. Hon. Sir Clifford Sifton, K.C., purchased the Winnipeg *Free Press* in 1889. He was a noted statesman, publisher and member of the Laurier cabinet (his brother, the Rt. Hon. Arthur Lewis Sifton was premier of Alberta and also a federal minister). His son, Clifford Sifton, Q.C., attended the Ottawa Model School, University of Toronto and Osgoode and is presently chairman of Armadale. He belongs to the Toronto Club and is brother-in-law to E. Llewellyn Gibson Smith, president of E.D. Smith & Sons, and director of Guaranty Trust. Michael C. Sifton, now president of Armadale is son of Clifford and attended Trinity College School and the University of Western Ontario. He ''was responsible for revival of polo in Toronto after the 2nd World War'' and is a member of the Toronto Club.

(xi) *The Southam-Selkirk Group*.

Almost equal to F.P. Publications in terms of the total daily newspaper circulation with 849,364 representing 18 per cent of all circulation for Canada, the Southam-Selkirk group is even more powerful because of its extensive holdings outside newspapers. In addition to the 14 dailies and 2 weeklies, there are three weekend magazines with a circulation of about 2-1/2 million, 34 business publications, 15 business annuals, eight television stations with 2,318,600 and 13 radio stations of which 10 have 709,700. They also have interests in four cable companies. "While it is estimated that no single interest holds more than 3.6 per cent, control over the company is exercised by a large number of persons related to the Southam family by birth and marriage" (II:101).

Founded in 1877 when an interest in the Hamilton *Spectator* was acquired by William Southam, the company has remained in family control. President since 1961 has been St. Clair Balfour, related to the family through his mother, Ethel May Southam. He attended Trinity College School and University of Toronto and is now a member of the Toronto and York clubs. Colin S. Glassco, son-in-law to St. Clair Balfour, is chairman of Southam Printing and director of Southam Press, as well as a director of Union Gas and Canada Trust. He too attended Trinity College School. Five Southam's are also on the board: W.J.H., Robert Wilson, William Watson, Gordon Hamilton and Gordon T. They have also had the advantages associated with private school education. Gordon T. is also a director of MacMillan-Bloedel and Gordon Hamilton, in addition to his journalism and diplomatic career, is director-general of the National Arts Centre. This does not exhaust the Southam interest on the board. Gordon Neil Fisher's maternal grandfather was Fredrick Neil Southam, one-time president of Southam Publications and son of William. His own father, Philip Sydney Fisher was president of Southam Co. while his father-in-law, William A. Arbuckle, is currently associated with Standard Life, Bank of Montreal, The Price Co., Petrofina Canada, and Canadian Pacific. Gordon Neil attended Lower Canada College School, Trinity College School and McGill and has memberships in the Toronto and York clubs. Robert Ross Munro, publisher of the Edmonton *Journal* is also a director and the "third generation of the family in newspaper work". Charles Hamilton Peters, nephew of Senator Robert Smeaton White, is president of Gazette Printing, a firm his father was also associated with, and also on the board of Southam Press. He belongs to the St. James' and Mount Royal clubs. Britton Bath Osler, Q.C., who with his brother, Peter Scarth Osler, Q.C., is a partner in his father's old law firm of Blake, Cassels and Graydon of Toronto, is also on the board. His father was also on the board of Southam in addition to National Steel Car, Bell Telephone, Woods Manufacturing, Imperial Realty, Mutual Life and the Steel Co. of Canada. His grandfather, Hon. Featherston Osler was a Justice of the Supreme Court of Ontario. He attended Ridely College, Royal Military College and Osgoode and is a member of the Toronto and York clubs. Frank Gustave Swanson, publisher of the Calgary *Herald* is a vice-president and director of

Southam Press and member of the Rideau Club. Additional corporate interlocks are provided by George L. Crawford, Q.C., who is a partner in Arnold and Crawford of Calgary and director of Canadian Utilities. His father, John Lydon, was an Alberta Judge and lawyer, as was his maternal grandfather, Hon. W.H. Biggs. Jean Jacques Pigott, vice-president and director, as are his brothers, William P. and Joseph Michael, of their father's and grandfather's firm of Pigott Construction. He is also a director of North American Life Assurance. He belongs to the National, St. James', and York clubs. Adam Hartely Zimmerman, Jr., son-in-law of Senator John S. Lewis, a lawyer and former editorial writer with the *Globe & Mail*, is on the board of Southam Press and British Columbia Forest Products. He is also vice-president and comptroller of Noranda Mines. He attended Upper Canada College, Ridley College and University of Toronto.

(xii) *Standard Broadcasting Corporation Limited.*

Argus Corporation holds controlling interest in Standard Broadcasting which operates five radio stations with four of these having circulation of 1,271,100. Argus is a powerful holding company operating in several sectors of the economy.

President of Standard Broadcasting is W.C. Thornton Cran. He is also an Argus director and member of the York and Mid-Ocean (Bermuda) clubs. John Angus McDougald is chairman of Standard Broadcasting and chairman and president of Argus. He is also a director and member of the executive committee of the Canadian Imperial Bank of Commerce and director of Domtar and Massey-Ferguson. His father, Duncan J., was a wealthy Toronto financier and investment dealer and director of the CNR and Trust & Guarantee Co. and brother of Senator W.L. McDougald. John Angus attended Upper Canada College and St. Andrew's College and is a member of the Toronto, Mount Royal, York, Rolling Rock (Pa.), Buck's (London), Seminole Golf (Palm Beach) and Metropolitan (N.Y.) clubs. W. Leo Knowlton, Q.C., attended St. Michael's College School, University of Toronto and Osgoode and is director of both Standard Broadcasting and Canada Permanent Mortgage. He is a member of the National Club. Pierre Paul Daigle, son of the Hon. Senator Louis Armand Daigle, director of Canadian Breweries, Montreal Life, RCA Victor, and other companies, attended Mt. St. Louis College and is a director of Standard Broadcasting, Confederation Life and Dominion Stores, as well as the Goodyear Tire & Rubber Co. and RCA. Alex E. Barron is director of Standard Broadcasting, Argus, Domtar, Huron & Erie Mortgage,

Great Canadian Oil Sands, London Life, Dominion Stores and chairman of Canadian Tire. He is also a member of the Toronto Club. Maj-Gen. A. Bruce Matthews, whose father, the Hon. Albert Matthews, was Lt.-Gov. of Ontario, president of Excelsior Life and director of Toronto General Trust, attended Upper Canada College and the University of Geneva. He is chairman of Excelsior Life, chairman of Canada Permanent Mortgage, executive vice-president of Argus and director of Standard Broadcasting, Dominion Stores, Massey-Ferguson and Domtar. He is a member of the Toronto, York and Mount Royal clubs. George Montegu Black, Jr. attended Appleby College and the University of Manitoba. His father-in-law is Conrad S. Riley, chairman of the Canadian Committee of the Hudson's Bay Co. and director of the Royal Bank and Great West Life. He is also brother-in-law to G.P. Osler. His own father was president of Western Breweries and director of the Union Bank of Canada. He is an Argus vice-president and director as well as holding directorships with Standard Broadcasting, Dominion Stores and the Canadian Imperial Bank of Commerce. He is a member of the Toronto, York, St. James', and Layford Cay (Nassau) clubs. G. Allan Burton, who attended the University of Toronto Schools, Lycee Jaccard in Switzerland and University of Toronto, is son of Charles Luther, who was chairman of Simpsons and director of H. Smith Paper and North American Life. G. Allan is also chairman of Simpsons in addition to holding directorships on Standard Broadcasting, Simpson-Sears and the Royal Bank. He belongs to the York, Toronto, Mount Royal and Rolling Rock (Pa.) clubs. Thomas Norbert Beaupre transferred from the bureaucratic elite to become chairman and president of Domtar, director of Standard Broadcasting, Argus, the Royal Bank, Hudson's Bay Co. and Hudson's Bay Gas and Oil. He is a member of the Rideau, Toronto, St. James' and Mount Royal clubs. Col. Maxwell C.G. Meighen who is the son of Rt. Hon. Arthur Meighen, former Prime Minister of Canada and director of Canadian Cellulose, Huron & Erie Mortgage, and vice-president and director of Canada Trust, is director of Standard Broadcasting, Argus, Huron & Erie Mortgage, Dominion Stores, Algoma Steel, Domtar, Massey-Ferguson, Canadian General Electric, and Canada Trust, as well as chairman of Canadian General Investments, a firm founded by his father in 1926. He attended Royal Military College and the University of Toronto and is a member of the Toronto Club.

(xiii) *Télémédia (Quebec) Limited*.

With three television stations, two of which have a circulation of

539,600 and 10 radio stations with 517,700, Télémédia is an important counterpart in broadcasting to Power Corporation in publications. Interestingly, the company is a recent offspring of Power:

> Phillippe de Gaspé Beaubien came to broadcasting in 1968 following four years as Chief Administrator of Expo facilities. For about two years he was the President of Québec Télémédia Inc., the broadcast holding company owned by Power Corporation. In 1970, Power Corporation determined to separate itself from all involvement in communications media. Beaubien agreed to purchase all the holdings of Télémédia Inc. and its name and gained C.R.T.C. approval on June 17, 1970 (II:108).

This is of interest because the transfer occurred prior to the Senate Report, thus reducing significantly Power Corporation's extensive control over all forms of private media in Quebec. It is interesting that with the December 31st, 1971 report filed with CALURA of the Consumer and Corporate Affairs, it is found that Philippe de Gaspé Beaubien indeed holds 42.1 per cent of the voting shares but the surprising fact is that Montreal Trust Company holds 57.9 per cent. Montreal Trust is now more than 50 per cent owned by Power Corporation. During the same time, the board of directors of Télémédia has not changed.

Interestingly, Télémédia has close state ties similar to those characteristic of Power Corp. Philippe de Gaspé is president of the company and director of GSW Ltd. and Dominion Bridge. His father was a vice-president of Canada Starch and director of Howard Smith Paper. Philippe de Gaspé graduated from the University of Montreal and Harvard School of Business Administration. He is a member of Mount Royal Club and has had an extensive career with the state as director of operations of Canadian Corporation for the 1967 World Exhibition and mayor of Expo 1967 from 1963 to 1967. He is chairman of the Sports Council and president of Sport Participation Canada. Nan-b. de Gaspé Beaubien is also a director of Télémédia. Another director is Pierre DesMarais II, who inherited his father's firm and attended College Jean-de-Brébeuf, College Ste.-Marie and the University of Montreal in business adminstration. He is also a director of Air Canada and the Canadian National Railway. Yves Jasmin, also a director of Télémédia is vice-president of public relations for Air Canada, previously being associated with Molsons Brewery and Ford of Canada as a public relations officer and director of public relations, information and advertising for The Canadian Corporation for 1967 World Exhibition from 1964-1967. Charles Leblanc, Q.C., a graduate of Scholarie De Sherbrooke, University of Ottawa and University of

Montreal, is an executive vice-president of Bombardier Ltd. and director of Télémédia.

(xiv) *The Thomson Group*.

Controlling 30 dailies and 11 weeklies, in addition to other interests,
Thomson Newspapers has the third highest control over total daily
distribution in Canada with 8.5 per cent, and circulation of 400,615.
"Lord Thomson has world-wide media interests. His North American
interests are linked in a highly complex corporate structure. There
interests are operated, in the main, by Thomson Newspapers Limited,
which is 72.6 per cent controlled by Lord Thomson's Woodbridge
Company Limited" (II:109).

Lord Thomson of Fleet is honorary chairman of the company and
founder of Thomson Newspapers as well as being director of the Royal
Bank, Imperial Life and Abitibi Paper. His son, The Hon. Kenneth R.,
is chairman and president of Thomson Newspapers as well as president
of Woodbridge and director of Abitibi Paper and Toronto-Dominion
Bank. He attended Upper Canada College and the University of Cambridge and is a member of the National, Toronto and York clubs. Ian H.
MacDonald, who was educated at Gordon College in Aberdeen and the
Edinburgh University, came to Canada at 22 and worked in the newspaper business becoming deputy chairman of Thomson Newspapers
and director of Woodbridge. He is a member of the Toronto and
National clubs. St. Clair Landerkin McCabe is a publishing executive
and executive vice-president, managing director and director of Thomson Newspapers as well as director of the Woodbridge Co. He is a
member of the National Club. The Hon. Walter Harris, Q.C., member
of the House of Commons from 1940-1957 and Minister of Citizenship
and later Finance, is a partner in Harris and Dunlop. In addition to his
Thomson Newspapers directorship, he is chairman and president of
Victoria & Grey Trust and member of the Rideau Club. Finally, John
A. Tory, Q.C., twin brother of James M. and son of John Stewart
Donald, who are both lawyers and hold multiple dominant directors-
ships. John A. and his brother both attended the University of Toronto
Schools, University of Toronto and Osgoode. In addition to being a
partner in Tory, Tory, Deslauriers and Binnington of Toronto, he is a
director of Woodbridge, Abitibi Paper, Royal Bank, Sun Life and
Rogers Broadcasting.

(xv) *Toronto Star Limited*.

Accounting for almost the same circulation as the Thomson Group, the
Toronto Star Limited has a circulation of 395,210 which means that it

controls 8.4 per cent of the total Canadian daily circulation. In addition, there are 11 weeklies and three weekend magazines with a circulation of 2-1/2 million. According to the Senate Report:

> Upon the death of Mr. [J.E.] Atkinson in 1948 his will provided that the shares in the capital stock of the two companies should ultimately belong to The Atkinson Charitable Foundation. The Charitable Gifts Act passed by the Ontario Legislature made it impossible to carry out the terms of the will, and, early in 1958, the Supreme Court of Ontario granted approval for the newly-formed Hawthorn Publishing Company Limited to purchase the predecessor companies. The name of the company was changed to Toronto Star Limited (II:112).

As was illustrated earlier, the Toronto *Star* became one of the main beneficiaries of the death of the Toronto *Telegram*. After this its circulation increased to 515,000 but its advertising rate has also increased by about a third over the year following the *Telegram*'s death. It has had the effect of rapidly increasing the value of stocks in the company. For example, Beland Honderich's 200,000 shares doubled in value to $10 million after the *Telegram* was gone (*Last Post*, 1972:33).

The publisher and president of the Toronto *Star*, since 1966, is Beland Hugh Honderich who began with the paper in 1943 becoming financial editor in 1946 and vice-president in 1961. Ruth A. Hindmarsh, daughter of Joseph E. Atkinson, publisher of the company from 1899 to his death in 1948, is currently a director of the Toronto *Star* and president of the Atkinson Foundation. Her husband, Harry C. Hindmarsh, took over as publisher upon the death of her father. Their son, Harry A. Hindmarsh is secretary and director. Burnett M. Thall, long-time employee of the company with a PhD. in engineering from the University of Toronto is also a senior vice-president and director as well as trustee of The Atkinson Foundation. The same is true for William J. Campbell who is also a long-time employee and director of the company. Alexander John MacIntosh, Q.C., a partner in Blake, Cassels, & Graydon of Toronto, is a member of the board for the Toronto *Star* as well as the Canadian Imperial Bank of Commerce, John Labatts, Brascan and Steel Co. of Canada, as well as deputy governor of the Hudson's Bay Company. Hon. Walter Lockhart Gordon is also a director of the company. Educated at Upper Canada College and Royal Military College, he is a brother of Duncan Lockhart, a partner in Clarkson & Gordon, their father's firm. Their father was also a graduate of Upper Canada College and Royal Military College, president of Canadian Land & Immigration Co., the Penny

Bank, and director of Canadian Locomotive and Consolidated Paper. Their maternal grandfather was Sir Walter Cassels, president of the Exchequer Court and through his father-in-law, J.L. Counsell, K.C., Hon. Walter is brother-in-law to Bud Drury, president of the treasury board and cabinet minister and to Anthony G.S. Griffin, chairman of Triarch Corp. and director of Canadian Industries, Consumer Gas and Victoria & Grey Trust; his grandfather was President of the Canadian National Railway. Hon. Walter, himself, was Minister of Finance and federal cabinet minister until his resignation in 1968.

(xvi) Western Broadcasting Company Limited.

As a relatively recent entrant, the conglomerate of Western Broadcasting controls four television stations with a circulation of 865,000 as well as having interests in five radio stations, four of which have a circulation of 455,300. It also controls a cable company. "Effective control is exercised by Frank A. Griffiths, President, through a voting trust agreement" (II:115).

Frank A. Griffiths, C.A., is president of Western Broadcasting and partner in Riddell, Stead & Co. of Vancouver. Walter S. Owen, Q.C., is a senior partner of Owen, Bird of Vancouver and vice-president and director of Western Broadcasting as well as director of Canada Permanent Mortgage, Imperial Life, Greyhound Lines of Canada and a variety of media subsidiaries. Peter Paul Saunders, who has a B. Comm. from the University of British Columbia, is also a director of Western Broadcasting and chairman and president of Cornat Industries. He was one of the Founders of Laurentide Finance and its president from 1950 to 1966.

The overview provided in this section suggests that there is a great deal of inheritance of social class within the dominant media complexes and that overall they are highly interlocked with the corporate world. Just how extensive upper class recruitment into the media elite is and how extensive the overlap with the economic elite will be the subjects of the following chapter.

Notes

[1]Throughout this chapter the Senate Committee Report on the Mass Media Reports will be identified by Roman numerals; I for Volume One, II for Volume Two, and III for Volume Three.

[2]The study uses "group" as opposed to "independent" in a rather strange way. They state: "For purposes of the study, 'group' has been taken to mean two or more media units under common ownership operating in more than one

community, whether or not these media units are the same kind. 'Independent' ownership may include two or more media units, but confined to one community'' (II:41). Using this definition, it was found that groups have interests in 52 per cent of the 485 mass media units in Canada.

[3]See Appendix XVI for a diagramatic presentation of this penetration.

[4]Generally, there has been very little content analysis work done on the mass media in Canada.

[5]For an interesting summary of the role played by the Southam family in getting this legislation through, see Bruce's biography of the Southam's (1968:396f). He shows some of the foreign threats perceived by the media elite and discussions between St. Clair Balfour of the Southam family and Prime Minister Pearson.

[6]For an excellent discussion of a system of controlled competition between the three giants in the magazine industry and the symbiotic relations between them, see *Last Post*, June 1970.

[7]This situation has recently changed with the monopoly charge on the Irving papers in New Brunswick. The effect of the conviction is not known at the time of this writing.

[8]The sale of *Le Soleil* was completed on January 14, 1974 to Jacques Francoeur, ''sometime partner of Desmarais and a fellow publisher'' for $8.425 million (*Financial Post*, March 30, 1974:Q12).

Chapter Nine

The Corporate Elite: Economic and Ideological Power

WHAT is the overlap between the economic elite and the media elite? How similar are the social background characteristics of the media elite compared to the economic elite? Can it, in fact, be said that the economic and media elite are actually one: the corporate elite? The rather detailed discussion of the media elite in the previous chapter suggested the answer to these questions through a series of examples. In this chapter the aggregate picture of the media elite will be analysed and compared with earlier findings reported for the economic elite. Actually, the overlap with the economic elite is extensive, almost one half the members are exactly the same people. Moreover, those not overlapped resemble very closely the economic elite. The conclusion must be that together the economic and media elite are simply two sides to the same upper class; between them they hold two of the key sources of power—economic and ideological—in Canadian society and form the corporate elite.

Of the fifteen dominant media complexes available and set out earlier, members of the executive and boards of directors were selected as the media elite. The total number of members selected on this basis was 133 of whom adequate biographical data was available for 105 or 79 per cent of the members of the elite. This is similar to the 82 per cent coverage of the economic elite for the same period[1].

(i) Overlap with the Economic Elite

Of the 105 members of the media elite for whom biographical data was available, 51 are simultaneously members of the economic elite. This means that 49 per cent of the media elite are also members of the executive or hold directorships in one of the 113 dominant corporations in the economic sector and, at the same time, hold one of these positions in one of the dominant media complexes. Of the 51 who overlap between the economic and media elite, 21 members or 41 per cent hold more than one dominant position within the economic elite, compared to 29 per cent for the entire economic elite. Of the 54 or 51 per cent who are not simultaneously in the economic elite, 21 hold corporate directorships which are not among the 113 largest corporations but nonetheless operate in the non-media sector of the economy. In other words, more than two thirds (69 per cent) of the members of the media elite simultaneously hold important corporate positions outside the media. Of the remaining 33, there are 10 who have close kin (fathers, brothers, fathers-in-law or uncles) within the corporate world. This leaves 23, of whom eight have directly inherited their posts within the media elite. The remaining 15 mainly have careers within journalism and have worked their way into the media elite as inside directors after being with the company for many years.

In light of the evidence that about one half of the media elite are simultaneously members of the economic elite while many others have close corporate ties, it becomes questionable whether the two spheres are separately controlled. Both the economic and media worlds represent major sectors of concern in Canadian society and each has as its major activity, aside from profit making, separate domains of power. One is power in terms of the economic functions of society and the other in terms of ideological functions but, in Canada, the two have become so merged that for 1972 it is found that about half of the media elite are also in the economic elite. Since the two groups—the one overlapping with the economic elite and the other "exclusively" media elite—are of interest, the distinction will be maintained throughout to see if there is an appreciable difference between them.

(ii) Career Patterns of the Media Elite

The media elite make decisions about investments, expansion, acquisitions of other corporations or media complexes, and about the appointments of publishers and editors. It would be incorrect to suggest that all publishers and editors are not themselves in the media elite. Actually, the trend is toward including people holding these positions in the major publication or broadcasting stations within media complexes on the board. The Southam Company has done this for some time now (Bruce, 1968:399) and only recently, Maclean-Hunter "included the editors of three of [its] national publications: Peter C. Newman of Macleans; Doris Anderson of Chatelaine; Paul S. Deacon of the Financial Post" on its board of directors (Annual Report for 1972). In additition, many of the complexes still have family members in these positions as well as on the board. For example, Robert Wilson Southam has remained publisher of the Ottawa *Citizen* since 1953 as was his father before him. The situation has not changed from Porter's 1961 study where he writes: "in a large number of cases, owners are also publishers and so retain the chief executive positions for themselves, or if the paper is family-owned some members of the family may have the position of publisher or managing editor or editor-in-chief" (1965:484).

In terms of career patterns, there is a significant difference between members of the media elite who overlap with the economic elite and those who do not. While 24 per cent of the entire media elite has had a journalist's position at some time, either as publisher, reporter or broadcaster, only six per cent of the overlap group are in this category but 41 per cent of the others have had this experience. Similar proportions appear for those whose main career avenue has been in the media. While the same six per cent of the overlapping group have had their main career paths within the media, 67 per cent of the non-overlapping have the media as their main career avenue. Seventeen per cent of the media elite have careers in law, seven per cent in other elites, six per cent in financial posts and four per cent elsewhere. However, when careers are examined in terms of whether or not members of the elite have had their main careers in family firms the differences become minimized. For example, 35 per cent of the overlapping group have had their main careers in family firms compared to 41 per cent of the non-overlapping group. In other words, family capitalism is even stronger in the media which does not overlap with the economic elite than in either the economic elite as a whole or that component which overlaps with the media elite.

Law firms remain important in the media elite as they were in the economic elite. In the non-overlapping group, 15 per cent are currently members of a law firm while 20 per cent of the other group belong to a firm. This represents a total of 18 members of the elite with law firm affiliations. In two separate law firms, there are two members of the media elite in each. In Tory, Tory, DesLauriers and Binnington of Toronto, both John A. Tory, director of Thomson Newspapers and Charles L. Dubin, director of Baton Broadcasting, have their practice. In Blake, Cassels and Graydon, also of Toronto, Alexander John MacIntosh is a director of the Toronto Star and Britton Bath Osler, like his lawyer father before him, holds a directorship in Southam Press.

Another way of addressing the question of careers is in terms of the current occupation of elite members. Using a self-reported definition of the "individual's principal occupation", Table 40 was produced for both groups.

This illustrates that about one half of the media elite regard their principal occupation to be association with the media while a little under a third have economic activities as their main occupation. Just under one fifth have law firms as their primary attachment. Once again, the higher media affiliation among the non-overlapping group, as would be expected, is apparent. The 24 per cent of the overlapping group with media affiliations as their primary activity indicates that those based in the media are highly regarded within the economic community, as is the economic community within the media. In other words, the overlap is not simply a one way penetration from the

TABLE 40

Principal Current Occupations of the Media Elite, 1972

	Economic Elite Overlap	Non-Overlap	All Media Elite
Media*	23.5%	70.3%	47.6%
Law Firms	19.6	14.8	17.1
Bureaucratic	2.0	3.7	2.9
Academic	—	1.9	1.0
Economic	54.9	9.3	31.4
TOTAL	100	100	100
N	(51)	(54)	(105)

* Counts Power Corporation as economic and not media in terms of principal occupation.

economic world but is a mutual relationship. Law firms, as indicated, are highly regarded within both sectors and their members move freely in each.

Before analysing class origins, it is worthwhile noting that some members of the media elite are able to make it into the elite after spending a relatively long time in journalism fields. Chalmers, in his biography of Maclean, provides some good examples of how this sometimes occurs. He says Maclean "demonstrated an aptitude for picking the right men, such as Horace T. Hunter, a brilliant executive. Thus freed from management problems, the Colonel could be the complete journalist" (1969:ix). In this case the vacancy left at the top of the organization because Maclean had no heirs paid off well for Hunter. It is important, however, to note the criteria used to determine who are defined as the "right men". The Colonel's definition included "the reporter who gradually worked up to the higher fields of journalism, commerce, finance and higher politics. . . . 'He is only successful [according to the Colonel] when he builds up, throughout the years, important connections. To make and maintain these connections in newspapers like mine involves especially heavy expenses', which meant gifts and entertainment for people who were important sources of information, club memberships and travel" (324). Of course, the Colonel himself would determine when the "right men" were to be promoted and what qualities were required. To be able to move in the circles he describes is a quality reserved only for the upper class. In other words, mobility required that the aspiring reporter already has to have the "right" class qualities.

There is another career path, some cases of which have been presented earlier, which is quite frequently followed and this is public relations. The individual could be attached to any type of organization but their contacts with the media bring them within that social circle and there are some who make the jump over. Some, like Yves Jasmin, remain in both. He began as a reporter after the war and becoming a public relations officer for Air Canada between 1952 and 1956 when he became an associate director of public relations for Molsons Brewery until 1961. He then became the regional director of public relations for Quebec and the Atlantic Provinces for Ford of Canada until 1964 when he was recruited as director of public relations for the 1967 World's Exhibition until 1967. From 1968 to 1970, he was president of Desroches, Jasmin et Assoc. in Montreal, returning to Air Canada to become vice-president of public relations. He is also a director of Télémédia (Quebec).

(iii) Class Origins of the Media Elite

A detailed breakdown of the class indicators is presented in Appendix XV and summarized in Table 41 for the media elite in both its overlapping and non-overlapping components.

Table 41 verifies the impression of very high upper class origin in the media elite derived from the earlier discussion of media complexes. There are, however, some interesting differences between the group which overlaps with the economic elite and those which are not overlapping. As would be expected, the overlapping group has a greater proportion whose fathers were directly in the economic elite at some period with 45 per cent of the overlapping group enjoying this advantage compared to 30 per cent of the other group. In the entire media elite, 37 per cent had this initial advantage. However, when fathers from other elites are included, the difference between the two components is reduced with 45 and 41 per cent, respectively, in the overlapping and non-overlapping groups who had a father in an earlier elite. When all those with upper class origins are examined, it is found that over three quarters of the overlapping group are included and almost two thirds of the non-overlapping group. This means just over seven tenths of the total media elite are from upper class origins. The group not simultaneously in the economic elite is somewhat more open to the middle and working class. It is also of interest to compare the class origins of the media elite to the overall economic elite. Table 42 presents the class origins of the media elite divided into its components

TABLE 41

Class Origins of the Media Elite in Canada, 1972

Class Origin	Overlapped with Economic Elite	Not Overlapped	Total Media Elite
Upper Class	78.4%	63%	70.5%
Middle Class	19.6	29.6	24.7
Working Class	2	7.4	4.8
TOTAL	100%	100%	100%
N	(51)	(54)	(105)

TABLE 42

Comparative Class Origins of the Canadian Born Media and Economic Elites, 1972

Class	Media			Economic	
	Overlapped	Separate	All	All	Multiple
Upper Class	78.4%	63%	70.5%	59.4%	72.8%
Middle Class	19.6	29.6	24.7	34.8	22
Working Class	2	7.4	4.8	5.8	5.2
TOTAL	100%	100%	100%	100%	100%
N	(51)	(54)	(105)	(673)	(230)

and compares this with the overall economic elite and those members with multiple directorships in dominant economic corporations.

Since the overlapping group is in both the economic and media elites, it is important to note what segment of the corporate elite is simultaneously in both elites. When compared to the overall economic elite, it is apparent that only a select group has mobility between the two elites. While 59 per cent of the overall economic elite has upper class origins, 78 per cent of the groups which simultaneously are in both elites have this advantage. In other words, almost twenty per cent more of the overlapping group had upper class origins compared to the economic elite as a whole, thus indicating that even within the elite class origins have an important part to play in mobility between the two elites. The overlapping group has very similar origins to that subset of the economic elite which has more than one dominant directorship in the corporate world; that is, they both have about three quarters from upper class origins. Those members of the elite who are able to move between dominant corporations and dominant media complexes are primarily those who have had upper class origins which gives them substantial advantages over others, particularly compared to the Canadian population but also within the elite itself.

Focusing on the media group which does not overlap with the economic elite, they have upper class origins which are somewhat higher than the economic elite as a whole and only about 10 per cent lower than those with multiple dominant economic directorships. Of all the divisions, however, the non-overlapping groups provides the greatest mobility for those from the working class. Although only 7.4 per cent of this group (four members) were able to make it into the media elite after long crawls through the journalism world without initial class advantages, this is still higher than for any of the other elite groupings.

From this it can be argued that the media elite not only overlaps significantly with the economic elite, but it also has very similar class origins to that group. It would be correct to say that the media elite overall is of the same class origin as the economic elite and they are hardly distinguishable in this respect. It is worthwhile noting, however, that those of upper class origin are able to move around within the various elites and between them much more readily than other members of the corporate elite.

It can be concluded, as did Porter for his 1961 study of the media elite, that "inheritance through kinship, rather than upward social mobility, is now the principal means of recruitment to that group which owns the major mass media instruments" (1965:483-484). Indeed, in 1972, 38 members of the media elite inherited positions directly which brought them into the elite. As Porter has said: "Only the very wealthy, or those successful in the corporate world, can buy and sell large daily newspapers which become, in effect, the instruments of an established upper class" (463). The high class origins of the members of the media elite are the product of selection by earlier elite members.

When the criteria for selection of directors is like that used in Southam Press, it is obvious why they are typically upper class in origin. Bruce, in outlining these criteria for Southam's, says there are "some special considerations. One was the family background. In looking at any younger member of the family for possible membership, Fisher thought there were two tests: that either through share ownership or executive position, or both, he should have an interest in the company and an ability to contribute to its operation" (1968:373-374). To ignore ascriptive characteristics would be to ignore the reality of inheritance and the importance of class origin in a capitalist economy. Accumulated privileges become transferred intergenerationally and are reflected in the high proportions of the current elites with upper class origins. This is evident even within the media elite who do not overlap with the economic elite. There are, for example, exactly half of the members of this group who have close kin who are or have been in the elite.

(iv) Sex, Religion and Ethnicity

Women have traditionally been excluded from elite positions in Canada. For example, only six members of the economic elite are women (.6 per cent). This exclusion is also reflected in the 51 members of the economic elite overlapping with the media elite and contains no women. There are, however, four women in the media elite who do not overlap with the economic elite, representing 7.4 per cent of the membership of that group. Thus, of the media elite as a whole, women represent 3.8 per cent of the membership. Although this is far from their representation in the population, it does appear that a very few women have been able to use the media as a means into the elite. Doris Anderson is editor of Chatelaine and director of Maclean-Hunter since 1972. The Hon. Jeanne Sauvé, now a minister in the federal cabinet succeeding her husband in that position, has been a freelance broadcaster and journalist and director of Bushnell Communications. Ruth A. Hindmarsh, wife of Harry Hindmarsh, publisher of the Toronto *Star* and, daughter of Joseph E. Atkinson, also publisher of the Toronto *Star*, is now a director of that company. Kathleen Griffith Laing, wife of Peter M. Laing, also a director of the Montreal *Star*, is daughter of J.W. McConnell, president of Montreal *Star* and she is now a director.

It is difficult to separate differences between religion and ethnicity as they affect mobility in Canada. It is clear, however, that together they have a significant impact on mobility possibilities for Canadians. There are only three Jews in the media elite (2.9 per cent) and this is a somewhat lower proportion than the 4.1 per cent representation they have in the economic elite. Catholics, on the other hand, have a greater representation in the media elite than in the economic but are still well below the 46.2 per cent of the Canadian population declaring this affiliation. While they make up only 12.7 per cent of the economic elite, 20 per cent of the overall media elite is Catholic. An explanation for this difference is apparent when the different proportions of over-lapping and non-overlapping groups are compared. While only 13 per cent of the overlapping group is Catholic, almost identical to the economic elite overall, 27.5 per cent of the non-overlapping group is Catholic. In other words, that section of the media elite separate from the economic elite permits greater mobility for Catholics than does the corporate world. As will be seen, this relates to the higher proportion of French-Canadians in the non-overlapping group. Because the media in Canada is divided into the two charter languages, it is necessary that the public be reached in their own language. Therefore, the different types of relationships between the economic elite and the media elite to their publics account for much of this difference. This will be returned to under ethnicity.

Anglicans are the most over-represented of all religious affilia-tions. While making up only 11.8 per cent of the population, they accounted for 25.3 per cent of the economic elite. It was also noted that of the multiple directorship holders, they represented 32 per cent of the membership. This becomes reflected in the media as well. Overall, they account for 29.5 per cent of the media elite but of the group which overlaps with the corporate world, they represent 38.9 per cent, more than three times their proportion in the population. In the non-overlapping group, they represent 19.6 per cent. Other religious affilia-tions are similar to their representation in the economic elite and the population at large.

Ethnicity, as Porter has stressed, is so strongly tied into class in Canada that the existence of ethnic enclaves creates, within Canada, a "vertical mosaic" of class bound ethnic groups. French-Canadians have somewhat higher representation in the media elite compared to the economic; while only 8.4 per cent of the economic elite was French, 13.3 per cent of the elite in the mass media are classified this way. This is still well below their one third representation in the population. The difference between the media and economic elites is also reflected in their different representation in the group which overlaps with the economic elite and the one which does not. While making up 17.7 per cent of the non-overlapping group they are only 9.3 per cent of the overlapped group, less than one per cent difference with their represen-

TABLE 43

Ethnic Representation in the Corporate Elite, 1972

	Media Elite			Economic Elite	Population (1971)
	Overlapping	Separate	All		
Anglo	85.2%	78.4%	81.9%	86.2%	44.7%
French	9.3	17.7	13.3	8.4	28.6
Other	5.5	3.9	4.8	5.4	26.7
TOTAL	100%	100%	100%	100%	100%
N	(51)	(54)	(105)	(775)	

tation in the economic elite as a whole. In other words, almost double the proportion French can be found in the non-overlapping group compared to the group in common with the economic elite.

Aside from the exclusively French-owned media, the extent of power for French-Canadians in the Anglo-controlled media is questionable. For example, "Originally *Le Magazine Maclean* was produced by a completely separate editorial staff based in Montreal. . . . But Maclean-Hunter isn't a philanthropic organization. By 1969 it was clear that an independent French language edition of *Maclean's* wasn't going to make any money. And so a decision was taken to make *Le Magazine Maclean* largely a translation of the English *Maclean's*. The editor, Mario Cardinal, resigned in protest" (Wolfe, 1973:21). This suggests that as rationalization of production along capitalist profit making lines occurs, the Anglo media no longer considers it valuable to produce separate French-language editions. If the French-Canadians are to have a separate media, they will have to own and control it themselves. They cannot expect the capitalist media of English Canada will carry the costs.

It has already been noted that Jews have a lower representation in the media elite than in the economic elite. Members of other "third" ethnic groups are virtually non-existent in the corporate world (only 10 of 673). The 1.5 per cent of other "third" ethnic groups in the economic elite is mirrored by the 1.9 per cent in the media elite, even though they represent over a quarter of the Canadian population. There is little difference between the groups. The Anglos, of course, dominate both the economic and media elites, representing 85.2 per cent of the overlapping group and 78.4 per cent of the exclusively media group.

Implications of Ethnic Representation in the Corporate Elite

Ethnic representation in the corporate elite satisfies neither the "official" bicultural nor multicultural models of Canadian society. Neither in the economic nor mass media elite is there even anything close to approaching the proportions required to say there was sufficient French representation for the bicultural model; nor was there sufficient "third" ethnic participation for the multicultural model. The conclusion must be that the corporate elite is represented by Anglo dominance in both its mass media and economic forms. The limited "third" ethnic penetration which has occurred with Jewish-Canadians has not been through integration with the dominant Anglos; rather, it has been by creating a parallel elite within a few dominant corporations for the most part separate from the mainstream of economic power. Members of other "third" ethnic groups remain virtually absent from both elites, never reaching over two per cent while comprising about one quarter of the population.

There is an important difference which should be noted between the economic and media elites with respect to French participation. While only 8.4 per cent of the economic elite, French-Canadians reach 13.3 per cent of the overall media elite and 17.7 per cent of the non-overlapping component. The difference reflects the different base of power for the two elites. The economic elite is primarily controlled through access to capital while the media elite—although also organized in corporate bodies—requires considerably less capital than the economic elite. Moreover, there are two separate language groups served by the media elite so the "market" reached by the media more closely reflects the two official languages since the "commodity" of advertising is surrounded by two distinct languages. Being based on a population of which nearly one third are French, the media elite must serve this population in its own language thus leaving this primarily as a Francophone domain isolated from the English media. The economic market with its commodities and services knows no language barriers and the population base is not protected in the same way as with the mass media. The media elite with an enclosed French-speaking population base resembles, in this respect, the political elite and, indeed, its proportion of French, particularly the non-overlapping component, is more similar to that found for the political elite than for the economic elite.

Two further pieces of data, one regarding longevity in the elite and the other concerning the preponderance of lawyers, suggest the primary difference between the Anglos and French is in control over capital. It was noted earlier that only 3.9 per cent of the economic elite lasting over twenty years in the elite was French, less than half their overall representation in this elite for 1972. Besides insuring access to the elite, capital in the form of stock holdings has the effect of allowing those in control to enter the economic elite at an early age and stay in the elite for a long period of time. The fact that the French tend not to stay for as long as the Anglos suggests, although by no means conclusively, that they lack the same stockholdings. The second piece of evidence suggesting this is the fact that over two fifths (43 per cent) of the French-Canadians were trained in law compared to less than one fifth of the overall elite. Law has been, and is increasingly, the key avenue for French-Canadians into the economic elite. Access through law is not linked to capital in the same way stockholdings are; in fact, law has characteristics more resembling the base of power for the mass media. Since law is a provincially controlled institution in terms of access (provincial bar associations such as the Law Society of Upper Canada and the Quebec Bar) and particularly the presence of the Quebec civil law, this tends to protect a base of power also established in terms of language. It appears that whenever access to the elite depends on a language base, the French are able to gain higher participation in the elite than when the base is primarily on capital. To arrive at a conclusive answer to this suggested interpretation would, however, require a detailed analysis of both stock ownership and the institution of law[2]. Focusing on these two means of access to the economic and media elites would provide a much broader and informed understanding of both the processes of access and exclusion from elite positions.

"Third" ethnic groups, given the above implications of the role of an "enclosed" language base and control over capital, are doubly disadvantaged. With Anglo dominance in finance, they lack access to capital and without a traditional control of blocks of shares, the Jewish cases noted being an important exception, this avenue of access is blocked. Furthermore, with a system of two official languages, they even lack the one advantage French-Canadians have as a base of power. These disadvantages are reflected in their low proportions in both the economic and media elites. Without any existing traditional avenues to the corporate elite, such as the language and legal avenues for French-Canadians, it is difficult to suggest any way of "opening" the existing corporate structures to members of "third" ethnic groups within the current mobility avenues available.

(v) Regionalism

In an examination of the economic elite, it was found that by comparing place of birth for members of the elite with the regional distribution of population in 1921, the census year closest to their mean year of birth, that the Center (Ontario and Quebec) was over-represented while the East and West were under-represented. The same pattern emerges when this procedure is repeated for the media elite but the differences are even more pronounced. While the Center for the economic elite was over-represented by eight per cent, this increases to 18 per cent for the media elite. Similarly, while the East was under-represented by three per cent, it is under-represented by six per cent for the media elite. The most inequitable distribution occurs in the West, where the under-representation of five per cent increases to 12 per cent with the media. Put another way, while there was a 13 per cent differential between the Center and the West in the economic elite, this increases to a 30 per cent differential in the media elite and the 11 per cent difference between the Center and the East for the economic increases to a 24 per cent difference with the media. In the relationship between birth place and regional representation in the media elite has any effect on the ideological position presented by the media, the dice are clearly loaded to the advantage of those born in either Ontario or Quebec and against those in the western or eastern areas. Given the known under-representation of French-Canadians, it is evident that the view from the Center is that of Anglos.

(vi) The Private World of the Media Elite

Private Schools and University

Private schools—those bastions of upper class breeding—remain important in the media elite. For the economic elite it was shown that their attendance had become more prevalent within the elite over the past twenty years, increasing from 34 per cent in 1951 to 40 per cent in 1972. This proportion increased to 65 per cent of those whose main careers were in family firms. Examination of the media elite finds that, overall, 46 per cent of the media elite attended one of the fee-paying private schools, particularly those of the Headmasters' Association. Those with economic interlocks fared somewhat better in this respect with 51 per cent having attended but even the non-overlapping group had a slightly greater proportion than the economic elite as a whole with 41 per cent. Among them, Upper Canada College again stands out as most important with 10 members of the media elite attending, including four who were there at the same time. Trinity College School also had four there at the same time and six altogether while Ridley College and the University of Toronto Schools each had four. Lower Canada College had five.

University attendance remains almost compulsory for membership in the media elite, as it was in the economic. While less than 10 per cent of the population of the age group characteristic of the media elite had attended university, 83.8 per cent of the media elite had this advantage. This includes 85.2 per cent of the overlapping and 82.4 per cent of the non-overlapping group. When other training beyond the secondary level is included, the corresponding proportions increase to 94.4 per cent and 88.2 per cent, respectively, with 91.4 per cent overall. This is somewhat higher than the 80.5 per cent of the economic elite attended university and 84.5 per cent including other postsecondary. The University of Toronto again stands out as the pre-eminent university for elites with 22 members of the media elite having gone there. McGill is also important with 11 members. Many members of the elite also have post-graduate degrees, including one third of the overlapping group and almost two fifths of the non-overlapping group. Again law is most important with most having attended the University of Toronto and Osgoode.

National Private Men's Clubs

Just over half (51.1 per cent) of the members of the economic elite belong to one of the six national exclusive men's clubs (the Toronto, York, National, Mount Royal, St. James', or Rideau Clubs). This is repeated for the media elite where almost one half belong to at least one (46 per cent). This includes 36 per cent of the non-overlapping group and 56 per cent of the overlapping group. The average number of club memberships among those belonging is 1.74 out of the six, with this increasing to an average of almost two each for the overlapping group. This includes 21 who belong to the Toronto, 15 to the York, 15 to the St. James', 14 to Mount Royal, eight to the Rideau and seven to the National.

The importance of private clubs and private schools is evident in two important biographies of the media elite: Bruce's history of the Southam family and Chalmers' of Col. Maclean. In each, the authors talk of large sums of money given to Upper Canada College (Chalmers, 1969:324-325, 329; Bruce, 1968:412-413). In this way the wealth of the rich is used to insure that future generations of upper class sons will receive the best of education and privilege.

Private clubs also appear in these biographies as the meeting place for the elite (see Bruce, 1968:386). Chalmers' reference is worth repeating at length. He writes of the occasion when Winston Churchill came to speak to the people of Canada. It is worth noting which people and where his encounter took place:

> With characteristic zeal and careful detailing, Maclean had organized a brilliant setting for the lecture, with appropriate social events before and after. Colonel E.A. Whitehead, leading militiaman and successful insurance executive, would be the host at a special luncheon in the *St. James's Club*. Senator (later Sir) George Drummond agreed to move the vote of thanks after the evening lecture and also to use his influence in ensuring a distinguished platform group of high court judges, business leaders, top military men and others. His Worship, the Mayor accepted the duty of chairman. And after the speeches, *this handpicked roster of Montreal's best* would move to the *Mount Royal Club*, where millionaire banker Edward S. Clouston had offered to entertain at supper (emphasis added, 1969:121).

This interesting passage captures some of the essence of purpose for the exclusive national men's clubs. They serve as a solitary meeting place for entertainment and social contact. Their exclusiveness insures that only the wealthiest and most important can belong. They average about 700 members each, but as the high overlapping illustrated suggests, this does not mean that 700 different faces could be expected to appear in each. In fact, within the circle of six clubs, Canada's upper class circulates forming and reinforcing their friendships.

(vii) Political Connections

Only 24 of the 105 members of the media elite declared a political affiliation, including 15 Liberals and nine Conservatives. Because of the low coverage, little can be said concerning party support. However, 12.4 per cent of the media elite have at some time held key offices in the state system, including six from the overlapping group and seven from the strictly media group. Included among these are members of the political elite such as Hon. Walter Harris, Hon. John Robarts, Hon. Walter Gordon and the Hon. Jeanne Sauvé. When examined in another way, it is evident that the media elite travels in very similar social circles as the state elite. More than one fifth of the members of the media elite have close relatives who have held important political or bureaucratic offices. This includes eight members of the overlapping group (15.7 per cent) and 14 members of the separate group (25.9 per cent). In other words, about one third of the media elite have either themselves held important state positions or close relatives have held these positions. Perhaps Weber's statement that "every politician of consequence has needed influence over the press and hence has needed relations with the press" (1946:97) can be taken more literally than he originally intended[3].

(viii) Summary

These last three chapters began with the position that ideologies arise from existential conditions people find themselves in but this is often counteracted by dominant ideologies which create within the lower classes a type of subordinate ideology. It was argued that the structure of the mass media is such that it is a powerful instrument for projecting ideologies and that those who control these means of mental production control, in large part, the ideological predisposition of the population. For this reason it is important to analyse who controls the mass media and with that, who acts as gatekeepers to that media. The evidence presented illustrates that the mass media in Canada are highly concentrated and becoming increasingly more so. Control over the media, it was shown, is exercised primarily by men of upper class origin who have attended one of the Headmasters' Association Schools, attended university, typically the University of Toronto or McGill, belong to one or more of the six exclusive national men's clubs, was born in Ontario or Quebec, is Anglican in religion, and Anglo by ethnicity. In other words, the profile of the media elite is the same as that for the economic elite. Indeed, it was shown that half of the media elite are themselves simultaneously members of the economic elite and others who are not frequently have kin who are. The mass media in Canada are class institutions run by, for and in the interest of the upper class. More than that, they are instruments of the corporate elite because the media elite and the economic elite turn out to be the same people occupying the uppermost positions in two functionally defined domains of life in Canada.

For class based action to occur, there must be an element of consciousness of class. While there is general agreement that this consciousness is evident in the upper class, it is absent as a general characteristic of all other classes in Canada. Part of the process by which consciousness can emerge is through communication within the membership of various classes. As long as the means of communication remain monopolized by a select few members of the upper class and remain "mass" in structure, the possibility of this communication is dramatically reduced.

The pattern of ownership and selection of personnel to fill key decision making positions within the media in Canada is heavily biased in favour of the upper class. Given that existential position affects the ideology of people, the content of the mass media as screened by these gatekeepers is also biased in favour of the existing arrangements of power. Porter was able to observe from his study of the media elite in 1961 that:

> There is no effort, for example, to prevent links between the corporate world and the major components of the ideological system, particularly broadcasting and newspaper publishing. Corporation directors control the mass media enterprises because these enterprises are viewed as economic units rather than ideological ones. However profitable as economic enterprises they may be, they are also important instruments of opinion-making and they establish the climate of thought in society. Thus where the mass media are considered to be primarily economic units there is an accruing of power to the corporate elite (1965:216).

Based on the data presented in this study, his findings can only be confirmed. Indeed, there is a greater interpenetration than even Porter suggests. Not only do the media elite coincide as overlapping social circles and have common class backgrounds with the economic elite, they are in very large part identical people.

The Senate Report's arguments regarding class control of the media are phrased in a "could be" or "becoming" format:

This tendency could—but not necessarily—have the effect of reducing the number of "diverse and antagonistic sources" from which we derive our view of the public world. It could also—but not necessarily—lead to a situation whereby the news (which we must start thinking of as a public resource, like electricity) is controlled and manipulated by a small group of individuals and corporations whose view of What's Fit to Print may closely coincide with What's Good for General Motors, or What's Good for Business, or What's Good for my Friends Down at the Club. There is some evidence, in fact, which suggests that we are in that boat already (I:4).

Indeed, the evidence of this study illustrates that the "could be's" in fact, have become "are's". It is interesting that the Senate Committee, with all its resources, was confined to an examination of media corporations and not to the people who control them. They have accepted the legal fictions and ignored the fact that these corporations are indeed controlled by people. It occurred to them to speculate about class control of the media but not to study it. If they had done so, as was done here, they would have found that upper class control in the interest of corporate capitalism is, indeed, characteristic of the mass media in Canada. They would have had to show that, in fact, the "diverse and antagonistic sources" are actually different faces of the same upper class and its elite.

Appendix XVI summarizes, in diagramatic form, the interlocking directorships between dominant corporations and selected media complexes. The extensiveness and complexity of these interlocks are readily perceivable from this diagram. In fact, almost one half (49) of the 113 dominant corporations have at least one interlocking directorship with one of the dominant media complexes. It is difficult to argue that these media complexes are any more than individual entities within the complex whole of the corporate elite.

The following statements summarize the three main points derived from this study of Canada's mass media: (i) the media elite is, in large part, a subset of the economic elite and increasingly becoming more so, (ii) the basis of revenue for dominant media complexes is primarily advertising, thus their profitable survival depends upon their relationships to major advertisers who are also the economic elite and, (iii) through appointments and active participation in publication and broadcasting, the media elite are able to act as "gatekeepers" to the management of news.

The media, through the ideology they present, reinforce the existing political and economic system. The mass media are not the pillars of capitalist society; they do, however, add important support to the structure and serve to reinforce the continuation of existing inequalities. An anti-capitalist, anti-existing socio-political order media would remove one of the bases of legitimacy upon which the prevailing order of inequality is founded. Under the existing system of concentrated and capitalist dominated media, the corporate elite will continue to maintain control over the means of mental production. In summary, only the words of A.J. Liebling seem appropriate to the present situation of the mass media in Canada: "Freedom of the press is guaranteed only to those who own one".

Notes

[1] With one exception, the list was drawn from the *Directory of Directors*, 1972. Members from Télémédia (Quebec) had to be drawn from the Annual Report to CALURA but it covered the same period.

[2] Indeed, a grant applications for just such a study has been submitted (Clement and Olsen, 1973).

[3] As with the economic elite, philanthropic activities are also important to the media elite, with 25.7 per cent belonging to a university or private school board of governors or equivalent and 24.7 per cent belonging to a board of a major city hospital.

Chapter Ten

Public and Private Power in a Liberal-Democracy

THIS concluding chapter will be used to summarize various findings presented earlier, elaborate some of the implications for Canadian society, and address two major issues raised earlier but not resolved within the present study. Because of the decision to confine the analysis to a detailed examination of the corporate system's development and the corporate elite within Canada, this necessarily limited the study by abstracting it from both the state system and the continental economic system. In addition to the central purposes of the study, important aspects of these two relationships have, nevertheless, become apparent and in this conclusion some frameworks useful for their analysis will be discussed. This will be organized into three sections: Relations Between Elites, Canada in the Continental Context, and Canada as a Liberal-Democracy.

(i) Relations Between Elites

Elites in liberal-democracies, John Porter suggests, are arranged into "several sub-systems" with functionally and structurally differentiated power roles. "The fused power roles of earlier societies give way, with social development," he says, "to separate elite groups at the top of separated institutional orders" (1965:207). Furthermore, "specialization" within particular institutions continues to promote increasing separation of the elites; this "reduces the possibility of interchange between the respective institutional orders". He identifies two aspects of "specialization" which promote this separation: one is knowledge and the other values. "Institutional orders are systems of interrelated roles with their own peculiar sets of values. Both instrumental norms (knowledge) and value norms (rules of the game) have to be learned. A high ranker in one institutional order finds it difficult to fit into the normative system of another institution". This theoretical explanation for separate institutional orders *and* plural elites is, however, qualified by an empirical rider—"The question of interchanges of elite personnel between the institutional orders is one to be answered by empirical analysis" (209). Empirically, his theoretical explanation fails for some institutions and his own theory of "specialization" by elites is also seriously questioned by his own analysis—namely, his argument presented earlier that "while it is correct to describe the modern corporation as a vast bureaucracy . . . its highest government is not in the hands of men best described as bureaucratic'' (281). The problem with Porter's analysis of relations between elites does not lie only with his theoretical formulation but also his empirical work because—except in a peripheral way—he was not able to put his theory to the test. This was not possible because his empirical analysis covers various years between 1951 and 1961. Again, this study is unable to answer precisely one of the crucial issues of relations between the economic and political or bureaucratic domains, although some evidence has been produced which suggests greater interpenetration than twenty years ago. Two institutions, however, have been examined and it was found that, indeed, they are barely distinguishable at the level of elites although they are functionally distinct domains; that is, the economic and mass media worlds are two separate institutional bases of power controlled by the same corporate elite.

These findings indicate that two or more functionally distinct domains established on separate bases of power are not necessarily operationally separate: hence, the use of the term corporate elite to encompass both the economic and media elites. There are, however, different ''sets of rules'' governing separation of elite members between the corporate, political and, usually, bureaucratic elites. But these do not cover (i) elite switchers, (ii) all positions held by members of the corporate elite in the state system, (iii) kinship ties across elites, (iv) associates (such as law partners) holding memberships in more than one elite or, (v) common class origins. Each of these aspects of possible relationships between elites refers to increasingly general ties for particular elite members, but do not encompass the institutional relationships between various domains. These will be discussed later in the chapter.

It will be possible to analyse some of these relationships in detail upon Dennis Olsen's completion of the state elites (1973), but for now some data relevant to this question from the perspective of the corporate elite will be summarized from earlier chapters. Before this is done, it is necessary to define the parameters of what is meant by ''the state''; that is, what institutions, when considered together, can be called ''the state system''? Miliband identifies key institutions which make up the state system, including the government, administration including ministerial departments, public corporations, central banks and regulatory commissions, the military, the judiciary, the sub-central government and parliamentary assemblies (1969:54-53). The people who fill the uppermost positions in these state institutions are called the state elite. This he distinguishes from the political system which ''includes many institutions, for instance parties and pressure groups, which are of major importance in the political process, and which vitally affect the operation of the state system. And so do many other institutions which are not 'political' at all, for instance, giant corporations, Churches, the mass media, etc.'' (54). This is an important distinction. By maintaining that ''the state system is not synonomous with the political system'', Miliband draws the distinction between political influence and state power. Political influence is the ability to affect state power while state power is the ability to activate the resources of the key state institutions. None of the positions in the domain of the political systems are *popularly* elected and only a few of those within the state system fall within this auspice.

At various points in earlier chapters it was shown that there has been an increasing interpenetration between the corporate elite and both the state and political systems in the last twenty years. For instance, in terms of main career patterns it was shown that while only 1.8 per cent or 14 members of the economic elite in 1951 had their main careers in the political, bureaucratic or military elite; by 1972, this had increased to 5.8 per cent or 45 members from the political, bureaucratic or academic elite. Including only the 1972 political and bureaucratic elite switchers, it was shown that there were 17 from the political and 20 from the bureaucratic elites—more than twice the interpenetration evident twenty years earlier. Moreover, if the media elite was included as a main career in another elite, the proportion would increase to 8.2 per cent. Although ''switching'' has become increasingly confined to the elite levels, it was shown that 52 members of the economic elite were on the boards of crown corporations, 24 on Royal Commissions and 78 on various other important boards and commissions such as the Advisory Council to Industry, Trade and Commerce. When this was combined with the 49 members who held key positions in the federal bureaucracy during the war, it was found that 31.1 per cent had held important posts within the state system at some time in their careers. Considered in light of the 32 who had close kin in the political elite, 20 in the Senate, eight in the bureaucratic elite and the total of 95 with close kin in important positions in the state system, a total of 39.4 per cent of the current economic elite members either were themselves or had close kin in the state system. This was replicated in the media elite where over one fifth had close relatives in important political or bureaucratic offices—including 26 per cent of the non-overlapping group—and over a third were either themselves or had close kin in these positions.

This did not exhaust the connections because it was also shown that members of the corporate elite were active in the political system through such associations as the Canadian Banker's Association, the Canadian Tax Foundation, or the various Chambers of Commerce. Various elite forums such as the Canadian Executive Overseas Service, the Canadian-American Committee, the Ontario Research Foundation, the Conference Board in Canada, and the Institute for Public Policy Research were also discussed and shown to be dominated by members of the economic elite. It is clear that the corporate elite is very active in both the state and political systems. They are not so neatly separate as the rules prohibiting simultaneous holding of elite positions in the corporate and state systems would make it appear on first glance. In order to undertake a thorough going analysis of this relationship would require a detailed study of associates and class origins in each direction (from and to the state and corporate elites). An analysis of associates would include, for instance, examination of the key law firms that so many members of the corporate elite belong to and see if other menbers of the firms belong, or have beloned, to the state elite. Analysis of class would compare the class origins of the state and corporate elites to see if they are drawing from a similar recruitment base and, if they are similar social types[1].

In terms of the high overlapping and similar upper class recruitment for the economic and media elites, plus the preliminary findings concerning the state system, it may well be that the major divisions in Canadian society are better understood along class lines than in terms of autonomous elites. That is to say, elites are functionally defined in terms of independent bases of power ("vertically") while classes are defined in relationship to sources of power ("horizontally") and individuals with various class origins fill elite positions. If it is found that the upper class provides the main recruitment base for various functionally defined elites, then it could be said that one class dominates these particular elites. It may, however, control some elites and not others. For instance, it would appear that the labour elite in Canada has a preponderance of persons from working class origins (Porter, 1965:344), thus indicating that there is at least separation between the corporate and labour elites in terms of their class of origin. As in 1951, there are no elite switchers from the labour to corporate elite. This is not the case for the political and bureaucratic elites but a complete comparison must wait.

To this point, only the flows between institutional elites and formal interactions have been discussed but there are, of course, other important indicators such as informal interaction through common private and university education or membership in exclusive national men's clubs which would also have to be taken into account. It would also be important to specify the circumstances and conditions which lead to coalitions or conflictual relationships between the various elites[2]. In part, this enters an area of research very difficult to analyse; Porter, for instance, suggests that: "There develops a confraternity of power in which the various institutional leaders share attitudes and values'' (1965:522). Although it is difficult to prove this statement in terms of values and attitudes, it is possible to document it, at least in part, by analysis of the behaviour of elites and the way they use their resources to affect other elites. Later, some examples of relationships between public and private power in Canada will be examined.

Labour Unions

Labour will be introduced here in only the most cursory manner. A more detailed analysis would require placing the role of labour within the context of state and corporate power and exploring the variety of ways, historically and cross-nationally, this relationship has been established. For present purposes, the relationship will simply be raised as problematic and as an important aspect to be taken into account.

Labour is one of the motor forces pressing for the expansion of production in order to keep up total outputs. The ''expansion of needs'' has been historically created in labour—in large part through the media to broaden the capitalist market—and their satisfaction requires continued economic expansion or redistribution of income. It is in the interest of dominant elements in society to attempt the former since the latter necessarily cuts into the dominant groups' resources.

But where does labour stand in the structure of power in liberal-democracies? Some time ago, Michels suggested that: ''The ruling classes in the countries under a democratic regime have hoped to impose obstacles in the way of the revolutionary labor movement by conceding posts in the ministry to its most conspicuous leaders, thus gaining control over the revolutionary impulse of the proletariat by allowing its leaders to participate in power, though cautiously and in an extremely restricted measure'' (1962:181). It appears that in some liberal-democracies, Michels' prediction has been borne out to some extent, while in others these developments have not occurred[3].

In Canada, Porter argues labour leaders are ''on the periphery of the over-all structure of power'' (1965:540). In his 1958 survey of labour leaders, he found that only ''14 per cent of the elite indicated that they had served on . . . federal or provincial labour relations boards, workmen's compensation boards, the Unemployment Insurance Commission, and industrial commissions of one kind or another'' (360). This peripheral role of labour in the direction of the state is reinforced by Presthus' findings regarding unions as interest groups. He finds a ''tendency of labour groups to seek access mainly at the secondary level of power, i.e. the legislature. . . . labour in Canada fails to enjoy the legitimacy imputed to other economic groups such as business, agriculture, and professional groups including law, medicine, and accountancy'' (1973:168-169). To the extent labour does enter into the state in Canada, it is restricted to lower levels of power. On the basis of the cursory review here, it appears labour in Canada falls somewhere between the relatively high interaction with the state in the United Kingdom and low association in France. Regardless, at the elite level the labour elite has a different recruitment base in Canada's class system than does the corporate elite and at the institutional level, labour is sufficiently autonomous to consider it an independent base of power. It is evident from Presthus' study that it does not have the same impact, at least on the state, that other institutions enjoy.

The State

The inequality evident throughout liberal-democracies favouring the corporate elite generates disproportionate strength for their association with the state. This requires much more analysis than can be provided here, but some illustrations will indicate the nature of the relationship between the state and corporate worlds. The state provides indirect subsidies to corporations through a variety of mechanisms; for example, while industry consumes 70 per cent of electrical energy in Canada it provides only 60 per cent of the sales revenue from this utility thus leaving either the state or private user to provide 40 per cent of the cost for 30 per cent of the use (Deaton, 1972:17). More direct examples of state support of industry could be illustrated; for instance, the cabinet forgave Ford duties of over $75 million early in 1969, and this certainly was not because Ford was in a difficult financial situation: its profits increased from $7 million in 1964 to over $50 million in 1968 (Zuritsky, 1972:131-133).

Government and business come together on a number of fronts in Canada but one of the most effective is through the advisory councils and associations already discussed, created by both business and government; for instance, the Canadian Manufacturers' Association and Canadian Chamber of Commerce created by business or the National Committee on Petroleum and the Business Advisory Committee created by government. Through these elite forums, and in a variety of other ways, government and industry relate to one another and discover each other's views, form alliances and plan strategies of development not open to the great majority of people.

Just as the Canadian government after Confederation used enormous funds to finance the likes of the CPR, government is still forced, within the framework of corporate capitalism, to try and manipulate the economy through corporations—DREE is a classic example of this. In an attempt to reduce regional inequalities, the government is forced to use incentives to corporations to encourage them to locate where they are needed. However, when government is dealing with corporate capitalists, particularly multinationals, they are not in a position to dictate the results of their expenditures. There are many examples which illustrate that corporations are in a position to by-pass many of the stated aims of the government incentives and use these programs for their own ends[4]. Working within the framework of the assumptions of corporate capitalism and in the economic environment of multinational corporations, the state is not in a position to establish national goals and insure that they will be followed. Indeed, it appears the alliance between government and business is not an alliance of equals but one dominated by the interests of corporate capitalism. Using corporations as the main means of conducting programs, like DREE, necessitates an alliance and use of business representatives on boards which decide these grants. This leads to a situation where business is deciding where it will spend government money and often results in cases of "conflict of interests" with board members giving grants to their own or associated companies (Chodos, 1972:146-149). In other areas government establishes agencies which provide support to corporations in dealing with international trade; for example, the Canadian Commercial Corporation and International Programs Branch. The state is in the position of providing and supporting agencies, services and incentives which are designed to strengthen corporate structures while profits from these services go into private hands.

It is frequently argued that government also serves the function of regulating business in the public interest but the government's ability, and even motivation, to regulate is questionable. Some examples of "government regulation" will illustrate. The Bank of Canada was established by the federal government to regulate the Canadian economy through various financial manipulations by means of controlling currency, issuing and holding bonds, but the most effective mechanism of control, as used by the U.K. and U.S. central banks, is the primary reserve ratio. Although the Bank of Canada between 1954 and 1967 had these powers, it never once used them, preferring instead to use "moral suasion" as a regulating device (Drummond, 1972:73). The efficacy of "moral suasion" is questionable, especially within the framework of Canada's concentrated banking system. In fact, what this means is that chartered banks are left to regulate the economy as they see fit and when it is to their advantage to do so. The Bank of Canada is dependent on the "good will" of the chartered banks to respond to their requests and lacks the teeth to demand conformity.

Another example of "government regulation" are anti-combines laws, first introduced in 1889, which have:

always kept two principles in mind. First, the law should not be a law against combines and mergers in general. Hence it is totally different in intent from U.S. antitrust law. Second, the law should emphasise publicity as a regulatory device. Canadian scholars have suggested a third principle, implicit in the law and in government behaviour. Rosenbluth and Thornburn believe that the law has always been meant to inflict the minimum inconvenience on business, consistent with government's need to convince ordinary citizens that it is against monopoly (Drummond, 1972:101).

The inactivity and failure to enforce existing anti-combines legislation reflects the alliance of business and government and the lack of control Canadian political men have chosen to exert over business. Again, perhaps "moral suasion" is considered a more effective policy.

Crown corporations, it is sometimes suggested, signify the government's willingness to enter the economy but the history of crown corporations would indicate otherwise. They have traditionally been established in areas of the economy where private business has failed or does not find it profitable to engage in business activity. The crown corporations in Canada reflect the state's willingness to provide essential support services to business when businessmen themselves feel it unprofitable to do it themselves (Mathias, 1971:12).

One area the government has shown a willingness to regulate is foreign take-overs of financial companies[5]. Government has tried, sometimes unsuccessfully, to keep banking and insurance as Canadian controlled (Rae & McLeod, 1969:194-195). This reflects the close traditional alliance between politics and finance in Canada since its origins. Focusing on financial control and commercial activities, the Canadian economic elite established a close hold on these areas of the economy and has called on the political leaders to help maintain this position. Finance, as earlier statistics indicate, provides a striking contrast to manufacturing and resource industries; foreign ownership and government legislation, or lack of it, in these areas reflect the relative power differential between financial and industrial capitalists historically in Canada.

One other area where the state has an important role is in terms of providing legal support and reinforcement to the corporate entity. By maintaining the legal sanctity of private capital, the state is crucial to the reproduction of the capitalist system. As Parkin suggests:

The state plays an important role in preserving the structure of class inequality by giving powerful institutional and legal backing to the rules and procedures which decide the distribution of advantages and the process of recruitment to different positions (1971:27).

The structure of corporate capitalism is a political formation, as is the institution of private property. The state preserves and legitimizes these economic relationships. It provides legal sanction aimed at the preservation of private property and regulates incorporation procedures and requirements. In some cases government fixes the prices a corporation can charge and indirectly determines their profit rate, as in the case of Bell Canada. Economic dominants are able to relate to the state at least on equal terms since they represent the best organized and most powerful influence with which the state must contend. Because the economic sphere is accorded such an important place in modern industrial societies, it is able to determine in large part government goals and policy (Galbraith, 1972a:17). It is primarily through corporations that the government must initiate its economic policies thus requiring cooperation and agreement on broad goals[6].

The practice of party funding by the corporate world usually comes to light as a scandal and is seldom examined as a community of interest with common views about how the economy should be run. Some have argued that campaign financing is directly related to some type of "pay-off" for specific legislation or favours (*Globe & Mail*, March 31, 1972). Although this type of activity obviously does go on and when discovered does produce "scandal", it would be incorrect to analyse contributions strictly in this way. Contributions represent capital flows between people who share the same ideology and should be seen more as an "insurance policy" against having legislation counter to the interest of corporate capitalism brought forward or having an "undesirable" party elected which would not be as sympathetic to them. This is the normal basis of corporate contributions not the deviant case. Evidence that this is considered "normal" is the openness with which the practice is discussed (*Toronto Star*, April 15, 1972: *Ottawa Journal*, July 5, 1973).

Numerous other examples of "corporate outreach" can be provided from the Canadian experience, for example the *Time-Reader's Digest* case (Levitt, 1970:8), the corporate and political careers of men like Robert Winters (Cramer, 1966), the concessions of John Turner to the Canadian Manufacturers' Association (*Globe & Mail*, June 7, 1972:B3) and scads of others. Each illustrates the political power of corporate power. Because the corporation is a powerful institution in modern industrial society it commands power which extends well beyond the corporate sphere and into society as a whole.

But to say the corporate elite has a disproportionate impact on the state system is not to say they are not distinct institutional domains and bases of power. On the other hand, as a model of liberal-democracies, these distinct domains of power do not mean that power should be viewed "piecemeal". Rather, it should be analysed as a whole by placing these distinct bases in relationship to each other—both in terms of class recruitment and their structural relationships—by examining their relative powers. Lynd has argued that: "The most characteristic feature of power in society is that separate power, however based, tend to flow together in working arrangements and so to become a structure of power co-terminous with society" (1968:105). But what is interesting is the way these powers tend to come together, which classes are represented in the coalitions, and what the consequences of their actions are for the society. Using this approach allows for a variety of historical combinations which can be empirically examined and evaluated. This is not to belittle the power of property in capitalist society; it is, however, to place this type of power within the constella-tion of other types of power. It is to recognize that the power of unions through the right to strike is, indeed, a power with importance or the power of military leaders to command their armies, even against the wish of the political executive, is of consequence. There are a wide variety of relationships which can and do exist and any satisfactory model of society should be able to take these into account. It forces the analyst to delve into the empirical realities and historical antecedents. It is also necessary for an adequate understanding to place the various components within the context of the whole. Miliband's work is a good example of this since he explicitly examines the state in liberal-democracies as part of capitalist society and not as some autonomous functioning apparatus. He says, for instance: "The enormous *political* significance of this concentration of private economic power in ad-vanced capitalist societies, including its impact upon the state, is one of the main concerns of this study" (1969:13). He may not deal adequately with all important aspects of social life, for example trade unions and working class movements, but this does not mean his model of society would not permit him to do so. In the final section, some of the implications of organizing society as a liberal-democracy will be ex-plored but before this is done, one further issue raised in this study, but not adequately dealt with, will be examined.

(ii) Canada in the Continental Context

The question of boundaries was raised at several points earlier and it was argued that Canada's economic development was best understood within the "North Atlantic triangle". In the post-war era, this has shifted primarily to the continental context. There are a number of indicators that Canada is actually part of the North American economy rather than self-contained within the Canadian nation-state. In other words, Canada's economic and political boundaries do not always coincide.

To undertake an analysis which places Canada in the continental context requires repeating the procedures used here with corporations operating in Canada for the United States[7]. This would allow an identification of the U.S. parasite elite and it would be possible to place this section of the economic elite within the context of the total U.S. economic elite. Moreover, it would then be possible to analyse the opportunities for mobility by Canadians within the parent multinationals with dominant subsidiaries operating in Canada. This would be important for specifying more clearly the relationship between comprador and parasite elites. Equally important is placing the indigenous Canadian elite within this continental context. For instance, it was shown that at least 15 of the top 80 Canadian born elite sit on the parent boards of multinationals, between them holding some 26 directorships in these foreign corporations. This type of study would also be able to place the 195 U.S. resident directors who hold directorships in dominant corporations operating in Canada.

Some of the findings from the present study suggest the importance of extending the analysis into this larger framework. The process of structural compradorization has been proceeding steadily over the last twenty years. Indeed, it was found that 29.2 per cent of the dominant positions in the Canadian economy are either within U.S. controlled subsidiaries or held by persons born in the U.S. The evidence from the present study illustrates that the Canadian indigenous elite have had an active role in U.S. controlled companies operating in Canada. While 29.2 per cent of the dominant positions are U.S. comprador, only 15.8 per cent of the Canadian born elite are. Conversely, three quarters of the Canadian born elite are indigenous with autonomous Canadian controlled bases of power. In other words, the Canadian indigenous elite is also recruited to sit on U.S. controlled branch plants. A good deal of evidence was provided which illustrated that this indigenous elite remains viable. For instance, the proportion with their main careers in family firms has increased over the past twenty years, the youngest group of elites are more likely to be indigenous than the middle age group, and almost 20 per cent fewer of the comprador elite are of upper class origin with half the comprador elite coming from the middle class while almost two thirds of the indigenous elite are upper class, with this rising to almost three quarters for the multiple directorship holders.

The Canadian economic elite is, however, a specialized elite. As was documented, the traditional elite has chosen to center itself in transportation, utilities, finance and the mass media. In so doing, it has stifled the development of indigenous social forces in most manufacturing and resource activities—the sectors which are actually engaged in the creation of surplus in a capitalist society. In the process it has become allied with foreign capitalists in these surplus-creating sectors. The scope of the traditional indigenous elite's power within the continental context remains to be examined but it should not be surprising to find that they have an important place in this larger context. Their viability within the Canadian context, as an expression of the upper class, has been illustrated but if they do not have a powerful position within the continental context they are vulnerable to U.S. industrial capitalists. This rather unique development of elite configurations makes the Canadian corporate elite atypical compared to other industrialized liberal-democracies. Panitch and Whitaker have summarized some recent work on Canada's development saying: ". . . from the start it was a resource hinterland within a mercantile-imperialist framework. The kind of bourgeoisie which emerges from this political economy is a conservative mercantile and financial type which inevitably is dependent upon the dynamic, creative, *productive* industrial bourgeoisies of the metropolis, first British, then American. Canadian capitalists are typically bankers who today make their profits by channeling Canadian surpluses into American takeovers. In other words, finance *capital* has led to industrial *capital*, but financial *capitalists* have not become industrial *capitalists*; instead they have provided Canadian funds for American industrial capitalists. Thus Canada lacks a *national* bourgeoisie in the sense that the U.S.A., Britain, Germany, France, and Japan have national bourgeoisies" (1974:52). But to say Canada ''lacks a national bourgeoisie'' like other liberal-democracies is not the same as saying it does not have a national bourgeoisie. The difference is that the Canadian bourgeoisie is primarily a commercial one, engaged in circulation rather than production while in other nations the bourgeoisie is typically both industrial and financial. The fragmentation which has resulted does not mean the total bourgeoisie is not powerful—indeed, it may be more powerful because of the continental context. It does mean, however, that the Canadian component must commit itself to the continental context to remain strong. In the meantime, indigenous industrial forces are restrained, their mobility limited, and the independence of the Canadian nation-state by-passed. The power of the indigenous commercial elite and the foreign industrial elite reinforce one another in the continental context. The following passage provides some insight into the way a representative of this indigenous elite perceives Canada's place in international capitalism:

Canada should rely on its comparative economic advantages in determining which economic sectors to develop and how to pace that development, W. Earl McLaughlin, president and chairman of the Royal Bank of Canada, said yesterday. "Let our comparative economic advantages speak for themselves, and let us avoid any artificial diversion of our economic structure into costly and inefficient forms", Mr. McLaughlin told the Canadian Club. . . . The Royal Bank chief executive added: "Let us try to avoid the misjudgment—or personal vanity—which proclaim one form of activity to be intrinsically superior to another, whether that be resource development, high technology manufacturing, or service industries" (*The Ottawa Journal*, April 18, 1974:9).

In other words, just because the Canadian corporate elite has chosen to extract its surplus as mediators in the sphere of circulation, this should not be judged as being somehow "inferior" to extracting surplus through production. This ideology of the traditional financial elite certainly fits well with its historical and contemporary role in the Canadian economy. It certainly fits well with W. Earl McLaughlin's position: he has the best of both worlds, his ancestors having sold out to General Motors of the U.S. in the early 1900's, he now has six dominant directorships plus a directorship on General Motors Corp. (Detroit).

By developing a powerful national base in the circulation sectors, the indigenous Canadian elite has been able to operate internationally among the most powerful world capitalists. By servicing U.S. control of most of the resource sector and much of the manufacturing, the indigenous elite has reinforced its position within Canada and in the international capitalist system. They have accepted an international "division of labour" and their role in it as mediators. To say that Canada's bourgeoisie is not like most other liberal-democracies is certainly correct; to say there is no national bourgeoisie fails to acknowledge the powerful position Canadian financial capitalists have had and continue to enjoy.

The question of "dependency" on the U.S. is much more complex when the important place of Canadian financial capitalists is introduced. For instance, is the bourgeoisie "dependent" on the workers because they create surplus? Are the Canadian commercial capitalists "dependent" on U.S. industrial capitalists because they control the creation of surplus? Of course, the parallels are not synonomous because U.S. industrial capitalists obviously have a better organized base of power than do Canadian workers, but it does serve to illustrate that the notion of "dependency" is, at least, paradoxical. If the indigenous Canadian elite were to suffer severe losses to its "turf" in finance, transportation, utilities and the media, then it could be said it was being drawn into a "dependency" relationship but as long as it maintains control over these key institutions, then it has an independent base of power with which it can enter into an alliance with foreign capitalists. This subservience has not yet arrived and, in the face of threats, it has been successful in using its political power to ensure protection. Again, to say the traditional elite has entered into a "partnership" with U.S. industrial capitalists is probably correct; to say this is a "junior partnership" is to underestimate the power this elite wields nationally and internationally.

The existence of a powerful Canadian commercial elite controlled by the upper class and of a predominantly foreign elite in production, means that Canada remains a "low mobility" society. Concentration and centralization in commercial sectors has been the result of indigenous forces while these same processes in the productive sectors have been imposed from outside. The result is an economy which is highly structured with few mobility avenues for those outside the upper class. A few middle class Canadians have experienced individual mobility with compradorization but even this avenue has had many of its uppermost positions filled by the indigenous elite. In light of the earlier finding that few from outside the upper class are able to make the shift from insider positions to the executive or outsider positions, it is probable that this middle class comprador elite is trapped in the branch plants of U.S. subsidiaries but a conclusive answer to this must await an analysis of the continental economy.

(iii) Canada as a Liberal—Democracy

To use C.B. Macpherson's words, the "democracy" of a liberal-democracy is not a "kind of society" but simply a "system of government". As has been evident throughout this book, neither the economic nor mass media domains in Canadian society are in any sense democratic. The "freedom" of liberal-democracy is limited since it must be placed within the framework of gross inequalities pervasive throughout society which confine that freedom. The structured inequality evident in the corporate world becomes reflected in the inequality of access to decision making positions. Mediating between structure and opportunity in capitalist society is ownership of property. Laski indicates, in part, how the selection and screening process under corporate capitalism operates when he says: "Once the right of employment is dependent upon the will of the owner of property, it is in his power to make occupation a function of orthodoxy" (1935:208). It can be expected that acts of firing or, more subtly, "freezing-out" the undesirable by promoting those deemed suitable, will lead to the perpetuation of similar social types and privileged status for those similar to the power holders. This should be viewed as a consequence, rather than a cause, which follows from the way a society is organized. That it exists, should cue the analyst to examine stable patterns of relations which encourage and permit its development.

It is important to understand that social classes transcend the individual in at least two crucial ways. First, since classes are the product of relationships between structures, they continue as long as the structures continue. Consequently, classes have a continuity which lasts over generations because the structures and relationships which create them have continuity. Second, class positions are typically transferred intergenerationally and here, for instance, Poulantzas would agree: "It is true that in the capitalist mode of production and a capitalist social formation, social classes are not castes, that agents are not tied by their origin to determinate places. . . . But it is also true that the effects of distribution show themselves in the fact that . . . the vast majority of bourgeois (and their children after them) remain bourgeois and the vast majority of proletarians (and their children after them) remain proletarians" (1973b:54). Poulantzas is arguing that education is not itself social class but does, in fact, serve to transfer class positions intergenerationally within families, but the cause of social class is "the positions themselves" within capitalist production. An alternative way used earlier to express these two dimensions of social class is through the concepts of condition and opportunity where condition refers to the structure of society based on relations of production and opportunity to the intergenerational transfer of positions within the structure of relationships. Within liberal-democracies there is no attempt to achieve equality of condition. As a result, their stated goal of equality of opportunity is severely limited. Even if Canadian society is highly structured and if there is unequal opportunity, some would still argue that everyone is "protected" by the variety of interest groups operating in the great "pluralist arena"—balancing each others' particularistic interests against the general good. This argument will now be examined.

The Pluralist Arena?

It has been argued by some observers of liberal-democracies that a great variety of "interest groups" operate to ensure that everyone gets a "fair" voice in the management and direction of society. Connolly identified two "types" of pluralism, one which "views the government as the *arena* where major group conflicts are debated and resolved" and another which "sees major social associations, especially organized labour and the corporation, involved in a balancing process which operates largely outside the government; the government acts more as *umpire* than as participant, setting rules for conflict resolution and moving in to redress the imbalance when one group goes too far'' (1969:8). Pluralists generally focus on "consensus" and the idea of a "balance" of social forces. It ignores the systematic biases evident in class based societies and the reflection these have on relations between the state and corporate worlds. The pluralist model assumes ''free willed'' individuals who will come together when they detect injustice and voice their concerns through the many "access points" in the state. What this ignores is the fact that individuals are not ''free willed'' but subject to dominant ideological systems; what it fails to acknowledge is the unequal allocations of resources necessary to mobilize and realize concerns.

Pluralists assume that the state will be an unbiased mediator of interests but fail to recognize the possibility, as Miliband argues, ''that the state might be a rather special institution, whose main purpose is to defend the predominance in society of a particular class'' (1969:3). Schattschneider has summarized the critique quite poetically when he writes: ''The flaw in the pluralist heaven is that the heavenly chorus sings with a strong upper class accent'' (1960:35). There is little reason to assume that the existence of several institutional bases of power (such as corporations, the state or mass media) necessarily lead to a ''countervailing'' or even competitive system. It needs to be demonstrated that various segments of society are organized into roughly equally powerful agencies and further that these are indeed competitive with one another. Neither of these positions has been empirically verified and evidence presented earlier indicate that some segments of society, such as the dominant Anglo upper class, have much more pervasive power than any other segment. Indeed, as Paul Sweezy has wittily remarked: ''Some of the alleged countervailing powers may veil more power than they counter'' (1959:71). Common ideologies, class backgrounds and relationships serve to solidify power holders, not bring them into opposition. Structured interlocks, combined with social ties, serve to create a system of mutual benefit and dependence between leaders of dominant corporations and other institutions. By failing to conceptualize dominant organizations as part of, and intimately involved in, the larger social system, pluralists fail to understand that these dominant organizations are not simply passive conductors of values; rather, they shape values and activate the values of those in control. Values are not ''free-floating'' variables but a part of life that changes and is changed by social situations. Large organizations represent values in themselves and further act to shape and develop other select values.

Interest group theorists, a version of pluralists, have a long theoretical and empirical history in social studies but one of their greatest difficulties is the tendency to identify organized pressure groups as a sign of strength rather than weakness. As Nettl has argued, many are simply "shells" engaged in a form of "shadow-boxing" (1969:291-302). The powerful have direct access to state leaders and do not have to be organized into "interest groups" which provide a façade of importance but lack the substance of direct access. One such study by Robert Presthus of interest groups in Canada is subject to such a critique. He says: "Although our sample includes a cross-section of virtually all types of interest groups, one common characteristic is that none of them are 'profit making'. Many, of course, are creatures of activities which are themselves profit-making" (1973:73). Only those groups which hang out their shingles and call themselves "interest groups" are defined as important for the power process of Canadian society. He eliminates, by definition, those sectors of corporate power which deal directly with the state and defines in the very groups Nettl argued are engaged in "shadow-boxing". It would be wrong to conclude that Presthus is not capturing an important aspect of the power process in Canada. What is important, however, is to recognize that he is only including one aspect—the formal interest group level—while ignoring direct interaction by corporations and their elite with members of the state elite. Moreover, it is not correct to place on the same level the Canadian Manufacturers' Association and other interest groups such as the Lions' Club, the Loyal Orange Lodge, or Association Cyclists Canadienne. The consequences of these latter groups "getting their own way" is on a totally different level, as is the weight they carry in the political domain.

In spite of limitations outlined, Presthus was able to detect "the tendency of governmental elites to reinforce the going distributive system" in Canada such that "the consequences include a virtual monopoly of access by established groups which tend to enjoy major shares of political resources". This, Presthus argues, is because of "the vital issue of practical politics which, all else being equal, compels governmental elites to defer to those who command the most powerful institutional structures in finance, industry and the mass media" (1973:350, 352). Inequality inherent in a class-based society, particularly in one which has concentrated power in a few dominant institutional orders, becomes reflected in the political domain whereby those with the most in turn are able to command the most advantageous arrangements with the state.

Presthus' position is that "elite accommodation" acts to "ensure some rough equilibrium among the contending group interests. . . . elite accommodation may be regarded as a structural requisite of any democratic society in which policy decisions are the result of negotiation and consultation among the elites concerned. . . . Elite accommodation is inherent in the process of democratic government" (4).

Moreover, he claims this reflects "an underlying pluralism" which offers "the hope of finding some way to overcome pervasive modern schisms between labour and capital, social classes, and indeed, between government and the governed" (24-25). These may be the aspirations of "elite accommodation" but the consequences have been of quite a different nature. Indeed, Presthus' own findings show that the "consequence of the going system of elite accommodation is a reinforcement of the *status quo* in terms of the existing pattern of distribution of public largesse and political power. Functional ties and established clientele relationships tend to crystallize existing power relationships. As we have seen, it is understandably difficult for new or substantively weak interests to penetrate the decision-making process. . . . The perhaps inevitable inequalities in political resources among interest groups mean that government, to some extent, is pushed into the anomalous position of defending the strong against the weak" (349). It is difficult to understand how Presthus can characterize such a system as "ensuring some rough equilibrium"; rough indeed! To argue as Presthus does, that this structure is "inherent" and "inevitable" does not justify his calling it "democratic" without twisting the use of that word so badly as to leave it without meaning. It is one thing to identify a structure and its consequences; it is yet another to advocate and celebrate the inequalities of liberal-democracies.

The Nexus of Public and Private Power

Collegiality as a principle of decision making by elites was considered earlier as it was elaborated by Weber (1947:392ff). Following this, Porter has identified two main aspects of collegiality: "First, it greatly increases the range of knowledge which can be brought to the making of major decisions and policies. . . . Secondly, collegiality helps to reduce power by requiring that it be shared among colleagues who represent the various and often conflicting interests of the larger group". The importance of these groups is stressed by Porter when he says that "within institutional systems and between them, control crystallizes within the ambit of these relatively small collegial groups" (1965:218-220).

The way collegial groups are formed and particularly the relative power of their components should be placed within the context of Laski's notion of how dominant interests respond to emerging social forces: "a class which controls the power of the state will not surrender it if surrender involves the abdication of its privileges. It will reform when it must if reform does not mean the destruction of what it regards as essential. But it will only reform when it believes that concessions can be made without essential sacrifice. On any other terms, a ruling

class will fight'' (1935:316). Within this framework, it can be anticipated that collegial groups formed in the post-war era between the state
and corporate interests will attempt to operate on the level of reforms
which do not involve ''essential sacrifice'' to the prevailing order. The
rudimentary principle which is left unchallenged is that of private
power as expressed in capital—the same principle which confines
equality of opportunity and condition in liberal-democracies.

The state is a major candidate as a location for collegial activity
because it has two advantages. First, it has the power to tax the
population thus providing such surplus as may be necessary to undertake its policies, although the capacity of the corporate world in this
respect should not be understated, and second, the state is also backed
by what Weber and Laski both called ''coercive authority''. While it is
correct to argue that dominant elements in society are forced to respond
to underlying social forces and movements, it is also important to
remember Laski's point that it is the dominant elements which usually
choose how to respond and their response is conditioned by some basic
issues for which they will be willing to fight.

How is it that collegial decisions are worked out and what are the
consequences for the populace? In a period of optimism, W.L. Mac-
Kenzie King, later to become Prime Minister of Canada, argued: ''It is
altogether probable that Collectivist ideals, and in particular what they
represent of the community idea and improvement in the status of
Labor, will vastly expand their influence in the years to come. This is
but continuing a natural evolution which experience has wholly jus-
tified. A belief in the wisdom and justice of a measure of State
interference succeeded the older conception of *laissez faire*, which
looked to unrestricted competition as the ideal in matters of industrial
organization. Regulation, especially as respect a minimum of social
well-being, is more and more the accepted order of to-day''
(1918:230). King's optimism has not been totally borne out in Canada,
although the collectivist structure he envisioned does bear some re-
semblance. The essential harmony of interests between the state,
labour and industry is a model more resembling the top of society than
its base. Michels' prediction seems much more accurate: ''Sooner or
later the competition between various cliques of the dominant classes
ends in a reconciliation which is effected with the instinctive aim of
retaining domination over the masses by sharing it among themselves''
(1962:343).

Structurally, both King's and Michels' frameworks resemble one
another but the anticipated consequences are radically different. King's
image is of harmony among all people while Michels' is of a basic
division between ruler and ruled with harmony limited to the rulers.

Even today the debate is a relevant one with the critics arguing that the elite accommodation or collectivist models really mean a coalition of the powerful dominating others while its defenders say this "balanced" coalition is the wave of the future and of benefit to all. Both agree that it means concentration of power in the hands of a few.

What then are the roles of public and private power in a liberal-democracy like Canada? Louis St-Laurent, as Prime Minister of Canada, represented the way he saw the role of the state in these terms: "I don't think that free enterprise requires that governments do nothing about economic conditions. Government can—and I believe governments should—pursue fiscal and commercial policies which will encourage and stimulate enterprise and wise government policies can do a lot to maintain the right kind of economic climate" (quoted by Lamontage, 1969:69-70). O'Connor has offered an explanation which goes a long way in explaining why the state "should", in St-Laurent's terms, "encourage and stimulate enterprise". O'Connor says that the state has succeeded in socializing a number of aspects of production in liberal-democracies, particularly risk, but what it has not socialized are private profits or control over private decision making. His argument is that the fiscal policies of the state in liberal-democracies are tied to the tax base of corporate activity such that "state expenditures remain integral to the process of private accumulation. In the event that state spending is not tied to the needs of private capital, there will occur a reduction in the rate of economic growth, and, hence, the tax base and the possibility of financing future expenditures" (1970:79). The fiscal policy of the state is tied to the prosperity of private capital since it is growth which generates taxation revenues, a basic ingredient of policy implementation. However, the long-term productivity of the corporate sector "requires the expansion of the state sector" O'Connor maintains, thus making them interdependent in their relationship (1972:25). The political economy of the state is such that it requires higher levels of involvement in order to meet demands made on it. To do so continues to require higher levels of revenue. The critical point appears when its revenues can no longer support escalating demands.

But who benefits? As long as production expands, at least that component of labour tied to big unions and large corporations gains in real income terms but it is not so clear that the rest of labour gains. Given the biased way state subsidies are offered to corporations, big corporations gain while smaller ones are allowed to pass by the way. But it is not enough to say big corporations gain; it is actually those at the top of these corporations who gain through higher salaries and through dividends from profits. Without explaining that there are people involved in these processes, there is a failure to understand how the major instruments of income and wealth distribution in capitalist societies operate. The distributive mechanism of the prevailing system serves to reinforce and perpetuate existing inequalities. To the extent that the state encourages and supports these mechanisms, public capital is used to promote private gains.

To argue that liberal-democracies are characterized by a "mixed economy" of public and private capital is to miss the point of how they are "mixed" and in what proportions. When public capital is used to support private capital the mixture is not "balanced" but has the effect of reinforcing and maintaining inequalities. The gains to be made are still private gains and the power is still private power.

The pressure by dominant interests within the state and corporate worlds has been toward increasing the stability of society through planning but given the existing inequalities, it is evident that this means further consolidation of already concentrated power centers and the reduction of boundaries between public and private power. To argue that the state has become more involved in economic activities without specifying the character and purpose of these activities fails to see the complementarity of these actions with those of private capital. State expenditures have been directed toward stabilizing relationships within the population and as a means of funneling surplus to dominant economic interests. In other words, what has frequently been understood as encroachments by public power on private power turns out in practice to reinforce and strengthen private interests. The future of the state and private capital have become identified as complementary and each has become mutually dependent upon the other. In order to coordinate these coincidental interests, there have evolved a series of forums and associations, created by and for the state and corporate elites. The majority of benefits from these types of arrangements accrue to those most capable of demanding them—the already powerful.

Top decision making positions in the economy and mass media in Canada are dominated by a small upper class. Through dominant corporations they maintain a hierarchically ordered corporate system by which they are able to extract surplus allowing them to continue and expand their control. This same surplus provides them with a life style much different than that experienced by the vast majority of Canadians and the privileges that accrue to them are passed on to their children. Despite severe erosion of the Canadian economy by U.S. based corporate capitalists since the early 1950's, the Canadian upper class remains intact. In fact, it has further consolidated its traditional commercial forté while compradorization has been a phenomenon primarily affecting the middle class. With all the changes which have been experienced over the last two decades, Canada has not fulfilled its promise as a society with equal opportunity. As long as corporate power is allowed to remain in its present concentrated state, there is no hope for equality of opportunity or equality of condition in Canada.

Notes

[1] Each of these undertakings is planned; see Clement and Olsen, 1973.

[2] The evidence provided earlier suggests, for instance, that during wartime, the "barriers" between public and private power are lifted. In the elite this is reflected in the high proportion of the current corporate elite who were recruited to top state positions during that time.

[3] Parkin, for example, points out that in Britain "trade union leaders . . . have been absorbed into the apparatus of the state. . . . union leaders were represented on only twelve government committees in 1939; by 1948 they were on sixty, and by the early 1950's they were on more than eighty. . . . This is understood to mean that they will act to safeguard the 'national interest', and not the class interests of their members" (1972:135). Hayward, on the other hand, says "union leaders in France refuse to accept more than an armistice in the class war against the capitalist system . . . unless the leaders follow their rank and file and reject the role of industrial salesmen, which they are encouraged to assume by government, plant level wild-cat strikes will effectively destroy the agreements negotiated at the summit (1972:297). These two accounts suggest that there is rather wide variance in the way labour "fits" into the dominant power structure.

[4] See, for instance, the ITT—Rayonier case in Quebec (Levitt, 1972:8; Auf der Maur, 1973:25).

[5] Examples of government legislation protecting against foreign ownership in finance include the Investment Companies Act of 1971 for sales finance companies, the Bank Act (1967), Loan Companies Act (1970) and Trust Companies Act (1964).

[6] Philip Mathias has provided some classic illustrations of the relationships between the state and corporate elites in *Forced Growth* (1971). One of the cases he presents is between Brinco and Newfoundland in which Joey Smallwood (premier) went to some merchant bankers, the Rothschild's, in 1952 to ask them to form Brinco. In 1953, "Brinco was granted mineral rights to 50,000 square miles of Labrador, 40% of its surface area. Only 24,000 square miles of crown land remained uncommitted. . . . Brinco was also granted mineral rights over 10,000 square miles of Newfoundland, which amounted to almost all the uncommitted crown lands on the Island. Brinco's 60,000 square miles of mineral rights were greater in extent than the whole of England and Wales". Addtional rights, granted through a subsidiary, included gas and oil concessions, timber rights, and water power rights on all Newfoundland and Labrador rivers (1971:46-47). In the case of Parsons and Whittemore, in Saskatchewan, the government guaranteed $157 million in loans and paid $1.5 million in equity while Parsons and Whittemore paid $7 million in equity for the development of

pulp mills. In return, Saskatchewan received 30 per cent of the equity, for 80 per cent of the risk, while Parsons and Whittemore received 70 per cent of the equity. Ironically, Parsons and Whittemore made back their original investment in profits dreived from constructing the mills (81-93). Parsons and Whittemore is a U.S. company owned entirely by Karl Landegger and represents capital investment of over $1,000 million throughout the world. The company had sales in 1971 almost equal to the entire budget of Saskatchewan (85-86). Both the cases of Brinco in Newfoundland and Parsons and Whittemore in Saskatchewan represent instances where the "host" was in an extremely weak bargaining position since each province needed economic development and was "forced" to make serious concessions to do so. Political pressures favoured, in each case, the company coming in to invest and left the provinces with little choice but to meet them on their own terms. In these cases governments were used by the corporations to gain economic power and certainly were not limited or countervailed in any sense.

[7]This study is now in its preliminary stages and I hope to have it complete toward the end of 1975.

References

Aaronovitch
  1955—Monopoly. London: Lawrence & Wishart.
  1961—The Ruling Class. London: Lawrence & Wishart.
Acheson, T.W.
  1969—"The Nature and Structure of York Commerce in the 1820's".
  Canadian Historical Review, L (December).
  1972a—"The Social Origins of the Canadian Industrial Elite,
  1880-1885".Canadian Business History, Selected Studies, 1497-1971,
  Macmillan, D.S., ed. McClelland & Stewart.
  1972b—"The National Policy and the Industrialization of the Maritimes,
  1880-1919". Acadiensis I (Spring).
  1973—"Changing Social Origins of the Canadian Industrial Elite,
  1880-1910". Business History Review, XLVII, no. 2 (Summer).
Aitken, H.G.J.
  1967—"Defensive Expansionism: The State and Economic Growth in
  Canada". Easterbrook & Watkins, ed.
  1965—"Government and Business in Canada". Deutsch, et al, ed.
Archibald, Bruce
  1971—"Atlantic Regional Underdevelopment and Socialism". Lapierre, et
  al, ed.
Armstrong, Jill
  1972—"Canadians in Crisis: the Nature and Source of Support for Leadership in a National Emergency". Canadian Review of Sociology and Anthropology 9, 4 (November).
Arnold, Truman
  1937—The Folklore of Capitalism. New Haven: Yale University.
Auf der Maur, Nick
  1971—"The trigger was the 'La Presse' affair". The Last Post, 2, 3 (Dec-Jan
  1971-72).
  1973—"ITT: Now the experts on Catch—22 move in on Canada". Last Post,
  3, 4.
Baran, P. and P. Sweezy
  1966—Monopoly Capital. New York: Monthly Review.
Beckhart, B.H.
  1964—"Fewer and Larger Banks". Neufeld, ed.
Behrman, J.
  1972—"The Multinational Firm and the Nation State: Another View".
  Paquet (1970).
Berger, Brigette
  1966—"Vilfredo Pareto and the Sociology of Knowledge". Social Research, XXXIV:261 - I.
Berle, A.A.
  1957—Economic Power and the Free Society. New York.
Berle, A.A. and G. Means

1968—The Modern Corporation and Private Property. (originally published in 1932) New York: Harcourt, Brace & World.

Bierstedt, Robert
1950—"An Analysis of Social Power". American Sociological Review, Volume 15, No. 6 (December).

Blau, Peter
1956—Bureaucracy in Modern Society. New York: Random House.

Blau & Scott
1962—Formal Organizations. San Francisco: Chandler.

Blishen, et al (eds.)
1968—Canadian Society. (Revised Edition) Toronto: Macmillan.

Bliss, Michael
1972—" 'Dyspepsia of the Mind': The Canadian Businessman and His Enemies". Macmillan, ed.
1970—"Canadianizing American Business: the roots of the branch plant". Lumsden, ed.

Block, Fred
1970—"Expanding Capitalism: The British and American Cases". Berkeley Journal of Sociology, Volume XV.

Bond, D.E. and Shearer
1972—The Economics of the Canadian Financial System. Prentice-Hall, Scarborough.

Brady, R.A.
1943—Business as a System of Power. Columbia University Press.

Brinkerhoff & Kunz
1972—Complex Organizations and Their Environments. Iowa: WM. C. Brown.

Bruce, Charles
1968—News and the Southams. Macmillan: Toronto.

Burnham, James
1941—The Managerial Revolution. Indiana University Press (new Preface, 1959).

Canadian-American Committee
1969—"US-Canada Free Trade". Rae & McLeod, ed.

Canadian Manufacturers Association
1969—"Tariff Policy in Canada." Rae & McLeod, ed.

Canada Year Book
Dominion Bureau of Statistics. Ottawa. various years.

Careless, J.M.S.
1972—"The Business Community in the Early Development of Victoria, British Columbia". Macmillan, ed.

Chalmers, Floyd S.
1969—A Gentleman of the Press. Doubleday: Toronto.

Child, Arthur
1970—"The Problem of Imputation Resolved". Curtis & Petras, eds.

Child, John
1969—The Business Enterprise in Modern Industrial Society. London: Collier-Macmillan.

Chodos, Robert

1972—"Why the CPR Doesn't Like You". Starowicz and Murphy, ed.
Christoffel, T. et al (eds.)
1970—Up Against the American Myth. New York: Holt, Rinehart & Winston.
Clark, S.D.
1970—"The Sociology of Frontier Religion". Cross, ed.
Clement, Wallace
1974a—"The Changing Structure of the Canadian Economy". Canadian Review of Sociology and Anthropology, *Aspects of Canadian Society*.
1974b—"Inequality of Access: Characteristics of the Canadian Economic Elite". Canadian Review of Sociology and Anthropology, Vol. 12, no. 2.
Clement, Wallace and Dennis Olsen
1973—"Canadian Power Elites and Ethnicity: A Research Proposal". Carleton University, mimeo (August).
1974—"The Ethnic Composition of Canada's Elites, 1951 to 1973". Report submitted to the Secretary of State (May).
Concentration in Manufacturing
1971—Department of Consumer and Corporate Affairs. Ottawa
Connolly, Wm. E.
1969—The Bias of Pluralism. Atherton Press: NY.
Conway, G.R.
1970—The supply of and demand for Canadian equities. Toronto Stock Exchange.
Chodos, Robert
1972—"Why the CPR Doesn't Like You". Starowicz and Murphy, ed.
Cramer, Alex
1966—"Canada's Power Elite". Sanity (September).
Creighton, Donald
1970—Canada's First Century. Macmillan: Toronto.
1965—"The Economic Background of the Rebellions of 1837". Easterbrook & Watkins, ed.
Cross, M.S., ed.
1970—The Frontier Thesis and the Canada. Copp Clark: Toronto.
Curtis, James & John W. Petras, ed.
1970—The Sociology of Knowledge: A Reader. Preager Publishers: NY.
Daly, William G.
1972—"The Mobility of Top Business Executives in Canada". Unpublished Master's Thesis, University of British Columbia.
Davey, Keith
1973—"Exactly What has Emerged Since 1970? (if anything)". Content (December).
Davis, A.K.
1971—"Canadian Society and History as Hinterland versus Metropolis" in Ossenberg (ed).
Deaton, R.
1972—"The Fiscal Crisis of the State". Our Generation, Vol. 8, No. 4.
Denison, Merrill
1955—The Barley and the Steam: The Molson Story. McClelland & Stewart: Toronto.

Deutsch, J.J., et al (ed.)
1965—The Canadian Economy: Selected Readings. Revised Edition. Macmillan: Toronto.

Dibble, Vernon K.
1970—"Occupations and Ideologies" in Curtis & Petras.

Dion, Léon
1969—"An Hypothesis Concerning the Structure and Function of Political Theory." Wadsworth Publishing: Belmont, California.

Domhoff, G.W.
1967—Who Rules America? Prentice-Hall: New Jersey.
1970—The Higher Circles. New York: Vintage.

Drache, D.
1970—"The Canadian bourgeoisie and its national consciousness." Lumsden (ed).

Drummond, Ian M.
1972—The Canadian Economy: Structure and Development. Revised Edition. Irwin-Dorsey. Georgetown.

Earl, D.W. (ed.)
1967—The Family Compact: Aristocracy or Oligarchy? Copp Clark: Toronto.

Easterbrook, W.T. and H.G.H. Aitken
1956—Canadian Economic History. Macmillan: Toronto.

Easterbrook W.T. and M.H. Watkins (ed.)
1967—Approaches to Canadian Economic History. McClelland & Stewart: Toronto.

Eisenstadt, S.N.
1959—"Bureaucracy, Bureaucratization and Debureaucratization". Administrative Science Quarterly, 4:302-320.

Elkin, Frederick
1971—"Mass Media, Advertising and the Quiet Revolution" in Ossenberg (ed).

Etzioni, A. (ed.)
1969—A Sociological Reader on Complex Organizations. 2nd Edition. New York: Holt, Rinehart & Winston.

Financial Post
1972—Survey of Industrials 1972. Toronto.
1972—Directory of Directors 1972. Toronto.

Fitch, Robert
1971—"Who Rules the Corporations?: Rejoiner to O'Connor". Socialist Revolution, Volume 7.

Fitch and Oppenheimer
1970—"Who Rules the Corporations?" (Three Parts) Socialist Revolution, Volume 4, 5, 6.

Ford, Henry II
1963—"An Incentive-For-Everybody Economy", in Stavrianos (ed).

Fossum, E.
1970—"Political Development and Strategies for Change". Journal of Peace Research, Vol. 1.

Frank, A.G.
1966—"The Development of Underdevelopment". Monthly Review (Sept).
1967—Capitalism and Underdevelopment in Latin America. Monthly Review Press: NY.
Galbraith, J.A.
1970—Canadian Banking. The Ryerson Press: Toronto.
Galbraith, J.K.
1952—American Capitalism: the Concept of Countervailing Power. Boston: Houghton Mifflin.
1967—The New Industrial State. New York: Signet.
1968—The McLandress Dimension. New York: Signet.
1973—Economics and the Public Purpose. Boston: Houghton Mifflin.
Gerth, H. and C.W. Mills (ed.)
1946—From Max Weber. New York: Oxford University.
Gilchrist, John
1972—"Exploration and Enterprise: The Newfoundland Fishery c. 1797-1677". Macmillan, ed. (1972).
Gitlin, Todd
1965—"Local Pluralism as Theory and Ideology". Studies on the Left, Vol. 5, No. 3.
Godfrey, D. and M. Watkins
1970—Gordon to Watkins to You. New Press: Toronto.
Goldthorpe, John
1966—"Social Stratification in Industrial Society" in Bendix & Lipset, editors, Class, Status and Power. Second Edition. Free Press: New York.
Gonick, G.
1970—"Foreign ownership and political decay". Lumsden, ed. (1970).
Gordon, R.
1961—Business Leadership in the Large Corporation. University of California (originally published 1945).
Guindon, Hubert
1968—"Two Cultures: An essay on nationalism, class, and ethnic tension" in Leach (ed.) 1968.
Hacker, Andrew (ed.)
1965—The Corporate Take-Over. Garden City, New York: Anchor.
Hall, Oswald
1971—"The Canadian Division of Labour Revisited". Ossenberg (1971).
Hammond, Bray
1967—"Banking in Canada Before Confederation, 1792-1867". Easterbrook & Watkins, ed. (1967).
Harbison, F. and C.A. Myers
1959—Management in the Industrial World: An International Analysis. New York.
Hartung, Frank E.
1970—"Problems in the Sociology of Knowledge", in Curtis & Petras.
Hayward, J.E.S.
1972—"State Intervention in France: The Changing Style of Government-Industry Relations". Political Studies, Vol. XX, no. 3.

Heap, James
    1973—"Conceptual and Theoretical Problems in *The Vertical Mosaic*".
    Canadian Review of Sociology and Anthropology, Vol. 9, no. 2 (May).
Hendricks & Struggles, Inc.
    1973—"Profile of a Canadian President". Chicago, Illinois.
Hobsbawn, E.J.
    1971—"Class consciousness in history" in Mészaros, ed.
Hutcheson, John
    1973—"Class and Income Distribution in Canada" in Laxer, ed.
    (1973).
Hymer, S.
    1972—"Multinational Corporations". Paquet (1972).
Information Canada
    1970—Report for the Royal Commission on the Status of Women in Canada.
    Ottawa.
    1970—Advertising Expenditures in Canada (June). Ottawa.
    1970—Incomes of Canadians. Ottawa.
    1972—Foreign Direct Investment in Canada. Ottawa.
    1972—Household facilities and equipment (May). Ottawa.
    1973—Printing, publishing and allied industries (September). Ottawa.
    1973—Economic Review. Ottawa.
Innis, Harold A.
    1956—Essays in Canadian Economic History. University of Toronto: To-
    ronto.
    1967—"The Fur Trade". Easterbrook & Watkins, ed. (1967).
Johnson, Leo A.
    1972—"The development of class in Canada in the twentieth century," in
    Teeple, editor.
    1973—"Incomes, disparity and impoverishment in Canada since World War
    II". New Bytown Press: Toronto.
Juran, J.M.
    1964—Managerial Breakthrough. New York: McGraw-Hill.
Juran, J.M. and J.K. Louden
    1966—The Corporate Director. New York: American Management Assoc.
Kalbach, W.E. and W.W. McVey
    1971—The Demographic Basis of Canadian Society. McGraw-Hill: To-
    ronto.
Katz, D. and R. Kahn
    1966—The Social Psychology of Organizations. New York: Wiley.
Keegan, W.J.
    1968—"Acquisition of global business information". Columbia Journal of
    World Business, Vol.1, No. 2.
Kennedy, J. deN.
    1950—History of the Department of Munitions and Supply. Volumes 1 and
    2. King's Printer, Ottawa.
Kesterton, Wilfred
    1973—(forthcoming) "Social Currents and the Printed Media" in The

Sociology of Communication in Canada. Benjamin O. Singer, ed. Copp Clark (forthcoming).

Kilbourn, W.
1960—A History of the Steel Company of Canada. Toronto.

King, W.L. Mackenzie
1918—Industry and Humanity. Macmillan: Toronto.

Labrie & Palmer
1967—Ziegel, ed. (1967).

LaMarsh, Judy
1969—Bird in a Guilded Cage.

Lamontage, Maurice
1969—"The Role of Government" in Rae & McLeod (ed.) 1969.

Lapierre, L. et al, ed.
1971—Essays on the Left. McClelland & Stewart: Toronto.

Laski, H.J.
1935—The State in Theory and Practice. Allen & Unwin: London.

Last Post
1970—"An Anatomy of the Time, Canada Lobby and How it Controls What is Published". Vol. 1, No. 4 (June).
1972—"Deals Behind the Toronto Star". Vol. 2, No. 5 (May).
1973—"Brascan, Brazil and the Liberal Party". Vol. 3, No. 2.

Lawrence, P. and J. Lorsch
1967—Organization and Environment. Boston: Harvard Graduate School of Business Administration.

Laxer, James
1970—The Energy Poker Game. New Press: Toronto.
1973—"Introduction to the Political Economy of Canada". The Political Economy of Dependency, Robert Laxer, ed. (1973).

Laxer, Robert (ed).
1973—(Canada) Ltd.: The Political Economy of Dependency. McClelland & Stewart: Toronto.

Leach, Richard H. (ed.)
1968—Contemporary Canada. University of Toronto Press: Toronto.

Lenin, V.I.
1969—Imperialism: The Highest Stage of Capitalism. Peking Press.

Levitt, Kari
1972—"Decolonizing Canada and Quebec". The Canadian Forum, March.
1970—Silent Surrender, the Multinational Corporation in Canada. Macmillan: Toronto.

Lewis, D.
1972—Louder Voices: The Corporate Welfare Bums. James, Lewis and Samuel: Toronto.

Lieberson, S. and J. O'Connor
1972—"Leadership and Organizational Performance: A Study of Large Corporations". American Sociological Review, 37:2 (April).

Littleton
1972—Dimension, Vol. 8, Nos. 4 & 5.

Litvak, I.A., & Maule, C.J.

1971—Dual Loyalty. Toronto: McGraw-Hill.
Lumsden, I. (ed.)
1970—Close the 49th Parallel, etc. University of Toronto: Toronto.
Lynd, Robert S.
1968—"Power in the United States" in Domhoff and Ballard (eds.).
Macmillan, D.S. (ed.)
1972—Canadian Business History, Selected Studies, 1497-1971. McClelland & Stewart: Toronto.
Macpherson, C.B.
1965—The Real World of Democracy. CBC Publications: Toronto.
1969—"Revolution and Ideology" in R.H. Cox, ed. Ideology, Politics and Political Theory. Wadsworth Publ. California.
Mandel, Ernest
1971—"Workers and Permanent Revolution" in George Fisher, ed. The Revival of American Socialism. Oxford: NY.
Mann, W.E. (ed.)
1968—Canada: A Sociological Profile. Copp Clark: Toronto.
Mannheim, Karl
1936—Ideology and Utopia. Harcourt, Brace & World: NY.
1953—Essays on Sociology and Social Psychology. Harcourt, Brace & World: NY.
Marx, Karl
1967—Capital (Three Volumes). International Pub.: NY.
1970a—A Contribution to the Critique of Political Economy. Progress: Moscow.
1970b—The German Ideology. International Pub.: NY.
Maslove, Allan M.
1972—The Pattern of Taxation in Canada. Economic Council of Canada. Information Canada. Ottawa (December).
Mason, E.S. (ed.).
1959—The Corporation in Modern Society. Mass.: Harvard University.
Masters, D.C.
1965—"Reciprocity, 1846-1911". The Canadian Historical Association Historical Booklet, Number 12.
Mathias, Philip
1971—Forced Growth. James, Lewis & Samuel: Toronto.
Mauer, J. (ed.)
1971—Readings in Organization Theory. New York: Random House.
McCalla, Douglas
1969—"The Commercial Politics of the Toronto Board of Trade, 1850-60" Canadian Historical Review, L (March).
McDayter, Walt & Russell Elman
1971—"In the Shadow of Giants" in McDayter, ed. A Media Mosaic. Holt, Rinehart & Winston: Toronto.
McDougall, W. and G. Fogelberg
1968—Corporate Boards in Canada. London: University of Western Ontario.
McDougall, W. (ed.)
1969—The Effective Director. London: University of Western Ontario.

Merton, R.K., et al (ed.)

    1952—Reader in Bureaucracy. Glencoe.

Mészaros, Istvan, ed.

    1971—Aspects of history and class consciousness. Routledge & Kegan Paul: London.

Michels, Robert

    1962—Political Parties. (First published 1911). New York: Free Press.

Miliband, Ralph

    1969—The State in Capitalist Society. Weidenfeld and Nicholson: London.

    1971—"Barnave: a case of bourgeois class consciousness", in Mészaros, ed.

Mills, C.W.

    1948—The New Men of Power. New York: Harcourt & Brace.

    1951—White Collar. New York: Oxford University.

    1956—The Power Elite. New York: Oxford.

    1959—The Sociological Imagination. New York: Oxford.

    1963—"The Cultural Apparatus" in Horowitz, ed. Power, Politics and People. Oxford: New York.

Minified, James Macdonald

    1971—"Mass Media and Their Control" in Ossenberg.

Monroe, John

    1967—"Sovereignty and Canadian Broadcasting". Reprinted in Canadian Dimension. Kit No. 3 "Canadian Nationalism".

Moore, Barrington, Jr.

    1966—The Social Origins of Dictatorship and Democracy. Beacon.

Monthly Review (editors)

    1969a—"Notes on the Multinational Corporation". Vol. xxi, No. 5 & 6 (October and November).

Morton, W.L.

    1963—The Kingdom of Canada. McClelland & Stewart: Toronto.

Mosca, G.

    1939—The Ruling Class. (originally published 1895 with part II added 1923) New York: McGraw-Hill.

Myers, G.

    1972—History of Canadian Wealth. (original 1914) James, Lewis & Samuel: Toronto.

Naylor, R.T.

    1972—"The rise and fall of the third commercial empire of the St. Lawrence". Teeple, ed. (1972).

    1973—"The History of Domestic and Foreign Capital in Canada" in Laxer (ed.) 1973.

Nettl, J. P.

    1969—"Consensus or Elite Domination: The Case of Business" in Rose (ed.) 1969.

Neufeld, E.P. (ed.)

    1964—Money and Banking in Canada. McClelland & Stewart: Toronto.

    1969—A Global Corporation, A History of the International Development of

Massey-Ferguson Limited. University of Toronto Press.

1972—The Financial System of Canada: Its Growth and Development. St. Martin's Press: New York.

Newcomer, Mabel

1955—The Big Business Executive. New York: Columbia University.

Newman, Peter C.

1959—Flame of Power. McClelland & Stewart: Toronto.

1972a—"The Bankers", Part 1. Macleans (February).

1972b—"The Bankers", Part 2. Macleans (March).

O'Connor, James

1970—"The Fiscal Crisis of the State". Socialist Revolution, No. 1 and 2.

1971—"Who Rules the Corporations?: Rejoiner to Fitch & Oppenheimer". Socialist Revolution, Number 7.

1972—"Inflation, Fiscal Crisis and the American Working Class". Socialist Revolution, Number 8.

Oliver, M. (ed.)

1961—Social Purpose for Canada. University of Totonto: Toronto.

Olsen, Dennis

1973—"The State Elite in Canadian Society: A Thesis Proposal". Unpublished PH.D. Proposal. Department of Sociology and Anthropoloty, Carleton University. Ottawa. Mimeo.

Ossenberg, R.J. (ed.)

1971—Canadian Society: Pluralism, Change and Conflict. Scarborough: Prentice-Hall.

Packard, Vance

1957—The Hidden Persuaders. David McKay Co.: New York.

Palmer, E.

1967—"Directors' Powers and Duties". Ziegler (1967).

Panitch, Leo and Reg Whitaker

1974—"The New Waffle: From Matthews to Marx". Dimension, Vol. 10, No. 1.

Paquet, Gilles (ed.)

1972—The Multinational Firm and the Nation State. Don Mills: Collier-Macmillan.

Park, Libbie & Frank

1962—Anatomy of Big Business. Toronto.

Park, Robert

1940—"News as a Form of Knowledge: A Chapter in the Sociology of Knowledge". American Journal of Sociology, XLV:669-686.

Parkin, Frank

1971—Class Inequality and Political Order. London: Paladin.

Parsons, Talcott

1947—Introduction to Social and Economic Organization. New York: Free Press.

1970—"Equality and Inequality in Modern Socity or Social Stratification Revisited" in Social Stratification, E.O. Laumann, ed. Bobbs-Merrill Company: New York.

1968—(ed.) American Sociology: Perspectives, Problems, Methods. New York: Basic Books.

Patman, W.
   1968—Commercial Banks and Their Trust Activities: Emerging Influence on
   the American Economy. Washington: House of Representatives.
Pease, John, et al
   1970—"Ideological Currents in American Stratification Literature". The
   American Sociologist, May:127-237.
Peers, Frank
   1970—"Oh say, can you see?". Ian Lumsden, ed. Close the 49th Parallel,
   etc. University of Toronto Press.
Pelton, Richard
   1970—"Who Really Rules America?" Progressive Labour, Vol. 7 (Feb).
Pen, J.
   1971—"What About the Managers". Rothschild (1971).
Perlo, Victor
   1957—The Empire of High Finance. New York: International.
Perroux, F.
   1971—"The Domination of Effect and Modern Economic Theory".
   Rothschild (1971).
Pinard, Maurice
   1970—"Working Class Politics: An Interpretation of the Quebec Case".
   Canadian Review of Sociology and Anthropology, 7, 2 (May).
Popper, Karl
   1970—"The Sociology of Knowledge" in Curtis & Petras (ed.)
Porter, John
   1955—"Elite Groups: A Scheme for the Study of Power in Canada".
   Canadian Journal of Economics and Political Science. Vol. XXI, No. 4.
   1956—"Concentration of Economic Power and the Economic Elite in
   Canada". Canadian Journal of Economics and Political Science. Vol. XXII,
   No. 2.
   1957—"The Canadian Economic Elite and the Social Structure in Canada".
   Canadian Journal of Economics and Political Science. Vol. XXIII, No. 3.
   1961—"Freedom and Power in Canadian Democracy". Oliver, ed. (1961).
   1965—The Vertical Mosaic. University of Toronto Press: Toronto.
Poulantzas, Nicos
   1973a—Political Power and Social Classes. N.L.B. and S & W London.
   1973b—"On Social Classes". National Left Review, No. 78 (Mar/Apr).
Presthus, Robert
   1962—The Organizational Society. New York: Vintage Books.
   1973—Elite Accomodation in Canadian Politics. Macmillan: Toronto.
Pritchard, James
   1972—"Commerce in New France". Macmillan, ed. (1972).
Rae, K.J. and J.T. McLeod (ed.)
   1969—Business and Government in Canada. Methuen: Toronto.
Reynolds, Lloyd G.
   1940—The Control of Competition in Canada. Harvard University Press:
   Cambridge, Mass.
Rioux, M.
   1971—Quebec in Question. James, Lewis & Samuel: Toronto.
Rose, Richard (ed.)

1969—Studies in British Politics. Macmillan: London.

Rosenberg, Louis
1939—Canada's Jews: A Social and Economic Study of the Jews in Canada. The Bureau of Social and Economic Research, Canadian Jewish Congress.
1971—The Jewish Community in Canada. Two Volumes. McClelland & Stewart: Toronto.

Rosenbluth, G.
1961—"Concentration and Monopoly in the Canadian Economy". Oliver, ed. (1961).
1970—"Foreign Control and Concentration in Canadian Industry". Canadian Journal of Economics, 3.

Ross, Aileen D.
1968—"Philanthropic Activity and the Business Career". Mann, ed.

Ross, H.I.
1969—Untitled. McDougall (1969).

Rothschild, K.W. (ed.)
1971—Power in Economics. Middlesex, England: Penguin.

Rotstein, A.
1970—"Binding Prometheus". Lumsden, ed. (1970).

Rowell/Sirois Report
1963—Book I. McClelland & Stewart: Toronto.

Russell, Bertrand
1938—Power. Unwin Books: London, U.K.

Ryerson, S.
1968—Unequal Union. Progress: Toronto.
1972—"Quebec: concepts of class and nation". Teeple, ed. (1972).

Sampson, Anthony
1965—Anatomy of Britain Today. Harper & Row: New York.

Saunders, R.E.
1967—"The Compact as an Economic and Social Group". Earl, ed. (1967).

Schattschneider, E.E.
1960—The Semisoveriegn People. New York.

Scheinberg, Stephen
1973—"Invitation to empire: tariffs and American economic expansion in Canada" Business History Review XLVII.

Selznick, P.
1948—"Foundation of the Theory of Organizations". American Sociological Review, Vol. 13 (February).

Senate Report
1970—(I) "The Uncertain Mirror". Report of the Special Senate Committee on Mass Media. Information Canada.
1970—(II) "Words, Music, and Dollars: A Study of the Economics of Publishing and Broadcasting". Report of the Special Senate Committee on Mass Media.

Sheehan, Robert
1970—"Proprietors in the World of Big Business". Zeitlin (1970).

Singer, Jacques
1969—Trade Liberalization and the Canadian Steel Industry. University of Toronto Press.

Starowicz, M. and R. Murphy (ed.)
1972—Corporate Canada. James, Lewis & Samuel: Toronto.

Starowicz, M.
1972—"Eaton's: An Irreverent History". Starowitz & Murphy, ed. (1972).

Statistics Canada
1970—Incomes of Canadians. Ottawa.
1971—Canada's International Investment Position, 1926 to 1967. Ottawa.

Stavrianos, L.S. (ed.)
1963—Readings in World History. Allyn & Bacon: Boston.

Stephen
1938—Private Schools in Canada; A Handbook of Boys' Schools Which are Members of the Canadian Headmasters' Association. Clark: Toronto.

Surette, Ralph
1972—"Why the Farmer's Dying" is Starowitz and Murphy (ed.) 1972.

Sweezy, Paul
1959—"The Theories of New Capitalism". Monthly Review, Vol. 11, No. 3 & 4 (July and August).
1971—"Resurgence of Financial Control: Factor Fancy". Monthly Review (November).

Tawney, R.H.
1920—The Acquisitive Society. Harcourt and Brace: NY.

Teeple, Gary (ed.)
1972—Capitalism and the National Question in Canada. University of Toronto Press.
1972—"Land, Labour and Capital in pre-Confederation Canada". Teeple, ed. (1972).

Trebling, H.M. (ed.)
1970—The Corporation in the American Economy. Chicago: Quadrangle.

Tugendhat, Christopher
1972—The Multinationals. Random House: New York.

Tulchinsky, G.
1972—"The Montreal Business Community, 1837-1853". Macmillan, ed. (1972).

Turner, Louis
1970—Invisible Empires. Harcourt, Brace & Janovich.

Underhill, Frank
1964—The Image of Confederation. Massey Lectures: Toronto.

Van Loon, Richard
1970—"Political Participation in Canada: the 1965 Election," Canadian Journal of Political Science, III (Sept.)

Warner, W. Lloyd and James Abegglen
1955—Big Business Leaders in America. Atheneum: NY.

Warnock, John W.
1970—"All the news it pays to print". Ian Lumsden, ed. Close the 49th Parallel, etc. University of Toronto Press.

Watkins, M. and Forester (ed.)
1963—Economics: Canada. McGraw-Hill: Toronto.

Watkins, Mel

1967—"A Staple Theory of Economic Growth". Easterbrook & Watkins, ed. (1967).

1970a—Address the Eleventh Annual Meeting of the Western Association of Sociology and Anthropology in Canadian Confrontation, A.K. Davis (ed.) Alberta.

1970b—"The dismal state of economics in Canada". Lumsden, ed. (1970).

1973—"Resources and Underdevelopment" in Laxer (ed) 1973.

Weber, Max

1946—From Max Weber. Gerth & Mills, ed. Oxford Press: NY.

1947—Social and Economic Organization. Parsons, ed. New York: Free Press.

Wolfe, Morris

1973—"Empire in print: Maclean-Hunter". The Canadian Forum (Sept).

Whyte, D. and F. Vallee

1968—"Canadian Society: Trends and Perspectives". Blishen et al, (1968).

Young, Michael

1958—The Rise of Meritocracy. Penguin: England.

Zartisky, John

1972—"Ford Has a Better Idea" in Starowicz and Murphy (eds.).

Preface To Appendices

The following tables and notes contain a detailed set of data which others may find useful in their own research. Appendix V through XII can be especially useful for additional analysis of corporations operating in Canada while some (V, VI and VIII) attempt to set out problems researchers may encounter in pursuing this type of study. Because of the costs and time involved in gathering this data, it was felt worthwhile to make this detailed information available.

Appendix I

Some Charters Issued by the Canadian Government to Sitting Legislators (1845-1858)

(1845) St. Lawrence & Atlantic Railroad Co.—A.T. Galt, P. McGill
(1847) New Brunswick & Nova Scotia Railway—A.N. McNab, J. Ross & four other members of the legislature
(1848) Western Telegraph Co.—F. Hincks, M. Cameron
(1849) Canada Life Assurance Co.—A.N. McNab, M. Cameron, J. Young
(1849) Ontario Marine Fire Insurance Co.—A.N. McNab, J. Young
(1849) Quebec Warehousing Co.—J. Young
(1849) Montreal & Vermont Junction Railway—R. Jones, J. Young
(1850) Quebec & Richmond Railway Co.—L. Massue, L. Methof, J.B. Forsyth, F.R. Angers
(1850) Quebec & St. Andres Railroad Co.—J.B. Forsyth
(1850) Kinston Fire & Marine Insurance Co.—J.A. Macdonald, J. Hamilton
(1851) Montreal & Kingston Railway—J. Young, G. Moffatt, A.N. Morin, L.H. Holton, A.T. Galt, G.E. Cartier, I. Gould
(1852) Grand Trunk Railway—A.T. Galt, P. McGill, G. Pemberton, G.E. Cartier, L.H. Holton
(1853) Dalhousie & Thorold Railway—J.A. Macdonald, W.H. Merritt
(1853) London & Sarnia Railway—J. Young, A.N. McNab
(1853) Hamilton & Port Dover Railway—A.N. McNab
(1854) Quebec & Saguenay Railway Co.—P.J.O. Chauveau
(1855) Niagara District Bank—J. Morris, J. Ross, J.A. Macdonald, W.H. Merritt
(1855) Molson's Bank—W. Molson, J. Molson, G. Moffatt, S. Gerrard, J. Ferrier
(1855) Hamilton & South Western Railway Co.—J. Young, A.N. McNab
(1856) Canadian Marine Insurance Co.—J.J.C. Abbott, G. Moffatt, H. Allan
(1856) Canadian Western Railway Co.—W. Cayley, H.H. Cameron, J.B. Robinson, and other members
(1857) Strathroy & Port Frank Railway Co.—M. Cameron
(1858) Bank of Canada—W. Cayley, J. Ross

Selected Individuals From Above.

A.T. Galt:—St. Lawrence & Atlantic Railroad, Montreal & Kingston Railroad, Grand Trunk Railway (also commissioner of British North America Land Co., Bank of Montreal, Northwest Coal & Navigation Co., chairman of the Select Committee of Public Accounts, Minister of Finance), President of Canada Guarantee Co.

J. Ross:—New Brunswick & Nova Scotia Railroad, Niagara District Bank, Grand Trunk Railway, Bank of Canada (also member of the executive, speaker of the legislature, Solicitor General).

J. Young:—Canada Life Assurance Co., Ontario Marine Fire Insurance Co., Quebec Warehousing Co., Montreal & Vermont Junction Railway, Montreal & Kingston Railway, London & Port Sarnia Railway, Hamilton South Western Railway (legislative member and later Governor General).

A.N. McNab:—New Brunswick & Nova Scotia Railway, Canada Life Assurance Co., Ontario Marine Fire Insurance Co., London & Port Sarnia Railway, Hamilton & South Western Railway (also Great Western Railway and leader of the opposition and Prime Minister in 1854).

J.A. Macdonald:—Dalhousie & Thorold Railway, Niagara District Bank (also executive member of the legislature and Prime Minister).

M. Cameron:—Western Telegraph, Canada Life Assurance, Strathroy & Port Frank Railway (also executive member of the legislature and Grand Trunk Railway).

P. McGill:—St. Lawrence & Atlantic Railway Co., Grand Trunk Railway (also British American Land Co., President of Bank of Montreal and member of the legislative executive).

(Sources:—Myers (1972), Ryerson (1968), Morton (1963).

Appendix II (a)

Foreign Capital Invested in Canada, Selected Year Ends
(Book Value of Assets in Million $)

	1867	1900	1913	1926	1939	1946	1952	1960	1965
U.K. Direct	—	65	200	336	336	366	544	1,535	2,013
U.K. Portfolio	185	1,000	2,618	2,301	2,110	1,333	1,340	1,824	1,485
Total	185	1,065	2,818	2,637	2,476	1,668	1,884	3,359	3,498
U.S. Direct	15	175	520	1,403	1,881	2,428	4,532	10,549	13,940
U.S. Portfolio	—	30	315	1,793	2,270	2,729	3,466	6,169	9,365
Total	15	205	835	3,196	4,151	5,157	7,998	16,718	23,305
Other Direct	—	—	50	43	49	63	144	788	1,255
Other Portfolio	—	35	147	127	237	290	358	1,349	1,449
Total	—	35	197	170	286	353	502	2,137	2,704
All Direct	15	240	770	1,782	2,296	2,826	5,220	12,872	17,208
All Portfolio	185	1,065	3,080	4,271	4,617	4,352	5,164	9,342	12,299
GRAND TOTAL	200	1,305	3,850	6,003	6,913	7,178	10,384	22,214	29,507
Direct as % of total foreign investment	7.5	18.5	20.0	30.0	33.5	39.0	50.0	58.0	58.3
U.S. as % of total foreign investment	7.5	15.5	21.5	53.0	60.0	72.0	77.0	75.0	79.0

(Adapted from Levitt, 1970:66. Table 3)

384

Appendix II (b)

Changes in Canadian Long-Term Indebtedness, Selected Periods

(in millions)

	U.K.	U.S. Direct	U.S. Portfolio	Other	Total
Formative years 1867-1900 (33 years)	+ 880	+ 160	+ 30	+ 35	+ 1.105
Wheat economy 1900-1913 (13 years)	+ 1.753	+ 345	+ 285	+ 162	+ 2.545
First World War 1913-1926 (13 years)	− 181	+ 883	+ 1.478	− 27	+ 2.153
Breakdown of world economy 1926-1939 (13 years)	− 161	+ 478	+ 477	+ 116	+ 910
Second World War 1939-1946 (7 years)	− 808	+ 547	+ 459	+ 67	+ 265
Early postwar boom 1946-1952 (6 years)	+ 216	+ 2.104	+ 737	+ 149	+ 3.208
Late postwar boom 1952-1960 (8 years)	+ 1.475	+6.017	+2.703	+1.635	+11.830
The Sixties 1960-1965 (5 years)	+ 139	+ 3.391	+ 3.196	+ 567	+ 7.293
Total Inflow (1867-1964)	+ 3.498	+13.940	+ 9.365	+ 2.704	+29.507
Inflow 1952-1965 (13 years)	+ 1.614	+ 9.408	+ 5.899	+ 2.202	+19.123

(Levitt, 1970:67, Table 4)

385

Appendix III

Canadian Chartered Banks

No. of Banks:

1868	21	
1875	36	
1901	34	
1920	18	
1928	10	
1953	11	— Mercantile Bank
1955	10	— Bank of Toronto & Dominion Bank to Toronto-Dominion
1956	9	— Barclays Bank with Imperial Bank
1961	8	— Bank of Commerce & Imperial Bank as Canadian Imperial Bank of Commerce
1968	9	— Bank of British Columbia

(Sources: Canada Year Book 1970-71, 1231-32; Beckhart "Fewer and Larger Banks" originally 1929, reprinted in Neufeld, ed., Money and Banking in Canada 1964).

Comparative Position of Chartered Banks, 1951-1971

	'51 Rank	'51 Assets (000,000)	'71 Rank	'71 Assets (000,000)	Founded
Royal Bank	1	2,516	1	13,710.5	1869
Bank of Montreal	2	2,222	3	10,397.6	1817
Can. Bank of Commerce	3	1,734	2*	12,062.7	1867
Bank of Nova Scotia	4	874	4	7,285.4	1832
Imperial Bank	5	536	2*	—	1875
Bank of Toronto	6	489	5**	6,578.1	1855
Banque Can. Nationale	7	464	6	2,395.7	1873
Dominion Bank	8	458	5**	—	1871
Provincial Bank	9	186	7	1,514.1	1900
Mercantile Bank	—	—	8	296.2	1953
Bank of British Columbia	—	—	9	184.2	1967

* Amalgamation 1961 to form Canadian Imperial Bank of Commerce.
** Amalgamation 1955 to form Toronto-Dominion.

(Sources: 1951 data Porter, 1965:589; 1971 data *Globe & Mail*, Feb. 16, 1972:B12; founding dates Financial Post Survey of Industrials, 1972).

Appendix IV

Relative Position of Canadian Corporations
As Identified by Porter C 1950 and Position in 1971

BANKS	1951	1971
Royal Bank		Dominant
Bank of Montreal		Dominant
Canadian Bank of Commerce		(1961) amalgam. Dominant
Bank of Nova Scotia		Dominant
Imperial Bank		(1961) amalgam. Dominant
Bank of Toronto		(1955) amalgam. Dominant
Banque Canadienne Nationale		Middle range
The Dominion Bank		(1955) amalgam. Dominant
Provincial Bank		Middle range

INSURANCE

	1950	1970
Sun Life		Dominant
Manufacturers Life		Dominant
Canada Permanent		Dominant
Great West controlled by Power Corp.		Dominant subsidiary
Mutual of Canada		Dominant
London Life		Dominant
Confederation Life		Dominant
Imperial controlled by Power Corp.		Dominant Subsidiary
North American Life		Dominant
Crown Life		Dominant
Metropolitan Life*		Dominant
Prudential*		Dominant
Standard Life*	*Added as dominant*	

* Reported by Porter but not included although comparable to Canadian controlled insurance companies which were included.

CORPORATIONS

1948-50	*1972*

Iron and Its Products

Canadian Pacific Railway	Dominant
Ford Motor Company	Dominant
Massey-Harris name changed to Massey-Ferguson (1958)	Dominant
Steel Co. of Canada	Dominant
Dominion Steel & Coal bought out by Quebec-owned Sidbec (1969)	Crown Corp.
Algoma Steel	Dominant
Canada Steamship Lines Power Corp. holds 99.6%	Dominant sub.
Dominion Foundries & Steel	Dominant
Dominion Bridge Algoma Steel holds 44%	Dominant aff.
Canadian Car & Foundry Sidbec, a Quebec crown corporation holds 100%	Crown Corp.
Page-Hersey Tubes Steel Co. of Can. holds 100%	Dominant sub.
Cockshutt Plow sold to White Motor C. (US) (1962)	<50 m. ass.
Canada Iron Foundries name changed to Canron (1968)	Middle range
General Steel Wares	<50 m. ass.
Montreal Locomotive Works name changed to MLW-Worthington	<50 m. ass.
National Steel Car acquired by Dominion Steel & Foundries (1961)	Dominant amalg.
Russell Industries sub. of Seaway Multi-Corp.	Middle range
Canadian Fairbanks-Morse Co. name changed to Robert Morse (1963)	Middle range
Atlas Steel takeover by Rio Algoma (1963)	Middle range
Burrard Dry Dock takeover by Cornat Industries	<50 m. ass.
Canadian Vickers Ltd.	<50 m. ass.
Beatty Bros. sub. of General Steel Wares	<50 m. ass.
Canadian Ingersoll-Rand bought out by Ingersoll-Rand (US)	U.S.
Mailman Corp. became private in 1964, Mailman family	
Moffat Ltd. 100% held by Avco	Dominant
Hayes Steel Products name changed to Hayes-Dana (1966)	<50 m. ass.
Ontario Steel Products acquired by N. A. Rockwell (1969)	U.S.

Ingersol Machines & Tool acquired by Ivaco (1970)	Middle range
DeHavilland Aircraft sub. of Racier 99%	Dominant sub.
General Motors of Canada	Dominant
International Harvester	Middle range
Chrysler Corp.	Dominant
Canadair	Middle range
Remington Rand	DK
Union Carbide	Middle range
Crane Canada US sub. Crane Co. 100%	<50 m. ass.
Otis Elevator US sub. Otis Elevator 100%	
American Can US corporation	
Continental Can	Middle range
Motor Products Corp. liquidated (1956)	
Electric Autolite	DK
Thompson Products US sub. TRW Inc.	
Singer Manufac. US sub. 100%	
Standard Stationary & Dominion Radiator	DK
Torrington Co.	DK
John Deere Plow now John Deere	Middle range
Outboard Marine & Manuf. US sub. 99.8% Outboard Marine	
Ontario Malleable Iron US sub. 100% Grinnell Corp.	
National Cash Register	Middle range
A. V. Roe sub. Racier	Dominant sub.
Sunshine-Waterloo	DK
Marine Industries sub. of Que.-owned SGFO 56.9%	
Babcock-Wilcox & Goldie McCulloch sub. US Babcock & Wilcox 58%	
Morton Engineering & Drydock	DK
Walker Metal Products sub. of Bombardier	Middle range

Wood & Paper Products

Abitibi Power & Paper name changed to Abitibi Paper (1965)	Dominant
Consolidated Paper name changed to Consolidated-Bathurst (1967)	Dominant
St. Lawrence Corp. sub. Domtar 98.1%	Dominant sub.
Price Bros.	Dominant
Powell River Co. Ltd. merged with Macmillan Bloedel	Dominant
Howard Smith Paper Mills amalg. with Domtar (1971)	Dominant amalg.
Minnesota & Ontario Paper merged with Boise Cascade (U.S.) 1965	
Alaska Pine & Cellulose sub. of Rayonier (1954)	Middle range
Macmillan & Bloedel	Dominant

Maclearn Power & Paper	Middle range
Anglo-Newfoundland Devel. Corp. acquired by Price Bros.	Dominant amalg.
Fraser Cos.	Middle range
Pacific Mills sub. Crown Zellerbach	Dominant
Anglo-Canadian Pulp & Paper	Middle range
BC Forest Products	Dominant
Bathurst Power & Paper sub. Consolidated Bathurst	Dominant sub.
Canadian Western Lumber sub. Crown Zellerbach (1953)	Dominant sub.
Mersey Paper acquired by Bowater Corp. UK Sub.	<50 m. ass.
Great Lakes Paper CP Investments holds 51.6%	Dominant sub.
E. B. Eddy sub. George Weston (1952)	Dominant sub.
Dryden Paper acquired by Anglo-Can. Pulp & Paper	Middle range
Building Products sub. Imperial Oil	Dominant sub.
Can. International Paper sub. International Paper Co. (US)	
Spruce Falls Power & Paper sub. Kimberly-Clark (U.S.)	
Tribune Co. US holding Co. for Ontario Paper	
KVP Co. now Eddy Forest Products sub. G. Weston	Dominant sub.
Brown Corp. acquired by Can. International Paper (above)	
Canadian Forest Products	DK
Great Lakes Lumber	DK

Vegetable Products

Distillers Corp.-Seagrams	Dominant
Hiram Walker-Gooderham & Worts	Dominant
Imperial Tobacco name changed to Imasco (1970)	Dominant
Canadian Breweries	Dominant sub.
George Weston	Dominant
Canadian Canners sub. Del Monte (US)	Middle range
Goodyear Tire & Rubber	Middle range
Canada & Dominion Sugar	Middle range
Dow Breweries acquired by Canadian Breweries (1963)	Dominant acq.
Ogilvie Flour Mills J. Labatt holds 99.7%	Dominant sub.
Acadia-Atlantic Refineries named changed to Atlantic Sugar Refin. (1962) sub. Glengair 62.3%	Dominant sub.
Canada Malting	<50 m. ass.
Molson's Brewery name changed to Molson Industries 1968	Dominant

Maple Leaf Milling amalg. with Maple Leaf Mills (1961)	Middle range amalg.
Dunlop Tire & Rubber sub. Dunlop Holdings UK	
Western Canada Breweries acquired by Can. Breweries (1963)	Dominant acq.
John Labatt	Dominant
Lake of the Woods Milling sub. Ogilvie Flour Mills (1954)	Dominant sub.
Consolidated Bakeries sub. Ogilvie Flour Mills (1966)	Dominant sub.
Walter M. Lowney acq. by Standard Brands (1968)	Middle range acq.
Moirs Ltd. acq. by Standard Brands (1967)	Middle range acq.
Dominion Rubber	
Firestone Tire & Rubber	Middle range
B. F. Goodrich Rubber	Middle range
Christie Brown & Co. sub. National Biscuit (US)	<50 m. ass.
B. C. Sugar Refining	<50 m. ass.

Textiles

Canadian Industries Ltd.	Dominant
Dominion Textile	Middle range
Can. Celanese	Middle range
Can. Cottons acq. Can. Corporation Management (1959)	Middle range
Dominion Oilcloths & Linoleum	DK
Bruck Mills	<50 m. ass.
Woods Manufacturing closed down (1963)	
Wabasso Cotton	<50 m. ass.
Cosmos Imperial Mills	<50 m. ass.
Hamilton Cotton name changed to Hamilton Group (1970)	<50 m. ass.
Courtaulds (Canada) Ltd. affiliate of International Paints (UK)	<50 m. ass.
Associated Textiles of Canada sub. United Merchants and Manufac. (UK)	

Animal Products

Canada Packers	Dominant
Burns & Co. now Burns Foods	Middle range
Silverwoods Dairies name changed to Silverwoods Industries (1970)	Middle range
B. C. Packers G. Weston sub. (71.3%)	Dominant sub.
Dominion Dairies	<50 m. ass.
Borden Co. sub. Borden Inc. (US)	<50 m. ass.
Swift Canada	Middle range
Connor Bros. sub. G. Weston (98%)	Dominant sub.

Non-Ferrous Metal

Bell Telephone	Dominant
International Nickel	Dominant
Aluminum Co. of Canada sub. of Alcan Aluminum	Dominant
Canadian General Electric	Dominant
Noranda Mines	Dominant
Canadian Westinghouse	Dominant
Phillips Electrical Works sub. Phillips Cables (UK)	<50 m. ass.
John Inglis	<50 m. ass.
Kelvinator of Canada	<50 m. ass.
Can. Marconi General Electric (UK) holds 51.7%	<50 m. ass.
RCA Victor	Middle range
Rogers Majestic	DK
Smith & Stone sub. PPG Industries (US)	
Ferranti Electric Ferranti Ltd. (UK) holds 100%	

Non-metallic Minerals

Imperial Oil	Dominant
British American Oil name changed to Gulf Oil Can.	Dominant
McColl-Frontenac Oil name changed to Texaco Can. (1959)	Dominant
Canadian Oil Companies acq. by Shell Investments (1962)	Dominant acq.
Consumers' Gas	Dominant
Dominion Glass Power Corp. holds 63%	Dominant sub.
Consumers' Glass	Middle range
Norton Co. of Canada	DK

Chemicals

Shawinigan Water & Power takeover by Hydro Quebec (1963)	Crown Corp.
Dominion Tar & Chemical name changed to Domtar	Dominant
Sherwin-Williams sub. Sherwin-Williams (US)	<50 m. ass.
North American Cyanamid now Cyanamid of Canada	Middle range

Crown Corporations

Canadian National Railways	Dominant Crown Corp.
Polymer Corporation	Middle range Crown C

Metals*

Hudson Bay Mining & Smelting	Middle range
Hollinger Consolidated Gold Mines now Hollinger Mines (1968)	Middle range

Industrial Minerals

Canada Cement	Dominant
Asbestos Corp.	Middle range
Gypsum Lime & Asbestos acq. Domtar (1959)	Dominant acq.

* Several companies are listed by Porter under more than one sector and repeats in Metals, Industrial Minerals, Fuels, Central Electric Stations, Telephones and Retail have been omitted.

Fuels

International Utilities now Canadian Utilities	Dominant
Union Gas	Dominant

Central Electric Stations

British Columbia Power Corp. acq. B. C. Government (1963)	Crown Corp.
Gatineau Power Co. acq. Hydro-Quebec (1963)	Crown Corp.
Saguenay Power Co. Ltd. acq. Hydro-Quebec (1962)	Crown Corp.
Winnipeg Electric acq. Manitoba (1952)	Crown Corp.
Calgary Power	Dominant
Nova Scotia Light & Power acq. Nova Scotia (1972)	Crown Corp.
Power Corporation of Canada	Dominant
Great Lakes Power Corp.	<50 m. ass.

Telephones

Maritime Telephone & Telegraph sub. Bell Canada	Dominant sub.
New Brunswick Telephone sub. Bell Canada	Dominant sub.
Anglo-Can. Telephone	Dominant

Retail & Distribution

T. Eaton Co.	Dominant
Simpsons Ltd.	Dominant
Hudson's Bay	Dominant
Loblaw Gros. sub. G. Weston 60.3%	Dominant sub.
Dominion Stores	Dominant
Zellers	Dominant

INDEX to Appendix IV:
— sub. — Subsidiary
— aff. — Affiliate
— ass. — Assets
— acq. — Acquired
— amalg. — Amalgamate
— DK — Don't Know

Appendix V

Some Problems With Industrial Classifications and Statistics

CALURA uses two methods of aggregating financial data on corporations. The first, reported in *Corporation Financial Statistics*, used smaller units based on individual legal entities as compiled from individual tax returns and aggregated by Standard Industrial Classifications (SIC). Parent companies may be classified separate from their subsidiaries, particularly when a holding company is involved, although all of the activities of the parent may be directly related to one sector or the major part of its activities are in one sector. This tends to reflect more the way in which capital is organized, for example use of a holding company, than any actual functional difference between the activities of corporations. This method also promotes double counting in specific instances when making comparisons across sectors. The second method, reported in *Industrial Corporations* and in *Financial Institutions*, uses the concept of corporate complexes or "families" thus grouping corporations under the sector of their major activity[1] regardless of the way capital is organized. This is analogous to use of unconsolidated statements for the first method and consolidated statements for the second. The first method is more appropriate to the study of specific detailed sectors while the second method lends itself more to the study of corporate control (the first being "activity" oriented and the second being "ownership block" oriented). By using the second method a company like Massey-Ferguson would be classified as an industrial because this is where its major activities are rather than as a holding company which reflects the way it organizes its capital. The second method requires some reallocation (from SIC) of corporations to match categories used to collect aggregate data and unlike the first method, requires that in some instances subsidiaries be integrated into categories where consolidated statements by parents are incorporated. An advantage of the second method is that data is published on a quarterly basis and more current, than publications using the first method. There are some minor problems involved. For example, in some cases classification is not as "fine" as the first method, as in the case of transportation where there is no separation of pipelines from other types of transportation such as railways, but divisions generally correspond to those used in the first method and do not require serious departures. Another problem is the way foreign holdings of Canadian companies are dealt with. Published statements typically consolidate foreign controlled enterprises with the parent but taxation statements over-state the amount in these categories as compared to aggregate statistics[2]. Since the amount of foreign assets and sales are not usually made public, it is not possible to systematically separate these in detail, although allowance can be made in cases where estimates can be obtained. One final problem is that *Financial Institutions* does not yet publish data on SIC category 756, investment companies. This is somewhat ameliorated by the fact that a number of the major holding companies in this sector have been reallocated and placed in the sector of their major activity by using the corporate complex approach but this does not completely eliminate the problem of establishing aggregate data for this category.

Both Mr. J.D. Wilson, who is in charge of publishing *Industrial Corporations*, and Mr. Albert Dorland, have cooperated with these problems and insured that the corporate complexes match the aggregate categories. This insures a "clean" set of individual corporations to be compared with aggregate data. Since the aggregate data for year end 1971 is now published, the same year as individual statements were gathered for, there is no error factor in projecting from 1970 data as would have been the case with *Corporation Financial Statistics*. None the less, it would be appropriate to regard the percentages as good estimates rather than precise figures because of the slight over-counting as outlined and the counter factors of non-disclosure by some corporations and not counting corporations with assets under $50 million which are controlled by dominant parent companies.

Appendix VI

Introduction To The Corporate Statistics Tables

EACH table represents an industrial division based on the Standard Industrial
Classification. These have been revised to integrate some sectors, e.g.,
mortgage and trust, while fine distinction have been maintained in other
cases, e.g., three mining divisions, because of the significant numbers of
large corporations which appear within each of these sectors. SIC classification was provided by CALURA. Some difficulties with the classification
distinguishing establishments or legal reporting units from corporate complexes are discussed in Appendix V.

COMP RANK represents a composite ranking of assets and sales constructed by ranking assets and sales within sectors and then combining
these two rankings to form the composite. Traditional measures have used
either sales or assets as a measure of relative corporate power. Each
individual statistic has its particular bias with sales giving more weight to
production-oriented companies and assets to finance-oriented companies.
This composite attempts to minimize either bias. As used in this context,
the label "sales" refers to either or both sales and revenue. Each financial
statistic measures quite distinct aspects of corporate power. Sales or operating revenue indicates power in terms of a "market" whether that market is
in terms of ownership claims on corporate stock or transactions on a
commodity market. In this sense, sales measures the relative position of a
particular corporation in terms of other corporations engaged in the same
market and as such, the degree of control exercised by a particular corporation or set of corporations, within that market. Assets measures corporate
power in terms of the "resources" at its disposal, whether these are in
relatively liquid state such as cash or stock holdings or mixed like land or
capital equipment. Used comparatively, this can also be a relative concept
and is more readily compared across sectors than is sales. Net income is
reported but not integrated into the composite index with sales and assets
because it is more volatile and subject to yearly conditions and stage of
corporate expansion. By using sales and assets, a more stable measure of
corporate power is derived, since these are not as subject to fluctuation as is
net income. This fits with the goal of presenting a general outline of
corporate power during this historical period rather than concentrating on a
particular year's activities. The high correlation between the composite
index and net income is to be expected but its fluctuating tendencies would
tend to distort the index in some places.

It should be noted that the statistics which are reported may or may not
consolidate sales or assets of subsidiaries. This has been allowed for in two
ways. First, the reclassification of some companies, particularly those
originally classified as investment companies, consolidates the assets and
sales of major subsidiaries wherever possible, this being one major advantage of working with aggregate data based on corporate complexes. The

other allowance is by using the parent company in cases where its subsidiaries are dominant within particular sectors, for example, Power Corporation, by using the subsidiary in terms of relative assets and sales within the sector but using the parent in terms of decision making. This is necessary when corporate complexes cut across several sectors, as Power Corporation does.

One weakness is that a method of comparing the relative importance of various sectors is difficult to develop. It is possible to argue that a set of corporations is dominant within a given sector in terms of the degree of control it exercises over sales and assets of that sector, but simple comparison across sectors is not that advisable because of the lack of homogeneity between sectors. For example, it is not advisable to compare the sales of a retail firm with the revenue of a bank although these comparisons within homogeneous sectors do indicate relative positions. This also follows, to some extent, from the different degrees of concentration within sectors. By definition, dominant corporations exist in dominant sectors and would not appear in sectors which do not command a large portion of the economy. like hunting and trapping, or in sectors where large numbers of small firms dominate, as in agriculture (although this appears to be changing). This problem will require more careful analysis before a suitable method can be established.

In the tables, SUB refers to a subsidiary defined as a holding by a single parent corporation of more than 50 per cent. AFF refers to an affiliated company with holdings of over 10 percent but less than subsidiary. An investment is less than 10 per cent. In most cases, an affiliate relationship indicates control (see "ownership/control"), with exceptions being cases where another corporation controls a greater percentage of the voting stock. For example, in the case of Hudson's Bay Oil & Gas, 21.9 per cent of the stock is held by Hudson's Bay Investments thus giving it affiliate status but Continental Oil holds 54.9 per cent of the stock, allowing it to actually control the company. As long as stock ownership is examined to see if another larger block exists, it is reasonable to assume that affiliate status indicates control.

Sources for the financial statistics used in the tables included: *The Financial Post Survey of Industrials, 1972*, *The Financial Post Survey of Mines, 1972*, *The Financial Post Survey of Oils, 1972*, *The Financial Post Survey of Investment Funds, 1972*, various issues of *The Financial Post* and *Globe and Mail* "Report on Business" and financial statements, particularly those of private companies, filed with Consumer and Corporate Affairs under the Corporations and Labour Union Return Act and The Canada Corporations Act. Aggregate data is from *Industrial Corporations*, *Financial Institutions* (both CALURA publications) and the three-volume *Report to the Superintendent of Insurance*.

Appendix VII, Corporation Statistics Tables

CANADIAN CHARTERED AND SAVINGS BANKS, 1971 year end

RANK 1951	FOUNDED	CORPORATION TITLE	RANK 1971	ASSETS (000,000)	CUM. %	INCOME (000,000)	CUM. %	NET INCOME (000,000)	CUM. %
1	1869	Royal Bank	1	12.954	24	873.077	24	44.052	
3 & 5	1867 & 1875 amel. 1961	Canadian Imperial Bank of Commerce	2	11.400	46	751.564	45	40.937	
2	1869	Bank of Montreal	3	10.165	65	682.197	64	38.366	
4	1832	Bank of Nova Scotia	4	7.085	78	552.434	79	28.300	
6 & 8	1855 & 1871 amel. 1955	Toronto-Dominion Bank	5	6.549	90	438.458	91	23.342	
		TOTAL: ALL DOMINANT BANKS		48.153		3,097.730		174.997	
		ALL BANKS		52.945		3,616.606		191.084	
		DOMINANT AS % OF ALL		90%		91%		91%	
7	1873	Banque Canadienne Nationale	6	2.281		152.060		7.096	
9	1900	La Banque Provinciale du Canada	7	1.416		90.253		4.428	
na	1871	Montreal & District Savings Bank	8	628		47.019		2.577	
na	1953	Mercantile Bank*	9	289		19.161		1.785	
na	1967	Bank of British Columbia	10	178		10.383		.201	
		TOTAL: ALL MIDDLE RANGE BANKS		4.792		318.876		16.007	
		MIDDLE RANGE AS % OF ALL		10%		9%		9%	

* First National Bank of New York held 64.5% of the Mercantile Bank as of March 1972. This is the only foreign controlled bank (First National is ranked 2nd on *Fortunes* top 50 Commercial Banks list).

LIFE INSURANCE

RANK 1950	EST.	CORPORATION TITLE	COMP RANK	ASSET RANK	ASSETS (000,000)	INCOME RANK	INCOME (000,000)	NET INCOME (000,000)	NATION
1	1865	Sun Life	1	1	3,643	1	567,129	11,376	CAN.
2	1887	Manufacturers Life	2	2	2,039	2	352,661	22,704	CAN.
6	1874	London Life	3	3	1,614	3	350,028	5,863	CAN.
4	1891	Great West Life*	4	4	1,470	4	273,480	4,740	CAN. SUB
3	1849	Canada Life	5	5	1,308	5	270,368	(4,997)	CAN.
7		Metropolitan Life	6	6	1,243	6	241,062	46,056	U.S.
	1871	Confederation Life	7	7	799	7	171,465	2,202	CAN.
5		Prudential Life	8	8	741	9	156,005	30,367	U.S.
10	1878	Mutual Life of Can.	9	9	1,216	11	118,498	3,071	CAN.
9	1900	Crown Life	10	10	729	8	169,733	(1,541)	CAN.
8	1879	North American Life	11	11	701	10	140,703	2,605	CAN.
		Standard Life	12	12	727	12	107,464	51,040	U.K.
	1896	Imperial Life**	13	13	498	13	88,084	(657)	CAN. SUB
		TOTAL DOMINANT (13)			16,728		2,935,620		
		DOMINANT AS % OF ALL			85.5%		80.5%		
		ALL LIFE INSUR. IN CAN. (139)			19,543		3,648,854		
	1889	Prudential Assur.	14	15	307	14	74,171	29,085	U.K.
	1897	Dominion Life	15	14	354	15	59,105	1,591	CAN.
	1897	Excelsior Life	16	17	248	17	48,885	1,379	CAN.
		National Life	17	16	232	16	50,621	594	CAN.
		New York Life	18	19	105	19	23,319	3,306	U.S.
		Travellers Insur.	19	18	109	21	21,068	7,733	U.S.
	1917	Alliance Mutuelle	20	21	91	20	21,102	728	CAN.
	1903	Comp. d'Assur.	21	27	86	23	16,344	691	CAN.
	1959	Assur.-Vie Desjard.	22	20	59	18	30,171	583	CAN.
		Northern Life	23	24	93	15	16,130	(900)	CAN.
	1894	Zurich Life	24	25	69	24	13,440	216	CAN.
	1899	Norwich Union Life	25	28	68	27	12,742	4,317	U.K.
	1902	Aetna Life	26	26	54	24	16,254	3,181	U.S.
	1936	Sovereign Life	27	23	63	28	11,483	258	CAN.
		Equitable Life	28		78	22	18,231	222	CAN.
		TOTAL MIDDLE RANGE (15)			2,016		433,066		
		MIDDLE RANGE AS % OF ALL			10.3%		11.9%		
		ALL CANADIAN (45)			15,963		2,911,281		
		ALL FOREIGN (84)			3,580		773,577		
		ALL LIFE INSURANCE			19,543		3,648,854		
		FOREIGN AS % OF ALL			18.3%		21.2%		
		CANADIAN AS % OF ALL			81.7%		79.8%		

* Controlled 50.1% by Investors Group, which in turn is 63.4% controlled by Power Corp.

** Controlled 51.2% by Power Corp.

INVESTMENT COMPANIES 1971 year end

(millions)

	COMP RANK	ASSET RANK	ASSETS	SALE RANK	SALES	NET INC.	OWNERSHIP & CONTROL
1928 Alcan Aluminum	1	1	2,297	2	1,381	60.2	51.2% O/S Can: 39.4% US
1956 Loblaw Cos. Ltd.	2	5	561	1	2,559	2.2	CAN. SUB: G. Weston 60.3%
1912 Brascan	3	2	1,180	4	425	83.8	CAN. AFF: Jonlab 10.5%
1939 Anglo-Can. Tel.	4	4	892	6	246	15.0	U.S. SUB: Gen T&E 100%
1962 Can. Pacific Invest.	5	3	1,071	8	165	86.8	CAN. SUB: Can. Pac. 90.1%
1938 Moore Corp.	6	9	342	3	449	39.8	33% O/S Canada
1947 Woodward Stores	7	15	142	5	332	9.0	U.K. AFF: 85% O/S Can.'
Racier	8	12	210	9	160	1.1	U.K. SUB: Hawker Sidd. 100%
1944 Woodbridge Co.	9	11	215	11	130	12.8	U.K. SUB: Thomson holds 100%"
1960 Trizec Corp.	10	6	516	16	77	4.5	U.K. SUB: Star Holdings 61%
1955 Shell Invest. (2)	16	7	493	27	15	14.8	NETH. SUB: Shell Pet. 100%
1925 Power Corp. (3)	17	8	383	28	14	10.0	
1945 Argus Corp. (4)	23	20	105	31	7	5.7	
TOTAL DOMINANT CORP.			8,407		5,960		
1960 BACM Industries	11	13	145	10	149	6.7	DOM. SUB: Genstar 99.2%
1960 Delsina	33	29	71	29	9	7.3	DOM. SUB: Royal Tr. 100%
Imasco Int'l	35	22	101	39	9	.7	DOM. SUB: Imasco 100% (UK)
Anglo-Can. Min. & R.	36	30	71	32	6	4.2	DOM. SUB: Int'l Nick. 100%
TOTAL DOMINANT SUBSIDIARIES			388		165		
1971 Placer Develop.	19	14	143	24	22	4.0	DOM. AFF: Noranda 26.2%
1957 SB McLaughlin	22	25	87	25	21	4.0	DOM. AFF: Simpsons 13.1%'
TOTAL DOMINANT AFFILIATES			230		43		
TOTAL ALL DOMINANT			9,025		6,168		

NB: Footnotes begin on p. 429.

INVESTMENT COMPANIES (Cont'd)

(millions)

	COMP RANK	ASSET RANK	ASSETS	SALE RANK	SALES	NET INC.	OWNERSHIP & CONTROL
1956 Can. Int'l Power	12	10	244	17	61	13.4	U.S. SUB: United Corp. 52%
1952 Bowaters Canadian	13	16	131	12	93	1.3	U.K. SUB: Bowater Pap. 100%
1917 Gambles Canada	14	25	98	7	184	5.6	U.S. SUB: Gamble-Sko. 100%
1968 Starlaw Invest.	15	19	116	15	79	6.3	
1969 Westburn Int'l	18	24	91	13	109	3.1	
1930 Maclearen Pow. & P.	20	26	87	22	42	2.7	
BNA Holdings	21	34	59	16	72	.1	
1961 Miron Co.	24	33	60	20	46	1.7	BELGIUM SUB: Cimenters 53.3%
SBC Financial	25	18	110	36	2	.1	SWITZER. SUB: Swiss Bank
1951 White Pass & Yuk.	26	37	53	18	36	2.3	AFF: Anglo-Amer. 26.2%
1930 Can. Gen. Invest.	27	21	104	34	3	2.6	
1954 Gt. North. Cap.	28	32	62	23	35	2.6	
Edper Invest.	29	19	108	37	2	1.3	
1969 Ivaco Indust.	30	36	53	21	43	3.7	Directors & Officers hold 62%
1962 Block Bros. Ind.	31	31	63	26	18	1.1	
Warnock Hersey	32	38	51	19	25	.4	Seaman family holds 16.4%
1954 Principal Group	34	27	77	33	6	.4	
1933 United Corp.	37	28	74	35	2	2.0	
1953 Can. Equity & Dev.	38	35	57	30	8	1.4	
1961 Siemens Overseas	39	39	51	38	1	.5	GERM. SUB: Siemens AG 100%
TOTAL MIDDLE RANGE			1,749		867		

Footnote: Since two CALURA Departments use SIC classifications differently (see Appendix V) "Investment Companies" remain a residual category not making it possible to provide percentages based on the aggregate.

403

SALES FINANCE & CONSUMER LOANS 1971 year end

(millions)

	COMP RANK	ASSET RANK	ASSETS	SALE RANK	SALES	NET INC.	OWNERSHIP & CONTROL
1925 IAC Ltd.	1	1	1,233	1	139	19.4	CAN. AFF: Acres 44.2%
1926 Traders Group	2	3	632	3	106	7.9	
1953 General Mot. Acc.	3	2	655	5	57	2.8	U.S. SUB: Gen. Mot. 100%
1971 Avco Fin. Serv.	4	4	463	4	88	10.0	U.S. SUB: Avco Fin. 100%
1962 Glengair Group	5	8	151	2	129	3.1	
1922 Can. Acceptance	6	5	307	7	46	7.6	U.S. SUB: CIT Fin. 100%
1933 Benef. Finance	7	7	209	6	48	9.2	U.S. SUB: Beneficial 99.8%
1950 Laurentide Fin.	8	6	287	8	.44	6.4	CAN. SUB: Power 53.7%
TOTAL DOMINANT CORP.			3,937		657		
1944 Union Accept.	12	12	66	10	10	1.0	DOM. SUB: Laurentide 98.6%
TOTAL DOMINANT SUBSIDIARIES			66		10		
1954 Assoc. Accept.	9	9	133	9	25	1.5	U.S. SUB: Associates 100%
1970 First City Fin. '72	10	10	113	11	10	1.1	
1954 Transamerican Fin.	11	11	75	12	10[1]	1.7	U.S. SUB: Transamer. 100%
1937 United Dominions	13	13	63	13	7	.8	U.K. SUB: United Dom. 51%
TOTAL MIDDLE RANGE			384		52		
TOTAL SALES & CONSUMER LOANS			5,595		723		

Footnote: According to Neufeld three Canadian companies, IAC Ltd., Traders Group, and Laurentide Finance, alone accounted for 54% of all assets for sales finance companies while an additional seven (of which four are included here as dominant and dominant subsidiaries) foreign companies accounted for (an additional) 46% and the ten largest companies together accounted for 90% of the total industry (1973:335).

TRUST COMPANIES 1971 year end
(millions)

		COMP RANK	ASSETS RANK	ASSETS	SALE RANK	SALES	NET INC.	OWNERSHIP & CONTROL
1892²	Royal Trust²	1	1	1,912	1	179	10.1	Bank of Montreal 9%
1898	National Trust	2	3	636	3	57	4.7	
1925	Guaranty Trust	3	2	757	4	56	3.8	CAN. AFF: Traders 40.2%
	Montreal Trust	4	4	545	2	58	3.7	CAN. AFF: Investors 23%ᵃ
1950	Victoria & Grey	5	5	541	5	43	3.5	CAN. AFF: Investors 23%ᵃ
	TOTAL DOMINANT TRUST COMPANIES			4,391		392		
1970	Trust General	6	6	238	6	23	1.9	
	Central Trust	7	7	180	7	16	1.3	
1962	Metropol. Trust	8	8	161	8	14	.7	
1897	Crown Trust	9	10	128	9	14	.5	
	Ontario Trust	10	9	141	10	13	—	U.K. AFF: Humbro 42%ᵃ
1962	City Sav. & Tr.	11	11	65	11	7	.6	CAN. SUB: First City 76.5%
1910	Farmers & Merch.	12	12	65	12	6	.6	CAN. SUB: St. Maurice Cap. 50.1%
1912	Nova Scotia Trust	13	14	62	13	6	.6	CAN. SUB: Central Trust 98%
1911	Sterling Trust	14	13	64	14	5	.4	
1963	Hamilton Trust	15	15	55	16	4	.4	
1964	Lincoln Trust	16	16	59	17	4	.3	
1913	Premier Trust	17	17	51	15	5	.3	
1929	Guardian Trust	18	17	53	18	1	.0	
	TOTAL MIDDLE RANGE			1,322		118		

Footnote: Classification of trust & mortgage companies remains problematic because CALURA data separates each financial unit by its particular function while public statements consolidate. For example, Canada Trust is a major company but its financial statistics are consolidated with Huron & Erie Mortgage, its parent, and similarly with Canada Permanent Trust and its parent company Canada Permanent Mortgage. Neufeld notes this problem but tries to separate out trust activities finding that the two largest companies, Royal Trust and Montreal Trust accounted for 58.7% of the assets of all trust companies in 1969 and the four largest, including Canada Permanent Trust and National Trust as well, accounted for 74.9% (1973:306-7). Based on these calculations the dominant trust companies included here, and the subsidiaries of dominant mortgage companies operating in the trust field would account for over 80% of all assets.

MORTGAGE COMPANIES 1971 year end
(millions)

		COMP RANK	ASSET RANK	ASSETS	SALE RANK	SALES	NET INC.	OWNERSHIP & CONTROL
1898	Can. Permanent Mort.	1	1	1,552	1	139	9.5	CAN. AFF: 2 banks 24.7%[1]
1864	Huron & Erie Mort.	2	2	1,475	2	129	10.2	
1940	Investors Group	3	3	494	3	38	9.7	CAN. SUB: Power 63.4%
1880	Credit Foncier	4	4	325	4	25	3.8	FR SUB: 8 of 13 directors reside in France
	TOTAL DOMINANT CORP.			3,846		331		
1912	Royal Trust Mort.	6	6	199	6	17	1.6	DOM SUB: Royal Trust 100%
1950	Traders Homeplan	8	8	76	8	9	1.0	DOM SUB: Traders 99.9%
	TOTAL DOMINANT SUBSIDIARIES			275		26		
1887	Eastern Can. Sav.	5	5	208	5	18	1.6	
1969	Nova Scotia Sav.	7	7	110	7	10	1.2	
	TOTAL MIDDLE RANGE			318		28		

(see footnote. "Trust Companies")

OTHER FINANCE 1971 year end
(millions)

		COMP RANK	ASSET RANK	ASSETS	SALE RANK	SALES	NET INC.	OWNERSHIP & CONTROL
1965	Wood Gundy	1	1	529	1	39	3.9	
	TOTAL DOMINANT			529		39		
1962	RoyNat	2	3	152	2	15	1.5	DOM. AFF: Consortium Bank[1]
	TOTAL DOMINANT SUBSIDIARIES			152		15		
1952	Harris & Partners	3	2	260	4	10	1.0	U.K. AFF: 42% by 2 companies[2]
	Maidstone Essex	4	4	115	3	11	9.4	U.S. SUB: Pac. Gamble 100%
	SFC1	5	5	72	5	4	.8	FR. SUB: 100%[3]
	TOTAL MIDDLE RANGE			477		25		

406

RETAIL TRADE 1971 year end
(millions)

	COMP RANK	ASSET RANK	ASSETS	SALE RANK	SALES	NET INC.	OWNERSHIP & CONTROL
1921 Loblaw Groceterias	1	2	529	1	2,559	3.7	CAN. SUB: Loblaw Comp. 99%[?]
T. Eaton Co.[2]	2	3	500	2	1,000	—	
1952 Simpsons-Sears	3	1	543	5	766	19.0	CAN./U.S. AFF: 50:50[3]
1930 Steinburg's	4	6	267	3	793	9.5	Steinberg family 100%
1670 Hudson's Bay Co.	5	4	367	6	559	13.3	80% in U.K.: Brascan 7%
1929 Simpsons Ltd.	6	5	357	9	335	17.2	
1907 F. W. Woolworth	7	7	238	7	459	12.5	U.S. SUB: F. W. Woolworth 100%
1919 Dominion Stores	8	10	157	4	769	3.3	CAN. AFF: Argus 24.7%
1929 Canada Safeway	9	8	217	8	346	15.0	U.S. SUB: Safeway 100%
1931 S. S. Kresge	10	11	120	10	259	10.4	U.S. SUB: S. S. Kresge 100%
Zellers Ltd.	11	12	94	11	202	7.8	U.S. SUB: W. T. Grant 51%
TOTAL DOMINANT			3,389		8,317		
1955 Can. Hydrocarbon	12	9	143	13	92	3.9	FOREIGN CONSORTIUM[1]
1928 Dylex Diversified	13	14	58	12	108	2.6	Kay & Posluns family 64.6%
1954 Allarco Develop.	14	13	66	14	39	.1	CA Allard, chm. 48%
TOTAL MIDDLE RANGE			267		239		
MIDDLE RANGE AS % OF ALL			3.1%		1.3%		
TOTAL RETAIL SECTOR			8,622[*]		18,273		
TOTAL DOMINANT AS % OF ALL			39.3%		45.3%		

* see "Correction Factors for Aggregate Industrial Data", p. 436.

WHOLESALE TRADE 1971 year end

(millions)

	COMP RANK	ASSET RANK	SALE RANK	ASSETS	SALES	NET INC.	OWNERSHIP & CONTROL
1925 B.P. Canada Ltd.	1	1	3	357	258	13.0	U.K. SUB: BP Hold. 79.8%?
1957 Oshawa Group	2	3	2	188	490	6.1	
1928 M. Loeb	3	8	1	78	532	.8	B. Loeb & assoc. 22.2%
1927 Can. Tire Corp.	4	5	5	137	245	12.7	
1929 Irving Oil	5	4	6	149	140	4.8	U.S. Control: 6 of 10 directors
James Richardson	6	2	12	232	77	2.5	
TOTAL DOMINANT CORP.				1,141	1,742		
1906 Kelly, Douglas	8	12	4	62	249	2.5	DOM. SUB: G. Weston 66%?
TOTAL DOMINANT SUBSIDIARIES				62	249		
1907 John Deere	7	6	10	83	95	4.4	U.S. SUB: Deere & Co. 100%
1905 Acklands	9	9	7	73	124	1.1	
Pilkington Bros.	10	7	13	79	56	.9	U.K. SUB: Pilkington 100%
1933 Finning Tractor	11	10	11	68	92	3.3	JE Barker & MM Young contr. [2]
1905 Robert Morse	12	13	8	56	97	.9	U.S. SUB: Gen. Tire & Rub. cont.
1906 Emco Ltd.	13	14	9	50	96	1.7	
BASF Canada	14	11	14	65	30	1.1	GERM. SUB: BASF Overzee 90%?
TOTAL MIDDLE RANGE				474	590		
MIDDLE RANGE AS % OF TOTAL				5.7%*	3.1%		
TOTAL WHOLESALE SECTOR				8,257*	18,851		
DOMINANT CORP. AS % OF TOTAL				13.8%	9.2%		
DOMINANT SUB. AS % OF TOTAL				.8%	1.3%		
TOTAL DOMINANT AS % OF TOTAL				14.6%	10.5%		

* see "Correction Factors for Aggregate Industrial Data", p. 436.

COMMUNICATIONS 1971 year end
(millions)

	COMP RANK	ASSET RANK	ASSETS	SALE RANK	SALES	NET INC.	OWNERSHIP & CONTROL
1880 Bell Canada	1	1	3,726	1	1,018	147.3	U.S. SUB: Anglo-Can. 50.7%[1]
1916 British Col. Tel.	2	2	705	2	200	20.4	
TOTAL DOMINANT			4,431		1,218		
1910 Maritime Tel & Teleg.	3	3	169	3	48	7.2	DOM. SUB: Bell Can. 52.2%[2]
1888 New Bruns. Tel.	4	4	142	4	45	6.4	DOM. SUB: Bell Can. 50.4%
1927 Queb. Teleph.	5	5	129	5	31	3.7	DOM. SUB: Anglo-Can. 55.2% (U.S.)[1]
Nfld. Teleph.	6	6	63	6	19	3.0	DOM. SUB: Bell Can. 99.7%
TOTAL DOMINANT SUBSIDIARIES			503		143		
TOTAL COMMUNICATIONS SECTOR			5,094		1,470		
DOMINANT AS % OF ALL			87.0%		82.9%		
DOMINANT SUBSID. AS % OF ALL			9.9%		9.7%		
TOTAL DOMINANT AS % OF ALL			96.9%		92.6%		

ELECTRIC POWER, GAS AND WATER UTILITIES 1971 year end

(millions)

	COMP RANK	ASSET RANK	ASSETS	SALE RANK	SALES	NET INC.	OWNERSHIP & CONTROL
1954 Northern & Central	1	1	607	1	193	15.9	CP Invest. 2.4%
1848 Consumers Gas	2	2	484	2	171	21.6	
1927 Canadian Utilities	3	4	328	4	101	12.9	U.S. SUB: Int'l. Util. 87%
1911 Calgary Power	4	3	377	5	63	12.9	
1911 Union Gas	5	5	276	3	122	12.7	
TOTAL DOMINANT CORP.			2,072		650		
1955 Gaz Metropolitain	6	6	195	6	55	5.1	DOM. SUB: North & Cent. 81.6%
1923 Northwestern Util.	7	7	90	7	39	4.7	DOM. SUB: Can. Util. 100% (US)
1911 Can. Western Natural	8	8	78	8	31	3.4	DOM. SUB: Can. Util. 87.7% (US)
1953 Gtr. Winnipeg Nat.	9	9	69	9	28	3.7	DOM. SUB: North & Cent. 99.7%
TOTAL DOMINANT SUBSIDIARIES			432		153		
1952 Inland Nat. Gas	10	10	57	10	16	2.7	
TOTAL MIDDLE RANGE			57		16		
MIDDLE RANGE AS % OF ALL			1.5%		1.8%		
TOTAL ELECT. POWER, GAS & WATER			3,803*		878		
DOMINANT CORP. AS % OF ALL			54.5%		74.0%		
DOMINANT SUBSID. AS % OF ALL			11.4%		17.4%		
TOTAL DOMINANT AS % OF ALL			65.9%		81.4%		

* see "Correction Factors for Aggregate Industrial Data", p. 436.

RAILWAYS (1970)
(millions)

EST. CORPORATION TITLE	ASSETS (000,000)	INCOME (000,000)	NET INCOME (000,000)
1923 Canadian National	5,550	852,178	(30,348)
1881 Canadian Pacific	3,487	616,846	52,360
TOTAL	9,037	1,469,024	
TOTALS ALL RAILWAYS	10,182	1,679,759	
Dominant as % ALL	89%	87%	

(Source: Statistics Canada. Railway Transport pt. II Financial Statistics, 1971)

SHIPPING

1913 Can. Steamship Lines	184	143	10.9	DOM. SUB: Power Corp 99.6%

PIPELINES 1971 year end
(millions)

	COMP RANK	ASSET RANK	ASSETS	SALE RANK	SALES	NET INC.	OWNERSHIP & CONTROL
1951 Trans-Canada	1	1	985	1	318	22.3	CAN. AFF: CP Invest. 16.6%[1]
1949 Interprovincial	2	2	507	2	144	35.6	U.S. AFF: Imperial 33%[2]
1949 Westcoast Transm.	3	3	500	3	98	7.5	U.S. AFF: Pac. Petro. 27%
1954 Alta. Gas Trunk.	4	4	430	4	56	11.4	CONSORTIUM[3]
TOTAL DOMINANT CORP.	6	6	2,422	(35.2)	616	(13.8)	
1971 Westcoast Pet.	6	6	79	7	12	4.0	DOM. AFF: Westcoast T. 40.2%[1]
TOTAL DOMINANT AFFILIATES			79		12		
1951 Trans Mountain	5	5	115	5	46	14.3	Shell & Imper. each 8.6%
1971 Alta. Natural Gas	7	7	64	6	14	1.8	U.S. SUB: Pacific G & E 66.6%
1971 Pembina Pipelines	8	8	57	8	10	2.6	CAN. AFF: Loram 48.6%
TOTAL MIDDLE RANGE			236		70		
MIDDLE RANGE AS % OF ALL			3.4%		1.6%		
TOTAL TRANSPORTATION SECTOR*			6,891		4,464		
TOTAL DOMINANT AFFILIATE AS % OF ALL			1.2%		.3%		
DOMINANT CORP. AS % OF ALL			85.8%	(35.2)	27.6%	(13.8)	
TOTAL DOMINANT AS % OF ALL			89.7%	(37.4)	31.1%	(14.1)	
* see also Railways. Shipping:							
CP			3,487	(50.6)	617	(13.8)	
Can. Steamship			184	(2.7)	143	(3.2)	

Pipelines have been separated from railways and shipping in order to clarify their relative importance. however, aggregate data from CALURA combines all of these under "Transportation". The bracketed figures show the total percentage by each of the sectors while the other percentages are for all transportation.

CONSTRUCTION 1971 year end
(millions)

	COMP RANK	ASSET RANK	ASSETS	SALE RANK	SALES	NET INC.	OWNERSHIP & CONTROL
Comstock Int'l.[1]	1	1	200	1	178	—	U.S. AFF: Holiday Inns 30.7%
1957 Bramalea Cons. Dev.	2	2	93	2	45	(.1)	
TOTAL MIDDLE RANGE			293		223		
SERVICES 1971 year end							
1964 Commonwealth Holiday	1	1	66	1	43	1.7	FOREIGN CONSORTIUM AFF.[1]
1953 Brinco	2	2	64	3	3	(2.3)	
Famous Players	3	3	54	2	30	1.5	U.S. SUB: Gulf & Western
1920 Can. Cablesystems	4	4	52	4	4	1.8	
TOTAL MIDDLE RANGE			236		80		
TOTAL SERVICE SECTOR			4,246		4,346		
MIDDLE RANGE AS % OF ALL			5.6%		1.8%		
STORAGE 1971 year end							
1929 Federal Grain	1	1	150	1	255	4.2	CAN. AFF: Searle Sec. 29%
1911 United Grain	2	2	119	2	36	1.7	
TOTAL MIDDLE RANGE			269		291		
TOTAL STORAGE SECTOR			804		751		
MIDDLE RANGE AS % OF ALL			33.5%		38.8%		

METAL MINING 1971 year end
(millions)

	COMP RANK	ASSET RANK	ASSETS	SALE RANK	SALES	NET INC.	OWNERSHIP & CONTROL
1916 Intern'l Nickel	1	1	2,095	1	789	94.2	69% o/s Can; 50% plus in US
1922 Noranda Mines	2	2	1,023	2	484	61.5	CAN AFF: Hollinger 10%
1906 Cominco	3	3	554	3	264	13.5	CAN SUB: CP Invest. 53%[1]
1928 Falconbridge	4	4	449	4	154	17.5	U.S. AFF: McIntyre Porc. 37%[2]
TOTAL DOMINANT CORP.			4,121		1,691		
1952 Brunswick M & S	7	7	138	7	51	(12.2)	DOM SUB: Noranda 50.8%
1947 Gaspé Copper	9	11	89	9	39	9.9	DOM SUB: Noranda 99%
1951 Pine Point Mines	11	15	71	8	47	20.8	DOM SUB: Cominco 69.1%[3]
TOTAL DOMINANT SUBSIDIARIES			298		137		
1958 Mattagami Lake	13	17	48	10	37	5.7	DOM AFF: Noranda 31.4%[4]
1963 Kerr Addison	16	14	74	16	18	3.8	DOM AFF: Noranda 44%
TOTAL DOMINANT AFFILIATES			122		55		
1927 Hud. Bay M & S	5	5	216	6	61	3.8	S.A. AFF: Anglo-Amer. 28%[5]
1927 Sherritt Gordon	6	9	125	5	74	8.8	U.S. AFF: Newmont 39.4%
1911 McIntyre Porc.	8	6	194	12	24	(3.3)	U.S. AFF: Superior 39.4%[6]
1916 Hollinger Mines	10	8	133	13	21	12.9	CAN. AFF: Argus 20.3%
1961 Patino Mines	12	12	76	14	19	4.4	NETH. SUB: Patino, NV
1960 Denison Mines	14	10	96	18	11	10.2	CAN. AFF: Roman Corp. 25%[7]
1955 Bethlehem Copper	15	17	58	11	25	7.4	FOREIGN CONSORTIUM[7]
1939 Steep Rock Iron	17	16	64	15	18	2.1	
1960 Preston Mines	18	13	75	19	4	.2	U.K. SUB: Rio Tinto 80.9%
1923 Dome Mines	19	19	47	17	18	3.4	U.S. AFF: Dome Petro. 17.6%*
TOTAL MIDDLE RANGE			1,084		275		
TOTAL METAL MINING SECTOR			8,065*		2,928		
DOMINANT CORP. AS % ALL			51.1%		57.8%		
DOMINANT SUB. AS % ALL			3.7%		4.7%		
DOMINANT AFF. AS % ALL			1.5%		1.9%		
TOTAL DOMINANT AS % ALL			56.3%		64.4%		
MIDDLE RANGE AS % ALL			13.4%		9.4%		

* see "Correction Factors for Aggregated Industrial Data"

OTHER MINING 1971 year end

(millions)

	COMP RANK	ASSET RANK	ASSETS	SALE RANK	SALES	NET INC.	OWNERSHIP & CONTROL
1925 Asbestos Corp.	1	1	143	2	52	6.0	U.S. SUB: Gen. Dynamics 55%
1918 Can. Johns-Manville[1]	2	2	130	1	130	—	U.S. SUB: Johns-Man. 100%
1951 Cassair Asbestos	3	3	79	3	41	4.6	FOREIGN CONSORTIUM CONTROL[2]
TOTAL MIDDLE RANGE			352		223		
TOTAL OTHER MINING SECTOR			1,683		985		
MIDDLE RANGE AS % OF ALL			20.1%		22.6%		

415

MINERAL FUELS 1971 year end
(millions)

	COMP RANK	ASSET RANK	ASSETS	SALE RANK	SALES	NET INC.	OWNERSHIP & CONTROL
1939 Pacific Petrol.	1	1	448	2	144	23.2	U.S. AFF: Phillips 48.6%[1]
Amaco Can. Petrol.	2	2	414	3	106	11.7	U.S. SUB: Standard 100%
1926 Hudson Bay Gas & O.	3	3	331	4	95	23.2	U.S. SUB: Continental 54.9%[2]
Mobil	4	6	277	1	191	43.0	U.S. SUB: Mobil Oil 100%
1970 Texaco Exploration	5	4	330	5	93	45.6	U.S. SUB: Texaco 99%
1953 Gt. Can. Oil	6	5	293	9	51	(8.3)	U.S. SUB: Sun Oil 96.1%
TOTAL DOMINANT			2,093		650		
1947 Pan Can. Petrol.	11	8	204	16	39	14.1	DOM SUB: CP Invest. 81.7%[3]
1965 Can. Indust. G & O	13	15	128	11	42	9.9	DOM SUB: Northern & Cent. 62%
1955 Brenda Mines	18	20	75	18	30	(.3)	DOM SUB: Noranda 50%
TOTAL DOMINANT SUBSIDIARIES			407		111		
1929 Home Oil	10	7	271	17	34	5.2	DOM. AFF: Consumers' 49%[4]
TOTAL DOMINANT AFFILIATES			271		34		

(continued)

(Mineral Fuels, continued)

1956	Total Petrol.	7	13	134	6	88	2.2	FR. AFF: CFP 42.4%
	Kaiser Resources	8	11	170	7	69	(15.4)	U.S. SUB: Kaiser 75%
1950	Dome Petrol.	9	9	202	13	42	10.2	U.S. AFF: Dome Mines 18%*
1921	Union Oil	12	12	146	10	48	9.8	U.S. SUB: Union Cal. 86.5%
1943	Canadian Superior	14	14	128	12	42	9.8	U.S. SUB: Superior 53.6%
1970	Ashland Oil Can.	15	17	107	8	64	8.1	U.S. SUB: Ashland 90%
1963	Aquitaine	16	10	186	20	19	15.6	FR. SUB: SNP 74.7%
1950	Bow Valley	17	23	56	14	40	.6	
	Tenneco Oil & Min.	19	18	88	10	48	5.8	U.S. SUB: Tenneco 100%
	Atlantic Rich.	20	16	126	15	40	12.9	U.S. SUB: Atl. Rich. 100%
1971	Can. Occidental	21	21	71	19	27	3.8	U.S. SUB: Occid. Pet. 82%
1950	Gt. Plains Dev.	22	19	77	23	11	4.4	U.K. SUB: Burmah Oil 70%
1954	Scurry-Rainbow	23	22	66	24	8	1.0	
1965	SE Commonwealth	24	24	51	22	17	2.2	U.S. SUB: SEDCO 66%

TOTAL MIDDLE RANGE		1,608	532
MIDDLE RANGE AS % OF ALL		26.7	26.8
TOTAL MINERAL FUELS		5,818*	1,986
DOMINANT (INC. SUB. & AFF.) AS % OF ALL (sub.)		7.0%	5.6%
(aff.)		4.7%	1.7%
TOTAL DOMINANT AS % OF ALL		47.7%	40.0%

* see "Correction Factors for Aggregated Industrial Data"

PAPER PRODUCTS 1971 year end
(millions)

	COMP RANK	ASSET RANK	ASSETS	SALE RANK	SALES	NET INC.	OWNERSHIP & CONTROL
1911 MacMillian Bloedel	1	1	856	1	704	22.0	CAN. AFF: CP Invest. 11.4%[1]
1929 Domtar Ltd.	2	2	510	2	516	10.4	CAN. AFF: Argus 17%
1931 Consol-Bathurst	3	3	457	3	343	.4	CAN. AFF: Power 36.5%
1914 Abitibi Paper	4	4	380	5	279	4.1	U.K. AFF: Daily Mail 17.8%
1920 The Price Co.	5	5	296	4	184	1.1	U.S. SUB: Cr. Zellerbach 90%
1914 Crown Zellerbach	6	6	237	6	206	8.8	
TOTAL DOMINANT CORP.			2,736		2,232		
1930 St. Lawrence Corp.	7	8	159	7	148	5.0	DOM SUB: Domtar 98.1%
1928 Bathurst Paper	11	11	100	10	80	(2.3)	DOM SUB: Cons-Bath. 100%
1936 Great Lakes Paper	13	13	87	12	81	3.2	DOM SUB: CP Invest. 51.6%[2]
TOTAL DOMINANT SUBSIDIARIES			346		309		
1924 Anglo-Can. P & P	8	9	140	8	114	2.1	U.K. SUB: Reed Paper 90%
1925 Rayonier	9	10	109	9	73	1.6	U.S. SUB: IT&T 100%
1946 Columbia Cellulose	10	7	195	13	84	(17.0)	U.S. SUB: Celenese 91%
1917 Fraser Co.	12	12	98	11	63	(4.9)	
1921 St. Regis Paper	14	14	54	14	4	2.4	U.S. SUB: St. Regis 100%
TOTAL MIDDLE RANGE			596		338		
MIDDLE RANGE AS % OF ALL			10.1%		7.5%		
TOTAL PAPER PRODUCTS			5,911		4,489		
DOMINANT CORP. AS % OF ALL			46.3%		49.7%		
DOMINANT SUB. AS % OF ALL			5.9%		6.9%		
TOTAL DOMINANT AS % OF ALL			52.2%		56.6%		

418

WOOD INDUSTRIES 1971 year end
(millions)

	COMP RANK	ASSET RANK	ASSETS	SALE RANK	SALES	NET INC.	OWNERSHIP & CONTROL
BC Forest Prod.	1	2	254	2	133	5.4	AFF. CONSORTIUM[1]
Wellwood of Can.	2	2	137	1	151	2.6	U.S. SUB: US Plywood 74%
AL. DOMINANT CORP.			391		284	(3.8)	
Crestbrook Forest	3	3	69	3	36		JAPAN SUB.[2]
AL. MIDDLE RANGE			69		36		
AL. WOOD INDUSTRIES SECTOR			2,909		2,627		
INANT CORP. AS % OF ALL			18.7%		10.8%		
DLE RANGE AS % OF ALL			3.3%		1.4%		

PETROLEUM 1971 year end
(millions)

	COMP RANK	ASSET RANK	ASSETS	SALE RANK	SALES	NET INC.	OWNERSHIP & CONTROL
Imperial Oil	1	1	1,648	1	1,907	136.0	U.S. SUB: Standard NJ 69.7%
Gulf Oil	2	2	1,169	3	774	53.8	U.S. SUB: Gulf 68.5%
Shell Canada	3	3	1,003	2	788	61.5	NETH. SUB: Shell Pet. 86.5%
Texaco Canada	4	4	396	4	401	31.3	U.S. SUB: Texaco Inc. 68.2%
BP Can. Holdings	5	5	389	5	195	8.7	U.K. SUB: Br. Petrol. 100%
Petrofina Can.	6	6	318	6	189	18.1	BELG. SUB: Petrofina 71.9%
Husky Oil	7	7	306	7	185	10.9	56% O/S Can: 23.2% US CONT[3]
TAL. DOMINANT	x	x	5,202	x	4,439		
Sun Oil			190		109	5.1	U.S. SUB: Sun Oil 100%
...TAL MIDDLE RANGE	x	x	190	x	109		
MIDDLE RANGE AS % OF ALL			3.3%		2.3%		
TOTAL PETROLEUM SECTOR			5,794		4,742		
DOMINANT CORP. AS % OF ALL			89.9%		93.6%		

* See "Correction Factors for Aggregate Industrial Data", p. 436.

NON-METALLIC MINERALS 1971 year end
(millions)

	COMP RANK	ASSET RANK	SALE RANK	ASSETS	SALES	NET INC.	OWNERSHIP & CONTROL
1951 Genstar	1	1	1	374	277	10.8	BELGIUM AFF: AFE 19.6%
1927 Can. Cement Laf.	2	2	2	278	156	7.9	FR. SUB: Cement Laf. 50.1%
TOTAL DOMINANT CORP.				652	433		
1913 Dominion Glass	4	4	5	86	74	(1.3)	DOM. SUB: Power Corp. 63%
TOTAL DOMINANT SUBSIDIARIES				86	74		
Can. Gypsum	3	6	3	68	79	8.5	U.S. SUB: US Gypsum 99.4%
Consum. Glass	5	5	4	83	79	2.3	CAN. AFF: Brockway 20%
1951 St. Lawrence Cem.	6	3	7	88	68	3.1	SWITZERLAND SUB: Holdenbank[2]
1951 Minn. Mining & Mun.	7	7	6	40	73	6.1	U.S. SUB: Minn. M & M 100%
TOTAL MIDDLE RANGE				279	294		
MIDDLE RANGE AS % OF ALL				16.7%	17.4%		
TOTAL NON-METALLIC MINERALS				1,672	1,689		
DOMINANT AS % OF ALL				39.0%	25.6%		
DOMINANT SUBSID. AS % OF ALL				5.1%	4.4%		
TOTAL DOMINANT AS % OF ALL				44.1%	30.0%		

FOOD & BEVERAGES 1971 year end

(millions)

	COMP RANK	ASSET RANK	ASSETS	SALE RANK	SALES	NET INC.	OWNERSHIP & CONTROL
1928 Distillers Corp.	1	1	1,326	1	1,236	60.1	Brofman family 42.3%
1928 George Weston Ltd.	2	3	457	2	1,037	15.1	
1926 Hiram Walker G & W	3	2	642	4	642	51.1	23% o/s Canada
1927 Canada Packers	4	7	187	3	919	9.6	
1930 Molson Industries	5	6	249	5	376	16.7	
1930 John Labatt	6	5	260	7	337	16.1	CAN. AFF: Brascan 32.2%
1930 Can. Breweries	7	4	266	9	251	9.1	S.A. SUB: Rothmans 50.1%
TOTAL DOMINANT CORP.			3,387		4,798		
1942 Ogilvie Flour Mills	14	14	80	16	141	1.9	DOM. SUB: J. Labatts 99.7%
1939 Atlantic Sugar Ref.	15	11	95	20	96	4.8	DOM. SUB: Glengair 62.3%
1912 Westfair Foods Ltd.	16	21	53	10	246	3.2	DOM. SUB: G. Weston 100%
1928 B. C. Packers	18	15	73	19	98	2.1	DOM. SUB: G. Weston 71%
TOTAL DOMINANT SUBSIDIARIES			301		581		
1961 Maple Leaf Mills	8	8	118	11	202	1.7	CONSORTIUM[2]
General Foods	9	10	109	12	182	7.9	U.S. SUB: Gen. Foods 100%
1902 Swift Canada	10	13	81	8	281	4.4	U.S. SUB: Swift 100%
1928 Burns Foods	11	17	68	6	359	2.9	R. H. Webster holds 41%
Standard Brands	12	9	117	15	149	5.9	U.S. SUB: Standard B. 100%
1920 Kraft Foods	13	16	70	13	161	8.5	U.S. SUB: Kraftco 100%
1930 Can. & Domin. Sugar	17	12	85	21	86	4.3	U.S. SUB: Tate & Lyle 56.4%
1928 Silverwoods Indust.	19	20	55	10	163	1.5	
Coca-Cola Ltd.	20	18	60	17	110	6.8	U.S. SUB: Coca-Cola 100%
1930 Robin Hood Multi.	21	19	52	18	105	2.7	U.S. SUB: Int'l. Multi. 100%
Campbell Soup	22	19	57	23	71	5.1	U.S. SUB: Campbell 100%
1940 H. J. Heinz	23	23	44	22	81	4.2	U.S. SUB: HJ Heinz 100%
TOTAL MIDDLE RANGE			916		1,850		
MIDDLE RANGE AS % OF ALL		16.4%			19.1%		
TOTAL FOOD & BEVERAGE			5,589		9,695		
DOMINANT CORP. AS % OF ALL		60.6%			49.5%		
DOMINANT SUB AS % OF ALL		5.4%			6.0%		
TOTAL DOMINANT AS % OF ALL		66.0%			55.5%		

RUBBER PRODUCTS 1971 year end
(millions)

	COMP RANK	ASSET RANK	ASSETS	SALE RANK	SALES	NET INC.	OWNERSHIP & CONTROL
1927 Goodyear Tire & R.	1	2	119	1	185	7.8	U.S. SUB: Goodyear 84%
Firestone T & R.	2	1	141	3	148	5.6	U.S. SUB: Firestone 100%
1906 Uniroyal	3	3	91	2	157	5.6	U.S. SUB: Uniroyal 100%
1922 B. F. Goodrich	4	4	62	4	99	2.8	U.S. SUB: BF Goodrich 100%
TOTAL MIDDLE RANGE			413		589		
TOTAL RUBBER PRODUCTS SECTOR			600		923		
MIDDLE RANGE AS % OF ALL			68.8%		63.8%		

TEXTILES 1971 year end
(millions)

	COMP RANK	ASSET RANK	ASSETS	SALE RANK	SALES	NET INC.	OWNERSHIP & CONTROL
1910 DuPont of Can.	1	2	106	1	288	11.3	U.S. SUB: E. I. DuPont 74.9%
1926 Celanese Canada	2	1	207	3	132	3.4	U.S. SUB: Celanese 57.1%
1922 Dominion Textiles	3	3	178	2	191	5.2	
TOTAL MIDDLE RANGE			491		551		
MIDDLE RANGE AS % OF ALL			19.6%		14.0%		
TOTAL TEXTILE SECTOR			2,506		3,937		

PRINTING & PUBLISHING 1971 year end
(millions)

	COMP RANK	ASSET RANK	ASSETS	SALE RANK	SALES	NET INC.	OWNERSHIP & CONTROL
1947 Thompson Newspapers	1	1	193	1	129	18.3	U.K. SUB: Woodbridge 78.5%
1927 Southam Press	2	4	72	2	124	10.1	
F. P. Publications	3	2	95	4	64	6.7	
1958 Toronto Star	4	3	76	5	56	3.7	
1891 Maclean-Hunter	5	5	54	3	69	3.5	
TOTAL MIDDLE RANGE			490		442		
MIDDLE RANGE AS % OF ALL			42.1%		37.8%		
TOTAL PRINTING & PUBLISHING			1,164		1,169		

423

PRIMARY METAL 1971 year end
(millions)

	COMP RANK	ASSET RANK	ASSETS	SALE RANK	SALES	NET INC.	OWNERSHIP & CONTROL
1910 Steel Co. of Can.	1	2	966	2	730	66.7	
1902 Aluminum Co. of Can.	2	3	499	1	862	36.8	U.S. SUB: Alcan Alum. 100%
1917 Dominion Foundries	3	2	603	3	381	28.0	
1934 Algoma Steel	4	4	448	4	272	12.8	GERM. AFF: Mannesmann 25%
TOTAL DOMINANT CORP.			2,516		2,245		
1960 Rio Algoma Mines	5	5	251	6	168	9.7	U.K. SUB: Rio Tinto 51.2%
1915 Canron	6	6	122	5	205	4.2	
1922 Anaconda Amer. Brass	7	7	73	7	66	2.0	U.S. SUB: Anaconda 100%
TOTAL MIDDLE RANGE			446		439		
MIDDLE RANGE AS % OF ALL.			9.7%		11.1%		
TOTAL PRIMARY METAL			1,580		3,974		
TOTAL DOMINANT AS % OF ALL.			54.9%		56.5%		

METAL FABRICATION 1971 year end
(millions)

	COMP RANK	ASSET RANK	ASSETS	SALE RANK	SALES	NET INC.	OWNERSHIP & CONTROL
1912 Dominion Bridge	1	1	153	1	235	6.2	DOM. AFF: Algoma Steel 44%
TOTAL DOMINANT AFFILIATE			153		235		
Continental Can	2	2	115	2	170	8.9	U.S. SUB: Cont. Can 100%
1965 Can. Corp. Manage.	3	3	60	3	115	3.1	
TOTAL MIDDLE RANGE			175		285		
MIDDLE RANGE AS % OF ALL.			8.0%		8.4%		
TOTAL METAL FABRICATION SECTOR			2,202		3,412		
TOTAL DOMINANT AFFILIATE AS % OF ALL.			7.0%		6.9%		

TRANSPORTATION EQUIPMENT 1971 year end

(millions)

		COMP RANK	ASSET RANK	ASSETS	SALE RANK	SALES	NET INC.	OWNERSHIP & CONTROL
	General Motors	1	2	706	1	2,493	79.8	U.S. SUB: Gen. Motors 100%
1911	Ford Motor Co.	2	1	987	2	1,458	75.8	U.S. SUB: Ford Motors 85.2%
1968	Chrysler Canada	3	3	383	3	1,292	26.5	U.S. SUB: Chrysler 100%
	TOTAL DOMINANT CORP.			2,076		5,243		
1945	Hawker Siddeley	5	4	206	6	158	1.9	DOM SUB: Racier 56.4% (UK)¹
	TOTAL DOMINANT SUBSIDIARIES			206		158		
1942	Bombardier	4	5	134	5	183	11.6	U.S. SUB: Ford Motors 100%
	Ensite	6	6	127	4	291	11.2	U.S. SUB: Gen. Dynamics 99.7%
1944	Canadair Ltd.	7	7	123	8	85	.1	U.S. SUB: United Air. 90.6%
1928	United Aircraft	8	9	67	7	106	1.3	
1963	Seaway Multicorp.	9	8	110	9	75	0.0	
1965	Budd Automotive	10	10	65	10	70	1.5	U.S. SUB: The Budd Co. 81%
1944	Levy Industries	11	11	52	11	55	.3	CAN. SUB: Seaway M-C. 83%
	TOTAL MIDDLE RANGE			568		865		
	MIDDLE RANGE AS % OF ALL			5.3%		9.4%		
	TOTAL TRANSPORTATION EQUIPMENT			3,866		9,214		
	DOMINANT AS % OF ALL			53.7%		56.9%		
	DOMINANT SUB. AS % OF ALL			5.3%		1.7%		
	TOTAL DOMINANT AS % OF ALL			59.0%		58.6%		

CHEMICALS 1971 year end
(millions)

	COMP RANK	ASSET RANK	ASSETS	SALE RANK	SALES	NET INC.	OWNERSHIP & CONTROL
1954 Canadian Industries	1	1	257	1	349	9.4	U.K. SUB: Imperial Chem. 73.4%
TOTAL DOMINANT CORP.			257		349		
1922 Union Carbide	2	2	196		198	9.6	U.S. SUB: Union Carb. 75%
1942 Dow Chemical	3	3	171	3	147	1.3	U.S. SUB: Dow Chem. 100%
Proctor & Gamble	4	4	159	4	117	5.0	U.S. SUB: Proctor & G. 100%
1934 Cyanamid of Can.	5	5	99	6	87	3.1	U.S. SUB: Amer. Cyan. 99.5%
Lever Bros.	6	7	61	5	114	4.5	U.K. SUB: Unilever 100%
Allied Chemical	7	6	94	7	84	6.0	U.S. SUB: Allied Chem. 100%
Can. Pittsburg	8	8	52	8	64	.7	U.S. SUB: PPG Indus. 100%
TOTAL MIDDLE RANGE			832		811		
TOTAL CHEMICALS SECTOR			2,698		3,391		
MIDDLE RANGE AS % OF ALL			30.8%		23.9%		
DOMINANT AS % OF ALL			9.5%		10.3%		

MACHINERY 1971 year end
(millions)

	COMP RANK	ASSET RANK	ASSETS	SALE RANK	SALES	NET INC.	OWNERSHIP & CONTROL
1891 Massey Ferguson	1	1	1,011	1	1,029	9.3	CAN. AFF: ARGUS 15.7%
IBM Canada	2	2	323	2	429	30.7	U.S. SUB: IBM 100%
TOTAL DOMINANT CORP.			1,334		1,458		
1913 Internat'l Harvest.	3	3	135	3	282	8.2	U.S. SUB: Int'l Harv. 100%
Nat'l Cash Register	4	4	50	4	60	2.8	U.S. SUB: Nat'l Cash 100%
TOTAL MIDDLE RANGE			185		342		
MIDDLE RANGE AS % OF ALL			9.1%		13.7%		
TOTAL MACHINERY SECTOR			2,024		2,500		
DOMINANT CORP. AS % OF ALL			65.9%		58.3%		

ELECTRICAL PRODUCTS 1971 year end
(millions)

	COMP RANK	ASSET RANK	ASSETS	SALE RANK	SALES	NET. INC.	OWNERSHIP & CONTROL
1892 Can. Gen. Electric	1	1	413	2	496	14.5	U.S. SUB: Gen. Elec. 91.9%
Northern Electric	2	2	366	1	576	12.6	CAN. SUB: Bell Can. 100%
TOTAL DOMINANT CORP.			799		1,072		
1903 Westinghouse Can.	3	3	136	3	267	4.1	U.S. SUB: Westinghouse 76.6%
RCA	4	4	97	4	140	2.7	U.S. SUB: RCA Corp. 100%
TOTAL MIDDLE RANGE			233		407		
MIDDLE RANGE AS % OF ALL			10.5%		11.7%		
TOTAL ELECTRICAL PROD. SECTOR			2,211		3,495		
DOMINANT CORP. AS % OF ALL			35.2%		30.7%		

OTHER MANUFACTURING 1971 year end
(millions)

	COMP RANK	ASSET RANK	ASSETS	SALE RANK	SALES	NET. INC.	OWNERSHIP & CONTROL
1912 Imasco	1	2	243	1	570	17.7	U.K. SUB: 58.5%¹
1956 Rothmans	2	1	410	2	336	10.0	S.A. SUB: Rembrant 59.4%
TOTAL DOMINANT CORP.			653		906		
Neonex Int'l	3	5	69	3	146	3.0	U.S. residents hold 17.2%
Kodak Canada	4	3	86	6	100	8.9	U.S. SUB: Eastman Kod. 100%
Bensen — Hedges	5	7	56	4	129	2.5	U.S. SUB: Phillip Morris 100%
1949 GTE Sylvania	6	5	72	7	90	2.8	U.S. SUB: Gen. Elec. & T. 100%
Honeywell	7	4	80	8	83	2.0	U.S. SUB: Honeywell 100%
Westburn Indust.	8	8	51	5	104	.7	
TOTAL MIDDLE RANGE			414		622		
TOTAL OTHER MANUFACTURING			2,251		2,123		
MIDDLE RANGE AS % OF ALL			18.4%		29.3%		
DOMINANT AS % OF ALL			29.0%		42.7%		

REAL ESTATE 1971 year end
(millions)

	COMP RANK	ASSET RANK	ASSETS	SALE RANK	SALES	NET INC.	OWNERSHIP & CONTROL
1968 Campeau Corp.	1	2	297	2	61	3.3	DOM. SUB: Power 52.2%
Can. Interurban	4	5	105	5	14	1.1	DOM. SUB: Campeau 98.5%
T. Eaton Realty	7	6	94	7	11	2.0	DOM. SUB: T. Eaton 100%
TOTAL DOMINANT SUBSIDIARIES			496		86		
1968 E-L Financial	2	4	193	1	63	2.2	3 officers hold 57.1%
1964 Cadillac Dev.	3	3	272	3	35	3.1	FOR. AFF: Brinco 57%
1968 Churchill Falls	5	1	628	11	1	.5	4 officers hold 64.9%
1969 Western Realty	6	8	88	4	17	2.6	CAN. SUB: Metrop. Est. 70.1%
1954 MEPC Can. Prop.	8	7	95	9	11	1.6	
1969 Y & R Property	9	11	54	6	12	1.0	CAN. SUB: Hollinger 59.9%
1936 Lab. Mining & Exp.	10	10	61	8	11	9.5	
1965 Markborough Prop.	11	9	76	10	8	.5	
TOTAL MIDDLE RANGE			1,467		158		

Appendix VIII

Notes To Corporation Tables

Investment Companies

1 Elmswood Ltd. holds 19.3% with approximately 85% held outside Canada.
2 Shell Investments holds 86.5% of Shell Canada which is dominant in the Petroleum sector. For purposes of analysis of decision making the board of Shell Investments is included rather than Shell Canada.
3 Power Corporation holds 51.2% of Great West Life, a dominant insurance company; 63.4% of Investors Group, a dominant Mortgage company which in turn holds 63.4% of Imperial Life, another dominant insurance company; 53.7% of Laurentide Finance, a dominant Credit Agency; 52.2% of Campeau Corporation, dominant in Real Estate. For purposes of analysis of decision making the board of Power Corporation is included rather than each of the above subsidiaries. Power Corporation has additional holdings of 36.5% in Consolidated-Bathurst, 10.4% in Argus Corporation, 99.6% in Canada Steamship Lines and 56.7% in Dominion Glass.
4 Argus Corporation is included as a dominant corporation even though its own assets would not place it in this category nor does it have any subsidiaries which would. Because of the practice of minority control used by Argus it effectively controls B.C. Forest Products, dominant in Wood; Dominion Stores, dominant in Retail; Domtar, dominant in Paper; Hollinger Mines, a major Metal Mining corporation with sizable holdings; Massey Ferguson, a dominant Machinery corporation, as well as 47.9% of Standard Broadcasting. In each case the directors of the dominant affiliates of Argus are included along with the directors of Argus. The high degree of interlocking between these corporations will reflect these ownership links.
5 Officers and directors of S.B. McLaughlin hold 44%.
6 Woodbridge Co. of England holds 78.46% of Thomson Newspapers Ltd.

Sales Finance And Consumer Loans

1 Revenue estimate of $10 million for Transamerican Finance is based on known assets of $75 million and compared relative to other companies in this sector.

Trust Companies

1 Revenue estimate for Ontario Trust is based on known assets of $141 million and compared to others in the same sector. The Bank of Montreal is the second largest investor in the company with 6% compared to 42% of Hambro of the U.K. Ownership of this company is currently under question (see "Foreign-ownership rule broken?" by Philip Mathias in *The Financial Post*, May 5, 1973).
2 The actual assets commanded by trust companies is underestimated, for example, "in addition to its own assets of $1,912 million at the end of 1971

(Royal Trust) was also administering estates, trusts and agency accounts of $9,325 million'' *(The Financial Post*, August 5, 1972, pg. 9).

3 Investors Group, a subsidiary of Power Corporation, increased its holding in Montreal Trust to 51% early in 1973 (The Investors Group 32nd Annual Report).

Mortgage Companies

1 The two banks which are affiliated with Canada Permanent Mortgage are the Bank of Nova Scotia with 12.4% and the Toronto-Dominion Bank with 12.3%.

Other Finance

1 RoyNat is controlled by a consortium of financial institutions: Royal Bank holds 41.5%, Banque Canadienne Nationale holds 34%, Montreal Trust holds 13.5% and Canada Trust, a subsidiary of Huron & Erie Mortgage Corporation, holds 10%. The company was established to provide business loans to corporations ''in amounts of $25,000 and up to Canadian companies for purchase of land, building assets, expansion etc.'' *(The Financial Post Survey of Industrials* 1972, pg. 68).

2 Two U.K. companies, Morgan Greenfield & Co. and Barring Brothers together hold about 42% of Harris & Partners.

3 Banque National du Paris holds approximately 75% and Banque de P'Union Parisienne about 13% of SFCI (Société Financiére pour le Commerce et l'Indsutrie).

Retail Trade

1 Loblaw Companies is 60.3% held by George Weston which is dominant in Food & Beverages.

2 T. Eaton Co. estimate of $1,000 million sales is a Financial Post estimate and $500 million assets is an estimate based on this compared to other companies in that sector. Eaton's does not release financial statistics; it is one of the few remaining large companies for which data is not available.

3 Stock in Simpsons-Sears is evenly split between Simpsons Ltd. of Canada and Sears-Roebuck of the U.S.

4 ''Elwin Developments Ltd. owns 56%. Elwin is owned: Elican Development Co. 67%, a U.S. institutional investor 8%, two U.S. residents, Raymond A. Rich and David R. Williams, Jr., 10% and 15% respectively. About 5% of Elican is owned in Canada, the remainder in Europe, mainly by Belgium and German interests'' (Financial Post).

Wholesale Trade

1 BP Holdings is wholly owned by The British Petroleum Co. of the U.K.

2 ''Finning Securities Ltd. and Tractor Holdings Ltd. *each* hold 35.9% (697,235 shares) in the company. J.E. Barker and M.M. Young *each* hold 3.3% interest in the company (64,765) and *each* equally owns *all* voting shares of Finning Securities and Tractor Holdings'' *(Financial Post)*.

Communications
1 Anglo-Canadian Telephone is 100% controlled by General Telephone and Electronics, U.S.
2 Bell Canada has 52.2% of the o/s common shares in Maritime Telephone and Telegraph representing over 2 million shares but "Amendment to Nova Scotia Company's Act limits any one share-holder with more than 1,000 shares to 1,000 votes at shareholders' meetings" (*F.P.S.I.*, 1972).

Pipelines
1 Home Oil also owns 8% of Trans-Canada Pipelines.
2 Imperial Oil is 69.7% held by Standard Oil (N.J.); Shell Canada also holds 2% of Interprovincial Pipelines.
3 Alberta Gas Trunkline is controlled by a consortium which makes the following appointments: Group I (utility) 1 director—Canadian Western Natural Gas, Northwestern Utilities Ltd. Group II (gas export) 1 director —Alberta & Southern Gas Co., TransCanada Pipelines. Group III (gas producer or processor) 3 directors—Gulf Oil Ltd., Shell Canada. Group IV, 2 government appointments (Based on information filed with Consumer and Corporate Affairs). In 1971 Pacific Gas Transmission Co., a subsidiary of U.S.-based Pacific Gas & Electric held 66.6% which was to be reduced to 45%.
4 Westcoast Transmission also holds 44.8% preferred shares.

Services
1 Rio Tinto-Zinc of the UK and Bethlehem StellSteel of the U.S. hold 49%.

Metal Mining
1 Canadian Pacific Ltd. holds 90.1% of Canadian Pacific Investments.
2 Superior Oil Co. (US) has a 14.6% "Indirect interest through McIntyre Porcupine Mines Ltd., which owns 37% of Falconbridge. Superior directly and through its 53.6% owned Canadian Superior Oil Ltd., has 39.4% interest in McIntyre" (*Financial Post*, August 5, 1972).
3 Canadian Pacific Investments hold 53% of Cominco.
4 In addition to the 31.4% interest of Noranda Mines in Mattagami Lake Mines, 27.2% is held by Canadian Exploration, 12% by Tech Corp Ltd., 6.5% by Dome Mines and 4.2% by Iso Mines.
5 Anglo American Corp. of Canada Ltd. is controlled in South Africa through Ammercosa Investments Ltd.
6 An additional 7.4% is held by Falconbridge Nickel Mines.
7 Granges Aktiebalag of Sweden holds 25% and Sumitomo Metal Mines of Japan, 24%.
8 About 75% of the shares are held outside Canada, mainly in the U.S.

Mineral Fuels
1 80% held outside Canada.
2 British controlled Hudson Bay Investments also holds 21.9%.
3 Canadian Pacific holds 90.1% of Canadian Pacific Investments.
4 "In 1971 Consumers' Gas Co. agreed to acquire from R.A. Brown, Jr. (now deceased) and his family approximately 50.33% of the outstanding

class B shares of Gygnus Corp. Ltd. (Cygnus in turn holds 43.5% voting control of Home). Consumers' also purchased additional Home shares directly. These transactions gave Consumers' 65% voting control of Home" (*Financial Post*).

5   42.4% common voting and 38% preferred voting stock controlled by Compagnie Fraç0aise des Petroles, France; about 66% of all voting stock is held outside of Canada.

6   About 66% voting stock held outside Canada, mainly in the U.S.

7   "Société Nationale des Petroles d'Aquitain (SNPA) of France holds 74.7% of the company's outstanding stock; SNPA is in turn 51% owned by a state agency, Enterprise de Recharcea et d'Activites Petroliéres" (*Financial Post*).

Other Mining

1   Estimate based on known sales and percentage of parents assets (*Financial Post Survey of Mines*, 1972).

2   Bell Asbestos Mines (UK) holds 23.4%, Newmont Mining (US) holds 13.2%, Paybestos-Manhattan Inc. (US) holds 10%, James Hardies Asbestos Ltd. (Australia) holds 8.8%, Conwest Exploration Canada holds 10%.

Paper Products

1   About 23% held outside Canada, mainly in the U.S.

2   Canadian Pacific Investments is 90.1% controlled by Canadian Pacific Ltd.

Wood Industries

1   Noranda Mines and Mead Corp. (US) each hold 29% while Argus Corp. also holds 13.4%.

2   Honshu Paper Manufacture Co. Ltd. and Mitisubishi Corp. own all preferred and 50.2% common.

Petroleum

1   Held through Shell Investments which is wholly owned by Shell Petroleum (Netherlands).

2   The G.E. Nielson family (US) holds 23.2%; Canadian Pacific Investments holds 50.4%.

Food & Beverages

1   Rothmans of Pall Mall Canada is 59.4% controlled by Rothmans Controlling Investments of South Africa.

2   Upper Lakes Shipping holds 28.6%, Overwaitea Ltd. 14%, Leitch Transport 11% and Norris Grain (US) 10%.

Transportation Equipment

1   Racier Ltd. is wholly owned by Hawker Siddeley Group Ltd., England.

Non-Metallic Minerals

1   Société Generale du Belgique and an officer hold 19.6%.

2   All outstanding class B shares (control) held by Holden Bank Financiere.

Machinery
1   Approximately 40% held outside Canada.

Other Manufacturing
1   44.2% by British American Tobacco and 14.3% by Tobacco Securities Trust.

Appendix IX (a)

Distribution of Sales and Assets for Industrial Corporations by Sector Expressed in Dollars and Percentages, 1971 year end

	ASSETS		SALES	
	(000,000)	%	(000,000)	%
Metal Mines	7,465	7.7	2,928	2.6
Mineral Fuels	5,818	6.0	1,986	1.8
Other Mining	1,683	1.7	985	.9
TOTAL MINING	14,966	15.4	5,899	5.2
Food & Beverage	5,289	5.5	9,695	8.6
Rubber Industries	600	.6	923	.8
Textile Industries	2,506	2.6	3,937	3.5
Wood Industries	2,090	2.2	2,627	2.3
Paper, Allied Indust.	5,831	6.0	4,489	4.0
Printing & Publishing	1,164	1.2	1,169	1.5
Primary Metal	5,280	5.4	3,974	3.5
Metal Fabricating	2,202	2.3	3,412	3.0
Machinery Industries	1,724	1.8	2,500	2.2
Transportation Equip.	3,566	3.7	9,214	8.2
Electrical Products	2,211	2.3	3,495	3.1
Non-metallic Miner. Prod.	1,672	1.7	1,689	1.5
Petroleum & Coal Products	5,484	5.7	4,742	4.2
Chemicals & Products	2,698	2.8	3,391	3.0
Other Manufacturing	2,051	2.1	2,123	1.9
TOTAL MANUFACTURING	44,368	45.8	57,910	51.3
Transportation	7,291	7.5	4,464	4.0
Storage	804	.8	751	.7
Communication	5,094	5.3	1,470	1.3
Utilities	3,372	3.5	878	.8
Wholesale Trade	8,607	8.9	18,851	16.7
Retail Trade	8,182	8.4	18,273	16.2
Services	4,246	4.4	4,346	3.9
TOTAL ALL INDUSTRIES	96,930	100.0%	112,842	100.0%

(Source: Calculated from *Industrial Corporation*, 4th Quarter, 1971 by CALURA Division of Statistics Canada. CAT. #61-003)

Appendix IX b

Correction Factors For Aggregate Industrial Data

CALURA calculations are based on Canadian operations of companies only but published statements by corporations typically consolidate all operations. For present purposes the consolidated data more accurately reflects the economic power of Canadian based corporations since it is indicative of the total capital and market base at their command. This requires that a correction factor be introduced to make the individual corporate groupings compatible with aggregated data. In some cases this involves adding greater assets to the set of corporations in sector because the CALURA data aggregates more than public statements but usually it involves adding to the aggregate data to account for foreign operations. Sales are not affected to the same degree as assets and in the opinion of CALURA representatives do not require correction factors.

It should be noted that this adjustment refers only to the set of corporations listed within each sector and not all corporations within the sector although there is a tendency for only the larger corporations to have significant holdings outside Canada.

(Corrections were calculated by Mr. J.D. Wilson, Industrial Corporations Section of CALURA).

CORRECTION FACTORS

(millions)

SECTOR	ORIGINAL ASSETS	CORRECTION	CORRECTED ASSETS
Metal Mines	7,465	add 600	8,065
Mineral Fuels	5,818	nil	5,818
Other Mining	1,683	nil	1,683
Food & Beverage	5,289	add 300	5,589
Rubber Industries	600	nil	600
Textile Indust.	2,506	nil	2,506
Wood Industries	2,090	nil	2,090
Paper & Allied	5,831	add 80	5,911
Printing & Pub.	1,164	nil	1,164
Primary Metal	5,280	sub 700	4,580
Metal Fabrication	2,202	nil	2,202
Machinery Indust.	1,724	add 300	2,024
Transport. Equip.	3,566	add 300	3,866
Electrical Prod.	2,211	nil	2,211
Non-metallic Min.	1,672	nil	1,672
Petroleum & Coal	5,484	add 310	5,794
Chemicals	2,698	nil	2,698
Other Manufac.	2,051	add 200	2,251
Transportation	7,291	sub 410	6,891
Utilities	3,373	add 430	3,803
Wholesale Trade	8,607	sub 350	8,257
Retail Trade	8,182	add 440	8,622

It should be noted that this adjustment refers only to the set of corporations listed within each sector and not all corporations within the sector although there is a tendency for only the larger corporations to have significant holdings outside Canada.

(Corrections were calculated by Mr. J. D. Wilson, Industrial Corporations Section of CALURA.)

436

Appendix X

*175 Selected Prominent Corporations and Institutions
and Their Interlocks with the Economic Elite 1972*

CORPORATION	ELITE DIR.	#BD. MBRS.	INCLUDING	CONTROL
Acadia Life Insur.	4	13		CAN
Acadia Pulp & Paper	8	12	chmn; pres & ceo (1)	DOM SUB: Glengair Group
Acres Ltd.	5	9	chmn; pres; v. pres of finance (3)	DOM AFF: Traders Group
Air Canada	7	9	chmn & ceo (2)	Crown Corp.
Algoma Cent. Rlwy.	6	11	chmn; depy chmn; pres (2)	
Alliance Mut. Life	7	12	pres; v. pres (3)	MR CAN
Aquitaine Co. of Can.	2	8	(1)	MR CAN
Asbestos Corp. Ltd.	4	12	v. chmn; v. pres & gen. counsel (4)	MR FR SUB
Atlantic Sugar Refin.	8	12	chmn; pres & ceo (1)	MR US SUB*
Atomic Energy of Can.	2	10		DOM SUB: Glengair
BC Sugar Refinery	3	9	chmn (2)	Crown Corp.
BNA Holdings Ltd.	3	7	chmn & pres (2)	S. CAN*
Bank of British Colum.	1	18		DOM SUB: Nat'l Trust
Bank of Canada	4	15		MR CAN
Banque Canadienne Nat.	7	22	chmn & pres; v. chmn (2)	Crown Corp.
Ben's Holdings Ltd.	4	9	chmn; pres (3)	MR CAN
Benson & Hedges (Can)	3	12	(1)	S. CAN
Bombardier	2	8	pres & ceo	MR US SUB
Bramalea Consol. Dev.	3	10	chmn (2)	MR CAN*
Brenda Mines	3	9	exec v. pres (2)	MR CAN
T. G. Bright & Co. Ltd.	2	7	(2)	DOM SUB: Noranda
				S. CAN

437

Company			Position	Affiliation
Brinco	7	22	chmn; pres & ceo (5) (6 others for.)	FOR. AFF; S. CAN
British Amer. Bank Note	4	11	(2)	
British Colum. Teleph.	8	11	chmn; pres & ceo (5)	DOM SUB: Anglo-Can. Telephone
Brunswick Min. & Smelt.	4	14	chmn; v. pres (3)	DOM SUB: Noranda
Budd Automotive Co.	2	7	(1)	MR US SUB
Burns Foods	3	15	pres & ceo (1)	MR CAN*
CAE Industries	7	11	chmn (6)	S. CAN
CFRB Ltd.	7	8	chmn (5)	DOM AFF: Argus
Cadillac Devel. Corp.	3	14	(1)	MR CAN
Campeau Corp.	2	14	v. chmn (3)	CAN
Canada Devel. Corp.	7	21	chmn; pres (8)	Crown Corp.
Canada Perm. Trust	29	42	chmn; pres (8)	DOM SUB: Can. Perm. Mortgage
Can. Steamship Lines	5	12	pres & ceo (4)	DOM SUB: Power Corp.
Canada Trust	20	50	chmn & pres; depy chmn & v. pres; v. pres & gen. mgr. (10)	DOM SUB: Huron & Erie
Canada Wire & Cable	6	11	chmn (4)	DOM SUB: Noranda
Canadair Ltd.	2	13	v. pres & gen. couns. (2)	MR US SUB*

( ): number of directors which hold multiple dominant directorships.

* : corporation included by Porter, or a predecessor company which has merged. in 1948-50 but which is not included in the present study.

Company		Position		Affiliation
Canadian Breweries	6	chmn (3)	13	DOM SUB: Rothmans*
Canadian Gen. Insur.	11	chmn (6)	13	DOM SUB: Traders Group
Canadian Gen. Invest.	7	chmn; pres (5)	13	MR CAN
Canadian Gypsum Co.	3	(3)	6	MR US SUB
Canadian Indus. Gas & Oil	5	chmn exec. comm; pres (3)	9	DOM SUB: Northern & Central
Canadian Int'l Paper	8	chmn (4)	12	US SUB
Canadian Marconi Co.	2	(2)	11	*
Canadian Pacif. Air.	5	chmn (4)	10	DOM SUB: Can. Pacif.
Canadian Pacif. Invest.	6	chmn & ceo; pres (4)	9	DOM SUB: Can. Pacif.
Canadian Salt Co.	3	(2)	9	S. US SUB
Canron Ltd.	7	chmn & ceo; v. chmn (4)	14	MR CAN*
Celanese Canada Ltd.	4	chmn (2)	13	MR US SUB*
Cemp Investments	5	chmn; pres (2)	5	
Churchill Falls (Labrador) Corp.	5	chmn & ceo (3)	13	MR FOR
Cominco	9	exec v. pres; v. pres (6)	14	DOM SUB: Can. Pacif.
Commonwealth Holiday Inns of Canada	3	sr. v. pres (2)	8	MR US SUB
Consumers' Glass Co.	3	(1)	11	MR CAN*
Crown Trust	8	(2)	25	MR CAN
Crush Int'l	4		13	S. CAN
Cygnus Corp.	5	chmn & man. dir. (2)	7	DOM SUB: Consumers' Gas
Denison Mines	4	chmn & ceo	13	MR CAN
Dome Mines	4	sec (3)	9	MR (US)
Dominion Bridge	7	chmn & pres; v. pres (2)	13	DOM AFF: Algoma Steel

Company			Position	Location
Dominion of Can. Gen. Insurance	5	13	v. chmn	CAN
Dominion Glass	7	11	pres (4)	DOM SUB: Power Corp.
Dominion Coal	6	9	chmn & pres (3)	DOM SUB: Racier
Dominion Tanners	4	8	pres (1)	
Dominion Textiles	5	11	(3)	MR CAN*
Dupont of Canada	3	12	(3)	MR US SUB
E-L Financial Corp.	5	13	pres (1)	MR CAN
Eddy Match	5	10	chmn	S. UK SUB
Eldorado Nuclear	4	7	(1)	Crown Corp.
Emco Ltd.	2	12	(1)	MR CAN
Empire Life Insur.	5	12	chmn; hon. chmn (1)	MR CAN SUB: E-L Finance
Excelsior Life	6	12	chmn (3)	MR CAN
Federal Grain	5	12	chmn; chmn exec comm (3)	MR CAN
Finning Tractors & Equipment	3	9		MR CAN
Fraser Companies	10	14	chmn & ceo; sr. v. pres (8)	MR CAN*
GWG Ltd.	2	6	(1)	S. US SUB
Gaz Metropolitain	6	10	chmn; v chmn (4)	DOM SUB: Northern & Central
General Foods Ltd.	3	9	(1)	MR US SUB
Goodyear Tire & Rubber	4	12	pres & ceo (3)	MR US SUB*
Grafton Group	4	13	chmn; pres (3)	S. CAN
Great Plains Dev. Co.	2	10	pres (1)	MR (UK) SUB
Great-West Life	10	16	chmn; v..pres (3)	DOM SUB: Power Corp.
Greater Winnipeg Gas	7	11	(3)	DOM SUB: Northern & Central

440

Company			Position	Affiliation
Greyhound Lines of Canada	2	10	(1)	S. US SUB
Halifax Insur. Co.	3	15	chmn (3)	CAN
Harding Carpets	3	8	chmn (3)	S. CAN SUB
Hawker Siddeley Can.	5	12	v. chmn: v. pres of finance; v. pres & sec (2)	DOM SUB: Racier
Hollinger Mines Ltd.	5	10	chmn; pres & ceo; v. pres & chmn exec comm (3)	MR CAN*
Holt Renfrew & Co.	4	11	(1)	US SUB
Home Oil	10	16	chmn (6)	DOM AFF: Consumers' Gas
Hudson Bay Mining & Smelting	2	10	(2)	MR SOUTH AFRICA*
IGA Canada	2	5	chmn; v. pres (1)	DOM AFF: M. Loeb: Oshawa Group
Imperial Life Assur.	11	20	chmn & ceo; v. pres & chmn exec comm (5)	DOM SUB: Power Corp.
Industrial Dev. Corp.	3	14		Crown Corp.
Investors Group	8	17	chmn; v. chmn (4)	DOM SUB: Power Corp.
Kaiser Resources	5	14	v. chmn (3)	MR US SUB
Kelly Douglas & Co.	3	9	pres (2)	DOM SUB: G. Weston
Kerr Addison Mines	5	10	(3)	DOM AFF: Noranda
Laurentide Fin. Corp.	4	13	chmn (3)	DOM SUB: Power Corp.
Lever Brothers	4	8	pres	MR UK SUB
Liquid Carbonic Can.	3	11	(2)	US SUB
MLW-Worthington	3	11	(3)	S. US SUB*
Maple Leaf Mills	4	12	(2)	MR CAN*

Marathon Realty Co.	3	8	chmn (2)	DOM SUB: Can. Pacif.
Marine Industries	6	13	chmn; pres; v. pres (2)	MR CAN
				S. CAN
Maritime Electric Co.	4	9	chmn; pres (2)	
Maritime Telegraph & Telephone	2		(1)	DOM SUB: Bell Can.*
Markborough Propert.	8	20	pres (1)	MR CAN
Mattagami Lake Mines	3	10	pres; v. pres (1)	DOM AFF: Noranda
McGraw-Hill Ryerson	2	14	(1)	S. US SUB
McIntyre Porcupine Mines	3	12	chmn; v. chmn (2)	MR CAN
McLarens Foods	2	4	pres & treas (1)	US AFF
Melchers Distilleries	2	10	chmn; v. pres (2)	S. CAN
Mercantile Bank	6	13	v. pres	MR US SUB
Minas Basin Pulp & Pa.	5	13	pres (3)	S. CAN
Miron Co.	7	13	chmn & pres (5)	MR BELGIUM SUB
Monsanto Canada	1	5	chmn	US SUB
Montreal Refrigerating & Storage	4	7	chmn; v. pres (2)	S. CAN
Montreal Stock Exch.	2	13	chmn (1)	
Morgan Trust	4	14	chmn (1)	
Robert Morse	5	12	(2)	MR US SUB*
National Agri-Services	2	7	pres & ceo (1)	US SUB
National Life Assur.	7	14	chmn (6)	MR CAN
New Brunswick Teleph.	2	15	pres; chmn	DOM SUB: Bell Can.*
Newfoundland Light & Power	5	12	chmn (1)	MR CAN
Newfoundland Teleph.	3	11	chmn (1)	DOM SUB: Bell Can.
Northern Electric	7	14	chmn & ceo (5)	DOM SUB: Bell Can.

442

Norwich Union Life Insurance	4	6	chmn (3)	MR UK SUB
Ogilvie Flour Mills	5	8	pres (3)	DOM SUB: J. Labatt*
Ontario Jockey Club	11	26	chmn; hon. pres; v. pres (6)	CAN
Ontario Research Foun.	13	22	chmn; v. chmn; v. chmn (7)	
Pacific Press	3	9	chmn (2)	MR SUB: Southam Press
PanCanadian Petroleum	5	12	chmn; pres; v. pres (1)	DOM SUB: Can. Pacif. / S. CAN
Pigott Construction	2	6	pres; exec v. pres	DOM AFF: Noranda Crown Corp.*
Placer Develop. Ltd.	8	11	chmn; pres & ceo (5)	S. CAN
Polymer Corp.	5	11	(3)	
Provigo Inc.	3	12	(2)	MR CAN
Provincial Bank of Canada	4	20	chmn; v. pres & gen. mgr (1)	DOM SUB: Angl-Can.
Quebec-Telephone	4	11	(1)	
Quebecair	3	11	chmn; pres (1)	MR US SUB*
RCA Ltd.	4	19	(2)	US SUB
Ralston Purina of Can.	4	10	(4)	S. CAN
Reed Shaw Osler	3	24	(3)	
Rio Algoma Mines	5	15	(3) (6 other for. dir.)	MR UK SUB*
Rolland Paper	6	12	pres (5)	S. CAN
Rolls-Royce Holdings North America	2	7		UK SUB
Royal Insur. Group	8	13	chmn (5)	UK SUB
RoyNat Ltd.	3	8	(2)	DOM CONSORTIUM
St. Lawrence Cement	3	10	(3)	MR SWITZ SUB

Company				Affiliation
Salada Foods	3	9	(1)	US SUB
Scott Paper	3	9	pres & ceo (1)	S. US SUB
Selkirk Holdings	3	10	v. pres; ass't sec (2)	S. CAN
Sicard Inc.	4	9	(3)	US SUB
Sidbec	3	12	pres & gen. mgr (1)	Crown Corp.*
Sobeys Stores	4	13	chmn; pres (1)	DOM AFF: G. Weston
Southam Press	5	17		MR CAN
Sovereign Life Assur.	5	14	chmn	DOM SUB: IAC
Standard Brands	4	13	chmn (3)	MR US SUB*
Standard Broadcasting	10	10	chmn; pres (8)	DOM AFF: Argus
Tech Corp.	3	12	(1)	
Thomson Newspapers	5	7	chmn & pres; depy chmn; exec v. pres & man. dir. (2)	
Toronto Harbour Comm.	3	4	chmn (2)	MR US SUB
Trans Mountain Pipe.	3	8	(3)	MR CAN
Triarch Corp.	4	9	chmn (4)	FOR SUB
UAP Inc.	3	8	chmn (3)	S. CAN
Union Carbide Canada	4	11	pres (3)	MR US SUB*
Uniroyal Ltd.	3	13	(3)	MR US SUB
United Aircraft of Can.	5	14	pres (3)	MR US SUB
United Corpor.	4	10	v. pres (2)	MR
United Domin. Grp. (Can)	3	5	(2)	MR UK SUB
Wabasso Ltd.	3	14	chmn & pres (7)	S. CAN*
Warnock Hersey Int'l	7	9	chmn; pres & ceo (3)	S. CAN
Westinghouse Can.	4	11	exec v. pres admin & finances	MR US SUB
Westcoast Petroleum	4	8	chmn (1)	DOM AFF: Westcoast Transmission
TOTAL	839	2,066	(40.6%)	

L E G E N D for Appendix X

CAN	— Canadian
DOM	— Dominant
SUB	— Subsidiary
AFF	— Affiliate
MR	— Middle Range
US	— United States
FR	— French
UK	— United Kingdom
SWITZ	— Switzerland
S	— small
FOR	— Foreign
chmn	— chairman
pres	— president
ceo	— Chief Executive Officer
v. pres	— Vice president
depy chmn	— deputy chairman
gen. counsel	— general counsel
man. dir	— managing director
sec	— secretary
exec comm	— executive committee
treas	— treasurer
hon.	— honourary
gen. mgr.	— general manager

Appendix XI

*INTERLOCKING DIRECTORSHIPS OF DOMINANT CORPORATIONS,
BY SECTOR and CONTROL, 1972 year end*

	CONTROL**	Banks*	Insurance	Invest. Co.	Trust & Mort.	Other Finance	TOTAL FINANCE	TRADE	UTILITIES	Metal Mines	Mineral Fuels	Petroleum	Wood & Paper	Non-met. Miner.	TOTAL RESOURCE	Food & Beverage	Primary Metal	Transport. Equip.	Other Industrial	TOTAL INDUSTRIAL	ALL DOMINANT INTERLOCKS
BANKS																					
Royal	CN	XX	10	7		2		4	10	1	3	4	9	3	20	1	5	1	4	10	63
Can. Imper.	CN	XX	10	9		1		2	12	7	1	4	8	4	25	4	3	3	6	6	90
Montreal	CN	XX	16	4	2	1		6	15	4	2	4	8	2	19	4	3		5	13	73
Nova Scotia	CN	XX	9	4	1			6	3	2		3	3	1	9	5	3			5	34
Tor.-Dom.	CN	XX	8	4				3	4	2	2	3	3			2	1		4	10	46
TOTAL		XX	59	27	3*	4	92	28	47	15	8	19	32	10	84	16	15	4	19	54	306
LIFE INSURANCE:																					
Sun Life	CN	14	XX	5	2	1	22	1	11	3	3	3	7	2	17	1	3	1	5	9	60
Manuf. Life	CN	4	XX		1	1	17		4	1	1	1	1		3	1	2			4	18
London Life	CN	2	XX	1	5		8	1	3	1			3		6	1	1		1	4	22
Canada Life	CN	2	XX	1	2		17	1	4	4		1	2		6	1	1		1	5	30
Metro. Life	CN	8	XX	6	1		8	1	3		1		1		2	1	2			4	9
Confed. Life	CN	3	XX	2			4	2	2	4	1	2			3					3	21
Prud. Life	CN	1	XX	1	1		9			1		1			1		1				15
Mutual Life	CN	6	XX				3		1	1		1				1	1		1	3	9
Crown Life	CN	7	XX		3		6		3			1									17
N.A. Life	CN	5	XX		1		6		1	1	1		1		1						15
Stand. Life	CN	5	XX				6		3								2		3	3	17
TOTAL		59	XX	18	21	2	100	6	32	13	5	8	19	4	49	11	12	2	8	33	220

* The three interlocks are between banks and mortgage companies only. Banks and trust companies are now restricted by legislation (since 1971) from interlocking directorships.

** Control abbreviations are — CN: Canadian; US: United States; UK: United Kingdom; CS: Consortium; US/CN: joint venture with equal Canadian and United States participation; GR: Germany; BE: Belgium; FR: France; SA: South Africa; NE: Netherlands.

Interlocking Directorship (Cont'd)

	CONTROL*	Banks*	Insurance	Invest. Co.	Trust & Mort.	Other Finance	TOTAL FINANCE	TRADE	UTILITIES	Metal Mines	Mineral Fuels	Petroleum	Wood & Paper	Non-met. Miner.	TOTAL RESOURCE	Food & Beverage	Primary Metal	Transport. Equip.	Other Industrial	TOTAL INDUSTRIAL	ALL DOMINANT INTERLOCKS
INVEST. CO.																					
Alcan Alum.	US	2	2	—	—	1	4	—	1	—	—	1	—	1	—	1	—	1	1	—	6
Brascan	CN	2	2	—	2	1	2	3	3	1	—	2	2	—	3	3	—	—	2	3	31
Ang-Can. T.	US	6	—	—	3	—	9	—	—	1	—	—	—	—	3	—	4	—	—	4	10
Moore Corp.	CN	—	—	—	1	—	3	—	1	—	1	1	—	—	—	—	—	—	—	—	9
Woodward St.	UK	2	—	—	—	—	—	—	—	—	—	—	—	—	—	—	—	—	—	—	5
Racier	UK	2	—	—	—	2	1	1	—	—	—	1	2	—	3	1	—	—	—	1	—
Woodbridge	UK	—	—	—	2	—	2	—	—	—	—	—	1	—	—	—	—	—	—	—	1
Trizec	NE	1	1	—	3	—	3	—	2	—	—	3	1	—	3	1	—	—	—	—	2
Shell Inv.	CN	2	2	—	1	2	3	1	1	—	—	—	—	—	—	1	1	—	1	2	2	28
Power Corp.	CN	4	3	—	2	1	10	1	2	1	1	—	3	1	—	3	—	1	—	1	1	28
Argus	CN	7	3	1	3	3	13	8	6	1	3	3	3	—	1	7	3	1	1	7	8	36
TOTAL		27	18	2	12	3	62	12	19	3	3	8	14	2	30	3	6	2	10	21	144
OTHER FINANCE																					
IAC Ltd.	CN	4	2	2	2	—	10	—	2	—	—	—	—	—	—	—	—	—	—	1	16
Traders Gr.	CN	—	—	1	6	—	6	—	—	—	—	—	—	—	—	—	3	—	—	—	6
GM Accept.	US	—	—	—	—	1	1	—	1	—	—	—	—	—	—	—	—	—	—	—	—
Avco Fin.	US	—	—	—	—	—	—	—	—	—	—	2	—	2	1	—	4	—	—	2	2
Glengair	CN	—	—	—	—	—	—	—	—	—	—	—	—	—	—	—	—	—	—	—	1
Can. Accep.	US	—	—	—	—	—	—	—	—	—	—	—	—	—	—	—	—	—	—	—	0
Ben. Fin.	US	—	—	—	—	—	—	—	—	—	—	—	—	—	—	—	—	—	—	—	0
Wood Gundy	CN	—	—	1	1	—	1	4	1	—	1	2	2	—	1	5	—	1	1	1	11
TOTAL		4	2	—	9	—	18	5	3	—	0	2	2	—	6	3	—	1	1	5	37
TRUST																					
Royal	CN	—	3	—	—	2	5	2	4	1	—	1	—	—	3	3	3	—	2	5	19
National	CN	—	3	3	3	6	8	3	3	3	1	—	2	1	—	6	4	4	—	1	7	27
Guaranty	CN	—	4	—	—	—	7	3	—	—	3	—	3	—	1	—	1	—	—	1	9
Montreal	CN	—	—	1	4	—	5	1	1	—	—	1	3	2	—	6	1	1	—	—	2	17
Vict. & Grey	CN	—	—	—	—	—	1	1	2	—	—	—	2	—	3	—	—	8	—	1	3
TOTAL		0*	9	7	0	9	25	8	11	4	—	2	6	3	16	8	—	5	15	75

* Banks and trust companies have been prohibited from interlocking directorships since 1971.

Interlocking Directorships (Cont'd)

	CONTROL*	Banks*	Insurance	Invest. Co.	Trust & Mort.	Other Finance	TOTAL FINANCE	TRADE	UTILITIES	Metal Mines	Mineral Fuels	Petroleum	Wood & Paper	Non-met. Miner.	TOTAL RESOURCE	Food & Beverage	Primary Metal	Transport. Equip.	Other Industrial	TOTAL INDUSTRIAL	ALL DOMINANT INTERLOCKS
MORTGAGE																					
Can. Perman.	CN		3	2			4	3	4				1		3	3			1	4	28
Huron & Erie	CN		8	3			11	3	2				4		6	3	1		4	8	30
Crédit Fonc.	FR	3	1				4		4					1	3	1				1	13
TOTAL		3	12	5	0	0	19	6	10	1	2	2	6	1	12	7	1	0	5	13	61
ALL FINANCE		93	100	62	45	18	316	65	122	37	19	41	79	21	197	40	43	10	48	141	843
RETAIL TRADE																					
T. Eaton Co.	CN	4		1			5	3	2			1	1	1	3	1			1	4	7
Simp-Sears	US/CN	2	1	1	1	1	6				2	1	2	1	6	1	1		1	3	16
Steinberg's	CN	1		1	1		3	1					2		2				1	1	6
Hudsons Bay	UK	8	1	3	1	1	21	3	1	1	2	1	4	2	9	3	1		1	5	25
Simpsons	CN	4					8		1		1		1	1	2				4	4	17
Woolworth	US	2					2	1	1						1						2
Dominion	CN	4	1			1	6		1				1		1	1			2	3	13
Can. Safeway	US																				
S.S. Kresge	US	2	1	1	3		3	1	1						1						3
Zellers	US	1					1														1
TOTAL		27	4	11	10	5	57	14	7	4	4	4	12	5	29	5			6	12	119
WHOLESALE TRADE																					
Oshawa Gr.	CN		1	1				1	1			1	1		1						2
M. Loeb	CN	1			3		4														13
Can. Tire	CN		1	1	1			1	1				1		2						7
Irving Oil	US		2				1														0
James Rich.	CN	1																			3
TOTAL		1	2	1	4	0	8	2	1			1	1		4					0	15

448

UTILITIES.																					
Bell Canada	CN	10	5	7	4	—	26	1	6	1	1	1	3	1	7	2	2	—	2	6	46
North. & Cen.	CN	3	2	2	1	—	8	—	1	1	—	1	3	—	5	1	—	1	—	2	16
Consum. Gas	CN	1	1	1	6	—	9	—	1	—	—	—	—	—	—	—	1	—	1	2	12
Can. Utili.	US	—	—	1	1	1	3	—	—	—	—	—	—	—	—	—	—	—	—	—	3
Calgary Pow.	CN	1	1	—	1	—	3	—	2	—	—	—	1	—	1	—	—	1	—	1	7
Union Gas	CN	2	1	—	1	1	5	—	1	—	—	—	—	—	—	—	—	1	—	1	7
Can. Nat'l	CN	2	1	—	—	1	4	1	1	1	—	—	—	1	2	—	—	—	1	1	9
Can. Pacif.	CN	12	10	2	5	—	29	3	4	5	1	3	6	2	17	3	5	—	—	8	61
TransCanada	CN	8	7	4	1	—	20	1	6	2	—	1	3	—	6	1	—	2	—	3	36
Interprov.	US	2	2	2	1	—	7	2	2	1	1	3	1	1	7	1	1	—	—	2	20
Westcoast Tr.	US	2	—	—	—	—	2	—	—	—	3	—	1	1	5	—	—	—	—	—	7
Alberta Gas	CS	4	2	—	—	—	6	—	—	—	1	—	—	—	1	—	—	—	—	—	7
TOTAL		47	32	19	21	3	122	8	24	11	7	9	18	6	51	8	9	5	4	26	231
METAL MINES																					
Int'l Nickel	US	8	7	2	2	—	19	2	5	—	—	—	2	—	2	2	2	1	1	6	34
Noranda	CN	5	3	—	1	1	10	3	3	—	—	1	3	1	5	1	—	—	—	1	22
Falcanbridge	US	2	3	1	2	—	8	—	3	—	—	—	2	—	2	1	—	1	—	2	15
TOTAL		15	13	3	5	1	37	5	11	0	0	1	7	1	9	4	2	2	1	9	71
MINERAL FUELS																					
Pacific Pet.	US	2	1	—	—	—	3	—	4	—	—	—	1	—	1	—	—	—	1	1	9
Amoco Can. P.	US	—	—	—	—	—	—	—	—	—	—	—	—	—	—	—	—	—	—	—	0
Hud. Bay G & O	US	4	2	1	2	—	9	3	2	—	—	—	3	1	4	1	1	—	—	2	20
Texaco Expl.	US	—	—	—	—	—	—	—	—	—	—	1	—	—	1	—	—	—	—	—	1
Mobil Oil	US	1	—	—	—	—	1	—	—	—	—	—	—	—	—	—	—	—	—	—	1
Grt. Can. Oil	US	1	2	2	1	—	6	2	1	—	—	—	1	—	1	2	1	—	—	3	13
TOTAL		8	5	3	3	0	19	5	7	0	0	1	5	1	7	3	2	0	1	6	44
PAPER PRODUCTS																					
MacMillan B.	CN	5	4	1	1	—	11	1	5	1	—	1	—	1	3	1	—	1	—	2	22
Domtar	CN	8	5	5	3	1	22	8	—	—	3	1	3	1	8	1	1	—	6	8	46
Consol. Bath.	CN	6	4	5	3	—	18	—	8	2	1	1	—	1	5	—	1	—	—	1	32
Abitibi Pa.	CN	7	4	3	2	1	17	2	3	2	—	—	1	2	5	—	—	—	1	1	28
	UK	2	1	—	2	—	5	—	2	—	—	2	1	—	3	1	—	—	—	1	11
Crown Zell.	US	1	—	—	1	—	2	—	—	—	—	1	2	—	3	1	—	—	—	1	6
TOTAL		29	18	14	12	2	75	11	18	5	4	6	7	5	27	4	2	1	7	14	145

	CONTROL*	Banks*	Insurance	Invest. Co.	Trust & Mort.	Other Finance	TOTAL FINANCE	TRADE	UTILITIES	Metal Mines	Mineral Fuels	Petroleum	Wood & Paper	Non-met. Miner.	TOTAL RESOURCE	Food & Beverage	Primary Metal	Transport. Equip.	Other Industrial	TOTAL INDUSTRIAL	ALL DOMINANT INTERLOCKS
WOOD INDUS.																					
B. C. Forest	CS	2	1	—	—	—	3	2	—	2	1	1	1	—	5	1	—	—	—	—	11
Weldwood	US	1	—	—	—	—	1	—	—	—	—	—	1	—	1	—	—	—	—	—	2
TOTAL		3	1	—	—	—	4	2	0	2	1	1	1	—	6	1	0	0	0	—	13
PETROLEUM																					
Imper. Oil	US	2	—	3	—	—	5	2	3	1	—	—	2	—	3	—	—	—	—	—	4
Gulf Oil	US	8	2	—	2	—	15	—	—	—	—	—	1	—	2	1	—	—	1	4	25
Texaco Can.	US	4	2	—	—	—	6	—	—	—	—	—	—	—	—	1	—	—	1	2	11
BP Can. Hol.	UK	—	—	3	—	—	4	—	2	—	—	—	4	—	5	2	—	—	—	2	8
Petrofina	BE	—	—	—	—	1	4	1	2	—	—	—	—	—	—	—	—	—	—	—	4
Husky Oil	US	5	—	4	—	1	14	2	2	—	—	—	—	2	5	—	—	—	—	—	22
TOTAL		19	8	8	4	2	41	5	9	1	—	0	7	2	11	4	0	0	0	8	74
NON-MET. MINERALS																					
Genstar	BE	3	2	—	—	—	8	—	5	—	—	2	—	—	4	—	1	—	2	3	19
Can. Cem. Laf.	FR	7	2	—	3	—	13	5	—	—	—	—	5	—	5	—	—	—	1	3	28
TOTAL		10	4	—	4	—	21	5	6	—	7	2	6	0	9	18	11	0	2	5	47
TOTAL RESOURCE		84	49	30	28	6	197	33	51	9	7	11	33	10	68	18	11	3	11	43	394
FOOD & BEVERAGE																					
Distil. Corp.	CN	2	—	—	—	—	2	—	—	—	—	—	1	—	1	—	—	—	3	3	3
Geo. Weston	CN	—	—	—	—	—	—	—	1	—	—	—	—	—	—	—	—	—	2	2	13
Hiram Walker	CN	1	—	—	—	—	—	—	—	2	4	1	2	—	3	—	—	—	1	—	2
Can. Packers	CN	2	4	2	—	—	8	—	—	—	—	—	2	—	7	—	1	—	1	1	2
Molsons Ind.	CN	7	5	2	3	1	14	4	6	3	3	4	2	—	6	—	—	—	1	2	25
John Labatt	CN	4	—	3	4	1	14	5	8	4	3	2	5	2	18	—	1	3	3	4	30
TOTAL		16	11	3	8	2	40	5	8	4	4	4	5	2	18	0	1	3	6	4	75
PRIMARY METAL																					
Steel Co. Can.	CN	7	6	3	4	—	20	—	5	2	2	—	—	—	5	—	—	—	2	2	32
Dom. Foundry	CN	5	5	3	4	—	12	—	2	—	2	—	—	—	3	—	—	—	3	3	19
Algoma Steel	GR	3	1	—	1	—	11	1	2	2	—	2	2	—	3	—	—	—	1	2	20
TOTAL		15	12	6	9	—	43	1	9	2	4	2	2	—	11	—	0	0	6	7	71

Interlocking Directorships (Cont'd)

	CONTROL*	Banks	Insurance	Invest. Co.	Trust & Mort.	Other Finance	TOTAL FINANCE	TRADE	UTILITIES	Metal Mines	Mineral Fuels	Petroleum	Wood & Paper	Non-met. Miner.	TOTAL RESOURCE	Food & Beverage	Primary Metal	Transport. Equip.	Other Industrial	TOTAL INDUSTRIAL	ALL DOMINANT INTERLOCKS
TRANSPORT. EQUIP.																					
Gen. Mot.	US	—	—	—	—	1	1	—	—	—	—	—	—	—	—	—	—	—	—	0	1
Ford Mot.	US	3	2	2	—	—	7	—	—	2	—	—	1	—	3	—	—	—	—	0	12
Chrys. Can.	US	—	—	—	—	—	2	—	—	2	—	—	—	—	—	—	—	—	—	0	5
TOTAL		4	2	1	—	1	10	—	—	5	—	—	1	—	3	—	—	—	—	0	18
CHEMICALS																					
Can. Ind.	UK	4	2	1	3	—	11	—	1	—	—	—	—	—	3	—	—	—	—	0	15
MACHINERY																					
Massey-Fer.	CN	5	3	7	3	—	18	5	1	—	1	—	6	—	8	—	2	1	2	4	36
IBM Can.	US	3	1	—	3	—	7	—	1	—	—	—	—	—	1	1	1	—	1	3	11
ELECTRIC PROD.																					
Can. Gen. E.	US	4	—	—	2	—	7	1	1	—	—	—	—	—	1	—	—	—	1	5	14
OTHER																					
Imasco	UK	1	1	—	—	—	1	—	—	—	—	—	—	—	1	3	—	—	—	—	1
Rothmans	SA	2	1	—	2	1	4	—	1	—	—	—	—	—	—	—	3	—	1	—	5
TOTAL		19	8	10	10	1	48	6	4	1	1	0	7	2	11	3	6	0	4	13	82
TOTAL INDUSTRIAL		54	33	21	28	5	141	12	26	9	6	8	15	5	43	4	7	0	13	24	246
ALL.		306	220	144	136	37	841	134	231	71	44	74	146	47	392	71	18	82	82	246	1848

451

Appendix XII

DISTRIBUTION OF DIRECTORSHIPS
BY CORPORATION, RESIDENCE AND BIRTH, 1972

BANKS	control	RESIDENCE				total	BIRTH*			
		CAN	US	UK	OTH.		CAN	US	UK	OTH.
Royal	CN	36	1	2	3	42	31	5	3	3
Can. Imperial	CN	55	2	2	3	62	51	5	3	3
B. of Montreal	CN	51	1	2		54	40	8	4	2
B. Nova Scotia	CN	29	1	3		33	26	3	4	
Toronto-Dominion	CN	37	2	1		40	30	6	4	
Total Banks		208	7	10	6	231	178	27	18	8
INSURANCE										
Sun Life	CN	18	1	1		20	14	3	3	
Manufacturers	CN	12	2			14	10	2	2	
London Life	CN	12				12	12			
Canada Life	CN	13	2	1		16	11	3	2	
Metropol. Life	US	2	4			6	2	4		
Confeder. Life	CN	15	1			16	14	1	1	
Prudential	US	10				10	10			
Mutual Life	CN	18				18	17	1		
Crown Life	CN	19		2		21	16	2	2	1
N. Amer. Life	CN	16		1		17	12	2	2	1
Standard Life	UK	9				9	8		1	
Total Insur.		145	9	6	0	159	126	18	13	2
HOLDING CO.										
Alcan Alum.	US	6	7	1	1	15	4	8	2	1
Brascan	CN	10	6	1	5	22	10	6	1	5
Anglo-Can. Tel.	US	3	6			9	2	7		
Moore Corp.	CN	8		1		9	6		3	
Woodward Stores	CN	18	1			19	18	1		
Racier	UK	3		3		6	3		3	
Woodbridge	UK	6				6	5		1	
Trizec	UK	16		2		18	14		3	1
Shell Invest.	NETH	7	1	1		9	4	2	3	
Power Corp.	CN	17	1			18	16	1		1'
Argus Corp.	CN	15	1		1	17	10	4	2	1
Total Holding Co.		109	23	9	7	148	92	29	18	9

* Canadian birth is defined as born in Canada or to parents temporarily resident outside Canada (e.g., schooling, temporary placement). The assumption is made that those for whom data is not available are born in Canada and a further assumption is made that foreign residents were born in the country of present residence.

	control	RESIDENCE				total	BIRTH*			
		CAN	US	UK	OTH.		CAN	US	UK	OTH.
SALES FINANCE										
IAC Ltd.	CN	15				15	13		2	
Traders Group	CN	16				16	12	2	1	1
GM Accept.	US	6	3			9	4	5		
Avco Financial	US	2	10			12	2	10		
Glengair Group	CN	10				10	9		1	
Can. Accept.	US	7	3			10	6	4		
Benefic. Fin.	US	7	2			9	7	2	.	
TOTAL SALES FINANCE		63	18	0	0	81	53	23	4	1
TRUST CO.										
Royal	CN	28				28	25	1	2	
National	CN	32	1	2		35	30	2	3	
Guaranty	CN	30				30	25		3	2
Montreal	CN	31				31	28	1	2	
Victoria & Grey	CN	27				27	26		1	
TOTAL TRUST CO.		148	1	2	0	151	134	4	11	2
MORTGAGE										
Canada Perm.	CN	30				30	29	1		
Huron & Erie	CN	15				15	15			
Crédit Foncier	FR	5			8	13	1	1	2	9
Total Mortgage		50	0	0	8	58	45	2	2	9
OTHER FINANCE										
Wood Gundy	CN	23		1		24	23		1	
Total Other Finance		23	0	1	0	24	23	0	1	0
TOTAL FINANCE		745	58	28	21	852	651	103	67	31
RETAIL										
Eatons	CN	11				11	9	1	1	
Simpsons-Sears	US/CN	8	6			14	7	7		
Steinbergs	CN	10				10	7			3
Hudson's Bay	UK	13		5		18	13		5	
Simpsons	CN	14				14	14			
F. W. Woolworth	US	9	6			15	9	6		
Dominion Stores	CN	12				12	12			
Can. Safeway	US	7				7	7			
S. S. Kresge	US	5	10			15	5	10		
Zellers	US	10	3			13	9	4		
TOTAL RETAIL		99	25	5	0	129	92	28	6	3

	control	RESIDENCE				total	BIRTH*			
		CAN	US	UK	OTH.		CAN	US	UK	OTH.
WHOLESALE										
Oshawa Group	CN	12				12	12			
M. Loeb	CN	9				9	8			1
Can. Tire	CN	10				10	10			
Irving Oil	US	4	6			10	4	6		
J. Richardson	CN	4				4	4			
Total Wholesale		39	6	0	0	45	38	6	0	1
TOTAL TRADE		138	31	5	0	174	130	34	6	4
COMMUNICATIONS										
Bell Canada	CN	21	1			21	17	3	1	1
ELECTRICITY, GAS & WATER										
Northern & Cen.	CN	11	3		1	15	11	3		1
Consumers' Gas	CN	15				15	13	2		
Can. Utilities	US	8	2			10	7	2	1	
Calgary Power	CN	11				11	11			
Union Gas	CN	12	1			13	12	1		
RAILWAYS										
Can. National	CN	14				14	12			2
Can. Pacific	CN	18	2	2	1	23	13	4	5	1
PIPELINES										
TransCanada	CN	15	1			16	12	3	1	
Interprovincial	US	11				11	8	3		
Westcoast Trans.	US	8	1			9	5	3		1
Alberta Gas Trunk	CS*	11				11	10	1		
TOTAL UTILITIES		155	11	2	2	170	130	25	8	6
METAL MINING										
Int'l Nickel	US	8	12	3	1	24	4	15	4	1
Noranda Mines	CN	11	1			12	11	1		
Falcanbridge	US	7	4	1		12	7	4	1	
Total Metal Mining		26	17	4	1	48	22	20	5	1

* Consortium

	control	RESIDENCE				total	BIRTH*			
		CAN	US	UK	OTH.		CAN	US	UK	OTH.
MINERAL FUELS										
Pacific Petrol.	US	5	2			7	3	4		
Amoco Can. Pet.	US	4	2			6	3	3		
Hudson Bay G & O	US	7	5			12	6	6		
Texaco Explor.	US	1	9			10	1	9		
Mobil Oil	US	4	1			5	3	2		
Gt. Can. Oil Sands	US	8	2			10	6	4		
Total Mineral Fuels		29	21	0	0	50	22	28	0	0
PETROLEUM										
Imperial Oil	US	9				9	8	1		
Gulf Oil	US	11	1			12	·10	2		
Texaco Can.	US	10	3			13	9	4		
BP Canada	UK	8		4		12	7		5	
Petrofina	BELG	11	1		4	16	8	1	1	6
Husky Oil	US	6	6			12	5	7		
Total Petroleum		55	11	4	4	74	47	15	6	6
NON-METALLIC MINERALS										
Genstar	BELG	9	1	1	5	16	6	3	1	6
Can. Cement L..	FR	15			3	18	15			3
Total Non-Met.		24	1	1	8	34	21	3	1	9
WOOD INDUSTRIES										
B. C. Forest	CS	9	5			14	9	5		
Weldwood	US	8	2			10	7	2		1
Total Wood Prod.		17	7	0	0	24	16	7	0	1
PAPER PRODUCTS										
MacMillan Bloedel	CN	15	4			19	15	4		
Domtar	CN	17	2			19	15	3	1	
Consol. Bath.	CN	14	1			15	13	2		
Abitibi Paper	CN	14	4			18	13	5		
Price Co.	UK	11		5		16	12		4	
Crown Zeller.	US	15	1			16	14	1	1	
Total Paper Prod.		86	12	5	0	103	82	15	6	0
TOTAL RESOURCES		237	69	14	13	333	210	88	18	17

	control	RESIDENCE				total	BIRTH*			
		CAN	US	UK	OTH.		CAN	US	UK	OTH.
FOOD & BEVERAGE										
Distillers Corp.	CN	6	5		1	12	6	5		1
George Weston	CN	10		1		11	9	1	1	
Hiram Walker	CN	7	5			12	7	5		
Can. Packers	CN	11	2	1		14	11	2	1	
Molson Indus.	CN	15	1			16	15	1		
John Labatt	CN	16				16	16			
Total Food & Bev.		65	13	2	1	81	64	14	2	1
PRIMARY METAL										
Steel Co. of Can.	CN	13	2			15	9	3	3	
Dominion Found.	CN	12				12	11	1		
Algoma Steel	GERM	11	1		2	14	9	2	1	2
Total Primary Metal		36	3	0	2	41	29	6	4	2
TRANSPORT. EQUIP.										
Gen. Motors	US	3	4			7	1	6		
Ford	US	8	4			12	7	5		
Chrysler	US	5	4			9	5	4		
Total Transp.		16	12	0	0	28	13	15	0	0
CHEMICALS										
Can. Indust.	UK	10	1	1		12	9		2	1
MACHINERY										
Massey-Ferg.	CN	11	4	3		18	9	6	3	
IBM Can.	US	9	2			11	8	2		1
Total Machinery		20	6	3	0	29	17	8	3	1
ELECTRICAL PROD.										
Can. Gen. Elec.	US	10	5			15	8	7		
OTHER MANUFACTURING										
Imasco	UK	8	1	1		10	8	1	1	
Rothmans	SA	8		1	1	10	7		2	1
Total Other		16	1	2	1	20	15	1	3	1
TOTAL INDUSTRIAL		173	41	8	4	226	155	51	14	6
ALL DOMINANT CORP.		1448	210	57	40	1755	1277	301	113	64

Appendix XIII

Number and Cumulative Per Cent of Corporate Interlocks by Area of Control, 1972

	CANADA			UNITED STATES			UNITED KINGDOM			OTHER		
	#	%	Cum. %	#	%	Cum. %	#	%	Cum. %	#	%	Cum. %
Over 50	5	8.6	8.6	—	—	—	—	—	—	—	—	—
40-49	3	5.2	13.8	—	—	—	—	—	—	—	—	—
30-39	11	19.0	32.8	1	2.9	2.9	—	—	—	1	14.3	14.3
25-29	5	8.6	41.4	1	2.9	5.8	1	10.0	10.0	2	28.6	42.9
20-24	4	6.9	48.3	2	5.7	11.5	—	—	10.0	1	14.3	57.2
15-19	10	17.2	65.5	1	2.9	14.4	2	20.0	30.0	1	14.3	71.5
10-14	3	5.2	70.7	5	14.3	28.7	2	20.0	50.0	2	28.6	100.0
5-9	9	15.5	86.2	6	17.1	45.8	2	20.0	70.0	—	—	—
0-4	8	13.8	100.0	19	54.3	100.0	3	30.0	100.0	2	28.6	100.0
TOTAL*	58			35			10			7		

* Total of this table is 110 of the 113 dominant corporations, the three joint ventures have been excluded. The average number of director interlocks by country of control is: Canada 23.4, United States 7.0, United Kingdom 9.6, and others 16.3.

Appendix XIV

Class Origins of the Canadian Born Members
of the Economic Elite, 1951 and 1972

CLASS INDICATORS	ALL, 1972 No.	Cumulative No.	%	TOP 100, 1972 No.	Cumulative No.	%	1972 MULTIPLE DIRECTORSHIP No.	Cumulative No.	%	1951 Cumulative % All	Top 100	Mult.
Upper[1]												
Father in corporate Elite	192	(192)	28.5	26	(26)	32.5	86	(86)	37.4	22	30.3	17.6
Father in other Elite	16	(208)	30.9	1	(27)	33.8	7	(93)	40.4	24	37	21.8
Wife from Elite Family	39	(247)	36.7	5	(32)	40	16	(109)	47.7	31	46	30.6
Father in substantial corp.	68	(315)	46.8	12	(44)	55	30	(139)	60.4	37.8	54.4	36.8
Upper/Middle[2]												
Attended private school	85	(400)	59.4	8	(52)	65	27	(166)	72.2	50	67	52.9
Middle												
Father in Middle Class occupation	57	(475)	67.9	7	(59)	73.8	15	(181)	78.7	}		
Attended University[4]	177	(634)	94.2	16	(75)	93.8	37	(218)	94.8	82	85.2	82.9
Working[5] (left)	39	(673)	(5.8)	5	(80)	(6.2)	12	(230)	(5.2)	(18)	(14.8)	(17.1)
N	(673)			(80)			(230)			(611)	(88)	(193)

458

Appendix XV

Class Origins of the Media Elite, 1972

CLASS INDICATOR*	CORPORATE OVERLAP			NON-OVERLAP			ALL		
	No.	Cumulative (No.)	%	No.	Cumulative (No.)	%	No.	Cumulative (No.)	%
Upper									
Father in economic elite	23	(23)	45.1	16	(16)	29.6	39	(39)	37.1
Father in other elite	0	(23)	45.1	6	(22)	40.7	6	(45)	42.9
Wife from elite family	1	(24)	47.1	4	(26)	48.2	5	(50)	47.6
Father in substantial business	9	(33)	64.7	4	(30)	55.6	13	(63)	60.0
Upper-Middle									
Attended private school	7	(40)	78.4	4	(34)	63.0	11	(74)	70.5
Middle									
Father in middle class occupation	1	(41)	80.4	2	(36)	66.7	3	(77)	73.3
Attended University	9	(50)	98.0	14	(50)	92.6	23	(100)	95.2
Possibly lower than middle class	1	(51)	100.0	4	(54)	100.0	5	(105)	100.0

* Since the categories are presented as mutually exclusive from top to bottom, some people in higher categories could also be placed in lower ones.

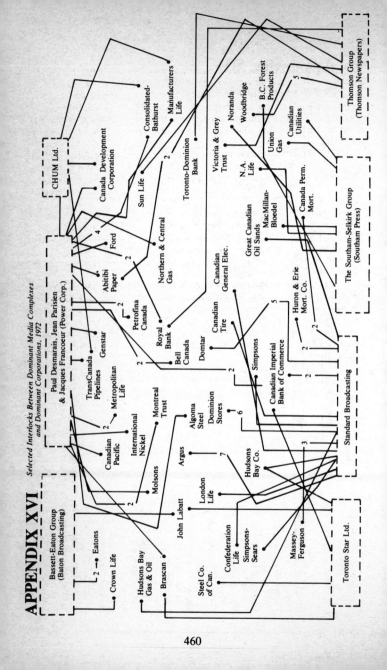

APPENDIX XVI

Selected Interlocks Between Dominant Media Complexes and Dominant Corporations, 1972

Bassett-Eaton Group (Baton Broadcasting)

Paul Desmarais, Jean Parisien & Jacques Francoeur (Power Corp.)

Thomson Group (Thomson Newspapers)

The Southam-Selkirk Group (Southam Press)

Standard Broadcasting

Toronto Star Ltd.

CHUM Ltd.

Eatons
Crown Life
Hudsons Bay Gas & Oil
Brascan
Steel Co. of Can.
Confederation Life
Simpsons-Sears
Massey-Ferguson
John Labatt
London Life
Hudsons Bay Co.
Argus
Algoma Steel
Dominion Stores
Canadian Imperial Bank of Commerce
Simpsons
Huron & Erie Mort. Co.
Canadian Pacific
International Nickel
Molsons
Montreal Trust
Metropolitan Life
Genstar
TransCanada Pipelines
Petrofina Canada
Royal Bank
Bell Canada
Domtar
Canadian Tire
Canadian General Elec.
Great Canadian Oil Sands
MacMillan-Bloedel
Canada Perm. Mort.
Abitibi Paper
Northern & Central Gas
Ford
Canada Development Corporation
Sun Life
Consolidated-Bathurst
Manufacturers Life
Toronto-Dominion Bank
Victoria & Grey Trust
N.A. Life
Union Gas
Noranda
Woodbridge
B.C. Forest Products
Canadian Utilities

Notes to Appendix XIV

[1]Since the categories are presented as mutually exhaustive from top to bottom, some in higher categories could also be placed in lower ones.

[2]'UPPER/MIDDLE' refers to the fact that although private schools are not exclusively the preserve of the upper class, they are upper class and the values as well as life-styles are those of the upper class. It should be remembered that most current members of the elite would have attended private schools during the 1930's.

[3]Middle Class occupations refer to that section of the population with the advantages of high skills and income. This includes fathers who were doctors, lawyers, engineers or managers and also ministers who are special cases since they have high status and advantages such as reduction in their son's tuition fees at private schools.

[4]Since only about eight per cent of the male population in the age group of the current elite had even some university training, it is reasonable to assume that using this as an indicator of middle class origin is still confining the class of origin to fairly near the top of the class structure.

[5]Elite members in this category have none of the above attributes and are considered to be of working class origin.

[6]For a detailed breakdown of Porter's findings for 1951, see *The Vertical Mosaic*, 1965:292, Table XXVIII. Porter collapsed "father in middle class occupation" and "attended university" while these have been reported separately here.

[7]Porter did not include multiple directorship holders as a category of analysis but by going back to the original data, this calculation was made for comparison with 1972.

Index

463

THE CARLETON LIBRARY